whistle while

you work

RICHARD J. LEIDER
DAVID A. SHAPIRO

whistle while you work

HEEDING YOUR LIFE'S CALLING

BK

BERRETT-KOEHLER PUBLISHERS, INC.
San Francisco

Berrett-Koehler Publishers, Inc.
450 Sansome Street, Suite 1200
San Francisco, CA 94111-3320
Tel: 415-288-0260   Fax: 415-362-2512
Website: www.bkconnection.com

ORDERING INFORMATION

Individual sales. Berrett-Koehler publications are available through most bookstores. They can also be ordered direct from Berrett-Koehler Publishers by calling, toll-free: 800-929-2929; fax 802-864-7626.

Quantity sales. Special discounts are available on quantity purchases by corporations, associations, and others. For details, contact the "Special Sales Department" at the Berrett-Koehler address above.

Orders for college textbook/course adoption use. Please contact Berrett-Koehler Publishers toll-free: 800-929-2929; fax 802-864-7626.

Orders by U.S. trade bookstores and wholesalers. Please contact Publishers Group West, 1700 Fourth Street, Berkeley, CA 94710; 510-528-1444; 1-800-788-3123; fax 510-528-9555.

Printed in the United States of America

Printed on acid-free and recycled paper that is composed of 85 percent recovered fiber, including 10 percent postconsumer waste.

Library of Congress Cataloging-in-Publication Data
Shapiro, David A., 1957–
    Whistle while you work : heeding your life's calling / David A. Shapiro, Richard J. Leider
        p.   cm.
    ISBN 1-57675-103-1
    1. Vocational guidance.   2. Vocation.   I. Leider, Richard.   II. Title.
    HF5381.S53 2000
    331.7'02—dc21   00–011404

06   05   04   03   02   01   10 9 8 7 6 5 4 3

Designed by Detta Penna

contents

preface

Repacking *Our* Bags

Six years ago, we embarked on a life-changing adventure. Having completed *Repacking Your Bags,* our first book together, we found ourselves faced with the opportunity to put into practice the ideas and suggestions we had written about. Our message in *Repacking* was that each of us needs to develop his or her own vision of the "good life"—which we defined as "living in the place you belong, with people you love, doing the right work, on purpose"—and having done so, must then "repack our bags" so the only burdens we carry are those that really assist us in getting where we want to be.

Walking this walk for us meant examining our own lives and asking ourselves the initial question in *Repacking:* "Does all this really make me happy?" What we discovered, individually and together, was that many of the choices we had made around place, work, relationships, and purpose were indeed contributing to our overall sense of well-being. But some of them needed to be re-evaluated and discarded. As a result, we both made a few fairly significant changes in our lives—some external and others of a more introspective nature.

Dick reconceptualized his vision of both his career coaching practice and his work as partner in *The Inventure Group* to focus more on writing and speaking. His deepening understanding of his own sense of purpose and direction led, in part, to his 1997 book, *The Power of Purpose: Creating Meaning In Your Life and Work.*

Dave gave up his career as a corporate consultant in favor of graduate school in philosophy. He has subsequently become deeply involved in doing philosophy with elementary and middle school students, work that, in part, inspired his 1999 book, *Choosing the Right Thing to Do: In Life, at Work, in Relationships, and for the Planet.*

In the six years since *Repacking* came out, we have each done a good deal of repacking ourselves. We have both moved; Dick has gotten married; Dave has become a father. Our lives have continued to present us with new opportunities for shaping our own visions of the good life.

Through it all, we have continued the discussion that led to *Repacking.* We have remained deeply intrigued by what it means to live a good life and what people really need in order to be happy. Our conversations on these issues have ranged far and wide; we've talked with each other, with colleagues and clients, with young children and older adults. Surprisingly, the one component of the good life that has consistently come to the fore has been work. While we've seen that relationships, place, and purpose contribute greatly to people's overall sense of satisfaction, we've been somewhat taken aback to discover the degree to which people's feelings that they are—or are not—doing the work they were "meant to do" makes a difference in their overall sense of fulfillment.

This observation, coupled with what we have learned by talking to a number of people who *are* doing what they were meant to, has led to this book, *Whistle While You Work: Heeding Your Life's Calling.* Whereas *Repacking* was centered around an examination of all four components we considered necessary to the good life, *Whistle* focuses on the singular issue that has emerged in our lives— and the lives of those we have spoken to—as essential: *the challenge of discovering meaningful work.*

You may find *Whistle* to be helpful if you are asking yourself questions like:

- "What do I want to be when I grow up?"

- "How can I make a living doing what I love?"

- "What was I born to do?"

- "What is my life's work?"

Our intent in *Whistle While You Work* is to help readers discover their own answers to such questions, answers that reveal to a person's own innate sense of *calling*—what we define as the "the inner urge to give our gifts away." Calling is not unlike purpose, but it's more vocationally focused. Purpose is characterized in terms of *who we are*; calling is more about *what we do*. So it's natural that, along with our examination of calling, we should spend most of this book exploring the world of work. People who have a powerful sense of calling about their work tend to love what they do and to experience a level of joy on the job that most of us only dream of. You will meet a number of these people in the following pages. We hope their stories illustrate how a life lived in alignment with calling is well within our reach.

Writing this book has been an incredible opportunity to express our callings. Each of us, in conducting interviews, facilitating seminars, teaching classes, having discussions, and putting our thoughts on paper has had the great good fortune of giving away our gifts in service to something we care deeply about. It has been a joyous experience even when—perhaps *especially when*—we were working the hardest. We offer this book as a token of our gratitude for being able to experience the power of calling in our own lives.

Heeding one's life's calling is a lifelong process. Our ongoing dialogue about calling has enriched our lives immeasurably and promises to keep doing so. We welcome you to participate in this conversation yourself and to experience the joy and fulfillment that follows from heeding your life's calling.

Richard J. Leider, Minneapolis, MN
David A. Shapiro, Seattle, WA

Introduction

if you can't get out of it, get into it!

Look around: How many people do you know who are living their lives on hold, just biding time until the right job comes along that will magically fulfill all their hopes and dreams?

Look within: How often do you find yourself longing for "something more," fantasizing about suddenly getting the perfect job, relationship, or living situation?

Look again: How many of us feel trapped? How many see no escape from jobs and lives we never chose?

Dick has seen firsthand how people get stuck in situations that they feel are inescapable. He recalls an incident that showed him what we believe is the only way out.

Africa—at last!

I have always dreamed of coming here. And now, I've finally made it, invited by Derek Pritchard, Executive Director of the Voyageur Outward Bound School, and former director of the Kenya Outward Bound school on the slopes of Mount Kilimanjaro. Derek is leading a group of seasoned outdoorspeople—Outward Bound leaders and board members—on this East African adventure. Little do I know that the real excitement and growth on our trip will be the inner journey—the "inventure."

We are taking a route that probably should not be taken—it is that challenging. But this group wants to "push the envelope," to have an authentic wilderness experience. And so, we find ourselves with full backpacks in a remote area along the eastern edge of the Serengeti Plains, climbing up from the Rift Valley—scrambling along the great rift itself— as we make our way forward under the brutal African sun. Our goal is to hike across the Salei Plain to the Ngorongoro crater where we will meet the truck that left us several days ago. None of us have taken this route before; it is new even to our Masai guide. And so, we are unsure of what lies ahead, nervous about our limited water supplies holding out.

Animals are everywhere; their screeches, growls, and yelps are a constant counterpoint to our own sounds of labored breathing and heavy footfalls. There are ten people in our group—men and women—and we are mostly silent, conserving our energy for the trek ahead. Our thoughts do not stray far from the experience at hand; ancient fears of the wild and savage continent lie just beneath the surface for us all.

And at the moment we have good reason to be on edge. We are hiking through tall grass that obscures our view beyond just a few paces. It is called, appropriately enough, "lion grass," because it is a favorite habitat of lions on a hunt. They hunker down in the dry stalks to hide from their prey, ready to spring when an unsuspecting animal comes across their line of sight.

Our group is spread out in a line behind our guide. I am near the rear, taking my time, trying to experience each moment of our trip as fully as I can. The only other member of our brigade that I can see—and I glimpse him only occasionally through the tall grass—is a man I'll call "Tom," a fairly experienced hiker, an Outward Bound board member, who in the "real world" is an extremely successful New York City attorney. Tom is on his first trip to Africa, too, and seems even more blown away by the experience than I am. He has certainly prepared well for the journey; his gear is brand-new and of the highest quality. If nothing else, he certainly looks the part of the intrepid African explorer.

Suddenly, though, out of the corner of my eye, I see him freeze. He stands, still as a statue, then sits down heavily, the tall stalks swallowing him up from my view. I swim through the grass to where he now sits. As I come upon him, he is trembling.

"Lion," he whispers, pointing off into the distance behind us. I scan

the area where he is pointing but can't see anything. "Lion," says Tom again, his eyes saucering.

Still unable to see anything, I try to get Tom to move, but he won't budge. He is paralyzed with fear. Leaving Tom, I rush ahead to our group and fetch Derek. He tells our guide to hold up the march and returns to Tom with me, who is still sitting where he was, shaking like a leaf.

Derek, an Englishman, questions Tom with the stereotypical straightforwardness of the classic British explorer. "What it is, old chap? You can't sit out here in the sun all day, you know."

Derek's right. It's late afternoon; the temperature is well over 100 degrees. Even standing still, we can feel the sweat pouring off our bodies. Tom just purses his lips and stares into space.

"Dick tells me you saw a lion. Not surprising, really." Derek brushes a clump of the tall grass with the back of his hand. "They call this stuff lion grass after all, don't you know?"

Tom is not amused. He shakes his head and mutters something.

Derek leans closer to the sitting man. "What's that?" he asks.

Tom is silent a moment and then repeats himself. "This is insane."

"I'm not sure I'd go that far," replies Derek, assuming Tom is talking about his reaction. "But I would agree that it's not the most useful response to seeing 'Simba' in the bush."

The mentioning the lion again seems to send shivers through Tom's body and loosen his tongue. "No. It's us. Here. This is crazy. Too dangerous. We shouldn't be here."

"Well, be that as it may," says Derek, "we ARE here. And there's only one way out—the way we're headed."

"I'm not going," insists Tom. "No way. No."

Tom's intransigence has brought home the seriousness of the situation not only to Derek and me but also to the rest of the group, who have filtered back and are now standing near us in various states of concern and disbelief. They are wondering whether our expedition will—or should—continue.

Derek tries reasoning with Tom. "Listen, old chap, you can't just sit here. It will be getting dark soon and if we don't find a camp near water tonight we'll all be in serious trouble tomorrow. Lions or no lions."

"I just want out of here," says Tom. "I want to go back."

Derek reminds Tom that we've already come two days' walk from *where the truck dropped us off. And besides, it's no longer there. At present, it should be making its way in a big semi-circle to where we plan to rendezvous next week. "There's nothing to go back to, Tom," says Derek, rather mildly.*

"I just want out," repeats Tom. "Out of this. Right now."

Derek kneels down next to the group. He speaks to Tom, but what he says is clearly meant for us all. "Tom, you can't get out of it. There's no getting out—this is what it is." He pauses a moment and then continues, louder, as if announcing to everyone: "We have a motto at Outward Bound precisely for this sort of situation: 'If you can't get out of it, get into it!'"

Derek's words have an immediate impact on the entire group—Tom included. "If you can't get out of it, get into it!" When there's no way out of a situation, there's only one thing to do: get into it.

At that point we realize that we're in so deep that our only recourse is to dive even deeper. Our situation is inescapable and so, instead of trying to escape it, we must embrace it. To get out of it, we have to get into it.

And so, we do.

After only a few words, the group decides to press on. We realize that heading back to where we came from is not an option; our only way out is to get into it.

Derek's motto becomes our group's mantra for the rest of the trip. We face other near-crises in the days ahead, but with each one, we accept that the only way around it is through it. By the end of our trek, we need only give each other a look which says it all: "If you can't get out of it, get into it."

In the years since that first trip to Africa, Derek's words have come back to me often. The motto never fails to create a shift in my perspective. I have been involved in wilderness experiences—whether in the plains of Africa, the mountains of Colorado, or even the boardrooms of corporate America—and whenever I find myself or my group becoming stuck, I am reminded of this simple truth: "If you can't get out of it, get into it."

We recall these words now because we see so many people who are "stuck" in their current career situation. They want out of where they are. They fantasize about winning the lottery, about becoming a millionaire, about meeting someone who will hire them and solve all their problems, about space aliens making contact with humanity and changing the entire world as we know it. In short, they fantasize about getting out of it.

But the simple fact is this: there is no getting out of it. The difficulties and dissatisfactions of work are only met in one way: head on. If we want to get out of our current situation, if we want to experience real joy in our work, there's only one thing to do: get into it.

And for us that means getting into the process of hearing and heeding our calling.

So then, let's get into it.

The Call

Calling is the inner urge to give our gifts away. We heed that call when we offer our gifts in service to something we are passionate about in an environment that is consistent with our core values.

Considering the concept of "calling" metaphorically, one of the great success stories is the telephone. What else comes so quickly to mind when we think of hearing a call?

The story of the telephone's success depends in no small part upon its simplicity. The fact that it doesn't (or at least historically didn't) require a number of complex steps to operate has made the telephone accessible to everyone. People with little or no technological sophistication are easily able to make and receive calls. The simplicity of the telephone has given people everywhere access to connections. Had it not been so easy to use, it's unlikely that its impact would have been felt so powerfully today.

As explorers of a different concept of "calling," we also hold simplicity in high regard. It's our belief that the message of calling is best presented in a manner that is straightforward and uncomplicated. It ought to be as easy to use as the telephone.

Thus, we would like to dial in four guiding principles of calling:

1. The Call comes from a Caller.

Each and every one of us is called. Where does the call come from? There is no calling without a Caller. Calling is an inherently spiritual concept that challenges us to see our work in relation to our deepest beliefs. The concept of calling is founded on the recognition that we are all born with God-given gifts to fulfill specific purposes on earth. Our calling emanates from a Source much larger and more powerful than we are. No one fully understands all that is "hard-wired" into newborns, but it is clear that we come into the world already endowed with unique gifts. These gifts have the potential to enrich our lives immeasurably if they are unwrapped and given away. And yet, calling is not revealed to us automatically at birth. Heeding our calling requires an effort on our part. It is an effort, though, that can be performed almost effortlessly. Quite simply, we must *listen*. We must choose to hear what summons us. We must open ourselves to that inner urge to share our gifts with the world in a meaningful way. When we are clear about our life's calling—when we have heard the call and can heed it—our full potential for joyful work can be realized.

2. The Call keeps calling.

Calling is revealed to different people at different times in different ways; it may not come to us in a time or a form we expect. And yet we become aware of it in consistent themes that run through our lives: those things we remain passionate about, the work that we continue to believe needs doing in the world. Discovering our calling is a process that has stages, much like the process by which we learned to walk. Each stage—rolling over, crawling, walking, running—had to be experienced in turn. Likewise, we move from *jobs* which pay the bills, to *careers* which help us grow, to *callings* which give us meaning. All three—job, career, and calling—are related, but at different levels and stages. And the common theme that ties them together is the gradual revelation of our calling over time.

3. The Call is personal.

There are as many callings in the world as there are people on the planet. This isn't to say that other people might not do the same things we do or that they can't be passionate about the identical issues that compel us. It does, however, mean that each of us is called directly; no one else is called to do the same things we are *in the same manner we are*. Our calling is our embedded destiny; it is the seed of our identity. The emphasis here is on *being*. We express calling not only through the work we do, but more importantly, through *who we are willing to be* in our work. *Heeding* our calling involves a conscious choice to be ourselves—to uncover in the here and now our God-given nature. Our calling is like our signature or thumbprint, uniquely ours. Heeding our calling means we realize that we are here to contribute to life on earth something that no one else can contribute in quite the same way.

4. The Call is long-distance.

Heeding our calling is a deliberate choice to use our gifts to serve others and make a difference in the world. Our calling is made manifest through service to others. We come alive when our efforts make a difference in other people's lives. It's paradoxical but true: we are more likely to receive the satisfaction and fulfillment we seek when we enable *others* to achieve the satisfaction and fulfillment *they* seek. When what we do is grounded in a sense of calling, we experience a special joy—a whistle—in our work. As a result, we are even more willing and able to give our gifts. We are in it, then, for the long-term; the overall meaning of our lives is revealed though the long-term expression of our calling. Calling is thus the active source of our legacy.

These four guiding principles represent the essence of our message about calling. Of course, there's much more to be said about how calling is revealed to us and the ways we can bring a heightened sense of calling into our lives and work, but the basic idea is quite basic—as we hope to show in the following chapters.

In *Chapter 1: What Do I Want To Be When I Grow Up?* we provide a framework for reflection upon a question we all need to revisit sooner or later. We also explore how our answers contribute to our fulfillment on the job—that is, the degree to which they put a whistle in our work.

Chapter 2: What Is My Calling Card? features the "Calling Card" exercise, a powerful interactive way of developing a clear sense of one's calling. Once we discover the "golden thread"—our embedded destiny—we can then begin to examine it in light of our current or future work.

Chapter 3: Gifts—Is My Job My Calling? asks us to think about the work we were doing the last time we were so absorbed that we lost all track of time. This provides us with a way to explore the *gifts* component of calling. We also begin to look at ways in which people can take charge of their current work lives in order to express their calling. This is intended to illustrate that heeding our calling does not necessarily mean that we change jobs; another alternative is to change the job we have.

Chapter 4: Passions—What Keeps Calling Me? explores the *passion* component of calling. Passions are the specific questions that obsess us constantly; they are the particular issues, interests, and problems that attract us—at work, in our lives, and with the people around us. Understanding our passions gives us insight into the many arenas where we can put our gifts to work.

Chapter 5: Values—Where Do I Make the Connection? gets at the *value* component of calling by exploring calling in a wider context than just on the job. Values frame the sort of environment in which we are most likely to flourish. Consequently, this chapter offers guidance and direction for figuring out what environments we're mostly likely to thrive in.

Chapter 6: How Do I Heed the Call? centers around an exploration of the challenges associated with heeding our calling. We share many examples of how people have dealt with the frustration of hearing a "busy signal" when trying to connect with their calling. This broadens the discussion of calling, and helps us to keep listening in spite of the inevitable missed connections we all experience.

Chapter 7: Legacy—Did I Answer the Call? explores the *legacy* we leave through the choices we make around calling. What do we want our lives to have been about? How do we want to be remembered? Who will we see when we look back upon ourselves? In this chapter, readers will have an opportunity to reflect on others' stories to draw lessons for their own lives and legacies.

Through these chapters, we hope to provide a process for readers to hear and heed their own unique calling. Ultimately, the discovery of calling is about connecting who we are and what we do. So our own exploration of calling can perhaps best begin by connecting with the question that, for most of us, is the source of our current experience: *"What do I want to be when I grow up?"*

Chapter 1

what do I want to be when I grow up?

Everything Happens for a Reason

I'm already late for my plane. The alarm in my hotel room didn't go off—or maybe I slept right through it. I'm stressing hard; if I miss this flight, I'll be two hours late for my meeting, not to mention deeply embarrassed in front of my clients when I finally do show my face.

Traffic is awful. My taxi driver coughs and shifts in his seat as he faces the long line of cars ahead of him. I see his reflection in the rear-view mirror. He looks like he's straight from Central Casting's cab driver department: the big, red, Karl Malden nose, the watery bloodshot eyes, the few greasy strands of hair sticking out from under the flattened wool cap.

"What time's your flight?" he asks, glancing up at the mirror to meet my gaze.

I tell him—the hopeful, pleading tone of my voice all too apparent.

The driver shakes his head. "You ain't gonna make it. Sorry. This traffic's outta control."

I sigh involuntarily and mumble something about the meeting I'm going to miss.

My driver waxes philosophical. "Everything happens for a reason," he says. "You wanna know why I'm a cab driver?"

Why not? I've got time to kill now.
"Because the Japanese bombed Pearl Harbor."
This I've gotta hear.
"Yeah," continues the driver. "You ever hear of the Sullivan Act?" He doesn't wait for me to answer. "Four brothers—all Navy—got killed in the bombing. So Congress passes a law that if you have a brother on active duty, you can't be drafted. Okay. My brother, who's a cop, is in Vietnam. And back in 1969, I'm just outta high school, and because I always do everything he does, I'm gonna enlist and go over there, too. I write him a letter telling him my plans and he writes back saying don't do it, this place is a mess, so I stay home, get into some trouble with the law and disqualify myself from following my brother's footsteps onto the police force. 'Course I wouldn't have that option if it wasn't for the Sullivan Act—I'd a been drafted. My number's already called. So you see, if it wasn't for Pearl Harbor, I'd be a cop today. Instead, here I am."
Sounds like he was fated to drive a cab.
"It's a good thing, too," says the driver, smiling wryly. "If I were a cop, I'd be dead. I got the kind of personality, you put me on the street with a gun, I'm not so sure things would work out, know what I mean? So, you see? Everything happens for a reason. If it wasn't for Pearl Harbor, I wouldn't be driving this cab. And if weren't for missing your wake-up call, you wouldn't have met the best taxi driver in town."

Think about your own life and the complex turn of events that led you to where you are today. Perhaps you can't trace the origins of your current career all the way back to the Second World War, but you probably recognize that a few key events played a major role in determining who and what you are today. The question to ask is "How involved was I in the course of those events?" Did you make choices that reflected what you really care about or were you pretty much borne along by forces outside your control? Are you, in other words, being what you wanted to be when you grew up?

Whistle While You Work

The Disney classic, *Snow White and the Seven Dwarfs,* features the unforgettable song, "Whistle While You Work." The tune, sung by

Snow White and the forest animals who come to her aid, captures the feeling of work done with a sense of joy, commitment, and focus. As Snow White works and whistles, we are reminded that, ultimately, the way we work is an expression of who we really are. And we share in Snow White's feelings of accomplishment and satisfaction as she busily completes her many tasks.

In doing so, we are naturally led to wonder about our own jobs. Like Snow White, many of us have too much to do. And like her, we are bothered by many troubles. How many of us, though, are able to put on a grin and start right in? How many of us find ourselves really able to whistle while *we* work?

Of course, Snow White's whistle is only half the story. Behind the scenes, the movie offers an even clearer model for joyful, committed work: the model of Walt Disney himself. Through his movies, his artwork, and his vision for the fantasy kingdom, Disneyland, Walt Disney created a legacy that any of us could hope to aspire to. An incredibly gifted animator, director, and businessperson, he was also incredibly passionate about his work; his values for high-quality family entertainment came shining through in all he did. Who can doubt that Walt Disney, as he created the many characters and stories that are now so deeply a part of our culture, whistled while he worked?

Naturally, we can't all be Walt Disney. Most of us, in fact, probably have jobs more like Snow White's friendly dwarfs. But this doesn't mean we can't bring to them the powerful sense of calling that Walt Disney did. And it certainly doesn't mean that we can't find a way to whistle while we work.

This feeling of doing what we were meant to do—of performing the work that we were born for—is something every one of us craves. We have a deep hunger to feel useful and to know that our natural abilities are being employed to their fullest potential. The desire is especially powerful because we've all had a taste of it; we've all had the experience of being deeply connected to what we're doing—that sense of timelessness and flow that fills us when we're doing exactly what we were meant to do.

When we were kids, we imagined work would be like this when we grew up. When parents and teachers asked us what we wanted to be, we usually had a ready answer. "An astronaut. A fire fighter. An explorer." We envisioned a life of excitement and challenge on the job—a life in which we'd employ our best-loved talents on projects we were passionate about.

For many of us, though, it hasn't exactly worked out that way. We find ourselves in working situations that are far from what we envisioned as children. Our jobs are *just jobs*. They pay the bills, but they don't provide us with the joy that, in the end, is what really matters. We've lost the whistle in our work. Even worse, we've forgotten what we wanted to be when we grew up.

So maybe it's time to ask ourselves again:

What do I want to be when I grow up?

Maybe it's time to take a lesson from a group of sixth-graders Dave worked with in a Seattle middle school. They all had very strong feelings about what the future ought to hold for them—and even stronger feelings about what it ought not. Each of them had already answered the question that we're still asking:

What do I want to be when I grow up?

Dave tells a story that made this abundantly clear to him, in a way that helped him realize what his own answer finally was.

| David A. Shapiro
Writer | | *Fostering*
Understanding |

We're playing a game called "Hand Dealt," which explores the question, "Is life fair?" by providing each player with a predetermined "life." Students are each dealt three cards; one card determines a fictional relationship they are in, one establishes a fictional job or jobs; the third tells them where they live. There is a wide range of relationships, occupations, and accommodations, from the quite affluent to the extremely poor. Thus, one player may end up having been dealt a "life" of two parents, one of whom is a chemical engineer making $80,000 a year, the other of whom is a banker earning $125,000 annually, two kids, living in a four-bedroom house, while another player is dealt a "life" of an unemployed single parent of 4 children living in a one-bedroom apartment. Not surprisingly, the kids who get the "good" lives tend to respond to the question of life's fair-

ness in the affirmative while those who are dealt less desirable lives usually respond that life is horribly unjust. This gives us the opportunity to wonder aloud about the relationship between monetary success and happiness, and ultimately, about just what it means for life to be fair or unfair.

But that's not all. It also gives us a chance to explore what it feels like to be dealt a life we didn't choose. And this, more than anything else, is what energizes our discussion. The kids are adamant about the injustice of having to live with choices they didn't make.

"I wouldn't mind being a janitor," says a boy I'll call Carlos, whose bleached-blond surfer look belies an unusual level of thoughtfulness for an 11 year-old, "if being a janitor is what I wanted to be. But since it isn't my choice, I don't think it's fair."

But the cards were passed out fairly, weren't they? Didn't everyone have an equal opportunity to be whatever they ended up being?

"That's not the point," says Miranda, a rather small girl with a rather large personality. "What makes it fair or not is that it's your own life and that nobody's forced you into it."

"Yeah. Some people are actually happy being, I dunno, schoolteachers. But that for me would be like worse than prison." This comment from Will, one of the class's several class clowns, elicits a humorous grimace from his teacher and chuckles from his classmates.

"Could you imagine coming to school for the rest of your life?" shouts curly-haired Maya with a theatrical shiver. "What a disaster!"

Amidst the general assent of her fellow students, I wonder out loud what kinds of things these 11- and 12-year-olds could imagine doing for the rest of their lives. I'm taken aback at the assurance with which they respond.

"When I grow up, I'm going to be a movie director," says Erin, a seemingly shy girl who spends much of her time drawing. "I'm going to start by doing commercials and then videos and then feature films."

Ryan, who collared me the moment I entered the classroom to show me his daily journal, in which he is recording tidbits for the autobiography he is working on, pipes up that he's going to be a writer. "Maybe I can write your movie scripts," he says to Erin.

Other students have similarly well-formed notions of what they love doing. I'm enjoying immensely talking to them about what they plan to do, how they plan to do it, and the philosophical implications of their choices—and their freedom to make those choices. I'm wondering how they manage to have such optimism and clarity about their lives at this young age. I'm wondering how—at this age—they seem to know themselves so well. When did they have the discovery that so often eludes adults: the discovery of what they want to be when they grow up?

And suddenly, I come to understand that I am having that same discovery myself. As I stand in a classroom, doing philosophy with children, I realize that finally, after years of searching, I am at last doing what I most love to be doing. All the other jobs I've ever had—from busboy to videodisc designer to corporate training consultant—have been merely steps upon the way to where I am now. I feel completely connected to the process of inquiry we're conducting; I'm immersed in the subject matter and delighted by my young colleagues and their inquiring minds. Time flies by. What I notice is how authentic it feels for me to be helping these students to better understand the questions and answers we are exploring and in the process, to better understand themselves. And it occurs to me that in all the other jobs I've ever had, this is the common theme that has given me satisfaction. At some level, "fostering understanding" has consistently been key.

And I realize that after all these years, I've finally become what I always wanted to be when I grew up. It's taken me more than 40 years to rediscover the answer to the question that my young friends in this classroom have found for themselves in just over a decade.

What do you want to be when you grow up?

The Roots of Calling

At a fairly young age—by fifth or sixth grade, certainly—most of us have a pretty good sense of what we love to do—and what we don't. Of course, we usually can't put a job title on it at that point; for an 11-year-old, loving to draw doesn't translate into being an art director; nor is finding math class fun a sign that a youngster should think about becoming an accountant. Moreover, given that well over half of the jobs that kids will grow up into haven't even been invented yet, it's obvious that we can't expect too much specificity in career choice at such a young age.

Still, the essential core is already there. Our gifts, though nascent, have already begun to take shape. Deep within, a part of us knows that we are here on this planet for a reason. A sense of destiny, unformed as it is, lies just beneath the surface of our awareness. And, even as children, we naturally incline towards the experiences that allow us to express this.

Somewhere along the line, though, we get sidetracked. We silence that voice within that speaks to us about what really matters. We make choices—or have them made for us—that are driven by practical concerns. We set aside "childish" dreams in the interest of making a living or satisfying someone else's plans. We seem to forget what we knew as boys and girls—what we most love to do.

But that wisdom never really goes away. It can be revived. We can open ourselves to that innate knowing that guided us when we were young: the inner urge to give our gifts away.

The roots of calling in our lives go back very deeply—to even before we were born. Calling is an expression of our essence; it's our embedded destiny. The seed of this destiny lies within us; one way or another it seeks to fulfill itself in the world. So the question we need to ask ourselves is whether we're doing all we can to bring the fruits of our calling to bear.

Seeds of Destiny

One unmistakable conclusion that Dick has drawn from a lifetime of coaching individuals about life and career design is this: *we all possess seeds of destiny.* Each of us has within us God-given natural gifts—unique potential for creative expression. From birth we have what we need to become all we can be. The challenge, of course, is to figure out how to make a living with our uniqueness; how to connect who we are with what we do.

But often we don't have to look very far to find our life's calling. We can simply start doing whatever we are already doing—driving a taxi, being a lawyer, raising a child, waiting on tables—with greater reverence for and attention to our natural gifts.

On a day-to-day basis, most jobs can't fill the tall order of making the world a better place, but particular incidents at work can have real meaning when we make valuable contributions, genuinely help someone in need, or come up with creative solutions to difficult problems. These transactions are meaningful because we do them with good will rather than simply to earn a paycheck. They are naturally rewarding and often occur effortlessly. Such moments put a whistle in our work. They fill purposeful lives—lives that are apt to be happier than lives that lack such moments.

The way we approach our work depends on our "big picture" of life. Unfortunately, many of us lose that perspective; we get so focused on the particulars at hand that we make decisions impulsively, losing touch with what is really important to us.

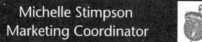

| Michelle Stimpson Marketing Coordinator | | *Creating Joy* |

Michelle Stimpson, Marketing Coordinator at the Minneapolis-based Carlson Companies is committed to helping people reconnect with what really matters to them. Too often, she has seen the "busyness" of business crushing people's spirits; in response, she has made it her special mission to help lift that heavy weight. She makes time on a daily basis to get to know the people she works with as *people,* not just co-workers. "I feel obligated to create a positive first impression with everyone who comes to work here—showing them how they fit into the big picture, why they're important."

Michelle's parents must have known intuitively that their daughter's calling was *creating joy*—her given middle name is Joy. Michelle's joy has always been to build bridges between people. Even as a small child, she loved to listen to people's stories, particularly stories about how they overcame obstacles. She recalls, "I've always loved to touch people's lives, to be a friend who was there. My gift is to surround myself with positive energy and give it off to other people."

Throughout her life, Michelle has chosen activities in which she could cheer people on and get them excited about things. As an intern at the Courage Center for the physically challenged, she researched patients' stories and sent them to their hometown newspapers. In college, she volunteered for the "welcome committee." *Creating joy* has been the common theme for her; she has expressed this destiny in many variations along the way. Michelle carries a small card in her billfold to remind herself of her true priorities: family, joy, simplicity, peace, and love. She and her husband Bill work hard at living these values every day—and, as Michelle's joy demonstrates, they are succeeding.

Michelle's embedded destiny to create joy illustrates the depth of calling within us. Each of us is, you can say, like an acorn. Somehow, almost magically, the acorn knows how to grow up to be an oak tree. It doesn't matter where you plant it, whether you put it in an oak forest, an orange grove, or even a junkyard, as long it gets the necessary sunlight and water, the acorn will develop into an oak tree. The acorn's destiny to flourish as an oak is implanted within itself. Attempting to make the acorn grow into a pine tree, for instance, will be—at best—fruitless; more likely, it will destroy the tree altogether.

The same can be said for our own destinies. Like the acorn, each of us contains within us the power to realize the fullest expression of who we are. Naturally, we need a good environment in which to grow and thrive, but assuming we can cultivate that, we can grow our roots down and reach up to become tall and mighty in our own way.

Sadly, many of us spend our lives trying to grow our acorns into pine trees—or palms or sycamores or something even more exotic and unlikely. And this stunts our growth. Yet our destiny continues to seek fulfillment in becoming an oak tree. Small wonder so many of us grow up feeling rather gnarled and twisted. Small wonder so many of us end up making work or lifestyle choices that hinder our natural growth.

One of the most common messages many youngsters receive is that they should rein in their natural creative capacities. How many of us have heard "You can't sing," "You can't draw," or "You're not a writer"? How many of us were told we were not good in one or all of the creative arts? And even those of us lucky enough to have had our creativity supported were likely to have been told that we could never make a living as a singer or artist or poet. Each time these limitations were imposed upon us, most of us acted as if they were the truth. We accepted the limitations, imposed them upon ourselves, and thus the limitations became real.

The lesson is that when we are given strong positive messages about our creative abilities, we tend to bring them forth quite successfully. Those of us fortunate enough to have had parents or mentors who encouraged our creative expression often find ourselves using those very abilities in our work lives as adults. Dick, for instance, who now makes a good deal of his living by giving speeches, had programmed into him from a very young age this simple message: "You can speak." He bought it.

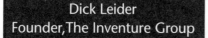

| Dick Leider Founder, The Inventure Group | *Uncovering Callings* |

"When I was in my pre-teens," says Dick, "my father strongly encouraged me to get up early every morning and look up a new word in the dictionary. At breakfast, I would share from memory my new word with him. I always picked ones that I thought would impress him—words like 'ameliorate' or 'erudition.' He believed that to be successful in any work or in life you needed to be able to express yourself clearly and articulately. For him, having the vocabulary to say precisely what you meant with a certain poetic flourish was a vital component of success. Encouraging me to learn a 'word a day' was how he impressed upon me the importance of this.

"His next push was for me to take elocution lessons. I dreaded this. My friends would be playing hockey at the corner playground on Saturday mornings while I sat with Miss Loker learning how to speak. Miss Loker was a dowdy gray-haired woman in her 70s who seemed plucked directly from the musty volumes of English literature that she carried with her for my lessons. Always perfectly put together and freshly coiffed, she showed up on Saturdays with poems to be memorized and lessons on pronunciation and inflection to be learned. I would avoid the work she gave me all week long and try to cram it all in Friday afternoon. Consequently, I dreaded her visits and the inevitable humiliation of having to stand before her, in my own living room, reciting the week's lesson over and over and over.

"The true terror, though, was the recital, six months out, where she brought all her students together in an auditorium to recite a selected piece. For months, I came up with every conceivable excuse to avoid this event. Unfortunately, there was no way out. I ended up on stage before scores of expectant parents, reciting my piece under the stark glow of the theater lighting. Much to my surprise, though, I liked it. Hearing my voice reverberate through the hall and seeing the smiles and hearing the applause of the audience gave me a thrill I never forgot.

"As a sensitive and mostly introverted 13-year-old, elocution lessons did not help me get picked for hockey games on Saturday afternoons or be able to talk to girls at school. But they did teach me to be comfortable speaking in front of groups. In fact, after two years of lessons, I found within me a natural enjoyment for sharing stories in front of a live audience. I discovered that I had a gift for communicating my thoughts and feelings to groups of people.

"Today I make my living sharing stories and lessons learned with audiences of all sizes. Speaking in public is a part of my occupation that I truly enjoy. It brings forth the whistle in my work.

"I often wonder if my parents saw this natural inclination of mine for public speaking or whether they just felt it would be a good skill for me to acquire. In any case, they nurtured my gift for it, and in doing so, helped make it possible for me to make a living doing what I love to do."

Doing What You Love, Not What You Should

How many of us ended up where we are because someone—probably a parent or a teacher —"should'ed" us? Somewhere along the line, an adult or mentor of some sort told us that we *should* go into some line of work or some course of study "to make a good living" or because some other occupation "isn't practical," or so we can have "something to fall back on," if what we *really* love to do doesn't work out?

This is common with college students. An eighteen year-old freshman loads up his schedule with lots of math and sciences, even though what he really loves is theater. If he's lucky, about the time he's a junior, he realizes he's made a mistake and changes his major. If he's not, he ends up graduating and taking a job that makes him miserable.

Dave remembers a young woman who took an Intro to Philosophy course from him. "She was quite good at it. She had a natural knack for understanding the often abstruse arguments of the philosophers we were reading. She seemed to really enjoy the interplay of ideas in the classroom; she wrote great papers, and often came to my office hours to discuss philosophical questions. Given her enthusiasm for the material, I naturally assumed she was majoring in Philosophy. But no, she said, she was pre-med. "Well, then, you'd better watch out," I joked, "given your talent, if you're not careful, you're going to end up a philosophy major." She just laughed.

"After the class, I lost track of her and didn't see her again until about two years later, when we happened to meet by chance in the library. I asked her how her studies were going, what courses she was taking, and so on. She listed the classes she was enrolled in that quarter—they were all upper division philosophy courses!

"'I thought you were pre-med,' I said.

"'I switched to philosophy,' she told me.

"I kidded her about the comparative job prospects of a philosopher and a physician. 'Well, your parents must have been delighted about that!'

"She laughed, 'Yeah, I thought when they found out I changed, they were going to kill me.' Then she got serious. 'But I thought that if I didn't change, I might kill myself.'"

The message is this: we limit ourselves by doing what we think we *should do*. But by doing what we *love to do,* we expand our potential and increase the likelihood that the work we do will be consistent with our gifts. We maximize our chances for whistling while we work.

Nobody but you knows what your path should be. Maybe it means taking a job as a taxi driver. Perhaps it's the seminary or teaching philosophy to children. Maybe expressing your calling means to form a collectively owned organic farm; maybe it is to run for mayor of your small town. Or perhaps you will heed your calling to become a chef, a poet, or an adoptive parent. There are thousands of callings and limitless ways to express them—and only we can name our calling and act upon it.

People who whistle while they work tend to have exercised choice in getting where they are. They tend to have—at some point or another—taken the proverbial "bull by the horns" and set a direction for their lives. They tend to have pursued that direction, using their intuition as a compass to navigate with. This isn't to say they necessarily travel in a straight line—they may change course many times along the way—but the mere fact of choosing their life's course enables them to pursue their dreams energetically. And the sense of power that comes from knowing that their direction is freely chosen provides them with the impetus to keep choosing throughout their lives.

It's a useful exercise, therefore, to look back on our own lives and think about the twists and turns that led us to where we are today. What were the key decisions we made—or didn't make—that resulted in our becoming the person we are, with the work we have, living in the place we do, with the people we know?

Parents at Work

Our parents' attitudes toward work are the foundation upon which we build our own. The way Mom and Dad work—and talk and think about work—are the first images we have of the world of work and, therefore, have a deep and powerful influence on our own attitudes.

Growing up, we formed opinions about work by observing the behavior and listening to the words of our elders. Our parent or parent figures—the most important people in our lives—modeled for us the meaning of work. Our own relationship to work evolved from that starting point.

For some of us, Father was the parent who most clearly characterized the nature and meaning of work. For others, it was Mother, and for many, it was both. If our parents whistled while they worked, and saw work as joy, we are more likely to seek enjoyment in our own work. If they saw their jobs as drudgery, as only a way to pay the bills, we are more likely to want to avoid it ourselves.

Of course, our beliefs and attitudes about work are complex and have their origins in many sources, but our basic pattern was formed by observing the work lives of our parent figures.

Dick observed his father and formed the foundation of his perspective on calling. "My father was a banker, an executive who worked for the same organization for 39 years. He worked hard— got up early in the morning six days a week to go to the office. He did so not simply to make a living, but because he believed that his efforts had a positive effect on individuals and the St. Paul, Minnesota community. This symbolic message, that work is a way to make a difference in people's lives, is deeply programmed into me. The bright side of what my father modeled to me about work was his masterful ministry to people. When I went to his office and saw him relate to people or we walked together down the streets of St. Paul, it was obvious that he was very skillful and enjoyed what he was doing. He whistled while he worked. He created the aura of an artist when he worked, echoing the words of Suzuki, who wrote, "I am an artist at living and my work of art is my life. I learned from my father that through giving yourself away you find your true self."

The Message We All Want to Hear

Our family, through parents and other significant elders, communicates a strong sense of limitations and possibilities as to what our work might be for each of us. We hear the message, "You're not good at this; you ought to do that . . ." These limitations and possibilities are often the projections of our parents' own fears and dreams.

Many of us were brought up to believe that we can't possibly make a living doing what we enjoy. We have a choice: either we can enjoy what we do or we can eat!

Step back for a moment and ask yourself if this makes sense. Is it true? Are all the people you know who enjoy their work starving?

Growing up, most of us were told by well-meaning parents that work is not something to be enjoyed. "It's not supposed to be fun; that's why they call it work," we were told. That early message made a powerful impression which was reinforced by seeing grown-ups drag themselves to their jobs, complaining all the way. Those of us lucky enough to have adult role models who whistled while they worked probably came to consider those people anomalies. Certainly, popular culture images—from Ralph Kramden to Archie Bunker to Homer Simpson—don't represent most people as particularly joyful in their work.

Probably very few of us heard a message like this when we were young:

"Welcome, my child! You've been born into an exciting era with unlimited potential. We don't know what your God-given gifts are, but we're committed to helping you discover them. We could never see the world thorough your eyes because God designed you to be you and to live a life that is yours alone to live. You have gifts that will come to you so naturally that no one can teach you how to use them, not even us! Your gifts will give you untold joy and will be as easy for you as breathing. We will give you plenty of chances to explore what you really enjoy doing in order for your gifts to truly flourish. We'll be proud of and celebrate whatever calling you choose for yourself, whatever it is that makes you happy."

Nevertheless, many people *have* found a unique, life-inspiring calling. Few, if any, were given the kind of support illustrated in the above paragraph. They had to discover for themselves the work that made them whistle.

Our callings exist within us; they are inborn, a natural characteristic, like our hair color or whether we're right- or left-handed. But until we heed our calling, we're not living authentically; we're adopting someone else's model for who we should be. Perhaps it's who our parents thought we should be; perhaps it's a false image that we ourselves have opted for. In any case, that false image must be examined, re-evaluated, and, if necessary—discarded if we're to whistle while we work.

Each of us has a unique and special calling. *What's yours? What are you here to do that no one else in the world can do in the way you can? What is your special role to perform in life's great drama?*

Chapter 2

what is my calling card?

Doing What You Do

I settle into the taxi, hoping to get a bit of work done before my upcoming meeting. As the driver pulls away from the curb, I open my briefcase and take out a folder. Even as I try to focus on my papers, I can see from the cabbie's face in the rear-view mirror that he wants to talk.

"So, whattayou in town for?" he asks.

"I'm giving a speech. A presentation to some businesspeople," I say, hoping to make it sound uninteresting so the driver will leave me alone.

He doesn't take the hint. "Oh yeah? What's it about?"

I'm not interested in giving the speech twice, so I offer the Reader's Digest abridged version. "Hearing and heeding your life's calling—doing the work you were born to do."

My cabbie scoffs. "That's a good one. You gotta section on how to make a million bucks while you sleep, too?"

Now he's hooked me. "You sound skeptical."

"Hey look, what am I supposed to say? Your life's 'calling?' C'mon, I drive a cab here. What's that got to do with a calling?"

I close my folder and catch the driver's eye in the rear-view. "You weren't born to drive a taxi?"

He just laughs.

"But you like your work well enough?"

He shrugs. "I guess it has its moments."

"I'm interested. What are those moments?"

"You mean besides quittin' time?"

I lean forward and put my hand on the front seat. "I'm serious. What is it about this job—besides the money—that you find satisfying? What is it that gets you out of bed in the morning?"

He smirks like he's going to say something sarcastic but then stops. Gradually, his face softens. He laughs a little and says, "Well, there's this old lady."

I stay silent and he continues. "A couple times a week, I get a call to pick her up and take her to the grocery store. She just buys a couple items. I help her carry them into her apartment, maybe unload them for her in her kitchen, sometimes she asks me to stay for a cup of coffee. It's no big deal, really; I'm not even sure she knows my name. But I'm her guy. Whenever she calls for a taxi, I'm the guy that goes."

I wonder why. "Does she tip well?" I ask.

"Not really. Nothing special, anyway. But there's something about helping her that, I dunno, just makes me feel good. I guess I feel like I'm making a difference in somebody's life, like somebody needs me. I like to help out."

"There's your calling right there," I say.

"What?" The smirk returns. "Unloading groceries?"

"You said you like to help out. That's a pretty clear expression of calling."

A smile spreads across his face. "Well, I'll be damned. I guess that's right. Most of the time, I'm just a driver, but when I get that chance to help somebody—as long as they're not some kinda jerk or something—that's when I feel good about this job. So, whattayou know? I got a calling."

He is silent for the rest of the short trip. But I can see his face in the rear-view mirror and even when we hit the mid-town traffic, he's still smiling.

Each of us, no matter what we do, has a calling. Of course, some jobs fit more naturally with our calling, but every work situation provides us with some opportunities for fulfilling the urge to give our gifts away. Satisfaction on the job—and ultimately, in life—

will be due in part to how well we take advantage of those opportunities. What this requires, though, is that we *hear* our calling, that we learn what to listen for. We need to recognize, as the taxi driver did, what our calling really is. We need to identify our Calling Card.

Connecting Who You Are with What You Do

Calling is proactive. It seeks expression in the world.

Historically, calling has been about the ministry. Preachers, evangelists, missionaries, and clergypeople speak about being "called" to do God's work. "Calling" in this sense is deeply rooted in a theological tradition and excludes people who are not similarly motivated.

But there is a more inclusive sense of calling, a sense to be found in the word "vocation." Vocation comes from the Latin, *vocare,* meaning "to summon." We are referring to the inner urge, or summoning, we have to share our uniqueness with others. In this sense, everyone has a calling, not just those in the ministry. Each of us has something—or perhaps several things—that we are, it seems, quite literally called upon to give. We feel a strong pull in a certain direction and our lives seem incomplete unless that direction is pursued.

In this way, calling is *active*. It's a summons to play our part. Calling is a present moment notion; it is constantly alive, tugging on us during our entire lifetime.

Although calling runs through our whole lives, we are not called once for life. Responding to our call is something we do every day. Calling breaks down into daily choices. In responding, we ask ourselves again and again: "How can I consistently give my gifts away?"

We bring our calling to our work every single day, by expressing our gifts, passions, and values in a manner that is consistent with the legacy we want to leave.

People who have discovered their calling and choose to bring it to their work tend to be phenomenally energized about what they do. They have an almost childlike passion for their projects and a great sense of gratitude for their good fortune. They have answered the eternal question we face every day: "Why do I get up in the morning?" They have answered it by aligning who they are with what they do.

"It's for You"

Inside each of us right now is a call waiting to be answered. It has been with us throughout our lives. The call was placed the moment we were born; it has been ringing in the background every day we have lived.

Taking that call—hearing and heeding our calling—is not the easiest path through life, but it is a path filled with joy. It is a path of joy quite different from the traditional conception of jobs and careers most of us grew up with. If we are going to find joy in our work, we will do so by approaching our work as a calling. And if we feel no such joy, it's clear that we have yet to make that approach.

Many people discover a sense of calling in fairly dramatic ways: through sensing an inner voice, in a vision, from a dream, as a result of a near-death experience, from a shamanic journey, or in meditative insight. For others, the call comes more subtly: through an inner knowing, a sense of inner peace, a realization that "it fits," or an overall perception of "rightness." Sometimes calling is revealed by a process of elimination, through the turn-offs and dead-ends of life. In some instances, a teacher's influence is central; sometimes it's a book or a lecture or the example of others. Many people report gaining insight about their calling through religious revelation or while traveling to new places. In many instances, our calling comes once we are removed from everyday routine—when we have the opportunity to listen to what authentically moves us inside.

All callings are, ultimately, spiritual in nature. Each one of us has unique potential—distinct, God-given gifts—with which to serve the world. These gifts provide us with a source of identity in the world. But until we connect who we are with what we do, that source remains untapped.

Some people are lucky enough to hear their calling easily and to find work that allows them to express it fully. But what about the rest of us who listen for our calling but don't hear a thing? Or hear conflicting things? What if I'm in a job that pays well, but brings me little joy? Or a job that pays poorly and provides a sense of fulfill-ment? What good is a calling if I'm trapped in a dead-end job?

All of us go through periods when our work feels dead and life-less. All of us have dreamed of winning the lottery and never having to work again. Similarly, most of us have also had some opportuni-ties to feel the joy that follows from doing work that is an expres-sion of our deepest nature. Yet when it comes to heeding our calling, most of us have the cards stacked against us. Naming our calling—and more importantly, getting *paid* for living it—seems as unlikely as winning the lottery.

Nevertheless, right here, right now, there are ways to bring your calling to your work. The challenge is to find or create aspects of your work that express your calling—even if the work as a whole leaves something to be desired.

Should I Quit My Day Job?

Discovering our calling doesn't mean that we should immediately quit our day jobs. It does, however, require us to work the process of connecting who we are with what we do.

Ultimately, the realization of our calling can occur anywhere. No special circumstances are necessary; what matters is a willingness to recognize the call when it occurs, even if our intu-ition seems to be guiding us in an unexpected direction.

Heeding our life's calling means thriving, not just surviving. It means that we refuse to accept less than full employment of our God-given talents. It means not settling for a relationship with our work that lacks passion.

It means asking, "How do I find my life's work?"

The moment we start asking this question and exert the energy to answer it, we make a commitment to the expression of our birthright gifts. We begin to clarify our calling when we sincerely ask:

- What gift do I naturally give to others?

- What gift do I most enjoy giving to others?

• What gift have I most often given to others?

The Calling Cards exercise described later in this chapter is a systematic way to go about developing your own answers to these questions. It is designed to prompt you to detect the theme of your life's work. Using the cards provides you with a framework to name your own personal Calling Card—that precious gift within you seeking expression in the world.

You can read through the Calling Cards casually for some insight into the concept of calling and how it applies to you. Or, you can make a serious commitment to working the Calling Cards process in the hope of having a breakthrough experience and seeing how far you can take it. This will require more than just a casual read, though. It will take serious self-study and input from others.

We believe it's worth it, however. And we're not alone. Many people have found the Calling Cards extremely liberating in overcoming blocks to the expression of their natural gifts. Using the Calling Cards has helped them trust their intuitions, take risks, and bring forth inner wisdom in the ongoing quest for meaning and fulfillment in their work.

Labor of Love

A calling is not something you do to impress other people or to get rich quick. It's a labor of love that is intrinsically satisfying. It's something you would happily do even if it never makes you rich or famous. Of course, there's nothing wrong with making money or being widely acclaimed. But we should also recognize that there are other ways to pursue a calling: helping others, learning, promoting change, or dedicating oneself to an art form.

No one more clearly exemplifies a life lived in accordance with calling than Arne Anderson, now 83, a physician from Scandia, Minnesota. Arne's calling reminds us of the possibility of pursuing a stewardship orientation to life, of shifting our commitment from personal success to serving others. Looking back upon his life, we see how Arne's calling has continually been a labor of love in the form of service to others.

| Arne Anderson
Physician | | *Seeing*
Possibilities |

Born into a first-generation Norwegian immigrant family, Arne had the importance of a good education drilled into him from the earliest age. But he had a hard time staying focused on what was happening in the classroom. "School was easy for me," he says. "I had a very curious mind. I was always seeing possibilities in everything." And seeing possibilities became his life's work.

After finishing college, Arne went straight to work in his father's company, E.B. Crabtree. He was a natural promoter of Crabtree's line of cigars, candies, and gift items. In just a few months, Arne knew every corner store and bar in Minneapolis and his father wanted him to take over the company. "I had little doubt about my capacity to earn money," he recalls, "but I wanted to do something that was of service not measured by money."

On a drive between customers late one evening, Arne had a revelation: "I could become a doctor." And the rest, as they say, is history. After passing all the pre-med requirements in nine months' time, Arne enrolled in medical school. "The first year was like going to heaven!" he says. "I couldn't get enough of medicine. I loved it!"

During his residency in San Diego, seeing many children in dire need of medical care, Arne decided to specialize in pediatrics. He was called, as a physician, to provide care to children. After a stint in the Army, where he served as Chief of Pediatrics at U.S. Army Headquarters in Frankfurt, Germany, Arne came to the Mayo Clinic. One of the big draws to that institution was the Rochester Child Health Institute and the breakthrough thinking of Dr. Benjamin Spock and his colleagues. "It was the finest faculty of child development experts in the world," recalls Arne.

Not everyone finds a calling during his or her lifetime; even those who do usually pass through significant periods of seeking before achieving clarity about the central work of their lives. Arne and his wife Rusk were genuine seekers. They partnered the whole way. "Arne has a gift of seeing the potential in people and things," says

Rusk. "And he was always willing to put his body where his mouth was."

After founding the innovative Park Nicollet Clinic, Arne went on to help found Children's Hospital in Minneapolis. As President and CEO of both organizations, he had a unique leadership style. He believed that to be a leader among physicians one had to be competent in both disciplines—leadership and medicine. So, he kept a half-time practice in pediatrics, despite his grueling schedule of meetings and fund-raising.

Always "seeing possibilities," Arne pioneered the concept of human ecology. He recognized how children were affected emotionally when they were ill and hospitalized. "We changed the hospital experience completely," he says, "from a trauma experience to a growth experience."

When he was 60, Arne decided to "retire." This meant keeping his half-time practice and retaining his role as Medical Director at Children's. It also meant expanding his opportunities to care for a wider constituency of children.

With the encouragement of colleagues and children, Arne and Rusk traveled to Togo on a six-month medical mission. Together, they saw new opportunities to be of service to humanity. After creating the Minnesota International Health Volunteers, they embarked on medical missions to Thailand, India, Laos, and Africa. As a team, Rusk and Arne were able to effect a cut in infant mortality rates and to expand the resettlement options in a camp of 35,000 refugees.

Arne says, "I wasn't doing these things out of choice. I was always called by the situations themselves. They chose me. We were just seekers."

Early in their careers, Rusk and Arne went to a Quaker Friends meeting and discovered what was, for them, a very practical means of living with their Christian ethics. Friends define themselves as seekers of truth. Arne and Rusk had difficulty accepting spiritual absolutes, but they fully understood the value of seeking. They also believed that life is all one piece, that the life of the spirit should find expression in all of one's relationships: at work, at home, and at play. Everyday pursuits could be just as surely a form of worship as

Sunday morning services. For Rusk and Arne, the whole of life is sacramental; it is all an expression of calling.

Calling Cards

Arne Anderson illustrates how our callings are made manifest in our choices and through the serendipitous events that take place in our lives. Unless we bring our calling to light, though, it remains hidden from the world. As Arne put it, "If I died, they couldn't find my calling in the autopsy." Our calling is invisible except in action.

Discovering that calling, though, can be made easier through the use of the Calling Cards—a list of natural preferences that have emerged in our discussions and research with hundreds of people over the last few decades. Each of the callings describes a core gift. Each calling comes directly from someone's experience. We have been collecting callings in seminars, workshops, and coaching sessions with individuals and groups from all walks of life. The list of 52 callings we have come up with represents the "essence of essences" in our research. (This doesn't mean that there are not callings other than our 52; it does, however, mean that these 52 represent those that have best withstood real-world testing.)

Using the Calling Cards in a simple self-examination helps us name our calling—that gift which is invisible but wants to be unwrapped and given away.

The lives we live emerge from the words we choose to define our lives. So, as you examine the Calling Cards, listen carefully to what you're telling yourself. To find joy in our work, we need a clear, simple way to name our calling. We need to reframe our concept of calling until the words feel natural and come to us easily. We must settle for nothing less than a description of calling that fits us and no one else exactly the same way. No one can choose our calling for us; no one else can tell us how to express our calling once it is found. Each of us, individually, must hear and heed our role in the world. Each of us must choose or create the Calling Card that expresses the gifts we feel an inner urge to give away.

So . . . go within. Examine the Calling Cards. Explore the possibilities of calling. Name your calling.

List of Calling Cards

REALISTIC

Building Things
Fixing Things
Growing Things
Making Things Work
Shaping Environments
Solving Problems

CONVENTIONAL

Doing the Numbers
Getting Things Right
Operating Things
Organizing Things
Processing Things
Straightening Things Up

INVESTIGATIVE

Advancing Ideas
Analyzing Information
Discovering Resources
Investigating Things
Getting to the Heart
   of Matters
Making Connections
Putting the Pieces Together
Researching Things
Translating Things

ENTERPRISING

Bringing Out Potential
Empowering Others
Exploring the Way
Making Deals
Managing Things
Opening Doors
Persuading People
Selling Intangibles
Starting Things

SOCIAL

Awakening Spirit
Bringing Joy
Building Relationships
Creating Dialogue
Creating Trust
Facilitating Change
Getting Participation
Giving Care
Healing Wounds
Helping Overcome Obstacles
Instructing People
Resolving Disputes

ARTISTIC

Adding Humor
Breaking Molds
Creating Things
Composing Themes
Designing Things
Moving Through Space
Performing Events
Seeing Possibilities
Seeing the Big Picture
Writing Things

Calling Cards Instructions

Step 1:   Your Natural Preferences

Examine the entire list of 52 callings. As you study them, arrange the callings in three groups according to your natural preferences.

Group 1: Those that fit your gifts and talents.

Group 2: Not sure if they apply to you or not.

Group 3: Those that don't feel like you at all.

Don't rush. Use your intuition. What does your hand turn to naturally? What calls to you? Continue to look through the first two groups to identify those callings that fit you best.

Ask yourself: What gift do I naturally give to others?

Step 2:   Your Five Most Natural Preferences

Concentrate on the Group 1 callings. Explore them more carefully. Which ones seem to be the "best of the best?" Without thinking too much about it, identify the ones that seem to call to you automatically. Select the top five callings from this group—those that best describe what you naturally enjoy doing.

Ask yourself: What gift do I most enjoy giving to others?

Step 3:   Your Single Most Natural Preference

Consider the five callings you have selected. Knowing yourself as you do, which one card seems to "call to you"; which is the one that, throughout your life, you have most consistently given to others? If you were forced to pick just one, which one would it be?

Ask yourself: What gift have I most often given to others?

An alternative way to arrive at Your Single Most Natural Preference is to work through the callings, pairing them two-by-two, and choosing which of the pair you think more accurately reflects your calling. This works especially well with a partner.

> Set the callings down between you and your partner. Have your partner name the first two callings. Quickly—within 3 seconds or so—choose which is a better expression of your calling. Put the "winner" in one group, set the "loser" aside. (If you honestly can't decide—that is, if they're both "winners," put them both in the "winning" group. If neither seems appropriate for you at all, discard them both.)

> Having gone through the callings once, you will have a group of 26 winners. Repeat the process from above, going through all 26. Now you will have 13 winners. Repeat the process with this group. You'll have 6 winners. Then 3. Then 1. This final "winning" card is your Calling Card.

Step 4:   Your Calling Card

> Study your number one card. If the words do not fit exactly, feel free to edit so your own calling describes you accurately. You may find it useful to use words from your top five callings to perfectly describe your single calling.

Step 5:   Make a Call

> Discuss your Calling Card with a close friend or family member. See if others have insight into your calling that can help you refine it further.

Step 6:   Imagine a Call

> Imagine that you could do any kind of work in the world, anything at all—*as long as it fits your Calling Card.* Jot down three or four things you can see yourself doing. What does this list tell you about your calling?

Step 7:   Heed the Call

Perhaps you're thinking: "This Calling Card looks great. But it's not my job! Moreover, I don't have the financial resources or personal freedom to do the work I love the most. How do I heed the call when I first have to heed my bills, my boss, and my family?" If you're asking questions like that, ask yourself these questions instead:

- Does your work give you a small opportunity—like the taxi driver at the beginning of this chapter—to express your calling? Does it ever let you do what you most enjoy doing?

- While you're working, do you ever get the sense that you're in the right place doing the right thing? How often does it happen? When it happens, what are you doing?

- What's one thing—a little thing—you could do right now to express your calling at work? What's stopping you?

Get Into It!

Having chosen our Calling Card, we are faced with the unavoidable choice of whether to heed it. Either we do or we don't—and the time to decide has arrived. Since it *is* unavoidable, however, we may do well to recall the words of Derek Pritchard: "If you can't get out of it, get into it!"

Any kind of work can provide us with opportunities for expressing our calling if only we "get into it." Calling isn't our job, it's what we *bring to* our job. The core idea of calling is a simple and liberating truth: "It's not what you do that matters, it's how you do it."

In order to understand this aspect of calling more fully, it's helpful to ask yourself two questions. The first is *"What do you do?"* What kind of work are you currently performing? How consistent is it with your stated calling? Should you stay or leave your current job? The second question is *"How do you do it?"* What part of your job fulfills your sense of calling? How can you give away your gifts even if you're in a job that isn't exactly what you want to be doing? How can you express your calling, even if it's only partially?

Elements of our calling can be expressed in almost any job. When we begin to see what we do as an opportunity for heeding our calling, nothing changes—but everything changes. We still have our cab to drive, our patients to care for, our clients to serve. We still have our up days and down days, empowering colleagues and irritating colleagues, interesting projects and boring projects. We still have days when it's hard to get out of bed in the morning. Nothing seems to have changed.

But on the other hand, everything has changed. By expressing our calling, even in small, partial ways, our work is suddenly more fulfilling. We find meaning in what we do, even when it's not exactly what we were meant to be doing. On occasion, throughout the work day, we feel that we're in the right place, with the right people, doing the right work, on purpose.

When this happens, even for an instant, we experience who we are and what we do as one. We experience the power of heeding our calling, the feeling of aliveness which comes from giving our gifts away to someone who needs them, in order to create something that wouldn't have existed without us. It's the joyful feeling that we strive to make common in heeding our calling: the feeling of whistling while we work!

Your Calling Journal

From time immemorial, reflective observers—writers, artists, travelers—have kept journals to put their thoughts about life into written form. A Calling Journal is a place to put our thoughts about calling into words. It's a personal place to listen, sort through our feelings, analyze our yearnings, and get ideas for connecting who we are with what we want to do. In our Calling Journal, we can give our thoughts free rein, free from the influence and advice of others.

A Calling Journal is a place to connect with ourselves and what's really important in our lives. When we record the details of our yearnings, we are more likely to connect at a deeper level with the Source of our calling. Keeping track of our dreams, ideas, and insights can give us the extra push we need to heed our calling. Christina Baldwin, a well known author of books on journaling, writes in *Life's Companion: Journal Writing As a Spiritual Quest* that a journal is "an intermittent recorder of the inner life, written consistently, but not necessarily on a daily basis." Consistently keeping a Calling Journal keeps us in touch with our calling and connected to our inner life.

Day One

Starting today, you can take a significant step toward heeding your life's calling. And you don't have to quit your job, move to another city, or even tell your boss what you really think of him or her. You simply have to start writing.

Make today Day One of heeding your calling. Get a blank journal book and keep it near your bed. Every morning, jot down a few sentences about how you might express or expand your calling in the day ahead. A line or two is enough. Don't turn the exercise into a huge and daunting task that you can't fulfill. Just take a change and put a few thoughts on paper. Trust the process and see what happens. If you need a push, ask yourself these questions:

- How am I going to express my Calling Card today?

- What will put a whistle in my work today?

Attend to your Calling Journal for a month. Go back at the end of each week and look at what you've written. At the end of the month, reread the entire journal. Do any of your thoughts call to you about work? Do your writings provide you with any new ways of putting a whistle in your work?

If this process proves worthwhile, continue to do it for another month. And then, another. The Calling Journal gives substance and permanence to the Calling Card exercise. Heeding our calling means being aware, listening and living one day at a time. Rather than trying to get it perfect the very first time, do something every day to attend to your calling.

Consider the following three principles of effective journaling.

Keep It Simple

Dick is on the board of directors of Graywolf Publishers, a small, values-driven publisher of poetry and literature. Board meetings often begin with a reading from a Graywolf author's work. One of the favorites is the poet William Stafford. Stafford had the habit of writing a poem each day before breakfast. When asked how anyone could accomplish such a feat, he replied, "Simple. Lower your expectations."

Journaling is all about lowering one's expectations; in fact, it's about having no expectations at all. The journal page is your page. Write for yourself. The page is intended for your eyes only. Don't worry about spelling or grammar. Write from your heart, not from your head. Free yourself to express whatever you feel about your calling—honestly and simply.

Keep It Short

How can we be expected to take even more time from life's hectic schedule to write in a journal? Don't we already have too much to do? And even if we can, how can we possibly find time to reflect on what we've written? Most of us don't even have time to reflect on what we want for dinner, much less what we want for our lives.

The most common excuse people give for not attending to their calling is lack of time. But the reality is that if a task is important and satisfying to us, we can make time.

You can record your daily thoughts about calling in no more than five minutes. Just one less press of the snooze button on your alarm clock. Is five minutes of dozing worth more than a lifetime of work satisfaction? Try it for a month. You decide.

Keep It Going

The easier ideas come, the more likely we are to make journaling a habit. Try to stick with the two questions for comparison on different days. The great value in journaling is the path it leaves. Each day, by itself, appears as an isolated footprint on the page. But as the days add up, they form a path that not only shows where we've been but also points to where we are headed. The path shows us how we arrived where we are and shows us where we can go if we're lost. Over time, we start to see the consistent pathway of our calling; our Calling Card points the way.

Recall the definition of calling: "an inner urge to give your gifts away." As your reflect upon the path you've left in your Calling Journal, ask yourself whether this definition rings true. Does it clarify ways to help you whistle while you work?

Your New Calling Card: Who You Are *and* What You Do

From the early part of the nineteenth century, people trying to be accepted into "society" commonly carried cards—much like today's business cards—but engraved only with their names. The practice of carrying and sharing calling cards evolved from people who wanted to claim members of the elite as their friends, people who wanted to be part of the social world of those who *were* the social world.

Calling cards also served as a discreet way to keep these social aspirants forever at distance, or at least, to hold them off for a while so as to screen those who would be seen from those who would not. Accordingly, in the Victorian world, with its complex social etiquette and mores, calling cards flourished.

In that era of formality and high manners, the exchange of calling cards was *de rigeur* socially, and played an essential role in developing friendships. It was customary to drop one's card at the homes of new neighbors, and to leave one for the hosts of balls, private recitals, and dinners on the day after the events. Leaving cards for one another was as meaningful as personal visits between acquaintances.

The origin of the practice can be traced to eighteenth-century France. By the end of the eighteenth century, the practice had spread throughout Europe and was popular in America. Handmade cards were inscribed with the bearer's name, a greeting, and a spot of ornamentation. More elaborate cards were embellished with the romantic detailing of hand painted vines, flowers, and fruits, or collaged with paper lace. By the mid-nineteenth century, printers were offering cards designed to order.

The protocol for leaving cards became as elaborate as the cards themselves. When you came to town, you presented yourself at the homes of those you wished to notify of your arrival. At each home, you sent in your card so that the master or lady of the house could decide to see you or not. If he or she was not home, you left your card to signal that you had come calling.

Eventually complex rituals arose, in which people often called at homes not to visit, but simply to leave a card. Subtle messages were communicated depending on which corners of the card were turned down. If the top left corner was folded down, it meant the caller came in person; an unfolded card meant a servant was sent. A folded top-right corner sent congratulations; the lower-right fold meant sympathy. If the lower left of a card was folded, it meant that the visitor was leaving town on a journey of more than a few months' duration. A card left for a particular person was folded in half diagonally, but if the visitor had wished to see the entire family, the card was folded in half like a book. Upon leaving town, you sent a card with "PPC" written on it, short for *pour prendre congé,* meaning "I'm leaving." If you were really new in town, you might avoid the whole process—or begin it—by getting a letter of introduction from a friend to someone of prominence in the community. This letter was referred to as a "ticket for soup," since it required, as a typical minimum, that the person receiving the letter invite the holder of the letter to dinner.

Women had their own calling cards without their husbands' names. Men, however, did not receive cards from a woman unless she was willing to risk earning a dubious reputation. Socially conscious individuals abided strictly to the rule that no lady ever called on a gentleman except for business or professional matters. To do otherwise, as a nineteenth-century etiquette book put it, "would be not only a breach of good manners, but of strict propriety."

Clearly, calling cards have come a long way since the nineteenth century. Their contemporary cousins, business cards, are used by men and women in all walks of life. Everyone in the world, it seems, leaves cards.

But even today, most people's cards only give the scantiest picture of them. Generally, they provide the person's title; at most, this provides information about *what they do.*

Your Calling Card, the one you've chosen through the calling cards process, however, provides insight into *who you are.* This, we think, is the next step in the advancement of calling card protocol.

Imagine that your calling is printed on the back of your business card. The front side, as usual, displays the company you work for and your title—what you do. But the back displays your Calling Card—who you are. In this way, your business card now communicates *both* your form and your essence. Your title is the form of your work—it's what you do. Your calling is the essence of your work—it's who you are.

If you were to change jobs, the front of your business card would change; you'd get a new title. But the back of your card—your essence—would remain the same. Your calling is something you bring to your work; it stays with you wherever you go.

Did You Choose Your Work or Did Your Work Choose You?

Very few people have always known what they wanted to be. Sure, you hear stories about artists or writers who, upon first picking up a paintbrush or pen, never looked back. Picasso, for instance, began drawing seriously at age 10 and was already exhibiting his work in galleries by the time he was 13. For most of us, though, the realization of what we were meant to do is quite elusive. Few young people stop to think about what their life's work is—and even among those who do, they usually don't think that they can make a living at it.

So most of us essentially drift into our occupations. Our lives unfold in a certain manner, and as they do, we make choices from among the options presented to us. There's nothing wrong with this, and some of us are lucky enough to fall into the perfect thing via this process, but it's pretty obvious that this is not the best way to hear and heed our life's calling.

And it's also obvious that many of us *fail* to discover our calling in this haphazard way. And when we do, we find ourselves at some point in our lives—usually around mid-life—asking ourselves the *big* questions. Questions like: "Who am I?" "What was I really meant to do?" "What would truly make me happy?"

That sense of being disconnected from our authentic self is pervasive. It's why so many people feel so lost. Sidetracked. Stuck. We wonder if we can possibly change course and find our way back to the person we really are.

How do we choose a life that expresses our calling?

The answer lies in a exploration of three essential qualities that go into the formation of our Calling Card: gifts, passions, and values. A good job, career, or life and work decision blends together all three.

Gifts

Our *gifts* are those special aptitudes that we were born with. They're the force behind those things we enjoy and do well—those that we never needed to learn. Our gifts are God-given, but we naturally feel compelled to give them away; we simply want to *give back* through them. Expressing our gifts is what we do naturally, effortlessly, and without regard for what we might receive in return. Gifts are deeper aptitudes than talents. Take, for example, a phenomenally gifted businessperson like Steve Jobs of Apple. His special ability would seem to be inspiring people to organize themselves around a vision for the future. Many individual skills and talents go into this; he's obviously an excellent speaker, motivator, product designer, and so on. But his gift, and the gift of others who are similarly successful in galvanizing support for visionary efforts, is greater than the sum of these parts.

When we explore our own gifts, therefore, we want to think in deep terms. We want to look beneath our talents to what motivates them. We want to explore what we are consistently and enjoyably giving to others.

There is a natural connection between our gifts and the most satisfying aspects of our jobs. So, one way to get at the nature of our gifts is to ask ourselves the following question: *What "work" was I doing the last time I was so absorbed that I lost all track of time?*

Spend a few moments writing your answer in your Calling Journal.

When we're expressing our gifts, we tend to get into what Mihaly Csikszentmihalyi, in his book, *Flow: The Psychology of Optimal Experience,* calls a state of "flow." We become deeply involved in what we're doing, so much so that the clock seems to melt away. Time becomes irrelevant. An hour, even an entire day can go by in a single instant. We are so absorbed in the moment that the moments fly by.

Think about the last time you experienced this sense of flow. What were you doing? More importantly, *what was it about* what you were doing that made it so satisfying? You might, for instance, have been making a presentation to team members or clients. *What was it about* presenting that turned you on? Communicating? Motivating? Selling? Look behind the presentation itself to discover what your gifts are. And then notice that expressing these gifts forms a common thread in the activities that really move you—your Calling Card.

It's also quite illuminating to wonder how your natural gifts were or were not encouraged. If we were lucky, our parents, schoolteachers, and colleagues nurtured our gifts. Many people, though, have had to fight to express their gifts—and, for many, the struggle has proven too much. Rather than find ways to make their gifts come alive, they have chosen to let their natural abilities lie dormant. While this is quite practical, it's deeply unfortunate. Our gifts continually *seek* expression; a life lived without allowing our gifts to flourish is a life less than fully lived.

It's never too late, though, to uncover and revitalize our gifts. And by working with our Calling Card to do so, we can begin to put a whistle in our work.

Passions

What issues or causes really move you? What problems in the world or work world do you think need solving? When you lie awake at night obsessing over the state of the universe, what obsesses you most? In the answers to questions like these we discover our passions. Our passions are the issues we care most deeply about. When we connect our gifts to our passions, we have a clear reason to get up in the morning.

Passions can take many forms. They can be quite specific: you may be passionate, for instance, about bicycles. You may feel that the bicycle represents the savior of humanity and spend a good deal of your free time working on bicycle-related causes. Passions may also be rather broad: you may be passionate, for instance, about spirituality. You may feel deeply committed to expanding people's spiritual awareness around the world. You may spend your free time working against oppression and injustice wherever it is found. Passions may be somewhere in the middle, too: you may be passionate, for instance, about community. You may spend your free time working to strengthen the connections between people in your neighborhood or town. You may be drawn to any number of organizations or activities that share this driving passion of yours.

What's important to realize about passions is that they are only passions if they are "alive." That is, they only count as passions if we feel them deeply. This doesn't mean we have to evangelize whenever their subject comes up; it does mean, however, that we have to feel strongly about them and have an inclination—realized or not— to act in their support. It doesn't make sense to say, "Oh, one of my passions is the environment, but I don't feel any desire to do anything about it." Our passions have to move us or they're not really passions. Moreover, they must ignite us consistently; passions run as an undercurrent throughout our lives.

So, to get a better sense of your own passions, ask yourself:

What do I think is worth doing in the world? What do I obsess about? What problems do I think need solving? What am I constantly reading about and talking to people about?

Spend a few moments writing your answers in your Calling Journal.

The common themes that emerge from this inquiry will give you a better sense of what your passions really are.

Values

What are the underlying impulses behind the choices you make? What working environments fit for you best? What consistent behaviors form the foundation of your character?

Answers to these questions point you in the direction of your values. Values are the expression of our deepest concerns. They're the fire that ignites our passions. As such, they determine how committed we'll be to particular causes or outcomes and in what environments we're likely to be most successful and fulfilled. When we're involved in projects and working environments that are consistent with our core values, we feel energized and enthusiastic about what we're doing—and our energy and enthusiasm is infectious.

It's important to keep in mind that values are active; valuing is something we *do*. If one of your values is, say, nature, then that means you actively care about the natural world. This care consistently colors everything you do. Values are only values *because* they are acted upon. If we stop acting on something, then it no longer counts as a value. If you're not concerned about what happens to the planet, if you don't feel an interest in protecting ecosystems and habitats, then it's inaccurate to say that you value nature.

Our values are expressed through the work we do and the manner in which we do it. Notice again the *active* aspect of values.

What's important to keep in mind about values is that they—more than any of the other components of calling—expose our individuality. Our values reflect the characteristic way we express ourselves; consequently, two people may have very similar gifts and passions but still have quite different values.

Legacy

"What did I give to the world?" "How will I be remembered?" "Did I live a good life?"

The answers to questions like these reveal our legacy—our "leave behind," our footprint, the picture that remains of us after we're gone. When we explore our legacy we ask, "What do we want our lives to have been about?"

When older adults look back upon their own lives, they consistently express a hope that their existence has made a difference. Most are not terrorized by the prospect of dying; rather, their greatest fear is of having lived a meaningless life. We all want to have made some "small dent" in the world. The prospect that no one will remember us after we're gone, or worse, that no one will even notice we're gone, is devastating.

Our legacy emerges from a life lived in a manner consistent with our calling. When we have given our gifts away in service to something we are passionate about in an environment that supports our values, we leave a legacy that is meaningful and makes a positive difference to us and our loved ones over time.

To explore your thinking about legacy more fully, ask yourself:

Isn't there something larger than my own life that I'm concerned about? Don't I want to feel that my life has made a difference somehow? When I reflect on my accomplishments as a human being, wouldn't I like to say that I have affected the world—even a small part of it—in some positive way?

Spend a few moments writing your answers in your Calling Journal.

Oliver Wendell Holmes said, "Most people go to their graves with their music still inside them." This is a crying shame; every one of us has a song to sing, a melody to contribute to the world's symphony. That anyone should miss the opportunity to contribute his or her unique voice is heartbreaking; that so many do miss it is nothing short of tragic.

Why then, do so many people die with their songs unsung? The reasons are many—lack of time, lack of resources, lack of confidence all contribute to the collective silence. Unexpected responsibilities, illnesses, or changes in family situations cause many people to remain mute. But the most common reason that people go to their graves with their music still inside them is that they never really come to know what their music is. They remain unclear, in other words, about their calling. Thus, they may, in fact, be whistling—loud and hard—but the tune they're following isn't their authentic melody at all.

In the movie *Mr. Holland's Opus,* Richard Dreyfus plays Glen Holland, a high school music teacher who begins his career thinking of it as nothing more than a way to make money while he works on his "real work," composing. As the film follows him through some 30 years of teaching, we come to realize—and more importantly, Mr. Holland comes to realize—that his true opus is the contribution he makes to his students' lives. His song is not so much to be a composer of music as to be a composer of dreams. Although it takes him many years to understand this, the revelation, when it does come, is a source of deep satisfaction and pride.

To discover our own music and then, eventually, to whistle it requires some of the discipline required to play any song proficiently. We have to acquaint ourselves with our own internal score and practice diligently. We have to explore new themes and modes of expression on a regular basis. And we have to be willing to make the sometimes less than perfectly harmonious sounds that are produced by the instruments of beginning musicians.

What is your "music" to play? Are you playing it or is still inside? How can you let it out more consistently? How can you whistle your own tune?

Spend a few moments answering these questions in your Calling Journal.

Understanding of our calling—the blending of our gifts, passions, and values—is heightened by focusing on these three qualities in greater depth. Our Calling Card helps us envision where our lives are headed; exploring our gifts, passions, and values helps us guide ourselves forward in a manner that will be as natural and fulfilling as possible.

In the chapters that follow, then, we undertake that exploration, beginning first with gifts.

Chapter 3

gifts—is my job my calling?

"This Is What I Do"

I'm coming back from my longtime friend's fiftieth birthday party, so I'm feeling no pain as my taxi snakes through the streets back to my hotel. My driver, though, isn't doing so well. He's describing to me the difficulties he faces, as a first-generation American, in raising his second-generation teenage son.

"Yesterday, I come back home at 2:00 in the morning and his mother tells me that he hasn't said his prayers before bed. So what do I do? I have to wake him up and stand over him while he says them." He looks up and catches my eyes in the rearview mirror. "And this is not the first time, you know?"

I murmur something about the difficulties of child-rearing, no matter what one's situation is.

"He is a good boy," continues my driver. "But he has no appreciation for our traditions."

"I'm sure all parents, in all ages and places, have had that same complaint," I say, trying to keep the discussion less personal.

But my driver wants to get into it. "It is not the same as now, though. Now it is more important than ever that the young do not stray."

"Why is that?" I wonder aloud.

"The world is a more difficult place than ever before. There are temp-tations and dangers that we did not face, that our fathers did not face."

"You are worried for your son," I say. "You're afraid that if he doesn't follow the traditions you did, he will be hurt or something."

"That is it, exactly," says my driver. He has pulled over to the curb by my hotel; I haven't even noticed. He drapes his arm over the front seat and swivels around to look at me directly. "So you think I did the right thing?"

"You mean about the prayers?"

"Yes. Should I have awakened him and forced him to recite them?"

I think of all the things people regularly do for their children's "own good"—things the kids hate at the time but come to appreciate years later. "Did your son know why you made him do it?" I ask.

"He knows that I love him if that is what you mean."

My taxi driver's eyes look very tired, but at the same time, very kind and compassionate. "Then how could you have done anything wrong?" I ask.

"Thank you," he replies. "Thank you very much."

I thank him and reach for my wallet to pay the fare.

"No. No charge," he says.

"You're kidding." I try again to pay.

"I insist." He is adamant. "We have talked. You have helped me. That's enough."

"Yes, but—"

"No," he says, opening my door from the inside. "This is what I do. When I talk with someone like this—on my job—it is worth enough. This is what I do. Now go, my friend."

With a gentle nudge he urges me out the door. I find myself on the street and begin walking into my hotel. I turn around to look but the taxi—my friend—is already gone.

"This is what I do." My friend's words stick in my head. When we think about what we do, what is it that makes it worthwhile? What aspects of our work transcend the financial reward? If we were driving a taxi, when would we give away rides for free? In our own jobs, when and how do we freely give of ourselves? The answers to these questions draw us deeper into an exploration of gifts—that which our calling consistently urges us to give away. In this chapter, we'll continue that exploration and examine the relationship between our gifts and our work as we ask "Is My Job My Calling?"

Seeing Life as a Set of Possibilities

Bill Strickland		*Seeing*
Executive Director		*Possibilities*

If you were just going on appearances, you'd probably be surprised to discover that Bill Strickland is a true visionary. A plain-spoken middle-aged man with gentle eyes, he seems more like a high-school science teacher than someone who is absolutely serious about changing the world in his lifetime. But this would be just the first of many ways that Bill would surprise you. You'd also be surprised by his story: how an inner-city kid from one of Pittsburgh's worst neighborhoods found direction in his life through ceramic arts and ended up as Executive Director of two world-class organizations— the Bidwell Training Center and the Manchester Craftsmen's Guild (MCG)—which provide vocational, technical, and arts education to young people and adults from throughout Western Pennsylvania. You'd shake your head in wonder to find out he convinced the Carnegie Foundation to finance the construction of Bidwell's warm and welcoming campus building—designed by Frank Lloyd Wright's protégé, Tasso Katselas. And you'd be amazed to learn that Bill was the entrepreneurial driving force behind the creation of the MCG's state-of-the-art concert hall and recording studio, a venue that has attracted the world's top names in jazz music, including Dizzy Gillespie, Betty Carter, Herbie Hancock, McCoy Tyner, and many, many more. You'd have to conclude that Bill Strickland is a man who deals in surprises—surprises of the positive sort, surprises that not only open people's eyes but also their hearts.

And you'd be right.

Bill states his calling with pinpoint clarity: *seeing life as a set of possibilities, not as a set of limitations.* He believes that if you provide people with a range of human experiences, intelligently presented and administered properly, they'll change their lives. "Because they'll see themselves as contributors," he says. "As assets instead of liabilities."

Most of the students at Bidwell have been told at one time or another that they are liabilities. Bill's school gives them—often for the first time in their lives—the sense that they matter. That they're worthwhile. That they have a future. You walk into the building and you can sense this. There are some 400 students hard at work in a dozen classes. But the hallways are quiet. The building hums with focused activity. You peek into the classrooms—a state-of-the-art chemical laboratory, a fully equipped computer facility, one of the world's only culinary amphitheaters, a complete digital recording studio—and you see students paying rapt attention to instructors or working independently on projects of their own. The place is immaculate, with beautiful paintings and sculptures throughout, and an in-house art gallery showcasing the work of world-renowned artists. A bright atrium welcomes you as you enter; hallways spider out gracefully from this center space. A large dining area with impressive windows lies beyond; it resembles an executive conference center at a four-star resort. The food, prepared by gourmet chefs, completes the picture. You feel you are in a successful high-tech corporation, not a vocational school, and the sense of respect that permeates the environment translates into how students and teachers treat each other and themselves.

In overseeing Bidwell's design, Bill made these choices quite consciously. His ambition was to build a magnificent place in the inner city for people whose lives often aren't very pretty. "I wanted to build a building like this, to show people that it could be done anywhere. I built the whole school around that philosophy: a beautiful place with good food, lots of light, with people who care. To show that the experience I had was transferable to others. The ghetto is not the neighborhood," he says. "It's a state of mind."

Bill escaped that state of mind as an adolescent when he discovered ceramic arts under the guidance of his high school teacher, Frank Ross. "My life changed when I made a big old pot. The arts saved my life," he admits. "Before that, I didn't have a focus. And, as a black kid growing up in a neighborhood like I did, you've got three career choices without a focus: jail, drugs, or death. The arts gave me a bridge to walk across to a new life. They gave me a new relationship to myself and to the community. When I invested in the arts, I invested in life."

At the Manchester Craftsmen's Guild, Bill helps young people make that same investment every day. "My constituency is here," he says. "I've got the guys walking around with the shoes untied and the pants falling down to here. I've got white working-class kids here. Hispanic teens. Unemployed adults. They're all here. The representation of the world is in this building. And I made that a point before I got this far. I decided that people biologically are built the same. We have different complexions, but on the inside, we're alike. And we all respond universally to the same things. Whether it's a poor black kid or a poor white kid or a middle-class adult, they all need affection. And they all need good food. And they all need an aesthetic in their life. And the ability to feel like they're worth something."

Sometimes young people come to Bidwell or the Craftsmen's Guild having had that essential ability to feel that they're worth something driven out of them. That's when, Bill says, you have to revive it in them. "And that's what," he adds, "this place does as well or better than many I've seen around the country."

And Bill has seen a lot. He's constantly in demand from major corporations, social service agencies, and private foundations to consult with them about how they can re-create the success he has achieved. His theory, though, is really quite simple. "Things grow out of things," he says. "You put bright people together, give them enough to eat and a good building and the funding and then get out of the way—because that's where you'll get innovation. A lot of the things we do grow out of the learning and innovation that come from one set of experiences."

Bill's work and his calling are one. He knew he had made his decision to stay where he is some years ago when he turned down the opportunity to fly commercial jets. (He's an airline pilot, too—another one of those surprises.) Flying was something he wanted to do very much, but he decided not to go. He wanted to continue making his dream for Bidwell and the Guild a reality. It became obvious to him that the true expression of his calling was to be found on the ground, not in the air.

The truest gauge of someone's alignment with calling is the "one-year test." When we asked Bill what he would do if he found out he had just one year to live, he responded without hesitation. "I'd do the same thing I did before. I wouldn't change anything. I'd probably do more of it. But the thing would be the same. I'd get up and come to work here. And I'd be selling the same bill of goods I'm selling now. Which is all the stuff that I do. The clay. Photography. Music. Architecture. So nothing would change in that regard. I wouldn't say, 'Well, I've only got a year left, so I'd better stop and go on to what's really happening. This *is* what's happening."

And Bill is deeply committed to making it happen around the world. His vision for the future is to build at least a hundred centers like his in the U.S. and a similar number around the world—centers characterized by high-quality architecture, world-class facilities, world-class staff, world-class food, great music, lots of art, and lots of technology. Bill's plan is to build them right on the edge of the worst neighborhoods and start using the centers as a way to revital-ize those communities and the lives of the people in them. He says he has no intention of changing that vision and is absolutely confi-dent he has the know-how and connections to make it happen. When you realize this know-how grows out of his current success and that those connections include places like Harvard, Kellogg, IBM, Bayer, Starbucks, American Express and more, you begin to be-lieve. And you begin to understand the power of calling in one's work.

This powerful sense of calling resonates through Bill's life. He says he would like to be remembered as a guy who absolutely re-fused to see life as anything but hopeful and as a wealth of human possibilities. In spite of the difficulties life presents all of us, Bill says, "I believe that there is something very special and very precious and very transforming about engaging life in terms of dreams rather than nightmares." He sees his contribution as helping to let every-one know that they can do the kind of work he does—work that is life-affirming and positive and which gives back to community. "That's my contribution to enhancing life on the planet, which I believe is what your ultimate stewardship is. The ultimate way of thanking life for being what it is, is to help pass it on to the next group."

Obviously, Bill is passing on a lot. His initial dream for Bidwell/MCG has become a reality and has made dreams come alive for countless numbers of students as well as the community at large. And it all started with that initial sensation of calling, that sense Bill first had when art saved his life back in high school.

What about you? Do you have a sense of calling about your work? Do you believe you're doing what you were always meant to do? If you had a year to live, would you keep doing what you're doing? Would you give it away for free? Or are you called to something else entirely?

Fully Absorbed and Immersed

There's an exercise called "the egg-drop game" that you may have played in school or at work. Teams are given 10 drinking straws, some masking tape, and a raw egg; their challenge is to create a device—using only the straws and tape—that will enable the egg to be dropped from a height of 8 feet without breaking. It's a fascinating and, usually, quite fun activity. Participants really get into it and work hard on their designs. And it doesn't matter whether the teams are composed of sixth graders or corporate executives, the same thing happens: time flies. No matter how long teams are given to work on their projects, there are always a couple of groups who wish they had longer. What's interesting to see is how differently teams behave when they're making their egg-dropper and when they're not.

Students in Vicky Hutchings' sixth grade class at Whitman Middle School in Seattle, Washington are, like most sixth graders, notoriously squirrelly. Most of the time, they sit at their desks halfway paying attention to their teacher, whispering, writing notes, drawing pictures, and surreptitiously sneaking glances at comic books tucked inside the text they're supposed to be following. But when they're building their egg-droppers, they're all business. Each student is focused on the task at hand. They talk, but the conversations are about better ways to attach straws or more effective techniques to soften the impact on the egg. Discipline problems disappear; in fact, students tend to get annoyed if anyone acts disruptively. You pretty much have to tear them away from their projects when it's time to do the drop test. Some groups, given the freedom to do so, would spend all day designing and redesigning their egg-drop gizmo.

What is it about this activity that makes it so different than so much of what students do the rest of the time? Well, for one thing, it's not graded—and there's no homework. But more importantly, participants in the egg-drop game care about the process and the results. They want to do well, not because their teacher or parents say they should, but because *they want to*. Something about the activity compels them really to engage with it. For one thing, it's fun, and for another, it's hilarious to see a dozen eggs potentially smashed to smithereens in the classroom, but there's more to it than that. Students commit to the exercise because it gives them an opportunity to express themselves in any number of ways. Those with an engineering bent are drawn to the challenge of designing an effective safety device; those with a flair for the artistic like the chance to make something interesting looking; those who are more people-oriented appreciate the opportunity to work as a team. There's something in it for nearly everyone, something that appeals to something that's in every student: their calling—their inner urge to give their gifts away to something they're passionate about in an environment that fits their values.

The call to a particular way of work fulfills four essential needs. First, it fulfills the need to receive guidance from something larger than ourselves, a Caller. What's important is that we feel we are responding to a wisdom greater than our own. It is the experience of doing something that just "feels right," even if we don't know why. Second, being called fulfills our ongoing need to make a difference in the world. Bill Strickland felt this need powerfully at an early age; yet his call to work with young people in disadvantaged communities continued and continues to evolve in stages over his lifetime. Third, responding to calling fulfills our need to become as much as we can be. Whether we're conscious of it or not, we all have a strong desire to maximize our potential. Nothing satisfies this desire more fully than activities performed out of a sense of calling. Doing work that is consistent with our calling involves a conscious choice to be ourselves—to reveal to ourselves and the world our God-given nature. Finally, the call to a particular life's work fulfills our need to leave a legacy. Calling is a unifying story that brings together the social, individual, and sacred dimensions of our lives. It connects us to our communities, to ourselves, and to our own conception of life's spiritual center. As Bill Strickland's story illustrates, it connects us to all that really matters.

The question is: how can we experience a similar sense of connection to our projects on the job? And, perhaps more importantly, how will we feel when we do?

What Does It Feel Like from the Inside?

Anyone who has ever attended high school or waited in line at the Department of Motor Vehicles knows how time can slow to a crawl. And anyone who has ever taken a tropical vacation or enjoyed a stimulating conversation with a new friend knows how time can race by in a flash. What's ironic is that when we want time to go quickly—when we're praying for the staff meeting to end, for instance—it drags ever slower; and when we wish it would slow down—so we could savor a few more minutes before the alarm goes off, for example—that's when it gallops ahead most rapidly.

If you've ever had a job on which you watched the clock, you know what this is like. Dave remembers an office job he had in his early twenties. "It was interminable. My job, for days on end, was to alphabetize filled orders using one of those long plastic divider strips. I constantly had to pinch myself and stick fingers in my eyes to keep from falling asleep. Lots of times it wasn't enough; I would nod off at my desk at least two or three times a day. One of my co-workers, a woman in her 70s, used to poke me with a pencil and ask me if I was getting enough sleep. I assured her I was—but what I didn't say was that my job was just so boring that I couldn't stay awake.

"When 5:00 finally sounded, though, I was up and out the door in a heartbeat. You've seen those signs: 'If you don't believe the dead can come to life, you should see this place at quittin' time.' I was the complete embodiment of that attitude. My boss once met me for a drink after work; she couldn't believe I was the same person. 'What's in that drink?' she kept asking. 'How come you're so lively?'

"Thinking back on those days, I can't believe I was the same person, either. But mostly, I can't believe I put up with living that way as long as I did. I spent four months at that job, feeling awful the whole time. That's four months of my life completely wasted. And given how time moved, it was more like four years."

Compare that experience—which is probably familiar to most of us—to Dave's experience a few years later on a job that suited him much better.

"I was senior writer for a corporate training company that was developing some of the first computerized interactive multimedia training programs. The people I worked with were all deeply committed to the success of the enterprise; we quite literally believed we were inventing the future of learning.

"My task was to design and write scripts for the programs we were creating. But because there were so many production elements to keep track of, this also meant I was responsible for coming up with a whole new way of writing scripts. Consequently, I was challenged not only to design and write compelling videoscripts, but I also had to explore emerging technologies for creating them.

"The job drew upon my interests in writing, education, technology, community, and more. I felt completely connected to the work I was doing and the people I was working with. It was, at the time, truly a 'dream job.'

"Strangely, though, even on the longest days there—some of which, when we were busy, stretched far into the night—I never felt tired at work. The thrill of doing something I cared so much about, and which was so consistent with my calling—fostering understanding—completely energized me. It wasn't until I got up and out of the building that I felt the exhaustion set in—completely opposite from my experience at that other job not so many years before."

Which of Dave's experiences is closer to your own? And what can you do to make it more like the latter? Do you need to quit your job and start all over doing something new? Or can you do something new without having start all over?

A Brand-New Old Job

Most of us don't have the freedom to pick up and quit a job that's dissatisfying. We tend to have a good deal invested in the place we work and the people we work with. Pensions, seniority, familiarity, and more all figure in to keeping us where we are—even when where we are isn't where we'd like to be.

So what can we do short of casting caution and good sense completely to the wind? What can we do when we're legitimately frustrated by our work situation but at the same have good reasons for not wanting to quit?

The answer to this can be approached by exploring our gifts. Examining what we consistently have the urge to give away can often help us find new ways to conceive of our jobs that lead to greater satisfaction and fulfillment.

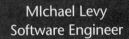Michael Levy
Software Engineer *Inquiring into Things*

Michael Levy, a successful software programmer we know, was promoted to manager of his engineering group. It seemed like a good career move at the time; his salary increased substantially and so did his visibility within the organization.

But within a few weeks, it became obvious to him that he had made a terrible mistake. He realized that he wasn't cut out for this position at all—especially given the personality conflicts he had to deal with. Three key employees in the department were unable to communicate; basically, they hated each other. This made the stress of being responsible for their work intense; Michael could never predict whether they'd be focused on the task at hand or plotting ways to undermine one another's efforts. To make matters worse, his manager refused to support him when he tried—with justifiable cause—to have one of them let go. Moreover, as consultants,

Michael's team was sometimes required to make radical shifts in direction. They had to pretend to be all things to all people; his boss would never tell anyone, "No, we don't do that." This further undermined morale, leaving Michael stuck in the middle, still beholden to deadlines that—unlike everything else—never changed. He constantly felt that there was something he ought to be doing to speed things up or improve productivity—but he wasn't sure what. Mostly, he just felt lousy; he wasn't sleeping well, his home life suffered, and he wished he had never agreed to the new position. But he felt trapped; he had made a commitment to his boss and didn't see any way of getting out of it.

Michael defined his calling as *inquiring into things*. He liked to ask questions. That's why he got into computers in the first place; he was an inveterate puzzler. From the time he was a little boy, he always wondered about how things worked; the gift that he consistently gave to the world was to be the person who asked the questions everyone else had but couldn't form or was afraid to pose.

Michael realized that, in his new job as manager, he felt unable to be a questioner. He didn't feel permitted to not have the answer. Consequently, he had completely stopped inquiring into things. He had become a "know-it-all," when what he really liked being was a "want-to-know-it-all."

So, instead of quitting his job—which he felt like doing on a number of occasions—Michael went to his boss and started asking questions. Could he get some assistance with some of the aspects of management—like dealing with interpersonal conflicts—that were hardest for him? Would it be possible to take over some of the programming work of one of his team members in exchange for that team member's helping out with some of the management chores? What options for flex-time and telecommuting could he propose to give team members more flexibility and control over their schedules?

He also stopped pretending he could solve all the problems team members came up with. His style become much more interactive. When programmers came to him with questions—technical or otherwise—he went into inquiry mode. Rather than trying to *answer* their questions, he made it a point to try to *understand* them better.

What he found was that, usually, as his understanding of the problem increased, so did the questioner's. Proceeding this way led, more often than not, to questioners themselves coming up with the solutions they were searching for.

This isn't to say that all of Michael's troubles were over. He still found management more difficult than he had expected it to be and sometimes he still wished he had remained just a programmer. But by reconnecting to his calling, by finding new ways to inquire into things, he at least managed to rediscover himself and his purpose within the context of his existing job. Instead of having to quit, he was able to recommit; instead of starting all over, he simply started anew.

No Whiners Allowed

There's no comparing suffering. A corporate executive who is unhappy in his job—even though he makes a good living and has a loving family—clearly isn't in as dire straits as someone who's out of work and all alone in the world. But it would be unfair to say that the executive has no reason to complain. Our feelings are, of course, based on our experience of the world, but it is *our experience*. If the executive in this case finds his work meaningless or deeply at odds with what he truly cares about, then it's perfectly understandable that he should be unhappy. No one should say that just because there are other people who live lives that, externally, are much more difficult, the executive is not justified in feeling the way he does.

On the other hand, those of us who enjoy certain privileges—even the relatively minor privilege of being able to read a book like this and think about issues such as calling—need to admit that we have more abundant options for doing something about undesirable situations in which we find ourselves. In contemporary society, people with skills and education have a greater degree of flexibility and freedom in their career choices than ever before. If we find ourselves complaining that we are hopelessly stuck in a job, then we probably haven't fully explored one of two options. Either we haven't examined all the possibilities for change within the job or we haven't looked carefully enough at what's available more broadly.

We live in the "free-agent" age. Millions of working people—and more every day—have chosen to go into business for themselves. The world today is full of independent contractors who work out of their homes or garages, having cast off the constraints of full-time organizational employment. Most of these people, especially the successful ones, don't work any less hard than they did when they worked for an organization. Most, in fact, work harder. But they experience a degree of freedom that they felt was lacking in a more structured environment. This can mainly be attributed to a closer connection to the value component of calling. Free agents have, in general, opted to pay particular attention to workplace values; usually, their choice to go independent was based in part on a decision about the environment in which they preferred to work.

This is no surprise. When people are asked what causes them stress and strain on the job, the most common answer is the environment. The physical and emotional place that people occupy on the job is the number one cause of discomfort and unhappiness. While this is certainly nothing to celebrate, there is a positive message that we can take from it: if we truly feel trapped in our jobs, it's probably that we feel trapped by the environment. The good news about this is that workplace environments can change. They can be changed incrementally from the inside or—as is the lesson from today's millions of free-agents—environments can be changed radically, by creating an altogether new one of our own.

In any case, the moral to be taken from this is that, while we all have every right and reason to be unhappy or dissatisfied in our jobs, most of us have little cause for complaint—at least, ongoing complaint. Instead of whining about how trapped we are, we should spend our energy exploring new avenues of freedom. Given the myriad options for internal and external change these days, the primary obstacle to real job satisfaction for most of us is *us*. We just have to get out of our own way and make it happen.

What Are You Good At?

A friend of ours is a very successful executive coach. He makes a six-figure income consulting with the senior management of Fortune 500 companies on issues of brand identification, marketing, and strategic planning. Remarkably, he is basically self-trained. Although his resume includes a stint as president of a respected corporate training firm, he has no formal business education, no college degree, and no MBA. Everything he's learned, he's learned by doing—and he's done incredibly well.

He tells a story about one of his early high-profile consulting gigs. A winter storm wreaked havoc with his travel plans and he arrived at his hotel after a 3-hour taxi ride through a blizzard (all flights were canceled for the last leg of his trip) at 4:00 in the morning. Scheduled to begin a training session for some twenty senior executives at 8:00, he set his clock for 6:00, figuring it would be better to be tired but prepared than having to rush around just to get an extra hour or so of sleep. Unfortunately, the alarm failed to go off. Our friend awoke with a start at 7:30. Leaping from bed, he washed his face, brushed his teeth, threw on his suit, and rushed unshaven to the meeting, arriving at 8:00 on the dot. The conference room was already packed. Nearly two dozen highly paid executives stared at him from their seats, waiting for him to perform.

Feeling unprepared, exhausted, and completely overwhelmed, our friend nevertheless managed to pull off a miracle. He introduced himself, and began soliciting input from the attendees about their expectations and goals for the upcoming workshop. His natural gift for facilitation kicked into high gear. Within the space of an hour, he had the executives deeply engaged in meaningful dialogue about their organization's most pressing needs, and before the day was over, the CEO of the corporation had pronounced the workshop to be the best training experience he had ever had the opportunity to be involved in.

When our friend told us this story, we marveled at his ability to turn this potentially disastrous situation into a major success. We tried to imagine ourselves in his shoes and cringed at the thought. How did he manage to do just what was needed with such minimal preparation and so few hours of sleep?

When we asked him he said he wasn't exactly sure. He felt that he instinctively knew the right thing to do. His lack of sleep made him less apt to censor himself and so he just did what seemed natural. Amazingly, it all worked out. As a matter of fact, he admits, he learned a lot from that experience about going with the flow. Ever since then, he's trusted his abilities a lot more. And it's really paid off, in financial as well as emotional terms.

Our friend's success is predicated on his understanding of what he's really good at. His calling is *creating dialogue*. He knows what his natural gifts are; this makes him more effective in his professional life. He's also happier and less stressed out. Instead of beating his head against the wall trying to succeed at something he's not really cut out for, he focuses on his strengths. And in doing so, he's managed to create for himself an incredibly successful and rewarding career.

What about you? Are you aware of what you do best? Do you have a clear sense of your natural gifts? And are you using these gifts to their fullest in your life and career? Doing so is an essential part of making the connection between your calling and your job.

Receiving Your Gifts

The important thing to remember about our gifts is that they are just that: *gifts*. They have been bestowed upon us; we are fortunate to receive them from a source outside ourselves. It is no understatement—and requires no particular theological perspective—to understand our gifts in terms of a blessing from beyond.

All of us have gifts; oddly, though, many of us have a difficult time identifying them. Ironically, the things we are best at are those which are most difficult for us to see. Most people can quite readily identify their weaknesses. Far fewer of us can say with assurance what our strengths are.

Part of this is because our gifts are things we perform with ease; generally, we haven't had to work to receive our gifts, so we're apt to overlook them. More importantly, since our gifts have come to us to easily, we tend to devalue them. All our lives we're told that only things that require hard work are valuable; since our gifts are things we do relatively effortlessly, they must not be worth much.

Identifying our gifts, therefore, can be difficult. (It's hard, after all, to identify something that we can't see and that we think is worthless.) So, one of the most effective ways to pick them out is to ask friends, family members, and colleagues. The people in our life often have a better handle on our gifts than we do. People who know us well can usually say quite easily what we do well. They recognize our gifts in action in ways that we don't. This is obvious if we think about our own friends and family; we often marvel at their abilities—feel jealous even—while they take them totally for granted. You probably have friends who can fix anything, or who are fantastic chefs, or who always seems to know the right thing to say to make someone feel better. But if you tell them about how impressed you are with what they can do, they'll just shrug their shoulders and say it's no big deal. And as a matter of fact, they'll probably go on to point out one of *your* gifts that impresses *them*. So it works both ways—and ends up providing you with an opportunity for getting to know your own gifts a little better.

Another way to identify our gifts is to work backwards from our Calling Card. Since we express our calling when we are using our gifts to do work we are passionate about in an environment that is consistent with our values, we might recall times that we felt particularly in touch with our calling. It will follow that, in such times, we were likely expressing our gifts. If we recall for example, Bill Strickland, whose calling is *seeing possibilities,* and think of times in which he was clearly expressing it, we'll see his gifts emerge—gifts like persuasive speaking, effective coaching, and artistic vision. Similarly, if we remember Dave's calling—*fostering understanding*—and his classroom experience of expressing his calling, some of his gifts will become apparent, notably facilitating discussions, listening actively, and, in general, teaching.

So go back to your own Calling Card. Reflect upon an occasion—in either your personal or professional life—when you were particularly attuned to it. What were you doing? What activities were you engaged in? Which of your gifts were you expressing? If the answer remains unclear, you might try writing a paragraph or two about the experience. Then share what you've written with a friend. Between the two of you, a fresh perspective on your gifts will emerge.

Is It Really Money?

One of the reasons people cite for failing to express their gifts is that they can't make money doing so. "I've got to make a living," they'll say. "And nobody's going to pay me for doing what I love to do."

But this gives rise to a few questions. First, what's the big deal about money, in the first place? And second, is money what it's really about, anyway?

In the ancient philosophical classic, *The Nichomachean Ethics,* Aristotle argues that the meaning of life is happiness. Everything we do, he observes, aims at some good. And all of these goods aim, in one way or another, at happiness. So, Aristotle concludes, happiness must be the highest good—in other words, the very thing that life is all about.

Aristotle's conclusion seems hard to dispute; after all, isn't the pursuit of happiness the primary motivation in our lives? Isn't everything we do intended—at least indirectly—to contribute to our sense of well-being and satisfaction? And if so, what else could the meaning of life possibly be?

Of course the challenge at this point is to identify what exactly makes us happy. Aristotle surveys the usual suspects—pleasure, honor, and money—and concludes that none of these can be the source of true happiness. Pleasure is fleeting and tends to make us feel lousy and dissipated when we overindulge. Honor is too dependent on other people; if our happiness depends primarily on what others think of us, we're going to constantly feel at the mercy of people's whims. Money is only a means to something else; moreover, it's usually the case that people undertake a life of money-making only because they *have* to; clearly, then, this can't be what really makes people happy, either.

Aristotle ultimately reasons that the authentically happy life is the virtuous life. The way he sees it, acting in accordance with virtue

is the best expression of what it means to be human. Virtuous behavior represents human excellence in action. Since excellence is
the manner in which anything best attains its ends, it follows naturally that virtuous behavior must be the manner in which human
beings will best achieve happiness.

Many people today probably wouldn't agree with Aristotle.
Often, when asked what would make them happy, people answer
money or material goods. Just look at the success of state lotteries or
get-rich-quick television programs. We tell ourselves that "if only"
we were rich, we'd be happy. And when we're dissatisfied with our
jobs, we tell ourselves that money is the only reason we're staying
where we are. Now, this may be. We may truly find ourselves in such
a bind that we have no choice but to grin and bear it to make a living. But chances are, if we think about it more carefully, we'll discover that we're not as tied down as we think we are—and that there
are considerations other than finances that are constraining our
choice.

Consider: aren't there any number of jobs that you wouldn't
do no matter how much they paid you? Imagine that you were
asked to be Hitler's press agent or an executioner in a country where
people were routinely put to death for simple expressions of free
speech. No doubt you would refuse, no matter how large the salary.

And it's not even necessary to take it to such extremes. We all
draw the line somewhere—whether it's at engaging in selling practices we find objectionable or having to submit to regulations or
policies we consider unfair or draconian. Dave remembers working
at a job—that, for the most part, he liked pretty well—but in an organization that tolerated what he considered an excessive use of
"position power" in people's interactions with each other.

"I was in a technical support role and provided computer assistance to a number of different departments. Given the corporate
culture, it wasn't uncommon for people to come into my office and
just start yelling at me about what they needed and how I'd better
drop everything and take care of their problem immediately. Often,
the only justification they had was that they held a more senior position in the organization.

"One day, one of these people collared me in the hall and

began berating me because the latest upgrade to our system was causing him some minor problems accessing files that he had stored on our server. I had sent out numerous e-mails about such problems and what could be done to correct them, none of which, apparently, he had read. He began calling me an incompetent idiot and demanded that I stop doing what I was doing and reinstall the older version of the server software so he could do his work as before.

"I tried to explain to him that I couldn't meet his request at *just this instant;* I would get to it as soon as I could.

"When he said that a 'low-level know-nothing peon' had no right to talk that way to his 'superior' I just decided I'd had it. I told him that he didn't have to worry about me ever speaking to him that way again—as a matter of fact, he didn't have to worry about me ever speaking to him *any* way again. I quit, effective immediately. I even told my boss to keep my last week's paycheck as combat pay for whoever it was they found to replace me."

Now, certainly, it's not always so easy to say "enough is enough;" and, of course, there is a certain amount of undesirable stuff we have to put up with in any job. It would be impractical—not to mention foolish and immature—to quit every time we felt things weren't going exactly as we wished they were. Still, there is only so much any of us can take. And if we're reached that point, then we shouldn't pretend that money is a sufficient reason for staying put. By the same token, though, if we *haven't* reached that point, then we shouldn't delude ourselves into thinking that the *only* reason we're staying where we are is because of a paycheck.

What *IS* Work, Anyway?

To explore the nature of meaningful work, we must confront the *big* philosophical question: "What is the meaning of life?" In *The Meaning of Life,* philosopher Hugh S. Moorhead collected statements on life's meaning from 250 writers and scholars. Novelist James Michener wrote: "The main purpose of life is: 1. to have a job in whose purpose you can believe; 2. to have friends whose immediate purposes you can trust; 3. to have some spot on earth which you can return to as home; and 4. to be at the same time a citizen of the world."

It is no surprise that Michener lists work first.

"We put our love where we have put our labor," wrote Emerson. "To work is to pray," said St. Benedict. "Far and away the best prize that life offers is the chance to work hard at work worth doing," said Theodore Roosevelt. Love, prayer, a prize—is this how you see work? And if you don't, isn't it a shame? Isn't there something pathetic about spending most of our lives, and certainly the greater part of our waking hours, engaged in something that isn't a gesture of love, a prayer, or a prize? Faulkner wrote that one of the saddest things is that the only thing people can do for eight hours a day, day after day, is work. He observed that we can't eat or drink or make love for eight hours—and literally, he's right. But when our work sustains us, when it becomes an act of love, then perhaps it isn't so sad at all. Perhaps it is something to celebrate. Perhaps we are, in essence, performing a sacred, life-affirming act for the time we are devoted to work.

Unfortunately, it's difficult to hold this attitude when we feel that what we're doing isn't connected to our most enjoyed gifts. Work becomes drudgery or worse when all we're doing is putting in our time to make money. Far from being love or prayer or a prize, our job seems like a forced march through a desolate and unforgiving landscape.

Clearly, though, work was meant to be satisfying. Evolution must necessarily have favored those creatures who naturally embraced the activities that helped them best survive. Our distant ancestors who enjoyed leaving their caves early and heading off to hunt and gather would have had a distinct adaptive advantage over those who had to drag themselves out from under the fur blankets to find something to eat. As human beings, we are built to find satisfaction in work; so it's more than a shame if our work is drudgery—it's unnatural!

Finding the natural satisfaction that our work potentially affords us involves, as we have seen, fully utilizing our natural gifts to support something we really care about. What's important to remember, though, is that this "something" doesn't have to be a matter of saving the world. It can be something much smaller, as long as the role it plays in our own lives is sufficiently large. It doesn't even have to involve the best aspects of people's lives; a perfectly satisfying—and meaningful—life can be derived from dealing on a daily basis with what most people choose not to deal with.

Our Love Affair with Our Job

Do you remember your first few days on the job? What was it like when you were just starting out and everything was new? How does that compare to where you are now? A job is like a love affair in some ways; as we become more familiar with it, we tend to overlook things—often the very things that drew us to it in the first place.

It can be helpful, therefore, to reacquaint ourselves with our jobs all over again. By re-examining our work with a fresh outlook, we can uncover opportunities for utilizing our gifts we may not have recognized. By looking at our jobs with a new—that is, old—perspective, we can sometimes discover unseen—or merely forgotten—pathways to where we would like to be.

This exercise, then, is quite simple. All it asks you to do is come to work with the perspective you had the first day on the job. Imagine that it's all new. Imagine that you haven't experienced the various events that affect your current attitudes about the things that you do. Imagine that you're sitting at your desk for the first time and that all the tasks you have to accomplish are the very first assignments you're undertaking on the job.

Now ask yourself: What really attracts my attention? Which of the things I'm doing do I especially enjoy? Which of my many responsibilities provides me with the fullest opportunity for expressing who I really am?

Your answers may surprise you. You may discover you've forgotten how much you enjoy some things that may have become routine. By the same token, you may be reminded that some of what you do most is what you like least. It may be that you've fallen into habits that are just habitual. You may be doing things not because they in any way express your calling but just because you're doing them.

Now, of course, some of this is likely to be beyond your control. No doubt some of your job responsibilities are requirements whether you want them to be or not. However, it's also likely that some potential dissatisfactions you may be experiencing are responsibilities you don't have to shoulder. You may be putting yourself in a negative situation unnecessarily. You may be bearing a burden that isn't necessary.

It really is like a love affair. We've all occasionally found ourselves doing things with friends or partners that we didn't want to do simply because we felt a responsibility to them. But then we've been surprised to discover that they never expected us to do it—or even worse, they never wanted us to do it, either. And if only we had discussed the matter beforehand, we could have saved everyone some measure of heartache or annoyance.

It's the same thing with our jobs. We want to make sure we keep asking questions that allow us to reflect upon our situation. We want to make sure we keep an open mind—and an open heart—about what we're doing and why. Calling is dynamic; it's an interactive process of hearing and heeding; if we allow that process to stagnate, so will our satisfaction. But if we keep it alive, our potential for renewed levels of satisfaction is enlivened as well—and so, ultimately, are we.

Chapter 4

passions—what keeps calling me?

Radiating Joy

I've just finished a delicious African feast at a favorite hole-in-the-wall hide-away in Nairobi, Kenya. My taxi driver, a laughing grandmother, is driving me slowly back to my hotel. Sitting in the cab, my belly full, watching the lights of the city pass by, I listen to her deep, mellifluous voice rising above the sound of the old car's engine.

She's telling me about her three grandchildren. They've been living with her since her daughter's husband was killed in an accident. That tragedy is mentioned almost as if in passing; her story focuses instead on the liveliness and energy of the three kids and what a pleasure—and a challenge—it is for her to keep up with them.

I express my condolences at her son-in-law's death and she nods sagely. Life is full of the unexpected, she says. Every day, she sees it, right here in her cab. To her, the opportunity to meet new people all the time is a source of great wonder; making connections with people, she says, is her undying passion. "What else matters in this world," she asks, "than people? I never tire of laughing with the happy ones and consoling the sad ones."

She tells me of the changes she's seen in Nairobi during

her life. It has become a strange and dangerous city, much different from when she was a little girl. But it still has its charms for her; it is her home, and she can't imagine living anywhere else.

"I am grateful anyway to be here and to have enough to eat and a job that I enjoy with its endless parade of people—young, old, rich, poor, all alone, newly married." She tells me that her own marriage didn't work out, but she is not bitter or angry about that. "Such is life," she shrugs. "We must look forward, not back."

Her focus is on the present; she lives very much for each day. She tells me that she drives long hours and always feels the pinch of many mouths to feed, but even when she is recounting these troubles, she radiates a joy that fills the cab. It's a joy that fills my soul as well.

It's doubtful that this taxi-driving grandmother will ever come across *Whistle While You Work*, but her spirit is never far from these pages. The echo of her laughter is a ongoing reminder that when we are passionate about what we do—when we believe our work is work that needs to be done in the world—we too, can radiate joy in our lives.

Reasons for Living

When older adults look back upon their own lives, they consistently express a hope that their existence has made a difference. Most are not afraid of dying; rather, their fear is of having lived a meaningless life. We all want to have made some "small dent" in the world. The prospect that no one will remember us after we're gone, or worse, that no one will even notice, is devastating.

Elizabeth Kübler-Ross, arguably the world's expert on people's attitudes about death and dying, summarized a life of research in three simple questions. When people look back upon their lives, she found, they ask three questions that determine their sense of whether it was meaningful:

- Did I give and receive love?

- Did I become all I can be?

- Did I leave the planet a little better?

How many of us will be able to answer "yes" to all three? How many of us will be able to look back upon our days and confidently say we lived the sort of life we intended to live? How many of us will be able to say we became what we wanted to be when we grew up?

Heeding our life's calling is no guarantee that we will be able to answer all of Kübler-Ross' questions in the affirmative. It is, however, a good start. When we're living our lives in a manner that expresses our calling, when we're doing work that we're passionate about, we tend to be more loving, more generous, and more committed to personal and professional development. In short, we're more apt to feel that our lives are meaningful.

In order to flourish, we need to discover and internalize an authentic reason for living that is bigger than we are. An artificial or self-absorbed reason fails to reflect who we really are and is destructive to our potential as persons. When we act on such a reason, we lack creativity and spirit, no matter how noble or self-sacrificing our motivation may seem to be on the outside. True creativity—real spirited passion—derives from our absorption in things we really care about. This energy, emanating from our very essence, tells us we are dialed into the right number, if we only listen. Our inner spirit—God within—provides us with the surest guidance for finding our true passions. Communicating with our inner spirit is the source of strength and insight into our special calling in life.

Carl Jung, in *Modern Man in Search of a Soul,* describes what he calls "the general neurosis of our time." He writes, "About a third of my cases are suffering from no clinically definable neurosis, but from the senselessness and emptiness of their lives." He continues, "The ordinary expression for this situation is: 'I'm stuck.'"

Is there any more succinct way of encapsulating the malaise that so many people feel today? How many people do we know who also feel stuck? How many of us feel stuck?

One of Dick's close friends tragically exemplified this experience of being stuck. For years, he denied—or failed to acknowledge—his deepest passions. Always ready to coach others, he refused ever to ask for help himself. Outgoing and ever willing to reach out to friends, he never let anyone reach in to him.

In the space of a few years, Dick watched him dissolve under the pressure of a life deferred. He hung on too long to a job that never gave him the opportunity to express his gifts, and a book that he had talked about writing for many years remained unfinished.

At just 50, still relatively young, and with his potential passion and creative genius still hidden inside him, Dick's friend died of cancer. For whatever private reasons, he remained unwilling to unleash his feelings with anyone and denied himself the passionate expression he so desperately needed. Quite literally, he ate himself up from the inside out.

His entire being was stuck, and although his work offered him little creative outlet, he hung onto the job, suffering years of frustration—usually with a warm, accepting smile. Even in attempting, near the end of his life, to write his book, he could not give voice to his inner feelings. Tears flowed, but the connection to a meaningful expression of his passionate nature had been severed by years of neglect. In the end, all he could feel was exhaustion.

During the final few weeks, Dick asked his friend what really mattered in life. "Being in nature and being with people," he answered. But, of course, at this point, it was too late for either. Dick's friend knew, in a profound and tragic way, that his denial of personal passion had cost him his life.

When Carl Jung pointed out, "It is difficult to treat patients of this particular kind because they are, in the main, socially well-adapted individuals of considerable ability," he vastly understated the problem. Patients "of this particular kind"—those who are "stuck"—are living a kind of spiritual death. The difficulty in treating them stems from the fact that their condition, though acute, may not manifest itself in any outward display of the problem. For years, people like Dick's friend can successfully pursue power, money, and recognition. But there comes a time when none of that matters anymore. At this point, we must journey to the core of our being and rediscover our passions; we must find a new reason to get up in the morning. Every day, 250,000 people in the U.S. die. This is a brutal reminder that each day we have the opportunity to live our lives fully and for a reason. And finding this reason begins with a brutally honest examination of our innermost feelings.

In *The Life Work,* poet Donald Hall describes his reason for getting up in the morning: "The best day begins with waking early—I check the clock: damn! It's only 3:00 a.m.—because I want so much to get out of bed and start working. Usually something particular beckons so joyously—like a poem that I have good hope for, that seems to go well. Will it look as happy today as it looked yesterday?"

Too absorbed to sleep, Hall wrestles with his impatience to get up and get at his life's work. He continues: "As I approach the end of *The Globe,* saving the Sports section until last, I feel work-excitement building, job-pressure mounting—until I need resist it no more but sit at the desk and open the folder that holds the day's beginning, its desire and its hope. Then I lose myself. In the best part of the best days, absorbedness occupies me from footsole to skulltop."

What is this "absorbedness"? And how can we achieve it in ourselves? Why do some people find passion in their life's work while others feel "stuck" in meaningless jobs?

Life Is Beautiful

The contrast between feeling "stuck" and feeling absorbed is poignantly illustrated in the Academy-Award winning film, *Life Is Beautiful.* The story centers on a loving father and his relationship with his young son. In the early years of the boy's life, the two are inseparable; they laugh, joke, play games, and delight in their mutual love for the boy's mother, for whom the father's love burns as brightly as when they first met.

Suddenly, one day, the father and son are dragged from their home and forced onto a train bound for the Nazi concentration camp, Auschwitz. The remainder of the film chronicles the intense passion the father has—not only to keep his son alive—but to keep the boy's spirit joyful through their dark ordeal. The father manages to convince his son that everyone at the camp is playing a complex game in hopes of winning a real full-sized tank as the prize. His inventiveness, humor, and dedication to his son's happiness are awe-inspiring and leave the audience deeply moved to both laughter and tears.

Although the father ultimately dies, *Life Is Beautiful* is a passionate reminder that meaning in life comes from a commitment to something outside of ourselves. When we are absorbed in something larger than our own lives, that's when we feel most alive ourselves.

Victor Frankl's "logotherapy," a theory that seeks to explain and treat human behavior on the basis of meaning in life, originated in Frankl's own survival of Auschwitz. He personally observed that the people who survived prolonged imprisonment in Hitler's death camps did so because they had something beyond themselves to live for. Those who somehow managed to live through the horrors of Auschwitz cared about something else than their own lives—they had a passion for a person or a cause that sustained them. In a sense, they became absorbed in something and committed to a life outside of themselves. Their survival vividly illustrates the notion that we are ultimately our brothers' and sisters' keepers. When we are passionately committed to a life other than our own, we are sustained in ways that are as powerful as they are unexpected.

Passion in Work

How do we find passion in work? How do we achieve the kind of absorbtion Donald Hall describes? How do we commit to something outside of ourselves such that we feel an overwhelming sense of aliveness and purpose?

Arthur Rouner's story answers these questions.

Arthur Rouner President		*Building Bridges*

At 70 years of age, Arthur Rouner cuts a handsome figure as he warmly takes your hand and pumps it, causing the 30 African bracelets he wears on his wrist to jangle merrily. Arthur calls them his "prayer beads" and explains how a friend from the Pokot tribe in Kenya gave him his first one. He has since added a new bracelet on every trip to Africa. "They remind me to pray for my friends there," he says.

Arthur is the founder and president of the Pilgrim Center for Reconciliation, based in Minneapolis, Minnesota. As he discusses the work of reconciliation—"most people have at least one relationship where there is a wound"—you get the feeling that you're with a man who knows who he is, why he's here, and where he's going—a man who has a powerful sense of his calling.

He says that his life of Christian ministry chose him. "My father made it clear," he states, "that he wanted me to be a minister, like him." But Arthur's real calling didn't come to him in church. It came to him as a 17-year-old, on a merchant boat returning from Greece. The oiler on the ship was in desperate shape after returning from a weekend of carousing on shore leave. Suffering from chronic syphilis exacerbated by dehydration, the oiler pleaded with Arthur and a small group of young men on the boat: "What is going to happen to me? What does it all mean?"

The oiler's pleas touched Arthur deeply. He didn't have answers to the sailor's questions, but they resonated powerfully with his own inquiries. That night, alone on the bow of the ship, Arthur heard his calling as clearly as he did the waves below: his own life's work was to serve the poor, to build bridges to people like the oiler. He vividly recalls that night and where it seemed the call came from. "I didn't hear a voice speaking to me across the ocean. It was an inner voice."

Arthur was called to Colonial Church in Edina, Minnesota, to do reconciliation work—to "build bridges." For 32 years, he was absorbed in a pioneering ministry, building bridges between rich and poor, inner-city and suburb, well-fed and hungry, Africa and America. Arthur's legacy at Colonial was, in his own words, "He loved the people." The feeling of absorbedness was overwhelming. "It was an awesome thing to feel that I was in the grip of God as His messenger," says Arthur.

Since leaving Colonial Church, Arthur has continued to build bridges around the world—usually in places where the chasms between people would seem insurmountable to most of us. There is no more vivid illustration of this than Arthur's work in the African nation of Rwanda. He shared the world's horror at the genocidal massacre of nearly a million people there during the mid-1990s. *Time* magazine reported that a depth of evil so searing to the soul as to be incomprehensible to our consciousness had overtaken that land. Rwanda's need—overlooked by many of the world's governments until it was too late—called to Arthur. He believed that, in the aftermath of the killings, what people were desperate for was forgiveness. For reconciliation to take place, both Hutu and Tutsi factions, perpetrators and victims alike, needed a way to forgive each other, and themselves. Unless the entire population could find a way to do this, the people in this small nation, with such a horrendous history of pain and suffering, could simply not live together.

Arthur felt that if the Church in Rwanda was to play a healing role, the church leaders themselves would need to have their own hearts healed. Their own grief and guilt and fear would have to be lifted if they were to lift those feelings from others. And in fact, as Arthur came in contact with more of these leaders, he heard a common refrain: "But how can we do the good work of reconciliation that we have been told to do if we are not healed ourselves?"

"It was precisely this healing of the inner heart that God has given to the Pilgrim Center," says Arthur. "And this call we have heard in our hearts."

It is a call to go to the killing fields in Rwanda and Burundi and to sit with the people, loving them and listening to their pain. It is a call to offer them whatever comfort is possible in the long process of healing a whole country. The Pilgrim Center invites healers in Rwanda—pastors, women's group organizers, youth leaders—"Come away from the struggle and rest awhile." As Arthur observes of these people, "They are so haunted. There is no rest for them."

A youth leader in Burundi confessed early in a Pilgrim retreat, "My brother was killed in the genocide. I know who killed him. I see him around the town. I hate him. I am tempted to revenge." But at the end of the retreat with the Pilgrim Center, he said, "I can hardly wait to get back home. I am going to seek out my brother's killer and tell him, 'I have forgiven you.'"

Arthur calls his life's work "a ministry of presence." His passion today is to be a genuine friend to those in need—to listen, to feel, to be reasonable and helpful to people. He sums up his ministry of presence by paraphrasing Edwin Markham: "I just want to be a house by the side of the road where I can be a friend to man."

Arthur's passion—the essence of his calling—is to build bridges. When he discovered he could no longer do this work in the Church, he realized he had to leave his parish. He had no choice but to honor this more basic and powerful spirit emanating from within. He says that this intimate contact with the source of his calling is his awareness of God. It has always been—and remains—more important than any institution or formal structure. Arthur's life work, and the mission of the Pilgrim Center, has no agenda, he says, other than the Holy Spirit's agenda. He describes it simply. "There are no fancy notebooks, no experts, no raised platforms for 'important people.' Instead, we all sit together in a circle, gathered literally around the cross."

Igniting Passion

"Passion" is a loaded word in our culture. Its connotes sexuality, emotion, lack of inhibition, uncontrolled self-expression, wildness; in short, it suggests danger. We are told from an early age to control our passions, to suppress them. Passion is like fire, goes the story. It burns brightly at first and then dies out. And unless we are cautious, passion will harm us. The fire is not to be toyed with; better to steer clear of passion altogether if we can.

None of these characterizations of passion capture the reality of passion as it relates to calling. When we refer to passion, we *are* referring to a kind of freedom, but it is a freedom that is life-affirming and positive. Rather than representing an expression of just a single part of our character, like sexuality, passion relates to the full expression of who we are. Moreover, passion is not something that ignites once, flares up quickly, and then dies away. Passion may not catch fire for some time; it may not take hold until there is a complete awareness of what we are passionate about. And, properly nourished, passion can burn throughout the entire course of our lives.

| Nancy Hutson
Senior Vice-President | *Helping Others*
Succeed |

Nancy Hutson, a biologist at Pfizer Pharmaceuticals, did not become an executive because she had a passion for the job; she did so originally to please her family. Plus, she wanted the money, prestige, and respect associated with the position. Most of all, she craved recognition. Today, she has the recognition—in spades. Nancy is senior vice-president and head of Pfizer's Groton Research Laboratory, and one of the company's leading advocates for "creating a culture of potential."

Over the past eight years, she has developed a passion for taking what she has learned to help others, particularly women, succeed. She says, "Helping others succeed is in my DNA!"

Nancy has intuitively blended her dual interests in science and spirituality with her passion for leadership. After completing her Ph.D. in biology, studying abroad for two years at Oxford, and working as a professional scientist for 10 years, she discovered that she was a natural organization builder—she cannot *not* lead. "I'm happiest when I see people succeed," she says, "when I see them grow and excel."

Nancy's interests range beyond the laboratory and boardroom, though. She balances her passion for blazing new trails at Pfizer's Groton, Connecticut research site with an abiding joy at heading out on the trail astride one of her beloved horses. In fact, she sees a number of similarities between the two. At Pfizer, she's building an organizational culture of potentiality that breaks the trail even when the trail does not lead in the general direction the rest of the organization is heading. She says, "I really love exchanging ideas— new paradigms of exploratory developments. I'm passionate about building an organization that allows people to be all that they can be and which exemplifies the Pfizer values."

Nancy's advocacy for and mentoring of women at Pfizer has earned her a national reputation. "I want to take what I've learned and help women succeed," she says. I want to realize my own potential and bring it out in others." Her passion for doing so burns as brightly as her future and the future of those she is helping.

There are millions of dispassionate people in the world who, unfortunately, are deaf to the passionate spirit that speaks within them. Yet their path to hearing and heeding their calling—though overgrown—is not indiscernible. It begins with paying attention to their feelings and listening to their inner voice. The encouraging fact is that it's never too late. Our inner voice does not grow silent unless we give up all hope. The embers of our passion do not die out unless we choose to neglect them altogether.

Jana Mohr Lone Director		*Instilling* *Confidence*

Jana Mohr Lone, director of the Northwest Center for Philosophy for Children, is passionate about helping people to make sense of the world for themselves by thinking and questioning. Through the efforts of the Center, a non-profit organization that brings philosophy into the lives of young people in schools and community forums, Jana has many opportunities to put that passion into action. In seminars and workshops with teachers and parents, but especially in classroom activities with children, she consistently encourages young people and adults to find new ways of figuring things out for themselves.

Jana's calling is *instilling confidence*. She does this through her passionate commitment to the power that philosophical thinking has for opening doors to self-directed learning. She is driven to help people keep alive the spirit of wonder and desire to learn new things. Kids have this spirit at age 4 or 5—but it is all too often extinguished by the time they hit 9 or 10.

The passion that Jana brings to her work is fueled in part by an overriding hopefulness that she has and that she seeks to imbue in others. "I want my life to be about helping others to create their own lives," she says. "There's a lot of hope in the way the world can be if we all have the freedom to do that."

We all can live with such hope. We can begin listening to ourselves at any point in our lives. In doing so, we can begin to realize the potential that has been living within us from birth. The call within us will last as long as we do; it only waits for us to turn our ears to its eloquent message. This call can lift us to a new level of passion and fulfillment in life if only we can hear and interpret its language.

But in order for this to happen we have to begin listening. We have to stop complaining about the past, fretting about the present, and worrying about the future. Each period of our lives has its own understanding, its own lesson to be learned. Each crossroad can represent an opportunity for passion, but we have to create the circumstances that make passion possible.

Chapter 5

values—where do I get connected?

Why Are You Doing This?

My taxi driver looks exhausted. I have to tap on the window three times to get his attention before he opens the door for me. Coming around to take my bags, he shakes his head and squints, clearing cobwebs from his brain. When he slides back into the driver's seat, I can see in the rear-view mirror how red and watery his eyes are.

"Where to?" he mumbles in a heavy accent made heavier by a thick sleepy tongue.

"Home," I say, leaning back into the seat, but—somewhat concerned about my driver—not quite relaxing. For one thing, it makes me nervous to see his eyelids droop as I give him directions to my house.

"Ah, home," says the driver wistfully, as he merges into traffic. "Very nice. I haven't been to my home in five years."

Figuring that he'll be more likely to stay awake if he's talking, I take the opportunity to engage him in conversation.

"Really? Where's home?"

"Far away," he tells me. "Far, far away."

A few moments pass. I can't tell if my driver is remembering his country or nodding off. I try to keep the conversational ball rolling.

"So what brings you here?"

"Many problems in my home country," he says. "I come here to get away. For a better life."

"And how has it worked out?"

A smile creeps across his face. "In my home country, I am a teacher. At University. Here, I am a taxi driver. I drive sixteen hours a day, some-times every day of the week."

"Not so well, then," I surmise.

"No," He laughs. "It is not so bad."

An eighteen-wheel semi looms large in the windshield. I hold my breath as my driver swings wide around him. When my heart returns to my chest, I ask another question.

"You ever think about going back?"

"Oh, I miss it," he replies. "But no. Too many problems there. Too much restriction. Here, at least, I can say what I think. And my family doesn't fear the knock on the door in the middle of the night."

"But what about your career? Your work? Don't you mind driving a taxi?"

The driver cuts across four lanes of traffic to my exit. He shrugs his shoulders and looks at me in the mirror. "It is only a job. Not so important. I cannot work as a teacher in this country and so this is how I make money for my family. That's all. What matters is that we are safe and free. When my son grows up maybe he will be a teacher himself. At least he has that chance. So I work this job. It is my choice."

"You don't feel cheated somehow? Like you're not getting what you want out of life?"

"On the contrary, my friend. Life is not so much about getting as it is about giving. And the choice I make now allows me to give what I must give. Other things are more important to me than being a teacher—being a fa-ther, a husband, a friend. With this job, I can do those, and so, it is good."

As I give the driver a few final directions and he pulls up at my house, I look at him more closely. There is a quiet calm about him I hadn't noticed before. His eyes contain a spark that even exhaustion cannot extinguish.

He helps me with my bags; I pay him. He ducks back into the cab and heads off. I think I would have liked to correct him about one thing: even in this country, he is still a teacher.

Try to imagine if you were in this cab driver's shoes.

Would you be so accepting of your situation? Would you have the same sense of perspective about life? Would you be as clear about why you're doing what you're doing and as positive about prospects for the future?

Would you, in other words, be as cognizant of your values as he is?

Many of us probably wouldn't be. We aren't nearly so settled in our understanding of why we're doing what we're doing. We make choices and compromises without feeling satisfied that these choices and compromises are worth it. This implies that we're disconnected from our values—and that it's valuable to reconnect to them in a deeper way.

Who's Dealing the Cards?

Think of how often we complain about the hand life has dealt us. But when we do, we forget who's dealing the cards—it's us!

Remember the game "Hand Dealt." The sixth-graders who played it considered the hands they'd been dealt unfair primarily because they weren't the ones dealing.

When we play the game with kids, though, we always follow up the initial round with two others. Players—especially those who were dealt undesirable lives—always insist we re-deal the cards. So, we do. We collect all the job, relationship, and living situation cards and, after shuffling them up, deal them out once more. Inevitably, the same dissatisfactions ensue as in the first round, just with different people. Players who have gotten bad jobs once again complain that life has dealt them a lousy hand; they chafe at having to settle for a life that isn't of their own making.

So, in the third round, we give them the opportunity to design their own cards. Instead of dealing the cards out, students create jobs, relationships, and living situations for themselves. Of course, this means we end up with an inordinate number of professional athletes and CEOs in the room, but that's just the point. When young people aren't forced to settle for situations that are imposed upon them, they tend to dream big. They tend to envision their lives as grand adventures to be lived to their fullest. They tend not to settle for the something small; rather, they imagine that they can be whatever they want to be, however unlikely it may seem as a real possibility. And their choices unabashedly reflect the thing they most love doing, whether it's art, sports, community service, you name it. Unconstrained by externally imposed limitations, the kids come up with their dream lives and at the core of these dreams is the internal fire we refer to as calling.

When they have the chance to deal their "lives" out to themselves—when they are allowed to choose the cards they are dealt—they feel that their "lives" are fair. But when their ability to make choices is constrained, they feel trapped. They feel that even a desirable life isn't really desirable.

Most of us aren't nearly so trapped in the game as we think we are. We *can* make choices and changes that more accurately reflect our deepest values. We don't have to live in a manner that is inconsistent with what we really care about. We have the freedom to structure our lives so that the burdens we accept are burdens we find acceptable. Like the taxi driver, we can learn to make choices that represent values we truly consider valuable.

The first step in doing that is to be absolutely sure what our values really are.

Do I Value My Values?

Values, as we mentioned earlier, are active. Valuing is something we *do*. The reason one of our values *is* a value is because we *live* it.

We express our values through the choices we make. Consequently, if we're living in a manner that is consistent with our values, our values will be apparent in the way that we live. The *environment* in which we work, for example, will reflect kinds of things we care about. The way we spend our time and money and the friendships we cultivate are other ways we make our values apparent in the world.

At least, this is the theory.

In fact, many of us at one time or another, have made choices that are decidedly at odds with our values. Many of us have found ourselves in situations that prevent us from being who we really are. The pressure to do well—that is, make money—gets in the way of our desire to do good—that is, express our core values. And when that happens, we tend to lose sight of the very values that could enable us to find ourselves. We end up in a self-reinforcing system that drags us farther away from our values, farther away from ourselves.

Dave experienced this very dynamic:

"In my early thirties, I tried my hand at a number of different jobs. At one point, I found myself doing computer network maintenance for a high-tech software development company. I'm not entirely sure how I ended up in this position; I guess I sort of fell into it through my interest in computers at the time. I had never intended to be a computer geek and, even when I took the job, I hoped it would be a stepping-stone to something else. But the money was great and I enjoyed helping people use the emerging technology to do their jobs more effectively.

"It didn't take long, though, for the gap between my values—what I really cared about—and my job—what I was doing—to widen.

"For one thing, the organization put an overriding emphasis on speed. Everything had to be done yesterday, so people were always rushing around, doing six things at once, and getting incredibly stressed out. This put a lot of pressure on my job because the inevitable network hiccups inevitably caused delays and, inevitably, people blamed me for missed deadlines—even if the delay caused by the network failure was only a minor part of the slowdown.

"So I was working seven days a week constantly trying to upgrade our system, and half the time I did upgrades, something else would go wrong, and we'd be no better—if not worse—off than before. People would complain and point fingers at me and, in general, make me feel pretty awful about myself. I was pretty unhappy, but oddly I didn't even realize it. I just kept pushing harder and harder, trying to make myself fit into an environment whose values were quite different than my own. While a sense of community and cooperation were of paramount concern to me, this organization valued individuality and competition above all else. I was constantly out of sync but I took it to be a failure on my part that things weren't working out. I remember one Sunday evening about 8:00 coming into an office where a program designer was working. He seemed to be having a grand time tweaking the color palette on an image he was processing. Obsessing over the subtlest of details in a part of the program which very few people were ever likely to see was, to him, a perfectly satisfying way to spend a Sunday night. I thought there must be something wrong with me because I was wishing I were at home reading a book.

"It was really just luck that I got out of this situation. My wife, Jennifer, was accepted into a graduate program in fine arts at a college in another city and we chose to move. I remember feeling awful about having to give my notice but I also recall that, as a soon as I did, I felt great. It was as if a huge burden was lifted from my shoulders. And, as a matter of fact, it was, for no sooner did I leave the job than I was able to stop carrying around a version of me that wasn't me. I was able to stop trying to force myself into a value system at odds with my own. I was able to be myself instead of someone I thought I ought to be, someone whose values were inconsistent with the things I held most dear."

Of course, Dave's situation isn't unique. Many of us, for one reason or another, find ourselves in working or living situations that are a poor fit for our values. The stories of how we end up like this are legion: money, family, and timing may all have something to do with it. Ultimately, though, these stories are secondary. It's not so important how we got into the situation. What really matters is what we can do to get out of it.

Getting Out and Getting Into It

How can we escape the feeling of being trapped and get into lives and work that are consistent with what we really care about? Obviously, it's easier said than done. Most of us have to make a living; consequently, we have to make compromises. We may value the natural setting of a sunny beach beside an azure sea above all else; unfortunately, though, there are only so many lifeguard jobs in paradise at any one time.

We can take heart from the knowledge that there are people—regular people in all walks of life—who *are* living in accordance with their values. Their lives aren't perfect, but they are nonetheless consistently fulfilling—at least on the job front.

Victoria Ingalls Medical Librarian		*Researching* *Solutions*

Consider the example of Victoria Ingalls, the medical librarian for a medium-sized hospital in the Pacific Northwest. Victoria's job is to research articles for physicians who need the most up-to-date information on emerging therapies and medications. It's not exactly thankless work, but Victoria rarely hears many thanks for the long hours she puts in rounding up articles, reprints, and journals for her hospital's medical staff. Even when she has to be a mind-reader—as when one young physician asked her to find an article that would broaden his understanding of a particular procedure without telling her what he knew already—Victoria approaches her work with enthusiasm and good humor. She just laughs at the suggestion that she's underappreciated.

"I appreciate me," she says. "So I don't get bent out of shape if these young kids—or even the older ones—don't recognize what I do for them sometimes. It's all part of their education. Mine, too. Besides, I just find it fascinating to search for the information they need. I think it's the natural detective in me. When I'm on the trail of some esoteric reference, I feel like the lead character in a mystery story. That's satisfaction enough—and why I got into this profession in the first place."

One of the reasons that people like Victoria tend to be fulfilled in their work is that they see the big picture. They recognize that the work they are doing makes a positive difference in the world—even if it's just a small difference. What matters to them is that their work matters. And it matters because it improves not just their own life, but, more importantly, someone else's life.

People like Victoria value what they do because they view what they do as a gift. They implicitly ask "what do I want to give to the world?" And they answer in a way that enables them to express their deepest values through an expression of their gifts and passions. This is why they whistle while they work.

Think of times in your own life when you have acted upon your values. Recall how it felt to stand up for what you believe in, even if it meant short-term hardship. Remember the sense of satisfaction that came from feeling connected to an idea or cause larger than yourself. There may have been financial implications; you may have had to sacrifice monetary success for successful expression of your values, but it was probably worth it. These are the experiences that make life worth living, the experiences that give meaning and purpose to our days.

To have such experiences more consistently, we have to do two things. We have to develop a deeper understanding of what our values really are and we have to begin to act in ways that express those values in our daily lives.

Keeping in mind that what makes a value into a value is that someone lives it, you might begin by considering some commonly held values. Some people cleave to what are usually thought of as traditional values like security, spirituality, order, community, wealth, work, family, and health. Others tend to hold values such as autonomy, newness, change, freedom, excitement, teamwork, and peace. And still others may share any of these as well as values such as cooperation, relaxation, friendship, power, learning, nature, and recreation.

Think of such values. Ask yourself which you value most highly. Which of those mentioned—or which others—would you list as your own values?

Then examine your answers more carefully to see if you've identified values you *really do* value.

One well-known way to ascertain what our values really are is to look at how we spend our money and our time. Review your checkbook and your calendar for the last three months. Where have your time and money gone? What are the five things you've spent most of your time on? What are the five things you've spent most of your money on? What does this say about your values? If, for example, community, cooperation, and friendship are your core values, wouldn't it be likely that your check stubs would include a number of entries for donations to social service organizations and dinners with friends? And wouldn't your calendar probably have dates for volunteer work groups and neighborhood parties?

If, on the other hand, you discover that the most common check you have written is to your travel agent and the most prevalent item in your datebook is an out-of-town meeting, then perhaps you *really* value something else—perhaps excitement, newness, or advancement at work.

Robert Fulghum, the best-selling author of *Everything I Need to Know I Learned in Kindergarten* and other contemporary classics, was once asked how the phenomenal success of his books had changed his life. The interviewer was obviously hoping for some juicy tidbit about how Fulghum, the former minister and longtime advocate of simplicity in word and deed, had developed expensive tastes or come to expect a level of luxury that his newfound wealth had made possible.

Fulghum surprised the interviewer by responding that success basically gave him the opportunity to put his money where his mouth was. He was able to help individuals and organizations he cared about in ways that he hadn't been able to previously. Instead of just providing moral support, he could provide financial support, too. In short, he was able to contribute to the success of what he valued. Money didn't change his values; it only gave him new ways to express them.

The question to ask yourself, then, is if the values you act upon—your demonstrated values—are indeed those you want to act upon. It may be that they are and that the disconnect is simply between what you think you value and what you say you value. If that's the case, then all you need to do is change your way of speaking.

Many of us may have experienced something like this when we've gone through a major life transition, such as having a child. We continue to tell ourselves and others that we're one way when our actions indicate that we're another. In the case of a new baby, for instance, we may loudly bemoan our pitiful social life while happily staying home every night playing with the new bundle of joy.

If, though, your demonstrated values are at odds with the values you would choose to live by, then it's necessary to make some life changes. It's necessary, at least, to begin spending your time and money in different ways. This means you actually have to do things differently—not just think about doing them differently. And that can be difficult.

Suppose, for instance, that, after reviewing your checkbook and calendar, you find you're spending far more time and money on shopping for new clothes, furniture, and computer gear than you would have expected—given that your stated values are simplicity and thrift. And suppose you believe that these demonstrated values—which seem to be more about complexity and wealth—are not what you want your life to be about; they aren't the gift you want to give to the world. In this case, you will have to find new interests, new ways of being. You won't be able to go to the mall as often; you won't be able to spend your time shopping on-line. It may be a painful transition; you may have to get some help or counseling to shift your life's direction. But if that's what you want you life to be about, then presumably, it's worth it.

Of course, no one—besides yourself—is forcing you to change. If you don't want to, you don't have to. But if you do...then what other choice do you have?

Well, It's Easy for You . . .

People who are dissatisfied with their jobs often say to people who love their work, "Oh, well, it's easy for *you*. You have the perfect job. You're a writer. Or an artist. Or you have your own company. No wonder you're happy. Me, I'm just a pitiful wage slave for a multinational cartel. If I were in your shoes, I wouldn't complain, either."

What these people don't realize, though, is that there are no perfect jobs. No matter what you do—even if you're a rock star or a supermodel—there will be aspects of your work that are less than thrilling. What makes a job great isn't so much *what* you do, but *how* you do it. It's a matter of "fit"—the alignment between your inner self and outer activities. In short, it's a matter of connecting who you are with what you do.

We know this intuitively. We're all aware that the same task, performed one day, can feel very different the next. Answering customer service calls on Monday morning gives us the sense that we're making a difference in the world; by Friday afternoon, it's all we can do to keep from diving into the receiver and strangling the person on the other end. So what's changed? Not the job—it's the same as ever. Not the customers—their questions and concerns are just as they were. No, it's something about *us* that's different, something about our attitude toward what we're doing that changes everything.

It's true that creative, self-directed people—artists, writers, entrepreneurs—are more likely to feel this way about their work than the average wage-earner, but that's not primarily because they're artists, writers, or entrepreneurs. (Think of examples like Van Gogh or Hemingway or Sylvia Plath, who, despite their artistic successes, were deeply dissatisfied with their lives.) Rather, it's primarily because they chose their life's work—they heeded their calling. Having a sense of creative control over our work and life makes us more likely to feel that our efforts are meaningful and worthwhile.

The challenge, then, is to develop that sense of volition and autonomy within the context of our job—even if we're not writers, artists, or entrepreneurs. Even if we're "just" customer service representatives answering consumer questions Monday morning through Friday afternoon.

One way to begin doing that is to reflect upon those moments within our working lives when we have felt particularly free and energized. Nearly everyone experiences—at least occasionally—that on-the-job sensation of connectedness and contribution to something truly meaningful. In these moments—however fleeting—we can begin to find the essence of our calling. And we can explore ways to expand the scope of these moments so they begin to occupy as much of our time at work as possible.

| Nathan Weller Subscription Clerk | | *Creating Dialogue* |

Consider the example of Nathan Weller, a 26-year-old subscription clerk in a theater ticket agency in San Francisco. Nathan doesn't exactly *love* his job; in fact, in many ways, he sees it as a stepping-stone to something better—although he's not exactly sure what that would be. Like most people, though, Nathan *needs* his job, he has rent to pay, bills to cover, little luxuries to indulge in. He works 8:00 to 5:30 five days a week in a shared office with fluorescent light at a small desk that he often bumps his knees on when sliding into his less-than-ergonomically-perfect chair. It's not an awful job; it's just a job: most of the time, Nathan does his work without thinking a lot about it. He answers phone calls, fills ticket requests, and issues refunds with an efficient detachment about what he's doing; he hasn't exactly "checked his brain at the door," but he's certainly not pushing the envelope of creative involvement as he goes through his day.

Occasionally, though, he really comes alive. His whole demeanor changes; Nathan goes from being a somnambulant wage-earner to an energetic entrepreneur. Instead of doing just what he has to, he does everything that's necessary—and more. He doesn't even feel as if he's working, but he gets more work done than at any other time on the job.

Nathan is responsible for working with non-profit organizations to make theater subscriptions available at a reduced rate so those organizations can use them to raise money. He contacts organization directors as well as prospective donors in an effort to forge alliances that benefit the non-profits, to provide theater experiences for otherwise underrepresented constituencies, and to, not incidentally, increase the theater's subscription base. Nathan loves helping bring these diverse populations together. He finds it immensely satisfying to stimulate dialogue between individuals and groups who, under normal circumstances, would be unlikely to have much of anything to do with one another. He feels that he is a natural bridge-builder; one of the things he does best and most enjoys doing is to bring people together and facilitate communication. When he's making phone calls and writing letters to set up these alliances, he doesn't even feel as if he's working. The time flies by. Problems that come up aren't headaches to be avoided; they are interesting challenges to be overcome. When he talks about this part of his job with friends and family, he never complains. In many ways, it's this one aspect of the work that makes all the rest tolerable.

It's obvious that Nathan values bringing people together in some way. He sees himself as a communication facilitator and feels most creatively independent when he's engaged in activities that allow him to facilitate communication in a fairly direct and obvious way. But, since his job doesn't provide uninterrupted opportunities for doing so, he has to reinvent his work constantly so that the times when he isn't doing what he most likes to do feel more like the times that he is.

Of course, changing one's mindset is not as easy as changing one's clothes. Most of us can't suddenly decide to love something we were only recently ambivalent about. On the other hand, it's certainly not impossible to modify our outlook on things. We're all familiar with instances where we were able to change a barely tolerable situation into something fairly enjoyable just by adjusting our attitude. Dave says, "I worked at a company that had a one hour staff meeting every Friday afternoon at 3:00. I hated them because they seemed like such a waste of time; I thought of them as unnecessary and boring bitch sessions. My boss, though, sensing my discomfort with them, suggested that I view the meetings as opportunities for increasing my understanding of the challenges people were facing and for learning more about the way individuals responded to business challenges in real time. He also assigned me the task of writing a one-page summary of the meeting to be distributed company-wide. I so enjoyed that task that it eventually developed into an organizational newsletter of which I became editor. What had once been an onerous burden eventually transformed into one of the central—and most enjoyable—aspects of my entire job."

As this example illustrates, there are at least two parts to changing our mindset about the less desirable aspects of our jobs. First, and probably most importantly, we have to *want* to change. Desire is key, and can make all the difference. In Dave's example, he was asked by his boss to modify his perspective. The possibility of letting his superior down provided some impetus for looking at things differently. He wanted to make a good impression on the person who signed his checks; it's not surprising that it wasn't particularly difficult for him to find the desire to change his attitude about the meetings. The incentive was right there in the form of his paycheck. It's not so difficult to learn to like something when doing so is so obviously in our self-interest.

What's useful to recognize, therefore, is that—in the broadest sense—it's *always* in our self-interest to learn to like better the less likable aspects of our jobs. This doesn't, of course, include any aspects that are illegal or abusive, but it does pertain to the vast majority of the slightly annoying or uncomfortable parts of our work days. Our lives, after all, are all that we have. If we're spending our precious hours feeling half-alive as we drag ourselves through tasks that we abhor, then we're wasting our most precious commodity of all: time. If, by contrast, we can shift our perspective on things so that those hours are expended on something that—at least—is in keeping with our deepest convictions and desires, then we'll feel more alive and more integrated into our daily activities. So, the incentive exists to make a positive change in our attitudes about all parts of our jobs—even without our bosses telling us to.

The second part about changing our attitudes towards the less desirable aspects of our jobs—or our lives, for that matter—is that we need to develop some sort of plan for doing things differently. If we don't change our behavior, then nothing will change. As Larry Wilson, corporate training guru and master salesperson, puts it, "If you always do what you've always done, you'll always get what you've always gotten." And if what we've always gotten is dissatisfaction, then, by all means, we'll continue being dissatisfied if we still behave in the ways that have led us to dissatisfaction—no matter how differently we think about them.

The Dalai Lama, in his book *Ethics for the New Millennium,* says we can classify the actions we take in pursuit of happiness into those which make a positive contribution to that pursuit and those which make a negative contribution to it. He then points out that those activities which foster happiness have, as their ultimate basis, concern for both the short-term benefit to us and the long-term effects on others' happiness. In short, he argues, genuine peace of mind is only possible when we undertake actions that are inspired by the wish to help others. We also find, he writes, that when we act out of concern for others, the peace this creates in our own hearts brings peace to our families, friends, workplaces, communities, and the world. Our ability as humans to feel compassion and love, says the Dalai Lama, is a precious gift, perhaps the most precious of all.

Surprisingly, this is fairly easy to see within the context of our working lives. When we feel as if we're helping others—customers, co-workers, or prospective clients—our levels of work satisfaction increase significantly. By contrast, when we're doing something that seems as if it benefits only ourselves, we tend to feel less than completely fulfilled.

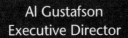

| Al Gustafson Executive Director | *Creating Meaning* |

Al Gustafson, Executive Director of the Crossroads Center at Old St. Patrick's Church in Chicago, reveals his values through an examination of the gifts he seeks to bequeath to the world. The mission of the Crossroads Center is to help people integrate their deeper values, including their faith and spirituality, into their work. And here "work" refers to work in the largest sense of the word, encompassing career, community, and family involvement. As Executive Director, Al's responsibilities are myriad; he does everything from developing programs to editing the Center's magazine, *The Works,* to fundraising. He even admits he occasionally takes out the garbage.

Al defines his calling as *creating meaning.* The thread that weaves through everything he does at Crossroads is helping others find a deeper sense of meaning in their personal and work lives. His own gifts, which he says center around an innate sensitivity and compassion for other people's cares and concerns, are utilized to their utmost in all aspects of his job.

The Crossroads Center environment is perfectly consistent

with Al's own deepest values. He remembers that, as a young man, searching for meaning in his own life, he had an unformed dream that someday he would be able to work in a situation that was entirely voluntary. That is, he imagined working entirely for something he believed in, quite apart from any financial compensation. Now, two decades later, he finds himself in just that position. Al is quite literally doing what he would do "if he won the lottery." Having achieved a level of financial success he believes is "enough" for himself and his family, Al made the decision to go off salary. He considers himself amply blessed in other areas of life and views his work at the Crossroads Center as his special opportunity to give back to the world and, in his own small way, make it a better place.

As Al's example illustrates, it comes back again to a question of values: if we're fulfilling the urge to give our gifts away to others in an environment that is consistent with what we really do value, then we feel most fulfilled. When we live our lives in conscious connection with our calling, we truly come alive.

Chapter 6

how do I heed the call?

"It's Not My Trip, Man"

I'm experiencing the most harrowing taxi ride of my life. My driver has already cut off half a dozen cars on his way out of the airport; now he's driving down the shoulder of the highway to get around the traffic jam.

"Hey, I'm not really in a hurry," I say, trying to drop a hint. My driver doesn't take it. He swings wildly from the shoulder back onto the road and then the passing lane, narrowly missing the back of a pick-up truck.

"Hey. Listen. Please." I knock on the plastic divider between the our seats. "Could you slow down? This is making me nervous."

The driver doesn't even acknowledge me. "Asshole!" he growls at a minivan blocking our way. Then, leaning on the horn, he cuts back across the right lane and onto the shoulder, the car's wheels spitting gravel behind us.

I fumble for the seatbelt but there isn't one, so I grab hold of the strap hanging down by the window. My arm is practically wrenched off as my driver swerves onto the exit ramp and into city traffic.

Here, it's no better. My driver is constantly leaning on his horn and swearing. He punches the gas and jams on the brake; I'm getting whiplash every half a block.

A couple of times I try to engage him in conversation,

105

hoping that this will calm him down, but I have no luck. He has no interest whatsoever it talking to me; his entire focus is on all the "assholes" that crowd our way.

Finally, we arrive at my hotel. The driver pulls over to the curb with a squeal of tires and one more whiplash for the road.

As I'm paying him, I try one last time to connect. "Man, that was a wild ride," I say, still feeling my heart throbbing in my chest. "I would have liked it lot better at about half the speed."

"Well, that's nice for you," he says, taking the money I hand over.

"Don't you care that you're scaring your customers half to death?"

"That's not my trip, man."

I watch him peel off my change from a wad of bills. "Your customers aren't your trip?"

"What? You from the Taxi Commission or something?" he says, counting out my bills. "Look, I drive the friggin' cab, okay? All that other crap? It's not my trip, man. You want a calm ride? Rent a limo."

He hands me my change. I consider how much to tip him. And then, I decide not to at all. I'm sure he'll understand—it's not my trip, man.

Is your job "your trip?" Or do you just "drive the friggin' cab"? Have you found work that provides you with reasonable opportunities to give your gifts away? Or are you still struggling to figure out what you want to be when you grow up?

Assuming you've heard your calling, how can you heed it?

That's something to think about—and, in this chapter, we will.

A Life of Your Own

In Richard Yates' best-selling 1961 novel, *Revolutionary Road,* the protagonist, Frank Wheeler, tells his friend what he's looking for in a job:

> All I want is to get enough dough coming in to keep us solvent for the next year or so, till I can figure things out; meanwhile, I want to retain my own identity. Therefore the thing I'm most anxious to avoid is any kind of work that can be considered 'interesting' in its

own right. I want some big, swollen old corporation
that's been bumbling along making money in its sleep
for a hundred years, where they have to hire eight guys
for every one job because none of them can be expected
to care about whatever boring thing it is they're supposed to be doing. I want to go into that kind of place
and say, Look. You can have my body and my nice col-
lege-boy smile for so many hours a day, in exchange for
so many dollars, and beyond that we'll leave each other
strictly alone.

Almost a decade later, still stuck in that same "uninteresting"
job, Frank tries to explain to his colleague, Ordway, why he's planning to quit so that he and his wife and family can sell everything
they own and move to Paris to live:

"My God, are artists and writers the only people entitled to lives of their own? Look. The only reason I'm in
this half-assed job is because—well, I suppose there's lots
of reasons, but here's the point. If I started making a list
of all the reasons, the one reason I damn sure couldn't
put down is that I like it, because I don't. And I've got
this funny feeling that people are better off doing some
kind of work that they like."

"Fine!" Ordway insisted. "Fine! Fine! Don't let's get all
defensive and riled up, please. My only simple-minded
question is this: What kind do you like?"

"If I knew that," Frank said, "I wouldn't have to be
taking a trip to find out."

Ironically, Frank never takes that trip. Events conspire to keep
him in his "uninteresting" job. Life takes hold of his plans and shuf-
fles them around. In the end, we wonder whether Frank ever finds a
life of his own, or if he just accepts the hand life has dealt him.

And of course, Yates' novel is just one of countless dramatiza-
tions of the soul-numbing effects of lives lived without a sense of
calling. From Sloan Wilson's literary classic *The Man in the Gray
Flannel Suit* to the Academy Award-winning Best Picture *American*

Beauty, we've seen what happens to people when their jobs suck the life out of them. We're drawn to these stories for the same reason we can't help rubbernecking at traffic accidents: we imagine ourselves in the same situation and have to find out what it's like. We see ourselves in Yates' Frank Wheeler or Wilson's Tom Rath or *American Beauty's* Lester Burnham and don't know whether to laugh or to cry or both.

Sometimes such stories function as a wake-up call; after reading or seeing them, we want to take stock of our lives and make changes. Sometimes, they depress us for days; we just want to stay in bed with the covers over our heads. Usually, though, they filter through our consciousness like a light rain; we're affected by them but then we carry on, pretty much the same as before. Any dissatisfactions they may have stirred up are quickly set aside and we go on with our lives and our jobs, "uninteresting" and "half-assed" as they may be.

Is this any way to live, though? Isn't there more to life than avoiding any sense of involvement in what we do? Shouldn't we be looking for a stronger sense of connection between who we are and what we do? If Frank Wheeler is right and people are better off doing something they like to do, how come more of us aren't doing it? How come *all of us* aren't heeding our calling?

And more importantly, if we're not, how can we?

What's Your Story?

The contemporary philosopher Alisdaire Macintyre argues that human beings are essentially story-telling animals. We become who we are through the telling of stories that aspire to truth. It is through the hearing of fables, myths, fairy tales, gossip—all manner of conversation—that we learn what it means to be a child and, ultimately, an adult. Deprive children of stories, says Macintyre, and you leave them unscripted, anxious stutterers in their actions as in their words. Our status as heroes and heroines in our own narratives is so important that our entire personal identity must be understood in terms of the stories we hear and tell.

Macintyre may be overstating it, but there's no doubt that our stories—what we tell ourselves about our choices and our actions—form the foundations of our identities. The way we process the events in our lives through language makes a huge difference. The same incident, described in two different ways, becomes two different incidents.

Think about the story you tell yourself about a day at work. To the question, "What are you doing?" you may answer in any number of ways: "Making a living," "Contributing to the success of my organization," "Just putting in time," "Supporting my family." All of these may be equally true depending on the story you're telling. But what's critical to notice is that your description of what's happening will contribute to that description's accuracy. The story we tell ourselves makes that story come true.

What this means is that we can effect real change in our personal and professional lives by changing the stories we tell ourselves. We can understand ourselves better by better understanding our personal narratives. By rewriting the stories we tell ourselves about who we are and what we do, and we can reconceptualize our lives in ways that make it possible to write in more happiness, success, and fulfillment.

An effective first step in this rewriting process is to retrace our steps. How did we get where were are? What choices did we make or not make? How did events transpire such that we're doing what we're doing today? Did we choose our work or did it choose us?

Dave's story illustrates what we mean.

I can't say I ever made a conscious decision to become a writer. Writing was just something I'd always done. From the time I was about 11, I kept a journal; I always liked corresponding by mail with friends; and in school, I was that weird kid who actually enjoyed English composition class. But it never really occurred to me that I could make a living writing, that doing what came so naturally could actually be a career choice. So, for the first part of my life, I considered writing more of an avocation than a vocation; I wrote for fun, without any real prospect of making money off it.

In my early 20s, more or less on a lark, I wrote a few pages of jokes for a stand-up comedian who was appearing at a club near my apartment in Los Angeles. Much to my surprise, he liked some of them, and eventually paid me for a few. It wasn't much, but it gave me a taste of earning money for doing what I liked best.

So it was basically an accident that I started writing for a living and even more of a fluke that I ever got a full-time job doing it. Struggling to make ends meet as an aspiring comedy writer, I usually read the entertainment trade paper, Daily Variety, *looking for leads of one type or another. One day there was an ad from a corporate training company in Santa Fe, New Mexico that was looking for a writer with experience in interactive multimedia. I reckoned that, having supported myself for nearly three years on various odd and sundry writing gigs, from jokes to press releases to an article on gambling for an in-flight magazine, I could call myself a writer; as for the multimedia experience—well, I had spent many hours and countless quarters playing a video game called Dragon's Quest. So, in my letter of application, I emphasized how this gave me a unique perspective on the effectiveness of multimedia and tons of ideas about how to employ it effectively as a tool for learning.*

Apparently I was convincing, because about two months later, I was hired. Suddenly, I was a professional writer in the corporate training business, an industry that, two months earlier, I didn't even know existed. I liked getting a regular paycheck for writing and I loved the people I worked with and so, for a couple of years, it seemed pretty great. Occasionally, I had a nagging suspicion that I wasn't really expressing what I cared most about by developing materials to help salespeople sell more effectively but it wasn't until a consultant named Dick Leider came to speak to us that my underlying feelings were revealed to me.

Hired at no small expense to inspire employees of our company to discover their purpose and, in doing so, recommit to the corporate mission, Dick inspired me to discover that I wasn't really satisfied doing what I was doing. Although I felt that my talents as a writer were being well-employed, I came to realize that I lacked any real passion for the problems our company was devoted to solving.

So I left the company; my wife and I sold everything we owned, and we moved to Paris where I tried to live the expatriate writer dream of Hemingway and Fitzgerald. Although it was wonderfully romantic, I eventually came to see that this wasn't me, either. The lack of regular contact with colleagues and co-workers got to me. Although I was pretty passionate about what I was doing, I ultimately found the environment oppressive. I valued human contact in a way that being a writer in a garret didn't fulfill.

We moved back to the States and I started my own free-lance writing company. It seemed for a while that I had found my perfect job. I was using my gifts; I was generally passionate about the projects I chose to work on; and, usually, my values of teamwork and shared purpose were met in dealings with clients and colleagues. But still, there was something missing. It was something bigger, something that had to do with the manner in which I was (or wasn't) giving back to the world.

It was through the writing of Repacking Your Bags *with Dick that the disconnect around my calling emerged for me. I realized that while I loved writing and that while putting words together represented the primary manner in which I sought to make a difference in the world, a writer wasn't actually what I wanted to be when I grew up. Writing was part of it—a big part—but it was really just a means to an end that, for me, was really about promoting understanding. I came to see that what I was consistently drawn to wasn't actually the wordsmithing, it was what those words could do. And when I had the experience of helping people to understand things that helped them understand themselves better, this is when I really came alive. Oddly enough, this "aha" led me to, among other things, graduate school in philosophy and the work I currently do exploring philosophy with children. More importantly, it led me to the feeling I described earlier in this book of finally having become what I wanted to be when I grew up.*

Looking back over my life—retracing my path—enables me to see the steps and missteps that led me to where I am today. It gives me insight into the manner in which I made choices—or let them be made for me— and helps me consider ways I might have chosen differently, or better. Above all, it's clear to me from looking back that I made a lot of mistakes. I often took jobs that didn't suit me. Time and again I found myself involved in projects that were a poor match for my skills and interests. A lot of time and energy was wasted; a lot of sleep was lost.

I often wonder what would have happened had I been clearer about what I was looking for from the start. It's easy to imagine the struggles I would have avoided had I not spent so much time spinning my wheels. I might have arrived where I am today with many fewer difficulties and far more satisfaction. It's all worked out in a way, but it could have happened with a lot less confusion and effort.

What Is Your Life Project?

Some people, like Dave, arrive at a sense of calling gradually; others experience it in a flash; still others are lucky enough to have always known. The key point is that, while calling may not correspond to our primary means of earning a living, it always refers to a "life project" that is central to our identity—and which enables us to fulfill our place in the world.

Coming to identify and embrace that life project is a process that occurs from the inside out. As Dave's story illustrates, trying to impose a life project on ourselves from the outside guarantees dissatisfaction. We have to come to hear and heed our calling through a personal process of self-examination and exploration. Nobody can do it for us.

You can facilitate that process by asking yourself two core questions that get at your life project from the inside out. These are:

- *What do I want?*

- *How will I know it when I get it?*

Your Calling Journal is a good place to write down and reflect upon your answers to these questions. We encourage you to take some time to sit down with these questions, and as you do so, structure your answers around a number of explorations that support the overall inquiry.

As you answer the "What do I want?" question, ask yourself how you would rate yourself on a 1–10 scale in the areas of leisure/play, learning/growth, career/work, money matters, romance, spirituality, friendships, and health. Think about what it would take to be a 10 in each area. Additionally, reflect upon what question that, if answered, would cause an immeasurable change for the better in your life. Ask yourself the same question about your work. Finally, think about who you would like to be your "life's work advisors." Imagine that you are a corporation and you have a board of directors. Who are the people you would count on to listen, give advice, inspire you and guide you?

Exploring the question more deeply, think about the kind of family you were born into. What characteristics of your childhood family life still influence you today? What were your parents' expectations of you? What did they want you to be when you grew up? Compare their desires to your own. What did you want to be when you grew up? Reflect upon your answers in light of your current situation. Think back to your Calling Card. What does your calling tell you about the life work you are engaged in? Where is the fit good and where can it be improved? How can you make what you do more consistent with who you are?

As you answer the "How will I know it when I get it?" question, reflect again on how you ended up doing the work you currently do. Draw a map or diagram if it helps. Spend some time reflecting on what work means to you. Why do you work? How would you describe your feelings about your work at this moment? Think about what makes the good days good at work and the bad days bad. Imagine your life and your work life on a timeline. What is it too late for you to do? What is it too early for? What is it the right time for? What would you most like to happen in the next twelve months? What do your answers to these questions tell you about yourself?

"What Have They Got That I Don't?"

Lots of people—perhaps most—have jobs that, at least on the face of it, are not expressions of their true calling. One friend who's *actually* a poet works as a bank teller. Another is a successful advertising executive when what she loves best of all is staying home doing art projects with her kids. And of course *every* waiter in *every* fancy restaurant is *really* an actor waiting for his break.

Why do people put up with this? Why do so many of us choose to live lives that aren't *really* our own. Is it money? Is it fear? Is it laziness or bad luck?

Perhaps it's a combination of all of these and more. Perhaps it's just "the way things are." Perhaps we aren't meant to experience a consistent sense of joy and commitment to what we do.

But this would belie the fact that many people do lead lives where satisfaction and fulfillment at work is commonplace. What we need to ask ourselves then, is "What do they have that I don't?" And more importantly, "How can I get it, too?"

Naming our calling and approaching our day-to-day activities in light of it is what heeding is all about. Seeing oneself as someone who "brings joy," for example, rather than someone who "fills orders" or "makes deals" enables us more consistently to achieve what we set out to do. It improves our likelihood of success in our endeavors and allows us more often to get what we want while simultaneously wanting what we get.

This doesn't mean, however, that we refrain from making real changes when real changes are called for. At some point, we need to stop thinking and talking about what we want and make the effort to attain it—even if it means making some tough choices. Of course, we risk failure if we do so; but if we don't, we guarantee it.

Robert Schulman Physician		*Giving Care*

For years, a doctor friend of ours, Bob Schulman, had a vision of having his own private practice in which he would combine his training in Western medicine with his longtime interest and expertise in complementary care, including Chinese medicine and acupuncture. The challenges of building a non-traditional practice, however, were daunting. Moreover, faced with the necessity of paying back the huge debt he accumulated over the course of his medical education, Bob felt reticent to take the risk necessary to branch out on his own.

So, for a number of years, he endured salaried positions in various hospitals and clinics—positions that paid handsomely, but which never really gave him the opportunity to express his calling as a physician. Bob is a healer in the full sense of the word. He is interested in a holistic approach to medicine. The jobs he held at other people's clinics usually required him to be a technician of sorts; at best, he was asked to focus specifically on a patient's illness or injury as opposed to their whole person; at worst, he was asked to simply perform "procedures" to maximize "patient throughput."

Bob felt deeply dissatisfied in these jobs. There were, of course, aspects he enjoyed—the patient contact, the opportunity to learn new things, the money—but he felt as if he were stagnating. He certainly wasn't doing the sort of work that drew him to medicine in the first place. He wasn't expressing his natural calling to be a healer.

And yet he put up with it for quite a while. It was almost ten years after he finished his residency before he finally opened his own practice. During that time, he held at least half a dozen different positions, some concurrently. Occasionally, he almost managed to convince himself that this was all there was—that compromise was necessary, that his vision was impractical and unattainable.

But calling cannot be silenced so easily. For Bob, the voice within continued to speak to him. Even in traditional hospital settings, he remained fascinated by alternative approaches to medical care and pain relief. Breaks and weekends would find him with his head in a book or journal about non-Western treatments and philosophies of care. Most of his vacations were taken up by workshops in acupuncture or Chinese herbology.

At some point, the pain of *not* doing what he really wanted to do outweighed the difficulties associated with doing it. Finding office space and negotiating with realtors was a nightmare, but not nearly as bad as coming in every day to an office where he didn't want to be. Putting together a marketing plan and taking steps to build up his practice was challenging, but it sure beat the challenge of working to build someone else's clientele. And, although the fear of striking out on his own was intense, it paled in comparison to the fear that he was wasting his life.

So Bob finally stopped working for other hospitals and clinics. It took more than a year to disengage himself from existing responsibilities and contracts and get fully set up on his own, but he did it. The first few months on his own were pretty dicey; sometimes he only saw two or three patients a day. But, through word of mouth and professional connections, his practice expanded. Of course, it's still difficult. Given his non-traditional approach, there continue to be challenges with getting insurance companies to cover certain procedures. Also, some potential patients are turned off by his holistic approach, which requires them to take some degree of responsibility for their own care. Consequently, his practice hasn't expanded as rapidly as he had hoped.

What this means is that Bob's lifestyle has taken a few hits. Renovating his apartment was put on hold. Renting a beachhouse for the summer is out. That new car he'd had his eye on is going to have to wait. But the trade-off has been worth it: Bob may not have the lifestyle he once had, but now, at last, he has his life.

Or to put it another way, he has found what—individually and collectively—we are all seeking: to be at home in the universe.

A Place in the World

Humans lived as hunter-gatherers for almost all of human history. It is only relatively recently in our time on earth that most of us moved to an agricultural society; it's for an even shorter duration that we have organized ourselves into an industrial society; and the emerging knowledge society is a mere blink of an eye in the overall story. Doesn't it make sense, therefore, to assume that we have something to learn from people who still live in the most natural and enduring of all human societies? Isn't it likely that they have wisdom that can assist us in our own quest for authentic fulfillment—our own effort to hear and heed our life's calling—even in the contemporary knowledge society? Since they are the true "elders" of humanity, shouldn't we pay attention to what their experience can teach us?

Hunter-gatherers, like the Hadza people in Tanzania, East Africa, have lived with almost no material possessions for hundreds of thousands of years, enjoying lives that are in many ways richer and more purposeful than our own. The Hadza have structured their lives so they need little, want little, and for the most part have all the means of fulfilling their needs around them. Life for them is a process of collaboration with nature in which there is no separation between who they are, what they do, and where they live.

The lack of preoccupation with acquiring material goods gives the Hadza unrestricted freedom to enjoy life, to follow their passions. Most of a hunter-gatherer's life is not spent in the workplace, away from family and friends, but rather, in talking, playing, resting, sharing, and celebrating—in short, in *being human*. This is an ideal in contemporary affluent societies, but it is an ideal that is largely unattained.

The Hadza, for example, spend only about 15 to 20 hours a week "working," that is, getting food. But even their methods of hunting and gathering are convivial and joyful. You don't see any Hadza tribe members dreading Monday mornings or being stressed out over upcoming deadlines or complaining about the number of meetings they have to attend. They spend their abundant leisure time doing the very things we associate with happiness. They enjoy an amazing degree of personal freedom. They also live in harmony with their environment, protecting, rather than destroying, the resources on which their lives depend.

For some reason, we were taught a myth that only after the discovery of agriculture did humans have enough leisure time to create culture; only then did we become truly human. But the more we learn about the Hadza, the more we realize that our affluent lifestyles do not fully reflect human nature. In a very real sense—the sense of having happiness and unlimited access to all one needs—the Hadza are far more affluent than we are.

In addition, the idea that work is drudgery and that its purpose is to earn us enough money so that we can enjoy our "real" lives is non-existent in the Hadza and other hunter-gatherer societies. For the Hadza, work is social and cooperative; it's as much a part of "real" life as anything else they do. The work of hunting and gathering is integrated with ritual, social life, and creative expression to a degree unknown to most of us in the contemporary world.

The Hadza are at home in the world. They have a genuine passion for and connection to the world around them. Their lives have a spiritual core that infuses everything around them with value and meaning. For the Hadza, all things participate in life and consequently everything—human, animal, plant, rock—is viewed as having intrinsic worth. Walking with the Hadza, one never comes across anything that does not belong, that does not fulfill a function. Be it a bird, a berry, or a tree, everything occupies an essential place in the natural world.

Obviously, we cannot return to a hunter-gatherer way of life. We can, however, incorporate some of the world view of hunter-gatherer societies into our own. Many of our trials and tribulations arise from our inability to discern our place in the overall scheme of things. The Hadza seem to be free of such difficulties. They consider themselves *a part of,* not *apart from, the* natural world. They have no questions about how they fit in, what they are doing here, or why.

Dick says, "For years, I have seen my friends, colleagues, and clients struggle with the very questions that the Hadza have naturally answered. I have coached literally hundreds of people who are looking for answers about their place in the world, about what they should be doing with their lives, about who they are and what their purpose on earth is meant to be. As I have worked with them through their evolutionary struggles, I have also seen events happening in their lives—and my own—that have given me faith in a process much greater than the coaching relationship we're engaged in. By becoming aware of the cycle of life, I have been able to help my clients realize the profound and spiritual connections among all of us. Coming to appreciate the Hadza perspective on life, I have been better able to communicate our essential place in the overall scheme of things. Seeing life through their eyes has been my guide to seeing and feeling these connections. To be part of this natural discovery process with my clients and share in their developing awareness is my passion as a career coach. Helping others to uncover their calling and having faith in a greater process that leads us all to understand ourselves and each other has taught me about my own place in the world."

And finding our own place, to feel at home in the world, is what heeding our calling is all about.

Chapter 7

legacy—did I answer the call?

Are You Driving a Taxi?

My taxi driver snakes through traffic effortlessly. He cuts down sidestreets and through alleyways, missing one tie-up after another. At this rate, I'll be in my hotel room half an hour early and snug in bed that much sooner than I expected. I marvel at my driver's ability to avoid delays and keep moving forward.

"How long have you been driving?" I ask, appreciating his expertise.

"'Bout nine hours," he cracks. "Still got three more hours before I cash out."

"No, seriously. You're quite a driver. I was wondering how long it's taken you to learn all these shortcuts."

He chuckles and makes a sharp right to avoid a truck unloading down the street. "Ten years. Right after I got laid off from my teaching job."

"You were a teacher? What grade?"

"Hmmm . . . 13th through 20th, I guess you'd say. Mostly undergrad, some graduates." He taps his ID card rubber-banded to the sun visor. "See this? I don't put the Ph.D. after my name here. But I'm a doctor; professor of sociology for 25 years."

"No kidding. So how come you're driving a taxi?"

"You know a better place to study sociology?" he asks rhetorically. He steers around a couple of construction sawhorses in the street and proceeds to answer his own question. "I see all types here: rich, poor, young, old, folks like you on business trips, people on vacations, one time I had a guy propose to his girlfriend, another time, a lady almost gave birth right in my back seat."

"You're still doing sociology, then?"

"Hell, yes!" announces the driver, honking his horn at a jaywalking pedestrian for emphasis. "I'm writing a book." He picks up a sheaf of papers on the seat next to him. "I mean, what else can I do? I've been interested in this stuff ever since I was a kid. Just because I'm not in the classroom doesn't mean I'm not still a sociologist."

I think about my own efforts at extra-curricular study. "Yeah, but isn't it tough to stay motivated when you're not in that environment?"

He shrugs. "For some people, maybe. And for me maybe if it were some other subject. But this is what I do. It's what keeps me going."

My hotel appears at the end of the block. I start to gather up my briefcase and coat. One of my business cards falls from a pocket. My job title stares me in the face; I wonder what is it about what I do that keeps me going.

"Look," he continues. "Nobody's gonna remember me as a taxi driver after I'm gone. Anything I do that lasts, that's what matters. So, I write a book, I get my ideas out, I'm immortal as far as that goes."

He pulls up to the corner to let me out. "Here you go. Have a good stay."

I pay and climb from the taxi. As I begin to close the door, my driver holds up his manuscript pages again.

"It's what you leave to the world that really matters," he says. "All the rest is just taxi driving. Know what I mean?"

In that moment, I think I do—and I know that my taxi driver has given me much more than just a ride.

What about you? How would you compare your experience to that taxi driver's? Are you leaving something meaningful to the world? Or just driving a taxi?

It's a question that gets to the heart of calling. What do you want to leave behind as the legacy of your years of work? What would you like people to say about you and what you did? When we heed our life's calling, we make something more of our life than just our life. We spill over the edges of our allotted time and make a difference for the ages. In short, we leave a legacy that carries on after we're gone.

Actually, to be honest, we leave a legacy no matter what we do. The choices we made define the person we were whether we like it or not. It's just that some people leave legacies that express their *true* selves, while others simply leave a husk of a life that signifies little of what they were really about.

Replacing Selfishness with Selflessness

Many voices call to us during our lives; most will not resonate with the sound of our calling. We are challenged, therefore, to decide which call to heed, and when.

The idea of calling includes a commitment to be moved by something other than simple self-interest. Calling, by its definition—the inner urge to give our gifts away—is a dedication to something larger than ourselves. Calling means replacing selfishness with selflessness.

How does your work help others? How is your work an expression of service?

No matter what people do for a living—taxi driver, physician, shopkeeper, consultant, executive—we all want to feel good about our work. We want it to count for something. We want it to express who we are—our gifts, our passions, our values. We don't want to waste our precious time on earth doing something meaningless. We want to feel that, at least in some small way, our work contributes to making the world a better place. This urge is fulfilled only when what we do makes a positive difference in someone else's life.

As we search to hear and heed our life's calling, we are apt to make many false starts and wrong turns. All of us will experience embarrassing failures at some point. Most of us will change jobs and careers many times as we seek expression of our vocational voice. All of these steps and missteps, seen from the point of view of our legacy, represent an unfolding of our calling in the world.

When we come to heed our calling, we find ourselves becoming aware of the legacy we leave through our work. We develop a deeper appreciation for the ways we can serve others. We feel free to bring our values to work, to take a stand for what we believe, to be the same person on the job as we are away from it. We simply refuse to check any meaningful part of ourselves at the office or factory door. As we grow whole through heeding our calling, we bring our whole selves to our work.

Think of people who have brought their true selves to their life's work: Gandhi, Einstein, Eleanor Roosevelt, Mother Teresa. Think of how their legacies extend far beyond the scope of their lives. The effect that they have had—and continue to have—on people's lives cannot be measured in terms of a single lifetime. Their contributions to humanity ripple out and touch people in ways that no one person could possibly imagine doing. But because they have left a *legacy,* their abilities to make a difference are virtually unlimited. The tune they whistled during their lives continues on after they're gone, touching people's lives in truly unexpected ways.

Of course, you don't have to be Gandhi or Mother Teresa to leave a legacy. Individuals from all walks of life lead lives whose positive influence resonates after they're gone. Many of us recall parents or grandparents, none of them famous, whose model we aspire to and whose legacies guide us. What most of these people have in common is a strength of calling and a commitment to a way of living that guides us. And the source of this is a powerful spirit in their lives—articulated or not—that all life is sacred.

Matt Johnson, Sole Proprietor MR Johnson's Antiques		*Creating* *Beauty*

Matt Johnson, the 28 year-old owner of MR Johnson's Antiques in Seattle, understands this spirit and is moved by it in profound ways. Matt characterizes his calling as *creating beauty.* He is passionate about helping to create environments that allow people to experience a sense of security, a sense of belonging, a sense of home. This is the legacy he is creating and it comes from an appreciation of what has been bequeathed to him. "I've lived an incredibly charmed life," he says. "And I want to give others the opportunity to experience what I have."

"I think the first antique I purchased was when I was 9," he says, "It was a wristwatch. And from then on, it was really just the positive responses I got—not only from my parents, but from their friends, and other people. When I try to explain why I have always collected stuff, it isn't materialistic, it was just that I always loved to have a lot of things and know a lot about a lot of things." That love for things and their histories eventually led to Matt's opening his own antiques, art, and collectibles store. His shop, overflowing with curios and "uniquems," has earned a reputation as the place to go in Seattle to find one-of-a-kind gifts or to fill out a collection—whether it be fountain pens, baseball cards, salt and pepper shakers, bakelight radios, or even Pez dispensers. And Matt, although decades younger than most antique store owners, has already earned a reputation as the person to talk to with questions about antique and collectable items.

He remembers the many road trips he took with his family as a child. He and his parents and sister used to take several car vacations a year on which they would stop at garage sales and junk shops looking for unusual items. It was here that Matt developed his love for strange and beautiful things. He even managed to cajole his mom and dad into giving him an "antique allowance" on their travels to augment his burgeoning collections. They encouraged him to find his own treasures. "I collected all sorts of things: baseball cards, bottle caps, and knives, and rock collections. I had thirty hobbies by the time I was nine or ten. Then, when I was 15 or so, I started going garage sale-ing with my Uncle Jim every weekend. We would pull up in his Cadillac—this baby-faced kid and this sorta scruffy-looking hippie guy—and people would basically just give us stuff to get us to go away."

It was just natural, then, that Matt would end up in the line of work he is in. "On one of our road trips, I drew a picture of a giant mansion in the country that was my antique store. It was more a kind of fantasy about having a place to house my own stuff. I hadn't thought through the retail aspect of it until right before I opened the shop." In fact, it took Matt's good friend to point out the obvious to him. "Why don't you just open a store?" he said. And from that point, it all fell into place.

These days, Matt says he often has to remind himself that he's working. "I feel that I work a fraction of the time I actually do. I might put in a 90-hour week, but it only feels like 30 or so. I love what I'm doing and that's what gives me the high-burn intensity to be moving furniture all the time, delivering things, picking things up, acquiring all these little things, cleaning them, dusting them, re-arranging them, and all that energy just comes right out of my feelings of joy to be doing this."

Think about your own work. Can you say the same? Do you feel like you work a third of the time you do? Or is more like three times the amount?

When we're operating, as Matt is, out of a deep sense of calling, our energy and joy border on limitless. The hours fly by; work doesn't seem like work at all. The challenge, though, is to sustain this sense of calling over time, and in doing so, begin to craft a legacy that distinguishes the life we have led. Responding to this challenge lies in a re-investigation of calling, an exploration that takes us beyond the boundaries of our own life and examines how our lived sense of calling carries on after we're gone.

What Really Matters, Anyway?

In the end, what really matters, anyway? We're born, we live, we die; a thousand years from now, it's highly unlikely that any of us will be remembered. A million years from now, it's probable that the entire human race will be forgotten.

In spite of this, though, most of us feel that our lives matter. We generally think it makes a difference whether we do one thing or another. The choices that present themselves to us are real choices. Even though they might not affect our distant ancestors many centuries in the future, they do affect us and those around us. Our happiness, our satisfactions, our concerns—small as they are in the "grand scheme of things"—fill the universe, at least from our perspectives. The attention we pay to sports or fashion or even politics is evidence of how deeply we care about things that are ephemeral, if not downright insignificant.

Given, then, our ability to make mountains out of molehills combined with our perfectly reasonable concern for what happens in our lives, it might be difficult to determine what really matters and what doesn't—even within the context of our own lives. How can we tell whether a choice is really important or if we're just making a big deal out of something that's going to seem pointless in just a few years?

The answer is: we can't! Or at least, we can't say for certain. All any of us has to do is reflect back upon how bent out of shape we got over an event in junior high school to remind us that what we take to be very important now will seem laughably petty one day.

On the other hand, we can make some fairly good predictions about what sorts of things will have staying power. We can be pretty confident that some things we care about now will still seem important to us years from now. We may not be able to say with certainty that *everything* that's currently at the top of our lists will always be, but—if we think about it—we're apt to do a better job of devoting ourselves to those things that really matter to us in the long run.

So what sorts of things tend to seem lastingly important?

When people look back upon their lives, nearly everyone agrees that relationships are paramount. The choices we make that sustain and nurture our caring connections with others are typically those that are least regretted. Few people look back upon their lives and wish they had spent less time with their loved ones. When all is said and done, what we cherish most, what gives our life meaning—what really matters—is the experiences we've shared with family members, friends, and colleagues.

Think about your life and work. Don't the highest highs—and the lowest lows—include others? Certainly there is much satisfaction to be taken from our own accomplishments, but those that we will take to our graves with us more often than not involve the participation of at least one other person. Our first kiss, our first heartbreak, the time our team won (or lost) the league championship, when our work group pulled an all-nighter to prepare for a major presentation, helping our children with their schoolwork, a last vacation with an aged parent—these are the events that stick with us.

Even money-making lags behind. A recent study revealed what Americans think is most important in life. Just 27 percent of those surveyed said earning a lot of money was "absolutely necessary" for them to consider their lives a success, placing it far behind having strong family relationships (94 percent), having good friends (87 percent), helping people in need (87 percent) and becoming well-educated (82 percent). Clearly, those intangibles make a bigger difference to our satisfaction than how much money we make.

What this seems to suggest is that—given a choice between doing almost anything and furthering a relationship with someone we care about—we ought to do the latter. We ought to take risks when it comes to letting people know how we feel about them. We should, in general, make that visit or place that phone call we've been meaning to. On Sunday afternoon, when we have to choose between going into the office or staying home with the family, we should—all other things being equal—favor our families.

Again, reflect upon your own experience. Which do you tend to regret more—the times you put yourself out on a limb with someone else or the times you failed to? When you lie in bed at night, turning over all the "mistakes" you've made in life, don't you tend to agonize more about what you didn't say than what you did? Isn't it usually true that the only regrets we really have are the risks we *didn't* take?

If I Could Do It All Over Again, What Would I Do Differently?

Some years ago, Dick conducted dozens of interviews with older adults—men and women in their 70s and 80s—in which he asked them to reflect back upon their lives. He explored their memories of work and family as well as their attitudes about the choices they'd made or not made in their lives. Many regretted that they had not taken enough risks in their relationships; they expressed remorse that they hadn't been as fearless in love as they could have been.

Looking back over their lives, many expressed a common fear: they worried that their lives would not, in the end, count as truly meaningful. Their number one fear was not of death; rather, what frightened them most was the prospect of having lived a meaningless life. The prospect of being forgotten after they were gone was far more troubling than the prospect of being gone. They were, by and large, relatively resolved about their deaths; only a few, however, were as equally comfortable about their lives. Given a second chance, they would have done more to ensure that they had left their distinctive marks on the world, marks that others would remember them by after they were gone. What emerged as a common theme was legacy; they wanted to leave behind something unique, something that would demonstrate that their time spent on earth wasn't in vain.

Many of us will admit that we share the feelings of these older adults. Their concerns are remarkably consistent with our own. Death is indeed a frightening prospect, but not nearly as frightening as the prospects associated with living—in particular, the prospect of not having lived our own unique lives. Like the poet Dylan Thomas, we want to not go gently into that good night; we want to rage against the dying of the light by having created a light of our own that can illuminate the way for others.

The question, of course, is how exactly do we do that? How do we truly shine so that others can light their own way forward by following our path?

Think about light for a moment and how it is generated. Any time there is illumination, something somewhere must burn. Whether it's sunlight, candlelight, even electric light, the source is the same: excited electrons, radiation, heat. So, in order for any of us to generate our own light source, we too must burn—metaphorically, that is. We must feel a passion for something burning within us. We create light in our own lives—light that illuminates the way for others—by feeding this passion so that it burns ever more brightly.

Among the older adults that Dick interviewed, those who had a passion for their work were those who felt their lives mattered. Their sense of satisfaction and meaning went well beyond any financial rewards. They saw their work as spiritual, as a chance to serve others. They believed that what they did made the world a better place. It didn't just satisfy their pocketbook or ego; it satisfied their soul.

 Jim Gleason
Security Guard

 Getting to the
Heart of Matters

Consider the example of Jim Gleason. Although he perfectly embodies the Hollywood image of the successful corporate CEO—trim, tanned, and articulate—Jim actually works as a security guard in Dick's office building. But it isn't just his executive demeanor that sets him apart from most security personnel; what drew Dick's attention initially was Jim's reading material. Signing in on evenings and weekends under Jim's watchful eye, Dick couldn't help noticing the leather attaché case behind the guard desk filled with books on Zen and other Eastern philosophies.

Striking up a conversation, Dick learned that Jim has been on a kind of long-term spiritual quest; he has been searching for an answer to the "Who am I?" question in the works of Zen and Zen-influenced writers for years. The answer he is currently pursuing came to him in 1995. "An article about 'Constructive Living' (CL) appeared in a magazine and I ordered an audiotape and some books," says Jim. It changed Jim's life. He has been studying CL, as he calls it, ever since, receiving his certification as a CL instructor in 1999.

Jim explains that CL is a common sense "life skills" program developed by David K. Reynolds that helps people accept their feelings, know their purpose, and do what needs to be done. CL has been described as a way of looking at the world that combines straight talk and action as a guide to setting and reaching goals. From living economically to avoiding self-absorption, this provides a key to creating a behavior-centered lifestyle.

"I feel now like I did when I was 18 years old," says Jim, referring to his experience with CL. "I know what I'm doing and why I'm doing it. One of the principles of CL is 'you are what you do; to change who you are, change what you do." And that's precisely what Jim is doing with his life.

Jim believes that every moment is a fresh one. We are all changeable. Living constructively, he believes, is the cure for the confusion, self-consciousness, and dread that so many of us feel. So, Jim took that cure and became a CL instructor. He loves "doing what needs to be done" and feels, in fact, that this phrase captures the essence of his calling. "One of my motivators," he says, "is a deep sense of healthy guilt. If you look at the balance sheets, I haven't paid back a lot. Now, I'm going to be a promoter of CL in any way that I can."

Jim started his vocational journey as a Holy Cross brother, spending nine years in religious life, teaching math and science in parochial schools. He then migrated into the secular world, pursuing a career as a chemical sales engineer. For the next twenty years, he shifted back and forth between teaching, technical sales, and real estate. At one point, he left a position as a tenured professor to become a salesperson. "To go from a tenured professor to selling real estate was not a very intelligent thing to do," he admits. "But it had gotten to the point where I dreaded going back to the classroom every September."

"Today," he says, "I'm drawn back toward my original calling, the contemplative monastic life. I finally got hit on the head enough times by reality. Now I'm hoping to be active doing this work all the way into my eighties."

Right now, Jim is involved in a process he calls "creating a new past." He shares a quote from David K. Reynolds' book, *A Thousand Waves:* "The way we discover ourselves, the way we create our identity, is to look back on our past and see what kind of people we were. If we did timid things we see ourselves as timid; if we did adventurous things we see ourselves as adventurous. The way to change the way we see ourselves is to change our past." From security guard to CL instructor, Jim is truly changing who he is by changing what he does.

The passion that Jim has for his work burns so brightly that it lights the way for others to follow. He inspires his audiences who, in turn, inspire their friends and families, and so on. The effect he has upon the world he touches expands geometrically and, in turn, enables him to leave a legacy that is similarly far-reaching. But it all starts from within himself and is sustained by the passion he feels for his calling. And while Jim's individual legacy is quite unusual, his internal experience of passionate calling is available to all of us. We just have to draw upon our own passion for what we are called to do and stoke the fire on a regular, consistent basis through our daily living. In doing so, not only are we creating a legacy that distinguishes our life, we are ensuring that ours is a life of no regrets: if we had it to do all over again, differently, we wouldn't.

Leave a Little Heaven Behind

There is power in naming things. When we have a word for something, we can make sense of it in ways previously unavailable to us.

By putting a name on our own calling, we focus our energy and attention on what truly motivates us. In doing so, we naturally attract resources that make the attainment of our goals more likely. A life lived in conscious connection to calling affords us more opportunities for making a difference in the manner that makes the most difference to us. People who have identified their calling bring to their lives and work a sense of enjoyment that others lack. And from this enjoyment springs heightened success, satisfaction, and joy.

| Sean Gonsalves | | *Confronting* |
| Journalist | | *Suffering* |

A prime example of someone who brings a powerful sense of calling to his work—and who receives deep satisfaction from it—is newspaper columnist Sean Gonsalves. Sean writes a nationally syndicated column for the *Cape Cod Times* in which he regularly deals with issues of social justice, racial and economic equality, and human rights on a national and international scale.

It's not surprising that Sean finds himself occupied with communicating a vision of justice to people; from the time that he was about 10 years old, he had a sense that he was called to bear witness and tell the truth about things in some way. "Growing up in an African-American fundamentalist church," he says, "this usually means you are called to preach." But Sean heard a different call.

"I was influenced by what newspaperman George Will said: 'Being a columnist is the best job in the world. You make a living by reading, writing, and talking to people.'"

Sean defines his own calling as *confronting suffering*. He believes that there are certain purposes that undergird all we do. For him, this has to do with transforming suffering into joy. Through his writing about and speaking the truth, Sean consistently seeks to unleash the creative potential that lies within all of us. He sees himself in the tradition of freedom fighters who have enabled people to overcome the bonds—both external *and* internal—that have held them back. "I guess I would consider myself a 'freedom maker' and that's where the writing comes in, the truth-telling, which I see as central to democracy and the democratic process. If there is going to be self-rule and self-management and self-government, that requires work on the part of citizens. We need to make informed decisions, and journalists can play a role by holding leaders accountable for their actions—and that's key to a healthy democracy. And to freedom."

The legacy that Sean hopes to leave is informed and inspired by his calling. He says it is captured in an old saying by the female elders of his church, "You ought to leave a little heaven behind everywhere you go." That's what he says he's trying to do—to bring the heaven within out into the world—and what he would like to be remembered as doing. The question we ought to be asking ourselves, he says, is not what we can get *out of* life, but rather, what can we *offer to* life. What he hopes to offer is assistance to others—family, friends, readers—for transforming suffering into joy. Or even, he admits, if he's able to do that for himself, he will have conveyed the message the he feels so powerfully called to share.

Legacy? What Legacy? I'm Just One Person!

Arthur Schindler, WWII German industrialist, saved hundreds of German and Polish Jews from extermination. Now, *that's* a legacy.

Rosa Parks, civil rights activist: Her courage inspired generations of freedom fighters to take up the cause of racial equality in the United States and abroad. Now, *that's* making a difference.

But who am I? I'm just a simple working person. I have a job; I try to do my best; I pay my bills on time; I care for my family and friends. But that's about it. I'm not changing the world, that's for sure. So what is this talk of leaving a legacy? Who am I kidding?

As a matter of fact, we're kidding ourselves if we think we're *not* leaving a legacy. Everything we do touches the lives of other people. All of our actions make a difference somehow. The way we live, the way we love, the work that we do all have an effect that transcends the particulars of our day-to-day living. Whether we choose a legacy or not, the person we are stands as the difference we made when we die. It may be a small difference, but from the point of view of our own lives, it's *all* the difference there is. So we can't possibly under-estimate the importance of our legacy because, in the end, it repre-sents everything we were.

As Joseph Campbell put it so powerfully: "The call rings up the curtain, always on the mystery of transfiguration. The familiar life horizon has been outgrown; the old concepts, ideals, and emotional patterns no longer fit; the time for passing the threshold is at hand."

And this requires passing across a threshold into a deeper di-mension of ourselves. On a deeper, spiritual level, this is what is oc-curs when we heed our life's calling. When we find our voice we become agents of transformation. By expressing our calling, we make our contribution, however large or small it may be, to our time.

We should keep in mind how our effect upon the world ex-tends out in strange and unexpected ways. Most of us are familiar with the concept of "six degrees of separation." The idea is that each of us is separated from anyone else in the world by no more than six steps. We know someone who knows someone else who knows someone else and so on. So, while it may seem that Oprah Winfrey or Steve Jobs or the President of France occupies a world vastly dif-ferent from our own, it turns out that they are directly connected to us via no more than half a dozen people. It's the same thing with our legacy. We may think it's no big thing, but given the manner in which our lives indirectly touch others, it is. Thus, it behooves us— if we care about our lives at all—to make the most of the effect we have . . . and the effect *that* effect has upon others.

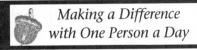

Tom Schultz
Senior Executive

Making a Difference
with One Person a Day

Tom Schultz understands that, just as his father, Jack, did before him. Tom is a second generation "Motorolan," following in the footsteps of his father, Jack, embodying—as did his father—Motorola's longstanding legacy of excellence in leadership. Jack was the first plant manager at Motorola's Mt. Pleasant facility, helping to bring out the special qualities of a small-town family-oriented workforce who had an absolute dedication to their jobs.

Tom, who now works at Motorola corporate headquarters in Schaumburg, worked summers and holidays at the plant, seeing firsthand how his father treated his employees as family. Tom considers his father's attitude typical of what Motorola is all about. "We are a family-oriented company. Legacy is a word we use a lot at Motorola."

Twenty-five years after his father's career ended, Tom is facing his own 25-year legacy. As part of a project he was working on several years ago, Tom issued a simple request to 25 of his colleagues: "How do you see me? What's my legacy?" He requested frank, honest responses from others about how they thought he might be remembered beyond retirement.

Within 48 hours, 19 people responded. Tom was surprised by the feedback, though. Hardly anyone mentioned his "hard skills"—his financial accomplishments; everyone talked about his "soft skills"—his interpersonal contributions. Like his father, the plant manager, Tom, a corporate vice-president and director of financial planning, was building a legacy about people. Tom says, "I always felt pretty good with people; the development of others is where I feel best."

Tom's legacy probably won't have much to do with Motorola's market share; rather, he will be remembered for his contributions to the "soft side" of the business. "I hate managing policies, procedures, and budgets," he admits. "But I get totally absorbed in people development discussions.

"I always ask myself, 'What impact will this decision have 100 years from now?'" His answers help Tom manifest his calling, which he defines as *making a difference with one person a day.* These days, the person with whom Tom makes the greatest difference is his daughter, Kelly, who daily faces the challenge of spina bifida. Kelly's treatments, which have included more than 40 surgeries, have, at times, tested Tom's resolve to keep making a difference at work.

As he spent more and more time with his daughter, Tom learned that the organization could get along fine without him. Exhausted by the pressures of caring for Kelly, he was ready to call it quits at Motorola. But a senior executive shocked him by saying, "Don't do it! You need us and we need you right now." Tom learned once again that the family-oriented culture, which his father had helped create, was now behind him 100%.

Tom stayed. Within the Motorola finance community, he has taken the lead in creating a world-class leadership development process. Fueled by his interest in the long-term direction of people's lives, he is creating a role for himself in which he can make a difference in, not just one, but many, people's lives a day. He says, "I love getting up in the morning to open up growth possibilities for people." Like his father, Jack, Tom is treating the people in the organization like family. And he is passing on the Schultz legacy of love and compassion to his daughter, Kelly.

Putting a Finish on Our Lives

James Hillman, in his book, *The Force of Character,* makes the point that we often misunderstand the word "character." As it is used in the media and popular press, "character" tends to refer only to those aspects of our personality that are desirable. We talk, for example, about how someone's character is defective or bad. But, as Hillman wants to point out, "character" originally referred simply to the person we are, no matter who or what that person is. Developing our character, therefore, is an activity of bringing forth *all* aspects of our personality, even those we might be less than thrilled with. Hillman also talks about the "finish" of our lives in a way that distinguishes "finish" from "end." Finishing our lives, says Hillman, is better understood as *putting a finish on* our lives—that is, burnishing our character to a high gloss. This means making all aspects of our personality shine—even those less desirable ones. For instance, if we have a cantankerous and curmudgeonly character, we can burnish this by using it for social activism and change. Or, if our character is shy and retiring, we can burnish it by taking time for deep reflection on what really matters.

The point is, there's a natural connection between finishing our lives—that is, putting a finish on our characters—and distinguishing the legacy we leave. Both require us to develop the most authentic expression of who we are. And there's no better starting point for this than our calling.

Listening with the Third Ear

There's more to life than meets the eye—and all of the senses, for that matter. Heeding our life's calling requires a mode of searching that isn't limited to the merely tangible. We need to connect with aspects of understanding that may be accessible only indirectly.

When theologians talk about this, they sometimes refer to it as "listening with the third ear." The idea here is that our calling comes to us through uncharted pathways. Our two ears alone aren't sensitive enough to pick up the subtle vibrations of calling.

Now this isn't as far-fetched or "woo-woo" as it may sound at first. We've all had the experience of "just knowing" that something was right—or wrong—for us. Sometimes our ability to understand *that* a choice is best is greater than our ability to understand *why* it is. This doesn't mean we should never think carefully about things and reflect thoughtfully about the best courses of action; however, it does suggest that we also pay close attention to our intuitive side, our "third ear."

Rocky Kimball President		*Awakening Spirit*

Take, for instance, the experience of Richard "Rocky" Kimball, president of Action Learning Associates, an extremely successful leadership training organization. Rocky's calling is to *awaken spirit*. He

creates direct experiences for teams and individuals to become architects of their own aliveness. Rocky's work is a combination of
outdoor initiatives and inward explorations that help people become one with who they are and what they are all about. He came
to his career and his calling through a roundabout series of explorations into schoolteaching, mountaineering, and personal development. The common thread that tied these disparate adventures
together was, for Rocky, a kind of innate knowledge of what he
ought to be—or ought not to be—doing. For instance, on the day
many years ago when Rocky was scheduled to take his law boards,
he had an opportunity to take a "road trip" to the Florida coast.
Now, for many people, this would hardly have qualified as a wise career move, but to hear Rocky tell it, he just had an "intuitive sense"
that this was the right thing to do. And as it turned out, it was. Not
only did missing the test prevent Rocky from embarking on a career
that ultimately wouldn't have suited him at all, the trip itself turned
out to be a stepping stone to the teaching job that started him on
the path to where he is now.

   And a similar thing happened some years later when Rocky
was contemplating leaving the Sante Fe Mountain Center, the
award-winning personal growth organization he founded, and
going to work for a larger organization doing pretty much the same
thing. Again, something stopped him right before he made the decision to go ahead. "I knew when to say 'no,'" he says. But at the time,
it wasn't obvious why he was doing so. The Mountain Center could-
n't compete with the salary he was being offered. "I didn't even
have a washer/dryer until I was 40," admits Rocky, and taking the
new job would have meant a quantum increase in his salary. But it
just didn't feel right. From somewhere within, his calling was speaking to him and urging him in a different direction. And it turned out
to be the wise choice, for it wasn't long afterwards that Action
Learning Associates really took off. Now he turns down more work
than he can possibly take and is compensated for doing what he
loves at a level that is best described by what Rocky humorously says
his epitaph should be: "He had a shit-eating grin."

   "Basically, I still do the work for free," he says. "Money is just
a way of making choices around time." And the choices that Rocky

makes continue to be informed by his calling—to *awaken spirit,* and not only others' but also his own.

Training Our "Third Ear"

Assuming that messages about our calling can come to us indirectly, how can we prepare ourselves to receive them? How, in other words, can we train our "third ear" to listen more attentively?

One possibility is to become more sensitive to the signs of readiness to listen. Chief among these is a kind of restlessness in work, at home, and in our relationships with family members and friends. When we find ourselves continually "champing at the bit" for no obvious reason, it may be a sign that our calling is seeking expression. When the familiar begins to feel fatiguing and the usual unusually uninteresting, it's probably time for self-exploration to discover what's at the root of the problem. It's time to recognize that we've probably got a "call waiting" and that it represents an opportunity to take our lives off hold.

Other signs that our calling is reaching out to us include a vague yearning for some different way of life, dreams of "chucking it all" and trying something completely different. Or we may find ourselves strangely obsessed with insignificant details; a hobby may take over our life in an unhealthy way. Procrastination, lack of energy, loss of focus, and just a general malaise are other indications that we are ready to embrace our calling in a new way.

What steps, then enable us to do this? What actions permit us to make the connection we intuitively are seeking to make?

Sandy Nelson Founder		*Designing Lives*

Consider the story of Sandy Nelson. Sandy is co-founder, along with his wife, JoAnne, of the Sonoma Institute. Headquartered in Healdsburg, California, the Institute is dedicated to helping people awaken their creative potential and see new possibilities for personal and professional growth. An innovative thinker and dynamic business coach, Sandy illustrates how our connection to calling can evolve over time: his calling has transformed from designing buildings to *designing lives.*

Sandy began his career as an architect. For more than 15 years, he created market-defining concepts such as the Atlanta Underground, winning international acclaim and producing over $2 billion dollars in commercial value. His work was featured in publications such as *The New York Times,* the *Washington Post,* and *Business Week.* As his success grew, though, his joy waned. Sandy recalls "I was very successful on the outside but living in a place of hubris on the inside. I was totally lost in my own arrogance."

His clients sensed Sandy had something else to give them, though, besides architectural designs. They began to seek advice from him on more than how to build buildings. They wanted to know how to be "architects of their own futures." Sandy shared their interest. He relates, "I had an intuitive sense it was time to move in a new direction. I walked out in front of my house one evening after a successful meeting and the recognition just hit me. In architecture school we learned that people spend their lives in 'built environments.' I decided right then that I wanted to help people spend their lives in 'built lives.'"

Sandy has devoted the last decade to doing just that—to helping people design their lives in a manner that maximizes their potential. Sandy says, "I always saw architecture as lifting the human spirit." Now he lifts human spirits through an architecture of life.

Sandy's work chose him and then he chose it. It took seven years for him to complete the transition from buildings to relationships. "I had a fear of letting go of my identity as an architect," he recalls. "So, at first, I started a smaller practice. I went from 200 architects to none. I used this practice as my studio until I was ready to move into the new world I was creating."

The Sonoma Institute has been a spiritual journey for Sandy. "My creativity," he says, "is a gift from God." The Institute helps high-performing individuals, like Sandy, sustain their success. He sees a lot of effective professionals, but a lot of unhappy people— and he wants to change that. His lifelong goal is to help his clients become—as he himself has become— "architects of their own lives."

Is It Worth It?

In the movement toward expressing our calling, nothing is more powerful than honesty: honesty with friends, family members, and colleagues—but, above all, honesty with ourselves. We need to be willing truthfully to face up to the facts of our situations and if we're unhappy, to do something about it.

Having those "courageous conversations" with oneself and others is never easy. But the alternative—living a life of regret—is ultimately even harder.

"I used to know this as a teenager," says Dave. "But for many years, I forgot it. I remember when I was 17, my favorite way to spend an evening was working out problems in my relationship with my girlfriend, or sitting around with a couple of my buddies trying to one-up each other at who could reveal their most intimate secret. In both cases, it felt as if I were entering a forest with a machete, working my way deeper and deeper into the heart of what really mattered. I recall one time, sitting in my father's car in my parents' driveway for three or four hours, where it seemed to me that my girlfriend and I had stripped away every vestige of illusion we had about ourselves and each other. Emotionally, we were totally exposed. It was terrifying in one way, absolutely exhilarating in another.

"As I went out into the world, though, I lost my courage. I became more and more self-conscious about revealing myself—not just to others, but to myself. So, for most of my twenties and thirties, I avoided the sort of intrepid self-examination that had been so important to me in my teens. While this saved me from the short-term pain associated with asking myself difficult questions, it resulted in countless hours agonizing about—but not doing anything to improve—undesirable situations in which I found myself. I put up with jobs I didn't like, relationships that weren't particularly satisfying, and friendships that left me feeling friendless. Had I only been willing to confront these situations honestly, I would have realized that they weren't consistent with my deepest values and, more importantly, weren't expressions of my true calling."

So the question we want to ask ourselves when we're balancing honesty and comfort is, "Is it worth it?" Are we willing to put up with the short-term pain of telling the truth to avoid the long-term dissatisfaction of a postponed life? Or is it simply too frightening to face the truth even though, in the long run, it will mean a greater chance of living a life of no regrets?

When it's put this way, most of us will probably agree that the former choice is preferable. It's easy to see that the long-term benefit justifies the short-term discomfort. It's worth wondering, therefore, how come so many of us so typically opt for the latter. Is it just our inability to see the big picture?

If so, thinking about our legacy is one way we may be able to meet this challenge and inspire our courage. If we conceive of our lives with the end in mind, then what's truly important is easier to see. Taking the long-term perspective allows us to see how—in a relative way—the short-term pains pale in comparison to the long-term consequences of our choices. When we look back over our lives, we're able to recognize that the bumps in the road are just that—bumps. By comparison, what really makes a difference to the quality of the life we've led is the road itself.

Did I Answer the Call?

We can explore the degree to which we're living in accordance with our calling by reflecting upon our lives now as we might reflect upon them in the future. Pretend you are in the twilight of your lifetime, looking back upon all that you did and were. How do you feel about the choices you made? How satisfied are you with the life you have led? How would you answer Elizabeth Kübler-Ross' three reflective questions?

- Did I give and receive love?

- Did I become all I can be?

- Did I leave the planet a little better?

Discuss your answers with a friend or family member. Examine together how you have lived—and how you might have lived differently.

Imagine you're putting your answers together in a letter to future generations. What will you say about how best to live? What insights can you share that will help people in the future heed their life's calling?

Take the time actually to write this letter in your Calling Journal. But substitute yourself—as you are right now—for future generations. What advice do you have from the person you will be for the person you are? How can that wisdom guide you as you make your way forward?

Remember Charles Dickens' classic, *A Christmas Carol*. Recall the scene in which Scrooge is taken to see his own tombstone by the Ghost of Christmas Future. Even though the Ghost emphasizes to Scrooge that what he is showing him is *not certain* to come to pass, the old miser is so affected by even the *prospect* of dying alone and unloved that he entirely changes his miserly ways overnight.

Now, of course, few of us face the sorts of regrets Scrooge was facing. But all of us have the potential for making changes in our lives that will result in fewer regrets and a greater sense of satisfaction and meaning in the long run.

Virtually all cultures on earth have a story about a shared quest for meaning and transcendence—the "heroic" journey. Throughout the world's indigenous peoples, religions, and myths, we find recognition of the journey toward legacy in human life. Our own individual legacies are a reminder that there is a vital spiritual dimension below the surface, a world of meaning that cannot be quantified, but can only be lived.

When we think of our lives in this larger context the core principles of calling re-emerge with greater impact.

• *The Call comes from a Caller.*

Here, we are reminded that each and every one of us is called and that turning our "third ear" to calling is a matter of turning to something larger than we are. Calling is heard inside, but it emanates from outside. Becoming attuned to this inner voice from outside as we move through life's stages will enable us to craft a legacy of calling that is consistent with our deepest sense of why we are here.

- ## *The Call keeps calling.*

  Here we are reminded that calling is revealed to different
  people at different times in different ways. When we keep in
  mind the unique and individual nature of calling, we naturally recognize that we will express our calling in our own
  distinct ways during our lives. Our calling is unique to us
  but the manner in which we make calling manifest in the
  world is multifold. This realization can make us more apt to
  explore new ways to make our calling come alive. It can
  help us to be more receptive to many alternatives for continuing to put a whistle in our work.

- ## *The Call is personal.*

  Here we are reminded that there are as many callings in the
  world as there are people on the planet. If we live our entire
  life in a manner consistent with our calling, we are likely to
  touch the lives of many other people. The opportunities for
  giving away our best-loved gifts to others will abound.
  Think of some of the people you have met in this book—
  people like Bill Strickland, Arne Anderson, and Michelle
  Stimpson. Each of them is consistently expressing his or her
  calling through a lifetime of service to others. As we take a
  big picture perspective on our lives, we recognize even more
  clearly that what *really* matters—what really puts a whistle
  in our work—is the chance to make a difference in the lives
  of others. And with this big picture perspective, we are better able to identify and take advantage of such opportunities
  when they appear.

- ## *The Call is long-distance.*

  Heeding our calling means making a deliberate choice to
  use our gifts to serve others and make a difference in the
  world. The legacy we leave is not created by a single act;
  rather, we will be remembered for the whole life we have

led. And a life lived out of a connection to calling is far more likely to be remembered in the way we would like it to be. It is far more likely to matter in a way that matters to us. As long as we continue exploring our gifts, passions, and values—we renew the potential to add meaning in our lives—and the lives of those with whom we come in contact—each and every day of our lives.

Taking the broad perspective also reminds us that the ongoing inquiry into hearing and heeding our life's calling is not something that can be answered with simple checklists or standardized formulas. Callings are inherently mysterious; they tend to come to us in the form of questions rather than answers.

Walt Whitman wrote, "Not I, nor anyone else can travel that road for you. You must travel it for yourself."

All of us must live in and learn from our own questions. We can, however, take guidance from the questions of others. We can refer to their stories and consider what they may teach us about our lives.

Perhaps in your own quest for calling, you can take some guidance from the stories of people in this book. If the voice of calling grows faint for you, you can reinforce it by recalling the voices of the people you have met here. They can reconnect you to that quiet place within from which the voice most important to you calls.

When you reconnect with that voice, listen to it. Let it help you heed your life's calling. Let it assist you in the creation of a fulfilling and distinguished legacy. Let it put a whistle in your work whose tune will carry on throughout your life and long after you are gone.

index

about the authors

Richard J. Leider is a founding partner of *The Inventure Group*, a coaching
and consulting firm in Minneapolis,
Minnesota devoted to bringing out
the natural potential in people. He is
a nationally known writer, speaker,
and career coach, and a pioneer in
the field of Life/Work Planning. A
National Certified Career Coach, he
has been helping people to hear and
heed their callings for more than 30

years. Author and co-author of five previous books, including the best-
sellers *Repacking Your Bags* and *The Power of Purpose*, he is also an online
columnist for *Fast Company*.

David A. Shapiro is a writer, philosopher, and educator whose work explores questions in ethics and meaning in life. He is the Education

Director of the Northwest Center for
Philosophy for Children, a non-profit
organization that brings philosophy
into the lives of young people in
schools and community groups
through literature, philosophical
works, and classroom activities.

David is the co-author of
Repacking Your Bags and the author
of *Choosing the Right Thing to Do*, a
practical guide for helping people
make educated decisions about matters of ethical import in all aspects
of their lives.

Congratulations!

By reading **Whistle While You Work**, you have just taken the first step in a life-enhancing journey—the journey of self-discovery. If you wish to further explore your calling or share this process with someone you know, Calling Cards is the ideal tool for you.

Calling Cards™: A Journey of Discovery

Illustrated in the book, **Whistle While You Work**, Calling Cards is a self-guided exercise that will help you discover how to align your special gifts and passions in a work environment that honors your values. This tool includes a deck of 52 cards, complete instructions to guide you through the exercise, a formal "Calling Card," on which to express your calling statement, and a decorative box to keep and display your cards.

We encourage you to continue discovering what it is that ignites your potential and makes you fulfilled both at work and in your personal life. To help you in the process, The Inventure Group offers a suite of interactive products that provides you with insights, information and direction.

To learn more about these products, visit The Inventure Group Web site at www.inventuregroup.com or call 952-249-5222.

Berrett-Koehler Publishers

BERRETT-KOEHLER is an independent publisher of books, periodicals, and other publications at the leading edge of new thinking and innovative practice on work, business, management, leadership, stewardship, career development, human resources, entrepreneurship, and global sustainability.

Since the company's founding in 1992, we have been committed to supporting the movement toward a more enlightened world of work by publishing books, periodicals, and other publications that help us to integrate our values with our work and work lives, and to create more humane and effective organizations.

We have chosen to focus on the areas of work, business, and organizations, because these are central elements in many people's lives today. Furthermore, the work world is going through tumultuous changes, from the decline of job security to the rise of new structures for organizing people and work. We believe that change is needed at all levels—individual, organizational, community, and global—and our publications address each of these levels.

We seek to create new lenses for understanding organizations, to legitimize topics that people care deeply about but that current business orthodoxy censors or considers secondary to bottom-line concerns, and to uncover new meaning, means, and ends for our work and work lives.

See next page for other books from Berrett-Koehler Publishers

Your Signature Path

Gaining New Perspectives
on Life and Work

Geoffrey M. Bellman

Your Signature Path explores the uniqueness of the mark each of us makes in the world. Bestselling author Geoffrey M. Bellman offers thought-provoking insights and practical tools for evaluating who you are, what you are doing, and where you want your path to lead.

Hardcover, 200 pages • ISBN 1-57675-004-3 CIP
Item #50043-346 $24.95

How to Get Ideas

Jack Foster, Illustrated by Larry Corby

In *How to Get Ideas,* Jack Foster draws on three decades of experience as an advertising writer and creative director to take the mystery and anxiety out of getting ideas. Describing eight ways to condition your mind to produce ideas and five subsequent steps for creating and implementing ideas on command, he makes it easy, fun, and understandable.

Paperback, 150 pages • ISBN 1-57675-006-X CIP
Item #5006X-346 $14.95

Bringing Your Soul to Work

An Everyday Practice

Cheryl Peppers and Alan Briskin

This book addresses the gap between our inner lives and the work we do in the world. Case studies, personal stories, inspirational quotes, reflective questions, and concrete applications navigate readers through the real and troubling questions inherent in the workplace.

Paperback, 260 pages • ISBN 1-57675-111-2 CIP
Item #51112-346 $16.95

Berrett-Koehler Publishers
PO Box 565, Williston, VT 05495-9900
Call toll-free! **800-929-2929** 7 am-12 midnight

Or fax your order to 802-864-7627
For fastest service order online: **www.bkconnection.com**

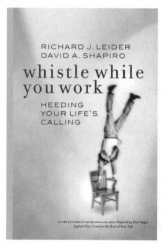

LIFE AND LEARNING IX

PROCEEDINGS OF THE NINTH UNIVERSITY FACULTY FOR LIFE CONFERENCE

JUNE 1999 AT TRINITY INTERNATIONAL UNIVERSITY DEERFIELD, ILL.

edited by
Joseph W. Koterski, S.J.

University Faculty for Life

Washington, D.C.

Published by University Faculty for Life
120 New North Building
Georgetown University
Washington, D.C., 20057

Printed in the United States of America
ISBN 1-886387-07-9

Table of Contents

Acknowledgments

John Hunt's paper, "Out of Respect for Life: Nazi Abortion Policy in the Eastern Occupied Territories," is reprinted from *Journal of Genocide Research* 1/3 (1999) 379-85.

Teresa Wagner's essay, "The Empty Promise of Contraception," is reprinted from *Family Policy* (The Charter Publication of the Family Research Council), 12/5 (Sept.-Oct.1999)1-4, 9-15. For further reference, consult their internet site: http://www.frc.org.

"The Critical Influence of the Prospective Father on Abortion-Decision Making" by Thomas W. Strahan first appeared in the November/December 1999 issue of the *Research Bulletin*, which has graciously granted permission for it to be reprinted here.

"Human Cloning: Never and Why Not" by Jorge L. A. Gracia is reprinted from *Human Cloning: Science, Ethics, and Public Policy*, edited by Barbara MacKinnon, forthcoming from the University of Illinois Press. Used with permission of the University of Illinois Press.

An expanded and revised version of John Crobsy's essay "Why Persons Have Dignity" will appear in a forthcoming issue of *Faith and Philosophy.*

The essay by Charles E. Rice ("Abortion: What Did the Supreme Court Do in *Roe v. Wade?*") is reprinted with permission from Ave Maria Press.

Preface

The present volume contains a selection of the many fine papers (chosen by peer review) which were presented at the ninth annual conference of the University Faculty for Life. We are deeply grateful for the kindly hospitality shown us at Deerfield, Illinois, on the campus of Trinity International University in June 1999.

Our sincere gratitude is due to our hosts at Trinity, Law School Dean Winston Frost and Prof. and Mrs. Frank Beckwith, as well as to Teresa Collett, UFL's indefatigable program chair. We would also like to thank all the benefactors who have supported our organization and made possible its annual meetings as well as the publication of its newsletter and of its annual volume of proceedings. Without their generous contributions this meeting would not have been possible.

This year's volume of proceedings features a wide range of papers on some of the most pressing issues relevant to the defense of human life, including cloning (Garcia), Anencephaly (Campion), and Multi-Pregnancy Fetal Reduction (Ring-Cassidy). We are also pleased to present a number of valuable papers on fundamental ethical theory (Crosby, Conley, Kalpakgian, Bracken) as well as on the moral analysis of medical issues (Ryan, Miller).

Legal perspectives have been a regular staple of our UFL volumes in recent years. David Reardon's essay on abortion risk factors as a fruitful avenue for new pro-life/pro-woman laws bears especially careful reading. We are also thankful to be able to present essays on a variety of other legal and political topics (Rice, Scaperlanda, Beckwith, Strahan, Gehringer, Frost), as well as a set of essays on historical and sociological themes (Cassidy, Dyer, Hunt, Wagner). Our pages are also graced by two fascinating essays from scholars of literature and drama (Koloze, Waterman-Ward).

Finally, let me offer special thanks to Prof. Jacqueline Nolan-Haley of the Fordham University Law School and to Rev. John J. Conley, S.J. of the Philosophy Department at Fordham for their invaluable help in the preparation of this volume.

Joseph W. Koterski, S.J.
Fordham University

Human Cloning: Never and Why Not

J. L. A. Garcia

INTRODUCTION[1] In one of Hegel's rare memorable passages, he remarks that the Owl of Minerva takes flight to paint its grey on grey at the end of day. He seems to have meant two things. That philosophy does little more than give intellectual expression to the spirit of the times and, second, that it does even that rather late, as the *Zeitgeist* is itself changing. Whatever the truth of the first as a general claim about philosophy, it certainly captures the discipline of bioethics. Practices that once outraged the common sensibility are now all the rage. Bioethicists, true to Hegel's vision, have entered the stage wringing their hands over some new practice, but quickly changed their tune as social attitudes changed from hesitation and disapproval to cheery contentment. Indeed, as the first wave of medically and theologically trained writers on medical ethics has been replaced by today's crop of lawyers, policy specialists, analytic philosophers, and those who revel in the neologism 'ethicists,' they have become so adept at this that they have now gotten ahead of the curve of attitudinal shift. That is not to say that they actually cause change, but they have removed an important cautionary voice, a brake against brash and sweeping transformations. In the past, intellectuals played an important cultural role in cautioning against haste, calling for reflection, reminding of past troubles, articulating traditional cultural commitments and a sense of continuity with forbears, and so on. In contrast, today's secularized clerisy of ethics intellectuals are among the most vocal in assuaging any lingering moral doubts about the new agenda pushed by researchers, and the increasingly consumer-driven, market-modelled medical industries. A recent *New York Times* headline caught this phenomenon nicely in the area that concerns us here: "On Cloning Humans, 'Never' Turns Swiftly Into 'Why Not?'." The story notes that after the initial near-unanimous outcry against cloning humans that immediately followed the announcement of the Dolly-experiment's

1

success, "scientists have become sanguine about the notion of ... cloning a human being."[2]   Bioethicists' uncharacteristically negative initial reaction to the renewed talk of cloning humans is now a cause of some embarrassment and, barely a year since Dr. Wilmut's announcement and less than a year after the Presidential Commission's report, we are already in the midst of a full-scale moral reconsideration.

This is not a bad thing. Medical ethics probably suffers from too little reconsideration, not too much. Indeed, I think that one of the problems in some of the new literature on cloning is precisely that it treats as definitively settled moral questions concerning the status of the embryo and so-called 'pre-embryo,' the moral legitimacy of abortion and *in vitro* fertilization done for more or less any reason, and other matters where some 'consensus' may or may not be emerging among secular elites, but where nothing has really been proven morally, even if there is such a thing as moral proof. There is no reason, then, to decry the raising of the question 'Why Not?' which the *Times* article heralds. The question, however, should not be treated as an impatient challenge to put up or shut up, lest some new medical agendum be delayed. The philosophical approach is to treat the question as an inquiry into the reasons for which human cloning might be morally objectionable.[3] This is the spirit in which I will treat it here. Where the *Times* article notes a shift in attitudes from 'Never' to 'Why Not?', the attitudes behind the two utterances are not in principle opposed. We can deny that cloning people is ever morally permissible and also inquire into what makes that true. Hence my title: never *and* why not.

I. PENCE'S SIGNIFICANCE

Gregory Pence's new work *Who's Afraid of Human Cloning?* is one of the first book-length treatments by a philosophically-trained bioethicist since the announcement of the Dolly-experiment's success which defends human cloning as ethical. For that reason, and the fact that it is being marketed to a mass audience as a general interest paperback on current affairs and science, it warrants attention. Most of the remainder of my treatment will focus on this text.

Professor Pence's book touches on a broad range of topics in the history of theology, Scriptural interpretation, literary criticism, social behavior, and cultural movements. Unfortunately, some of the things Pence says on these topics suggest a certain lack of depth. Pence reveals, for example, that the problem in Huxley's novel *Brave New World* was "the loss of reproductive choice by individuals."[4] We get no rationale for this bizarre interpretation and no sources are cited in its support. If you wondered what drove the Savage to suicide in a society of human hatcheries, of reverence for "our Ford" as Lord, where "Epsilons" were bred, reared, shaped, and stunted by the state to perform menial tasks for their betters and like it, now you know. It bugged him to live in a world before *Griswold*.

Pence's views on social controversy are also somewhat simplistic. You might have thought that, even if the initial reaction against human cloning was inadequately thought through, there nevertheless are serious problems about the practice. Yet, as Pence makes clear in his very title, this is not his view. Hesitation about its licitness is just a matter of fear, not reason. He warns us against "fear of a change, fear of changing human nature, fear of humans having more choice and control." This is just a struggle between the "fatalistic view...that everything is changing too fast" and those who distrust people, on the one side, and "voluntarists," on the other, who believe "we have the wisdom to use new knowledge to help people" and who are "more optimistic."[5] Fortunately, Pence's extensive research has equipped him to enlighten us: "There is nothing about change itself," we discover, "that is bad." With this hard-won *aperçu*, he thinks, we can "take a more assertive stance toward the future of humanity."[6] One might think that the end of humanity's most destructive and barbarous century calls for more caution than Pence's none-too-searching question, "So why not trust humans rather than fear them?"[7] Reflect for a moment on what Arendt called "the banality of evil." Recall what nice, ordinary people did or let happen in Germany, or Alabama, or Siberia, or Soweto, or Tibet, in the just the last few generations. Then follow the procedure Pence naively recommends in considering whether we might use the new technologies in ways that harm people: "Go to your local neighborhood meeting, Parents-Teacher Association night, or Kiwanis Club and ask yourself: are all those people the kind who have bad motives?"[8] Those with rather more self-knowledge than Pence seems capable of may not reach the answer he wants.

Pence's assurances are sometimes downright alarming. People always worry about new medical practices, Pence thinks, and the facts prove them wrong. After all, "Physician-assisted dying for competent, terminal adults in Holland was predicted to turn that peaceful country into an ethical hell, but the practice has been going on twenty-five years with hardly any bad results."[9] Justice Souter, whose concurring opinion in the recent assisted suicide cases, legal commentators saw as almost inviting opportunity to find a more limited constitutionally protected right, seems to have held back in these cases largely because of the widespread abuses of the rules putatively governing physician-assisted suicide in the Netherlands.[10] Perhaps Pence doesn't think involuntary euthanasia, for example, unreported and unpunished, counts as a bad result.

And sometimes his remarks are just weird. Despite those who worry about dangers should human cloning become widespread, we are not to worry: "for every high-minded couple who produced a superior child by NST there would be a Brazilian couple who produced nine children by normal sex."[11] Even within the often openly eugenicist discourse of the fans of human cloning, this explicit, bigoted contrast of the high-minded and superior on the one side and the Brazilian on the other, is shocking. But it is, presumably, O.K. to speak of Latin American reproductive customs with open contempt because these people are likely to be Christians, especially Catholics or evangelicals. Pence makes little effort to conceal his loathing for such people. Those who plead that human life should be protected and reverenced from its earliest stages he derides as "Keepers of the Holy Embryos" and "the embryo-saving crowd."[12] Catholic moral theology's objection to *in vitro* fertilization is "preposterous." Pence warns that "people who hear this view expressed ... think of the Vatican as bunch of old men in Rome who have some very foolish ideas."[13] Pence plainly has heard the view expressed, so the reader is left to draw her own conclusions about his own assessment of the Chair of Peter. Richard Lewontin has questioned the conspicuous absence of testimony before the President's Commission from Christian fundamentalists.[14] For Pence, however, there was too much heard even from mainline Protestant and Jewish thought, too much from religious people. Even governmental regulation of cloning and other techniques of artificial reproduction is to be avoided because government is too easily pressured by "extreme religious groups."[15] He does not seem to have in mind those whose views, like those of his intellectual hero, Joseph Fletcher, are extreme in their enthusiasm for new manipulations of and interventions in the beginning and end of life.

So, Pence's contempt is not unadorned ethnic prejudice; it is ethnic prejudice adorned with religious bigotry. For Pence, that apparently makes it quite comely. We need not agree.

However, Pence is probably at his worst on Scripture, theology, and religion. Of the stricture in Eden against eating from the Tree of Knowledge of Good and Evil, Pence reasonably asks, "What should we infer from this story?" At this point, one expects some discussion of Bible commentaries, Scripture criticism, the treatments of this passage by Doctors of the Church, perhaps some discussion of the old suggestion that what this text condemns is our arrogating that maker's knowledge of the moral realm indicated by Protagoras's dictum that man is the measure of all things. But one who expects that is disappointed. Pence continues, and then stops, with his own increasingly peeved questions: "What should we infer from this story? That humans should know nothing about morality? Perhaps humans made no moral judgments in the Garden of Eden, but how is that story relevant to a world where humans must constantly do so?"[16]

With Pence theologians fare no better than Scriptures. "For Augustine, having children within marriage was a license to sin."[17] This is remarkable since a sin would seem to be something forbidden by God and a license to do something would seem to render it permissible, so that Pence must think Augustine thought people were permitted to do some things that they were not permitted to do. Why he attributes this nonsensical doctrine to the great theologian is a mystery since Pence gives no reference to any of Augustine's texts.

The bishop of Hippo is not alone in drawing Pence's disapproval. Roman Catholicism is criticized for proclaiming its doctrine's continuity but also rejecting Augustine's view. (Pence does not trouble with the detail of whether Augustine's view was ever declared Church doctrine, on which hangs the question of whether rejecting it was a reversal of the Church's position.) In modern Catholicism, he informs us, "Sexual desire is no longer an evil force that lures young people to hell–it has now become an uplifting expression of love in happy marriages." It is hard to see why it cannot be both, but again Pence has no time for theological niceties when there are religions to be thumped.[18]

Lutheran theologian Gilbert Meilander worries that cloning might not comport with Genesis's picture of human beings divinely enjoined to sustain human life through procreation. Pence snorts, "the problem with Protestants justifying their views on biblical passages is that they only go there to justify what they already believe, not to find guidance."[19] It would seem rather harsh to accuse a believer of abusing his own Scriptures, seeking in them not the word of the God he thinks therein revealed but only endorsement of his own prejudices. No fair-minded person would make such a charge against a person, let alone a whole sect, without first entertaining the possibility that the thinker might indeed have sought and received guidance from the passage, might indeed have read and reflected on it many times before this citation. (Meilander is, after all, a theologian.) But Pence has no time for such stuff. Meilander piously holds that a child is a gift from God, and that we should strive so to see it, a striving he thinks cloning repudiates and makes more difficult. This is what Pence cannot brook. "If every pregnancy from sex is a gift from God, why not accept every 'gift' that comes along? Why not ban abortions? Contraception?" Actually, Meilander does find abortion morally objectionable, but for Pence the question is rhetorical, indeed, a *reductio*. No time for reconsideration here, no serious effort to engage another's thought.

Pence is a man in a hurry and Meilander's "gift"-talk threatens to slow things down. All this fretting about God and ethics is, after all, "holding hostage important medical research."[20] That Pence cannot abide. "When are we allowed to choose to have better babies?" he sneers, patience running out. "Never? When are we allowed to say to the Giver of the gift, 'Gee, couldn't you do any better than that?'"[21] "Better babies," "superior children," for the "high-minded" through cloning? Or Latinos rutting away–beneath garish images of Jesus on the bedroom wall, no doubt–turning out their litters of human inferiors?

The contrast latent in Pence's imagery is now manifest. We should turn to his more thematic discussion of the moral case against cloning. However, before we get to that, we must pause to clear up some confusions Pence introduces about moral reasoning.

II. ETHICAL THINKING

I have said that my interest here is to affirm the view that human cloning is not permissible morally (my 'never') and also to begin exploring some factors in virtue of which it is not (my 'why not'). If it is wrong, it is wrong for reasons. Notice, however, that nothing in this fact entails that in order for someone to know (or justifiedly to believe) that it is wrong she must first know why it is. It is an ontological point that has nothing to do with moral epistemology. Pence claims "Philosophers and bioethicists are very suspicious about 'knowing what you want to do' [in condemning something morally], but not knowing 'why' it is morally wrong." And plainly, he thinks their suspicions are right. In his view, "if the balance of reasons favors one side over another, we know that the right side is the one with the better reasons."[22] This may be right, but it is unwarranted. The reason for my doubt is precisely that Pence's view does not seem to permit us to say that a position may be right is unwarranted.

Notice, first, that Pence's principle here would be nonsense as a general epistemological claim. If I claimed never to know what color or figural qualities a thing had until I knew why it had them, I would merely be deceiving myself. What is supposed to make the moral case so radically different? As in many other matters, we come to moral knowledge through various combinations of perception, testimony, inference, reflection, analysis, and empirical investigation. Of course, when I know that something is wrong, I often (but need not) also know some respect in which it is wrong. Still, it hardly follows that the "balance of reasons" must always favor the position that is, in fact, correct. Certainly, it need not, if the reasons intended are merely the ones so far presented at a certain point in the discussion. Nor need the correct side even be favored by the balance of reasons available for our inspection. Maybe we just do not know yet what makes the thing wrong, as we do not know what grounds or causes many of its other qualities. Of course, there are forms of anti-realism according to which to say something is wrong is just to say how the discussion of it is proceeding. And there are forms of constructivism according to which what is wrong is made wrong by a process of moral deliberation. I doubt that any such metaethical theory is correct, but even if one proves true, that hardly warrants Pence's smug confidence that the correct moral position is always the one supported by the balance of reasons. So, as in other areas of inquiry, even if the moral arguments against human cloning were unpersuasive, weaker than those on the other side, that would not entail that the "right" view is that cloning is not wrong.

Part of Pence's reason for his confident overstatement is that he endorses Peter Singer's skeptical approach to so-called moral intuitions. Singer asks, why should we not distrust our intuitive moral judgments about particular cases as "derive[d] from discarded religious systems, from warped views of sex and bodily functions, or from customs necessary for the survival of the group in social and economic circumstances that now lie in the distant past? In which case," he continues, "it would be best to forget all about our particular moral judgments, and start again from as near as we can get to self-evident moral axioms."[23]

I cannot pursue the issue of moral epistemology here. Permit me just to observe, among other things, that Pence does nothing to show (i) that the discarded religious systems are in fact false, (ii) that, whatever their truth or falsity, these systems' moral views did not capture important truths about human beings and their needs, service to which may explain the endurance of those moral intuitions, (iii) that warped views of sex are more likely to be found in traditional views than in more modern ones, or (iv) that we are likely to come closer to self-evidence at the level of general principles than we are at the level of judgments about particular forms of behavior, such as human cloning. Indeed, Mill himself conceded that we are more certain about such particular judgments as we make about this lie or that assault than we are about such generalizations as the utilitarians' own happiness principle.[24] My own view is that the lesson to be learned from thinking about intuitions–general and particular, old and new–is that we should be distrustful of the least reliable of intuitive judgments, *viz.*, those that have recently arisen to allow us to feel all right about ourselves as we engage in practices long recognized as perverse. That, however, does much to undercut a line of reasoning popular among the fans of human cloning and other new medical practices. They argue, for example, that cloning for sex selection, or to tailor children to parents' (or others') design specifications, or as source of tissue donations, is not wrong, because something similar is sometimes done using IVF, where (they say) it does not elicit the horror it used to.[25] That frequency has eroded the sense of moral horror that some people feel over such practices does not mean that they now pass some test of being acceptable before respectable intuitions. I should say the same about the view that we have somehow generally now come to know that human life does not exist *in utero* or, if it does, that it deserves no protection there, that we have a right to decide exactly how and when to die. (What of the man who chooses to go out mid-orgy with the Spice Girls in the Super Bowl half-time show?) Where is our distrust of received moral opinion when we need it?

Pence makes other strange claims about moral thinking and theory; I will criticize just one here. He claims that Mill's famous "harm principle," which holds that state prohibitions on liberty are permitted only when the prohibited behavior harms someone, "does not merely champion an area of personal life free from governmental interference, but also an area free from moral criticism."[26] It is difficult to see how this could this be right as an interpretation, but what is more important is that it is difficult to see how it could be a correct moral principle.[27] If a range of my actions is free from *all* moral criticism, then how can I undertake moral reform by acknowledging my own past wrongdoing in that area and seeking to avoid such behavior in the future? Quite possibly, what Pence means, though, is that the area of my conduct is to be free from other people's moral criticism. Still, if that is what he means, then what room is there for me to seek your moral guidance in a matter of my private life? Even if the state should not intervene, can it really be correct that there is nothing morally objectionable in conducting my private affairs from racial or ethnic or gender or religious prejudice? Or is it that such conduct is wrong, but Pence's point is that nobody has any business telling me that? If so, then how do I learn to reform morally? And what becomes of freedom of speech in this new gag-ruled liberalism?

In claims scattered throughout his book, then, Pence says things that manifest ignorance, bigotry, and a shallow mind. Moreover, his methodological claims about how to judge moral reasoning are unsupported, ill thought-through, and implausible. Still, this does not suffice to show that he has nothing to say about the moral status of human cloning or that what he does say is without value. I turn, at this point, to consider the chapter where Pence rebuts what he sees as the principal moral objections raised against human cloning. My focus throughout here is on Pence's book, so my aim in the next section is not to develop any of these arguments into decisive proofs of the immorality of human cloning, but merely to point out difficulties in Pence's efforts to counter them.

III. SOME REASONS *AGAINST* HUMAN CLONING

We need not stoop seriously to discuss Pence's contention that critics of the morality of human cloning are simply the "side [of] defeatism and fatalism" nor that they are driven by "fear of the new and different."[28] The former is merely name-calling and there is no more to the latter than to the complementary complaint that Pence, in his moral criticism of a government prohibition, must be motivated by fear. Certainly, there is good reason to find the prospect of human cloning troubling. It appears in several ways to endanger society and those involved as donors or in gestation.

It plainly poses a threat to the dignity and equality of women when, by plan, their child-bearing loses its normal and proper origin in an act of spousal love. Pence realizes this possibility but poses no serious response. Instead, it is at this point that he invokes his odd, perverse interpretation of Mill's harm principle. Beyond that, he simply affirms that "women fearing increased sexism from the introduction of NST [nuclear somatic transfer, that is, a type of human cloning] have a knock-down argument to any sexist fantasy about reproducti[ve exploitation]... they can simply refuse to get pregnant, refuse to stay pregnant, or refuse to gestate a fetus any more."[29] This misses the point of the objection several times over. The point is not about the conse-quences of de-sexed reproduction–whether it *will* increase sexism.

Rather, it is about whether reproduction by human cloning already treats the gestating mother in a demeaning way.[30] In any case, it is no response to this concern to say that women can escape the degradation. For one thing, such ways out as sacrificing her child prior even to its birth are already tragic. For another, a degradation eventually escaped is still a degradation and therefore something whose occurrence should not be tolerated in the first place.

Similarly, there is good reason to worry that human cloning as it becomes widespread even as an available option depreciates and denatures both sexual relations and reproduction by making the former merely one alternative among many for the latter. Pence, again, is tone-deaf here. He proudly sides with what he sees as a de-mystified view of the sexual which, following Alan Goldman, he calls 'plain sex.' This understands sexual activity in terms of sexual desire, itself conceived simply as desire for tactile bodily contact and its pleasures.[31] This sort of willful shallowness fails miserably to capture the sexual. It does not even successfully differentiate sexual activity from a vengeful desire to poke somebody. Understanding sex in terms of sexual desire is certainly preposterous in the etymological sense: it gets things backwards. It completely misses the sexual, because the very term and its cognates enter our vocabulary in differentiating groups, organs, and activities defined by their role in a certain mode of reproduction. Not all sex does or should result in reproduction, of course, but the idea that we can conceptualize the realm of the sexual without mention of reproduction is one of those ideas it seems only a modern intellectual could have.[32]

Again, there is ground for concern that, at a time when it is conceded all around that family life is strained, difficult, and damaging especially to children, cloning muddies the concepts of family and parenthood for those it touches. This is especially likely in some of the bizarre scenarios Pence imagines where, for example, a mother bears the clone of her own grandfather or of herself. Lewontin claims each clone will have two parents just like everyone else, apparently meaning the male and female whose chromosomes joined to shape the principal gene donor's genome.[33] Pence allows that a clone may have "four 'genetic' parents" plus two (or more) additional mothers.[34] I think Pence closer to the mark here. What matters is that the mother in one of Pence's cases may bear (and thus be gestational mother of) someone whose genetic parents (Lewontin's sense of 'parent') are her own great-grandparents. In another, she is the gestational mother of someone whose genetic parents are her own. In others, identical twins are born years, even decades, apart. What sense can we make of generations in such a family? Indeed, in what sense is it family when the relationships that constitute it no longer match those constitutive of family life? Some, of course, are sanguine that the family can easily be 'reconceived' or 're-visioned.' More sober minds will want to proceed with caution here about what, after all, Aristotle considered the fundamental unit of society. It is already broken in our culture, as even Pence more or less concedes, and there is every reason to suppose that cloning would only make it harder to fix. Strangely, though Pence's book touches on worries raised about the family here and there, he offers no sustained discussion of the impact of cloning on family. Instead, with characteristic ill-temper, he brands such concern "hypocritical" on the grounds that there are other, more immediate steps we could take to protect families and children without bothering about cloning.[35] This *ad hominem* may be good bullying, but it plainly does not rebut, or even address, the charge that human cloning could greatly exacerbate an already dangerously unstable social situation.

Human cloning may thus deprive the clone of real parents. She may have many quasi-parents, but one ground for worry is that none may be tied to her in the role of protector that a child's parents traditionally occupy. This danger is aggravated to the extent that the clone's parents may be more likely than those of other children to have had her (produced) merely as a means to their own projects (*e.g.*, providing tissue for donation to other children), and then to treat her accordingly.

There are other grounds for legitimate concern about particular forms of human cloning, but I will not pursue them here. Rather, I want to make a few remarks about one of the more serious objections to human cloning as intrinsically and decisively objectionable, a claim that Pence virtually ignores. That is the claim that it wrongs the person cloned by degrading her. It strikes me as so transparently demeaning to a human being to make her a product of technological manufacture that it is difficult to understand why some people claim not to see it. This is *not* the way we have ever treated human beings; it *is* the way we have always treated the subhuman things we regard as wholly subject to our will. Thus, in cloning a human person is treated in a way otherwise reserved only for subhuman beings. It is hard to know a better definition of de-grading, de-preciating. Consider a religious perspective. Trinitarians have, for half a millennium, praised God the Son as equal to the Father precisely as "begotten, not made." The clone, however, is made, not begotten.[36] Even some advocates of cloning consider it 'replication,' not reproduction. It is hard to see equal treatment or much acknowledgment of human equality in a situation where one person is planned and designed by another, and then manufactured to the latter's specifications. Of course, some people twist IVF and even sexual procreation in these directions. That shows not that such perversions are morally unproblematic, but that they should be avoided and condemned everywhere and that forms of reproduction that facilitate or encourage them have a heavy moral presumption against them.

Nevertheless, Ruth Macklin told the NBAC that "If objectors to cloning can identify no greater harm than a supposed affront to the dignity of the human species, that is a flimsy basis on which to erect barriers to scientific research and its applications."[37] The report does not reproduce the context of her remarks, but it is important to observe that this quotation is not an argument but merely an assertion of her value ordering. I should have thought that conducting and applying (supposedly) scientific research is a pretty flimsy excuse for affronting human dignity. Of course, the person produced by cloning would not have existed but for this degradation. Some have argued that this shows the act was not a net harm to her.[38] Even if that is correct, however, that cloning someone is not a net harm to her does not suffice to show that it is not a sufficient offense against her to render the act impermissible. Harm, after all, matters morally only insofar as it is a way of wronging someone. Yet, if harm is so narrowly defined that degrading someone is not harming her, then that only means that there are other ways of wronging people. So, failure to harm does not entail failure to wrong.

None of this is to say that the clone is subhuman, unequal, a thing to be used rather than a person to be respected. Rather, the argument presupposes just the opposite. That is why cloning is a degradation.[39]

In any case, pace Professor Macklin (and, as we saw earlier, Pence), scientific research is nice, but we can do without it, as we did for most of our history. In contrast, it is doubtful that there is any secure foundation for human rights except in the inherent dignity of the individual. Thus, the Preamble to the 1948 *Universal Declaration of Human Rights* begins, "Whereas recognition of the inherent dignity and of the equal and inalienable rights of all members of the human family is the foundation of freedom, justice, and peace in the world...." The first article, similarly, begins, "All human beings are born free and equal in dignity and rights."[40] The nature, source, limits, preconditions, and normative requirements of dignity, of course, could be made clearer, as most important moral concepts could. That is a large part of the work of analytical moral philosophy. However, any suggestion that, till this work is completed, we should banish this concept–or the related concepts of rights, respect, and deference–from our discussion of the morality of human cloning should be regarded as we would the parallel suggestion that we banish from this or other bioethical discussions such controversial and imprecise concepts as those of cause, benefit, harm, or health, till their conceptual clarification has similarly been completed. We should greet it with derision.

If, as I maintain, all human cloning is wrong as a degradation of the one cloned, it may still be that some special forms of cloning are worse for special reasons. Thus, cloning *for* sex selection, to create tissue donors, to make "better babies," to have another so-and-so (especially, another ME), etc., further demean the child to the extent that they value her simply for her use and characteristics rather than her nature. Cloning *of* human multiples is especially repugnant. Even Pence wants a temporary ban on this, though by the end of his book, he giddily celebrates his story of a rich man who arranges to produces multiple clones of himself.[41] Cloning *from* grandparents, and so on is odious for the harm, mentioned above, such arrangements may do this culture's already unstable family relationships.[42] Likewise, research toward human cloning should be rejected as immoral insofar as it destroys human "pre-embryos," encourages degrading views of humans as mere means to organs, pursues the loathsome eugenic project of "improving humanity" by manufacturing Pence's "superior children," and so on. This research is morally impermissible in part for the reason Paul Ramsey identified: it is research performed without informed consent from those experimented upon.[43] Pence dismisses Ramsey's objection as "silly" on the grounds that it is absurd to demand consent from someone to the very procedures that may bring her own consent into existence. Of course, he is right about that, as Ramsey presumably knew.[44] What is unclear is why Pence thinks this proves that such consent is inessential. There is no contradiction in saying that consent is required for morally acceptable research and also that it cannot be secured. What follows from this is simply what Ramsey said: the research is impermissible. Pence may not like this conclusion, but he needs to give some rebuttal to Ramsey's argument.

Perhaps Pence thinks he can use the commonly accepted principle that 'ought' implies 'can' to rebut Ramsey. After all, if this is principle is correct, and if informed consent to the experiment cannot be secured, then the experimenter cannot be accused of wrongdoing for failing to secure it. Again, this is correct, but it does not do the work Pence needs done to rebut Ramsey. For Ramsey's claim is not that the experimenter ought to (and, if the principle is correct, therefore can) secure consent. Rather, it is that the experimenter ought not to perform the experiment without consent. And the experimenter surely can refrain from performing the experiment without consent. She can abandon the experiment.

IV. PENCE'S CASE *FOR* HUMAN CLONING

I think Pence's case for human cloning is rather weak. Few of the reasons he adduces for cloning can be morally considered compelling. There is little here to show that cloning would do much to protect rights, alleviate injustice, avoid treachery, promote virtue or thwart vice. Pence does try to show that banning cloning would somehow be unjust. I will suggest that this effort fails rather badly. However, what matters is that even if it succeeded in demonstrating that position on the question of morally acceptable public policy, it could still be that human cloning itself is morally wrong–always, inherently, and indefeasibly. In short, the morality of public policy here, as elsewhere, underdetermines the central moral issue of whether the practice itself is morally permissible.

Pence defends human cloning on the grounds that it could help avoid genetic disease.[45] This would, of course, be good. However, until we have some evidence of the likelihood that it really helps and, moreover, helps in ways that could not otherwise be realized (or, not otherwise realized without great sacrifice), this reason is, to borrow, Macklin's term, "flimsy."[46]

The same holds for Pence's defense of human cloning as an aid to those afflicted with infertility.[47] How likely is it to help? How much? In what ways? What are the prospects for alternative approaches? Moreover, we should remember that, while infertility is a genuine health dysfunction, there are already *many* legally permitted, and some morally permissible, ways of compensating to a greater or lesser extent: adoption, social volunteering, assisted reproductive techniques, *etc.* Insofar as human cloning is proposed simply to assuage those unwilling or unable to find such alternatives reasonable accommodations, the case for it is still weaker. There is in general no compelling moral reason to make sure everyone gets what she or he wants. Sometimes the proper approach to dissatisfaction is to change one's desires, as the Stoics knew. It is a lesson our culture needs to relearn, not least in these matters.

Pence, like other eugenicist fans of human cloning, thinks it will improve the race.[48] This is no reason at all, for the supposed improvement is moral retrogression as its vicious rhetoric of "superior children," *etc.* should make manifest. This merely displays an insulting and socially dangerous view of illness and human limits. Healthier adults are not therein superior to others. The same holds for babies. The main reason some do not regard talk of "better babies" as offensive is that some people, offensively, view babies as functional items to be evaluated according to how well they serve others' purposes, especially, the purposes for which they were made. This instrumental view of people is deeply wrongheaded and ugly, yet it is the mentality that animates much of the push for cloning. There is a related point.

Sometimes talk of preventing disease is a smokescreen for eugenic improvements, as indicated by Pence's enthusiasm for "changing our [human] natures."[49] What is presented as a noble parental effort to avoid such illnesses as obesity will in fact sometimes be only parents refusing any child not up to their or societal standards of beauty.

He also endorses cloning as a reproductive right.[50] I do not know what the U.S. Supreme Court can be persuaded to affirm as constitutional rights these days. However, there is no good reason to see a *moral* right here. While people plainly have some moral rights over their reproductive activities, Pence's talk of a right over how one reproduces is fanciful. Somebody might as well argue that a right to vote entails that Internet voting must be made available because some people would choose to vote that way.

Pence claims that homosexuals have been "denied" genetic connection to their children and endorses human cloning as a mode of redress.[51] Again, this is not serious for the same reason it would be unserious to demand such redress for celibates, avowed or adventitious.[52]

Theoretically, the most interesting argument Pence offers in support of the morality of human cloning is his appeal to John Rawls's theory of justice. Pence, closely following Rawls, reasons that in the original position, behind Rawls's "veil of ignorance," a rational contractor unaware of which generation she belonged to would choose for those in any generation to seek "the best genetic endowment" for their successors.[53] From this, he concludes that justice requires that society take steps to secure that optimal inheritance, including research and ultimately employment of human cloning. Unfortunately for Pence, I think this argument is based on a misunderstanding of both Rawls's earlier and later understanding of his theory. Rawls's earlier version of his theory in his book *A Theory of Justice* makes it explicit that his theoretical apparatus is designed only to secure principles for insuring that what he calls "the basic structure of society" meets criteria for "social justice." So understood, the apparatus of the original position is misapplied when used, as Pence uses it, to derive conclusions about whether various practices are morally licit. So, even if one accepts Rawls's theory as he first proposed it, the most that Pence could show with it is that society should not interfere with human cloning, not that cloning itself is morally permissible. Of course, I doubt that Rawls's early theory, if itself correct, really shows even that. That the goal of eliminating genetic disease is justified does not suffice to show that such means as cloning are themselves permissible. Indeed, the deontological element in Rawls makes it more difficult to derive such conclusions about means from premises simply about ends.

As for the theory from Rawls's later book, it is still more narrowly circumscribed as a theory simply of political justice for reaching collective political decisions in societies with certain kinds of history, commitments, projects, self-conceptions, *etc.* Again, no conclusions about the permissibility of such non-political practices as human cloning.

On the whole, then, Pence's case for human cloning is hardly compelling. For the most part, it does not deal in the graver moral realms of freeing people from injustice, ending vicious conduct, attaining a deeper appreciation of what is valuable. Nor is it at all established that human cloning is likely to free real people from what any reasonable, objective observer would see as serious health deficits in someone's functioning as a human being. Rather, Pence's case largely reduces to the claim that human cloning may make some things go somewhat better for some people, largely by making things go more to their liking. In light, among other things, of the affront to human dignity and equality that human cloning appears to constitute, I should think a much stronger kind of defense is needed to vindicate it morally.

CONCLUSION

Human cloning can appear to be a great affirmation of life. In fact, I think Pence is more revealing, if not in the way he wants to be, when he ties the drive for human cloning to the earlier and continuing push for radical revision of medical ethics to legitimize abortion, physician-assisted suicide, and active and passive euthanasia.[54] In the end, human cloning merely presents us with a different face of what has rightly been called the "anti-life culture" that infects our medicine and has long ago turned many of our more prominent ethicists into carriers of the contagion. It is another way of attacking human life, this time by degrading it rather than destroying it, by treating human life as something for us to bestow, and therefore of subordinate and only instrumental value. That other practices manifesting this mentality have won wide public acceptance in the last few decades does nothing to justify them, let alone human cloning.

Pence delights in tying himself to the late Joseph Fletcher. That is appropriate, as it is that, at one point, Pence refers to Fletcher with what he must mean to be an avuncular term of affection: 'Old Joe.'[55] That vaguely Stalinist sobriquet fits, because Fletcher was ahead of his time in his enthusiasm for breaking eggs to cook up his omelette: mercy-killing, abortion, fetal and pre-fetal experimentation, manufactured people–all were ingredients in his recipe.[56] Fletcher's contribution to ethical theory was to discover utilitarianism two centuries after Bentham, and then to baptize it, before even he eventually realized that he and his body-count simulacrum of moral thinking had no place in a Church whose founder was murdered in service of the supposed greater good. Pence insists near the beginning of his book that discussion of the ethics of human cloning needs to be "Fletcherized," that is, informed with the spirit and thought of Joseph Fletcher.[57] As his book builds to its finale, Pence gets wilder and wilder. He refashions the commandments from the downbeat "Thou Shalt Not" to something more like the sunny, more contemporary slogan, "Just Do It!"[58] He rejoices in the multiple clones he has fretted over just a chapter before. He calls for a day when cloning can help us match babies to parents as we can dogs to owners. He affirms people to be "compassionate monkeys." He rhapsodizes over the day when a baboon, goosed up with human genes, will instruct us verbally. We were warned that the sleep of reason breeds monsters, and finally, Pence proclaims in his book's last sentence, "Call me Joe Fletcher's clone." By this work's close, he has lived down to that aspiration.

SELECTED BIBLIOGRAPHY

Doerflinger, Richard. National Conference of Catholic Bishops' statement at U.S. Capitol (Jan. 29, 1998).

Dworkin, Ronald. "Assisted Suicide: What the Court Really Said." *New York Review of Books* (Sept. 25, 1997), pp. 40-44.

Fletcher, Joseph. *Ethics of Genetic Control: Ending Reproductive Roulette.* Buffalo: Prometheus, 1984.

Hendin, Herbert. *Seduced by Death: Doctors, Patients, and the Dutch Cure.* New York: Norton, 1996.

Johnson, George. "Ethical Fears Aside, Science Plunges On." *New York Times* (Dec. 7, 1997), p. 6.

Kass, Leon. "Wisdom of Repugnance." *New Republic* (June 2, 1997), pp. 17-26.

Kolata, Gina. "On Cloning Humans, 'Never' Turns into 'Why Not?'." *New York Times* (Dec 2, 1997), pp. A1, A24.

Kolata, Gina. "With an Eye on the Public, Scientists Choose Their Words." *New York Times* (Jan. 6, 1998), p. F4.

Lewontin, Richard. "Confusion over Cloning." *New York Review of Books* (Oct. 23, 1997), pp. 18-23.

Lewontin, Richard, Harold Shapiro, *et al.* "Confusion over Cloning: an Exchange." *New York Review of Books* (Mar. 5, 1998), pp. 46-47.

McCormick, Richard. "Blastomere Separation: Some Concerns." *Hastings Center Report* (March/April 1994), pp. 14-16.

Moraczewski, Albert S. "Cloning Testimony." *Ethics and Medics* 22 (May 1997) 3-4.

National Bioethics Advisory Commission (NBAC). *Cloning Human Beings.* Rockville, 1997.

Pence, Gregory. *Who's Afraid of Human Cloning?* Lanham: Rowman and Littlefield, 1998.

Pontifical Academy for Life. "Human Cloning Is Immoral." *The Pope Speaks* 43 (Jan./Febr. 1998) 27-32.

Ramsey, Paul. *Fabricated Man.* New Haven: Yale University Press, 1970.

Ramsey Colloquium. "On Human Rights." *First Things,* No. 82 (April 1998) 18-22.

Robertson, John A. "The Question of Human Cloning." *Hastings Center Report* (March/April 1994), pp. 6-14.

Scarre, Geoffrey. *Utilitarianism.* London: Routledge, 1996.

Zallen, Dorothy. "We Need a Moratorium on 'Genetic Enhancement'." *Chronicle of Higher Education* (March 27, 1998), p. A64.

NOTES

1. This paper was presented at a University of San Francisco conference on "Human Cloning: Science, Ethics, and Public Policy." I am grateful to the audience at this conference, and to Victoria Wiesner and W. David Solomon for bibliographical materials.

2. Kolata (1997), p. A1. Also see, for example, Johnson.

3. A usage note: throughout, I talk simply of 'human cloning.' This is not as clear as it could be since it is a term that can be applied to many different things. (On this, see Pence, p. 11.) However, many of these differences make little moral difference and it is important to resist the urge to drift into technical obscurity and lose the resonance of the more familiar term. Pence and others now prefer the term "nuclear somatic transfer" (Pence, p. 49). I demur, concerned lest this move, like the insistence on the term 'pre-embryo' and similar moves, form part of a strategy of obfuscation and euphemism. On the strategy, with special reference to the terms 'pre-embryo' and 'nuclear somatic transfer,' see Kolata (1998), p. F4.

4. Pence, p. 56.

5. Pence, pp. 123-125, 139, 165, and *passim*.

6. Pence, p. 7.

7. Pence, p. 65.

8. Pence, p. 66.

9. Pence, p. 70.

10. See Dworkin. On Holland's troubles, see Hendin.

11. Pence, p. 130.

12. Pence, pp. 94, 165.

13. Pence, p. 166.

14. Lewontin (1997), p. 23; (1998), p. 47.

15. Pence, pp. 35, 153.

16. Pence, p. 121.

17. Pence, p. 74.

18. See Pence, p. 121 for his unsubtle (and typically citation-free) analysis of the Old Testament as "just stories." Given the simple-mindedness of his interpretation of Huxley's relatively straightforward dystopia, I suppose we should not have expected him to get much from a text as elusive as the opening of Genesis.

19. Pence, p. 80.

20. Pence, p. 97.

21. Pence, p. 81.

22. Pence, pp. 5, 6.

23. Singer, "Sidgwick and Reflective Equilibrium" in *The Monist* 58 (1974) 516; quoted from Pence, p. 64.

24. Note, too, that whatever Mill may have thought, it is no longer plausible to maintain that utilitarianism can stand without support from our intuitions either in its consequentialist account of what actions are right, its aggregative and sum-ranking account of what distributional schemes or states of affairs are better, or its account of the maximand. Indeed, the very decision to interpret its central principle as that of maximizing what is good rather than one of minimizing what is bad is itself usually decided on the basis of intuition nowadays. There is no obvious warrant for Singer's–and by implication, Pence's–confidence that all these intuitions will be trustworthy and pristine, while intuitions about the immorality of such practices as cloning are corrupted. (For an introduction to some of the issues over utilitarians' competing understandings of happiness as pleasure or preference-satisfaction, negative utilitarianism, act-utilitarianism versus rule- and other forms of indirect utilitarianism, whether the happiness principle should be used by agents in practical deliberation or only by critics in retrospective assessment, and other related issues, see Scarre.)

25. See, for example, Robertson, p. 11. (Also see the response in McCormick.)

26. Pence, p. 142.

27. As an interpretation of Mill, the problem is that it is not consistent with the utility principle to maintain that there are actions immune from moral assessment.

28. Pence, p. 122.

29. Pence, p. 145.

30. It is not fully clear that this makes it sexist because, while the gestating mother must be a woman, of course, even males involved in de-sexed reproduction and child-rearing will similarly be demeaned by their participation.

31. Pence, p. 79.

32. Or still worse, I suppose, a postmodernist one. As an example, see Michel Foucault's multi-volume history of sexuality.

33. I ignore the complication of mitochondrial genes.

34. Lewontin, p. 21; Pence, pp. 122-123.

35. Pence, pp. 139-140.

36. See Moraczewski, p.3; Pontifical Academy.

37. NBAC, p. 71.

38. See the discussion at NBAC, pp. 65f.

39. Moraczewski, p. 3.

40. See, for example, the text reproduced in the periodical *First Things,* No. 82 (April 1998), pp. 28-30. For a discussion, especially on the importance and ground of human dignity, see the Ramsey Colloquium. Also see Doerflinger, Moraczewski, and the Pontifical Academy.

41. Pence, chaps. 10, 11.

42. It may be that cloning *for* male or female homosexuals, cloning the superannuated, *etc.* are also to be condemned for similar reasons.

43. See Ramsey; also Pence, p. 52.

44. Notice, however, that it begs an important question about the moral status of the embryo (and 'pre-embryo') to assume that there is no person at all involved in cases of experimentation on a human embryo. I am grateful to Al Howsepian for focusing my attention on this element in the dispute between Ramsey and Pence. The common ground in such cases is that there is no person in a position to give or withhold consent.

45. Pence, pp. 101-06.

46. At least here it can be said that human cloning would pursue this end in a less morally outrageous way, *viz.*, by genetically healing those with genetic disease markers, as compared with IVF, where the effort is not to help any real person but to prevent conception of the diseased or, viciously, to destroy those marked before they can be born.

47. Pence, pp. 106ff.

48. Pence, pp. 166-170.

49. "A frequent corollary to the fatalist viewpoint is that human nature is not to be trusted with any new knowledge. Any attempt to change our natures [on this view] will produce dark consequences..." (Pence, p. 124; see also p. 165.) Note that Pence here talks as if gaining new knowledge and trying to change human nature were the same thing.

50. Pence, pp. 44, 45, 101.

51. Pence, p. 114.

52. Moreover, it merely encourages irresponsibility thus to disconnect natural effects from causes in this way. In light of what we said above about the family, here bio-engineering can be seen as a partner in dangerous, unproven social experiments. Those who, like Pence, pride themselves on the empiricism of their approach need to attend more closely to the safety issues surrounding these social experiments.

53. Pence, pp. 112-114.

54. Pence, pp. 124, 126.

55. Pence, p. 125.

56. For a sample of Fletcher's thought on genetic issues, see Fletcher.

57. Pence, p. 35.

58. "That part of Western religions based on fear and control always approaches human reproduction with 'Thou Shalt Not!' What is needed is a vision of ideal reproduction that embraces new ways of making babies and that says, 'Thou May!'" (Pence, p. 166).

Abortion Risk Factors: An Avenue for New Pro-Life/Pro-Woman Laws

David C. Reardon

THE "PROTECTION FROM HIGH RISK and Coercive Abortion Act" is a bill that may dramatically change the national abortion debate. Sponsored by State Senator Richard White, it was introduced as Senate Bill 2677 before the Mississippi legislature during the 1998-99 session and is expected to come up again in the 1999-2000 session. Support for the bill has grown to the extent that other states, including Kentucky and Illinois, are considering introducing it in their legislatures as well.

If passed into law, the act will bring an end to assembly-line abortion practices and finally make it possible for women who have been injured by abortion to hold abortionists fully and properly accountable for failing to safeguard their health. A woman's consent to an abortion will be considered "informed, voluntary, and free from negligent and unnecessary exposure to risks" only if the following conditions have been met:

(1) Before the physician recommends or performs an abortion, a qualified person has evaluated the woman to identify the presence of any known or suspected risk factors and informed her and the physician, in writing, or the results of this evaluation....
(2) In the event that any risk factors were identified, the patient has been fully informed by a qualified person which risk factors exist, why these risk factors may lead to adverse reactions, and a detailed explanation of what adverse reactions may occur....
(3) In the event that any risk factors were identified, the qualified person who has provided the screening and counseling has provided a written statement to the patient and the physician certifying, to the best of the qualified person's knowledge, that the patient fully understands and appreciates the significance of the risk factors discussed and her increased exposure to the related adverse reactions....[1]

This new legislation will be difficult to challenge in the courts because it simply puts into law the standard of care presumed by the Supreme Court and endorsed by the medical community. According to the Supreme Court, "basic responsibility" for the abortion rests with the physician.[2] While a woman may request an abortion, it is the physician's obligation to determine if the abortion may be dangerous. If an abortion is contra-indicated for medical reasons, which can include physical, psychological, and social reasons, the physician has a right and duty, in the best interests of the patient, to refuse to perform the abortion.

These rights and duties of physicians are widely recognized in medical textbooks on abortion.[3] In addition, the American College of Obstetricians and Gynecologists,[4] the National Abortion Federation,[5] and the Planned Parenthood Federation of America[6] have all issued documents re-affirming or at least alluding to these duties. Indeed, Sylvia Stengle, executive director of the National Abortion Federation, has stated that at least one in five patients is at psychological risk from abortion due to prior philosophical and moral beliefs that are contrary to abortion. Regarding this "worrisome subset" of patients, Stengle states that there may be an ethical obligation for abortion practitioners to refuse to participate in the violation of a woman's conscience.[7]

Unfortunately for women, however, this obligation is seldom met. In practice, abortion in the United States is provided on request, without the type of screening or counseling that is necessary to protect patients' health.

It is ludicrous to believe that abortionists can make informed recommendations for abortion when no one even knows what benefits, if any, are associated with abortion. Every claim that abortion is beneficial is based solely on the presumption that because women are requesting it, it must be helpful to them. Perhaps worst of all, in the present system of abortions on request, many women are being pressured into unwanted and harmful abortions for the benefit, convenience, or profit of others.

A LARGE BODY OF RISK FACTORS IS KNOWN

Risk factors for immediate physical complications from abortion include uterine abnormalities, multiple gestation, cardiovascular disease, renal disease, asthma, epilepsy, diabetes, venereal infection, intoxication or drug use, obesity, and other pre-existing conditions.[8]

There are also a wide variety of risk factors for delayed physical complications–most notably, the association between abortion and breast cancer. The risk of subsequent breast cancer is associated with abortion of a first pregnancy, abortion at a younger age, abortion performed on a woman with a family history of breast cancer, or a history of multiple abortions.[9] A history of prior abortion (at least 45% of all abortion patients have had at least one abortion already) is also correlated with a wide variety of health risks, such as increased risks of sterility, miscarriage, and low birth-weight in future pregnancies.[10]

While the physical risks of abortion are significant, the published literature demonstrates that emotional and psychological complications following an abortion are even more common. Even the most dedicated of pro-choice researchers generally admit that "there is no virtually no disagreement among researchers that some women experience negative psychological reactions postabortion [sic]."[11] The degree, frequency, and duration of emotional complications are still unknown, however. The lowest estimate for adverse outcomes is 6%, with typical reports ranging from 12 to 25%, and the highest estimates ranging up to 80%.[12]

What is important for the purposes of this discussion, however, is not precisely how many women suffer post-abortion emotional problems,. Instead, it is important to recognize that there is general agreement concerning the risk factors that can *reliably predict* an increased risk of significant post-abortion psychological distress. Indeed, most of the research on pre-identifying risk-factors has been published by abortion proponents.[13]

The risk factors for post-abortion psychological maladjustments can be divided into two general categories. The first category includes women for whom there exist significant emotional, social, or moral conflicts regarding the contemplated abortion. The second category includes women who are experiencing developmental problems, which can include immaturity and pre-existing or unresolved psychological problems.

A summary list of established risk factors includes the following:

conflicting maternal desires; moral ambivalence; feeling pressured by others to abort; feeling that the decision is not her own or is her "only choice"; feeling rushed to make a decision; immaturity or adolescence; prior emotional or psychological problems, including poor development of coping skills or prior low self-image; a prior history of abuse or unresolved trauma; a history of social isolation, as indicated by having few friends or lack of support from one's partner or family; a history of prior abortions; or a history of religious or conservative values that attach feelings of shame or social stigma to abortion. Readers may refer to the addendum for a more complete list of these pre-identifying risk factors.[14]

These risk factors clearly suggest that a substantial number of women–most notably, the majority–are at risk of experiencing adverse psychological reactions to abortion.[15] The conscientious physician would be legally and ethically bound to consider these risk factors when forming a recommendation, to advise the woman of the existence of these risk factors, and, in at least some cases, to refuse to perform the abortion until these risk factors had been alleviated through appropriate counseling.

MEDICAL OBLIGATIONS FOR PROPER SCREENING

All physicians considering a course of treatment have a duty to screen their patients for any predisposing risk factors, to inform their patients of these risk factors, and to make an informed medical recommendation as to whether or not the presume benefits of the procedure outweigh the risks. If the physician believes that the risks outweigh the benefits of any particular procedure, he should decline to perform that procedure.

The same standards apply to physicians performing abortions.[16] According to the ideal standard of care, proper pre-abortion counseling should include screening for all of the risk factors listed above, notifying the patient of any existing risk factors, and providing appropriate counseling or a referral to resources outside the clinic where these risk factors can be addressed or treated.[17]

Furthermore, after this initial screening, patients should routinely be instructed about *all* pre-existing risk factors, even those that the patient does not report. It is well-known that patients seeking abortion are more likely than other types of patients to conceal relevant information, such as a history of prior abortions or the fact that they are being coerced into the abortion by others. In anticipation of such concealment, routine disclosure of all risk factors is necessary to ensure that the patient is given at least the opportunity to make an informed self-evaluation of her risk profile.

Proper screening, full disclosure of risks, and customized counseling for high-risk patients are time-consuming tasks. This is precisely why the standard of care in the abortion industry has fallen so low. Many abortion clinics are profitable because they depend on high volume and fast turnaround. This means that they operate on an assembly-line basis that allows 30 minutes or less for intake, screening, evaluation, and counseling of each patient. This violation of patients' rights must be stopped.

ENSURING THE LEGAL OBLIGATION FOR PROPER SCREENING

The Protection from High Risk and Coercive Abortion Act recognizes that inadequate screening clearly endangers patients' health. This alone is basis for recovery of damages for reckless endangerment. The Act also would correct numerous imbalances in laws and court rules governing abortion malpractice litigation. These imbalances provide an undue advantage to abortionists and tend to protect the abortion industry's low standard of care.

One such imbalance is the short statute of limitations that normally allows injured parties to sue only up to two years after undergoing a medical procedure. The new act would allow women to sue for abortion-related injuries for up to two years after they have *recovered* from any physical or psychological injuries related to the abortion. This provision recognizes that abortion is different from other medical procedures. It can cause psychological disabilities, such as intense feelings of shame, guilt, and self-punishing behavior, that make it difficult or impossible for injured women to seek compensation for their injuries while suffering from abortion-related trauma. It is only after a woman has achieve a significant emotional healing that she can effectively cooperate with her attorney in pursuing a malpractice claim.

Of special concern are cases in which a woman desires to have her child but is under pressure from her male partner, or from his or her parents, to have an unwanted abortion.[18] Clearly, physicians and counselors should be held accountable for failing to properly screen for coercion. In addition, if abortion counselors cooperate with the coercing parties by attempting to convince the girl or woman to submit to the unwanted abortion, the proposed law would allow her to hold the abortion provider liable for the wrongful death of her wanted child.

DUTY TO MAKE INFORMED MEDICAL RECOMMENDATIONS

While a woman may initiate a request for an abortion, it is the duty of the physician to evaluate her, identify the factors that make her pregnancy a problem in her life, examine all the options that may resolve the problem, and provide her with an informed recommendation as to what the most appropriate course of treatment should be.[19] A physician who ignores these duties and merely provides abortions on request should be held accountable for a serious malfeasance of duty.

In forming a medical recommendation for abortion, physicians should not only be aware of predictive risk factors for physical or psychological complications, but they should also have a sound medical basis for determining in what circumstances an abortion is likely to be beneficial. If a woman has one or more risk factors, and there is no clear evidence that she is likely to benefit from an abortion, it is difficult to see how a physician could justify proceeding with a contra-indicated procedure.

Very little research, if any, has been done to identify the situations in which abortion is most likely to improve a woman's life or well-being. Furthermore, there is little, if any, research that has attempted to measure the degree of any benefits. Instead, there is a widespread and untested presumption that if an abortion does not measurably hurt a woman's life, then it must have benefitted her life. But there is no logical basis for assuming that lack of harm correlates to positive benefit.

Humans are extremely adaptable. Some mothers who have been denied abortion will subsequently claim that they never wanted an abortion in the first place.[20] Speaking to a reporter from *The London Express* in 1967, British physician Aleck Bourne expressed his opposition to legalized abortion by saying that easy access to abortion would be a "calamity" for women: "I've had so many women come to my surgery and pleading with me [sic] to end their pregnancies and being very upset when I have refused. But I have never known a woman who, when the baby was born, was not overjoyed that I had not killed it."[21] Many crisis pregnancy counselors and other physicians who have successfully encouraged abortion-minded clients to choose birth have reported similar experiences.

In short, while an abortion can always eliminate a pregnancy, it is very unclear when, if ever, it helps to solve the problem that made the pregnancy problematic. For example, many women seek abortion in the hope of saving a relationship, but the bulk of the evidence shows that they seldom achieve this goal. Abortion is more likely to destroy relationships than to improve them. Other women abort to protect or advance their careers. But there is not even one published study that shows that abortion actually helps them to do so. Furthermore, it is possible and even likely that temporary career advantages, if any, are outweighed by the physical and psychological complications these women suffer from abortion.

CONCLUSION

The Protection from High Risk and Coercive Abortion Act would protect patients' rights simply by putting the ideal standard of care into statute and by making it easier for injured patients to hold negligent abortion providers liable for injuries. Juries would be given the opportunity to hear medical testimony that would support the view that abortion was contra-indicated and not medically justified. In short, the act would compel abortion providers to act like doctors who are obligated to use good medical judgment. In too many cases, abortionists are simply selling their skills to any desperate person who has enough cash, even if that person is totally ignorant of the risks she is facing.

In summary, the challenge this bill represents to abortion proponents has been well articulated by Dr. Philip Ney:

We should remember that in the science of medicine, the onus of proof lies with those who perform or support any medical or surgical procedure to show beyond reasonable doubt that the procedure is both safe and therapeutic. There are no proven psychiatric indications for abortion. The best evidence shows abortion is contraindicated [sic] in major psychiatric illness. There is no good evidence that abortion is therapeutic for any medical conditions with possible rare exceptions. In fact, there are no proven medical, psychological, or social benefits.... If abortion was [sic] a drug or any other surgical procedure about which so many doubts have been raised regarding its safety and therapeutic effectiveness, it would have been taken off the market long ago.[22]

TABLE 1

RISK FACTORS PREDICTING
POST-ABORTION PSYCHOLOGICAL SEQUELAE

(Reference Key: bold–statistically validated study; *italicized–clinical experience, soft data;* normal–literature review)

I. CONFLICTED DECISION
    A. Difficulty making the decision, ambivalence, unresolved doubts: 1,2, 3, **10**,13,**14**,*18,23*,**25**,**29**,**34**,37,**38**,**40**,**46**,**49**,**52**,53,55,**56**,**57**,61
        1. Moral beliefs against abortion: 61
            a. Religious or conservative values:
                1,2,**5**,*23*,**34**,39,**40**,*48*,**49**,54,**56**,**58**,**59**
            b. Negative attitudes toward abortion: 1,**8**,27,**57**
            c. Feelings of shame or social stigma attached to abortion:
                2,61
            d. Strong concerns about secrecy: 50
        2. Conflicting maternal desires: 1,**29**,**30**,**33**,**34**,**46**,*51*
            a. Originally wanted or planned pregnancy:
                1,13,*23*,27,**29**,53,**57**,**59**,61
            b. Abortion of wanted child due to fetal abnormalities:
                3,7,13,*18*,**19**,20,**26**,27,**28**,*41*,61
            c. Therapeutic abortion of wanted pregnancy due to maternal
                health risk: 3,13,15,*18*,20,**26**,27,37,42,**49**,54,55,61
            d. Strong maternal orientation: **34**,*48*
            e. Being married: 1, **10**
            f. Prior children: **25**,*48*,54,**58**,**60**
            g. Failure to take contraceptive precautions, which may
                indicate an ambivalent desire to become pregnant: **6**
            h. Delay in seeking an abortion: 1,2,**26**
        3. Second or third trimester abortion: 1,20,**26**,27,**39**,42,**49**

    4. Low coping expectancy: 1,27,**29,30**
  B. Feels pressured or coerced:
        13,*16,18*,27,**34**,*43,45,48*,**49**,50,*51*,**52**,55,61
    1. Feels decision is not her own, or is "her only choice": **14**,,*18*
    2. Feels pressured to choose too quickly: **17**,*24*
  C. Decision is made with biased, inaccurate, or inadequate
      information: **17**,*48*,**49**

II. PSYCHOLOGICAL OR DEVELOPMENTAL LIMITATIONS
  A. Adolescence, emotional immaturity:
      1,*4*,**9,11**,15,*16*,**17**,27,**29,32,33**,42,*48*,50,54
  B. Prior emotional or psychiatric problems:
      3,5,6,13,15,*18*,20,22,*23*,**25,26,34**,37,**40**,42,*47,51*,54,**57**,61
    1. Poor use of psychological coping mechanisms: 2,**29,34**,61
    2. Prior low self-image: **33,34**,*43,48*,**52**,61
    3. Poor work pattern or dissatisfied with job: **6,52**
    4. Prior unresolved trauma or unresolved grief: *48,51*
    5. A history of sexual abuse or sexual assault.: *23,31,51*,61
    6. Blames pregnancy on her own character flaws, rather
        than on chance, others, or on correctable mistakes in
        behavior: **29,30,36**
    7. Avoidance and denial prior to abortion: **12**,27
    8. Unsatisfactory or mediocre marital adjustment: **6**
    9. Past negative relationship with mother: **5,40**
  C. Lack of social support: 1,9,27,**33**,46,54,55,**56**,58,61
    1. Few friends, unsatisfactory interpersonal relations: **6,52**
    2. Made decision alone, without assistance from partner: **35**
    3. A poor or unstable relationship with male partner:
        6,25,34,40,*43*,53
    4. Single and nulliparous: **9**
    5. Separated, divorced, or widowed: **14**
    6. Lack of support from parents and family (either to have baby or
        to have abortion): 2,**8,9**,*18*,27,**29,33,35**,**52,56**
    7. Lack of support from male partner (either to have baby or to
        have abortion):: 2,**6,8,9**,*18*,**25**,27,**29,33,34,35**,42,**46,52**,53
    8. Accompanied to abortion by male partner: 21,**30**
    9. Living alone: **56**
  D. Prior abortion(s): 13,37,*43,48*,**52,58**
  E. Prior miscarriage: **58**
  F. Less education: **58**

References for the above table:
1. Adler, N.E., *et al.*, "Psychological Factors in Abortion: A Review" *American Psychologist* 47(10): 1194-1204 (1992).
2. Adler, N.E., *et al.*, "Psychological Responses After Abortion," *Science*, 248: 41-44 (1990).
3. **Ashton, J.R. "The Psychosocial Outcome of Induced Abortion," British Journal of Ob&Gyn., 87: 1115-22 (1980).**
4. *Babikian & Goldman, "A Study in Teen-Age Pregnancy," Am. J. Psychiatry, 755 (1971).*
5. **Barnard, C.A., The Long-Term Psychosocial Effects of Abortion (Portsmouth: Institute for Pregnancy Loss, 1990).**
6. **Belsey, E.M., et al., "Predictive Factors in Emotional Response to Abortion: King's Termination Study-IV," Soc. Sci. & Med., 11: 71-82 (1977).**
7. **Blumberg,B.D., et al., "The Psychological Sequelae of Abortion Performed for a Genetic Indication," Am. J. of Obstetrics and Gynecology 122(7): 799-808 (1975).**
9. **Bracken, M.B., et al., "The Decision to Abort and Psychological Sequelae" Journal of Nervous and Mental Disease, 158: 154-162 (1974).**
10. **Bracken, M.B. "A Causal Model of Psychosomatic Reactions to Vacuum Aspiration Abortion," Social Psychiatry, 13: 135-145 (1978).**
11. **Campbell, N.B., et al., "Abortion in Adolescence," Adolescence 23: 813-823 (1988).**
12. **Cohen, L. & Roth, S., "Coping With Abortion," Journal of Human Stress 10: 140-145 (1984).**
13. Council on Scientific Affairs, American Medical Association, "Induced Termination of Pregnancy Before and After *Roe v Wade*: Trends in Mortality and Morbidity of Women," *JAMA*, 268(22): 3231-39 (1992).
14. **David, H.P., "Post-abortion and Post-partum Psychiatric Hospitalization," 1985 Abortion: Medical Progress and Social Implications (London: Ciba Foundation Symposium 115, 1985) 150-64.**
15. De Veber, L.L., et.al., "Post-Abortion Grief: Psychological Sequelae of Induced Abortion," *Humane Medicine*,7(3): 203-08 (1991).
16. *Dunlop, "Counseling of Patients Requesting an Abortion," The Practitioner, 220: 847-52 (1978).*
17. **Franz, W., Reardon, D., "Differential Impact of Abortion on Adolescents and Adults," *Adolescence*, 27(105): 161-72 (1992).**
18. *Friedman, C.M. et al., "The Decision-Making Process and the Outcome of Therapeutic Abortion," Am J of Psychiatry, 131(12): 1332-37 (1974).*
19. **Furlong, R. & Black, R., "Pregnancy Termination for Genetic Indications: The Impact on Families," *Social Work in Health Care,***

10(1): 17 (1984).

20. Lazarus, A., Stern, R., "Psychiatric Aspects of Pregnancy Termination," *Clinics in Obs/Gyn,* 13(1): 125-34 (1986).

21. Gold, D., *et al.*, *The Abortion Choice: Psychological Determinants and Consequences* (Montreal: Concordia University Department of Psychology, 1984).

22. Heath, D.S., "Psychiatry and Abortion," *Can Psychiatr Assoc J,* 16: 55-63 (1971).

23. Hern, W. *Abortion Practice, (Boulder: Alpenglo Graphics, Inc., 1990).*

24. Landy, U. *"Abortion Counseling–A New Component of Medical Care," Clinics in Obs/Gyn, 13(1): 33-41 (1986).*

25. **Lask, B. "Short-term Psychiatric Sequelae to Therapeutic Termination of Pregnancy,"** *Br J Psychiatry,* **126: 173-77 (1975).**

26. **Lazarus, A. "Psychiatric Sequelae of Legalized Elective First Trimester Abortion,"** *Journal of Psychosomatic Ob&Gyn* **4: 141-50 (1985).**

27. Lemkau, J.P., "Emotional Sequelae of Abortion," *Psychology of Women Quarterly,* 12: 461-72 (1988).

28. **Lloyd, J. & Laurence, K.M., "Sequelae and Support After Termination of Pregnancy for Fetal Malformation,"** *British Medical Journal,* **290: 907-09 (1985).**

29. **Major, B. & Cozzarelli,C., "Psychosocial Predictors of Adjustment to Abortion,"** *Journal of Social Issues,* **48(3): 121-42 (1992).**

30. **Major, B., *et al.*, "Attributions, Expectations and Coping with Abortion,"** *Journal of Personality and Social Psychology,* **48:585-599 (1985).**

31. Mahkorn, S. K., *"Pregnancy & Sexual Assault," The Psychological Aspects of Abortion, Mall, D., & Watts, W.F., eds., (Washington, D.C.: University Publications of America, 1979), pp. 53-72.*

32. **Margolis, A.J.,et.al., "Therapeutic Abortion Follow-up Study,"** *Am J Obstet Gynecol,* **110: 243-49 (1971).**

33. **Martin, C.D., "Psychological Problems of Abortion for Unwed Teenage Girls,"** *Genetic Psychology Monographs* **88: 23-110 (1973).**

34. **Miller, W.B., "An Empirical Study of the Psychological Antecedents and Consequences of Induced Abortion,"** *Journal of Social Issues,* **48(3): 67-93 (1992).**

35. **Moseley, D.T., *et al.*, "Psychological Factors That Predict Reaction to Abortion,"** *J. of Clinical Psychology,* **37: 276-79 (1981).**

36. **Mueller, P. & Major, B., "Self-blame, Self-efficacy and Adjustment to Abortion,"** *Journal of Personality and Social Psychology* **57: 1059-68 (1989).**

37. **Ney, P.G. & Wickett, A.R., "Mental Health and Abortion: Review and Analysis,"** *Psychiatr J Univ Ottawa,* **14(4): 506-16 (1989).**

38. Osofsky J.D. & Osofsky, H.J., "The Psychological Reaction of Patients to Legalized Abortion," *American Journal of Orthopsychiatry,* 42: 48-60 (1972).
39. Osofsky, J.D., *et al.,* "Psychological Effects of Abortion: with Emphasis upon the Immediate Reactions and Followup," in H. J. Osofsky & J.D. Osofsky, eds., *The Abortion Experience* (Hagerstown, MD: Harper & Row, 1973), pp. 189-205.
40. Payne, E.C., *et al.,* "Outcome Following Therapeutic Abortion," *Archives of General Psychiatry,* 33: 725-33 (1976).
41. Rayburn, W. & Laferla, J., "Mid-gestational Abortion for Medical or Genetic Indications," *Clin Obstet Gynaecol 13: 71-82 (1986).*
42. Rosenfeld, J. "Emotional Responses to Therapeutic Abortion," *American Family Physician,* 45(1): 137-40 (1992).
43. Rue, V. & Speckhard, A., "Informed Consent & Abortion: Issues in Medicine & Counseling," Medicine & Mind 7: 75-95 (1992).
45. Senay, E., "Therapeutic Abortion: Clinical Aspects," Arch Gen Psychiatry 23: 408-15 (1970).
46. Shusterman, L.R., "Predicting the Psychological Consequences of Abortion," *Social Science and Medicine,* 13A: 683-89 (1979).
47. Sim, M., Neisser, R., "Post-abortive Psychoses: A Report From Two Centers," The Psychological Aspects of Abortion, Mall, D. and Watts W.F., eds. (Washington, D.C.: University Publications of America, 1979).
48. Speckhard, A. & Rue, V., "Postabortion Syndrome: An Emerging Public Health Concern," Journal of Social Issues, 48(3): 95-119 (1992).
49. Vaughan, H.P., *Canonical Variates of Post Abortion Syndrome* (Portsmouth: Institute for Pregnancy Loss, 1990).
50. Wallerstein, J.S. *et al.,* "Psychological Sequelae of Therapuetic Abortion in Young Unmarried Women," *Arch Gen Psychiatry* 27: 828-32 (1972).
51. Zakus, G. & Wilday, S., "Adolescent Abortion Option," Social Work in Health Care, 12(4): 77-91 (1987).
52. Zimmerman, M., *Passage Through Abortion* (New York: Praeger Publishers, 1977).
53. Zimmerman, M. "Psychosocial and Emotional Consequences of Elective Abortion: A Literature Review" in Paul Sachdev, ed., Abortion: Readings and Research (Toronto: Butterworth, 1981).
54. Zolese, G. & Blacker, C.V.R., "The Psychological Complications of Therapeutic Abortion" British J Psych 160: 742-49 (1992).
55. Gibbons, M., "Psychiatric Sequelae of Induced Abortion," J Royal College of General Practitioners 34: 146-50 (1984).
56. Hanna Söderberg, Andersson C, Lars Janzon, Nils-Otto Sjöberg,

"Emotional distress following induced abortion: A Study of incidence and determinants among abortees in Malmö Sweden" *Eur J Obstet Gynecol Reprod Biol* 79: 173-78 (1998).

57. Miller, W.B., Pasta, D.J., Dean, C.L., "Testing a Model of the Psychological Consequences of Abortion" *The New Civil War: The Psychology, Culture, and Politics of Abortion*, ed. Linda J. Beckman and S. Maria Harvey (Washington, D.C.: American Psychological Assoc., 1998).

58. Peppers, L. G., "Grief and Elective Abortion: Implications for the Counselor," *Disenfranchised Grief: Recognizing Hidden Sorrow*, ed. Kenneth J. Doka (Lexington: Lexington Books, 1989), pp. 135-46.

59. Lydon, J., Duncel-Schetter, C., Cohan, C.L., Pierce, T., "Pregnancy Decision Making as a Significant Life Event: A Commitment Approach" *Journal of Personality and Social Psychology*, 71(1): 141-51, 1996.

60. Gail B. Williams, "Induced Elective Abortion and Pre-natal Grief" PhD Thesis, New York University (1991), *Dissertation Abstracts Int'l*, Vol 53, No 3 (Sept. 1992), Order No DA9213205.

61. Anne Baker, et. al., "Informed Consent, Counseling, and Patient Preparation," A Clinician's Guide to Medical and Surgical Abortion, ed. Maureen Paul, *et al.*, (New York: Churchill Livingston, 1999) 29.

NOTES

1. The Protection from High Risk and Coercive Abortion Act, Section 3.

2. *Roe v. Wade*, 410 U.S. 113 at 166 (hereafter *Roe*): "[T]he abortion decision in all its aspects is inherently and primarily a medical decision, and basic responsibility for it must rest with the physician."

3. E. Friedman *et al.*, eds. *Obstetrical Decision Making* (Philadelphia: B. C. Decker, 1978), 2nd ed., esp. M. Borton, "Induced Abortion," p. 44, and Patricia S. Stewart, "Psychosocial Assessment," p. 30; Warren Hern, *Abortion Practice* (Boulder: Alpenglo Graphics, 1990), p. 86.

4. Committee on Professional Standards, American College of Obstetricians and Gynecologists, *Standard for Obstetric-Gynecological Services* (1981). Also, ACOG Executive Board, *Statement of Policy–Further Ethical Considerations in Induced Abortion* (Washington, D.C.: ACOG, 1977).

5. *Standards for Abortion Care* (Washington, D.C.: National Abortion Federation, 1987).

6. L. Saltzman and M. Policar, *The Complete Guide to Pregnancy Testing and Counseling* (San Francisco: Planned Parenthood of Alameda/San Francisco, 1985).

7. J. Woo, "Abortion Doctor's Patients Broaden Suits" in *The Wall Street Journal* (Oct. 28, 1994), p. B12.

8. Hern, pp. 67-74, 166.

9. J. R. Daling *et al.*, "Risk of Breat Cancer among Young Women: Relationship to Induced Abortion" in *Journal of National Cancer Institute* 86/21 (1994) 1584.

10. A. Tzonou *et al.*, "Induced Abortions, Miscarriages, and Tobacco-Smoking as Risk Factors for Secondary Infertility" in *Journal of Epidemiology and Community Health* 47, No. 36 (1993); A. Levin *et al.*, "Association of Induced Abortion with Subsequent Pregnancy Loss" in *JAMA* 243, No. 2495 (1980); M. T. Mandelson *et al.*, "Low Birth Weight in Relation to Multiple Induced Abortions" in *Public Health* 82/3 (1992) 391-94. These citations are examples only. Additional citations could be added.

11. Wilmoth, "Abortion, Public Health Policy, and Informed Consent Legislation" in *Journal of Social Issues* 48/3: 1-17. See also Anne Baker, "Counselor's Corner" in *Hope News* (The Hope Clinic for Women, Ltd., Granite City IL, Dec. 1994), pp. 2-4.

12. In 11 studies, reviewed by P. Dagg, searching for various long-term negative psychological effects of abortion, the lowest incidence-rate reported was 6% and the highest was 32%, the average reported rate being 15%. Dagg, "The Psychological Sequelae of Therapeutic Abortion–Denied and Completed" in *American Journal of Psychiatry* 148/5 (May 1991) 578-85 (Table 2). Another major study found that 49% of 360 women experienced psychological maladjustments post-abortion. E. M. Belsey *et al.*, "Predictive Factors in Emotional Response to Abortion: King's Termination Study–IV" in *Social Science and Medicine* 11 (1977) 71-82. Still other researchers have reported even higher rates by accounting for women who refuse to participate in follow-up programs precisely because they have had, or continue to experience, psychological stress related to the abortion and do not wish to aggravate this stress by participation in the study.

13. See, for example, N. E. Adler *et al.*, "Psychological Factors in Abortion: A Review" in *American Psychologist* 47/10 (1992) 1194-1204; Belsey *et al.*, *op. cit.*; H. P. David, "Post-Abortion and Post-Partum Psychiatric Hospitalization" in *1985 Abortion: Medical Progress and Social Implications* (London: Ciba

Foundation Symposium 115, 1985), pp. 150-64; and U. Landy, "Abortion Counseling–A New Component of Medical Care" in *Clinics in Obstetrics and Gynecology* 13/1 (1986) 33-41.

14. D. C. Reardon, "Predictive Factors of Post-Abortion Maladjustment: Clinical, Legal, and Ethical Implications" at the American Psychiatric Association Annual Meeting, San Diego CA, May 17-22, 1997.

15. Over 70% of women having abortions are doing so against their conscience, with 74% agreeing with the statement "I personally feel that abortion is morally wrong, but I also feel that whether or not to have an abortion is a decision that has to be made by every women for herself"–see *The Los Angeles Times* Poll, March 19, 1989. See also M. Zimmerman, *Passages Through Abortion* (New York: Praeger, 1977), and D. Reardon, *Aborted Women: Silent No More* (Chicago: Loyola Univ. Press, 1987). Some 30 to 55% report feeling pressured to abort by others, and a similar percentage express some desire to keep the child (Zimmerman, Reardon). Approximately 45% of abortions are for women with a prior history of abortion, and over one-fourth are for teenagers. In addition, some trauma experts estimate that as many as one in three women has been sexually abused in childhood–see Judith Herman, *Trauma and Recovery* (New York: Basic Books, 1992), p. 30. It is likely that the percentage of women having abortions who have a prior history of abuse, trauma, or other psychological problems is as high as, or higher than, that for the general population.

16. M. Borton, *op. cit.*; see also *Ambulatory Maternal Health Care and Family Planning Services Policies, Principles, Practices*, ed. F. Barnes (Committee on Maternal Health Care and Family Planning Planning, Maternal and Child Health Association, American Public Health Association, Interdisciplinary Books and Periodicals for the Professional and Layman, 1978).

17. Hern, pp. 84, 86-87.

18. Hern, pp. 80, 81.

19. ACOG Executive Board, *Statement of Policty–Further Ethical Considerations in Induced Abortion* (Washington, D.C.: ACOG, 1977), p.2.

20. See H. David *et al.*, *Born Unwanted: Developmental Effects of Denied Abortion* (New York: Springer, 1988).

21. Valentine Low, interview with Aleck Bourne, "The Rape that Really Changed Our Minds about Abortion" in *Evening Standard* (Feb. 28, 1992), p. 20.

22. P. G. Ney, "Some Real Issues Surrounding Abortion, or The Current Practice of Abortion is Unscientific" in *The Journal of Clinical Ethics* 4, No. 2 (1993) 179-80.

The Value of Life and its Bearing
on Three Issues of Medical Ethics

Peter F. Ryan, S.J.

T HIS PAPER WILL address three related questions of medical morality. First, what are we to make of arguments favoring assisted suicide? Second, how should we determine when, if ever, it is permissible to withhold, or withdraw, nutrition and hydration? Third, how ought we to determine when, if ever, it is permissible to induce the labor of a pregnant woman whose fetus is not yet viable? I will examine some of the problematic ways in which certain ethicists have addressed these issues in an effort to establish by contrast the principles necessary to deal with them properly. It will become evident that we should not only exclude all directly intended death but also carefully apply the principle of double effect in a way to exclude wrongly accepting death as a side effect. It will likewise become clear that one's position on the three issues at stake will depend on whether one regards human life as intrinsically or only instrumentally valuable, and whether one has a dualistic or an integralist view of the human person.

PHYSICIAN-ASSISTED SUICIDE

Before we consider physician-assisted suicide (PAS), we must distinguish it from a choice to use pain-relieving drugs that will have the side effect of ending the patient's life earlier than otherwise would have been the case. As the 1995 papal encyclical *Evangelium Vitae* makes clear, under certain circumstances the latter sort of choice is licit.[1] Such medication may be used only if there is no other medication adequate to deal with the patient's intense pain that will not have the additional effect of hastening his death and if the patient has fulfilled all outstanding responsibilities, such as making a will and, especially, preparing spiritually for death. Under those circumstances the patient's earlier

41

death can be accepted as a side effect of a legitimate effort to relieve pain. PAS, on the other hand, carries out a decision precisely to end the patient's life, generally as a means to ending suffering or removing the burdens his continued living imposes on others. With PAS, the drug used need not have any capacity to relieve pain other than by killing the patient.

Although the external behavior may be the same in the two cases, both the acts themselves and the attitude toward life they reflect are different. In the former case, the patient's life is recognized as intrinsically good and therefore worth living, despite the patient's inability to participate in the full range of human goods and the consequent emotional unattractiveness of staying alive. The hastening of the patient's death is accepted reluctantly as a side effect of using a medication designed specifically to relieve pain. In the latter case, the patient's life is treated as a mere instrumental good. When suffering increases and life no longer seems to serve as the condition for participating in *other* goods, it is presumed to be without value and therefore not worth living. The patient's life is considered expendable; the intention is to kill, and, morally speaking, there is no difference between intentionally prescribing an overdose of painkillers and suffocating the patient with a plastic bag.

It is important to note that despite the possibility that the external behavior may be the same, the acts discussed above are different because they are characterized by different proximate intentions. The agent's proximate intention shapes each human act and determines what that act is. The proximate intention is to be distinguished from the remote intention, which is the purpose the agent has for doing what he does. In both of the cases considered above, the purpose of the act is to relieve pain, but the different proximate intentions that shape the acts themselves make them specifically distinct in a morally significant way.

Sometimes those who support PAS disclaim the proximate intention and describe the act solely in terms of the agent's remote intention: to relieve suffering. They deny that PAS involves intentionally killing the patient and insist that it simply ends the patient's suffering. That is, some PAS supporters deny that PAS carries out a choice to end the patient's life as a *means* of ending his suffering, and describe the act exclusively in terms of stopping suffering. For example, at the trial in which he was convicted of murder, Jack Kevorkian told Judge Jessica Cooper: "My intent is not to kill. But it is my duty as a physician to ease suffering. My intent is tailored towards their ultimate goal, which some people call murder, some call assisted suicide."[2]

The claim that those who practice PAS do not seek death but only to end suffering is belied by two closely related considerations. First, there are almost always ways to end suffering without killing the patient. When such means are passed over in favor of lethal means, death is clearly intended. Second, it is hard to see how death would not be intended when the means chosen to end pain could never do so without bringing about the death of the patient. Many supporters of PAS overlook the significance of these points because they think of life as only instrumentally good and therefore do not hold that the death of a human person is always bad. They regard life as no longer worth living if it cannot serve as the condition for one's participating in other goods. As a result, though they may continue to deny that PAS means intentionally killing the patient, they see no moral problem with choosing to end such a life as a means of ending pain and removing burdens on society.

Of course, some who hold that the death of a human person is always bad nevertheless argue that PAS is sometimes morally acceptable, namely, whenever death is a lesser evil than the patient's continuing to suffer and/or the other bad consequences of keeping him alive. Some who argue in this way for the moral acceptability of PAS claim that when it is justified, death is not intended; others admit that it is intended but claim that that intention can be morally upright. Despite this difference, all such views are instances of proportionalist or consequentialist reasoning. These approaches have been subjected to cogent philosophical criticism and rejected by the Catholic Church.[3] It is worth noting that some who have adopted a version of consequentialism or proportionalism have argued that PAS is not morally acceptable. But their general theory excludes exceptionless moral norms, for they insist that all concrete factors must be weighed before judging the morality of particular choices. Hence, their arguments against PAS are merely prudential rather than principled and are inevitably open to exception.

Other ethicists, however, who oppose intentional killing on principle and reject every form of consequentialism and proportionalism, nevertheless seem to support intentional killing in certain cases, or at least unwittingly support accepting death as a side effect in cases in which doing so cannot be morally justified. This will become clear as we examine the issue of withholding or withdrawing artificial nutrition and hydration (ANH).

ARTIFICIAL NUTRITION AND HYDRATION

U. S. federal courts have treated legal issues concerning PAS. The Second Circuit Court of Appeals claimed that "New York law does not treat equally all competent persons who are in the final stages of fatal illness and wish to hasten their deaths."[4] The court was concerned that

those in the final stages of terminal illness who are on life support systems are allowed to hasten their deaths by directing the removal of such systems; but those who are similarly situated, except for the previous attachment of life sustaining equipment, are not allowed to hasten death by self administering prescribed drugs.[5]

This analysis treats PAS no differently from withdrawing burdensome treatment since both involve a person's doing something that results in death. Indeed, the court states that the "ending of life by [withdrawing life support systems] is nothing more nor less than assisted suicide."[6] This assessment ignores the significance of the means used and the agent's proximate intention shaping the act, and considers only the outward performance and the goal sought. The court reasons that by approving the withdrawal of burdensome treatment, society already has accepted PAS and should make that acceptance explicit as a standard for law.[7]

The Ninth Circuit Court of Appeals is even more explicit in its rejection of the significance of the proximate intention. It explains that according to the principle of double effect, "it is sometimes morally justifiable to cause evil in the pursuit of good" and interprets such causation as including intention. The court argues that when a doctor authorizes the disconnection of a respirator, "there can be no doubt that in such instances the doctor intends that, as the result of his action, the patient will die an earlier death than he otherwise would." The court further states that "[i]n the case of 'double effect' we excuse the act or, to put it more accurately, we find the act acceptable,...because the act is medically and ethically appropriate even though the result–the patient's death–is both foreseeable and intended."[8]

Kevin O'Rourke, O.P., opposes PAS and exposes the flawed moral reasoning behind the two federal appellate court rulings–subsequently overturned by the Supreme Court–that declared PAS legal. He rightly insists that the courts are wrong to

allow a good remote intention to justify an evil proximate intention. Killing an innocent person is never an ethically acceptable remote or proximate intention. Human life is a basic good, and we should never directly act in opposition to basic goods. Even though a remote intention to avoid ineffective therapy or to eliminate suffering is acceptable, this should not be accomplished by a proximate intention of directly hastening death or assisting suicide.[9]

So far, I agree with O'Rourke; the principles he sets out are sound. But problems arise because, despite his statement that "human life is a basic good," he fails to treat it as intrinsically good. That failure, along with a consequent misapplication of the principle of double effect, leads him to defend withdrawing ANH from patients in the persistent or permanent vegetative state (PVS)[10] even in the absence of a special circumstance. O'Rourke denies that such a decision is tantamount to PAS. He argues that "in the case of PVS, AH&N is an ineffective therapy for the pathology which causes the permanently comatose condition and it is burdensome as well. The proximate and remote intention would not be to kill the patient."[11] This argument is unsound for the following reasons.

First, ANH is not intended as a therapy for the pathology and should not be judged as ineffective because it does not remedy it. Its efficacy should be judged according to whether or not it really does serve to keep the patient alive by providing food and water, which it almost always does. Why does O'Rourke hold that ANH can only be justified if it remedies the pathology? He assumes that it is pointless to sustain a life burdened with the pathology that makes one a PVS patient. That assumption presupposes the further assumption that bodily life is not a value in and of itself. So, O'Rourke considers ANH inefficacious if it merely sustains bodily life apart from what he recognizes as beneficial to the patient. Thus, to justify withdrawing ANH from one's parent in PVS, O'Rourke says: "given the physiological condition of mom or dad, we cannot do anything beneficial for them."[12] On this basis, O'Rourke thinks that an intervention that does not resolve the underlying problem is futile. He fails to recognize that bodily life is intrinsically valuable; he regards it only as instrumentally valuable and considers it worthwhile only insofar as it enables a person to participate in other goods.

Second, the burdens of ANH are one thing and the burdens of all the other elements of the patient's care are quite another, and the two should not be confused. To remove a patient's feeding tube in order to avoid other burdens, such as the burden of keeping him clean and properly positioned in bed, is not to accept the patient's death as a side effect but to choose the patient's death as a means of avoiding those other burdens. When ANH is readily available at reasonable cost, as it is in developed countries, and when providing it does not trouble the patient, as it clearly does not in the case of a PVS patient, then the claim that the burden of ANH is excessive implies that preserving his life is of no benefit to the patient. The underlying assumption, again, is that life is not an intrinsic good but is good and worth living only if it enables the patient to participate in other goods.[13]

O'Rourke holds that there is no point in sustaining life unless doing so helps a person "strive for the purpose of life," which, "as described in the Catechism of the Catholic Church (I.1), is to know and love God." In order to pursue this purpose, "either a person must possess this capacity for cognitive-affective function or have the potential to develop this capacity." And he argues that the PVS patient lacks both the capacity and any possibility of developing it.[14] However, his conception of knowing and loving God is very narrowly drawn. Catholic pastoral practice treats those who apparently do not have that capacity or potential as apt recipients of the sacraments. Just as the severely retarded are regularly baptized, so also PVS patients, like patients in a coma and on the verge of death, are apt recipients of Baptism, Confirmation, and the Sacrament of the Sick. This pastoral practice presupposes that the relationship these recipients have with God can be affected by receiving these sacraments. Moreover, to agree that the purpose of life is to know and love God does not entail holding either that fundamental human goods, including the good of bodily life itself, lack intrinsic value or that the purpose of life does not include participating in those goods.

The line of reasoning O'Rourke proposes–that providing medical care to sustain the life of patients is useless and burdensome if it does not help them pursue the purpose of knowing and loving God–leads to implausible conclusions when applied to other situations. William May points out that "an infant suffering from Trisomy 13 will never be able to pursue the spiritual goal of life. Yet if such an infant should suffer a cut artery it would surely not be 'extraordinary' treatment to stop the bleeding, although doing so would be 'ineffective' in helping the infant pursue the spiritual goal of life."[15]

Against the position O'Rourke defends, I maintain that there are four reasons why ANH ordinarily should be provided to PVS patients.

First, ANH offers the benefit of warding off starvation and dehydration. In and of itself, sustaining the life of the patient is a benefit because human life is intrinsically, not only instrumentally, good.

Second, besides benefiting the patient by sustaining his life, ANH benefits both patient and caregiver with respect to the good of human solidarity. The very effort to sustain the life of another creates a bond that is beneficial to both parties. As many family members who have had the experience of caring for their loved ones with debilitating afflictions such as PVS have attested, conscientious caregivers enter into solidarity with the patients for whom they assume the burden of care. Caregivers with the gift of Christian faith who are motivated by charity can grow in holiness by treating the PVS patient as they would treat Christ himself and by uniting the sacrifices they make with his sacrificial passion and death. PVS patients also benefit from this care by sharing more profoundly in human community and in the community of faith. That is true, even assuming such patients have no conscious experience of that benefit. Just as we rightly say that a PVS patient suffers indignities when treated as a mere object–as, for example, when a female PVS patient is wronged by being raped–so also we rightly conclude that such a patient shares in the benefits of human community when treated with the respect due all human persons. Indeed, caregivers who conscientiously strive to ensure that Catholic PVS patients receive the Sacrament of the Sick implicitly acknowledge that the condition of such patients does not preclude their benefiting from goods other than that of bodily life itself.

Third, all competent physicians realize that diagnosing PVS is very difficult, if possible at all. The common view is that it can be diagnosed only when a condition of unresponsiveness continues for months or perhaps years. But some physicians have become convinced that it is impossible to diagnose PVS definitively. They argue that one cannot be sure that a patient has no conscious awareness whatever and will never emerge from that presumed state.[16] This difference of opinion grounds a reasonable doubt about the actual condition of so-called PVS patients. So, even those who think that only conscious life is worth living cannot reasonably maintain that ANH is useless for such patients.

Fourth, ANH generally imposes no significant burdens. The usual procedures required to initiate and maintain it are simple. Neither the nasogastric tube with smaller dimensions, which allows for non-operative access, nor the gastronomy tube, which often allows for operative access on an outpatient basis, are very costly. Moreover, the patient is either unconscious and therefore feels no pain, or the patient is conscious, in which case any discomfort caused by ANH hardly would exceed the excruciating pain of starving to death or dying of dehydration.

When, if ever, it is permissible to withhold or withdraw ANH from PVS patients? Any of three special circumstances can justify such a decision.

First, ANH obviously is not required if it is ineffective. For example, if a PVS patient cannot assimilate the nutrients provided, ANH is not providing the benefit of sustaining life and is therefore pointless. Despite a possible emotional motivation to continue ANH, human solidarity with such a patient is served by withdrawing it.

Second, it is conceivable–for example, in undeveloped countries–that ANH is out of the reasonable financial reach of some people. Those who cannot provide someone with ANH without using resources needed to fulfill other exigent responsibilities may not be morally required to provide it. Likewise, those in charge of health care and public officials generally in undeveloped countries could reasonably decide to allocate their very limited resources to patients with better prospects than those for whom ANH otherwise would be morally required. Of course, as I explained previously, the cost of providing ANH must be not be confused with the entire cost of patient care so as to facilitate rationalizing the intentional killing of patients.[17]

Third, the patient may decide, by means of some form of advance directive, to forgo all care so that the resources that would have been expended in providing ANH may be used for other purposes. One can reach such a decision morally only if one is confident that those resources will serve at least as important a purpose as they would in sustaining one's life. That norm is not easy to fulfill, because without being very costly or labor intensive, ANH provides the great benefit of allowing one to live. Here again, one must assiduously avoid rationalizing. One must not direct that the resources that otherwise would be expended to provide ANH be used for other purposes because one would rather be dead than in PVS. Moreover, because the choice to forgo care is an act of freely given mercy, no one can make this decision for the patient. It is impossible to be merciful on behalf of another.

ABORTING NON-VIABLE FETUSES WHEN THE MOTHER'S LIFE
IS NOT THREATENED

In a joint article entitled "Care for the Beginning of Life," Jean deBlois, C.S.J., and Kevin O'Rourke comment on the 1994 *Ethical and Religious Directives for Catholic Health Care Services* approved by the U.S. bishops. They claim that Directive 48 "succinctly defines the limits within which the moral assessment of treating extrauterine pregnancy must take place. The sole criterion proposed is that treatment must not constitute a direct abortion."[18] However, Directive 47 limits accepting death as a side effect. A medical intervention that will result in the unborn child's death is licit only if there is "a proportionately serious pathological condition of a pregnant woman."[19]

How does the principle of double effect bear on the case of a woman pregnant with an anencephalic child? An anencephalic infant lacks much of its brain, skull, and cap due to the neural tube's failure to close during the embryo's early development. If brought to term, the child will not be able to achieve normal cognitive or affective development because it has no functioning cerebral cortex; in fact, it will die very soon, probably within hours of birth.[20]

In "Anencephaly and the Management of Pregnancy," deBlois claims that anencephaly can be diagnosed in the first trimester and argues that "once the diagnosis is made, there seems to be no purpose in maintaining the pregnancy."[21] Since the pregnancy involves physical risks to the mother along with "the emotional trauma suffered by a couple upon diagnosis of anencephaly," deBlois concludes that "terminating the pregnancy" can be justified by the principle of double effect:

> The intervention which terminates the pregnancy is taken to avoid the continued risk to the mother posed by carrying an anencephalic fetus. The risks cannot be avoided in any other way. The death of the fetus, while unintended, is unavoidable. It is a matter of prudential judgment that the good being sought in this case is of due proportion to the evil permitted. While the mother's life is not in imminent danger, there is the real possibility of maternal harm as pregnancy advances. Since the condition of the fetus deprives it of any potential for development, the proportion seems adequate to justify terminating the pregnancy.[22]

This analysis is riddled with problems. DeBlois's presupposition that prenatal diagnosis can be moral even when it is done with a view to discovering candidates for abortion is not justified and is at odds with explicit Catholic teaching.[23] Her apparent assumption that it is possible to provide an absolutely certain diagnosis of anencephaly prior to birth ignores relevant medical findings.[24] Her representations about the risks to the mother of carrying an anencephalic child are misleading.

Unfortunately, this article cannot treat all of those issues. But the assumption that the abortion would reduce the risk to the mother's health and remove her psychological trauma should not go unchallenged. DeBlois says nothing of the physical risks associated with abortion itself, such as the risk of cervical muscle damage and damage to the uterine wall, which can lead to scarring, future miscarriages, and ectopic pregnancies. And it is by no means clear that psychological trauma is removed or even reduced when the unborn child is aborted. In exchange for a possible short-term release of tension, there is the daunting prospect of post-abortion syndrome, which has caused severe psychological trauma in many women who were advised to turn to abortion as a solution to their problem.

It is of inestimable value to both child and parents for the pregnancy to be brought to term, not least so that the parents can use what little time there is to bond with the child. A study of couples who learned that their pregnancy involved a lethal abnormality records the following poignant remark of one mother who gave birth to an anencephalic infant: "We saw him. If I had had a termination, we would have nothing to remember. And I would have wondered if the scans were wrong. I would have had that termination on my conscience for the rest of my life."[25] Besides drawing attention to the psychological benefit to the woman of bringing her child to term, this comment underscores the significance of the woman's spiritual welfare. As Mother Teresa of Calcutta puts it, abortion involves two deaths: the death of the unborn child and the death of the woman's conscience. To encourage a woman to prefer an illusory health advantage and a possible temporary respite from emotional trauma over the very life of her unborn child is to disregard not only the value of the child's life but the woman's spiritual welfare as well.

DeBlois's willingness to accept the physical and psychological risks of abortion undermines her claim that because it removes the physical and psychological risks of carrying an anencephalic child to term, the abortion would not be an intentional killing. It makes little sense to argue that one's intention is not the death of the child but the avoiding of risks when the child's dying entails greater risks. But even if one were to concede that the abortion would not be directly intended, it does not follow that it would be morally justifiable. Mother and child must be treated as persons with equal rights and dignity. When one bears that in mind and applies the Golden Rule, it becomes evident that it is grossly unfair to proceed with a treatment that will result in the death of one for any reason other than to save the life of the other. Even in such a conflict situation, which virtually never occurs in modern medical facilities, reasons must be given for choosing to save one rather than the other. But there is no conceivable justification for removing a minor risk to the mother's health and attempting to reduce her psychological trauma when doing so requires the death of her unborn child.

Why do ethicists like deBlois argue that the (alleged) removal of physical danger and emotional trauma can justify consenting to a procedure that would result in the death of the anencephalic unborn child? Given the approval of such procedures in some ostensibly Catholic hospitals, her argument is perhaps an effort to justify what those hospitals already are doing to accommodate women pregnant with anencephalic children. In any case, her analysis manifests the same attitude toward the value of life that characterizes the effort, criticized above, to justify removing ANH from PVS patients. The assumption once again is that bodily life is not valuable in itself but only as the condition for one's participating in other goods. Life is regarded not as intrinsically but only as instrumentally good.

DeBlois claims that "anencephaly makes integrated development impossible"[26] and notes that human development is significant only if it is integrated. She explains that "human life, while dependent upon a physiologic substrate, involves psychologic, social and creative capacities as well" and insists that "human life involves more than simply biologic life."[27] While the latter statement is true, in context deBlois's assertion plainly implies that she does not consider the anencephalic fetus to be a human person.

If deBlois really holds that the anencephalic fetus is not a person, one wonders why she bothers to insist that in aborting it one need not directly intend its death. She could simply argue that one has sufficient reason to justify intentionally killing a non-person. Moreover, if deBlois holds that the anencephalic fetus is not a person, consistency would require her to hold that if it were brought to term and born alive, there would be no point in baptizing it. But deBlois provides no credible basis for holding that the anencephalic fetus is not a human person. That its neural tube fails to close later on in gestation is no reason to deny that, as with all of us, such a fetus becomes a person at fertilization, when integrated development begins. And while the affliction of anencephaly hinders normal development, the development these infants do achieve—evident in their virtually perfect bodies—is by no means entirely unintegrated.

If, on the other hand, deBlois acknowledges that the anencephalic fetus is a person, then her observations about what constitutes significant human life provide no support at all for her claim that the abortion can be justified. She avoids dealing with these problems by failing to be explicit about the personal status of the anencephalic fetus.

The implication that it is possible for a human being not to be a person reveals an underlying dualistic anthropology that fails to recognize the inherent value of bodily life. On such a view, bodily life is not identified with the person and is considered valuable only if it enables one to participate in other goods.

CONCLUSION

A common assumption underlies the reasoning of many who hold the positions I have argued against. Those who justify PAS, those who support the withdrawal of ANH from PVS patients, and those who defend the abortion of anencephalic fetuses tend to suppose that bodily life is good only instrumentally and not in itself. Underlying that assumption is a dualistic anthropology, according to which the human person is not considered an integral unity of body and soul. Rather, the person's true self is thought to be somehow distinct from his body.

This dualistic perspective leads one to assume that when the body cannot sustain a person's satisfactory participation in human goods, he is better off dead. Those who hold this view often suppose that the body can be killed without compromising the person and that in death the soul is "freed" from the body. Such a perspective fails to recognize that death is a radical dissolution of an integrated unity rather than an event that in itself offers freedom. Christianity holds, to the contrary, that our full freedom comes only with the resurrection of the body, when death is overcome and the body is once again brought into personal unity with the soul.

The dangers of a dualistic anthropology extend far beyond the way it shapes attitudes on the specific questions we have considered. When society embraces the view that bodily life is valuable only when it enables a person to participate satisfactorily in a broad range of goods, then it is not only the lives of PVS patients and the anencephalic unborn that will be in peril. The lives of the severely disabled also will be considered expendable, as will many others, including newborns and even alert adults thought to have a very meager participation in goods other than life itself. Indeed, a proportionalist analysis will consider expendable all persons whose participation in human goods is judged not to offset the burden they pose to society. The inexorable and frightening logic of the view that human life is not intrinsically valuable should move us to respond convincingly to those who endorse that idea.

NOTES

1. John Paul II, *Evangelium Vitae* (Washington, D.C.: U.S. Catholic Conference, 1995), 65: *AAS* 87 (1995) 476, recalls that "Pius XII affirmed that it is licit to relieve pain by narcotics even when the result is decreased consciousness and a shortening of life, 'if no other means exist, and if, in the given circumstances, this does not prevent the carrying out of other religious and moral duties.' [Pius XII, Address to an International Group of Physicians (24 Feb. 1957) III: *AAS* 49 (1957) 147; *cf.* Congregation for the Doctrine of the Faith, *Declaration on Euthanasia*, III: *AAS* 72 (1980) 547-548.] In such a case, death is not willed or sought, even though for reasonable motives one runs the risk of it: There is simply a desire to ease pain effectively by using the analgesics which medicine provides."

2. Bryan Robinson, Mary Jane Stevenson, and Aldina Vazao Kennedy, "Kevorkian argues in opening statement that he did not intend to kill, says he did his duty as a doctor," *Court TV*, 22 March 1999, Online, Internet, available http://www.courttv.com/trials/kevorkian/032399_pm_ctv.html.

3. See John Finnis, *Moral Absolutes: Tradition, Revision, and Truth* (Washington, D.C.: The Catholic Univ. of America Press, 1991); Germain Grisez, *The Way of the Lord Jesus*, Vol. 1, *Christian Moral Principles* (Chicago, Franciscan Herald Press, 1983), 141-71; John Paul II, Encyclical Letter *Veritatis Splendor*, 71-83: *AAS* 85 (1993).

4. *Vacco v. Quill*, 80 F.3d 716, 727, 729 (2d Cir 1996).

5. *Ibid.*

6. *Ibid.*, 729.

7. See David Orentlicher, "The Legalization of Physician-Assisted Suicide," *The New England Journal of Medicine*, 335/9 (29 August 1996) 663-67.

8. *Compassion in Dying v. State of Washington,* 79 F3d 790 (9th Cir 1996).

9. "Ethical Issues in Health Care," *Saint Louis University Health Sciences Center, Center for Health Care Ethics*, 18/ 8 (April 1996) 2.

10. A vegetative state tends to be regarded as "persistent" if it lasts any time from one to three months and "permanent" after a year or more.

11. O'Rourke, "Ethical Issues," 2.

12. *Ibid.*

13. Apparently, many physicians in the United States share this mistaken view. In Payne *et al.*, "Physicians' Attitudes about the Care of Patients in the Persistent Vegetative State: A National Survey," *Annals of Internal Medicine*, 125/2 (15 July 1996) 104-10, researchers point to an emerging consensus of attitudes and beliefs among physicians who care for PVS patients. With respect to their attitudes, of the 319 doctors who responded, 89% consider it ethical to withhold ANH from PVS patients; 65% consider it ethical to transplant vital organs from PVS patients; and 20% consider it ethical to administer lethal injections to hasten the death of such patients. With respect to these physicians' beliefs about the condition of PVS patients, only 13% think such patients are aware and have the experience of hunger and thirst; and only 30% believe these patients feel pain. The report concludes: "When evaluating the appropriateness of treatments for patients in the PVS, neurologists and medical directors largely concur. Most physicians in both groups believe that patients in the PVS would be better off dead; that it is not necessary to provide aggressive therapeutic interventions; and that all therapeutic interventions, including artificial nutrition and hydration, can be withheld in certain circumstances. The areas of consensus are remarkable and suggest that an ethical standard that physicians believe should be followed when caring for these patients may be emerging" (104). Of particular interest is the revelation that almost half of the doctors who responded "agreed that patients in the PVS should be considered dead....Defining patients in the PVS as dead would eliminate the physicians' responsibilities to these patients and thus may, in some respects, appeal to some physicians" (108). If such patients were "defined as dead," all questions about care for PVS patients would be instantly resolved, and harvesting organs from them would not violate U.S. law that prohibits harvesting organs from living patients (108).

14. O'Rourke, "A Response to William E. May's "Tube Feeding and the 'Vegetative State,'" *Ethics and Medics*, 24/4 (April 1999) 3-4.

15. "Tube Feeding and the 'Vegetative State,'" *Ethics and Medics*, 23/12 (December 1998) 2.

16. Andrews *et al.*, "Misdiagnosis of the Vegetative State: Retrospective Study in a Rehabilitation Unit," *British Medical Journal,* 313 (6 July 1996) 13-16, report on a study of forty PVS patients at Britain's Royal Hospital for Neurodisability. The researchers found that seventeen (43%) had been misdiagnosed by their referring physicians as being in PVS; thirteen (33%) slowly emerged from the vegetative condition during rehabilitation therapy; and only ten (25%) remained in the vegetative state. This disturbingly high incidence of misdiagnosis occurred despite the fact that in most cases, the diagnosis was "made by a neurologist, a neurosurgeon, or rehabilitation specialist–all of whom could have been expected to have experience of the vegetative state" (15). The researchers point out that misdiagnosis can occur even when the patient is assessed regularly and the observations of family and caregivers are taken into account. The conclusions of this British study of PVS, which is among the largest and most comprehensive available, echo the findings of an earlier U.S study of PVS patients referred to the Healthcare Rehabilitation Center in Austin, Texas. Childs, et al, "Accuracy of Diagnosis of Persistent Vegetative State," *Neurology*, 43 (August 1993): 1465-67, report that "of the 49 patients referred in coma or PVS, 18 (37%) received a change in diagnosis at or shortly after admission"(1466).

17. One might ask what a financially strapped family is to do when it cannot afford a hospital room and basic nursing care. It seems to me that the members of such a family can make arrangements for the loved one in PVS to stay at home, with feeding tube intact. Their responsibility simply would be to do what they can to provide for the patient's basic needs without ignoring their other responsibilities. Since what they can do under such circumstances is likely to be quite a bit less than what a nursing staff could do in a hospital room, the situation can be distressing. Proceeding in this way may not be as neat and easy as removing a feeding tube, but neither does it involve the choice to kill or wrongly cut off care. Rather, it maintains solidarity with the patient.

18. "Care for the Beginning of Life: The Revised *Ethical and Religious Directives* Discuss Abortion, Contraception, and Assisted Reproduction," *Health Progress* (Sept.-Oct. 1995) 39.

19. National Conference of Catholic Bishops, *Ethical and Religious Directives for Catholic Health Care Services* (Washington, D.C.: U.S. Catholic Conference, 1995), directive 47.

20. Still, the extent of the pathology varies, and some anencephalic babies live a month or more. See D. Alan Shewmon, "Anencephaly: Selected Medical Aspects," *Hastings Center Report*, 18/5 (Oct.-Nov. 1988) 11-15.

21. "Anencephaly and the Management of Pregnancy," *Health Care Ethics USA* (fall 1993): 2.

22. *Ibid.*, 3.

23. See Congregation for the Doctrine of the Faith, *Instruction on Respect for Human Life in its Origin and on the Dignity of Procreation* (1987) 1,2: *AAS* 80 (1988); *Catechism of the Catholic Church*, no. 2274.

24. Stumpf *et al.*, "The Infant with Anencephaly," *The New England Journal of Medicine*, 322/10 (8 March 1990): 670, report that "it may not be possible in all cases to distinguish anencephaly from other very severe anomalies of the head...For purposes of genetic and reproductive counseling and epidemiologic reporting, the diagnosis should be confirmed by an experienced observer following delivery of an abortus or stillborn infant." Even after birth, "errors in diagnosis have been described in the literature, by surveillance programs, and by our task force in a survey of pediatric training programs." Also see Shewmon, 11-15.

25. Chitty *et al.*, "Continuing with Pregnancy after a Diagnosis of Lethal Abnormality: Experience of Five Couples and Recommendation for Management," *British Medical Journal*, 313 (24 August 1996) 479-80.

26. DeBlois, "Anencephaly," 3.

27. *Ibid.*, 2.

Ending Renal Dialysis:
Ethical Issues in Refusing
Life-Sustaining Treatment

Kevin E. Miller

INTRODUCTION: BACKGROUND AND ISSUES

As of 1991, approximately 230,000 people in the United States had end-stage renal disease (ESRD),[1] kidney disease that has irreversibly progressed to the point that there remains insufficient kidney function to sustain life. ESRD may result from a pathology affecting the kidneys alone, or it may be secondary to a systemic disorder, diabetes in the case of 35.8% of new U.S. ESRD patients in 1991.[2] For a multitude of reasons, many ESRD patients cannot receive transplants. For these patients, including 134,000 medicare recipients in the U.S. in 1991 (medicare recipients represented 93% of all U.S. ESRD patients), renal dialysis is the only option for sustaining life.[3]

While dialysis is no longer an experimental treatment, it uses complicated technology and is very expensive. The majority of U.S. dialysis patients receive hemodialysis, in which the patient's blood flows through a machine that filters out toxins (as opposed to peritoneal dialysis, in which fluid is infused into the abdomen and toxins filter from the blood into this fluid through the peritoneal membrane); the majority of these–58.8% of all U.S. medicare dialysis patients in 1991–receive it in a clinic on an outpatient basis (as opposed to at home).[4] Such hemodialysis, on which I shall focus in this paper, cost approximately $47,400 a year for each patient in 1991.[5] Because the Federal government has covered the cost of dialysis for most ESRD patients since 1972,[6] patients may not incur direct financial burden, but they do impose costs on society. Furthermore, when ESRD is consequent to a condition like diabetes, it will often be accompanied by other serious health problems that will sometimes impose more direct financial burdens on patients and their families.

Putting aside cost to patients and to society, dialysis is itself burdensome and its benefits may be limited. Most patients receive hemodialysis for three to four hours at a time, three times a week.[7] Patients may not only feel discomfort during dialysis, but may also begin to feel the effects of uremia, the buildup of toxins in their blood, before a dialysis session, and afterwards may feel tired or cramped.[8] Dialysis therefore requires a significant time investment, or, put differently, may provide the patient with only several fully functional days each week. Dialysis patients must observe a strict diet, including limitations on fluid intake.[9] Finally, dialysis cannot cure other complications of conditions like diabetes to which ESRD may be secondary. Therefore, the life that it sustains may be burdened by other such problems. Without denying that sustaining life can be a benefit even in such cases, one can still say that it is less of a benefit than it is when the life sustained is healthier.

For all of these reasons, patients may want to end dialysis, and the consensus among medical ethicists and health-care personnel is that ending dialysis can be acceptable in principle.[10] There are protocols for helping patients through the decision to end dialysis and its aftermath,[11] and approximately eight percent of U.S. patients ended dialysis in 1987, resulting in death after a mean of eight days.[12]

To make the issue more concrete, one can consider an especially "hard case." Last summer, in the Milwaukee area, an 85-year-old retired physician died after ending kidney dialysis after six years. The man's kidney failure was secondary to diabetes. Due to circulatory complications of his diabetes, his legs had been amputated three years before. His daughter wrote of the "suffering" that dialysis had caused him. The man's wife had been dying of cancer, and he decided that when she died and he was therefore no longer needed to support her, he would end dialysis. He did so with the support of his Catholic pastor, who, in his daughter's words, "wrote specifically in the parish bulletin that according to the Catholic Church, discontinuation of dialysis is not suicide." Reports of the case in the *Milwaukee Journal Sentinel* led to an exchange of letters to the editor concerning whether the man's decision should be termed "suicide."[13]

It is the purpose of this paper to consider the ethical issues raised by such cases. This is important not only because of the number of patients who might wish to end dialysis, but also because the use of life-sustaining treatment in general has, needless to say, led to many questions about what health-care personnel, families, and patients are ethically required, allowed, or forbidden to do, and what civil laws would be in keeping with ethical norms. In my discussion, I shall explain principles and draw conclusions that I hope will address some of these more general concerns as well as some of those peculiar to the use and ending of renal dialysis.

I shall argue that a patient's motives for ending life-sustaining treatment are of particular ethical importance. Great care must be taken to ensure that a patient is weighing the benefits of treatment against the burdens of that same treatment, rather than against the burdens of his medical condition that the treatment may not relieve. That is, patients must not end treatment in order to eliminate such burdens by means of the death that will result from ending treatment. This would be contrary to the spiritual meaning of human life. This same meaning of human life, however, also implies that, as the Catholic Church teaches, patients may forego treatment that does not offer benefits proportionate to the burdens it entails. This principle can be shown to be relevant for some dialysis patients. Furthermore, patients may take into account their underlying condition in assessing the total benefits to be weighed against the burdens of a treatment–a treatment that keeps a patient alive but in a condition like that of the Milwaukee-area dialysis patient I have mentioned offers fewer benefits than one that keeps a patient alive and generally well; therefore, in the former case, the benefits will not be proportionate to as great a burden as they would in the latter case.

It will as a matter of principle be impossible to specify in detail what sorts of benefits outweigh what sorts of burdens, and vice-versa. Much will depend on the individual patient. Each decision will therefore require prudence. However, since the possibility of burdens that are disproportionate to even the benefit of sustained life reflects the same spiritual meaning of human life that precludes choosing death as a means to relief from burdens, spiritual maturity will make a difference in patients' decisions, even though decisions reflecting spiritual imperfection are not necessarily blameworthy or unethical.

PRINCIPLES: THE MEANING OF LIFE, THE MEANING OF DEATH, AND
    RESPECT FOR LIFE IN THE FACE OF DEATH

What do reason and, for those who are Christians, faith tell us about the meaning and value of life, and about how to view death in a way that is consistent with the value of life?[14] To answer this question, it is necessary to consider first what kind of beings we are. We are material beings–our bodies are not extrinsic to our "selves," like clothing–but we are at the same time more than material beings; we are spiritual beings because we have spiritual souls. What makes it possible for us to be simultaneously material and spiritual is the intimate relationship between our bodies and our souls: the human soul is the "form" of the body; it is what makes it to be a living, human body.[15] Our body thus participates in the spiritual life of the soul.

Now the human soul is a spiritual soul because it is a rational soul; it is capable of knowing the true and loving the good. Yet it is really the person, body and soul, not only the soul, that knows and loves. This is what it means concretely to say that the body participates in the life of the soul.[16] We can therefore say that in a certain sense the purpose of life, including bodily life, is a spiritual purpose: to know and to love. A Christian can add to this that our purpose is to know and love absolute Truth and Goodness: to know and love God in communion with God's own knowledge and love of himself–that is, to participate by grace in the life of the Trinity.

At this point, we can see what it means to speak of the human body as having special value: the spiritual is more valuable than the material, and the human body shares in the value of the spiritual soul.[17] We can also see what it means to treat the human body and human life–that is, bodily life–in accord with its value. The body must not be treated as though it were to be valued only for its material value, for its ability to experience such material realities as pleasure, in isolation from or opposition to its spiritual value, for its participation in knowledge and love.

First, then, we must not cease to respect its integrity and life, conferred upon it by its participation in the life of the soul, when pain or sickness causes the fact that there is not perfect harmony between body and soul, and that our person's integrity is therefore not perfect, to intrude upon our consciousness.[18] Above all, we must not think of even severe pain or grave illness as destroying the entire value of our bodily life.[19] Pain and illness do not, after all, make it impossible to pursue spiritual goodness. To the extent that they make it difficult to do so, it is still incoherent to try more effectively to pursue such goodness by directly rejecting the body. For we come to pursue and live out spiritual goodness through our bodies–through our senses and through our bodily actions. Indeed, this is possible in the first place because of the intimate relationship between body and soul that I have described above. In other words, it is possible because the body shares in spiritual goodness. For these reasons, to reject the body as lacking in value is to reject spiritual goodness.

In fact, on the Christian view, suffering can be an occasion for living out the spiritual value of human life. For we must remember that spiritual goods cannot be effectively pursued by attempting to grasp them. Rather, it is necessary to surrender to them. We do not so much make truth and goodness our own as allow them to possess and form us.[20] This is above all true when we are thinking of how we attain communion with Truth and Being in Person, namely, God. Our status as creatures precludes our ever grasping such communion. We can only receive it as a gift and then live in accordance with it. Indeed, to attempt to grasp it would be effectively to reject it, since it would be effectively an attempt at self-deification, that is, a denial of our need to receive it as a gift.

It was such an attempt on the part of our first parents that led to the estrangement of the human race from God, and to the dis-integration of our humanity (and of all creation) when we thus lost communion with the one who is our integrating principle, and to death itself, the ultimate dis-integration.[21] And while God has restored communion with the human race, he has done so in such a way that we now accept it and allow it to penetrate our being, including our bodies, and therefore definitively to relieve the burdens of our condition, only by surrendering ourselves to God precisely through death.[22] Furthermore, if death can and must be such an act of self-surrender, so also must all the prefigurations of death we experience in illness and injury and pain. This is not to say that we may never try to relieve our own or others' suffering. The point concerns, rather, how we may do so. Actively to pursue death to escape the burdens of illness and injury and pain is the antithesis of suffering and dying in a spirit of self-surrender; as such, it actually subverts the communion with spiritual goods that is the meaning of our life.

Secondly, however, we must not value bodily integrity in such a way that we guard it at the expense of spiritual goods. While it is, as I have explained, always futile to try to pursue spiritual goods by means that directly attack and therefore reject the value of the body, it is sometimes helpful or necessary in pursuit of spiritual goods to forego actions that would help to maintain our bodily integrity, and therefore indirectly to give up such integrity and even our lives.[23] Most clearly, love of God or neighbor can allow or compel us to give up our lives. But attempts to postpone as long as technology will allow the death toward which one is irreversibly moving, even in ways that are not directly incompatible with justice or charity, can still reflect an attitude of grasping of life, this time of bare material life, rather than a willingness to allow this life to attain its meaning by surrendering it to God.

Perhaps most relevant for the purposes of this paper, it must also be recognized that, while the pain and other burdens that accompany illness and injury can be the situations in which we learn to accept, live out, and return God's self-communication and grow in knowledge and love of him and thus prepare for a genuinely "good death," this can at some point require an especially difficult act of will, one greater than that of which many people will be capable. In short, persevering can at some point require "heroic virtue." While we must trust that God will give each person enough virtue to avoid doing anything that is immoral–to persevere in treatment that does not itself significantly increase spiritual burdens, even when the burdens of his condition seem extreme, rather than seeking to end those burdens by withdrawing from treatment–we must at the same time not foreclose the possibility that some people will not have the ability to allow the spiritual benefits of remaining alive to outweigh the sometimes-significant burdens of life-sustaining treatment itself, since accepting death (as opposed to choosing it) is clearly not intrinsically immoral.[24] In such cases–when the burden of a treatment is not proportionate to the benefit that someone can gain from life–the treatment can be ended (or one may refuse to initiate it on the basis of its predicted effects), even when this would entail accepting death.

Furthermore, when a patient's underlying condition is bad and cannot be relieved by life-sustaining treatment, the treatment's benefits are lessened and its burdens will more quickly become disproportionate to those benefits.[25] As I have indicated, even though suffering does not preclude and in fact can and sometimes must be an occasion for pursuit of spiritual goods through self-surrender, suffering can also make pursuit of those goods more difficult and can therefore make life less beneficial than life without suffering would be. The burdens imposed by treatment itself will therefore become more than a patient can spiritually bear sooner if the treatment does not relieve the burdens imposed by the patient's condition.

To summarize the principles whose derivation I have outlined in this section: Since life is never without value, a treatment is never without benefit when it sustains life; and one cannot in any case refuse life-sustaining treatment in order to end the burdens of one's condition by means of death. This would be to ignore and even act contrary to the spiritual meaning of life. On the other hand, one need not and indeed should not seek to preserve life at all costs. A treatment that imposes spiritual burdens greater than the spiritual benefits of remaining alive may be ended, even when this would entail death, and the judgment of when this is the case can take into account the fact that the benefits of remaining alive can be lessened by the effects of one's condition.

APPLICATIONS: JUST MOTIVES AND PROPORTIONATE ACTIONS

What can be concluded about concrete cases, for example, those of dialysis patients? First, a patient's motives for wanting to end dialysis are important in an ethical assessment of his decision. As I have indicated, ESRD is often consequent to diabetes, which also has other severe effects that result in suffering. It is not difficult to see how a diabetic ESRD patient could be tempted to end dialysis and die as a way to end the suffering imposed by other effects of diabetes. And there is reason to suspect that this is in fact at least part of the motivation for some patients to end dialysis, just as in general some patients are tempted to end their lives in order to end suffering.

The Milwaukee-area case illustrates the problem of possibly-mixed motives.[26] The patient's daughter wrote, "My father...chose to continue dialysis for six years in spite of the suffering it caused him. He chose to live confined to a wheelchair for three years after his legs were amputated–a very painful process with a long recovery period." Suffering caused specifically by dialysis could certainly be a reason to end dialysis. The condition in which dialysis keeps someone alive could be relevant in a judgment of how much suffering caused by dialysis needs to be accepted, as I have explained. It is possible, however, based on his daughter's explanation, that the Milwaukee-area patient also saw as a reason to end dialysis the cessation of the suffering imposed by his condition that would accompany the death that would follow an end to dialysis; note the daughter's statement that her father had "chose[n] to live," perhaps as if the opposite choice–"to die," as a means to ending suffering–would be equally warranted.

It seems that the ethical guidance that patients receive sometimes contributes to this problem. Such guidance is often at best ambiguous. The Milwaukee man's pastor's advice as reported by the man's daughter, quoted above ("discontinuation of dialysis is not suicide") does not take into account the issue of motivation. Discontinuation of dialysis in order to die and thereby to relieve suffering is suicide. The man's daughter also reported that his physician had told him that "no one can be forced to take dialysis." This is true enough: no competent adult can legally or ethically be "forced" to receive any treatment. But again, it is not clear that the man received fully accurate guidance concerning what constitute ethically appropriate reasons for ending dialysis. Articles for renal professionals and publications for patients will mention "burdens" and "benefits" of treatments[27] and will recommend assessment for stressors in the patient's life and for depression before a patient makes a final decision,[28] but at the same time will focus primarily on question-begging statements about "rights"[29] and will suggest that failure to maintain "quality of life" suffices to justify ending treatment,[30] which could lead a patient to believe that he may rightly judge his life to be without value and choose to end it; indeed one textbook refers (not disapprovingly) to the decision to end dialysis as a decision that "it is better to be dead."[31]

The Milwaukee-area patient's situation was also complicated by the terminal illness and death of his wife. It seems that this might have entered into his decision in a problematic way. The man said, "I just know I want to be with her in life and in death. That's the kind of companion she was." This suggests that he was, at least in part, choosing his own death as a means to end his separation from her after her death. He was also quoted by one of his daughters as having told her and his other children, "I really have been doing dialysis and staying alive so that I could be a support to your mother...and it doesn't make any sense to continue without her." This could mean that he saw life as simply unworthy of being lived once he was no longer needed by another.[32]

It is, however, possible that someone could have a motive for ending dialysis that is at least formally good. Someone could, that is, judge that, taking into account his condition, dialysis is more of a burden than a benefit. The question then arises, when might this be true? Under what kinds of circumstances might continuing dialysis be contrary to the spiritual meaning and purpose of human life, as I have explained it? To answer, it is necessary to consider both what kinds of burdens of dialysis could become disproportionate, and what kinds of underlying conditions could render dialysis less beneficial.

Hemodialysis always imposes the burden mentioned above: it requires a significant portion of the patient's time, and patients must observe a strict diet. Suppose that a patient is generally in good condition and feels no significant burdens from dialysis apart from these. Would ending dialysis be an ethical option in such a case? It seems to me that it would not. As long as a patient does not need to invest the vast majority of his time in pursuing a course of treatment, it would seem that, objectively, the time he must invest is not dispropor-tionate to the benefit that he receives: life and a still-reasonable amount of time really to live it. Dietary restrictions can be very unpleasant, but it is difficult to see how they could objectively be the sort of burden that outweighs preserving one's life. (Compare someone who must observe a special diet as the sole treatment for a condition and means of preserving his life, for example, some diabetics.[33]) None of this is to say that no patients will experience these burdens as onerous. But I think it reasonable to expect that virtually anyone will be able to avoid being overwhelmed by them, with suitable support and counseling, both spiritual and psychological (the importance of which should not be minimized).

As has also been mentioned, however, dialysis can itself give rise to painful complications. When it does, it will impose a burden of a different kind, and perhaps one that would justify ending dialysis. Objectively, pain can be very difficult spiritually. This will be all the more the case when one has to prepare to face it on a regular basis, and for the rest of one's life (unlike in, for example, a chemotherapy regimen, which is usually of limited duration when successful). Subjectively, this is the sort of burden that it can sometimes require "heroic virtue" to face. Doing so will therefore be beyond the capacity of some patients.

A patient may wish to end dialysis in order to avoid being a burden to others, in this case to society as a whole, which will pay the costs of his treatment. Such a patient can have a good reason to end an expensive procedure. The primary concern would be to ensure that the patient's underlying motivation is really charity for others (perhaps especially for those who could use those resources to sustain their own lives) rather than a kind of pride that could make one unreasonably reluctant to accept others' acts of charity. In a certain sense, dependence on others can rightly be seen as a spiritual burden upon oneself–it prevents one from exercising a certain kind of charity toward those upon whom one is dependent. But it must not be seen as a burden upon oneself that is unmitigated or mitigated only extrinsically (that is, because it saves one's life). Dependence is certainly not intrinsically undignified.[34] Indeed, other's acts of charity are in a real sense the condition for one's own exercise of charity (above all, God's love precedes ours, and God's love comes to us through other human beings as well as directly). As long as this is recognized and one genuinely wishes to make one's own act of charity toward those in need of medical resources, one can in principle forego such expensive treatments as dialysis.

We must now consider what kinds of underlying conditions could render dialysis less beneficial, and whether in those cases it could be ended even if complications imposed no significant additional burden beyond time and dietary restrictions. Consider first a patient who is in severe pain. For such a patient, dialysis will be less beneficial: It will keep him alive but not relieve his pain. This could, I think, make even the burdens of uncomplicated dialysis disproportionate. While those burdens should not ordinarily be overwhelming in themselves, it is more easily conceivable that they could become so when added to the struggle that life with severe pain can become.[35]

A patient who is really dying would certainly be justified in ending dialysis.[36] There is a difference in kind between prolonging life and prolonging the dying process. While each of us will eventually die, and while in certain imperceptible or minor ways we may already be undergoing the "disintegration" that will culminate in death, it is sensible to resist death before the beginning of the dying process in a way that it is usually not once that process has really begun.[37] In the former case, one preserves the conditions for coming to participate in spiritual goods; in the latter case, one would be refusing to surrender for the sake of those same goods. Therefore, when the dying process has begun, the burdens of such treatments as dialysis are usually disproportionate to their benefits.

It could also be mentioned, especially since this was a factor in the Milwaukee-area case, that some obligations, especially to family, could warrant preserving life or prolonging the dying process in ways that would be unnecessary or inappropriate absent such obligations. Thus, one's spouse's need for care could make it reasonable or perhaps even obligatory to accept what otherwise would be a disproportionately-burdensome treatment. Similarly, one should settle one's affairs and make peace with or express one's love for one's family before dying, and it would be right to prolong dying until one has had a reasonable chance to do so. Once one has fulfilled justice or charity in these matters, one could end the treatment that has kept one alive to do so. It must only be borne in mind that one can then end treatment only because the treatment would in the first place have been disproportionate had the patient had no special obligations. Thus, one cannot settle the issue of whether treatment is disproportionate by pointing to the lack of such obligations–one cannot, for example, end life-sustaining treatment simply because one's spouse has died.

It should be obvious that this analysis does not suffice to settle every practical question, to tell us in each case, in detail, what treatments would be disproportionately burdensome. Burdens such as pain will be experienced differently by different patients, and it is in part, even mostly, how they are experienced that will be ethically relevant.[38] There will be some grey area about the beginning of the dying process and therefore between "prolonging life" and "prolonging dying." Therefore, while rules are necessary, prudence will also be necessary.[39] More or less detailed protocols for dealing with patients in general or dialysis patients in particular can be helpful in ensuring that patients' needs are met and even in ensuring that the guidance they receive is ethical, but they can only be seen as a help, not a substitute, for prudent health-care workers and indeed for prudent patients. And to develop prudence, one must develop an awareness and a right appreciation of the realities upon which one's actions bear,[40] including, importantly in matters of life and death (and in many other matters too), the spiritual realities of truth, goodness, and Truth and Goodness itself.

This is not only to say that one should be aware of the significance of how one happens to be able to cope with life, suffering, and death for one's participation in these realities. It is also to say that one should be open to growth in one's ability to appreciate them, growth that will transform one's attitude toward life, suffering, and death, making one more appreciative of the opportunities that life gives us to find fulfillment in these realities, of their power over suffering, and, at the same time, of their power over death. For someone who has matured spiritually in this way, life-sustaining treatments will more easily be seen as beneficial despite their burdens and despite the suffering they may not relieve–and will more easily be seen as burdens to be cast off when dying has really begun. Growth of this sort and the transformation of prudential judgment that it brings are important not because judgments and actions that reflect lack of full spiritual maturity are necessarily blameworthy, but because they are, in the long run, less conducive to human fulfillment and happiness; they are a holding-back of part of the self from participation in spiritual goods and, concretely, in the life of God that we receive when we have been crucified with him (Gal. 2:19–20).

Spiritual growth is also important for a more basic reason: To the extent that pain is experienced as an unmitigated burden, to that extent will one be tempted to end it even by death–tempted, that is, to the kinds of bad motives for ending treatment that I have discussed. This will be all the more a problem when one also has good reasons to end treatment, that is, when an action that could be described abstractly as "ending treatment" could be justified. For this will make the action seem more acceptable and will therefore make it more likely to be chosen, and therefore one's bad motives as well as one's good ones will more likely be chosen. In short, apart from spiritual growth, situations in which one is suffering and will die without treatment will more likely be near occasions of sin.

CONCLUSIONS

I have argued that patients may not end dialysis in order to bring about death and with it relief from the burdens of illness, but they may sometimes end dialysis because it imposes burdens disproportionate to the benefits it provides, even to the benefit of sustaining life. Both of these norms follow from an understanding of the meaning and value of human life: our bodies participate in the spiritual life of our souls and the spiritual goods to which our souls are open, so that (bodily) life may be treated neither as a mere means to the end of pleasure or the absence of pain, to be disposed of when these are not possible, nor as absolutely good, such that nothing could warrant giving up the measures that sustain it. One's judgments about when life-sustaining treatments impose burdens disproportionate to their benefits must also be informed by an appreciation of the spiritual meaning and purpose of life if they are to be prudent. Prudence requires taking into account what might be called the subjective factor of how different patients will experience different burdensome conditions. However, people should strive for a deeper appreciation of spiritual goods in order to be prepared for such situations.

All of this implies that ethical guidance dispensed only at a time of medical crisis is unlikely to be of much help to patients. Growth in prudence is a lifelong process. It is a matter of learning not abstract norms but the meaning of life–indeed, of learning from God who we are as we develop in our relationship with him. Ethical norms will seem arbitrary and themselves burdensome apart from such a relationship.[41] In general, no solutions to the myriad of problems that have arisen in our age of scientific medicine will be forthcoming unless people are formed as members of a "culture of life" that places technology at the service of the human person by placing the material at the service of the spiritual,[42] allowing the material to be formed by the spiritual and thus receive value, treating the material–our bodies and the ways we have learned to help them heal–as neither irredeemable nor as an end in itself. This will in turn not be possible until we appreciate that we have been made as spiritual beings in order that we might be given a share in the life of God, since it is our openness to that share as our end that integrates and gives meaning to all that we are and do. In other words, we cannot live in the integrity and justice conferred upon us by God's love until that love has been effectively revealed to us.[43] In short, preparing ourselves as a culture and as individuals to make appropriate use of the scientific and technological abilities God has given us, to share in God's mastery over creation (Gen. 1:28), requires being formed by the Gospel of Life, with which "the Gospel of God's love for man," the love he revealed on the Cross, is "a single and indivisible Gospel."[44]

NOTES

1. Anne Marie Mills and Eli A. Friedman, "Center and Home Chronic Hemodialysis: Outcome and Complications" in *Diseases of the Kidney,* 6th ed., ed. Robert W. Schrier and Carl W. Gottschalk, vol. 3 (Boston: Little, Brown, 1997), p. 2807.

2. Eli A. Friedman and Anne Marie Mills, "Dialytic Management of Diabetic Uremic Patients" in *Replacement of Renal Function by Dialysis,* 4th ed., ed. C. Jacobs, C. M. Kjellstrand, K. M. Koch, and J. F. Winchester (Dordrecht: Kluwer, 1996), p. 935.

3. Mills and Friedman, "Center and Home Chronic Hemodialysis," p. 2809.

4. Mills and Friedman, "Center and Home Chronic Hemodialysis," p. 2807.

5. Mills and Friedman, "Center and Home Chronic Hemodialysis," p. 2807.

6. Mills and Friedman, "Center and Home Chronic Hemodialysis," p. 2808.

7. Mills and Friedman, "Center and Home Chronic Hemodialysis," p. 2810.

8. Salim K. Mujais, Todd Ing, and Carl Kjellstrand, "Acute Complications of Hemodialysis and their Prevention and Treatment" in *Replacement*, p. 689; Mills and Friedman, "Center and Home Chronic Hemodialysis," p. 2831. Chronic complications also often arise; see *Replacement* and *Diseases, passim,* and esp. Peter G. Wilson, "Part A: Psychiatric Aspects of the Dialysis Patient" in *Replacement*, pp. 1455–65, and J. Ahlmén, "Part B: Quality of Life of the Dialysis Patient" in *Replacement*, pp. 1466–79.

9. For some details, see Joel D. Kopple, "Dietary Considerations in Patients with Advanced Chronic Renal Failure, Acute Renal Failure, and Transplantation" in *Diseases*, pp. 2913–62.

10. See, *e.g.*, Carl M. Kjellstrand, Ronald Cranford, and Michael Kaye, "Stopping Dialysis: Practice and Cultural, Religious, and Legal Aspects," in *Replacement*, pp. 1480–82, 1498; Nancy Boucot Cummings, "Ethical and Legal Considerations in End Stage Renal Disease," in *Diseases*, pp. 2851–53, 2869–70.

11. E.g., Kjellstrand *et al.*, pp. 1482–84; in more detail, Ramiro Valdez and Alex Rosenblum, "Voluntary Termination of Dialysis: When Your Patient Says, 'Enough Is Enough!'" in *Dialysis and Transplantation* 23 (1994), 567–70.

12. Kjellstrand *et al.*, p. 1482.

13. See "Waukesha couple's decision to die together nears quiet end, as planned," *Milwaukee Journal Sentinel*, 8 August 1998 [newspaper on-line]; available from http://www.jsonline. com/archive/aug98/news/wauk/980808 waukeshacouplesdecisi.stm; Internet; accessed 21 March 2000; "Waukesha man fulfills his wish to join his wife in death," *Milwaukee Journal Sentinel*, 14 August 1998 [newspaper on-line]; available from http://www.jsonline. com/archive/aug98/news/wauk/980814waukeshamanfulfillshi.stm; Internet; accessed 21 March 2000; "Suicide gets the spotlight," *Milwaukee Journal Sentinel*, 18 August 1998 [newspaper on-line], available from http://www.jsonline.com/archive/aug98/news/editorials/0818letters.stm; Internet; accessed 21 March 2000; "Suicide wasn't courageous," *Milwaukee Journal Sentinel*, 20 August 1998 [newspaper on-line]; available from http://www.jsonline.com/archive/aug98/news/editorials/0820letters.stm; Internet; accessed 21 March 2000; "Loving husband chose dialysis so he could

be with his wife" and "Stories show endurance of their strong love," *Milwaukee Journal Sentinel,* 25 August 1998 [newspaper on-line]; available from http://www.jsonline.com/archive/aug98/news/editorials/0825letters.stm; Internet; accessed 21 March 2000.

14. For fuller treatments of what follows, see Kevin E. Miller, "The Incompatibility of Contraception with Respect for Life" in *Life and Learning VII,* ed. Joseph W. Koterski (Washington, D.C.: University Faculty for Life, 1998), pp. 80–126, and for the role of faith specifically in anthropology and ethics, idem, "The Role of Mercy in a Culture of Life: John Paul II on Capital Punishment" in *Life and Learning VIII,* ed. Joseph W. Koterski (Washington, D.C.: University Faculty for Life, 1999), pp. 405–42.

15. See St. Thomas Aquinas, *Summa Theologiae,* I, q. 76, aa. 1, 3, 4, 5; *Catechism of the Catholic Church,* no. 365.

16. One can, in fact, see indications of the body's "form" (the rational soul) in its form or appearance. For an insightful discussion, see Leon R. Kass, *Toward a More Natural Science: Biology and Human Affairs* (New York: Free Press, 1985), pp. 276–98.

17. For the hierarchy of goods and its ethical relevance, see Karol Wojtyła, "On the Metaphysical and Phenomenological Basis of the Moral Norm," in *Person and Community: Selected Essays,* trans. Theresa Sandok, Catholic Thought from Lublin, vol. 4 (New York: Peter Lang, 1993), pp. 78–79. This view that I have adopted and defended elsewhere (see Miller, "The Incompatibility of Contraception with Respect for Life"), that the value of the body and bodily life and the ethical implications of this value follow from an account of the body-soul relationship, stands in contrast with the view of Germain Grisez that life is one of a number of "basic human goods" that are self-evident, irreducible, and incommensurable; see, e.g., Grisez, *Christian Moral Principles,* vol. 1 of *The Way of the Lord Jesus* (Quincy: Franciscan Press, 1983), pp. 115–228.

18. On the effects of sickness on the body and the body-soul relationship, see Kass, *Toward a More Natural Science,* p. 220.

19. Thus, while I deny that life is irreducibly or incommensurably good, I affirm on the basis of the body-soul relationship–an intrinsic relationship, not an extrinsic one as in dualism–that life is intrinsically good. Hence my view also stands in contrast to that implicit in the discussion of end-of-life issues in Benedict M. Ashley and Kevin D. O'Rourke, *Health Care Ethics: A Theological Analysis,* 4th ed. (Washington, D.C.: Georgetown Univ. Press, 1997), pp. 421–28; cf. especially their criticism (p. 423) of the view "that patients can so deteriorate as to be beyond the possibility of benefit," even

when they can be kept alive, and their contention (p. 426) that "when consciousness and freedom have been lost ... the artificial prolongation of life ... ceases to be of any real benefit." In the end, then, my practical conclusions concerning end-of-life treatment will be consistent with Grisez's (see, e.g., *Difficult Moral Questions,* vol. 3 of *The Way of the Lord Jesus* [Quincy: Franciscan Press, 1997], pp. 214–25), but for different reasons. The significance of these distinctions will become clear as the argument develops.

20. This is true notwithstanding the reality of self-determination (for discussion of which, see Wojtyła, "The Personal Structure of Self-Determination" in *Person and Community,* esp. p. 191). In fact, it is because our willing of a good is really an opening of self up to the good–an allowing of self to be possessed by the good—that it makes us good.

21. For this account of original sin and its consequences, see the *Catechism of the Catholic Church,* nos. 374–79, 397–400. It is rooted in the theological anthropology retrieved in this century by Henri de Lubac; see esp. *The Mystery of the Supernatural,* trans. Rosemary Sheed (New York: Crossroad, 1998), and my discussion of its ethical implications in Miller, "The Role of Mercy in a Culture of Life."

22. In brief, Christ turned the suffering and death that are the consequences of humanity's estrangement from God into an act of love for the Father, in which we can participate (in the Holy Spirit). See, *e.g.*, John Paul II, *Salvifici Doloris* (1984), nos. 14–18.

23. Cf. Pius XII's statement in his 24 Nov. 1957 Address to an International Congress of Anesthesiologists (in *Conserving Human Life,* ed. Russell E. Smith [Braintree: Pope John XXIII Medical-Moral Research Center, 1989], p. 315): "But normally one is held to use only ordinary means [of treatment]. ... A more strict obligation would be too burdensome for most men and would render the attainment of the higher, more important good too difficult. Life, health, all temporal activities are in fact subordinated to spiritual ends." See also the references to the distinction between "proportionate" and "disproportionate" means of treatment in the Congregation for the Doctrine of the Faith's *Declaration on Euthanasia* (1980), chap. IV. My contention is that Pius XII really does mean that spiritual goods are "higher" than material ones, which presupposes that neither are incommensurable, and that the CDF really does mean that one can determine whether the benefits of a treatment are "proportionate" to its burdens, which again presupposes that the goods at issue, including the good of human life, are not incommensurable–and that this presupposition is philosophically cogent and ethically significant, for the reasons I am indicating in the text. This is in contrast with Grisez's position, as I have noted, that the goods at issue in decisions about end-of-life treatments

are incommensurable. Grisez therefore claims that in general, "[w]hen the classical moralists required a 'proportionate reason' for freely accepting bad side effects [as when one accepts death as a side effect of rejecting burdensome treatment], they implied that the good sought and the evil accepted could be rendered commensurate. ... But the commensuration they required can be explained without admitting the commensuration of premoral goods and bads the proportionalist requires. For one can say that the reason for not accepting bad side effects is 'proportionate' if their acceptance does not violate any of the modes of responsibility [which govern pursuit of goods]. For example, by this criterion one who risked the death of healthy children in medical experiments would lack a proportionate reason, for to take such a risk would be unfair" (*Christian Moral Principles,* p. 300). More specifically, he holds that "when it is not wrong in itself either to accept some form of health care or forgo it, the benefits and burdens must be evaluated. Unless these are measured by moral standards [such as "fairness,"] however, there is no rational way to commensurate them, since they are diverse instances of values. Therefore, relevant moral standards must be employed" (*Living a Christian Life,* vol. 2 of *The Way of the Lord Jesus* [Quincy: Franciscan Press, 1993], p. 527). Accordingly, Pius XII's "teaching does not imply that there is a hierarchy of value among the basic goods considered in themselves, but that priorities among them are established by unfettered practical reason and reflected by the commitments which shape an upright person's life" (*Living a Christian Life,* p. 529, n. 119). It seems to me that these claims are gratuitous both exegetically, and, for the reasons I indicate in my argument, philosophically.

24. On the genuine spiritual difficulties that suffering can impose, see John Paul II, *Salvifici Doloris,* no. 26.

25. This is consistent with the CDF's teaching that judgments concerning means of treatment must be made "taking into account the state of the sick person and his or her physical and moral resources" (*Declaration on Euthanasia,* chap. IV).

26. For the record, my use of this case to illustrate the issues requiring analysis does not mean that I am questioning the motives of the man or his family. I am in no position to do this, since I cannot know these motives. Nor do I mean to question whether ending dialysis was objectively justified; I lack access to sufficient information to make this judgment. I mean only to analyze the ethical significance of what the newspaper accounts suggest as possible motives and as relevant factors–without passing judgment as to whether these motives were really operative or whether these factors would be dispositive.

27. *Cf.* Valdez and Rosenblum, "Voluntary Termination," p. 566.

28. Valdez and Rosenblum, "Voluntary Termination," pp. 567–68.

29. Valdez and Rosenblum, "Voluntary Termination," p. 567; National Kidney Foundation, *When Stopping Dialysis Treatment Is Your Choice* (New York: National Kidney Foundation, 1996), p. 1.

30. National Kidney Foundation, *When Stopping Dialysis Treatment Is Your Choice,* pp. 1, 3.

31. Kjellstrand *et al.,* p. 1480.

32. "Waukesha couple's decision."

33. On the centrality of dietetic measures in medicine, see Kass, *Toward a More Natural Science,* 232–33.

34. Here I disagree with Ashley and O'Rourke, *Health Care Ethics,* p. 427.

35. *A fortiori* this will be true when a patient is unconscious; hence in such cases a given burden will more likely be disproportionate. But contrary to Ashley and O'Rourke (*Health Care Ethics,* p. 426), to be disproportionate, the burden will still have to be significant; hence I agree with Grisez (*Difficult Moral Questions,* pp. 218–25) that nutrition and hydration in particular should be continued in such cases.

36. On the meaning of "dying" or "terminal," see Grisez, *Difficult Moral Questions,* p. 221, in contrast to Ashley and O'Rourke, *Health Care Ethics,* p. 423. Grisez's position is consistent with that of the Congregation for the Doctrine of the Faith, *Declaration on Euthanasia,* chap. IV ("When inevitable death is imminent in spite of the means used ...").

37. On this in relation to the purpose of medicine, see Kass, *Toward a More Natural Science,* pp. 203–9.

38. Classical criteria for distinguishing extraordinary means of treatment acknowledge this; see Daniel A. Cronin, "The Moral Law in Regard to the Ordinary and Extraordinary Means of Conserving Human Life" in *Conserving Human Life,* pp. 103–04.

39. On the need for prudence in medical practice, see Kass, *Toward a More Natural Science,* pp. 209–10. On the meaning of prudence in relation to moral virtue, see Josef Pieper, "Prudence," trans. Richard and Clara Winston, in *The Four Cardinal Virtues* (Notre Dame: Univ. of Notre Dame Press, 1966), pp. 3–9, 32–36.

40. On this as of the essence of prudence, see Pieper, "Prudence," pp.10–17.

41. *Cf.* John Paul II, *Evangelium Vitae* (1995), nos. 48–49.

42. *Cf.* John Paul II, *Redemptor Hominis* (1979), no. 16.

43. Cf. John Paul II, *Redemptor Hominis,* no. 10.

44. John Paul II, *Evangelium Vitae,* no. 2.

Why Persons Have Dignity

John F. Crosby

IN ALL OF OUR PRO-LIFE WORK we constantly appeal to the dignity of persons, arguing that this dignity is violated by abortion, euthanasia, and other crimes against life. If persons had no dignity, then these forms of killing would be morally unobjectionable. But the dignity to which we appeal is usually taken for granted by us. In this paper I propose to stop taking it for granted and to reflect on it and try to give an account of it.

1. SOME PRELIMINARIES

It may be useful for the pro-life cause to discuss the beginning and the ending of personal dignity in a human being. We all know how much mischief is caused by those who argue that a human being in the womb is not a person and so lacks the dignity of being a person. But I will not address the questions of beginning and ending.[1] My question today is rather this one: Granted that a given human person exists, why do we recognize dignity in the person? By trying to answer this question we gain something of great importance for our pro-life commitment. This will become especially clear when we encounter Peter Singer along the path of our argument.

When pro-lifers address the question of personal dignity, we are usually quick to invoke God as the source of it. But at the same time we are keen on finding moral foundations around which a broad consensus can form even in a pluralistic society. And so I propose to see how far I can get without invoking God. After all, believers say that the dignity of persons is intrinsic to persons and is not just extrinsically superimposed on them by God. But if we can recognize human beings as persons without direct recourse to God, and if dignity inheres intrinsically in persons, then we should be able to recognize their dignity as persons without recourse to God. Of course, if we think personal dignity through to the end and trace it back to its ultimate ground, we do arrive at God. Václav Havel, president of the Czech Republic, recently said: "I always come to the conclusion that human rights, human freedoms, and human dignity have their deepest roots somewhere outside the perceptible world. These values are as powerful as they are because...they make sense only in the perspective of the infinite and the eternal."[2]   A remarkable statement coming from one who is not a Christian believer! But before we can trace personal dignity to the infinite and the eternal, we must first see what this dignity is in its own right and how it grows out of the person. To this task I limit myself in the present paper.

Another important preliminary remark concerns the way in which I distinguish between personal dignity and the basic rights of the person. Havel uses these concepts interchangeably. Although such usage is common, I propose to distinguish them in two ways. First, the rights of a person have a social dimension that is foreign to dignity. Only *another* person can respect or violate my rights. If I commit suicide, one cannot explain the wrong I undeniably do in terms of me violating my own right to life; it takes a person other than myself to be capable of violating my rights. Just as I cannot steal from my own property or commit adultery with my own wife, so I cannot violate my own right to life. But my dignity as a person is there for me no less than for others; I can act against my own dignity just as much as others can act against it.   One might think of self-hatred, or of despair over myself, as examples of offending against my own dignity as person.

Secondly, my basic human rights, as they are called nowadays, are not as strictly inalienable as my personal dignity. I mean that if I ask another to take my life, then, although I act wrongly, I remove my right as a moral obstacle for the other, and the wrong he does has to be explained in terms other than the violation of my right to life. If I tell someone to help himself to my property, I thereby prevent him from being a thief and from violating my property rights–even if I act irresponsibly in offering him my property. In the same way, if I ask someone to take my life, I thereby prevent him from being a mur-derer–even though I act irresponsibly. Thus I can suspend or block my rights as a morally relevant factor in a given situation. But I cannot remove my dignity from a moral situation in this way. A prostitute may try ever so hard to make herself mere flesh for sale, but despite herself she forever retains her personal dignity, which is inevitably violated by all her customers. Since, then, my personal dignity is not just there for others but also for me in relation to myself, and since it is absolutely incapable of being suspended or in any way alienated by me, it shows itself to be something different from and deeper than the basic human rights of the person. My concern in this paper is with this dignity rather than with rights.

And one last preliminary. One commonly speaks of depriving a person of dignity by some unworthy or humiliating treatment of that person. But, in fact, unworthy treatment of another is absolutely powerless to abrogate the other's dignity. Dignity is, as I said, intrinsic to being a person, and you would have to first abrogate the other as person before abrogating his or her dignity. Besides, unworthy treatment *presupposes* dignity; a given treatment of another is qualified as unworthy just because it fails to give the other what is due to him or her as a person having dignity. If dignity in my sense were stripped away from a person, then so would be the reason for calling the treatment of that person unworthy. So by dignity I do not mean that treatment of a person which is appropriate to him or her as person, but rather that in a person by virtue of which some treatment is appropriate and other treatment is inappropriate.

2. TWO SOURCES OF THE DIGNITY OF PERSONS

With our preliminaries completed, let us turn to the traditional account of human dignity given by philosophers. The Greeks saw the unique dignity of man in his reason; man is a rational animal and in this he is superior to all subhuman animals. The Greek philosophers saw reason as the divine element in man; for Aristotle, man never lives in a more godlike way than when he exercises his reason in the way of philosophical understanding. Of course, Plato and Aristotle saw reason at work in nature and in the cosmos, but here creatures only passively undergo reason, being ordered according to a rational plan; man by contrast has an essentially more intimate relation to reason in that he understands the meaning of things with his own reason. Reason is internalized in man as it is in no subhuman being, so that he is not just governed by reason but governs himself with his own reason. (One sees that reason is here understood in such a way as to comprise what we call freedom, even though the Greeks did only partial justice to freedom.) The point for us is that man through his more intimate relation to reason has a greater share in the dignity of reason; since reason enters into his essential definition–man is a rational animal–he surpasses all sub-rational beings in dignity. Here we have a timelessly valid element of the philosophical heritage of the West.

The rationality of man is so rich and deep an idea that one might wonder whether anything more is needed for a full account of the dignity of persons. In explaining the ethics of the respect we owe to each other, in explaining the inviolability that others should recognize in us, do we need to do more than affirm the dignity flowing from the rationality of each human being? I think that we need to do vastly more, and I will now try to explain what this more is.

Notice that rationality is something common to all human beings. It belongs to human nature, the nature in which we all share. Reason is not my exclusive possession, for you too have it. This commonness of reason shows itself in the universal validity of rational activity; whatever I rightly understand as rationally necessary must also be understood by you as rationally necessary. The work of reason is supposed to be impersonal, the same for all, valid for all possible beings endowed with reason. You cannot say that some essential relation is rationally necessary for you but not for me, as if rationality varied from one rational being to the next, each having his own reason. This commonness goes so far that the idea has crept into Western philosophy more than once that human beings are plural only through their bodies, as if the rational spirit in them were literally one, so that each human being does not have his or her own reason in the same way that each has his or her own body. Against this view we have, of course, to say that each human being has his or her own intellect and rational powers, no less than each has his or her own body. And yet, true it is that the rational activities of each converge with those of all other human beings in the sense explained. Individual though reason be in each human being, it is also in some strong sense common to all; and the dignity of rationality is a dignity that we all share in.

But you will ask, why does this commonness of dignity represent a problem for a philosophy of human dignity? Well, consider this: in a human being there is not only that human nature which he has in common with all other human beings, but also something that he has as his own–his own and not another's–incommunicably his own. Obviously, a human being would not amount to an individual being if he were not, over and above all that he has in common with others, also incommunicably his own. And so we find that each of us is a certain composition of what we have in common with others and what we precisely do not have in common with others. Now, the dignity of human beings, as we have so far discussed it, is tied to our common human nature, which includes our rational nature. It is not because I am *this incommunicable* human being that I have dignity, but because I am *a human being* endowed with reason. What gives me dignity is not incommunicably my own but is found in every other human being. Some may see no problem for the philosophy of human dignity and may even point out an advantage that seems to be gained by deriving dignity from our common human nature. They will say that the much-celebrated equality of human beings as to dignity is secured by this route, for if that which endows me with dignity also endows you with it, then we are equal in dignity, a conclusion that seems to be of the first importance for the organization of the political community.

And yet there is a problem here if the account of dignity so far proposed is meant as a complete account. Notice that the incommunicable element in man belongs to man *as person*. One of the best known utterances of the Roman jurists about the person connects being a person with being incommunicable: *persona est sui iuris et alteri incommunicabilis*. It is precisely as person that I am myself and no other. St. Thomas Aquinas clearly teaches that personhood is not a common nature like human nature that can be shared in by many; personhood is rather a matter of being an incommunicable individual within some common nature (see his *Summa theologiae*, I.30.4). This means that the account we have so far given of human dignity does not ground dignity in man as a person; it is not because I am this incommunicable person that I have dignity, but because I share in the rational nature common to me and many others. This raises the question whether we have yet really taken the full measure of dignity. Is it really true that personhood has nothing to contribute to dignity, that our dignity does not also belong to us in virtue of our being persons?

These doubts grow on us if we consider the difficulty that we have in objecting to certain anti-life measures if we use only the account of dignity so far presented. Let us look at that notorious passage in Peter Singer's *Practical Ethics* that has received so much attention in the press. In defense of a certain case of infanticide he writes as follows:

[S]uppose that a newborn baby is diagnosed as a haemophiliac. The parents, daunted by the prospect of bringing up a child with this condition, are not anxious for him to live. Could euthanasia be defended here? Our first reaction may well be a firm 'no,' for the infant can be expected to have a life that is worth living, even if not quite as good as that of a normal baby.... His life can be expected to contain a positive balance of happiness over misery. To kill him...would be wrong.

Singer proceeds to say that there is a somewhat different utilitarian perspective in which the killing of this infant turns out, after all, to be the right thing to do.

Suppose a woman planning to have two children has one normal child, and then gives birth to a hemophiliac child. The burden of caring for that child may make it impossible for her to cope with a third child; but if the defective child were to die, she would have another.... When the death of a defective infant will lead to the birth of another infant with better prospects of a happy life, the total amount of happiness will be greater if the defective infant is killed. The loss of happy life for the first infant is outweighed by the gain of a happier life for the second. Therefore..., it would...be right to kill him.

Singer concludes this passage with the significant statement that his view "treats infants as replaceable, in much the same way as non-self-conscious animals were treated in Ch. 5."[3]

Our question is whether we can take a principled stand against Singer on the basis of the dignity born of our common rational nature. Let us see. Suppose I were to object to him like this: "the hemophiliac infant has human and hence also rational nature. The infant, having all the dignity that comes from this nature, stands before me as inviolable; no one may directly kill him for the utilitarian reason given by Singer or for any other reason." Is this a good and decisive response to Singer? Let us suppose, just for the sake of argument, that Singer does not object to ascribing rational nature to an infant that as yet performs no rational activities.

Is Singer left with no response to us? By no means. The statements of his just quoted need not prevent him from professing great admiration for the rational nature of man and saying many of the things that we say about the dignity flowing from it. He is at liberty to say that it would be a terrible crime to destroy the race of rational beings in the world and he might even say that it is wrong needlessly to reduce by even one the number of rational beings in the world. But he will point out that he is not reducing this number; whether one performs or does not perform the infanticide that he advocates, the number of human beings remains the same. Performing the infanticide simply lets Singer get a specimen of health that would otherwise not exist. He will exploit the fact that the dignity of persons depends on their common human nature. He will say that all that is lost when the hemophiliac infant is killed exists again in the healthier infant that he wants to make room for. For this new infant also shares in rational nature and so has dignity from exactly the same source and in exactly the same measure as the hemophiliac infant had it. One instance of rational nature succeeds the other; the first is replaced by the second. The loss in terms of dignity that comes from the infanticide is perfectly and exactly annulled by the gain in terms of dignity that comes from the new child who takes the place of the first child. But, in addition to this "wash" of gain and loss, there is also a gain not annulled by any loss, an absolute gain, namely, the gain of full health in the new child. People like Singer might even make bold to say that we are in fact *required* by our respect for human dignity to carry out this replacement, for we show respect for human dignity by seeing to it that human beings live in the greatest possible state of flourishing. I submit that if we cannot enlarge our account of human dignity, if we cannot find some way to let the incommunicable personhood of each human being play a role in the grounding of dignity, then we are left with no good answer to Singer. As long as the dignity of human beings is tied to that which is common to them all, they are replaceable one by another, and Singer has the last word.

Let us then turn our attention to human beings, not insofar as they share in the same nature but insofar as each is himself and no other. If we continue the tradition of using Socrates as a kind of logical dummy, then we can say that we are now turning our attention to Socrates, not as a human being but as Socrates, and we ask whether Socrates does not have some dignity just by being Socrates.

Let us consult those who knew and loved Socrates and ask them whether all that they knew and loved in Socrates could be repeated in some other human being. The human nature of Socrates is in a sense repeated in all other human beings; his being a Greek is in a sense repeated in all other Greeks; his being a philosopher is repeated in all other philosophers; even his famous irony was practiced by at least a few others, by some disciples who have been called "Socratic" thinkers. But those who knew and loved Socrates will not grant that everything that they knew and loved in him can be repeated in others; they will insist, as indeed anyone who loves another person will insist, that there was in Socrates something absolutely unrepeatable; they will say that there was the mystery of the man and that Socrates was not a mere instance or specimen of this mystery but that he *was* it, so that a second Socrates is impossible–strictly, absolutely impossible. When Socrates died, a hole was left in the world, such that no subsequent person could possibly fill it. It was not just that a great philosopher died, the likes of which were not likely to be seen again; with this approach one would push the incommunicable personhood of Socrates into the realm of unusual achievements and miss the mystery of it. The incommunicable Socrates was something ineffable, something too concrete for the general concepts of human language; something knowable through love but not utterable in words.

Let me try to bring out the unrepeatability of which I speak by means of a contrast. Take any copy of today's *New York Times*. Everything of interest in any one copy can be found as well in any other copy; no one copy has any point of interest that would distinguish it from the others. In fact, each copy exists simply for the sake of that which is common to all the copies of today's paper; each copy is well made just to the extent that it contains neither more nor less than the other copies contain. Of course, each copy is an incommunicable individual; one copy of the paper is not another. And yet that which is common to all the copies in some sense dominates each individual; the individuals exist simply for the sake of multiplying the common content. This is why any one copy is so easily replaceable by any other copy. If you lose the copy that you first bought, your loss is completely replaced by the purchase of another copy. In fact, the replaceability of one by another goes so far that under certain circumstances the difference between one and another is indiscernible. If I leave a copy of today's *Times* on my desk when I step away, I cannot tell when I return whether it is the same copy or a replacement copy that someone has secretly supplied. What is common to the individual copies is so strong that it may be impossible to tell one individual from another.

Clearly it is along just these lines that Singer is thinking when he proposes replacing one human infant with another. Killing the hemophiliac infant so as to make room for a perfectly healthy one is just like turning in a frayed copy of today's *Times* for a perfectly clean one. Even if that which is common to many individuals is not just the content of today's news but is the much grander thing of human nature with its wonder of rationality, the human individuals who are being treated as mere instances in relation to the common will still be subject to the same law of replaceability that we see with the newspapers.

What I have tried to show of Socrates, who here stands for every human person, is that there is something in him that can be known and loved that is not a mere instance of some kind, that is not common to him and others, that is incommunicably his own, that is too concrete and individual to be common to him and others. No hole is left in the world by the destruction of a copy of today's paper as long as other copies remain; but an irreparable, unfillable hole is left by the removal of a single human person. Not even God can fill it; it is not that He lacks power, but absurd things do not fall within the scope of His power, and completely replaceable persons, or persons who exist in duplicate or triplicate, are as great a metaphysical absurdity as there is.

And so we have developed the distinction between that which is incommunicably each person's own and that which is common to many persons. Before proceeding further, I should remind my readers that this is only a distinction and that in an integral personalist philosophy one would have to re-unite the things distinguished. This means that one would have to show that the very idea of a "mere specimen of rational nature" is absurd, that rational nature cannot be multiplied in interchangeable individuals in the way that today's newspaper can be multiplied, and that rational nature is such that it can exist only in incommunicable persons. This would, in turn, mean that the Greek idea of "man as rational being" already contains "man as person," and that the Christian idea of "man as person" does not overthrow but only serves to complete the Greek idea of "man as rational being." But I will not try to give a full account of this unity of the human person; the contribution that I want to make here to our understanding of the dignity of man requires above all that I focus attention on "man as incommunicable person."

Now, the dignity of a human being is grounded, or rather co-grounded, in this incommunicable personhood of each. It is not only because I share in the rational nature common to us all that I have dignity, but also because I am the unrepeatable person that I am. This unrepeatable person has value, for it awakens love when glimpsed by others. But it is not a value achieved only by some and not by others, for it goes with existing as a person. It is that aspect of dignity that we can with all precision call the dignity of the human person. And only when our understanding of the sources of dignity has been expanded to encompass the incommunicable personhood of each human being are we in a position to defend hemophiliac infants against the likes of Peter Singer. For now, but only now, can we say that this infant has dignity, not just as the bearer of rational human nature, but as this infant, as this incommunicable newborn person. The hemophiliac infant cannot be replaced because, as person, it is absolutely unreplaceable and is invested with dignity in its very unreplaceability. Only now does human dignity bring with it moral protection for the individual person. Only now can the invocation of dignity do the work in moral analysis that we expect it to do.

Those contemporary philosophers who, in speaking of personal dignity, stress the *otherness* of other human beings (for example, Levinas) are finding dignity precisely in the personal incommunicability to which I have been calling attention. They form a certain contrast to those who speak of the other as *alter ego,* who are approaching others in terms of what is common to themselves and the others; the advocates of radical otherness are approaching others in terms of what each person incommunicably is.

We may come to understand better this personal dignity and the inviolability of the individual person that follows from it if we see the "intimation of immortality" that it contains for individual persons. Let us assume that human beings really were mere instances of human nature. In that case an endless succession of human beings would provide all the immortality that anyone could wish. Their ability to replace each other would allow for an immortality accomplished through mortal individuals continually reproducing themselves. The immortality of man need not bring with it the immortality of any individual human being. But since human persons are precisely not mere instances of human nature and since the final destruction of any one of them would tear open a hole in being that could never be filled, there is a deep point to the immortality of individual persons. This is, of course, not a finished proof but only, as I put it, an "intimation of immortality" for persons. But it does add something to our understanding of personal dignity. The inviolability of persons known to us from our moral dealings with them becomes a promise of immortality when persons are considered in relation to death.

3. SOME OBJECTIONS

When in the past I have presented to other philosophers something like this account of personal dignity, I have received various objections.

According to the first, my view exaggerates the importance of that which is incommunicably each person's own. One says that what distinguishes one person from another is really peripheral to the person. Put together some things like the place of one's upbringing, the year of one's birth, one's IQ, and soon you will have a set of properties that serves to distinguish one person from all others. But these individuating factors are not central to a person; what is central to him is his having a soul, having free will, being made for God, and the like. These central determinants of a person are common to him and all other persons, whereas the determinants of him being himself and no other are, as was said, relatively peripheral. But that which is relatively peripheral to a person can certainly play no very large role in establishing the dignity of the person; if dignity is to depend on what belongs most centrally to a person, it will have to depend on what is common to him and all persons. Hence, the attempt to bring incommunicable personhood into the ground of human dignity is misguided.

I respond by saying that the objection quite trivializes what I mean by personal incommunicability. I do not mean merely a bundle of traits in a being, as if the whole bundle served to identify this being as this one and no other, even though each separate trait were common to that being and to many other beings. Such a bundle just provides a device for picking out one individual among other individuals and referring to it with precision; it does not capture that ineffable mystery of a person that engenders love in the one who know the person. Besides, many a bundle of traits that happens to pick out one individual could in principle be instantiated by more than one individual; however unlikely it is to be repeated in others, this could in principle happen, and hence the bundle falls short of the unrepeatable person.[4] It follows from my discussion in this paper that the whole conception of personal incommunicability as peripheral is fundamentally flawed; it is simply not true that the deeper we go into the center of a person, the more we find that which is common to all persons. Just the contrary is true: we arrive at the center of a person only when we encounter the person as unrepeatable.[5] It is, then, quite in order to let personal incommunicability play a large role in our account of human dignity.

According to a second objection, my view seems to compromise the unity of the human species. One suspects that I am saying of human persons what St. Thomas Aquinas said of the angels, namely, that each is its own species, and thus that human persons are not together in the unity of one human species. And there are indeed weighty reasons, including weighty theological reasons, for wanting to preserve the unity of the human species. I would say in response that the unrepeatability of human persons as I understand it does not prevent them from sharing a common nature. From the beginning to the end of this paper I have acknowledged this common nature. We can in fact express the unrepeatability of persons in terms which *presuppose* a common nature, as when I say that each human person has human nature in his or her incommunicable, unrepeatable way. This "adverbial" way of expressing personal incommunicability inserts it from the beginning within our common human nature.

More interesting, in my opinion, is a third objection, according to which the equality of persons seems to be jeopardized by letting dignity be based in part on persons as incommunicable. As we remarked above, we seem to secure this equality by letting dignity flow from our common human nature, for then dignity arises in each person from the same source. But if we let it also flow from the unrepeatable person-hood of each human being, then this dignity is no longer the same in each person but is one thing in one person and another thing in another. This might seem to open the door to persons differing in dignity, some having more of it and some having less. In this case the appeal to personal dignity could function in moral discussions in certain "elitist" ways that would yield some very suspicious moral conclusions.

To this objection I would first respond that the equality of human dignity is by no means secured by deriving dignity from our common rational nature. For one could say with Aristotle that man realizes this rational nature more perfectly than woman, that masters realize it more perfectly than natural slaves, that Greeks realize it more perfectly than barbarians, and one could thus be led to posit large differences in dignity among human beings. The equality of dignity is better pre-served by letting dignity also derive from personal unrepeatability. For you cannot say that one incommunicable person has more dignity and another has less without positing some common dignity-grounding quality possessed to different degrees by the two persons; but with such a common quality you abandon the incommunicability of persons who are being compared. The fact is that, by being incommunicable and unrepeatable, persons are incommensurable with each other and cannot be compared with each other, and with this a certain equality is established among them. They are alike in that each is incommunicable and unrepeatable. In addition, the comparisons that give rise to more or less dignity are blocked by the incommensurability of persons with each other. We have seen in this paper that dignity belongs to persons *both* because of their sameness in a common nature *and* because of their differences one from another. As for the equality of personal dignity, we get the surprising result that the differences among unrepeatable persons lend more support to this equality than the sameness does.

NOTES

1. I did address this question in my 1993 UFL paper: "The Personhood of the Embryo" in *Life and Learning III: Proceedings of the Third University Faculty for Life Conference*, ed. Joseph W. Koterski, S.J. (Washington, D.C.: UFL, 1993), pp. 177-99.

2. Václav Havel, "Kosovo and the End of the Nation-State," *The New York Review of Books* (June 10, 1999), p. 6.

3. Peter Singer, *Practical Ethics* (Cambridge: Cambridge Univ. Press, 1979), pp. 133-34.

4. For a penetrating criticism of this bundle theory of personal incommunicability, see Jorge Gracia, *Individuality* (Albany: SUNY Press, 1988), *e.g.*, pp. 64-69, to mention just one passage.

5. Max Scheler argues for just this thesis and in fact regards it as a thesis central to his ethical personalism; see the discussion of this whole theme in Scheler's thought in my "The Individuality of Human Persons: A Study in the Ethical Personalism of Max Scheler," *The Review of Metaphysics* 52/1 (1998) 21-50.

Against Capital Punishment:
A Teleological Argument

John J. Conley, S.J.

I N THE CATHOLIC COMMUNITY a strong opposition to the practice of capital punishment has emerged in the magisterium over the past decades. Since 1974, the U. S. Catholic Conference, the public-policy arm of the nation's Catholic bishops, has issued a series of statements condemning the resumption of judicial executions.[1] Numerous state Catholic conferences have opposed legislative initiatives to establish capital punishment in their respective states.[2] Pope John Paul II criticized the death penalty in *Evangelium Vitae* (1995): "It is clear that for these purposes [retribution and rehabilitation] to be achieved, the nature and extent of the punishment must be carefully evaluated and decided upon, and ought not to go to the extreme of executing the offender except in cases of absolute necessity; in other words, when it would not be possible otherwise to defend society. Today, however, as a result of steady improvements in the organization of the penal system, such cases are very rare, if not practically non-existent."[3] The Pope's opposition to capital punishment became even more categoric in his homily in Saint Louis, Missouri (1999): "I renew the appeal...for a consensus to end the death penalty, which is both cruel and unnecessary."[4]

The emerging opposition to capital punishment within the Catholic and other religious communities often operates on the level of a thin and opaque argument. The tone of the argument is often tentative if for no other reason than that the current rejection of the death penalty rests uneasily with the apparent support for the death penalty offered by religious authorities of several generations ago.

The degree of opposition varies. The New York State Catholic Conference (1998) categorically rejects the death penalty as unjustified violence, parallel to the recourse to abortion in the case of a problematic pregnancy.[5] The United States Catholic Conference (1980), on the other hand, opposes the death penalty as an unnecessary practice, but it recognizes that those Catholics who still support the death penalty are in conformity with Church tradition.[6]

The grounds of opposition also vary. Some statements opposing capital punishment criticize the practice in principle as immoral.[7] Others accept the legitimacy of the practice in principle but make a prudential case that the state should renounce the exercise of this power, at least in current circumstances.[8] Others focus on the inequities surrounding the current American practice of capital punishment: the presence of innocent people on death row; the arbitrariness of the decision to impose the penalty; the disproportionate burden upon the poor, especially poor racial minorities, in bearing the brunt of this punishment.[9]

The purpose of this paper is to develop a teleological case against capital punishment. It will attempt to demonstrate how capital punishment frustrates or destroys the three basic purposes of judicial punishment: retribution, deterrence, and reformation. It will argue that the convergence of these arguments can furnish a compelling, if not absolute, case against the death penalty.

RETRIBUTION

Retribution is civil society's imposition of a just penalty upon an offender who has violated the order of justice. The purpose of the punishment is to restore the order of justice so violated. The gravity of the penalty must reflect the gravity of the offense committed and of the degree of culpability of the person who committed the offense.

The concept of retribution is easily distorted in contemporary society. Retribution is not vengeance. Nor is retribution strict symmetry. A rapist is not punished by being raped by an officer of the court. A burglar is not punished by having his own home burgled by a police officer. A drunken driver guilty of vehicular manslaughter is not run over on a highway by jury members in a state of intoxication. Retribution is proportionate inasmuch as the severity of the civic punishment must vary according to the gravity of the crime committed.

Capital punishment poorly serves this end of retribution. First, rather than placing a penalty upon a person, capital punishment aims to destroy the person himself or herself. The death penalty does not impose a grave burden upon a criminal member of society. It literally removes a person from society. Rather than disabling the freedom and other goods of the criminal as a just punishment for violation of the order of justice, the death penalty removes the criminal from any further participation in the social order. It is paradoxical, to say the least, to attempt to restore the order of justice among persons by using a judicial weapon that aims at the very annihilation of the person by destroying the criminal's life.

Earlier natural-law theorists supporting capital punishment often use telling analogies that inadvertently manifest the depersonalization of the criminal who is considered properly condemned to death. In a typical argument, Vernon Bourke claims that capital punishment is a type of social surgery: "A state may kill a criminal who has seriously offended against the common good of the community. Just as it is reasonable to cut off a diseased member of the human body, when the member threatens the welfare of the whole body, so it is reasonable to permit the body politic to cut off a bad member of society for the sake of the good of the whole society."[10] This social-surgery argument clearly reduces the criminal to a means to an end. The personal dignity of the criminal, an ontological trait that cannot be destroyed by moral transgression, has evaporated in this image of the criminal as a diseased organ subordinate to the good of the whole.

Bourke deepens the anti-personalist traits of his argument by another consideration: "Capital punishment may also be justified on the reasoning that a serious criminal has receded so far from the order of reason that he is no longer worthy of treatment as a rational being."[11] This is an odd argument inasmuch as conviction of serious crime, such as first-degree murder, requires evidence of sanity. Indeed, conviction for the aforecited crime requires evidence of rational premeditation. An irrational agent should be in a state hospital for the criminally insane, not in a prison nor in the electric chair.

Nonetheless, this argument that the grave criminal is "no longer worthy of treatment as a rational being" indicates how easily the case for capital punishment rests upon a depersonalization of the criminal. In this instance, the foundation of personal dignity, human rationality, is denied the criminal. This refusal to recognize that the criminal is in fact a rational agent is precisely what grounds the abandonment of the inviolability of the life of a human person.

The retribution operated by the civil authority in punishment of the criminal is always a retribution proper to the order of persons. Capital punishment distorts this personalist structure of retribution by inflicting a sentence that both aims at the destruction of the person and that easily denies the very personality of the criminal.

Second, capital punishment fails to use death as a "last resort" in its treatment of the criminal. It has long been commonplace in ethical literature to argue that the state may only employ lethal force as a last-resort in defending the innocent against grave aggression. Hence, the recourse to war can only be justified after other, more pacific means of redress and negotiation have failed. The police use of lethal force is only reasonable when non-lethal means would probably not disable an imminent threat to the lives of police officers or innocent bystanders by an aggressor. Similarly, capital punishment cannot be justified when other, less lethal means of punishment can be used to restore the order of outraged justice. The capacity of contemporary penal practice to impose such punishments, as in the case of life imprisonment without parole for aggravated murder, would appear to rule out the use of capital punishment. As Pope John Paul II and other religious authorities have argued, it is difficult to see how capital punishment could function as a last-resort means of retribution when the methods of retribution open to the contemporary state are so ample and so effective.

The argument that capital punishment fails the "last resort" test presupposes a supreme, but not, absolute value placed upon life itself. It is the condition for the existence and development of all other goods of the human person. Its destruction can only be justified–and then tragically–when the very survival of innocent persons necessitates the destruction of a grave aggressor. One can imagine such scenarios in certain cases of self-defense, police action, and defensive warfare. However, it is difficult to imagine such a scenario in the case of the punishment of a criminal who is already disarmed, imprisoned, and subject to the substantial surveillance and punitive powers of the contemporary state.

Just as the state may not depersonalize the criminal in its effort to restore the order of violated justice, it may not employ lethal means of punishment when non-lethal means can clearly effect the work of retribution. The incapacity of capital punishment to serve as a last resort in the defense of the innocent against aggression disqualifies it as an appropriate punishment.

DETERRENCE

The second major purpose of judicial punishment is deterrence of future crime, both by the criminal and, more importantly, by other members of society. If the state is to employ this lethal punishment, it should be able to demonstrate that the use of capital punishment clearly deters the commission of violent crime. In the absence of such evidence, the state is obliged to use other non-lethal means of punishment as a method of educating and discouraging the public from the commission of grave assaults upon the order of justice.

To put it mildly, criminal statistical evidence for decades has indicated that capital punishment has little, if any, deterrent effect upon the commission of violent crime. States vigorously employing the death penalty, such as Texas and Louisiana, do not have lower rates of criminal activity than do those which have abolished capital punishment.[12] Many of the abolitionist nations of the world (Japan, Western Europe) enjoy comparatively low levels of violent crime, while many nations employing capital punishment have high rates of criminal activity.

Obviously, such statistical correlations should be studied with caution. Many abolitionist societies are affluent, highly educated cultures that enjoy a high level of civic concord for reasons other than the single one of suppressing the death penalty. Nonetheless, supporters of the death penalty who claim that it does deter violent crime should be able to make a strong empirical case for its effects in crime reduction, if indeed it is such a powerful deterrent. In lieu of such evidence, however, and with substantial evidence to the contrary, capital punishment loses one of its traditional justifications. If the lives, potential or actual, of citizens are not in fact protected by recourse to this lethal means, the state is obliged to confine itself to less violent methods of crime prevention.

The illusory allegiance to capital punishment as a deterrent often prevents society from endorsing less dramatic but more effective means of deterring the commission of serious crime. As recent criminological research has indicated, new penal practices (such as mandatory minimum sentences, greater difficulty in parole, firmer sentencing guidelines) and police practices (restoration of street patrols, community policing, "zero tolerance" approaches to non-violent crime) have contributed to the substantial reduction in violent crime witnessed by American society in the 1990s.[13]

The illusory embrace of capital punishment as an effective deterrent also risks the further brutalization of our society. A violent solution to crime is avidly endorsed, despite the pointed evidence that it provides no reduction in criminality. As Bishop Joseph A. Fiorenza, President of the National Conference of Catholic Bishops, recently argued: "We oppose the death penalty not just for what it does to those guilty of heinous crimes, but for what it does to all of us: it offers the tragic illusion that we can defend life by taking life."[14]

REFORMATION

The final purpose of judicial punishment is to reform the criminal so that he or she may again participate in social life in conformity with the order of justice. By its nature, the death penalty precludes any long-term reformation of life by the criminal. Not only does it prevent any re-integration into society by the criminal. It even pre-empts any durable amendment of life and commitment to work and friendship possible for a prisoner with a life sentence. No process of rehabilitation is possible.

By its destruction of the end of reformation, capital punishment introduces a certain despair into the process of judicial punishment. It radically forecloses the future in a way unparalleled by any other species of punishment. Not surprisingly, many religious opponents of capital punishment argue that it defies the fundamental gospel values of mercy and reconciliation by its refusal of any possibility of a redemptive future to the convicted criminal. It signals society's willingness to despair of the life of a criminal member of that society. By doing so, not only does capital punishment attack the rehabilitative purpose of all punishment. It assaults the values of repentance, amendment, and conversion that constitute the heart of a humane social order and, *a fortiori*, the order of grace.

CONCLUSION

Capital punishment's violation of the central purposes of judicial punishment—retribution, deterrence, reformation—constitutes a compelling case against this practice. I do not believe that it constitutes an absolute case, inasmuch as the only absolute (that is, universal and exceptionless) norm in this area of human action is: One many never directly kill an innocent human being. There is a gap—and it is steep—between Ted Bundy's killing of his victims and the State of Florida's killing of Ted Bundy.

The growing and, I believe, justified opposition to capital punishment is not based upon a global pacifism that condemns all deliberate homicide as wrong. Nor is it rooted in a categoric denial of the state's right and duty to exercise the power of the sword in the defense of the innocent against the aggressor. It springs from the conviction that this power of the sword can only be used as a last resort, given the supreme worth of the life of every human person, regardless of his or her moral status. It perceives no need to use this last resort in a society which can effectively punish the violent criminal through imprisonment. The moral unworthiness of this punishment emerges even more clearly, given its failure as a deterrent and its assault upon the good of personal reformation. Like many violent solutions to our social problems, its popularity outdistances its necessity.

NOTES

1. *Cf.* Administrative Board of the U. S. Catholic Conference, *A Good Friday Appeal to End the Death Penalty* (1999) (www.nccbuscc.org/sdwp /national/criminal/appeal): 1-3.

2. *Cf.* New York State Catholic Conference, "Statement on Capital Punishment" (1998) (www.nyscatholicconference.org/agenda/1H): 1.

3. Pope John Paul II, *Evangelium Vitae* (Boston: Pauline, 1995): # 56, 91.

4. Cited in USCC, *op. cit.*: 1.

5. New York State Catholic Conference, op. cit.: 1.

6. U. S. Catholic Conference, *USCC Statement on the Death Penalty*, 1980 (www.nccbuscc.org/sdwp/national/criminal/death/uscc 80): 1-7.

7. Cf. New York State Catholic Conference, *op. cit.*: 1.

8. Cf. U. S. Catholic Conference, *USCC Statement on the Death Penalty*, *op. cit.*: 2.

9. *Cf.* Joseph Cardinal Bernardin, "Testimony to the Judiciary Committee of the United States Senate" (1989) (www.nccbuscc.org/sdwp/national/ criminal/death/bern89): 2.

10. Vernon J. Bourke, *Ethics* (New York, Macmillan): 354.

11. *Ibid.*: 355.

12. *Cf.* Federal Bureau of Investigation, "Synopsis of FBI Uniform Crime Report" (sun.soci.niu.edu/~critcrim/crime/ucr.95): 1.

13. The research of political scientist John DiIulio indicates how certain penal practices can reduce crime and effectively isolate violent criminals from society. *Cf.* John J. DiIulio, Jr., *Governing Prisons: A Comparative Study of Correctional Management* (New York: Free Press, 1987) and *No Escape: The Future of American Corrections* (New York: Basic Books, 1991).

14. Bishop Joseph A. Fiorenza (1999), cited by Catholics Against Capital Punishment (www.igc.org/cacp/): 1.

The Right to Life and the Natural Law

Mitchell Kalpakgian

T HE NATURAL LAW is one of the oldest moral concepts in the history of civilization. In Western culture the idea of the natural law finds foremost expression in the literature and thought of ancient Greece and Rome. The discovery of the natural moral law on the part of Greek and Roman thinkers explains such great moral insights as Plato's ideas of the true, the good, and the beautiful; Socrates's teaching that it is better to suffer wrong than to do evil; Aristotle's notion of the golden mean in his definition of virtue as a form of moderation or balance that avoids the extremes of excess and deficiency; the concept of the cardinal virtues of prudence, justice, fortitude, and temperance; and the stoic ideal of duty and obligation as the highest good.

The natural law, however, transcends the classical civilizations of Greece and Rome and encompasses all men. As C. S. Lewis shows in *The Abolition of Man*, universal moral precepts abound in all societies and cultures throughout all the ages of history and reflect worldwide consensus. Lewis cites sacred writings, philosophical texts, and books of wisdom to illustrate the naturalness, universality, and timelessness of the natural law. To prove the existence of the natural law, Lewis examines the topic of "Duties to Children and Posterity" as but one illustration of natural law. From Hindu sources he cites the following passage: "Children, the old, the poor, *etc.*, should be considered as lords of the atmosphere." From the Roman writings of Cicero, Lewis quotes a passage from *On Duties*: "Nature produces a special love of offspring." From the *Analects* of ancient China Lewis selects this line: "The Master said, respect the young." From *An Account of the Battle of Wounded Knee*, Lewis cites this passage from the wisdom of the American Indian: "The killing of the women and more especially of the young boys and girls who make up the future strength of the people, is the saddest part... and we feel it very sorely."[1]   This one simple example of the existence of the natural law proves that it is indeed natural, inborn, and native to people of all nations and cultures. In other words, the natural law is not invented or formulated by man but discovered as inherent in the structure of reality, in the "nature of things." It is as real, constant, and universal as the laws that govern the sunrise and sunset. The natural law is independent of opinion and not relative to culture. It encompasses people of all nations, races, and religions, and it is the basis of international law, what the Founding Fathers call "the laws of nature and nature's God."

Frequently, advocates of abortion argue that we live in a multicultural, pluralistic society with a wide spectrum of opinions on many controversial subjects; therefore, no one individual or group should impose its opinion or morality on others. This attitude praises tolerance and diversity as the ultimate virtues and denies the validity of absolute truths and unchanging moral norms. In this view the meaning of good and evil become relative to political trends, the swing of the pendulum, ideological movements, and the will of those in positions of power and influence. Thus the Supreme Court in 1973 in *Roe v. Wade* legalized abortion in America and changed the traditional, time-honored meanings of good and evil, allowing the killing of pre-born children on the basis of a woman's right to privacy, reversing 2,000 years of custom, tradition, law, and religion and capitulating to feminist special-interest groups. This view of abortion, however, as a matter of opinion and relative truth avoids the reality of natural law that binds all men and transcends political trends.

To say "You are entitled to your own opinions on abortion; however, you should not try to impose your opinions, morality, or values on others" contains two errors. First, it implies that abortion is simply a matter of opinion rather than a question of truth or an issue of knowledge. Second, the statement suggests that the abortion question is non-debatable, so divisive and controversial a topic that it is not open to an appeal to reason or conscience or tradition or science or the authority of God's word. In other words, any person who defends the right to life or the unborn or argues that abortion is the killing of innocent, helpless children is accused of dictating like a tyrant, "imposing" or forcing his unwelcome personal views upon unwilling subjects who resent having their own ideas questioned. However, abortion is neither a matter of arbitrary opinion nor heavy-handed dictatorship. For two thousand years, from the beginning of the Roman Empire, the Christian tradition consistently defended the sanctity of life from conception until death. Historian John T. Noonan writes: "As soon as the Christian community in the Roman Empire became vocal (from the 2nd century on) ... they emphatically and unanimously proclaimed their complete rejection of abortion at any stage of pregnancy. The grounds were that it was a horrendous evil which would seriously lead to hell.[2]

Abortion is also condemned by all of the world's great religions, not merely by the Catholic Church or the Christian tradition. Vedic spiritual writings from India that date from about 1000 B.C., Hinduism, conservative and orthodox Judaism, and Islam have all acknowledged abortion as an heinous evil and grave crime. Even Hippocrates, a pagan Greek physician, writes in his famous Oath, "I will give no deadly medicine even if asked, nor suggest to a woman a pessary to produce abortion." This universal consensus about the evil of abortion, then, can hardly be termed a matter of subjective opinion, cultural bias, or relative truth. The Chief Justice of the Supreme Rabbinical Court of America, Rabbi Marvin S. Antleman, describes the problem of abortion as one of "universal morality," and he adds, "It is neither a Catholic problem, nor a Jewish problem, nor a Protestant problem. It involves the killing of a human being, an act forbidden by universal commandment."[3]

The basis for this universal agreement on the evil of abortion prior to 1973, however, is not merely religious but also philosophical. All people do not share the same religion, but all people possess the same human nature and the same desire for justice. All people belong to the human race and are endowed with the gift of reason and born with a conscience, an innate moral law that is God-given and natural, the basis for natural law. St. Paul says in his letter to the Romans that the Gentiles, having not the Law–that is, the Ten Commandments as revealed by God to the chosen people of Israel–"do by nature the things contained in the Law." That is, they honor the moral teachings found in the Ten Commandments: do not steal, do not murder, do not commit adultery, do not bear false witness. The explanation for the morality of

Gentiles and pagans who have not received the Mosaic Law or the Gospel from the revealed Word of God is the natural law that is "written in their hearts," as St. Paul says, adding that "their conscience bears witness to them" (Romans 2:14-15). The natural law, then, forms the basis for all morality and virtue, and it establishes the foundation for the higher truths of religion. Thus both the testimony of all the world's great religions and the universal evidence of the natural law argue that the pro-life position in the abortion controversy is not some eccentric, idiosyncratic, outdated, minority opinion but is founded on moral truth and ancient wisdom based on reason, experience, and authority.

For example, in the Greek tragedy *Antigone* Sophocles illustrates that the natural law is higher than any individual opinion, man-made law, or arbitrary ruling of a tyrant or political body. In the play King Creon has by decree forbidden anyone to bury the body of Eteocles, the brother of Antigone who fought against the king. In defiance of King Creon's arbitrary laws that imply that "might is right," Antigone feels obligated to give her brother the dignity of a decent burial and appeals to the natural law as having greater binding authority than man-made laws that do not conform to justice. As St. Thomas Aquinas explained in his treatise on law, *mala lex, nulla lex*: a bad or unjust law is no law at all. In her self-defense for breaking the official law of the land, Antigone appeals to "The infallible, unwritten laws of Heaven./ Not now or yesterday they have their being,/But everlastingly, and none can tell/ The hour that saw their birth."[4] The pro-life movement is essentially Antigone's argument: *Roe v. Wade* is an unjust law and therefore no law at all. Even though at the time all fifty states forbade or restricted abortion, the Supreme Court, in what Justice Byron White called "an exercise in raw judicial power," overrode the long-established decisions made for people in their own legislatures. The Supreme Court decision also subverted the whole Western Judeo-Christian moral tradition that forms the basis of American government: "We hold these truths to be self-evident, that all men are created with certain unalienable rights...that among these are life, liberty, and the pursuit of happiness." These famous words express the natural law. "We hold these truths to be self-evident" means that the moral law is clear to the light of reason and the voice of conscience. "Unalienable rights" means that humans are endowed by their Creator with natural, God-given rights that no government, tyrant, or man-made law can deny to them. Unalienable rights have priority over government policies and Supreme Court decisions. The legalization or institutionalization of a practice or policy such as abortion-on-demand does not make it moral because the natural law and God's justice have greater weight than Supreme court decisions. *Roe v. Wade* is just as immoral, cruel, and inhumane as the *Dred Scott* decision that sanctioned slavery and classified blacks as the "chattel" or property of slave-owners. As Sophocles's play *Antigone* illustrates, when human laws do not conform to the natural law, justice loses its meaning, man presumes to be God, and tyranny in the form of "might is right" or "raw judicial power" violates the most natural rights of all, such as Antigone's brother's right to a burial and the pre-born child's right to life.

To say that the pro-life argument is an attempt to impose, force, or dictate ideas upon others is just as preposterous as referring to the evil of abortion as a private opinion. The pro-life position is an appeal to reason, conscience, justice, and divine authority as the final arbiters of this issue. How reasonable is *Roe v. Wade* and legalized abortion in the light of the court cases cited by columnist George Will in the June 19, 1983 issue of *The Washington Post*? His first example shows that under the law the fetus has a right to protection. In Baltimore, a pregnant drug user was placed under court orders to protect the health of the fetus. She was ordered not to inflict harm upon the pre-born child through the use of drugs. However, while the court could hold her liable for impairing the health of the child in her womb, *Roe v. Wade* allowed her to kill this same child because of her right to privacy. Will's second example proves that under the law a fetus has a right to inherit property. In Maryland, if the fetus is conceived before the death of the person from whom the property is inherited, the fetus may be a beneficiary. The child that is entitled to an inheritance, however, is not entitled to the right to life if a woman chooses to abort. Will's third example demonstrates that a fetus has a right to prenatal medical care. He writes, "Malpractice cases are establishing that a child born injured as the result of negligent prenatal medicine can claim violation of rights it had as a fetus." In another case in 1983 in California a police officer who killed the fetus of a woman in a drug raid was convicted for the killing of the child in the womb. So how can a pre-born child have a right to protection, a right to inherit, and a right to prenatal care and yet have no right to life? *Non sequitur.* It is illegal to deny the pre-born child pre-natal care and criminal to shoot the child in the womb, yet it is perfectly lawful for a woman to pay an abortionist to destroy the very child that other laws protect. This is the kind of tortured logic that George Orwell in *1984* calls "doublethink" (such as the slogan that "War Is Peace"). Is it reasonable that Dr. Abu Hayat is convicted of malpractice for a botched abortion that resulted in a child's loss of one arm while his successful killing of the child would prove him innocent of crime? In asking these questions, the pro-life position is not expressing opinion or imposing morality but demonstrating the courage to think, the desire for justice, a love of the truth, and intellectual honesty.

How much thought or logic does the pro-abortion position reflect when it introduces such topics as overpopulation, rape and incest, unwanted children, the right to privacy, choice, and women's rights into the abortion debate but avoids asking the central moral questions, namely, is the fetus an innocent and living human being? Is the killing of innocent and living human beings wrong? The whole weight of scientific evidence, the discoveries in fetology, and the technology of ultrasound demonstrate the undeniable truth that the pre-born child in the womb is a unique human being. Dr. Bernard Nathanson states, "The life processes begin a fertilization, when the sperm unites with the egg to create a unique genetic entity for each fetus that can never be repeated." Is abortion the killing of a human being? The procedures of abortion themselves answer this question. In the technique known as Dilation and Curettage (D&C) a sharp loop-shaped knife is inserted, and "the placenta and the child are then dismembered and scraped out into a basin." In the technique known as Dilation and Evacuation (D&E), "a pliers-like pair of forceps is then used to crush the child's skull and snap its spine." In saline Amniocentesis "a solution of concentrated salt is injected. The child breathes in, swallowing the poisonous salt. After an hour of convulsing and struggling, the child is overcome and the mother goes into labor. About an hour later she will deliver a corpse."[5] Is the child innocent? The pre-born child, like the newborn infant, is helpless, weak, dependent, and in need of protection and nourishment. No one could be more innocent. The pro-abortion argument ignores these facts and self-evident truths, rejects common sense, evades reality, and suppresses the truth.

Is it just to deprive women considering an abortion truthful information regarding the fetal development of their children or to deny them a full knowledge of abortion techniques and their consequences? Is it reasonable to refer to abortion as a "safe, legal" procedure when it has caused a multitude of problems from infertility to infection to an increase in the risk of cancer, and is it honest to speak of abortion as "safe" when it often leads to such psychological disorders as post-abortion-stress syndrome that produces guilt, anger, despair, and nightmares? Is it fair-minded of the media to suppress the visual evidence of aborted babies and conceal from the public the bloodshed and violence of the Holocaust while the media graphically represent wars in all their carnage? How much sense does it make when abortion advocates like Planned Parenthood claim that the natural events of pregnancy and childbirth are more dangerous to a woman's health than the violent, unnatural act of abortion–the propaganda that killing children is safer than having them?

All these questions appeal to common sense, the power of reason, the natural law, and the dictates of conscience. They are not the questions of extreme religious bigots who are manipulating evidence to superimpose their narrow, unenlightened views and idiosyncratic personal opinions upon a pluralistic society. Rather they are *bona fide* and legitimate questions that honor the universal moral norms of civilization that recognize the blessing of children and the sanctity of human life. They are questions that expose the fallacies, contradictions, unreasonableness, propaganda, and immorality of the pro-abortion mentality.

If the pro-life position is firmly rooted in the natural law, in the inherited wisdom of the human race, and in ancient moral traditions, what is the basis or foundation of the pro-abortion view? First, it is rooted in the *Roe v. Wade* decision of 1973, a decision that is no more than 20 years old compared to the eternal nature of the natural law. *Roe v. Wade* has been consistently compared to the 1857 *Dred Scott* decision that legalized slavery by denying the personhood of black slaves just as *Roe v. Wade* rejects the personhood of the unborn. *Roe v. Wade* based a woman's right to an abortion on the so-called "right to privacy" that allows a woman and her physician to determine the death of the pre-born child without any choice or involvement on the part of fathers or grandparents. *Roe v. Wade* reversed 200 years of American moral tradition and 2,000 years of Western civilization. It deemed all state laws forbidding or restricting abortions as "unconstitutional," thus legislating new law and inventing a new morality instead of interpreting the Constitution as the Court was designed to do.

The pro-abortion position is also rooted in the politics of radical feminism that attacks the dignity and vocation of motherhood and blames patriarchy as the root of all evil, interpreting all of history and culture as the conspiracy of men to oppress women. Radical feminism does not acknowledge the inherent, natural God-given distinctions between men and women as complementary differences designed for the enrichment of husbands and wives and for the moral and emotional well-being of children who need the influence of both a mother and a father. Radical feminism argues that women have a right to their own body, disregarding the truth that the child in the womb is a unique being with a separate life and destiny of its own. Radical feminism is an ideology that attempts to alter the very structure of reality and to re-invent nature as it seeks to separate women from their gender, biology, and motherhood in the name of a false equality and a distorted sense of freedom. The politics of radical feminism that advocates the abortion pill RU-486 ("the first human pesticide") and also promotes the Freedom of Choice Act (abortion-on-demand) that prohibits any form of restriction such as 24- hour waiting periods or parental notification also promotes lesbianism, witnessed by the leadership of the National Organization for Women.

The pro-abortion view, however, has roots deeper than *Roe v. Wade* and radical feminism. It can be traced to the eugenics movement of Margaret Sanger, founder of Planned Parenthood and the author of the notion that only the "fit" should live and the "unfit" be eliminated. By "fit" Sanger meant white Anglo-Saxon Protestants and by "unfit" she meant Jews, blacks, Slavic peoples, and Italian immigrants. In her crusade to promote birth control, sterilization, and abortion her mottoes were "Birth Control: To Create a Race of Thoroughbreds" and "No Gods, No Masters"–phrases that appeared in magazines that she founded.[6] In a letter she wrote to Dr. Clarence Gamble dated December 1939, she wrote, "We do not want the word to go out that we want to exterminate the Negro population and the minister is the man to straighten that idea out if it ever occurs to any of their more rebellious members."[7] In her magazine *Birth Control Review* she wrote, "The most urgent problem today is how to limit and discourage the over-fertility of the mentally and physically unfit."[8]

Sanger's eugenics movement in the early 20th-century clearly influenced Hitler's ideas of the pure Aryan race and Hitler's eugenics policies of exterminating Jews and Poles as "vermin" or "lice" that contaminated the human race. Many black leaders today view abortion as a continuation of the eugenics movement and have referred to abortion as "black genocide." Indeed, of the 1.6 million abortions in the United States each year, the greatest victims are black children. Wherever the ideology of eugenics takes control, the methods of population control always involve contraception, sterilization, and abortion. In a 1942 conversation Hitler said, "In view of the large families of the native population, it could only suit us if the girls and women there had as many abortions as possible. Active trade in contraceptions ought to be actually encouraged in the Eastern territories, as we could not possibly have the slightest interest in increasing the non-German population."[9]

Beyond *Roe v. Wade*, radical feminism, and the eugenics programs of Margaret Sanger lie other historical precedents for unlimited killing of children. In the Old Testament the Bible lists child sacrifice, along with homosexuality, as one of the abominations practiced by people inhabiting the land of Canaan which the Israelites were to conquer. Likewise, in the Punic Wars the Romans waged war against the Carthaginians and their god Baal, who also required child sacrifices. In the Aztec empire of Mexico in the year 1487, the ruler Tlacaellel promoted the practice of human sacrifice to the devil god of the Mexicans called Huitzilopochtli. Every year the law of the Aztec empire required a thousand sacrifices to this god in every town with a temple. The total number was at least 50,000 sacrifices a year, and one early Mexican historian estimates that one out of every five children was a victim of this demonic practice.[10] Every day in America some 4,000 children are killed in the abortion mills of the nation, and every year some 1.6 million children are sacrificed on the altars of pleasure, greed, selfishness, convenience, and ideology. Despite its legal status and the support of such organizations as Planned Parenthood, the National Organization of Women, the American Civil Liberties Union, the American Jewish Congress, and the American Medical Association, abortion in 20th-century America is just as savage and demonic as the practices of the Canaanites, Carthaginians, and Aztecs.

The background of the history of abortion and its precedents are not as respectable or flattering as the terms "pro-choice," "right to privacy," and "equal rights" suggest. Abortion has no venerable, honorable tradition in religion, law, or custom. Unlike the natural law, whose defenders include great minds like Sophocles, St. Paul, Cicero, St. Thomas Aquinas, the Founding Fathers of America, Edmund Burke, and C. S. Lewis, abortion is related to radical left-wing movements, totalitarian policies, and demonic practices. The Supreme Court's exercise of "raw judicial power," radical feminism's will to power, and the eugenics policies of Sanger and Hitler all attempt to substitute ideology for truth and to subvert the ancient moral order with wild-eyed, unthinkable propositions.

Ideology, as Russell Kirk explains in *The Politics of Prudence,* regards politics as "a revolutionary instrument for transforming society and even transforming human nature," and he remarks that ideology opposes "religion, tradition, custom, convention, prescription, and old constitutions."[11] Whether it is Communist ideology that denies man's spiritual, religious nature or feminist ideology that rejects the maternal, nurturing nature of womanhood or abortion ideology that does not recognize the reality or personhood of the pre-born child, ideology defies the truth of things and the structure of reality. It attempts to remold human nature according to its own pre-conceived, arbitrary definitions and fabrications, and it invents new language, jargon, and euphemisms to change reality. Thus the reality of a mother or father paying someone to destroy their own flesh and blood becomes the euphemism of "the right to choice." The medical procedure of crushing the pre-born child's skull or ripping apart its arms and legs is euphemistically called "termination of pregnancy." Abortuaries that kill babies and then dispose of them in waste baskets and rubbish dumpsters prefer to call themselves "women's health services." This transformation of reality through the manipulation of language is called "newspeak" by George Orwell in *1984.* It is the age-old technique of making evil appear good and good evil through verbal ingenuity. Thus words like clean-up, removal, evacuation, cleansing, and disinfection were used in Nazi Germany to conceal the reality of extermination and genocide, and terms like "fetal tissue," "protoplasmic rubbish," "fetal-placental unit," and "product of pregnancy" become the "newspeak" of abortion rhetoric.[12]

Ideology, as Russell Kirk noted, not only attempts to transform human nature but also to redesign society–to restructure it by elimination of whole classes of people as in the French Revolution that attacked the aristocracy and the clergy, by the annihilation of certain races of people as in Margaret Sanger's eugenics movement and Hitler's Germany, and by the wholesale slaughter of the innocents in a world that accepts abortion as a way of life. In the name of promoting a brave new world in the march toward utopia, ideology has overturned the most venerable institutions of civilization. It has corrupted the practice of medicine, the meaning of law, the purpose of education, and the integrity of the family. The Hippocratic Oath is no longer honored, the words of the 14th Amendment ("nor shall any state deprive any person of life, liberty, or property without due process of law") are contradicted, the National Education Association has committed itself to the abortion lobby, and the family is in a state of crisis.

The ideology that has condoned the killing of innocent children has also contributed to the unprecedented rise in child abuse, to a view of children as financial burdens and inconveniences, to the rise of day-care centers where children are abandoned for most of their waking hours, and to the popularity of euthanasia and Dr. Kevorkian's death machine. This substitution of ideology for natural law, religious truth, and ancient wisdom has produced trends and practices that destroy the family and undermine civilization. Former U.S. Education Secretary, William

Bennett has formulated a list of cultural indicators that reveal this transformation of culture and society since 1960. Here are the facts: there has been a 560% increase in violent crime, a 419% increase in illegitimate births, a quadrupling of divorces, a tripling of the percentage of children living in single-parent homes, more than a 200% increase in the teenage suicide rate, and a drop of almost 80 points in the SAT scores.[13]

Ideology has attempted to re-invent human nature and to reconstruct society by altering language, changing laws, and eradicating old traditions and norms; the wreckage of a world in ruins is the result. The aftermath of legalized abortion, like the fallout from the horrors of the French Revolution, Communism, and the Holocaust, is a moral wasteland in which nothing is sacred or revered and in which good and evil lose their meanings. Evil in all its insidious forms multiplies. While ideologues promote the abortion pill RU-486 and discuss overpopulation, Western nations are barely replacing themselves and are suffering the problems of under-population. While the economies of many nations face severe financial problems and tax burdens, whole generations of workers, consumers, taxpayers, school children, and human talent—a society's greatest resources—are being destroyed through abortion and depleting nations of the power of renewal. While parents clamor for school choice and tuition vouchers or elect to home school their children, the National Education Association supports abortion rights and the killing of the very children who constitute the future of education. This is the madness and senselessness of ideology: it is utterly out of contact with reality.

"By their fruits you shall know them." The fruits of abortion are cruelty, lies, greed, selfishness, self-destruction, and a culture of death that has led to the cancerous multiplication of evil. We have progressed from illegal abortion to legalized abortion, from the Freedom of Choice Act that ensures unlimited abortion-on-demand with no restrictions to RU-486 and partial birth abortions (infanticide). We have progressed from the view that abortion is sinful, immoral, and evil to the idea that abortion is a right and a way of life around which people organize their futures and careers, an argument that appeared in the *Casey* decision in 1992. We have progressed from teaching the virtue of chastity that eliminates the need for abortions to providing sex education courses that encourage "safe sex," premarital sexuality, and the need for legalized abortion to deal with the problem of unwanted pregnancies. The words of Edmund Burke in *Reflections on the Revolution in France* apply perfectly to America since 1973: "France has bought undignified calamities at a higher price than any nation has purchased the most unequivocal blessings. France has bought poverty with crime."[14] America too has bought poverty–the poverty of the culture of death and the poverty of a moral wasteland–and paid for it by wasting the richest of gifts and its most valuable treasure, her own children.

In the 19th century a French visitor to America, Alexis de Tocqueville, wrote a classic work entitled *Democracy in America,* in which he offered this prophetic statement: "America is great because America is good, and if America ever ceases to be good, America will cease to be great." In August of 1993 a Polish visitor from Rome, Karol Wojtyła (Pope John Paul II) also visited the United States and made a similar prophetic statement:

The ultimate test of your greatness is the way you treat every human being, but especially the weakest and most defenseless ones. The best traditions of your land presume respect for those who cannot defend themselves. If you want equal justice for all, and true freedom and lasting peace, then, America, defend life! All the great causes that are yours today will have meaning only to the extent that you guarantee the right to life and protect the human person. These great minds were not imposing their French or Polish or 19th century or religious opinions on modern Americans but appealing to the natural law, to the light of reason, to the power of conscience, and to the love of truth found in all men and women of good will.

NOTES

1. C. S. Lewis, *The Abolition of Man* (New York: The Macmillan Co., 1967) pp. 107-08.

2. John T. Noonan, Jr., ed. *The Morality of Abortion* (Cambridge: Harvard Univ. Press, 1972) p. 8.

3. Brian Clowes, "Choice and the Jewish People" in *HLI Reports* II/5, p. 9.

4. Sophocles, *Antigone*, tr. Campbell, as quoted in *Catholic Morality* by John Laux (Rockford: Tan, 1990) p. 10.

5. Bernard Nathanson, *The Silent Scream* (videotape).

6. Robert Marshall and Charles Donovan, *Blessed Are the Barren* (San Francisco: Ignatius Press, 1991) pp. 9, 7.

7. *Ibid.*, p. 18.

8. *Ibid.*, p. 9.

9. Clarissa Henry and Marc Hillel, *Of Pure Blood*, tr. Eric Mossbacher (New York: McGraw Hill, 1976) p. 149, as quoted in *Rachel Weeping: The Case Against Abortion* by James T. Burtchaell (San Francisco: Harper and Row, 1982) p. 174.

10. Warren Carroll, *Our Lady of Guadalupe* (Front Royal: Christendom Press, 1983) p. 8.

11. Russell Kirk, *The Politics of Prudence* (Bryn Mawr: Intercollegiate Studies Institute, 1993) pp. 1, 3.

12. Burtchaell, p. 152.

13. Quoted by Kenneth D. Whitehead, "Family Values, Moral Values" in *Catholic League Newsletter* (July-August 1993) pp. 7-8.

14. Edmund Burke, *Reflections on the Revolution in France* (New York: Penguin, 1986) p. 124.

Is *In Vitro* Fertilization
in accord with
a Symbolic Concept of Natural Law?

W. Jerome Bracken, C. P.

U SING A NATURAL LAW ETHICS, Lisa Sowle Cahill and Bruno Schüller conclude that the use of a reproductive technology can be moral. It is so when it protects the spousal relationship and bestows benevolent and beneficial results upon the couple and the child that is born.

In this article I will present their natural law arguments for upholding the morality of *in vitro* fertilization. Since these arguments do not address the multiple dimensions of the person, I propose that a new conception of natural law is needed, a symbolic one. Rahner's "theology of symbol" provides the basis for conceiving natural law this way. Using his theology to formulate a symbolic conception of natural law, I then examine the use of IVF. I consider its impact, first, on the love relationship of the couple, then on the embryo, and finally on the child that is born and in need of ego development. Considering that a couple might decide to forgo IVF, I briefly examine, from a symbolic view, the possible and positive consequences that could result from this decision. I conclude with the argument that a symbolic concept of natural law goes beyond the intentionalities of the moral actors and embraces the substantial realities of their persons and the persons they affect.

THE POSITIONS OF LISA SOWLE CAHILL AND BRUNO SCHÜLLER

Both Cahill and Schüller hold that using a reproductive technology accords with the distinctive quality of human nature, namely, reason.[1] Schüller argues that, when nature can no longer fulfill its reproductive purpose, it is reasonable and thus ethical to utilize a technology to attain that purpose.[2]   Moreover, such action confers a benefit upon its recipient, the child, who is given life. Cahill, while admitting that the use of artificial technologies is not an ideal way of relating love, sex and procreation,[3] nonetheless argues that it is not immoral but moral.

Cahill builds her argument for this conclusion with the following series of proposals. Natural law comes from rational reflection on experience.[4] Since this reflection occurs within an historical context[5] of one's own way of questioning and understanding things, the experience upon which one reflects should be that of contemporary couples themselves and should be based upon what is supplied by today's empirical sciences and medicine. This reflection should be aided by refined philosophical analysis and, as Catholic, should occur within the Church's tradition.[6] When people carry out this reflection, they can see that the dignity of the person lies in an exercise of freedom which, in the case of marriage, concerns "the interpersonal relationship of the couple."[7]   Supported by the Church's own but incomplete[8] paradigm-shift from seeing marital consent in terms of the "right over one another's body" to seeing it in terms of a partnership of the whole of the spouses' lives,[9] couples can readily conclude from their own experiences that the "interpersonal relationship" is primary.[10] Of the three values (love, sex, and procreation), the love relationship takes precedence.[11] First, love is in itself a personal value while the other two are in the category of "physical goods and values."[12] Second, the relationship is obviously more important than any particular acts in that relationship.[13] Thus, the act of procreation, whether it is by *in vitro* fertilization, which is a "manipulation of reproductive biology," or by sexual intercourse, which is a "biological manipulation of one (or both) of two persons,"[14] is moral and in accord with natural law as long as it does not cause an imbalance in the couple's marital relationship and does not undermine the couple's shared relation to their children and to the society at large.[15]

In this regard, both Cahill and Schüller see the person's dignity as residing in the power to reason and choose.[16] From these powers come expressions of personal love or expressions of selfishness.[17] So the use of one's body, which they see as an instrument of a person's freedom,[18] can communicate one's love or one's selfishness.[19] The same can be said for reproductive technologies; they can be instruments of love and of benevolence or of selfishness. In other words, instruments of procreation can become signs of love or of selfishness. All depends on the reason and free choice of the persons acting. When a person finds good reason for acting and that reason is supported by the consensus of others,[20] then one is being guided by natural law.

However, one needs to ask whether this way of conceiving natural law is adequate to the issues at hand. As Cahill underlines, we are talking about relationships. They are the relationships between the spouses themselves and between the spouses and the child. These relationships are multi-leveled: physical, spiritual, moral, and emotional. So one has to ask whether it is morally adequate to speak of sex and the reproductive technologies as simply instruments of these relationships. If not, then is it morally adequate to say that it is the intentions of the actors that make these instruments into personal signs of love or of selfishness? Or do we need a fuller view of human nature and its mode of being and acting to adequately describe and evaluate the kinds of actions couples do as both spouses and parents?

USING THE NOTION OF SYMBOL TO UNDERSTAND NATURAL LAW

I think we need more. Instead of seeing sex as a sign or an instrument of love, as Cahill and Schüller do, would it not be better to see it in the fuller context of being a symbol? If we did, would we not be encouraged to conceive natural law in terms of the symbolic reality of things? By conceiving natural law in terms of the symbolic aspect of reality rather than in the rationalistic terms of intentionalities and uses of instruments and signs to produce effects and convey meaning, a person can gain a far richer way of understanding human nature and of evaluating human acts.

Rahner's "Theology of Symbol" lays the basis for doing just that.[21] Rahner writes that "the body can and may be considered as the symbol, that is, as the symbolic reality of man."[22] In other words, the human nature that is common to all human beings operates as a symbolic reality. Moreover, in this same treatise, Rahner lays the basis for differentiating what is a sign from what is a symbol. [23]

After presenting some of Rahner's basic ideas to show how he builds on these to speak about the person and the human body in terms of symbol, I will demonstrate some of the ramifications of using Rahner's notion of symbol in evaluating the use of reproductive technologies.

Like a sign, a symbol is a reality by which we can know something else. This happens because there is an agreement between the two, either in themselves or because someone arbitrarily establishes the agreement.[24] Thus the red octagonal stop-sign stands for the order that one should stop the car at the intersection. But a symbol is more than a sign, more than a representation of something else. A symbol is an expression of that something else as it makes that present whereby it can be known and possessed.[25] When the expression is self-conscious, then "[t]he expression, that is, the 'symbol'" is primarily the "way of knowledge of self...[and of] possession of self."[26] It is also the way by which the self is known and possessed by another.[27]

Having explained 'symbol' in this way, Rahner then writes: "[T]he body can and may be considered as the symbol, that is, as the symbolic reality of man."[28] This is because that which makes the material being a human being is its soul.[29] The human body does not just represent the soul *as* living and thinking and choosing. The body *is* the presence of the soul in its material counterpart, giving the body life and powers of thinking, choosing and feeling. We know this, for when the soul departs from the body, the body no longer lives, thinks, chooses or feels.

But the body is more than a symbol of the human soul.[30] It is a symbol of the human person. While Rahner does not say this explicitly, one can draw this conclusion from a statement that he does make. In explaining how "the body...may be considered as the symbol...of man," he says that this "follows at once from the Thomist doctrine that the soul is the substantial form of the body."[31] The soul, in other words, does not just give life to the body but makes it a substantial individual. A substantial individual who has intelligence, according to the commonly accepted definition in scholastic philosophy, is a person, namely, "an individual substance of a rational human nature."[32] One can conclude, therefore, that the body is a symbol of the person.

There are certain corollaries that follow from this. The body is a symbol of the person, because the connection between the body and the person is intrinsic, not extrinsic. So when the spouses use their bodies in sexual intercourse to procreate a child, they not only express themselves outwardly but also make their persons present to one another and to the act of procreation itself. This makes their action very different from the action whereby a child is procreated through the instruments of reproductive technologies. Whereas the use of a reproductive technology can be the means by which the couple effect what they intend, namely, to procreate a child, the use of this technology does not make their persons present to each other and to the act of procreating. It cannot do this, because there is no intrinsic connection between the reproductive technology and the spouses.

Consequently, when Thomas likens the members of the body to instruments, as Schüller indicates, Thomas calls them *quaedam animae instrumenta*, but he does not simply call them instruments. That is, they are "like" (*quaedam*) instruments insofar as they are directed by a person's choice the way an instrument is directed by the agent using it, but they are not instruments *per se*. Instruments *per se* receive a power and a direction from the agent that uses them, but they do not make the person present. They cannot do so because they are not intrinsically related to the person.

In addition, the members of the spouses' bodies and the instruments of reproductive technology receive their direction differently. In the case of the spouse's bodies, the direction is coming from the intrinsic principles of the bodily members of the persons themselves. In the case of the use of technologies, the direction is coming from agents extrinsic to the spouses. In the sexual intercourse of the spouses, the causes of the direction are formal ones. In the use of reproductive technologies, the cause of direction is an efficient one. In sexual intercourse, the direction is coming first from the human form of the spouses and then from their natural inclinations,[33] which are vital, sexual and intellectual.[34] Reproductive technologies have no such inclinations. To the natural inclinations of the spouses that come from their human form (the soul) come the inclinations or appetites that arise from the other forms inward to the spouses. These are the forms grasped by the external senses of sight, touch, and so on, the forms grasped by the internal powers of common sense, imagination, memory and estimation,[35] and the forms grasped by the intellect. From these forms, taken together, come affective movements that are natural, sensible, emotional, and intellectual.[36] Moreover, all of these movements are expressive of the persons whose bodies are performing these actions. These movements are therefore personal and not just "physical," to use Cahill's description, or "animal," as some describe the bodily movements of the person.[37] Thus, the body with all its natural movements is an expression of the person and the way by which the person will fully realize himself or herself.[38] These inclinations are not made personal by the choice of the person, since they are already expressions of the substantial individual who is this person. What the person's choice does, when made according to a rightly formed conscience, is to perfect these personal inclinations. The person perfects these inclinations by consciously directing them to what is truly beneficial to the person and the person's nature.

So, it is the intrinsic relationship between the symbol and what it symbolizes that makes a symbol very different from a sign. Because of this intrinsic relationship there are reciprocal influences and changes that take place. This is not the case with signs. Signs like a letter or a poem can be an expression of one's self and can convey something of one's self to the other person. But, once written, there is no reshaping of one's self, of the message or of the one to whom the message is given. Being extrinsically connected to the person, the letter or poem cannot make the person present. The body, on the other hand, as symbol, makes the person present. Because the body is intrinsically connected to the person and because the body is composed of active and passive principles,[39] the person is capable of not only giving something to the other but of receiving something as well. Because of this bodily presence to one another, we can express ourselves to the other, change the situation, shape ourselves and the other, and be reshaped in the process. Our minds and hearts, imagination and feelings, our whole body modifies and is modified by whatever world of meaning and action we enter. Consequently the expressions the person makes in and through his or her body have a four-fold effect. They communicate the person outwardly, shape the person inwardly, change the situation, and make the person capable of being shaped by the one with whom one is communicating.

There are further consequences. Since the body is a symbol of the being, and particularly of the human being, our attitude towards our own body-self affects our attitude towards other human beings and their body-selves and *vice versa*. This will be shown later when we discuss attitudes towards infertility.

Also, because our bodies are symbolic realities, they play a constitutive role in human relationships. They can forge bonds that intentionalities and "sign-instruments" cannot. This is especially evident in the case of marriage. While it is true that the Catholic Church has long settled on its teaching that marriage is essentially constituted by the consent of the couple,[40] it does not teach that this bond cannot be broken.[41] What the Catholic Church does teach is that, when the marriage bond is symbolized by sexual intercourse, the marriage bond then becomes "absolutely indissoluble." When this occurs, no human reason is sufficient for dissolving such a bond.[42] This is the importance of one's body-self and body-self union. From this we can conclude that it would be against nature, against the natural law, to ignore the importance of our bodies. Unlike the angels, willy-nilly, our bodies, our body selves, are involved in our acts. Even the greatest intellectual endeavors cannot be carried on without our bodies, and when they are carried out, we cannot escape the fatigue that is in our bodies. We are inextricably one.

With this conception of natural law, the paper will endeavor to show that even though the use of *in vitro* fertilization for reproduction can achieve the shared purpose of the spouses, it bypasses by that very fact their mutual acceptance and love of each other in their individual or combined infertility. It will attempt to show that their using their bodies to express love for each other while using *in vitro* fertilization to procreate can set up an imbalance in their love relationship to each other which can be disruptive of their union. Third, it will attempt to show how the decision to use *in vitro* fertilization not only puts the child being conceived at risk but also puts the child at risk in attaining his or her personal identity.

IN VITRO FERTILIZATION AND LOVING ACCEPTANCE

When we initially think of *in vitro* fertilization and other reproductive technologies, we naturally think of those couples who love each other dearly and long to seal that love with a child of their own but cannot do so because of infertility. Our heart goes out to them. Spontaneously, we look for some way of removing their pain. Even a miracle would do. It is no wonder, then, that we see this miracle in the reproductive technologies only recently developed. They provide a way of bypassing the couples' problem of infertility and of obtaining for them what they have longed for, a child of their own bodies. And so this technology, even though it involves injections, surgeries, repeated cycles, and substantial fees, is seen as the couples' savior. It is not hard to understand why couples, burdened with their own infertility, embrace this miracle of modern science and are willing to suffer the psychological and economic costs to pay for its promise of a child for them.

However, these costs are often more than the couples themselves realize. For instance, when they choose to bypass their infertility, they are bypassing a good part of themselves as well. They might think that one means of reproduction can be exchanged for another, but in the process of doing this they are making an implicit judgment about their own bodies. In order to provide the gametes for *in vitro* fertilization, the wife must put aside her feelings, undergo a series of injections to bring the eggs to maturity, submit to laparoscopy so that the eggs can be harvested for the fertilization process, and receive the newly fertilized egg as a transplant to her womb. On his part, the husband masturbates his genitals to provide the seed for the fertilization. In going through these processes the couples have to treat their bodies not as their own body-selves but as things to be mined and manipulated so that the precious gametes can be obtained and placed together to produce their child. In going through this, couples involve themselves in a whole series of bodily and emotional activities that treat their own bodies as if they were no different from the instruments that will be used to procreate their child. Taken together, these activities say back to the couple that what happens to their own bodies and psyche is not so important as long as the technological instrument of reproduction works. Symbolically, their body-selves are given less importance than the end-result.

In the process of doing this, they are putting aside the very pain that prompted them to do these things in the first place, their infertility. But infertility is not just a fact; it is a condition of their body-persons. When the husband and wife seek to get around this fact by a reproductive technology, they ignore this truth about themselves. It is a truth that can carry with it a very deep wound to their sense of self, as both the Hebrew and Greek Testaments testify in their stories of Sarah, Hannah, Elizabeth, and others. When couples seek to pass over this fact about themselves and to use a reproductive technology, they ignore a wound that lies deep within them. In doing so they experience neither their own love nor their spouse's love for them despite this fact. As least Hannah, in her infertility, heard Ilkanah tell her that he loved her more than the wife who bore him children. Without this acceptance from one's spouse and from one's self as well, the spouses can find themselves going through the difficult processes of *in vitro* fertilization not because of love but because of shame or guilt over their infertility.

By treating their bodies as an instrument and as one that has failed at procreation, couples symbolize, if not to their conscious level, at least to their unconscious a double alienation. There is their alienation from the truth about themselves and the alienation from their own body-selves as they treat them as instruments rather than as parts of themselves. In addition, when they ignore these truths about their own body-selves, they leave this particular wound of theirs untended. Neither spouse realizes that the wound is there and is in need of healing and neither spouse realizes that his or her partner is in need of healing as well. Should success come in their having a child this way, it will be difficult for them to acknowledge the wound that still remains.

There is another wound as well that can occur. It comes from the experience that couples have when there is a miscarriage after the embryo is transferred to the womb. This can happen two or three cycles in a row, each of which can cause real grief to the couples. But they push on, not realizing that they are going through two or three grievings within the space of time of one miscarriage of a fertile couple. One psychologist, speaking at a seminar in the Camden diocese, said that this has become a serious problem for couples trying to have a child by way of *in vitro* fertilization. In "Parental Grief Response to Perinatal Death," Smith and Borgers report that the tendency to blame self for death reaches a mean of 55.19 for mothers and 45.72 for fathers.[43] They also report that the type of loss, miscarriage, stillbirth, and infant death did not make a difference in grieving.[44] And John De Frain and associates report that recovery from a still-born death is very slow.[45]

What can cover over these experiences, however, is the couple's physical love-making itself. By it, they symbolize that they do love, accept, and care for each other. However, this act clashes with the symbolic meaning of their other acts directed to the use of the reproductive technology. On the one hand, they experience a closeness to one another in their love-making. On the other hand, they experience a distancing from their own body-persons and one another as they seek to procreate a child through the agency of others.

By the time the child is born, a serious imbalance can be set up within their shared loved experience. As spouses their love for each other is a body-and-soul person-to-person love. They act in complete freedom, towards themselves and towards each other. Theirs is not the payment of a debt but a freely offered gift. In their love relationship as parents, however, it is different. As parents their love for each other involves only their soul, that is, they agree on the same goal and means. As parents their love of the child involves only a bit more than their souls–besides their intention to procreate, they offer their gametes. They do not offer their bodies nor do they make themselves present in the act of procreation as they had done in their act of spousal love. Between the parents and the child there are other people who actually take over the procreative process. What binds parent and child together is not the loving act expressive of a gift between the spouses but a loving act that is expressive of a contractual duty between parents and procreators. Consequently, the two modes by which the couples express their marital relationships are vastly different. The spousal mode is wholly personal, self-giving, and free; the parental mode is partly personal, self-distancing, and financially obligatory. This can cause a serious imbalance in the way the couple relate to one another as they look toward the good of each other and their child. So, even according to Cahill's standard for ethical behavior, the use of the reproductive technology falls short of preserving and protecting the marital bond.

REPRODUCTIVE TECHNOLOGY AND THE BENEFIT TO THE CHILD

But what of the child that is begotten? Is the child's well-being the purpose of the act? Schüller says yes.[46] Without the use of this reproductive technology, there would be no child; with its use, the child receives the gift of his or her own existence.

But, before concluding that the use of reproductive technology is ethical from the standpoint that the child is benefitted, we must examine the kind of existence into which the child is brought. Abstractly we can say that being is always good; nonetheless, we do not recommend that a child be born without enough food to nourish him or her or without the security of caring parents who will not only beget the child but raise the child to adulthood. We do not recommend that unmarried couples beget children so that others who want a child but cannot have them can adopt them. We know instinctively that putting a child through this kind of experience is not good, no matter how much we want the adopting parents to have a child. Actually, when parents adopt, they are not acting to make it worse for the child but to overcome some of the things that were missing when the child was begotten–a secure home, parents who could not only love but raise the child, and so on.

Although the married couple who can afford to use the reproductive technology fall under neither of the above mentioned categories, we still have to examine what kind of environment the use of a reproductive technology places the child in.

With *in vitro* fertilization, the child comes into being in a petri dish, not in the mother's womb. Its environment is dangerous. Even if the possibility of contamination is lessened, the child as a fertilized egg is far from the mother's body and love and in the hands of those who are genetically strangers to him or her and whose commitment is neither parental nor familial but professional and contractual. Considering that all the embryos are human beings and not some other kind of living being, we have to look at the fate of not just the one who is brought to term by birth but at the fate of each one from the moment of fertilization. Each one is fated with many possibilities. Some of these possibilities are good, some bad.

Melissa Moore Bodin provides a personal account of what happens to the embryos in the *Newsweek* essay "My Turn: Eggs, Embryos and I."[47] After giving up contraception and then experiencing three ectopic pregnancies, she and her husband tried IVF.   Of the 11 embryos, she conceived one child, losing five and freezing five. A few years later she conceived twins, having started with 18 embryos. Of these, she lost ten, and had six frozen, waiting, as she describes it, to be destroyed or adopted. So, of the 23 conceived, 3 made it to birth (13%), 6 are still frozen (26%) and 14 were lost (60%). Mrs Bodin's 13% who made it, corroborates the 10-to-30% that Dr. Marian Damewood says are implanted in the mother's womb.[48] For a specialized group, those women under 40 and without male factor infertility, 25.6% of the embryos become live-birth deliveries.[49] *The Chicago Tribune* reports that in a survey of 300 centers in the U.S. 32% of the cycles of assisted reproductive technology issued in babies, in 1996.[50] Nonetheless, we need to pay attention to what is not said in these success figures. What is not said is the number of embryos actually created–it is presumably a much higher number than those actually transferred since not all embryos are transferred to the womb. Some are discarded, some frozen, some used for experimentation. But even if we ignore this fact, we need to also recognize that even with the high figures of success reported by Couvares and *The Chicago Tribune*, between 63.4 and 68% of the embryos involved in the transfer or reproductive cycle never make it to birth. Even when infertile couples are treated medically or surgically, their loss of pregnancy by miscarriage is only between 20 and 30%.[51] Deliberately to place a individual human being in a situation where it has a 63 to 68 % chance of not making it is unfair to the child.

And what of those who do make it? Are they affected psychologically by this? It would seem not, unless a protein within the embryonic cell becomes a memory-chip later on. Nonetheless, a child and later an adult can come to know of his or her beginnings. He can come to know that in his beginning his parents put him at great risk for survival. How would he feel in knowing that he was put at such risk so that his parents could obtain their goal of having a child of their own genes? Also, what happens when the child or the adult thinks of the embryos that were lost in the process? Were they not lost, they could be his brothers or his sisters. It has been shown that when the sibling who died was known, that sibling "was generally of great importance to the survivor."[52] It has also been shown that many siblings feel guilt over the loss of a brother or sister and that for some this has "arisen out of a basic belief that to survive was to do so at another's expense."[53] Could the child born by this process have similar feelings and be disturbed by them? Would he or she feel foolish at raising these problems, since it was only some embryos that were lost and many people consider them as non-persons anyway? To what extent this would cause suffering in the child born this way, we do not know. It would have to be studied.

THE CHILD'S EGO DEVELOPMENT

There is one more question to ask. Would such a process affect the child's ego development? The Vatican document *Donum Vitae* argues that it would.[54] While believing that one's origin came about because one's parents desired him so much that they were willing to procreate him through the agency of others, the child could still sense some negativity about his origins. Like others born of loving parents the child's birth would have been one of initial pain but final joy. However, the *in vitro* child's conception would have been different. Instead of arising from a joyful and pleasurable exchange between the parents, his or her conception would have been preceded by a contractual exchange between parents and the technicians and the inevitable discomfort and anxiety that comes from undergoing the reproductive procedures. While a child and later an adult can come to appreciate the value of something by knowing its great costs, the child and later the adult could well want to feel that his or her origin in the world was not a costly but a pleasurable and joyful experience. The child might prefer that his or her origin came from a loving act between his parents that was pleasurable and bonded them bodily rather than from an act that was not their own and was separate from them. The child might well feel more secure in knowing that the bond between himself or herself and the parents was not forged in the moral and financial commitments that the parents made to have a child, but was constituted by the sheer pleasure that his or her origin brought about. Just as a marriage bond is stronger when it is pleasurable as well as moral, so too can one expect that the parent-child bond is stronger for the same reasons.

But there might be some other reasons why the ego development of the child would be affected. To put this in perspective, we need to consider what Erik Erickson says about the child's ego development into adulthood and how it applies to people in general before seeing a particular application.[55]

According to Erickson, a child's personal identity depends on a series of interactions with others, beginning with his or her parents. In these interactions, the child learns to establish who he or she is and to situate himself or herself in the world. For this to happen the child must successfully resolve various conflicts about himself and his relationships to others and the world. When children are successful in resolving these conflicts and growing into adulthood, they come to a trust in themselves and in the world rather than a distrust, a sense of their own autonomy rather than a doubt about themselves, a desire to initiate relationships rather than a feeling of guilt for doing so, a resolve to be industrious rather than settling for inferiority, an establishment of their own personal identity and the roles they play in the world rather than a confusion about them, a movement towards intimacy rather than a flight into isolation, and finally an achievement of generativity for others rather than a sterile stagnation.

How the mother and father respond to their child in these interactions can either help or hinder the child in its ego development. But properly responding to their child is not just a matter of the parents thinking about what they should do and doing it. Much more is involved. These interactions are extremely subtle and often whole-body reactions. A mother's smile at her baby, for instance, can generate a smile in the child, whereas an expression of displeasure in the child can generate a similar reaction in the mother.[56] And such interactions are not limited to the mother; they can involve the father as well. Often the interactions are spontaneous—the smile on the face, the warm embrace, the words spoken and the feelings generated in the exchange. Whether subtle and spontaneous or patiently contemplated, these interactions between parent and child become the means by which the child resolves or does not resolve the conflicts involved in his or her ego development. The reason for this is that the child's conflict situations are unlike Kohlberg's moral dilemmas, which can be resolved by ever more sophisticated forms of reasoning. Rather, the conflicts are emotional in content. They are the result of the child encountering at the psychological level the symbolic nature of his being. Where spirit meets matter, meaning is joined to feeling so that they become inextricably one. So the parents must be ready to respond to their child in the same way. It is not enough for the parents to respond only intellectually and according to plan or only in terms of the feelings of the moment. The response has to be intellectual and emotional, both for the short and for the long term.

Consequently, parents who have never developed a total-person way of responding to situations are at a disadvantage. They can only respond to part of what is going on within their child and can provide guidance only for that part. Those who have developed full-body responses in life, on the other hand, can best help their child. They can provide simultaneously the sensitivity and the knowledge that the child needs.

Let me use an example of what I mean by examining what Erickson describes as the first stage in the child's ego-development. In this stage the child must negotiate between a trusting and distrusting stance towards the world. The child can come to a trusting stance towards the world when what he feels within corresponds with the outside world's response to him. Should his parents respond to his discomfort, he develops a sense that his inner world is connected with the world around him. Should his parents remedy his discomfort, he develops a sense that the world can be a friendly environment. Should his parents respond to him in a consistent way, even if not always immediately, he develops a sense that he can trust the world. Depending on what happens in these exchanges between himself and the outside, the child gains or loses the assurance that his "reading" of his inner and outer world is correct and trustworthy and that he as a person is "O.K."

Of the parents this requires not only a felt sensitivity of the moment but also a firmness of purpose in their multiple activities of raising their child, taking care of the household, earning a living, fulfilling social obligations, and worshiping God. If parents only respond at the feeling level, meeting the child's need when their own feelings are positive, but not meeting his need when they are not in the mood, the child becomes saddened and resentful. Such on-and-off responses to his needs confuse the child and undermine the child's assurance that he can trust himself and the world around him. On the other hand, if parents only respond at the planned and reasonable level but not at the feeling level, the child can experience that his or her feelings have no say in the world.

Consequently, to respond adequately to the child's need, parents have to shape themselves to the point where feelings and plans have equal value and make a whole. Then, when parents make spontaneous decisions about their child's needs, these decisions will intuitively address both the feelings of the child and the parents' own firm purposes.

Parents can develop this capacity of attending to both things simultaneously by making multiple little decisions in their own lives along these lines. But parents can also hinder this development in making full body responses when they themselves make decisions that separate thoughts from feelings or persons from goals. In other words, the decisions of our past not only can carry their external effects into the present but also can shape us and dispose us to make similar kinds of decisions in the present.

It is this possibility that leads me to argue that the kind of decision the parents make in order to have a child through *in vitro* fertilization not only can bring their child into being but also can condition them in the ways they respond to the child as they seek to help the child grow. I say this because we can shape ourselves into being a certain way not only by a series of similar decisions along the same path but also by very significant decisions. For instance, the engaged spouses shape themselves for marriage by all the little decisions they make through this engagement period. Nonetheless, there is one radical decision they make that can either seal their commitment or unseal it. And that is the decision to stand before others and make their vows to one another and before God. The wedding day becomes not just another day, but a day that sets their destiny.

It appears to me, from the descriptions that couples give about their decision and its execution in having a child through *in vitro* fertilization, that this kind of decision is one of those radical ones that can readily shape their attitudes and ways of acting. To carry out their purpose to have a child through a reproductive technology, the couple often have to separate their sexual feelings for one another from their plans to have a child. They have to separate their feelings about the procedures which at times can be quite negative from the goal that the procedure promises, having a child. While these separations are directed only to achieving the goal of having a child, they can perdure even after the goal has been attained. This can happen since couples must set aside their feelings as they go through the whole process of ovulation induction, oocyte retrieval, sperm procurement, oocyte fertilization, and embryo transfer. Setting aside their feelings for their goal is not something that is done only for a moment. Each fertility attempt takes from 48 to 72 hours. And couples repeat this for three to five fertility cycles. By steeling themselves to do this, they consciously and even unconsciously shape themselves into thinking and feeling that such a separation is acceptable since it is for a good goal. This disposes them to think and feel that the denial of one's feelings for the achievement of certain goals is something that can and should be done. They can carry this over when they spontaneously deal with their child's needs and their own purposes. In the same way that they accustomed themselves to set aside their own feelings to fulfill their plans, they can spontaneously set aside their child's feelings at that moment as they seek to fulfill the purpose at hand. Since so many exchanges between parent and child are spontaneous and not thought out, the parents can make these separations many times. So, when the responses are inconsistent, the child develops the sense that the world cannot be trusted. Or, if his feelings of the moment are so often ignored, he can come to believe his own feelings are unimportant in the scheme of things. This can carry over and be reinforced when the child goes through others stages of development, for instance, when he seeks to initiate a special relationship with mother or father and believes that performance, not feelings, are the only things that count. For these things not to happen, the couple would have to make concerted efforts to reverse their own tendency of separating feelings from plans.

THE DECISION OF THE CHILDLESS COUPLE

If a childless couple were to recognize that they should not use reproductive technologies, then what? What would be the good they would choose? To answer this question in a way that is proportionate to what has already been written would require another article. But some things, though needing elaboration, can be said that would be supportive of such a couple. First, by choosing not to harm themselves or the child for the sake of being parents, they would be establishing their own moral integrity. This would happen because they would be choosing what they judge to be true and good over what they judged to be more satisfying. It would not be easy, however. It would bring with it a great deal of sorrow for they would be giving up their goal of having their own genetically related child. But they could help each other in this sorrow. They would know what their sorrow was about and they would be able to sympathize with one another. In supporting one another in this sorrow, they would be giving each other the assurance that they are loved and accepted. This loving acceptance could have even deeper meaning for, as they express it to each other, they would be expressing it as regards their whole persons. It would even embrace the fact that their loss is due to their own infertility. But with the total body acceptance of their particular loss, they would be symbolically accepting the other in his or her particular loss. Such loving acceptance could be healing of the shame or guilt that either or both might be experiencing because of their infertility. Coming to this personal and mutual acceptance of one another can have other ramifications as well. In the eighth stage of growth, of which Erickson speaks, the stage after the intimacy and the generativity stages, there is the integrity stage. People come to this stage of development, writes Erickson, when they come to accept the whole of their past history, its successes and failures, its perfections and its defects. They integrate these opposites into a unity. No longer conflicted, such persons not only can experience a harmony within but can communicate it outwards. When they act, their thoughts and feelings are in harmony with what they judge to be good.

Consequently, people can trust them. Erickson sees people of this kind as able to foster growth in others. This is what he writes:

Trust (the first of our ego values) is here defined as "the assured reliance on another's integrity" (the last of our values).... And it seems possible to further paraphrase the relation of adult integrity and infantile trust by saying that healthy children will not fear life if their elders have integrity enough not to fear death.[57]

Couples who have come to terms with their own incapacity of begetting new life from their own bodies truly have "integrity enough not to fear death." Such couples can become for society a haven for trust. When these couples move beyond themselves and express their parenthood through their caring for others, their inner integrity will be a trust bulwark around which others can grow. When this occurs, something more than what is observed could be going on as well. Considering that St. Paul saw in the love of husband and wife for one another a symbol of Christ's love,[58] the couples who make a moral choice not to harm one another or expose any children to harm symbolically express Christ's love. By this I do not mean that they provide a modern example of self sacrifice; rather, I mean that their actions can be expressions of Christ's self-sacrificing and redeeming love itself. Such is Paul's conviction. To understand how it would be possible, we would have to elaborate the connections between the natural symbolism of marriage and its supernatural sacramentality. Nonetheless, infertile couples who forgo the natural satisfaction of having their own child for what is and what they judge to be morally right, open themselves to these good things: a moral and psychological integrity that can generate human develop- ment in another because of their trustworthiness and that can be saving for others, because the couples' lives express a divine as well as a human reality.

CONCLUSION

As we have seen, Cahill and Schüller have been able to construct natural law arguments that justify the use of *in vitro* fertilization by spouses who are infertile. For these two ethicists and theologians, acting according to natural law can be reduced to acting according to right reason. Using IVF accords with natural law, since it is reasonable to use it for procreation when couples are infertile. Morally speaking, they say, there is no difference between sexual intercourse and *in vitro* fertilizations. They are both apt instruments to effect the procreation of a child. When directed to loving and not selfish ends they constitute a good act. According to Cahill, this benefits the couple for they can realize their shared goal of having a child genetically like themselves; according to Schüller, it benefits the child by conferring life on the child. Provided the use of IVF is for love and not selfishness and provided that its use does not disturb the primary value of the marriage relationship, the partnership of love between the spouses, it is good.

In my response, I suggested that this rationalistic concept of natural law, which situates morality in the intentionalities of the actor and considers sexual intercourse or *in vitro* fertilization as instruments of these intentionalities, is not adequate to the situation at hand. Cahill intuitively recognizes this when she puts such emphasis on the marriage relationship. She is concerned about how the spouses lovingly relate to each other, to the child, and to the society at large. But relationships involve more than the free acts and good relationships involve more than love and the use of "physical goods" or "instruments" to achieve the goals of that love. Relationships involve the subjects in those relationships–not only the actors but those acted upon, not only the actors as acting but as acted upon. All of these things have moral significance. Moreover, besides the two spouses and their relationship to one another, there is the mutual relationship between them as parents and the child. The mutuality of this second relationship is underway long before the child reaches his own discernment and free choice. The child's body and his or her emotional and intelligent responses are deeply affected by the parents' choices even though they are not subject to any choice on the child's part. Something similar can be said for the spouses: their body and their emotional and intelligent responses deeply affect their own choices, and they are deeply affected by their choices and affect their future choices.

To describe sex as an instrument to achieve procreation and as a physical value that must be "...subsumed under the interpersonal meanings in order to have moral intelligibility..." does not adequately address the moral significance of the bodies and feelings of the child and the spouses as they relate to each other.[59] To describe sex as simply a physical value and as an instrument to be used does not match the long-standing notion in the Catholic tradition that persons are "individual substances of a rational nature," which is a body constituted by a spiritual and material principle.[60]

What does match this notion of person and what does address both the active and passive aspects of human nature and human actions are Rahner's two notions about the human body. First, that the "body...[is] the symbolic reality of man"[61] which "comes to...its self-fulfillment"[62] as "a being [that] realizes itself in its own intrinsic 'otherness' (which is constitutive of its being)." [63] Second, that the body is a symbolic reality of the person because the "soul is the substantial form of the body."[64]

From this symbolic concept of human nature, one can argue that whatever protects or advances the symbolic reality of the human person in his or her body and relationships to others is moral and that whatever undermines the symbolic reality of the human person and his or her relationships to others is not according to natural law. I have given reasons for saying that the use of *in vitro* fertilization undermines the symbolic nature of the human body, the symbolic reality of human love between the spouses, and the symbolic reality of human love between the parents and child.

Using IVF as just another instrument of procreation, alienates the persons from their own bodies. Ignoring the wound of infertility by going after the use of IVF for procreation alienates the person further from his or her own body and the body of the other person. While acts of sexual intercourse between the spouses build up the symbolic reality and understanding of their love relationship with each other, acts of using IVF in procreation do not build up the symbolic reality and understanding of their love relationship with their child. Subjecting their bodies to what has to be done in order for *in vitro* fertilization to take place and putting aside their emotions in the process symbolically expresses that the bodily and pleasurable aspects of love in procreation are not important. This dichotomy sets up a serious imbalance in the way the spouses love each other as spouses and love each other as parents. Regarding the child, the use of *in vitro* fertilization does not express care for the child because it puts the child at a vastly greater risk than a child conceived through sexual intercourse. The child's later knowledge of such action can undermine its feelings and even thoughts about his or her own self worth. Unlike adoption, which tries to make up for such losses, the use of IVF to have a child exposes the child to such losses. In addition, the spouses' attitudes about their own bodies and emotions when procreating a child can have an effect as they seek to raise the child and grow in his or her ego identity. Because the parents have symbolically expressed to themselves that the body and its pleasures are of secondary importance when it comes to begetting the child, they are disposed to approach raising their child with this same kind of attitude. Unless they make many conscious efforts to undo this way of thinking and feeling, they will be ill disposed when it comes to spontaneously helping the child develop his or her sense of self.

Should the couple accept themselves in their own infertility, then they lay the groundwork for healing each other of their losses and of establishing themselves as trustworthy carers and mediators of love for others.

In short, to preserve rather than harm the goodness of the spouses and to help rather than prevent the development of that goodness, we are called to attend to the full dignity of the person. The dignity of the person arises not only from that person's free choice's, as Cahill and Schüller affirm, but also from the person's own body and the bodies of others, as this paper has sought to demonstrate.

NOTES

1. Aquinas, *Summa theologiae*, 1-2. 94. 2

2. Bruno Schüller, "Paraenesis and Moral Argument" in *Gift of Life: Catholic Scholars Respond to the Vatican Instruction*, eds. Edmond D. Pellegrino, John C. Harvey and John P. Langan (Washington, D.C.: Georgetown Univ. Press, 1990). Reading what Schüller writes prior (pp. 87-92) and subsequent (pp. 92-98) to his question (p. 92: "Is it inconceivable that God has provided man with

reason and understanding also so that he, by himself, may endeavor to find out how to succeed when natural measures prove a failure?"), I gather that his answer is "No."

3. Lisa Sowle Cahill, "What is the nature of the Unity of Sex, Love, and Procreation? A Response to Elio Sgreccia" in *Gift of Life*, p. 141.

4. *Ibid.*, p. 144

5. *Ibid.*, p. 138.

6. *Ibid.*, p. 145

7. *Ibid.*, p. 139

8. *Ibid.*, pp. 140-142. Cahill sees this paradigm-shift as incomplete, for, although, *Gaudium et Spes* and the *Code of Canon Law* (1983) speak of marriage as a partnership directed to the whole of the couple's life, the Church still holds on to setting norms for particular actions of the body rather than for the marriage relationship itself. It should be pointed out, however, that Cahill goes further than *Gaudium et Spes* by giving primacy to the spousal relationship. She writes that "the procreative relationship of parent to child is...a great and precious good" but "not an absolute value," and so it is right that the "the love commitment of spouses sets reasonable humane and Christian parameters" to it *(ibid.*, p. 147). Cahill does not indicate that the love commitment to the offspring should also set parameters for the spouses, whereas *Gaudium et Spes* says that the "intimate union (of the spouses) as well as the good of the children imposes total fidelity on the spouses..."(#48).

9. *Ibid.*, p. 140

10. *Ibid.,* p. 142.

11. *Ibid.*

12. *Ibid.*

13. *Ibid.*

14. *Ibid.*, p. 143.

15. *Ibid.*, pp. 141, 142, 147. "The first feature of the emerging paradigm is that the partnership of the couple is the basic category; the partnership opens out onto family and society." "If there is an inviolable value in the triad of love, sex, and procreation, it is clearly the value which is in and of itself a personal one: love." The "valid unity among them...[is] the marital relationship." "Even

within marriage, the use of technology must be judged in relation to the love and commitment of spouses, and by its effects on their relationship."

16. *Ibid.*, p. 139.

17. Schüller, "Paraenesis and Moral Argument," p. 88.

18. Cahill, "The Unity of Sex, Love and Procreation," p. 143; Schüller, "Paraenesis and Moral Argument," p. 93. Schüller argues that not just "conception *in vitro*" can be described as a "biological technique" but so can sexual intercourse. He refers to a quote from Thomas's *Summa contra gentiles* III, 126, which speaks of a member of the human body as *quaedam animae instrumenta*.

19. *Ibid.*, p. 86.

20. Cahill, "The Unity of Sex, Love and Procreation," p. 144.

21. Karl Rahner, S.J., "The Theology of Symbol" in *Theological Investigations*, vol. 4: *More Recent Writings*, tr. Kevin Smyth (Baltimore: Helicon Press, 1966), pp. 231-52.

22. *Ibid.*, p. 246. Rahner also writes: "It is well known that in every human expression, mimetic, phonetic, *etc.*, in nature, the whole man is somehow present and expressing himself, though the expressive form is confined to one portion of the body to start with" (*ibid.*, p. 248). It appears that Rahner sees the body and its members as a symbol of the whole and substantial human being, rather than as an instrument of the person. Why then does Schüller characterize the reproductive parts of the human body as instruments if, according to Richard A. McCormick, S.J., Schüller follows Rahner's anthropology? See "Some Early Reactions to *Veritatis Splendor*" in *John Paul II and Moral Theology: Readings in Moral Theology, No. 10*, ed. Charles E. Curran and Richard A. McCormick, S.J. (New York/Mahwah, NJ: Paulist Press, 1998), pp. 9-10.

23. *Ibid.,* pp. 231-52.

24. *Ibid.*, p. 225.

25. *Ibid.*, pp. 224-25.

26. *Ibid.*, p. 230.

27. *Ibid.*, p. 225.

28. *Ibid.*, p. 246.

29. *Ibid.*, p. 247. "What we call the body," he says, "is nothing else than the actuality of the soul itself in the 'other' of *materia prima.*"

30. *Ibid.*

31. *Ibid.*, p. 246.

32. Thomas, *Summa Theologica*, 1.29.1. This definition is from Boëthius's work, *De Duabus Naturis*. Thomas also writes that although the soul of the human species "may exist in a separate state, yet since it ever retains its nature of unibility, it cannot be called an individual substance, which is the hypostasis or first substance, as neither can the hand nor any other part of man; thus neither the definition nor the name of person belongs to it." *Ibid.* 1.29.1.5m.

33. Thomas Aquinas, *Summa theologiae*, 1.80.1: "To make this evident, we must observe that some inclination follows every form; ...therefore this natural form is followed by a natural inclination, which is called the natural appetite."

34. *Ibid.,* 1-2.94.2.

35. *Ibid.*, 1.78.4.

36. Bernard F. Lonergan, who changed from speaking about psychological activity in terms of forms and movements to speaking about them in terms of the cognitive operations of experience, understanding, judgment, and decision, nonetheless recognizes that there is an affective movement that flows from these cognitional activities. See p. 65 when he speaks about feelings and p. 115 when he speaks about love being connected with a judgment of value in his book, *Method In Theology* (New York: Herder and Herder, 1972).

37. Rahner, "The Theology of the Soul," p. 247. While Rahner acknowledged that there are empirical objections to the affirmation of such a close unity between the body and the human person, he makes his final assertion: "Hence, we may formulate in our theory of symbols the principle that the body is the symbol of the soul, in as much as it is formed as the self-realization of the soul, though it is not adequately this, and the soul renders itself present and makes its' appearance' in the body which is distinct from it."

38. Rahner, "The Theology of Symbol," p. 234. "The symbol strictly speaking (symbolic reality) is the self realization of a being in the other, which is constitutive of its essence."

39. *Ibid.*, p. 245. Since Rahner sees his notion of the body as symbol as directly related to the Thomist concept of the body, it seems proper to use Thomas's other notions of the body as it relates to natural law, namely, his notion of the

active and passive qualities of human nature and of human operations. Thomas defines natural law as the human participation in the Eternal Law of God. He writes, "There are two ways in which a thing is subject to the eternal law...first by partaking of the eternal law by way of knowledge; secondly, by way of action and passion, *i.e.*, by partaking of the eternal law by way of an inward motive principle.... But since the rational nature, together with that which it has in common with all creatures, has something proper to itself inasmuch as it is rational, consequently, it is subject to the eternal law in both ways; because while each rational creature has some knowledge of the eternal law.... It also has a natural inclination to that which is in harmony with the eternal law" (*Summa theologiae*, 1-2.93.6). In regards actions, Thomas writes: "But a certain agent is to be found, in which there is both the active and passive principle of its act, as we see in human acts.... For everything that is passive and moved by another is disposed by the action of the agent: wherefore, if the acts be multiplied a certain quality is formed in the power which is passive and moved, which quality is called a habit" (*Ibid.*, 1-2.51.2).

40. In the chapter, "The Unity of Sex, Love, and Procreation," Cahill classifies "sex and procreation" as "physical goods and values" and sets in opposition to them, "love," which she classifies as a "personal" value. Consequently, she writes that "physical goods and values can have an important relation to human relationships, but they are expressive and contributory rather than fundamentally constitutive of such relationships" (p. 142).

41. *Codex Iuris Canonici (Code of Canon Law*, 1983), c. 1142.

42. Only for the supernatural reason of one's faith can a consummated marriage be dissolved and that is only on the condition that the original marriage was not between two baptized persons. *Ibid.*, cc. 1141, 1142, 1143, 1150.

43. Anne Clark Smith and Sherry B. Borgers, "Parental Grief Response to Perinatal Death," *Omega* 19/3 (1988-89) 297.

44. *Ibid.*, pp. 209, 212.

45. "The Psychological Effects of Stillbirth on Surviving Family Members," *Omega* 22/2 (1990-1991) 102-03.

46. Schüller, "Paraenesis and Moral Argument," pp. 89, 90. Begetting the child is an act of beneficence. Even when it is done through technicians, the child is still treated as a an end and not a means.

47. *Newsweek* (28 July 1997).

48. "Current Technology of *in vitro* Fertilization and Alternate Forms of Reproduction" in *Gift of Life*, p. 120.

49. John L. Couvares reported this figure on the Internet, February 10, 1997.

50. *Chicago Tribune* (May 5, 1999), Section 8, pp. 1, 2, 8.

51. Cvetkovich, "The Reproductive Technologies: A Scientific Overview" in *The Gift of Life: The Proceedings of a National Conference on the Vatican Instruction on Reproductive Ethics and Technology*, eds. Marilyn Wallace, R.S.M., Ph. D. And Thomas W. Hilgers, M.D. (Omaha: Pope Paul VI Institute Press, 1990), p. 8.

52. Joanna H. Fanos, *Sibling Loss* (Mahwah: Lawrence Erlbaum Associates, 1996), p. 34.

53. *Ibid.*, p. 113.

54. Congregation for the Doctrine of the Faith, *Instruction on Respect for Human Life in Its Origin and on the Dignity of Procreation: Replies to Certain Questions of the Day* [*Donum Vitae*, 1987] (Boston: St. Paul Editions, n.d.). Under the section on heterologous artificial fertilization the document states that "it is through the secure and recognized relationship to his own parents that the child can discover his own *identity and achieve his own proper human development*" (II, A, 1). In the section on homologous fertilization, the document states: "Such fertilization entrusts the life and *identity* of the embryo into the powers of doctors and biologists and establishes the domination of technology over the origin and destiny of the human person" (II, B, 5), italics mine.

55. Erik H. Erickson, "Eight Stages of Man," *Childhood and Society*, 2nd ed., revised and enlarged (New York: W. W. Norton & Co., 1963).

56. In *Developmental Psychology: Childhood and Adolescence,* 3rd ed. (Pacific Grove: Brooks/Cole Publ. Co., 1993), p. 410, David Shaffer (in referring to Hornik's and Gunner's study of social reference) writes: "A mother's pained expression and accompanying vocal concern might immediately suggest that the knife is one's hand is an implement to be avoided. And given the frequency with which expressive caregivers direct an infant's attention...or display their feelings about an infant's appraisal of objects and events, it is likely that the information inherent in their emotional displays will contribute in a major way to the child's understanding of the world in which he lives." See R. Hornik and M. R. Gunnar, "A Descriptive Analysis of Infant Social Referencing," *Child Development* 59/3 (1988) 626-34.

57. Erikson, *Childhood and Society*, p. 209.

58. Ephesians 5:32

59. Cahill, "Sex, Love and Procreation," p. 142.

60. Rahner, "The Theology of Symbol," p. 247.

61. *Ibid.*, p. 245.

62. *Ibid.*, p. 230.

63. *Ibid.*, p. 231.

64. *Ibid.*, p. 246.

Abortion: What Did the Supreme Court Do in *Roe v. Wade*?

Charles E. Rice

A MY GROSSBERG AND BRIAN PETERSON, aged 19 and 20, were sentenced to two-and-a-half and two years, respectively, for manslaughter for killing their baby boy after Amy gave birth to him in 1996 at the Comfort Inn in Newark, Delaware. The autopsy showed that the full-term, healthy boy died from "multiple fractures... with injury to the brain due to blunt force head trauma and shaking." Amy and Brian did not concede that they knew the baby was alive when they put him in a plastic bag which they put in a trash container in the hotel parking lot. It is unclear whether the injuries to the baby happened before or after he was put in the trash bin. After the birth, Amy and Brian returned to their colleges. The incident came to light when she was hospitalized for complications from the delivery.

Amy and Brian are criminals, not because they intentionally, or through indifference, killed an innocent human being, but because they waited ten minutes too long and used the wrong method. They would be in the clear if they had hired an abortionist to solve their problem, even during delivery, by a legal partial-birth abortion. The Supreme Court has decreed that abortion may not be banned, even in the ninth month, when it is sought to protect the mother's mental health as could be claimed in a case such as this. Had Amy and Brian exercised their "right to choose" in this way, the abortionist would have dilated the entrance to the uterus sufficiently to deliver the baby's body, except for the head. He would have delivered the baby, feet first, except for the head. He then would have inserted scissors into the base of the baby's skull and opened the scissors to enlarge the hole. He would have inserted a suction catheter and sucked out the baby's brains. The head would have collapsed and the abortionist then would have removed and disposed of the body. If they had chosen that course, Amy and Brian could have gone back to college, not as targets of a homicide prosecution, but as vindicators of the preferred constitutional "right to choose."

The attorneys for Amy and Brian chose not to use an insanity defense. In fact, Amy and Brian would seem to be more in touch with reality than are the Supreme Court of the United States and the State of Delaware. Their boy was no less a human being–and no less a person–during delivery, or at his conception, than he was when they killed him or put him in the trash bin. Yet the Court and the State would have mobilized the federal marshals to protect their right to kill him before birth and even during delivery. But because Amy and Brian waited for ten minutes and did not use an approved method of killing, the State charged them with murder and sought the death penalty. As columnist George Will put it: "Could Delaware choose to execute [Amy and Brian] by inserting scissors into the bases of their skulls, opening the scissors, inserting suction tubes and sucking out their brains? Of course not. The Constitution forbids choosing cruel and unusual punishments." So who's crazy?

The killing of newborn babies, who could have been legally and secretly aborted, is not all that rare. This case drew attention because Amy and Brian are children of wealth who could have easily had an abortion. But their case reminds us that legalized abortion will inevitably lead to infanticide and euthanasia. All three are founded on the denial of personhood to the victim. A "[r]eckless disregard for the value of human life has been transmitted through the culture for 25 years. The easy resort to abortion and the extremist rhetoric supporting the abortion regime have clearly cheapened the lives of babies.... There never was a clear dividing line between abortion and infanticide.... [I]t should not come as a huge surprise that young women from nice families don't quite see why prosecutors are knocking at their doors for performing very late abortions. Isn't it still a choice?"

THE SUPREME COURT RULINGS

The Supreme Court's abortion rulings include four principal elements:
1. The unborn child is a non-person and therefore has no constitutional rights;
2. The right of his mother to kill that non-person is a " liberty

interest" protected by the due process clause of the Fourteenth Amendment;

3. The states may impose some marginal restrictions on abortion but are barred from effectively prohibiting abortion at any stage of pregnancy;

4. Efforts undertaken in the vicinity of an abortuary to dissuade women from abortion are subject to more stringent restrictions than are other forms of speech, assembly and association.

A NON-PERSON

The Fourteenth Amendment, adopted in 1868, protects the right of a "person" to life and to the equal protection of the laws. The framers of that amendment did not consider the status of the unborn child but they intended that, "in the eyes of the Constitution, every human being within its sphere...from the President to the slave, is a person." This was in reaction to the *Dred Scott* case in 1857, in which the Supreme Court held that the free descendants of slaves were not citizens and said that slaves were property rather than persons.

In any society where personhood determines the possession of legal rights, justice mandates an inseparable connection between humanity and personhood. If that connection is broken, where does one draw the line? Peter Singer carries to its logical conclusion the separation of humanity from personhood:

We should reject the doctrine that places the lives of members of our species above the lives of members of other species. Some members of other species are persons; some members of our own species are not. No objective assessment can give greater value to the lives of members of our species who are not persons than to the lives of members of other species who are.

On the contrary, as we have seen there are strong arguments for placing the lives of persons above the lives of non-persons. So it seems that killing, say a chimpanzee is worse than the killing of a gravely defective human who is not a person.

Singer, an Australian ethicist, is the Ira W. DeCamp Professor of

Bioethics at the Princeton University Center for Human Values, which may tell us something about Princeton. "We can no longer base our ethics," says Singer, "on the idea that human beings are a special form of creation, made in the image of God, singled out from all other animals, and alone possessing an immortal soul." Singer's views are a consistent application of mainstream positivist jurisprudence. "The right to life," Singer thinks, "is not a right of members of the species *Homo sapiens*; it is...a right that properly belongs to persons. Not all members of the species *Homo sapiens* are persons, and not all persons are members of the species *Homo sapiens*." Singer believes that while chimpanzees, whales, dolphins, dogs, and cats can be persons, newborn infants and retarded humans are not. He even seems to think that chickens may be persons, raising the prospect that the greatest mass murderer in history is not Ghengis Khan, Hitler, or Stalin, but Colonel Sanders.

If all human beings are not entitled to be treated as persons before the law, the criteria for inclusion and exclusion will be utilitarian, political, and arbitrary. The denial of personhood was the technique by which the Nazis set the Jews on the road to the gas chambers. Under the Nuremberg Laws of 1935, the Nazis stripped Jews of their citizenship and political rights, effectively depriving them of personhood. Hitler's euthanasia program, designed to achieve "the destruction of life devoid of value," would later deprive them of their lives as well.

An innocent human being subject to execution at the discretion of another is, in that most important respect, a non-person. If a human being can be defined as a non-person at the beginning of his life and put to death at the discretion of others, the same thing can be done to his elder retarded brother or his grandmother. Abortion is merely prenatal euthanasia.

Before 1973, state and lower federal courts increasingly recognized the personhood rights of the unborn child with respect to his right to recover for prenatal injuries and wrongful death, to inherit property, and to get a court to compel his mother to get a blood transfusion to save his life. The precise question of the personhood of the unborn child, however, did not reach the Supreme Court until 1973. In *Roe v. Wade* and *Doe v. Bolton*, the unborn child's right to life was asserted against the mother's constitutional right to privacy, which the Court had discovered in 1965 in the "penumbras formed by emanations from" the Bill of Rights. The Court acknowledged that the right to life is superior, indicating that, if the unborn child were a person, abortion would not be permitted even to save the life of his mother:

> When Texas urges that a fetus is entitled to Fourteenth Amendment protection as a person, it faces a dilemma. Neither in Texas nor in any other state are all abortions prohibited. Despite broad proscription, an exception...for an abortion...for the purpose of saving the life of the mother, is typical. But if the fetus is a person who is not to be deprived of life without due process of law, and if the mother's condition is the sole determinant, does not the Texas exception appear to be out of line with the Amendment's command?

The Court stated that if the personhood of the unborn child were established, the pro-abortion case "collapses, for the fetus's right to life is then guaranteed by the [Fourteenth] Amendment."

After declining to decide whether an unborn child is a living human being, the Court ruled that he is not a person, since "the word 'person,' as used in the Fourteenth Amendment, does not include the unborn." Regardless of whether he is a human being, he is not a person. This ruling is the same, in effect, as a ruling that an acknowledged human being is a non-person. As a non-person the unborn child has no more constitutional rights than does a goldfish or a turnip.

Once the Court ruled out the rights of the unborn non-person, the only right remaining was the mother's right to privacy. While asserting that this right is not absolute, the Court defined it so as to permit, in effect, elective abortion at every stage of pregnancy up to the time of normal delivery. According to *Roe*, even after viability, when the state may regulate and even prohibit abortion, the state may not prohibit abortion "where it is necessary, in appropriate medical judgment, for the preservation of the life or health of the mother." The health of the mother includes her psychological as well as physical well-being. And "the medical judgment may be exercised in the light of all fac-tors–physical, emotional, psychological, familial, and the woman's age–relevant to the well-being of the mother." This is equivalent to a sanction for permissive abortion at every stage of pregnancy.

The essential holding of *Roe* is that the unborn child is not a "person" within the meaning of the Fourteenth Amendment which protects the right to life of persons.

BUT HASN'T THE COURT RETREATED FROM ITS HOLDING IN *ROE*?

No. Since 1973, the Court has upheld marginal restrictions on abortion, such as a requirement that abortions be performed by physicians. In 1992, in *Planned Parenthood v. Casey*, the Court upheld Pennsylvania requirements that the woman be given information about abortion 24 hours before the abortion; that a minor have the consent of at least one of her parents, or the approval of a judge, before she can have an abortion; and that abortion facilities comply with record keeping and reporting requirements. But the Court struck down a requirement that the woman notify her spouse before the abortion.

A "LIBERTY INTEREST"

The Court in *Casey* described the woman's right to an abortion as a "liberty interest" protected under the Fourteenth Amendment rather than as an exercise of the right to privacy." In the 1997 "right to die" case, the Court described its *Casey* ruling as follows: "There, the Court's opinion concluded that 'the essential holding of *Roe v. Wade* should be retained and once again reaffirmed.' We held, first, that a woman has a right, before her fetus is viable, to an abortion without undue interference from the State; second, that States may restrict post-viability abortions, so long as exceptions are made to protect a woman's life and health; and third, that the State has legitimate interests throughout a pregnancy in protecting the health of the woman and the life of the unborn child."

NO EFFECTIVE PROHIBITION OF ABORTION

Although the Court allows marginal restrictions on abortion, the Court will not allow the states to enact any effective prohibition of abortion at any stage of pregnancy. The Court requires that the states allow abortion for emotional as well as physical health even up to the time of normal delivery. The Court has also imposed severe restrictions on pro-life activities at abortion sites.

A UNANIMOUS COURT

Casey reaffirmed *Roe* by a 5-4 vote. That margin led some to conclude that we are only one vote away from overruling *Roe v. Wade.* That is not true. The *Casey* dissenters did say, in Chief Justice Rehnquist's words, that *Roe* was wrongly decided and that it can and should be overruled. However, when those dissenters (Rehnquist, White, Scalia, Thomas) say they want to overrule *Roe*, they mean they want to turn the issue back to the states to let them decide whether to allow or forbid abortion.

Such a states' rights solution would confirm, rather that overturn, the holding of *Roe* that the unborn child is a non-person who has no constitutional rights and who can therefore be legally killed at the discretion of others. In his *Casey* opinion, Justice John Paul Stevens explained this basic holding of *Roe*:

The Court in *Roe* carefully considered, and rejected, the State's argument "that the fetus is not a 'person' within the language and meaning of the Fourteenth Amendment." ... [T]he Court concluded that that word has application only postnatally.... Accordingly, an abortion is not the termination of life entitled to Fourteenth Amendment protection.' ...From this holding, there was no dissent, ...indeed, no member of the Court has ever questioned this fundamental proposition. Thus, as a matter of federal constitutional law, a developing organism that is not yet a 'person' does not have what is sometimes described as a 'right to life.' This has been and, by the court's holding today, remains a fundamental premise of our constitutional law governing reproductive autonomy.

In his *Webster* opinion, in 1989, Justice Stevens had stressed that "(e)ven the dissenters in *Roe* implicitly endorsed that holding [of non-personhood] by arguing that state legislatures should decide whether to prohibit or to authorize abortions.... By characterizing the basic question as a 'political issue,'...Justice Scalia likewise implicitly accepts this holding." In the *Thornburg* case, in 1986, Justice Stevens said that, "unless the religious view that a fetus is a 'person' is adopted...there is a fundamental and well-recognized difference between a fetus and a human being; indeed, if there is not such a difference, the permissibility of terminating the life of a fetus could scarcely be left to the will of the state legislatures."

When the *Casey* dissenters argue for a states' rights solution, they confirm the non-personhood of the unborn child. If an innocent human being is subject to execution at the decision of another whenever the legislature so decrees, he is a non-person with no constitutional right to live. Justice Rehnquist's bottom line is that, "A woman's interest in having an abortion is a form of liberty protected by the Due Process Clause, but States may regulate abortion procedures in ways rationally related to a legitimate state interest." Justice Scalia's bottom line is that: "The states may, if they wish, permit abortion-on-demand, but the Constitution does not require them to do so. The permissibility of abortion, and the limitations upon it, are to be resolved like most important questions in our democracy: by citizens trying to persuade one another and then voting. As the Court acknowledges, 'where reasonable people disagree the government can adopt one position or the other'."

The Supreme Court is unanimous in its endorsement of the proposition that the law can validly depersonalize innocent human beings so as to subject them to execution at the discretion of others.

WORSE THAN SLAVERY

The Thirteenth Amendment was adopted to eliminate slavery which, throughout history, has been based on a comparable denial of person-hood. In the Roman Republic, "the slave had no rights respected by the law.... The slave was property, not a person.... The owner of a slave was free to whip him, jail him, or kill him, with or without reason. He could send his slaves to death against beasts or against men in the arena or put them out to die of starvation." In the United States before the Civil War, "In the law's eye the slaves were chattels to be disposed of at their master's pleasure. The slave, therefore, had no political or civil rights.... If he was killed by a white the white would probably not be tried for murder."

However, there were cases in which whites were convicted of

murder for killing slaves in the pre-Civil War South. In this light, *Roe v. Wade*, because it allows him to be killed with total impunity, inflicts on the unborn child a status worse than American chattel slavery.

In 1854, William Lloyd Garrison, leader of a radical anti-slavery movement, described the United States Constitution as "a covenant with death, and an agreement with hell." A century and a half later, the Supreme Court's conversion of murder of the innocent into a constitutional right has again merited for the Constitution that same evaluation.

TO RESTORE CONVICTION

Roe applies precisely the principle that underlay the Nazi extermination of the Jews, that an innocent human being can be declared to be a non-person and subjected to death at the discretion of those who regard him as unfit or unwanted. The Justices who triggered the abortion avalanche by their own free decision, are no more defensible than the Nazi judges who acquiesced in the crimes of that regime and the functionaries who administered its decrees at Auschwitz and similar places. At least in some cases, those who cooperated with the Nazi exterminations did so under the impression that they would be subjected to serious sanctions if they did not cooperate. The most that our depersonalizing justices have to fear is that a pro-life vote could cost them favor in the media and the academy. And Pontius Pilate, as an operational positivist who executed the innocent for reasons of state and of his own convenience, would have found little to quarrel with in the philosophy of the Supreme Court.

The Court will allow states to enact marginal restrictions on surgical abortions but those abortions are becoming obsolete because of early abortifacient drugs and devices. As Pope John Paul II said at the Capitol Mall in 1979, "No one ever has the authority to destroy unborn life." Until that conviction is restored among the American people, there will be no chance of enacting the licensing and other restrictions and prohibitions which will be the only possibly effective ways of preventing the use of early abortifacients. Nor will there be any chance of undoing the legally sanctioned practice of euthanasia.

Membership: Reflections
on Abortion and Immigration

Michael Scaperlanda

T HOSE OF US WHO TEACH and write in the area of immigration law tend to agree, almost uniformly, that the Constitution inadequately protects noncitizens. (I stay away from the term "alien" because it conjures up in my mind images of Dr. Spock with his pointed ears and impeccable logic.[1]) We also tend to agree that Congress and the Executive often fail in providing appropriate substantive relief and procedural protection to noncitizens within the United States and to those knocking at our doors. In the scholarly literature, immigration law has been referred to as "a constitutional oddity," a "maverick," and the "neglected step-child of our public law."[2]   Yale law professor, Peter Schuck, suggests that "no other area of American law has been so radically insulated and divergent from those fundamental norms of constitutional right, administrative procedure, and judicial role that animate the rest of our legal system."[3]   Pro-lifers know that there is another area of our law that is even more radically insulated and divergent from those fundamental norms of constitutional right, administrative procedure, and judicial role that animate the rest of our legal system but more on that later in the essay.

At both constitutional and subconstitutional levels, immigration law scholars, often with great justification, bemoan the xenophobia and nativism present in American law.[4] A brief survey of recent titles in the scholarly literature makes this point: "Aliens as Outlaws,"[5] "Global Rights, Local Wrongs, and Legal Fixes: An International Human Rights Critique of Immigration and Welfare Reform,"[6] "Don't Give Me Your Tired, Your Poor,"[7] and "The First Time as Tragedy, the Second Time Farce: Proposition 187, Section 1981, and the Rights of Aliens."[8]

Immigration law is an interesting and rewarding discipline in and of itself. But when the horizon expands and immigration law is seen as

153

a small part of the legal structure, we discover that immigration law casts unique shadows on the broader legal terrain. For, you see, immigration law allows us to peer into the soul of the nation. The criteria upon which we judge others as worthy or unworthy of membership in our community and the procedures employed in making the determination tell us much about who we are as a people, about our values, our dreams, and how we live our common life together.

Abortion even more than immigration presents opportunities for a stark assessment of the nation's inner core as reflected outward by its membership regime. In some respects pre-born children and would be immigrants share a similar position in the America of the late 1990's. In *Roe v. Wade,* the Court concluded that "the unborn have never been recognized in the law as persons in the whole sense."[9] Justice Stevens, in *Planned Parenthood v. Casey,* draws the parallel between abortion and immigration in a rather startling footnote, suggesting that Haitians "have risked the perils of the sea in a desperate attempt to become 'persons' protected by our laws."[10] Both immigrants and the pre-born are knocking at membership's door, with neither guaranteed admission into the American community. These days the pre-born also have the additional burden of clamoring for recognition as members of the larger human family. As we all know far too well, this wasn't always the case. At an earlier time in our history, before *Roe v. Wade* created a constitutional license to terminate a pregnancy, the pre-born did not have to petition for membership in either the human family or the American political family. Entrance into the human family came, well, *naturally.* And, for those children born in the United States, entrance into the American family came by way of the Fourteenth Amendment.[11]

Ever since the infamous *Roe* decision, the pre-born have been relegated to the status of "outsider" who must be granted permission to join our community. With a little imagination, immigration law can help us see even more clearly, if that is possible, just how little our culture values the unborn. Normally, when we stare into the looking glass with the eyes of an immigrant, we are struck by the stark contrast between the generous substantive rights and procedural protections afforded members of the community for their protection and the absence of such rights and protections for the noncitizen–the nonmember or the partial member. If we adjust our viewpoint only slightly, the status of the would be immigrant or potential member of American society looks pretty good. Compared with the pre-born (or to use the Supreme Court's euphemism–"potential life"), the pre-American or "potential member of our political community" is granted a generous array of constitutional and subconstitutional safeguards offering protection and refuge.

In this essay, I contrast the rights granted noncitizens seeking admission to membership in the American community with the lack of protection afforded by any recognition of rights for the unborn child who silently and without counsel makes a similar claim. Although this essay revolves primarily around legal themes, it is not offered as a cogent legal analysis of the type a lawyer would argue in court. Instead, I offer it more as a reflection on our culture. Think of it as another count in the long indictment against a society that allows, as a matter of fundamental constitutional right, the slaughter of millions of innocent and helpless human beings. In short, I hope to spark your imagination as I place the unborn's struggle for life within the context of the types of membership issues that arise in the field of immigration law.

In this brief discussion, I will proceed by exploring three facets of the membership question as it pertains to immigration: (1) the substantive value choices we make in deciding who we will accept for membership; (2) the procedural protections afforded noncitizens seeking membership; and (3) specifically the substance and procedure driving our asylum and refugee law. I conclude by contrasting the constitutional and subconstitutional status of the noncitizen with that of the unborn focusing primarily on the issues of separation of powers and procedural due process.

SUBSTANTIVE VALUE CHOICES

The Constitution, at least as interpreted by the Supreme Court,[12] offers no substantive protection for would be immigrants or even aliens who face deportation. With broad deference granted the political branches by the judicial, noncitizens can be excluded or deported from this country on any grounds Congress deems appropriate, even on grounds that would offend our domestic constitutional norms. For instance, the

Supreme Court has acquiesced in congressional action providing for exclusion or deportation on the grounds of race,[13] gender,[14] unpopular speech,[15] and membership in unpopular organizations.[16]

Despite the instances when Congress has exercised its plenary immigration power in narrow and nativist ways, Congress and the American people generously allow hundreds of thousands of people to immigrate to the United States annually, including many persons who are considered human refuse by their own countries. Our membership scheme favors four types of aliens: (1) those with family ties in the United States; (2) those who possess skills in areas where the labor market demand outstrips the domestic supply, (3) those who come from countries that have contributed few immigrants over the years; and (4) refugees and asylum seekers who cannot safely remain in their country of origin. Current immigration law allows nearly a half a million people to immigrate to the United States annually for the purpose of family reunification, an additional 140,000 can immigrate annually based on employer petitions, and 55,000 immigrant slots are awarded annually through a lottery weighted heavily in favor of those coming from low sending countries.[17] Additionally, during the 1990's, the United States admitted on average more than 100,000 refugees and asylees annually.[18]

PROCEDURAL SAFEGUARDS

When a noncitizen seeks the partial membership that permanent residence status brings, the noncitizen is provided a wide array of procedural safeguards. These safeguards, which are considered woefully inadequate by immigrant rights advocates, are exceedingly generous when placed in stark contrast to our abominable human rights record with respect to the unborn.

For more than a century, the U.S. Supreme Court has recognized that noncitizens who are within the borders of the U.S., even if they are here illegally, cannot be deported or removed from the U.S., without being given a fair hearing in compliance with the due process clause of the 5th Amendment.[19] In part, procedural due process applies to protect these noncitizens because, as Justice Field said in 1893, "nothing can exceed a forcible deportation from a country of one's residence, and the breaking up of all the relations...there contracted."[20]

Similarly, a permanent resident alien (a person we may define as a partial member of our community) who has left the United States for a short time and is returning has a constitutional right to a fair hearing before she can be denied entry.[21] The procedural due process clause, however, does not protect a noncitizen who is (a) in a foreign country seeking a United States visa or (b) seeking entry at the border unless she is a returning permanent resident alien. Theoretically then, no judicially correctable constitutional violation would occur if, without a hearing, we cast potential immigrants into the shark infested waters off the Florida keys to prevent them from infiltrating our sovereign territory.

As you might imagine, even where no process is due under the Court's interpretation of the Constitution, the political branches of our national government through legislation and regulation provide a myriad of procedures to protect the interests of the noncitizen. Most people who desire to live in the United States permanently and become members of our community must successfully navigate a complex web of agencies and subagencies, possibly calling on the judiciary to help them past the most treacherous points on the journey. Within the Department of Justice two agencies, the Immigration and Naturalization Service ("INS") and the Executive Office for Immigration Review ("EOIR") with its immigration judges ("IJ") and Board of Immigration Appeals ("BIA"), play separate but major roles in implementing and policing the immigration regime. Additionally, the State Department's Visa Consular Offices independently review the files of most noncitizens seeking to immigrate. Finally, many applicants seeking employment based immigrant visa's must receive labor certification from the Department of Labor ("DOL"), which typically involves a state employment agency, a DOL certifying officer, and the Board of Alien Labor Certification Appeals ("BALCA"), an appellate body of administrative law judges.

Although we could contrast the substantive rights and procedural protections of any number of types of immigrants with those afforded the unborn, I'll focus, in the next section, on the contrasting legal positions of the asylum seeker and the unborn. The asylum applicant, like the fetus, knocks at our door begging entry and protection claiming that without our government's sanctuary her life will be imperilled.

ASYLUM

An alien, who presents herself at our border without documents or other evidence of admissibility can claim asylum, alleging that she has "a well founded fear of persecution on account of race, religion, nationality, membership in a particular group or political opinion."[22] Persecution includes "the infliction of suffering or harm, under government sanction, upon persons who differ in a way regarded as offensive (*e.g.*, race, religion, political opinion, etc.), in a manner condemned by civilized governments."[23] By way of example, a young woman, let's call her Monique, from a particular tribe in Africa who is subject to but opposed to female genital mutilation ("FGM) may be a member of a social group. And, if the government of her country will either subject her to FGM or stand by while her tribe or family performs FGM, she may have a claim for asylum on the basis that she has a well founded fear of persecution on account of her social group.[24]

     According to United States law, if Monique presents herself at the border seeking asylum, she will be detained, given the opportunity to consult an attorney, and then taken before an asylum officer who will make an initial determination as to whether she has a "credible fear" of persecution.[25] If she establishes credible fear defined as "a significant possibility...that the alien could establish eligibility for asylum," the asylum officer will then refer her for a full determination of her claim before an immigration judge.[26] If the asylum officers does not find credible fear, the officer must in writing summarize the facts and provide an analysis of why no credible fear was found. Monique can seek review of the asylum officer's decision before an immigration judge and after consulting an attorney. If the immigration judge finds no credible fear, then the alien is subject to removal from the U. S. without the benefit of judicial review of either the asylum officer or the immigration judge's decision.

     If Monique is already present in the U.S., her asylum application will be acted upon by an asylum officer in a nonadversarial proceeding. The asylum applicant has the right to counsel, the right to offer witness affidavits, and the right to offer evidence including live witnesses. If the asylum officer denies her asylum claim, she can renew that claim before an immigration judge as an affirmative ground of relief from deportation in a subsequent removal hearing. During the removal hearing, Monique has a right to be represented by an attorney, to a translator if her native language is not English, to have the immigration judge's decision (findings of fact and conclusions of law) made on the record, to put on her own witnesses, and to cross-examine government witnesses. She also has the right to appeal an adverse decision by the immigration judge to the Board of Immigration Appeals in Washington. If the BIA refuses to grant her the relief sought, she can appeal to the federal appellate court.

Even with these procedures, the risk of error abounds. Lack of money compounded by a lack of knowledge of our culture, the legal system, and the English language may cause Monique to miss the opportunity to effectively apply for asylum. At the border, Monique is subject to expedited removal if she fails to affirmatively ask for asylum. Even if she asks for asylum, she may not have the ability to obtain the services of an attorney who will help her navigate the uncertainties of a credible fear determination and subsequent hearing. And, Congress has denied her access to the courts to appeal an adverse credible fear determination. Although immigration lawyers and advocates detest for good reason the lack of procedural protection and review for would be members of our community, when contrasted with the unborn who make similar claims for membership in our political community and who also seek refuge from life threatening forces, the alien's position is enviable.

THE UNBORN–UNWORTHY OF PROTECTION?

"No society is free where government makes one person's liberty depend upon the arbitrary will of another."[27]

As we have seen, the Constitution as interpreted by the Supreme Court mandates certain protections for some immigrants, but in no case does the Constitution prohibit the political branches of the government from granting greater substantive and procedural protection to potential members. Through its substantive immigration policy the legislative branch has developed an immigration policy favoring family reunification, economic development, and refuge. Congress also specifies certain procedural guidelines for the executive branch to follow in determining whether an alien meets the specified substantive criteria. The executive branch, through the INS, acts in a dual capacity, as a service provider facilitating the entry of qualifying immigrants and as enforcer, attempting to police the border to keep out non-qualifying aliens. The executive branch, through the EOIR, also acts in a quasi-adjudicatory role, supplying immigration judges and the Board of Immigration Appeals to rule on whether the INS overstepped its bounds by denying entry or ordering the removal of noncitizens who are entitled to enter the United States. And, adversely affected noncitizens through the constitutional writ of habeas corpus[28] and through legislative grants of jurisdiction can, in many cases, seek limited judicial review of the executive's immigration decision in a particular case.

In contrast, when the unborn petition for membership in the American community, our Constitution, as interpreted by the Supreme Court in *Roe v. Wade* and modified by *Planned Parenthood v. Casey*, prohibits the American people from providing all substantive and most procedural protection. As we know all to well, the Court grants the mother the power to deny the child's humanity or to abort her child in spite of the child's humanity. This decision remains her's alone subject to no meaningful oversight. She possesses the absolute authority to determine whether the "distress, for all concerned, associated with an unwanted child"[29] outweighs the child's claim to membership. The mother acts in a legislative capacity as policymaker making the substantive determination with respect to the value of fetal life and the circumstances in which the unborn child will be allowed to enter into membership in our human and political community. During a pregnancy in which abortion is contemplated, the mother also acts in an executive capacity, carrying out her substantive policy as to whether this particular baby ought to be denied membership. Finally, she acts in an adjudicative capacity, reviewing the propriety of her legislative value choices and judging the executive application of that policy. In other words, the Court requires that she be the sole authoritative lawmaker, executive, and judicial officer in determining the membership status of her offspring. Investing this type of power in one person to determine the fate of an asylum applicant who is presently in the United States would clearly be unconstitutional. And, even for the arriving asylum applicant, Congress grants much more in the way of substantive and procedural protection.

The Court's abortion arrangement, which places with the mother complete sovereignty over this vital membership issue, violates basic constitutional concepts. Quite apart from the substantive question about the unborn child's right to life and whether and in what circumstances abortion might be justified, placing the legislative, executive, and judicial power over this important membership issue in the hands of a single person assaults our core values of separation of powers and due process. To borrow from Justice Cordozo, "this is delegation running riot."[30] Writing as Publius, James Madison stated that "[n]o political truth is certainly of greater intrinsic value, or is stamped with the authority of more enlightened patrons of liberty" than the proposition that the "accumulation of all powers, legislative, executive, and judiciary, in the same hands, whether of one, a few, or many, ... may justly be pronounced the very definition of tyranny."[31] Quoting Montesquieu, Madison explained, "[w]ere the power of judging joined with the legislative, the life and liberty of the subject would be exposed to arbitrary control, ... were it joined to the executive, the judge might behave with all the violence of an oppressor."[32] In the absence of separated powers with checks and balances, the interest and passions of the mother prevail over the interest of the unborn child and the interest of the community in protecting innocent human life.

The due process interests of the petitioning fetus also suffer jurisprudential genocide under the weight of the Court's mandate in *Roe* and *Casey*. Many years ago, Judge Henry Friendly listed eleven attributes of a fair hearing: "an unbiased tribunal," "notice of the proposed action and the grounds asserted for it," an opportunity to present reasons why the proposed action should not be taken," the "right to call witnesses," the right "to know the evidence against one," the right "to have the decision based only on the evidence presented," the right to counsel, "the making of a record," a "statement of reasons" for action to be taken, a proceeding open to the public, and judicial review.[33] Since *Planned Parenthood v. Casey*, a state can take a limited role in lobbying the women regarding the wisdom of her legislative formulation (providing her with information as to fetal development), it may also provide limited relief to the child during the prosecutorial phase of the membership hearing by requiring a 24 hour continuance before a final judgment is made, but unless the pregnant women is a minor, she is the ultimate judge as to whether her child will be admitted into membership in our society. In reality, the child receives almost no meaningful procedural protection. The child is entitled to neither a guardian ad litem nor an attorney to represent her interests. No unbiased tribunal waits to decide the fate of this youngest of asylum seekers. Instead, the Court insists that the mother, who as prosecutor has charged the fetus with inadmissability on grounds of inconvenience, distress, public charge, physical defect, or some similar ground that makes the fetus undesirable, acts as judge without much interference from any outside party, including the state and the child's father. In fact, each and every element of a fair hearing is denied the child seeking membership in our community.

Professor Kevin Johnson stresses that when we distinguish "between aliens and persons, [we are] able to reconcile the disparate legal and social treatment of the two groups" by institutionalizing and legitimating the alien as "other" or as a nonperson.[34] A similar process occurs within the abortion realm. As pro-choice philosopher Naomi Wolff remarked, by "[c]linging to a rhetoric about abortion in which there is no life and no death, we entangle our beliefs in a series of self-delusions, fibs and evasions."[35] Instead, she argues, we must confront the fetus "in its full humanity," admitting that abortion involves real death.[36] Pro-choice constitutional law scholar, John Hart Ely would also have us recognize that "[a]bortion ends...the life of a human being other than the one making the choice."[37]

Such honesty is fraught with consequences. If we set aside the legerdemain and correct the judicially sanctioned "fibs and evasions" about abortion and fetal life, tremendous pressure will be brought to bear on the constitutionality of the abortion license. The courts and/or the legislatures have a duty to protect this most innocent of human life. To articulate it in immigration terms, one could even imagine an unborn child seeking asylum through the assistance of a guardian, claiming that her government will do nothing to protect her from certain death, which will occur as a form of persecution on account of the unborn's social group defined as unborn children who desire to live but who have mothers bent on destroying that possibility. Our asylum policy requires the grant of asylum anytime an innocent noncitizen can prove that she will be put to death on account of her social group, and our abortion law should do no less.

At a minimum, however, recognition of the child's humanity should require the court to allow the legislatures discretion to offer the unborn greater procedural and possibly substantive protections. Ely suggests that "an unwanted child can go a long way toward ruining a woman's life."[38] Wolff says that women who seek abortion because of poverty, youth, marital rape, and incest have less moral culpability than those who seek abortion for other reasons."[39] Even assuming *arguendo* that morally justifiable abortions exist, Ely, in attacking what he calls the "frightening" *Roe* opinion, reminds the reader that "the Court requires of the mother" no showing that her desired abortion falls into an acceptable category.[40] As Wolff points out, "[o]f the abortions I know of, these were some of the reasons: to force a boy or man to take a relationship more seriously; and, again and again, to enact a rite of passage for affluent teenage girls. In my high school, the abortion drama was used to test a boyfriend's character."[41] In her own case, Wolff says, "there were two columns in my mind–'Me' and 'Baby'–and the first won out" because of "unwelcome intensity in the relationship with the father; the desire to continue to 'develop as a person' before 'real' parenthood; wish to encounter my eventual life partner without the off-putting encumbrance of a child."[42] In conclusion, she says, "I chose myself on my own terms over a possible someone else, for self-absorbed reasons."[43]

Abortion pits mother against child in a life and death struggle. Some argue that the abortion decision is "an intensely personal deci-sion" for the mother alone to make. To this Noami Wolff says, "No: one's choice of *carpeting* is an intensely personal decision" but not one's "struggles with a life-and-death issue."[44] We as a society must resolve these conflicts when presented to us. If we are not going to fully protect the weak and innocent in their quest for membership, we can surely enforce our concepts of separation of powers not allowing the mother to be law maker, prosecutor, and judge in a case in which she has an inherent conflict. We could also insist on fair procedures, allowing the unborn child an advocate and a forum to make the case for membership against the certain death if membership is denied.

Dissenting in the *Mezei* case, Justice Jackson severely criticized the majority for creating a legal fiction, which denied the alien's personhood. By pretending that Mezei was not a person for constitutional purposes, the Court held that he was not entitled to the protections given other's pursuant to the due process clause; therefore, the Executive under authority granted by Congress could hold him indefinitely as a prisoner on Ellis Island without ever disclosing the charges against him or giving him an opportunity to defend himself.[45] After concluding that basic "fairness in hearing procedures does not vary with the status" of the one subject to harm, Jackson suggested that the Court's logic could allow the United States to "eject [an alien] bodily into the sea."[46] While the Court's use of legal fiction might allow this outcome in immigration cases, the *Roe* and *Casey* mandate an even worse fate for the unborn. Yes, Professor Schuck is right, immigration law resides at the fringes of our public law. But, the law dealing with the distribution of membership benefits to the pre-born is even more "radically insulated and divergent from those fundamental norms of constitutional right, administrative procedure, and judicial role that animate the rest of our legal system."[47]

NOTES

1. See Kevin Johnson, "'Aliens' and the U.S. Immigration Laws: The Social and Legal Construction of Nonpersons," *Univ. of Miami Inter-American Law Review* 28 (1996-97) 263, 272.

2. Stephen H. Legomsky, "Immigration Law and the Principle of Plenary Congressional Power," *Supreme Court Review* (1984) 255, 255; Hiroshi Motomura, "The Curious Evolution of Immigration Law: Procedural Surrogates for Substantive Constitutional Rights," *Columbia Law Review* 92 (1992) 625,

1631; Peter H. Schuck, "The Transformation of Immigration Law," *Columbia Law Review* 84 (1984) 1, 1.

3. Schuck, *supra* n.2 at 1.

4. See, *e.g.*, Gabriel J. Chin, "Segregation's Last Stronghold: Race, Discrimination and the Constitutional Law of Immigration," *UCLA Law Review* 49 (1998) 1.

5. Gerald Neuman, "Aliens as Outlaws: Government Services, Proposition 187, and the Structure of Equal Protection Doctrine, *UCLA Law Review* 42 (1995) 1425.

6. Berta Esparanza Hernandez-Truyol & Kimberly Johns, *Southern Cal. Law Review* 71 (1998) 547.

7. Bill Ong Hing, "Don't Give Me Your Tired, Your Poor: Conflicted Immigrant Stories and Welfare Reform," *Harvard Civil Rights & Civil Liberties Law Review* 33 (1998) 159.

8. Stephen Knight, *UCLA Pacific Basin Law Journal* 15 (1997) 289.

9. 410 U.S. 113, 162 (1973).

10. *Planned Parenthood v. Casey*, 112 S. Ct. 2791, 2840 (1992) (Stevens, J., concurring in part and dissenting in part).

11. "All persons born or naturalized in the United States and subject to the jurisdiction thereof, are citizens of the United States and of the State wherein they reside." U.S. Constitution, Amendment 14 (1868).

12. See Michael Scaperlanda, "Who is My Neighbor? An Essay on Immigrants, Welfare Reform, and the Constitution," *Connecticut Law Review* 29 (1997) 1587, 1599 (suggesting that the responsibility for ensuring that our immigration law and policy is consonant with our constitutional norms lies with the citizenry and its elected representatives); and Michael Scaperlanda, "Partial Membership: Aliens and the Constitutional Community," *Iowa Law Review* 81 (1996) 707, 771 (same). See also Victor Romero, "Expanding the Circle of Membership By Reconstructing the 'Alien': Lessons From Social Psychology and the 'Promise Enforcement Cases," *Univ. of Michigan Journal of Law Reform* 32 (1998) 1 (taking this task of communal formation seriously).

13. *Chae Chan Ping v. United States* (the Chinese Exclusion Case), 130 U.S. 581 (1889); *Fong Yue Ting v. United States,* 149, U. S. 698 (1893).

14. *Fiallo v. Bell*, 430 U.S. 787 (1977).

15. *Kleindienst v. Mandel*, 408 U.S. 753 (1972).

16. *Harisaides v. Shaughnessy*, 342 U.S. 580 (1952).

17. 8 United States Code Annotated, Section 1151 (1999).

18. Stephen Legomsky, *Immigration and Refugee Law and Policy* (Foundation Press, 2nd ed., 1997), p. 762.

19. *Yamataya v. Fisher* (the Japanese Immigrant Case), 189 U.S. 86 (1903).

20. *Fong Yue Ting v. United States*, 149 U.S. 698, 759 (1893)(Field, J., dissenting).

21. *Landon v. Plasencia*, 459 U.S. 21 (1982).

22. 8 United States Code Annotated, Section 1158 (1999).

23. *E.g., Abdel-Masieh v. INS*, 73 F.3d 579, 583 (5th Cir. 1996).

24. See *Matter of Kasinga*, Int. Dec. 3278 (BIA 1996).

25. 8 Code of Federal Regulations Section 235.3 (1999).

26. 8 United States Code Annotated, Section 1225 (1999).

27. *Shaughnessy v. United States, ex rel.* Mezei, 345 U.S. 206, 217 (Black, J., dissenting).

28. See Lenni Benson, "Back to the Future: Congress Attacks the Right to Judicial Review of Immigration Proceedings," 29 *Connecticut Law Review* 29 (1997) 1411.

29. *Roe v. Wade*, 410 U.S. 113, 153 (1973).

30. *Schecter Poultry Corp. v. United States*, 295 U.S. 495, 553 (1935)(Cordozo, J., concurring).

31. *The Federalist Papers*, No. 47 (1788).

32. *Ibid.*

33. Henry J. Friendly, "Some Kind of Hearing," *U. Penn. Law Rev.* 123 (1975) 1267, 1279-95.

34. Johnson, *supra* note 1 at 273, 268 & 270. He draws a parallel between the alien and the fetus in this article. *Ibid.* at 278, n.73.

35. Naomi Wolff, "Our Bodies, Our Souls," *The New Republic* (October 16, 1995) 26.

36. *Ibid.* at 33 & 26.

37. "The Wages of Crying Wolf: A Comment on *Roe v. Wade,"* 82 *Yale Law Journal* 82 (1973) 920, 924.

38. *Ibid.* at 923.

39. Wolff, *supra* note 35 at 32.

40. Ely, *supra* note 37 at 924, n.26 & 935.

41. Wolff, *supra* note 35 at 32.

42. *Ibid.*

43. *Ibid.* at 33.

44. Wolff, *supra* note 35 at 34.

45. 345 U.S. 206 (1953).

46. *Ibid.* at 225 & 226.

47. Shuck, *supra* note 2 at 1.

Disagreement Without Debate:
The Republican Party Platform and
the Human Life Amendment Plank

Francis J. Beckwith

"John Stewart [sic] Mill once said, 'there is always hope when people are forced to listen to both sides of the issue'."
  Ann Stone, of Republicans for Choice, in an open letter to the delegates of the 1992 Republican National Convention in Houston

A S WE APPROACH the 2000 Republican National Convention in Philadelphia, the issue of abortion and the question of whether the pro-life plank should remain in the party platform will intensify. In the 1990s Republican pro-choice governors George Pataki (NY), William Weld (MA), Christie Todd Whitman (NJ), and Pete Wilson (CA) came out publicly in support of removing the pro-life plank. In fact, the 1996 platform included an Appendix that contained alternatives to the plank suggested by delegates. These alternatives, all of which were either rejected by the platform committee or withdrawn for consideration, ranged from acknowledging disagreement on abortion among party members to calling for the shoring up and nurturing of social and civic institutions that would result, according to its authors, in abortion becoming rare (RNC 1996, Appendix I). All the alternatives, however, fell short of what the platform language called for: a human life amendment (HLA) to the U.S. Constitution.[1]

The media, of course, enjoy this bickering. When I was a delegate from Nevada at the 1992 national convention in Houston,[2] I was approached by at least six network correspondents (including Dan Rather) who asked me if there was anything in the party platform or convention speeches which made me uneasy. I responded to them by saying that I was disappointed that there was nothing in the Republican party platform condemning the gagging of pro-life spokesmen (such as former Pennsylvania Governor Robert Casey) at the Democratic National Convention in New York.[3] Needless to say, the network correspondents moved on to search for more cooperative malcontents.

DISAGREEMENT WITHOUT DEBATE

What stands out about this intramural G.O.P. debate is that for all the talk about Republican disagreement about abortion, one rarely if ever *actually* sees or hears pro-choice Republicans arguing for the merits of their position, a position which, if correct, would entail that the *content* of any HLA, as called for by the platform, is mistaken. Although one may hear *affirmations* of the pro-choice position (*e.g.*, "A woman's right to choose is a fundamental right"), there is near total silence when it comes to proponents *actually defending* their position or the media requiring them to do so. Certainly, one hears, from both pro-life and pro-choice proponents, much about the political ramifications of their positions. For example, pro-lifers point out that Ronald Reagan's 1980 and 1984 landslides as well as George Bush's 1988 victory occurred while the party's presidential standard bearer stood firmly for the pro-life position. They also argue that in 1994 pro-lifers running for Congress were overwhelming victors as a result of a large number of pro-life voters who, through both their activism and their voting preference, played a large part in the Republican takeover of Congress. Of course, pro-choicers have a different interpretation of these and other political events. For example, some pro-choicers argue that the Republican takeover of Congress was the result of the American people's fondness for the "Contract with America," which was virtually devoid of any mention of "social issues" such as abortion. The consecutive presidential victories of Bill Clinton, a strongly pro-choice Democrat with moderate economic policies, as well as the decrease of the Republican Congressional majority resulting from the 1998 mid-term elections, are cited as evidence that the American people are rejecting the G.O.P.'s pro-life message. Making the political argument among party faithful, Ann Stone and her group, Republicans for Choice (RFC), maintain in their literature that over 71% of all registered Republicans are pro-choice.[4]

Although there is no doubt that political concerns are important, the very nature of the abortion question makes it nearly impervious to political resolution. Most partisans on the issue believe that their position is grounded in some fundamental non-negotiable right, whether it is the right to life (pro-life) or the right to personal autonomy (pro-choice). Non-negotiable perspectives do not lend themselves to the typical compromises that are necessary for the pacification of contrary factions in the rough and tumble world of party politics (see Hunter 1991). For instance, pro-choice Republicans William H. Hudnut III, former mayor of Indianapolis, and his wife, Beverly Hudnut, advocate an uncompromising and yet principled position: "It seems to us that under traditional minimalist Republican policy, government would choose *not* to interfere with a woman's right to make her own decision about whether or not to bear a child" (Hudnut and Hudnut 1996). The Hudnuts seem to be saying that even if espousing the pro-choice position were a political liability, the members of the Republican Party should *encourage* their elected officials to support this fundamental right.[5] Ann Stone affirms this principled position in the postscript of a 1992 open letter to Republican delegates to the national convention in Houston: "The Supreme Court...reaffirmed that a woman's right to choose is essential for women to participate equally in society. Our party platform is in contradiction with the Court" (Stone 1992).[6]

The pro-life position is equally resistant to political inoculation. For most pro-lifers, the fetus is a human person from the moment of conception or at least during virtually all of her development in her mother's womb.[7] Therefore, the fetus deserves at least as much protection (and perhaps more, because it is so vulnerable and defenseless) as those who were fortunate enough to have been born. This is why pro-lifers are unmoved by the typical arguments one hears propounded by pro-choice advocates. For example, it is often argued that prior to legal abortion, women resorted to unscrupulous doctors who performed illegal abortions on them, and consequently these women were harmed (and sometimes died). Therefore, abortion ought to remain legal. Of course, if the fetus is *not* a human person, this is a legitimate concern. But if the fetus *is* a human person, this argument is tantamount to saying that because people die or are harmed while killing other people, the state should make it safe for them to do so. Thus, the pro-choicer begs the question, since he has not refuted the one premise which, if true, makes virtually all his arguments unsound: the fetus is a human person.[8] But this flaw is found in nearly every popular pro-choice argument, whether it is the argument from poverty, from "choice," from familial inconvenience, from fetal handicap or from single parenthood. Without first begging the question as to the fetus's non-personhood, virtually none of the pro-choice arguments work.[9] This is why author and social critic Gregory P. Koukl is fond of saying, "If the unborn is not a human person, no justification of abortion is necessary. However, if the unborn is a human person, no justification for abortion is adequate."[10]

None of this means, of course, that political compromises are impossible. It just means that abortion is not *merely* a political issue. For it touches on the most important philosophical questions of our time, including but not limited to the meaning of liberty:what it means to be a human person, and whether law, with all its assumptions about property, freedom, and rights, can be divorced from metaphysical questions about the nature of such things. One does not ordinarily *choose* a position on abortion; it is typically thrust upon oneself by how one has *already first answered* (whether consciously or unconsciously) these metaphysical questions.[11]

WHAT THE "ABORTION PLANK" REALLY SAYS

Although the media continue to say that there is a plank in the Republican platform calling for "a constitutional amendment banning abortion,"[12] there is simply nothing in either the 1992 or 1996 platforms which calls for such an amendment. What is typically and incorrectly referred to as the "abortion plank"[13] is the section of the 1992 and 1996 platforms which calls for a constitutional amendment to protect all human life regardless of venue or level of maturity. The 1992 plank reads:

We believe the unborn child has a fundamental right to life which cannot be infringed. We therefore affirm our support for a human life amendment to the Constitution, and we endorse legislation that the Fourteenth Amendment's protections apply to unborn children. (RNC 1992, 39)

The 1996 plank provides a different reading:

We oppose the non-consensual withholding of health care or treatment because of handicap, age, or infirmity, just as we oppose euthanasia and assisted suicide, which, especially for the poor and those on the margins of society, threaten the sanctity of human life. The unborn child has a fundamental individual right to life which cannot be infringed. We support a human life amendment to the Constitution and we endorse legislation to make clear that the Fourteenth Amendment's protections apply to unborn children. (RNC 1996)

The text in which both the 1992 and 1996 planks reside deals with issues of race relations, bigotry, the civil rights of women, and the rights of the handicapped, as well as the rights of the unborn. In fact, this portion of the 1992 platform, which is under the general heading of "Individual Rights," begins with these sentences: "The protection of individual rights is the foundation of opportunity and security. The Republican Party is unique in this regard. Since its inception, it has respected every person, even when that proposition was universally unpopular. Today, as in the day of Lincoln, we insist that no American's rights are negotiable" (RNC 1992, 38).[14]

For the pro-life Republican, both the 1992 and 1996 planks call for extending our nation's moral progress toward the elimination of unjust discrimination to those who are the most vulnerable in the human family, the unborn. Consequently, when Republicans, such as the Hudnuts and Ann Stone, refer to this section of the platform as primarily referring to abortion and/or a woman's right to choose,[15] they simply are not speaking accurately, and they are clearly not addressing their criticisms to the essential claim put forth by the planks' authors: the unborn are members of the human community and deserve to be protected from unjust harm.

The remaining portion of the 1992 HLA plank reads: "We oppose using public revenues for abortion and will not fund organizations which advocate it. We commend those who provide alternatives to abortion by meeting the needs of mothers and offering adoption services. We reaffirm our support for appointment of judges who respect traditional family values and the sanctity of innocent human life" (RNC 1992, 39). The only time abortion is opposed in the 1992 platform is in terms of government funding, which is hardly a call for a total ban on abortion.

The 1996 platform, in comparison to its 1992 predecessor, has more to say immediately following its call for a human life amendment:

Our purpose is to have legislative and judicial protection of that right against those who perform abortions. We oppose using public revenues for abortion and will not fund organizations which advocate it. We support the appointment of judges who respect traditional family values and the sanctity of innocent human life.

Our goal is to ensure that women with problem pregnancies have the kind of support, material and otherwise, they need for themselves and for their babies, not to be punitive towards those for whose difficult situation we have only compassion. We oppose abortion, but our pro-life agenda does not include punitive action against women who have an abortion. We salute those who provide alternatives to abortion and offer adoption services. Republicans in Congress took the lead in expanding assistance both for the costs of adoption and for the continuing care of adoptive children with special needs. Bill Clinton vetoed our adoption tax credit the first time around–and opposed our efforts to remove racial barriers to adoption–before joining in this long overdue measure of support for adoptive families.

Worse than that, he vetoed the ban on partial-birth abortions, a procedure denounced by a committee of the American Medical Association and rightly branded as four-fifths infanticide. We applaud Bob Dole's commitment to revoke the Clinton executive orders concerning abortion and to sign into law an end to partial-birth abortions. (RNC 1996).

The only time abortion is opposed in the 1992 platform is in terms of government funding, which is hardly a call for a constitutional amendment to ban abortion. Although abortion is mentioned more explicitly in the 1996 platform, an anti-abortion constitutional amendment is nowhere to be found. Like its 1992 version, the 1996 platform both calls for the ending of public funding for organizations that advocate abortion as well as commends and supports those who provide abortion alternatives such as adoption. The 1996 platform, however, discusses the latter in greater detail and makes the point that the party's call for protecting the unborn will not translate into punishment for women seeking abortions if this protection were to become part of the

Constitution. The platform does call for the punishment of physicians and others who abridge the right to life of the unborn by performing procedures whose *sole* purpose is the destruction of prenatal human beings. In addition, the plank is critical of President Clinton's vetoing of the partial-birth abortion ban as well as his initial resistance to certain adoption measures put forth by the Republican-majority Congress.

It would certainly be correct to infer that if a human life amendment were to become part of our Constitution, statutes and court decisions (such as *Roe v. Wade*) which permit virtually unrestricted abortion would be unconstitutional. However, this is merely *an inference* from the passage of such an amendment.[16]

The reason why neither the 1992 nor 1996 platform mentions a direct ban on abortion is because its authors no doubt understood, and their opponents are reticent to admit, that what is doing the moral work in the question of abortion is the status of the fetus. Everything else is simply beside the point. This is why there was a call for a human life amendment to the Constitution in the 1992 and 1996 Republican platforms and *not* a call for a constitutional amendment to ban abortion totally.

WAYS TO AVOID DISCUSSING FETAL PERSONHOOD:
A CRITICAL ANALYSIS

It is clear that if pro-choice Republicans want to address the content of the plank with which they find disagreement, they must address the question of fetal personhood. There are, however, a number of tactics that pro-choice Republicans may employ in order to avoid confronting this question. These tactics seem to come in two varieties: (1) appeals to pluralism and/or tolerance, and (2) appeals to agnosticism concerning fetal status.

1. Appeals to pluralism and/or tolerance. In an attempt to maintain an apparently "neutral" posture on the question of fetal personhood, pro-choice Republicans may argue in the following way: since people disagree about abortion, we simply ought to permit each person to decide for himself or herself whether the fetus is a human person and/or whether abortion is immoral. Consequently, if pro-lifers believe that abortion is homicide, that is fine. They need not fear state coercion to have an abortion or to participate in the procedure. On the other hand, if some people believe that abortion is not homicide and/or it is morally permissible, then they need not fear state coercion to remain pregnant.[17] This, according to conventional wisdom, is the tolerant position one ought to take in our pluralistic society.

The problem with this reasoning is that it misses the point of why people oppose abortion. That is to say, it does not seriously engage the opposition's case. Perhaps an example will help. During the 1984 presidential campaign when questions of Geraldine Ferraro's Catholicism and its apparent conflict with her pro-choice stance were prominent in the media, New York Governor Mario Cuomo, in a lecture delivered at the University of Notre Dame, attempted to give the tolerance argument intellectual respectability (Cuomo 1984). He tried to provide a philosophical foundation for Ferraro's position. But it is not clear that Cuomo gained any ground, either politically or philosophically. For one cannot appeal to the fact that we live in a pluralistic society, as Cuomo argued, when the very question of *who* is part of that society (that is, whether or not it includes fetuses) is itself the point under dispute. Cuomo lost the argument because he begged the question.

To tell pro-lifers, as many Republican supporters of the tolerance argument do, that "they have a right to believe what they want to believe" is evidence of a failure truly to grasp the pro-life perspective.[18] Think about it. If *you* believed, as the pro-lifers do, that a class of persons were being unjustly killed by methods which include dismemberment, suffocation, brain-suctioning, and burning, wouldn't you be perplexed if someone tried to ease your outrage by telling you that you didn't have to participate in the killings if you didn't want to?[19] That's exactly what pro-lifers hear when pro-choice supporters tell them "Don't like abortion, don't have one" or "I'm pro-choice, but personally opposed." In the mind of the pro-lifer, this is like telling an abolitionist, "Don't like slavery, don't own one," or telling Dietrich Bonhoffer, "Don't like the holocaust, don't kill a Jew." Consequently, for the defender of the tolerance argument to request that pro-lifers "should not force their pro-life belief on others," while claiming that "they have a right to believe what they want to believe," is to reveal a gross misunderstanding of the pro-life position.[20] Keep in mind that for the pro-lifer, a fetus is no less a member of the human community simply because it happens to be living inside Ann Stone, Whoopi Goldberg, Eleanor Smeal, or Kate Michelman. All fetuses deserve protection, even if they happen to reside in the wombs of citizens who do not embrace the pro-life viewpoint.

Perhaps the pro-choice Republican will reply to this critique by giving his argument a theological twist and argue that the pro-life position is a "religious position" and that in the interest of "pluralism" the pro-lifer ought to refrain from imposing her religious views on others.[21] In fact, one piece of pro-choice literature claims that "personhood at conception is a religious belief, not a provable biological fact" (NARAL 1983). What could possibly be meant by this assertion? Is it claiming that no aspect of a religious worldview has scientific import? If it is, it is incorrect, for many religions, such as Christianity and Islam, maintain that the physical world literally exists, which is a major assumption of contemporary science. On the other hand, some religions, such as Christian Science (Eddy 1875) and certain forms of Hinduism (Hackett 1979), deny the literal existence of the physical world. Moreover, some of the arguments used to support the view that life begins at conception, or any other view on abortion for that matter, are not even remotely religious, since they involve the citing of scientific evidence and the use of philosophical reasoning and reflection.[22]

But maybe this assertion is claiming that biology can tell us nothing about values. If this is the case, it is right in one sense and wrong in another. It is right if it means that the brute facts of science, without any moral reflection, cannot tell us what is right and wrong. But it is wrong if it means that the brute facts of science cannot tell us *to whom* we should apply the values of which we are aware. For example, if I don't know whether the object I am driving toward in my car is a living woman or a manikin, biology is important in helping me to avoid committing an act of homicide. Running over manikins is not homicide, but running over a woman is.

Maybe this assertion is saying that when human life should be valued is a *philosophical* belief which cannot be proven scientifically.

Maybe, but this cuts both ways. For isn't the belief that a woman has *abortion rights* a *philosophical* belief which cannot be proven scientifically and over which people widely disagree? But if the pro-life position cannot be reflected in the Republican party platform and/or enacted into law because it is philosophical (or religious), then neither can the pro-choice position. The pro-choice advocate may respond to this by saying that this fact alone is a good reason to leave it up to each individual woman to choose whether she should have an abortion. But this begs the question, for this is precisely the pro-choice position, a disputed moral viewpoint. Furthermore, the pro-lifer could reply to this pro-choice response by employing the pro-choicer's own logic. The pro-lifer could argue that since the pro-choice position is a disputed philosophical position over which many people disagree, society should permit each individual unborn human being to be born and make up her own mind as to whether she should or should not continue to exist.

It seems, then, that the tolerance argument is not as neutral as its proponents believe. For to say that a woman should have the "right to choose" to terminate the life of the fetus she is carrying is tantamount to denying the pro-life position that fetuses are human persons worthy of protection. And to affirm that fetuses are human persons with a "right to life" that ought to be protected by the state is tantamount to denying the pro-choice position that a woman has a fundamental right to terminate her pregnancy, since such a termination would result in a homicide. Consequently, when pro-choice Republicans, in the name of tolerance and pluralism, call for the elimination of the HLA plank and to replace it with either nothing[23] or a pro-choice plank,[24] they are calling for the party to acquiesce to the legal *status quo*, namely, that fetuses are not full-fledged members of the human community and therefore are not entitled to protection by the state. It seems, then, that the tolerance argument is inadequate in resolving the current debate over the HLA plank in the Republican party platform.

   2. Appeals to agnosticism concerning fetal status. An example of such an appeal can be found in Justice Blackmun's often-quoted comments in *Roe v. Wade*: "We need not resolve the difficult question of when life begins. When those trained in the respective disciplines of medicine, philosophy, and theology are unable to arrive at any consensus, the judiciary, at this point in the development of man's knowledge, is not in a position to speculate" (U.S. Supreme Court 1973, 160).

Justice Blackmun is arguing that because experts disagree as to when life begins, the Court should not come down on any side. That is, since experts disagree about when and if the fetus becomes a human life, then abortion should remain legal.

In popular debate Justice Blackmun's claim is often put forth by pro-choice advocates when they affirm that "no one knows when life begins," and from that affirmation conclude that abortion ought to be legally permitted. Republicans for Choice, for example, maintains that the claim that human life begins at conception is "a fact still widely disputed" ("Oklahoma's Massive Challenge" 1992, 2). There is a difference, however, between claiming that "no one knows when life begins" and "experts disagree as to when life begins." My guess is that when people use the former in popular debate, they are in fact arguing that it is justified by the latter:

(1) Experts disagree as to when life begins, therefore
(2) No one knows when life begins.

Of course (2) does not necessarily follow from (1). It may be that experts disagree as to when human life begins but some of them are wrong while others in fact know when human life begins. This would not be surprising, since historically some faction of experts usually turns out to be correct about a disputed issue, such as in the cases of slavery, women's suffrage, and the position of the earth in the solar system. In some cases expert disagreement can be accounted for by some factions ignoring contrary evidence or alternate theories, for reasons having to do with a prior commitment to a worldview the expert judges to be properly basic to knowledge about the world and thus ought not be discarded unless an alternative worldview has more explanatory power.[25] In other cases expert disagreement may result from holding an irrational belief, clinging to a religious or secular dogma, or not wanting to appear politically incorrect. By treating all expert disagreement over fetal personhood as philosophically and scientifically indistinguishable, by giving the impression that all the arguments of all the factions in the personhood debate are equally compelling, and by simply appealing to expert disagreement rather than wrestling with the actual arguments put forth by these experts and evaluating these arguments for their logical soundness, the Court was able to simply discard the issue of fetal personhood while pretending actually to take it into consideration.

The claim, however, that "no one knows when life begins" is a misnomer, since virtually no one seriously doubts that individual biological human life is present from conception.[26] Thus, what pro-choicers probably mean when they say that "no one knows when life begins" is that no one knows when the personhood or full humanness is attained in the process of human development by the individual in the womb. That is to say, no one knows when the fetus becomes a member of the human community and worthy of protection.[27]

In light of this, it is interesting to note the conclusions of a U.S. Senate subcommittee, which interviewed numerous scientific and bioethical authorities in conjunction with its study and analysis of the 1981 Human Life Bill. It concluded that "no witness [who testified before the subcommittee] raised any evidence to refute the biological fact that from the moment of conception there exists a distinct individual being who is alive and is of the human species. No witness challenged the scientific consensus that unborn children are 'human beings,' insofar as the term is used to mean living beings of the human species." On the other hand, "those witnesses who testified that science cannot say whether unborn children are human beings were speaking in every instance to the value question rather than the scientific question.... [T]hese witnesses invoked their value preferences to redefine the term 'human being.'" The committee report explains that these witnesses "took the view that each person may define as 'human' only those beings whose lives that person wants to value. Because they did not wish to accord intrinsic worth to the lives of unborn children, they refused to call them 'human beings,' regardless of the scientific evidence" (U.S. Senate 1981, 11).

Thus, Justice Blackmun and pro-choice Republicans are likely to argue in the following way:

(1) Experts disagree about when human life becomes valuable (or becomes a person or becomes fully human, as some ethicists have put it), therefore,
(2) No one knows when human life becomes valuable (or "begins"), therefore,
(3) Abortion should remain legal.

There are many problems with this argument, but consider just the following two.

(A) The Argument from Agnosticism is difficult if not impossible to maintain in practice. Recall what Justice Blackmun said in *Roe v. Wade*: "We need not resolve the difficult question of when life begins. When those trained in the respective disciplines of medicine, philosophy, and theology are unable to arrive at any consensus, the judiciary, at this point in the development of man's knowledge, is not in a position to speculate" (U.S. Supreme Court 1973, 160). Hence, the state should not take one theory of life and force those who do not agree with that theory to subscribe to it, which is the reason why Blackmun writes in *Roe*, "In view of all this, we do not agree that, by adopting one theory of life, Texas may override the rights of the pregnant woman that are at stake" (U.S. Supreme Court 1973, 163). Thus for the pro-life advocate to propose that non-pro-life women should be forbidden from having abortions, on the basis that individual human personhood begins at conception or at least sometime before birth, is clearly a violation of the right to privacy of non-pro-life women.

But the problem with this reasoning is that it simply cannot deliver on it what it promises. For to claim, as Justices Blackmun does, that the Court should not propose one theory of life over another, and that the decision to abort should be left exclusively to the discretion of each pregnant woman, *is* to propose a theory of life which hardly has a clear consensus. For it has all the earmarks of a theory of life that morally segregates fetuses from full-fledged membership in the human community, for it in practice excludes fetuses from constitutional protection. Although verbally the Court denied taking sides, part of the theoretical grounding of its legal opinion, whether it admits to it or not, is that the fetus in this society is not a human person worthy of protection.

Thus, the Court actually did take sides on when life begins. It concluded that the fetus is not a human person, since the procedure permitted in *Roe*, abortion, is something that the Court itself admits that it would not have ruled a fundamental right if it were conclusively proven that the fetus is a human person: "If the suggestion of person-hood [of the unborn] is established, the appellant's case, of course, collapses, for the fetus's right to life is then guaranteed specifically by the [Fourteenth Amendment]" (U.S. Supreme Court 1973, 157-58).

Imagine if the Court were confronted with the issue of enslaving African-Americans and delivered the following opinion: "We need not resolve the difficult question of whether blacks are human persons. When those trained in the respective disciplines of medicine, philoso-phy, and theology are unable to arrive at any consensus, the judiciary, at this point in the development of man's knowledge, is not in a position to speculate." Suppose that the Court on that basis *allowed* white Americans to own blacks as property, concluding that slave ownership is a fundamental right. It would appear that although the Court would be making a verbal denial of taking any position on this issue, the allowance of slavery and the claim that it is a fundamental right would for all intents and purposes be morally equivalent to taking a side on the issue, namely, that blacks are not human persons. Likewise, the Court's verbal denial of taking a position on fetal personhood is contradicted by its conclusion that abortion is a fundamental constitutional right and that fetuses are not persons under the Constitution.

Republicans for Choice employs reasoning similar to the Court's in its commentary on a 1992 Oklahoma Initiative: "The Initiative, putting the rights of the fetus above those of the woman, declares 'The life of each human begins at fertilization'–a fact still widely disputed" ("Oklahoma's Massive Challenge" 1992, 2). But if we are to accept the Supreme Court's holding in *Roe*, as RFC does,[28] and agree with Justice Blackmun that the right to abortion is contingent upon the status of the fetus (U.S. Supreme Court 1973, 157-58), then the allegedly disputed fact about life's beginning means that the right to abortion is disputed as well. For a conclusion's support–in this case, "abortion is a fundamental right"–is only as good as the veracity of its most important premise–in this case, "the fetus is not a human person." So, RFC's admission that abortion-rights is based on a widely disputed fact, far from establishing a right to abortion, entails not only that it does not know when life begins but that it does not know when if ever the right to abortion begins.

(B) The Argument from Agnosticism is contrary to the Benefit of the Doubt Argument. If it is true that no one knows when life begins, this is an excellent reason *not* to permit abortion, since an abortion *may* result in the death of a human entity who has a full right to life. If one killed another being without knowing whether the being is a person with a full right to life, such an action would be negligent, even if one later discovered that the being was not a person. If game hunters shot at rustling bushes with this same mind-set, the National Rifle Association's membership would become severely depleted. Ignorance of a being's status is certainly not justification to kill it. This is called the Benefit of the Doubt Argument, since we are giving the fetus the benefit of the doubt.

The Agnostic Argument as employed by Justice Blackmun and pro-choice Republicans seems to imply that the different positions on fetal personhood all have able defenders, persuasive arguments, and passionate advocates, but none really wins the day. To put it another way, the issue of fetal personhood is up for grabs; all positions are in some sense equal, none is better than any other.[29] But if this is the case, then it is safe to say that the odds of the fetus being a human person are 50/50. Given these odds, it would seem that society has a moral obligation to err on the side of life, and therefore, legally to prohibit virtually all abortions.

CONCLUSION: WHAT THE PLATFORM DEBATE IS REALLY ABOUT

One could conclude from what has been written so far that the debate in the Republican Party over its platform is a dispute between two factions that hold incommensurable value systems. But one would be mistaken, for these factions hold many values in common.

First, each side believes that all human persons possess certain inalienable rights regardless of whether their governments protect these rights. That is why both sides appeal to what each believes is a fundamental right. The pro-life advocate appeals to "life" whereas the pro-choice advocate appeals to "liberty" (or "choice"). Both believe that a constitutional regime, in order to be just, must uphold fundamental rights.

Second, each side believes that its position best exemplifies its opponents' fundamental value. The pro-choice advocate does not deny that "life" is a value, but argues that his position's appeal to human liberty is a necessary ingredient by which an individual can pursue the fullest and most complete life possible.[30]

On the other hand, the pro-life advocate does not eschew "liberty." She believes that all human liberty is limited by another human person's right to life. For example, one has a right freely to pursue any goal one believes is consistent with one's happiness, such as attending a Los Angeles Lakers basketball game. One has, however, no right freely to pursue this goal at the expense of another's life or liberty, such as running over pedestrians with one's car so that one can get to the game on time. And, of course, the pro-life advocate argues that fetuses are persons with a full right to life. Since the act of abortion typically results in the death of the unborn, abortion, with few exceptions, is not morally justified, and for that reason ought to be made illegal.

The pro-choice advocate does not deny that human persons have a right to life. He just believes that this right to life is not extended to fetuses since they are not human persons. The pro-life advocate does not deny that people have the liberty to make choices that they believe are in their best interests. She just believes that this liberty does not entail the right to choose abortion since such a choice conflicts with the life, liberty, and interests of another human person (the fetus), which is defenseless, weak, and vulnerable, and has a natural claim upon its parents' care, both pre- and post-natally.

Thus, when all is said and done, the debate over the HLA plank is not even really about conflicting value systems. After all, imagine if the plank had said this: The Republican Party affirms a woman's right to terminate her pregnancy if and only if it does not result in the death of her unborn child. Disagreement over such a plank would not be over the morality of killing persons or even the morality of abortion; it would be over the metaphysical question of whether the unborn human is a full-fledged member of the human community.

What then is one supposed to conclude from this essay? First, most politically active Republicans, both pro-life and pro-choice, along with most members of the media and most Republican candidates, seem not to have read the national platform. This is why it is not surprising that most of them do not seem to understand what the platform debate is supposed to be about. It is supposed to be about *the plank*, a plank which calls for our Constitution clearly and unequivocally in its text to assert that the human community includes both born and unborn from the moment of conception until natural death and that for that reason unborn persons, like their postnatal brethren, should be protected from unjust harm.

Second, if pro-choice Republicans want to dislodge *that plank* from their party's platform, and if pro-life Republicans want their party's platform to retain *that plank*, and if the media want to report accurately the debate over *that plank* to their viewership, readership, and listenership, then the content of *that plank* is the only appropriate topic of debate. For, as we have seen, everything else is simply beside the point.

What, then, is the platform debate really about? It is about the nature and order of things. It is about who and what we are. It is, in the end, whether we like it or not, a testimony to that inescapable truth penned by Aristotle over two millennia ago, "Statecraft is soulcraft."

REFERENCES

"Attention." *Choice News: The Bi-Monthly Newsletter produced by Republicans for Choice*. 1.4 (July/August 1992)

Beckwith, Francis J. *Politically Correct Death: Answering the Arguments for Abortion Rights*. Grand Rapids: Baker, 1993

Beckwith, Francis J. "Personal Bodily Rights, Abortion, and Unplugging the Violinist." *International Philosophical Quarterly* 32 (March 1992).

Bedate, C. A., and R. C. Cefalo. "The Zygote: To Be or Not to Be a Person." *Journal of Medicine and Philosophy* 14 (1989)

Boonin-Vail, David. "A Defense of 'A Defense of Abortion': On the Responsibility Objection to Thomson's Argument." *Ethics* 107/2 (January 1997).

Brody, Baruch. *Abortion and the Sanctity of Human Life*. Cambridge: MIT Press, 1975

Clouser, Roy. *The Myth of Religious Neutrality: An Essay on the Hidden Role of Religious Belief in Theories*. Notre Dame: Univ. of Notre Dame Press,

1991

Cuomo, Mario. "Religious Belief and Public Morality: A Catholic Governor's Perspective." *Notre Dame Journal of Law, Ethics, and Public Policy* 1 (1984)

Dworkin, Ronald. *Life's Dominon: An Argument About Abortion, Euthanasia, and Individual Freedom.* New York: Knopf, 1993

Eddy, Mary Baker. *Science and Health with Key to the Scriptures.* Boston: The First Church of Christ, Scientist, 1875

Englehardt, H. Tristram , Jr. "The Ontology of Abortion." *Ethics* 84 (1973-74)

George, Robert P. "Public Reason and Political Conflict: Abortion and Homosexuality." *Yale Law Journal* 106 (June 1997)

Hackett, Stuart C. *Oriental Philosophy: A Westerner's Guide to Eastern Thought.* Madison: Univ. of Wisconsin Press, 1979

Hunter, James Davison. *Culture Wars.* New York: Simon & Schuster, 1991

Hudnut, Beverly G. and William H. Hudnut III. "We're Good Republicans–and Pro-Choice," *The New York Times* (29 May 1996)

Kamm, Frances M. *Creation and Abortion: A Study in Moral and Legal Philosophy.* New York: Oxford, 1992

Koukl, Gregory P. *Precious Unborn Human Persons.* San Pedro: Stand to Reason, 1996

Kuhn, Thomas. *The Structure of Scientific Revolutions.* 2nd ed. Chicago: Univ. of Chicago Press, 1970

Laudan, Larry. *Progress and Its Problems: Towards a Theory of Scientific Growth.* Berkeley: Univ. of California Press, 1977

Laudan, Larry. *Science and Values: The Aims of Science and Their Role in Scientific Debate.* Berkeley: Univ. of California Press, 1984

Lee, Patrick. *Abortion and Unborn Human Life.* Washington, D.C.: The Catholic Univ. of America Press, 1996

Marquis, Don. "Why Abortion is Immoral." *The Journal of Philosophy* 86 (April 1989)

McDonagh, Eileen. *Breaking the Abortion Deadlock: From Choice to Consent.* New York: Oxford, 1996

Moreland, J. P., and Scott B. Rae. *Body and Soul.* Downers Grove: InterVarsity Press, 2000

National Abortion Rights Action League (NARAL). "Choice–Legal Abortion: Pro and Con." Prepared by Polly Rothstein and Marian Williams. White Plains: Westchester Coalition for Legal Abortion, 1983

News Hour. "Campaign '96–Abortion Plank." <www.pbs.org/newshour/bb/election/june96/abortion_6-11.html>. April 4, 1999

"Oklahoma's Massive Challenge." *Choice News: The Bi-Monthly Newsletter produced by Republicans for Choice* 1.4 (July/August 1992)

Pavlischek, Keith. "Abortion Logic and Paternal Responsibilities: One More Look at Judith Thomson's Argument and a Critique of David Boonin-Vail's Defense of It" in *The Abortion Controversy 25 Years After Roe v. Wade*, 2nd ed., eds. Louis P. Pojman and Francis J. Beckwith. Belmont: Wadsworth, 1998

Pojman, Louis P. "Abortion: A Defense of the Personhood Argument" in *The Abortion Controversy 25 Years after Roe v. Wade*, 2nd ed., eds. Louis P. Pojman and Francis J. Beckwith. Belmont: Wadsworth, 1998

"Pro-Choice Minister Booed." *Choice News: The Bi-Monthly Newsletter produced by Republicans for Choice* 1.4 (July/August 1992)

Rawls, John. "The Idea of Public Reason Revisited." *University of Chicago Law Review* 64 (Summer 1997)

Republican National Committee (RNC). *The 1996 National Republican Platform.* <www.gopnm.org/gopnm/platform.html>. April 4, 1999

Republican National Committee (RNC). *The Vision Shared: Uniting Our Family, Our Country, Our World–The Republican Platform 1992.* Washington, D.C.: The Republican National Committee, 1992

Republicans for Choice (RFC) Home Page. <www.rfc-pac.org>. April 4, 1999.

Stone, Ann. "A Message from Ann Stone." Republicans For Choice Home Page. <www.rfc-pac.org/ann.html>. April 4, 1999

Stone, Ann. "Open Letter from Ann Stone to the Delegates and Alternates to the 1992 Republican National Convention."

Suarez, Antoine. "Hydatidiform Moles and Teratomas Confirm the Human Identity of the Preimplantation Embryo." *Journal of Medicine and Philosophy* 15 (1990)

Sullivan, Lynn K. "Gearin' Up for Houston." *Choice News: The Bi-Monthly Newsletter produced by Republicans for Choice* 1.4 (July/August 1992)

Sumner, L. W. *Abortion and Moral Theory.* Princeton: Princeton Univ. Press, 1981

Thomson, Judith Jarvis. "A Defense of Abortion." *Philosophy and Public Affairs* 1.1 (1971)

Tooley, Michael. *Abortion and Infanticide.* New York: Oxford, 1983

Tooley, Michael. "In Defense of Abortion and Infanticide" in *The*

Abortion Controversy 25 Years after Roe v. Wade, 2nd ed., eds. Louis P. Pojman and Francis J. Beckwith. Belmont: Wadsworth, 1998

    Tribe, Laurence. *Abortion: The Clash of Absolutes*. New York: W.W. Norton, 1990

    U. S. Senate. *The Human Life Bill–S. 158; Report Together With Additional and Minority Views to the Committee on the Judiciary, United States Senate, made by its Subcommittee on Separation of Powers*. Washington, D.C.: U.S. Government Printing Office, 1981

    U. S. Supreme Court. 1992. *Casey v. Planned Parenthood* 505 U.S. 833

    U. S. Supreme Court. 1973. *Roe v. Wade* 410 U.S. 113.

    Warren, Mary Ann. "On the Moral and Legal Status of Abortion" in *The Problem of Abortion*, 2nd ed., ed. Joel Feinberg. Belmont: Wadsworth, 1984

    "Welcome." 1999. Republicans for Choice Home Page. <www.rfc-pac.org/welcome.html>. April 3, 1999

    Wilcox, John T. "Nature as Demonic in Thomson's Defense of Abortion." *The New Scholasticism* 63 (Autumn 1989)

NOTES

1. An example of what such an amendment would look like is one proposed by the U.S. Congress in 1981. Here's a portion of S. 158: "SECTION 1. (a) The Congress finds that the life of each human being begins at conception. (b) The Congress further finds that the fourteenth amendment to the Constitution of the United States protects all human beings. SECTION 2. Upon the basis of these findings, and in the exercise of the powers of Congress, including its power under section 5 of the fourteenth amendment to the Constitution of the United States, the Congress hereby recognizes that for the purpose of enforcing the obligation of the States under the fourteenth amendment not to deprive persons of life without due process of law, each human life exists from conception, without regard to race, sex, age, health, defect, or condition of dependency, and for this purpose "person" includes all human beings. SECTION 3. Congress further recognizes that each State has a compelling interest, independent of the status of unborn children under the fourteenth amendment, in protecting the lives of those with the State's jurisdiction whom the State rationally regards as human beings...." (U. S. Senate 1981, 1-2).

2. I was also a delegate to the Nevada Republican state conventions in 1990 and 1992 as well as a delegate to the Clark County (Nevada) Republican conventions in 1992 and 1994. In the 1992 county convention I served as chair of the platform committee.

3. Ironically, some delegates suggested addressing this in the 1996 platform. Here is a portion of a suggested change that was considered but not accepted by the platform committee: "As Republicans, we acknowledge and respect the honest convictions that divide us on the question of abortion. Unlike the Democratic Party, we will not censor members of our party who hold opposing views on this issue. We are a party confident enough in our beliefs to tolerate dissent." (RNC 1996, Appendix I)

4. On its web site, RFC asserts: "71% of Republicans nationwide are pro-choice. That pro-choice majority wants to replace the plank with one which recognizes Republicans can differ on this issue, and [holds] that abortion should not be a litmus test for candidates or Party members." ("Welcome" 1999).

5. For a defense of abortion as a fundamental non-negotiable legal right, see Dworkin (1993) and Tribe (1990).

6. Although Stone's point is factually correct, it is not clear how her point would persuade those who think that the Court is mistaken about abortion. After all, these non-compliant Republicans can always argue that the G.O.P. came of age while resisting another controversial U.S. Supreme Court decision: the party's 1860 platform–the one on which Abraham Lincoln ran–contradicted the most controversial Court decision of Lincoln's time, *Dred Scott*.

7. See Beckwith 1993; Brody 1975; Lee 1996; Moreland and Rae 2000; Schwarz 1990.

8. There are some who challenge this claim that the nature of the fetus is what is doing or ought to be doing the moral work in the disagreement over abortion. For defenses of this perspective, see Thomson (1971); Tribe (1990), ch. 6; Boonin-Vail (1997); and McDonagh (1996). For replies to this perspective, see Beckwith (1992); Lee (1996), ch. 4; Pavlischek (1998); and Wilcox (1989). Although this is an important and influential perspective, it falls outside the scope of this essay, for the focus of this discussion is a plank in the Republican Party platform that calls for amending the Constitution to include a human life amendment. The purpose of such an amendment, as I understand it, is to directly respond to the conditional challenge put forth by Justice Blackmun in *Roe v. Wade*: "The appellee and certain amici argue that the fetus is a 'person' within the language and meaning of the Fourteenth Amendment. In support of this, they outline at length and in detail the well-known facts of fetal development. If this suggestion of personhood is established, the appellant's case, of course, collapses, for the fetus's right to life would then be guaranteed specifically by the Amendment. The appellant conceded as much on reargument. On the other hand, the appellee conceded on reargument that no

case could be cited that holds that a fetus is a person within the meaning of the Fourteenth Amendment" (U.S. Supreme Court 1973, 157-58). Consequently, the political and legal reality is that fetal personhood is doing all the moral work, even though some moral philosophers and legal and political theorists argue that it does not and/or should not.

9. See Beckwith 1993; Lee 1996; Schwarz 1990.

10. Koukl 1996, 4.

11. For an interesting defense of the view that political and social perspectives are the result of certain ultimate (or religious) commitments, see Clouser (1991).

12. Consider the following comments from Margaret Warner, in a story that appeared on the June 11, 1996 edition of PBS's News Hour: "Abortion is a potentially explosive issue for Republicans this year. The 1992 party platform called for a constitutional amendment banning abortion, and pro-life forces within the party want the '96 platform to remain the same, but pro-choice Republicans, including some powerful governors, have threatened a convention fight unless the anti-abortion plank is struck or radically amended." (News Hour 1996). Later on in the program in her interview with Ann Stone and Phyllis Schlafly, Warner makes the same mistake again in a discussion with Stone:

> STONE: ....We appreciate the fact that [Bob Dole's] welcoming the majority [*i.e.*, pro-choice advocates] back into the party, but we do have to go beyond this, and for his own sake, and we are very concerned about keeping the human life amendment in the platform as we look to fall because I think, as Bill Clinton laid out his strategy, there will be a fight over should there be a constitutional amendment or not, and that–
> WARNER: You're talking about an amendment to outlaw abortion?
> STONE: Right. Outlaw abortion, and if that is the discussion in the fall campaign, Bob Dole will lose that discussion. Once people understand what such an amendment would include, it would be a real problem for us. (News Hour 1996).

13. On numerous occasions during the 1996 presidential campaign, Republican candidate Bob Dole referred to the HLA plank as "the abortion plank." See, for example, Dole's comments in News Hour (1996).

14. This section of the 1996 platform reads a little differently, though the meaning is the same as the 1992 version: "We are the party of individual Americans, whose rights we protect and defend as the foundation for opportunity and security for all. Today, as at our founding in the day of Lincoln, we insist no one's rights are negotiable." (RNC 1996)

15. The Hudnuts (1992) write: "Why should political parties, our party in particular, stake out a position on abortion? Why borrow trouble on a matter on which people are so seriously divided? It seems to us that under traditional minimalist Republican policy, government would choose *not* to interfere with a woman's right to make her own decision about whether or not to bear a child." Stone writes (1992): "You see, to be Republican and Pro-Choice does not mean you are an advocate of abortion. It simply means that you feel the best way to solve the problem is through inspiration and leadership, rather than legislation." In an interview (June 11, 1996) on PBS's News Hour, Margaret Warner asks Stone the question, "You're talking about an amendment to outlaw abortion?" Stone replies: "Right. Outlaw abortion...." (News Hour 1996). The Republicans for Choice web page states: "We will fight at our Party's National Convention to remove the anti-choice plank and nominate a pro-choice Vice-Presidential candidate. We must be viewed as a Party of inclusion and not one of exclusion. Continuing to maintain the anti-choice plank in our Party's platform and ignoring GOP pro-choicers will continue to drive away many Americans who would normally support us" ("Welcome" 1999).

16. The Congressional authors of the failed 1981 Human Life Amendment (S. 158) understood the moral logic of this inference. After Sections 1 through 3 in which abortion is *not* mentioned (see footnote 2), the amendment reads:

SEC. 4. Notwithstanding any other provision of law, no inferior Federal court ordained and established by Congress under article III of the Constitution of the United States shall have jurisdiction to issue any restraining order, temporary or permanent injunction, or declaratory judgment in any case involving or arising from any State law or municipal ordinance that (1) protects the rights of human persons between conception and birth, or (2) prohibits, limits or regulates (a) the performance of abortions or (b) the provision at public expense of funds, facilities, personnel, or other assistance for the performance of abortions: *Provided*, That nothing in this section shall deprive the Supreme Court of the United States of the authority to render appropriate relief in any case.
SEC. 5. Any party may appeal to the Supreme Court of the United States from an interlocutory or final judgment, decree, or order of any court of the United States regarding the enforcement of this Act, or any such law or ordinance. The Supreme Court shall advance on its docket and expedite the disposition of any such appeal.
SEC. 6. If any provision of this Act or the application thereof to any person or circumstance is judicially determined to be invalid, the validity of the remainder of the Act, and the application of such provision to other persons and circumstances shall not be affected by such determination. (U.S. Senate 1981,

2)

17. Stone asserts (1992): "[W]e do not and will not ask President Bush, or anyone else, whose views differ from ours, to change their position. Nor do we advocate that our Party not welcome, or support candidates who represent the pro-life/anti-choice position. While *they* [*i.e.*, pro-lifers] have invited us [*i.e.*, pro-choicers] out of our party, *we welcome them* with open arms. We respect their right to hold a position that differs from ours. *That is their choice*" (emphasis is the author's).

18. Recall Stone's concession to pro-life Republicans (1992): "[W]e do not and will not ask President Bush, or anyone else, whose views differ from ours, to change their position.....*That is their choice*" (emphasis is author's).

19. Political and legal philosopher John Rawls (1997, 798-99) seems to be saying something similar when he writes: "Some may, of course, reject a legitimate decision, as Roman Catholics may reject a decision to grant a right to abortion. They may present an argument in public reason for denying it and fail to win a majority. *But they themselves need not themselves exercise the right to abortion.* They can recognize the right as belonging to legitimate law enacted in accordance with legitimate public institutions and public reason, and therefore not resist it with force. Forceful resistance is unreasonable: it would mean attempting to impose by force their own comprehensive doctrine that a majority of other citizens who follow public reason, not unreasonably, do not accept" (emphasis added). Of course, the pro-lifer (Catholic, Protestant, or whatever) believes that the state's allowance of feticide and its requirement that the pro-lifer not interfere with the performance of feticide is using its force to establish a particular comprehensive doctrine, one that entails certain philosophical conclusions about the nature of persons and the nature of things. Among these conclusions is the belief that the properties necessary to declare something a full-fledged person are absent from fetuses.

20. Stone seems to affirm both of these assertions: "[W]e do not and will not ask President Bush, or anyone else, whose views differ from ours, to change their position.... We respect their right to hold a position that is different from ours.... The Supreme Court just declined to overturn *Roe* and affirmed that a woman's right to choose is essential for women to participate equally in society. Our party's platform is in contradiction with the Court–a Court mostly selected by Republican Presidents. Let's return our Party Platform to the basic Republican Philosophy of less government in our lives" (Stone 1992).
    How can we reconcile our goal to take government out of the daily life of business, but yet thrust government into this most personal and private individual decision? (as quoted in Sullivan 1992, 5).

21. Pro-choice Republicans sometimes subtly make this argument when they describe their opponents in language that conveys the message that pro-life Republicans are *religious* extremists. In one article, pro-life Republicans are called "anti-choice fanatics" and "anti-choice zealots." ("Pro-Choice Minister Booed" 1992, 4)

22. See Beckwith 1993; Brody 1975; George 1997; Lee 1997; Moreland and Rae 2000; Schwarz 1990.

23. The Hudnuts write (1992): "Granted, we are pro-choice, but why not simply leave abortion out of the platform, which has opposed abortion in recent years. As soon as a party or politician or citizen takes a stand on abortion, an 'us against them' situation is set in place, leaving little room for dialogue or diversity of opinion." In an announcement for new members, RFC states, "Help us take abortion out of politics" (RFC Home Page 1999).

24. Sometimes it appears that pro-choice Republicans are not merely calling for the pro-life plank to be dropped, but to replaced with a pro-choice one. On the RFC web page, a portion of the welcome statement reads: "Republicans for Choice believes that in accordance with the basic fundamental principles of the Republican Party, we must protect individual rights, including a woman's right to choose" ("Welcome" 1999). Stone writes:

That Statement of Principles reads: The Republican Party wants "[a]n America with a smaller less burdensome government that trusts its people to decide what is best for them...[a]n America where freedom of expression, individual conscience, and personal privacy are cherished and respected." Apparently these principles apply only to men. The new Statement of Principles would be comical if it weren't so insulting. How can anyone take these principles seriously when the Platform abortion plank specifically says the Party doesn't trust a woman to make the right decision, disrespects her individual conscience, and intends to intrude into her private life with a Constitutional amendment that could help put her behind bars? It's no wonder the GOP has a female gender gap problem.

Stone, in her testimony before the 1992 Republican Platform Committee, asserted: "How can we reconcile our goal to take government out of the daily life of business, but yet to thrust government into this most personal and private individual decision?" (Sullivan 1992, 5). Although it is not clear from RFC literature whether it merely wants to remove the HLA plank or replace it with a pro-choice one, its rhetoric to justify the former sometimes seems to lead inexorably to an obligation to do the latter as well.

25. Some philosophers of science have argued that a scientist's worldview or scientific paradigm has a very strong influence upon the process of discovery and theory-making as well as other aspects of the scientific enterprise. See, for

example, Kuhn (1970), Laudan (1977), and Laudan (1984). It does not take much imagination to conclude from this that political, social, and legal theories may also be shaped largely by one's worldview or paradigm commitments. See Clouser (1991).

26. This has been challenged by Bedate and Cefalo (1989). Their case, however, is seriously flawed. See Lee (1996), 98-102; and Suarez (1990).
    Some have argued that the phenomena of twinning and possible recombination count against human individuality beginning at conception. Although there is good reason to believe this conclusion to be flawed (see Beckwith [1993], 97; and Lee [1996], 90-98), even if it were correct, its practical effect would be negligible, for virtually all pregnant women discover their pregnancy long after these phenomena would have occurred.

27. It should be noted that there are some pro-choice scholars who argue that they *do know* when human life becomes morally valuable. They maintain that at some decisive moment during pregnancy or after birth the fetus (or newborn) acquires certain properties that make him a human person (or moral human being) rather than merely a human being (or genetically human). For defenses of a variety of views on when after conception this decisive moment occurs, see Brody (1975), Englehardt (1973-74), Tooley (1983), Tooley (1998), Pojman (1998), Sumner (1981), and Warren (1984). For critiques of these and other views, see Beckwith (1993), Brody (1975), Lee (1996), Moreland and Rae (2000), Schwarz (1990), and Marquis (1989).

28. Stone writes (1992): "The Supreme Court just declined to overturn *Roe* and reaffirmed that a woman's right to choose is essential for women to participate equally in society. Our party platform is in contradiction with the Court–a Court mostly selected by Republican Presidents." See also the brief analysis of *Casey v. Planned Parenthood* (U.S. Supreme Court 1992) by RFC in "Attention" (1992), 1.

29. Even though this is a logical conclusion of the Court's reasoning, it is clear that the Court's permission of abortion, as I argued above, is inconsistent with this logical conclusion.

30. More sophisticated pro-choice advocates argue that fetuses are not human persons. And for this reason, fetuses do not have a right to life if their life hinders the liberty of a being who is a person (i.e., the pregnant woman). See Dworkin (1993), Englehardt (1973-74), Tooley (1983), Tooley (1998), Pojman (1998), and Warren (1984). Of course, in debate over the HLA plank in the Republican platform, one rarely if ever hears an argument that defends this sophisticated pro-choice claim and takes on the plank's content: fetuses are human persons entitled to the state's protection.

The Critical Influence of the Prospective Father on Abortion-Decision Making

Thomas W. Strahan

CONSPICUOUSLY ABSENT from most discussions of the abortion issue are considerations of third party interests, especially those of the father. A survey of the literature reveals an implicit assumption by most writers that the issue is to be viewed as a two-party conflict–the rights of the fetus versus the rights of the mother–and that an adequate analysis of the balance of these rights is sufficient to determine the conditions under which abortion is considered to be morally permissible.[1] The United States Supreme Court has held that even a husband has no legal right to be notified prior to his wife obtaining an abortion.[2]

Despite the fact that the prospective father may be lacking in legal rights, he is nevertheless very likely to be an important part of the decision for abortion or childbirth. For example, several studies have found that the attitude of the prospective father is an important factor in the stress, anxiety, or depression of the pregnant woman. One U.S. study found that the two most stressful conditions for pregnancy were situations in which (1) the woman is pregnant out of wedlock and receives no help from the father of the baby and (2) the husband doesn't want the baby she is carrying.[3] Another American study found that the most consistent predictor of anxiety throughout the pregnancy was the need for emotional support and the degree of satisfaction of her relationship with her partner.[4] Studies in Nigeria,[5] Japan,[6] and England[7] reached similar conclusions.

Anthropologist George Devereux, in his study of abortion in 400 pre-industrial societies, concluded that female attitudes toward maternity appear to be largely determined by the masculine attitude toward paternity even where children are ardently desired and fertile women are much esteemed. He concluded that this was true even when women abort of their own free will, including instances where they abort from spite, or as a result of a domestic quarrel, for they do so under the impact of a genuine or expected masculine attitude.[8] The importance of the male attitude in pregnancy outcome is not limited to pre-industrial societies. Teri Reisser, an experienced women's post-abortion counselor in Southern California, has stated, "It has been my experience in post-abortion counseling that most women desperately needed their partner to demonstrate a reassuring attitude that everything would work out, that the destruction of a baby that was the product of their love-making was out of the question, [and] that he would protect and care for her and the child.[9]

For many women, abortion appears to be a pressured pragmatic response to a pregnancy rather than an affirmative action in her life which is consistent with her highest and best aspirations. This appeared to be the case in interviews of 1900 women in a 1987 study conducted by the Alan Guttmacher Institute at U.S. abortion facilities. When women were asked why they were having abortions, 23% said their husband or partner wanted her to have an abortion, 68% said they could not afford a baby now, and 51% said they had problems with a relationship or wanted to avoid single parenthood.[10] Among the 790 women who stated they had relationship problems or wanted to avoid single parenthood, 25% indicated they were not in any relationship with their partner. This could include pregnancy resulting from casual or unwelcome sex or from relationships that broke up prior to the abortion. Some 29% of the women said that they were aborting because the partner did not want or was not able to marry. Included among these women are those who may have become pregnant to test the quality of the relationship and then had an abortion if the male failed to commit himself to the relationship. It would also likely include women who became pregnant from extra-martial affairs. Another 32% gave as a reason for abortion that "the couple may break up soon." This likely indicates that the abortion was a consequence of a conflicted or strained relationship.

In comparison to other types of relationships, a married couple is much less likely to seek abortion if the wife becomes pregnant. An Alan Guttmacher Institute survey of 9985 women who obtained induced abortions in the U.S. in 1994-95 found that women who were living with a partner to whom they were not married accounted for 20.2% of the women obtaining abortions but only about 5.8 % of the women of reproductive age in the general population. In contrast, married women only accounted for 18.4% of the induced abortions but 49.9% of the women of reproductive age in the general population. Never married women accounted for 64.4% of the abortions but were only 37.5% of the women of reproductive age in the general population.[11]

Similar findings have been made among Latin American and African women. A 1983-84 study of Bolivian women with induced abortions found that the abortions were much more likely to come from single women who were never in union (46.3%) or women who were divorced, separated, or widowed (54.8%), compared to women in consensual union (23.6%) or married women (18.0%).[12] An African study among 1077 women admitted to various hospitals for incomplete abortions in Kenya during 1988-89 found that the women who had induced abortions were much more likely to have been impregnated by a boyfriend and much less likely to have been impregnated by a husband.[13]

The mental and emotional state between women at the time they undergo abortions compared to women at the time of childbirth can be widely different. Many women who have had abortions perceived that they were all alone at the time when they had the abortion.[14] In contrast, women in a stable marriage may make a "gift" of the baby to her husband which satisfies her sense of femininity and her husband's sense of masculinity. Once this is accomplished, it has been observed that strong reassurance to the self occurred, producing a profound sense of security in the woman.[15]

Studies in several Latin American countries have also found that the partner's ability to provide emotional and financial support are important factors in determining whether or not the pregnant woman has an abortion or carries to term. In a 1974-75 study of Columbian women, if the male partner advised an abortion, the woman took steps to obtain an abortion in 70% of the cases.[16] In a 1988 Chilean study, 48% of the women who obtained abortions reported that they had relationship problems or could not afford a baby.[17] In a study of Mexican women who had abortions in 1980-88, 33% said they were pressured into the abortion by their partner, 21% of the women said they did not wish to marry the partner, and 18% cited economic reasons for having an abortion.[18] Brazilian women seeking abortion by use of misoprostol also appeared to do so primarily for socioeconomic reasons, including no stable partner and lack of income.[19] Other studies among such diverse populations as unmarried African-American women in the inner-city[20] or married Filipino women[21] have been found to be influenced for childbirth or abortion based on the economic status of the prospective father.

Research has identified some of the specific reasons for abortion in the context of the partner-relationship. These include a threat to abandon the woman if she gives birth, that the partner or the woman herself refuses to marry in order to legitimate the birth, that a break-up is imminent for reasons other than the pregnancy, that the pregnancy resulted from an extra-martial affair, that the husband or partner mistreated the woman because of her pregnancy, or that the husband or partner simply does not want the child. Sometimes women combined these reasons with not being able to afford a baby, suggesting the importance of a partner who can offer both emotional and financial support.[22]

Various Swedish studies have also confirmed the important role of the male. In one study of 120 unmarried Swedish women, all of whom had induced abortions, it appeared that many of the women who had abortions actually desired childbirth. In this study, 80% of the women who had abortions said they wanted children in the future. Two-thirds of those who said they wanted children in the future could accept a child with the same man who fathered the aborted child. Some 68% of the women were nulliparous. Many of the women said they decided more or less on their own to have the abortion. Men's reactions to the pregnancy were, "I support whatever you decide" or "It's your problem."[23] Thus, the lack of commitment on the part of the male appeared to be a major reason for the abortions. In another study of Swedish women, some of whom were applying for abortion while others were carrying to term, the women were asked what were the main motives for choosing an abortion. Some 53% said because of the relationship to the partner, 26% said an unstable life-situation for having a child, and only 15% said that they did not want more children. The women carrying to term were much more likely to be married or in a stable, established, long-lasting relationship with a perceived better economic situation compared to women applying for abortions.[24] A more recent Swedish study of 75 male partners of women who obtained abortions found that the most common reaction of males upon first becoming aware of their partners' pregnancy was that it was unrealistic and that they appeared to view abortion as an acceptable form of birth control. Although many men were ambivalent, only one wanted his partner to carry the pregnancy to term.[25]

Further evidence of influence is found in a study of 71 post-abortion women recruited from urban undergraduate colleges in the New York city area. The study found that women would often initially deny that their partners were influential in the decision. However, during the course of the interview, women would describe how they would evaluate the quality of the relationship or the partner's attitude toward the pregnancy. They would further describe how this evaluation was used in their decision to abort. It became evident that the partners were either directly or indirectly influential in the decision-making process.[26] A recent study among Vietnamese couples found that both husbands and wives considered the husband to be the main decision-maker regarding family-size, including the decision whether or not to have an abortion.[27] A German study found that an important factor in pregnancy decision-making was the general commitment of the involved man toward a relationship.[28]

VARIOUS SPECIFIC WAYS IN WHICH
THE MALE INFLUENCES A DECISION FOR ABORTION

One of the reasons for males urging abortion on women may be that the male has difficulty in seeing himself as a father. In a study of 55 expectant fathers by the U.S. Air Force, it was found that men with a previous history of impulsive or schizoid behavior often rejected the expected baby. Expectant fathers without identified psychiatric problems had a superior adaptation to fatherhood and had a "benign kind of identification with their pregnant wife or with the expected baby." However, those with psychiatric problems were unable to form a helpful or stable identification as a "good father or husband."[29]

Sometimes males influence a decision for abortion by being more dysfunctional compared to childbearing fathers. A Hong Kong study compared husbands of women who were applying for abortion with husbands of women who had completed their pregnancies. Significantly more abortion-husbands compared to childbirth-husbands reported poor relationships with either or both parents, a more unhappy childhood, more psychiatric illness in their families, and a higher incidence of alcoholism, drug dependency, neurosis, and compulsive gambling. Some 45% of the abortion-fathers compared to only 12% of the childbirth-husbands considered themselves as having financial, job, or relational problems.[30]

It is not necessary for a prospective father to have a psychiatric or mental illness in order to adversely influence the outcome of a pregnancy. An Australian psychiatrist has found that the unborn child is a potential recipient *par excellence* for projection and displacement. He developed a list of several risk factors for fetal abuse based on attitudes and personality characteristics of the pregnant woman as well as prospective fathers toward the child in the womb.[31] These risk factors also can be applied to fetal destruction as well, including the increased likelihood of abortion. Several identified risk factors specifically include the male partner. These include: low attachment to fetus; denial of pregnancy; passivity by both partners; psychological problems of pregnancy not being tackled or being overwhelmed by them; perception of the fetus as a threat by spouse or partner; marital dysfunction; or adopting an attitude of being only interested in the fetus rather than the mother.

OVERWHELMED BY PREGNANCY

If men are psychologically overwhelmed by the pregnancy of their partners, this may result in excessive daydreaming, heavy drinking, forgetting related events, doing things to avoid confrontation with the pregnancy, and having trouble making even the simplest of decisions regarding the pregnancy. These are all ways of fleeing from situations that create anxiety.[32]

When 25 year old Becky told her boyfriend she was pregnant, he panicked. "He just didn't know what to do. He didn't know how to react. He would hike in the hills all by himself." Becky saw that she had to fend for herself and had an abortion.[33]

Riana (27) faced a similar situation with her boyfriend. She said, "The whole thing was freaking him out far more than me. He waffled between extremes, from frightened but solid support, to getting drunk and high to try to make it go away." Riana obtained an abortion and the relationship broke up.[34]

Joan is in her early twenties and has one child from a relationship a few years ago. When she got pregnant by a new boyfriend, she was devastated by the idea of having two illegitimate children, but would have seriously considered another child if the father was in favor, and she wanted to build on the relationship. Joan said, "He has always said he doesn't want children. He has a very low opinion of himself and is convinced that any child he has will be as 'bad' as he is. He just went into a black depression when I told him, and wouldn't discuss it." Joan had an abortion.[35]

CHILD UNWANTED BY MALE

"I was surprised [to find out that my girlfriend was pregnant], for sure, but in my mind there was never any question of what she'd do. My response was automatic.... She wanted the kid, but it seemed totally unreasonable to me. There is no way I could handle a kid right now." (A 31-year-old garage mechanic who is now impotent three months after his girlfriend's abortion.)[36]

I was working as a bartender at a local pub when I met Jim. He managed a local band and was very handsome, intelligent, and determined. One night he showed up at my apartment, claiming he and his wife were through. Our love affair began, and he was helping me raise my two children. Once I found out I was pregnant, all of the band members were very excited for us, except Jim. He did not say anything about it for a week, but when I pressed him, he stated that he did not want me to have the baby, and that if I did he would leave me. So weighing the costs, and very much wanting to please him, plus being fearful of his leaving me... I had an abortion.[37]

These are not isolated situations. In a study of Hong Kong fathers whose wives had abortions, 44% of these fathers instigated the decision for abortion. In 20% of those cases, the mothers wanted to bear the child.[38]

In a survey of 252 U.S. women who were members of Women Exploited By Abortion (WEBA), one-half of the women said they were encouraged to have an abortion by a husband or boyfriend; others had also encouraged abortion in many instances. The vast majority (84%) stated that the outcome would have been different if they had been encouraged differently. Two out of three said their life was out of control at the time of their decisions.[39]

UNBORN CHILD AS A THREAT

There are men who struggle, and perhaps never manage, to accept the pregnancy.[40] This was the situation with the father in the case next described. It appears to have occurred because he believed that the unborn child was a threat:

May was not particularly happily married with two daughters, and lived in a small house in the suburbs. She worked part-time to supplement her husband's small income. At the time she became pregnant, he was investing the little money they had in a business venture (which later failed). May said: "My husband was furious and would not even talk about the idea of another baby. I pleaded with him that if I could have the child then I would be sterilized. I had never imagined having an abortion... but I knew there was no other alternative because I knew my husband meant it when he said that he would leave me if I didn't get rid of the baby. I couldn't face the idea of being alone, in poverty, trying to bring up three children."[41]

RELATIONSHIP CONFLICTS

Conflict in the relationship, which may involve third parties, is a risk-factor for abortion if the woman becomes pregnant, as the following situations illustrate:

"We don't know if I am the father of the child. She told me that if she knew for sure I was the father, she wouldn't want to have the abortion. I blame her and she blames me. She says that if I hadn't yelled at her and given her a hard time that night, then she wouldn't have gone out with another guy in the first place.... We have lived together for two years, off and on.. I will have a boy someday. I know his name." Later his girlfriend found out he was the father, but had the abortion anyway.[42]

Sally had been involved with her partner for only six months and they conceived while using the rhythm method. Her partner was very distressed because he had impregnated his previous partner, who claimed to have been using contraception. She gave birth around the time that Sally had conceived. Sally said: "My partner was totally traumatized and rushed out to obtain a vasectomy." Sally had an abortion.[43]

HOSTILITY/RESENTMENT

Men may have their own needs that are being neglected during the pregnancy. Invariably they feel resentment and anger, and these feelings find expression. Perhaps a man will subtly remind his wife of her vulnerabilities or withhold affection.[44] In the following case, the boyfriend contributed to the abortion decision by teasing his pregnant girlfriend at her point of vulnerability:

Ricki (20) was pregnant and preoccupied with her body shape. She recalled, "As soon as I found out, I always had this fascination with the mirror and thought one day I was going to wake up and I'd be showing. I was like, Oh no. People are going to know." She stared into her full-length mirror and thought, "Damn, I'm getting fat." Ricki was slender and small-boned and figured she couldn't possibly be showing. Her boyfriend, however, egged on her "paranoia about showing" and would rub her abdomen and say, "Oh, you are going to start showing in a minute." With new doubts, Ricki returned to the mirror. Ricki had her abortion when she was about three and a half months along. Just about the time when she would start to show.[45]

Sometimes the hostility of the male toward the unborn child will take the form of an obsession which may result in abortion. Simone (39) found herself pregnant, but recently had had a baby with her husband Vic some 17 months before. Both were in the middle of career changes and had planned to conceive in the next year once their lives had stabilized. Simone was ambivalent and relied heavily on her husband. Vic told her, "I am willing to be convinced by you and I am willing to go through it all" if she felt it was essential to give birth. Vic cautioned, however, that he saw "the future of this child as bleakness and darkness." Simone thought, "I just cannot do it alone" and so she reluctantly had an abortion. Later they began to fight about it. Each blamed the other for the decision.[46]

It is also possible that the unborn child may be seen as a rival by the prospective father and thus become a target for unconscious aggressive feelings. This was observed in a study of 60 battered women at the University of North Carolina School of Medicine. The women involved frequently reported changes in the pattern of family violence during pregnancy. There was increasing abuse for some, with the pregnant abdomen replacing face and breasts as the target for battering, which resulted in abortions or premature births.[47]

One reason for this resentment or hostility is that a pregnant woman may become more inward-looking and as a result may withdraw some of the affection she previously expressed to her husband or partner. In addition, there are some husbands or partners who are so immature, narcissistic, and demanding of attention that they tend to regard their offspring, even before birth, as rivals for their wives' or girlfriends' attention. This attention was demanded of their mothers and after marriage was demanded from their wives. In other words, the male continued to want another mother, not a wife.[48]

MARITAL DYSFUNCTION

An example of marital dysfunction as a risk-factor for abortion can be found in pregnancy resulting from an extra-marital affair:

Elissa, 24, a Caucasian, met Miguel 9 months ago when she began to work at her father's company. Miguel, a Spanish American, drove a company truck. Elissa's father forbade her to date anyone in the company, but Elissa and Miguel developed a "passion" so strong they became involved anyway. Miguel lived with a woman and was married to a third woman. Miguel and Elissa met once a week and after two months, Elissa believed she had conceived. She said, "The idea of carrying his baby seemed absolutely wonderful." They planned to go together to a clinic for a pregnancy test, but Miguel didn't show. Elissa was furious. Miguel said he wanted her to have the baby, but Elissa, feeling violated, very lonely, and crying at the clinic, had an abortion.[49]

DENIAL

One way that a man may attempt to deny a pregnancy is to attempt to trivialize it. This occurred in the following situation:

When Charles found out his girlfriend Suzy was pregnant he made a joke about it by buying a little bean-bag frog and put a sign on it saying: "It's not my fault,

I'm only a frog." Suzy left it up to Charles to make the arrangements for the abortion. Charles said, "At the time of the abortion I felt immensely sad. I felt I'd been shouldering an enormous burden. I'd made all the arrangements and worked everything out. Suzy just wanted to wake up and find it over, which was exactly what she did. Later we decided it was much more of a moral dilemma than we had realized."

Another way a man can deny or trivialize a pregnancy is by failure to acknowledge that there is human life present in the womb. Consider the following example:

Leo said Liane must have an abortion when he found out she was pregnant. Liane said "No, I'm carrying your child." Leo said, "Not a child, a blob of tissue" and said his family would be disgraced unless she had an abortion. Liane reluctantly had an abortion and their relationship was badly damaged as a result. Although they later married, it ultimately ended in a divorce.[50]

Based upon the few available studies, many men whose wives or girlfriends have abortions believe that a human life is not destroyed when an abortion occurs. One American study of male partners who accompanied women when they obtained abortions found that only one-third believed that life began at conception or within the first 12 weeks after conception, the period when most abortions take place.[51] A larger U.S. study found that 39% of the male partners thought the fetus was a person and 26% felt abortion was the killing of a child.[52]

PASSIVITY OR "NEUTRALITY"

There are some passive men who do not say anything or do not reveal their own attitudes when their wife or partner becomes pregnant. This may be because they believe that the decision on childbirth or abortion is solely that of the woman. But by relying on the legal status of abortion as the basis for the content of the communication with their partner, they may mistakenly convey an attitude of indifference or even abandonment to the pregnant partner. They will thus increase the likelihood of abortion:

Wanda (23) had her first abortion at age 19, mainly because her boyfriend at the time abandoned her. Later, she became pregnant again by Colin, her live-in boyfriend. She felt terrified. "He's going to walk. I really love this person and I've been so happy with him. I'm pregnant and now he's going to leave." Wanda told Colin she was pregnant and he responded, "Whatever you want to do, I'll be there." Colin kept his word. They talked over the situation at length and Wanda decided to have an abortion. However, Colin never told Wanda that a part of him was thrilled about the pregnancy because he did not want to influence her in any way. After the abortion Wanda developed various psychological problems, and it became clear that Wanda and Colin had different perspectives about the abortion. The relationship languished and may end soon.[53]

A 20-year-old man in the waiting-room of an abortion clinic whose girlfriend got pregnant the second time they had sex said: "It was real important to me for her not to have the abortion, but I didn't let on. I didn't want her to feel she was hurting me. I'm fairly religious, a Catholic. I'm totally against abortion. But it was what she wanted to do. And she's got to have the say, doesn't she?"[54]

A large study interviewed 1000 males who accompanied their partners to various U.S. abortion facilities in 1981. In this study, 45% of the men interviewed recalled urging abortion, while only 10% recalled urging adoption, and 17% had recommended childbirth, which the men said they would support financially and emotionally. Thus, the urging of abortion was the predominant reaction of the males to their partners' pregnancy. But perhaps more significantly, 83% of the men favored legal abortion, while only 9% favored a law to outlaw abortion.[55] In another U.S. study of 60 males who accompanied their partners to a Connecticut abortion facility in the early 1980s, only 12% were opposed to abortion.[56] The attitude of certain males about conforming to the legality of abortion may also convey to the female a perceived attitude of indifference or abandonment by the male. This can occur because the woman might fear that her partner will reject both her and the baby, though the degree to which her own fears are real or fantasy may depend on her own ability to accept the pregnancy. In other words, she is likely to project some of her own feelings of ambivalence onto her male partner.[57]

EROTIC ANTI-CHILD ATTITUDES

Abortion serves well the erotically compulsive male or one with such tendencies who strives to maintain his self-esteem and to gratify narcissistic needs through sexual achievements. Typically, this Don Juan male is minimally involved in the personality of his partner since his capacity to love is sharply limited. His sexual activity is invested in countering feelings of inferiority by proving an erotic success. After such a conquest, he loses interest in the chosen woman and reacts with hostility towards her after the successful conquest. Abortion is a handy passport for such adventure.[58] Consider the following two examples of erotic, anti-child males who were involved in multiple abortions.

Three years ago, Ralph, now 26, had a bad year during which he was responsible for three unwanted pregnancies with three different women. None of the women were important to him, and neither were any of the abortions. Rather than drawing him closer to any of the women, the abortions made him dislike them as they became emotional and dependent upon him. Ralph likes "superwomen" and dislikes children, and at this point in his life has no intention of marrying and settling down. He thinks he is lucky to have been involved in only three abortions, given his free-wheeling life style in New York, where he is in public relations.[59]

At age 51, Fritz is a successful insurance agent. He estimates he has been responsible for at least nine abortions. Each of his two wives had three abortions and various other casual encounters led to other abortions. He was not upset by any of them, nor did he feel much emotional responsibility, as he believes that birth control is in the woman's province. He provided some insight into his life. "My father was a frightfully irresponsible ne'er do well who saw me around five times in my life. He deserted my mother when I was three, and the only memory I have of him is being terrified of his booming voice. I rarely saw my mother either and can only remember her kissing me good night. I lived with my nanny while my mother was being supported by her various boyfriends. I was sent away to boarding school at age six and always had a terrible feeling of rejection. My mother subsequently remarried and became a drunk. What terrified me about having children was that it entailed for me a commitment not to reject them. And I still craved attention for myself.... If I did knock up another girl, I'd certainly go through with another abortion. It doesn't bother me at all. It's much easier to have an abortion than to have a child."[60]

Although the outward response of the male may strongly influence the decision for abortion, many males whose wives or girlfriends have abortions have considerable ambivalence toward abortion, and some are strongly opposed. A 1989 *Los Angeles Times* nationwide poll found that about two-thirds of U.S. males expressed guilt over their involvement in abortion.[61] This would offer some hope insofar as the expression of guilt would indicate that many males believed that they had not lived up to their ideals.

SUMMARY AND CONCLUSIONS

The various types of males involved in pregnancies frequently resulting in abortion include those with relational conflicts often involving third parties; male hostility or resentment of the unborn child, or seeing the child as a threat; confusion about or being overwhelmed by the pregnancy; attempting to deny or trivialize the pregnancy; timidity or passivity or attempting to remain "neutral"; or erotic, immature, anti-child males.

What will increase the possibilities for childbirth? The available evidence indicates that the more the male is committed to the female, especially in marriage, the less likely that an abortion will take place if pregnancy occurs. On the other hand, if the female perceives that she is all alone without an adequate sense of security and well-being because the male is not providing both economic and emotional support for childbirth, she is at increased risk for abortion.

NOTES

1. George. W. Harris, "Fathers and Fetuses," *Ethics* 56 (1986) 594.

2. *Planned Parenthood v. Casey*, 505 U.S. 833, 1992.

3. Malcomb M. Helper *et al.*, "Life Events and Acceptance of Pregnancy" in *Journal of Psychosomatic Research* 12 (1968) 183.

4. Joan Jurich, "The Relationship of Social Support and Social Networks to Anxiety During Pregnancy, Sociology, Individual and Family Studies" in *Dissertation Abstracts International* 48/1 (July 1987).

5. O. A. Abiodun *et al.*, "Psychiatric Morbidity in a Pregnant Population in Nigeria" in *General Hospital Psychiatry* 15 (1993) 125. Anxiety and depression were found in pregnant Nigerian women whose husbands were unsupportive.

6. T. Kitamura *et al.*, "Psychological and Social Correlates of the Onset of Affective Disorders among Pregnant Women" in *Psychological Medicine* 23 (1993) 967.

7. R. Kumar and K.M. Robson, "A Prospective Study of Emotional Disorders in Childbearing Women" in *British Journal of Psychiatry* 144 (1984) 35.

8. George Devereux, *A Study of Abortion in Primitive Societies* (New York: The Julian Press, 1955), pp. 135-36.

9. Teri Reisser, "The Effects of Abortion on Marriage and Other Committed Relationships," *Association for Interdisciplinary Research in Values and Social Change* 6/4 (1994) 1-8.

10. Aida Torres and J. D. Forrest, "Why Do Women Have Abortions?" in *Family Planning Perspectives* 20/4 (July/August 1988) 169.

11. S. K. Henshaw and K. Kost, "Abortion Patients in 1994-1995: Characteristics and Contraceptive Use" in *Family Planning Perspectives* 28 (1996) 140.

12. P.E. Bailey *et al.*, "A Hospital Study of Illegal Abortion in Bolivia" in *PAHO Bulletin* 22/1 (1988) 27.

13. V.M. Lema *et al.*, "Induced Abortion in Kenya: Its Determinants and Associated Factors" in *East African Medical Journal* 73/3 (March 1996) 164.

14. Carol Gilligan, *In a Different Voice: Psychological Theory and Women's Development* (Cambridge: Harvard Univ. Press, 1982), p. 74 (the woman focuses on herself because she feels that she is all alone); Eve Kushner, *Experiencing Abortion* (New York: Harrington Park Press, 1997) pp. xx (in a study of 115 post-abortion women almost all of them mentioned how isolated they felt when they had abortions).

15. Howard W. Fisher and I.C. Bernstein, "Pregnancy Fantasies" in *Minnesota Medicine* 57 (Feb 1974) 129.

16. Carole Browner, "Abortion Decision-Making: Some Findings from Columbia" in *Studies in Family Planning* 10/3 (March1979) 96.

17. Monica Weisner, "Induced Abortion in Chile, with references to Latin America and Caribbean countries," a paper presented at the annual meeting of the Population Association of America, Toronto, Canada, May 3-5, 1990 as cited in A. Bankole, "Reasons Why Women Have Abortions: Evidence from 27 Countries" in *International Family Planning Perspectives* 24/3 (1998) 117.

18. Susan Pick de Weiss and H. P. David, "Illegal Abortion in Mexico: Client Perceptions" in *American Journal of Public Health* 80/6 (1990) 715; H. P. David and Susan Pick de Weiss, "Abortion in the Americas" in *Reproductive Health in the Americas*, ed. A. R. Omran *et al.* (Pan American Health Organization/World Health Organization,1992), pp. 323-54.

19. H. L. Coelho *et al.*, "Misoprostol: The Experience of Women in Fortaleza, Brazil" in *Contraception* 49 (1994) 101; S. H. Costa and M. P. Vessey, "Misoprostol and Illegal Abortion in Rio de Janeiro, Brazil" in *The Lancet* 341 (1993) 1261.

20. Susan H Fischman, "Delivery or Abortion in Inner-City Adolescents" in *American Journal Orthopsychiatry* 47/1 (January 1977) 127.

21. A Ankomah, "Unsafe Abortions: Methods Used and Characteristics of Patients Attending Hospitals in Nairobi, Lima, and Manila" in *Health Care for Women International* 18 (1997) 43.

22. A. Bankole *et al.*, "Reasons Why Women Have Induced Abortions: Evidence from 27 Countries" in *International Family Planning Perspectives* 24/3 (Sept. 1998) 117.

23. Kristina Holmgren, "Time of Decision to Undergo a Legal Abortion" in *Gynecol. Obstet. Invest.* 26 (1988) 289.

24. M. Tornbom *et al.*, "Evaluation of Stated Motives for Legal Abortion" in *Journal of Psychosometric Obstetretical Gynecology* 15 (1994) 27.

25. A. Kero *et al.*, "The Male Partner Involved in Legal Abortion" in *Human Reproduction* 14/10 (1999) 2669.

26. Maria J. Rivera, "Abortion Issues in Psychotherapy" in *The New Civil War. The Psychology, Culture, and Politics of Abortion*, ed. Linda J. Beckman and S. Marie Harvey (Washington, D.C.: American Psychological Association, 1998) p. 337; Maria J. Rivera, "Conception, Pregnancy, Decision-Making, and Post-Abortion Response Among Women Who Have Undergone Single, Repeat and Multiple Voluntary First Trimester Abortions, *Dissertation Abstracts International* 56/10 (April 1996) 5780-B.

27. A. Johansson *et al.*, "Husbands' Involvement in Abortion in Vietnam" in *Studies in Family Planning* 29/4 (1998) 400.

28. H. Roeder *et al.* "Partnership and Pregnancy Conflict" in *Psychother. Psychosom. Med Psychol* 44/5 (1994) 153 (Abstract).

29. James Curtis, "A Psychiatric Study of 55 Expectant Fathers" in *United States Armed Forces Journal* 6/7 (July 1955) 937.

30. F. Lieh-Mak, "Husbands of Abortion Applicants: A Comparison With Husbands of Women Who Complete their Pregnancies" in *Social Psychiatry* 14 (1979) 59.

31. John T Condon, "The Spectrum of Fetal Abuse in Pregnant Women" in *Journal of Nervous and Mental Disease* 174/9 (1986) 509.

32. Sam Bittman and Sue Rosenberg Zalk, *Expectant Fathers* (New York: Ballantine Books, 1978, 1980), pp. 18-19.

33. Eve Kushner, *Experiencing Abortion* (1997), p. 287.

34. *Ibid.*

35. Angela Neustatter and Gina Newstrom, *Mixed Feelings. The Experience of Abortion* (London: Pluto, 1986).

36. Linda Bird Francke, *The Ambivalence of Abortion* (1978) and Francke (Harmondsworth: Penguin, 1979).

37. David C Reardon (1987).

38. Lieh-Mak *et al.* (1979).

39. Reardon (1987).

40. Bittman and Rosenberg, p.32.

41. Neustatter (1986).

42. Francke (1979).

43. Kushner (1997), p. 288.

44. Bittman and Rosenberg (1978).

45. Kushner (1997).

46. Kushner (1997).

47. Elaine Hilberman *et al.* "Sixty Battered Women" in *Victimology* 2 (1977-78) 460.

48. W. H. Trethowan, "The Couvade Syndrome" in *Modern Perspectives in Psycho-Obsetrics*, ed. J. G. Howells (EdinburghL Oliver & Boyd, 1972), pp.84-85.

49. Kushner (1997), p. 297.

50. *Catholic Women and Abortion*, ed. Pat King (Kansas City: Sheed & Ward, 1994), pp. 34-35.

51. David A Cornelio, "A Descriptive Study of the Attitudes of Males Involved in Abortion" in *Dissertation Abstracts International* 44/5 (Nov. 1983) 1592-B.

52. Arthur B. Shostak and Gary McLouth, *Men and Abortion: Lessons, Losses and Love* (New York: Praeger, 1984).

53. Kushner (1997).

54. Francke (1979).

55. Shostak (1984).

56. Cornelio (1983).

57. Bittman and Rosenberg, p.51.

58. Vincent M. Rue, "Abortion in Relationship Context" in *International Review of Natural Family Planning* (Summer 1985), pp. 95-121.

59. Francke (1979).

60. Francke (1979).

61. George Skelton, "Many in Survey Who Had Abortion Cite Guilt Feelings" in *Los Angeles Times* (March 19, 1989), p.28.

Discrimination Against Pro-Lifers
in Higher Education?
A Preliminary Survey

Edward F. Gehringer

THE POPULAR WISDOM, at least among conservative observers of the American university scene, is that "political correctness" reigns supreme. Feminism is a major component of political correctness, and support for abortion rights is often alleged to be one of the integral tenets of feminism. From this, one might assume that academe is an unfriendly place for a pro-lifer.

But the university is also home to academic freedom. There is a strong tradition of respect for free inquiry and the right of individual faculty members to speak out on controversial issues of the day without damage to their careers. When academic freedom meets political correctness, what is the result? How free *are* pro-lifers to take a public position on life issues?

To investigate this question, academics were surveyed over the World-Wide Web in late May and early June 1999. Participants in the survey were gathered by e-mail sent to the University Faculty for Life mailing list, and *via* an announcement on Steve Ertelt's Pro-Life Infonet, a daily digest of pro-life news sent to thousands of subscribers by e-mail. Forty-nine academics participated in the survey, a number that is large enough to gain a feel for the magnitude of discrimination, but not large enough to demonstrate statistical significance. About two-thirds of the respondents were UFL members.

ANECDOTAL EVIDENCE OF DISCRIMINATION

Two respondents to the survey painted a stark picture of discrimination. The first is from a natural scientist at a masters-level institution:

I have been told (by faculty and career advisors) *not* to list my research (on pro-life topics) in my resumé or CV. I have been told that I was not even allowed to first level interviews for college teaching positions because I had previously listed my pro-life medical and sociological work. I have been told that I would never get a job at certain Catholic and Christian colleges because of my previous pro-life biological, medical, and social research. I have been passed over as a candidate for college teaching positions because I was considered too Catholic (Catholic being equated as being pro-life and antithetical to liberal faculty agendas). I had one interview where I discussed my paper presented on cloning (animal and human scientific aspects) at a Catholic conference and the interviewing faculty were stunned and remarked that they thought Catholics were anti-science and just too pro-life (anti-abortion) to understand the scientific issues surrounding cloning. I never got the job.

The second is from someone at a medical school in a prominent private secular university who felt compelled to resign from her position within two months after responding to the survey:

I have to work in a family medicine clinic where abortions are done *in the clinic*. The nurses have been quite upset (on one occasion a nurse was just about compelled to participate and left the treatment room where the procedure was done in tears, saying she was a murderer). When I protested that this was not an appropriate venue, as we have a nearby surgical center, I was told I could leave the university if I didn't like abortions being done in the room next to those where I see infertility patients. On another occasion, I was told that I could not use my affiliation when I wrote pro-life or other pieces for papers unless these were reviewed for content. A high official in the medical school tried to get me fired (this anecdotally from a reliable source) for pro-life articles I wrote under my maiden name in the *LA Times*.

But were these anecdotes typical of the situation most pro-life academics face? The survey was designed to find out.

ATTITUDE OF THE SCHOOL ADMINISTRATION

The first question investigated the attitude of school administrators toward pro-life views. Results are given in Table 1. As can be seen, the administrations of church-related schools were markedly more sympathetic to pro-life views. Private secular schools did not differ much from public schools, nor was there much difference between denominations of church-related schools.

TABLE 1. HOW WOULD YOU CHARACTERIZE THE ATTITUDE
OF THE ADMINISTRATION OF YOUR SCHOOL TOWARD PRO-LIFE VIEWS?

	Very Pos.	Posi- tive	Neu- tral	Ten- ding Neg.	Neg- ative	Into- ler- ant	Aver- age.
All schools	3	11	19	6	8	2	2.8
Public	0	1	7	5	6	1	2.1
Private secular	0	0	3	0	1	1	2.0
Church-related	3	10	9	1	1	0	3.5
Protestant	0	2	2	0	0	0	3.5
Catholic	3	7	6	1	1	0	3.6
Other	0	1	1	0	0	0	3.5

Scale: Very positive = 5, Positive = 4, ... , Intolerant = 0

Representative prose responses included these on the negative side:

lack of funding/invitations for any speakers with pro-life views; support for protestors who aggressively interfere with pro-life poster displays; pro-abortion statements by faculty, administration; official invitations of pro-abort speakers, politicians; funding of abortions by campus medical plans; referrals for abortions by campus doctors, advisors, *etc.*; requirement that student groups who have pro-life speakers provide inordinate amounts of police protection. (From someone at a state university)

The President supports Planned Parenthood as a possible placement center for our students even though it is a major abortion provider. Many administrators, most faculty are publicly pro-choice. The new head of a program here in Community leadership is a minister who is a pro-choice defender and very anti-evangelical Christian and Catholic official teachings. (From someone at a Catholic college)

Those answering "neutral" cited conflicting loyalties of administrators:

The biggest concern of the current administration is the political fallout to the school from my pro-life activities. "Will it harm fundraising or negotiations with state officials regarding things the school wants," is the dominant question. (From a professor at secular law school.)

Although I believe most of the administrators are pro-life, they never speak about the issue... there is more of a "silence".... Once, when I said I would write a letter about a "life" incident, I was told I could write as a person...but not in the name of the college. (From someone at a Catholic college)

Some of the "positive" attitudes came from schools with obvious denominational loyalties. When asked what evidence there was for the positive attitude, our respondents answered this way:

Statements by visiting Church leaders in Devotional assemblies. Pro-life supplement carried in student newspaper. BYU President gave pro-life talk in August 1998 commencement address. Pro-life section to be included in new textbook for course on family values. (From someone at Brigham Young)

Their public statements; my personal knowledge of them; practical help for events in Washington like the annual March for Life, where students get excused from classes to attend the March, hospitality is given in University buildings for out-of-town marchers, *etc*. (From somone at Catholic University of America)

One particular incident was cited by a respondent from a masters-granting Catholic college:

Several years ago, when the pro-life group lost its funding due to an administrative oversight on their own part, the administration provided the year's funds. The Dean of Students has made every effort to give the group the opportunity to be provocative, as long as they provide an opportunity for dialogue with those who disagree. The school will not allow the establishment of a pro-abortion group, despite repeated requests. The administration has made certain to cut all ties, even purely incidental ones, with groups like Planned Parenthood, so as to avoid any appearance of scandal on this front. (They haven't been so successful avoiding scandal in other areas, but they've been pretty strong about abortion.)

A second question asked about the attitude of the administration or department to the respondent's own pro-life activities. On this matter there was less difference between church-related and secular schools, though church-related schools were again the more supportive. Table 2 summarizes the responses. We can see that the vast majority of respondents say that the administration has not expressed an opinion on their activities. Here are two representative comments about supportive departments:

TABLE 2. HAS YOUR ADMINISTRATION OR YOUR DEPARTMENT BEEN SUPPORTIVE OR CRITICAL OF YOUR PRO-LIFE ACTIVITIES?

	Supportive	No Opinion	Critical	Avg.
All schools	11	37	1	2.2
Public	1	19	0	2.1
Private secular	0	5	0	2.0
Church-related	10	13	1	2.4
Protestant	1	3	0	2.3
Catholic	8	9	1	2.4
Other	1	1	0	2.5

Scale: Supportive = 3, No opinion = 2, Critical = 1

My department chair has verbally and financially supported pro-life causes in the past. My dean supports the position of the Church against elective abortion and for upholding the sanctity of life. (From someone at a Catholic college)

My department chair has verbally and financially supported pro-life causes in the past. My dean supports the position of the Church against elective abortion and for upholding the sanctity of life. (From someone at a private college)

Surprisingly, only one person said his director was critical of his activities. He said simply, "The assoc. director had made disparaging remarks about Orthodox Catholics." However, it is probably a mistake to assume that the administration and the department speak with a single voice. The above-mentioned law professor commented,

I could mark all three answers to this question, depending upon which administration or which activity. My scholarly writing is generally supported regardless of the topic. My political activities are supported or criticized, depending on the individual in that administration or the manner in which it came to the attention of the administration.

COLLEAGUES' ATTITUDES

In addition to the attitudes of superiors, one's colleagues can also have a great influence on how welcome one feels in academia. The survey asked whether respondents' colleagues respected their right to speak out on life issues. It was discovered that they generally do, and it doesn't make much difference whether one is at a secular or a church-related institution. Generally those who say *yes* outnumber those who say *no* two to one. Only two candidates in the whole survey said their colleagues did not respect them. One might observe (though the questions do not correlate exactly) that colleagues might be more supportive than administrators.

TABLE 3. HAVE YOUR COLLEAGUES RESPECTED
YOUR RIGHT TO SPEAK OUT ON THESE ISSUES?

	Yes	?	No	Avg.
All schools	31	16	2	2.6
Public	13	6	1	2.6
Private secular	2	2	1	2.2
Church-related	16	8	0	2.7
Protestant	3	1	0	2.8
Catholic	12	6	0	2.7
Other	1	1	0	2.5

Scale: Yes = 3, ? = 2, No = 1

A representative remark came from someone in decision sciences:

They are professional scholars, researchers, and educators in a field that has never been politicized in the way that humanities and social sciences have, and we all treasure this too much to dare to impose political correctness of any stripe, left, right or sideways.

One of the two people who answered "no" said this:

Faculty at [this college] treated me with disdain and lied to me, when my book came out. I've been told by a fellow academic that he would have loved to have me come and speak at his (Catholic) University, but he would be fired if this occurred. (This individual is a tenured faculty member of 28 years at the university.)

PRO-LIFE VIEWS AND CAREER PROSPECTS

Another set of questions focused on the effect of pro-life views on an academic career. The first of these questions asked whether the respondent's own career prospects had been hurt. In general, respondents were about three times as likely to say "no" as "yes" and the affiliation of the university did not matter much.

TABLE 4. DO YOU BELIEVE THAT YOUR PRO-LIFE ACTIVITIES HAVE HURT YOUR ACADEMIC CAREER-ADVANCEMENT PROSPECTS?

	Yes	?	No	Avg.
All schools	10	10	29	1.6
Public	3	6	11	1.6
Private secular	2	1	2	2.0
Church-related	5	3	16	1.5
Protestant	1	0	3	1.5
Catholic	4	2	12	1.6
Other	0	1	1	1.5

Scale: Yes = 3, ? = 2, No = 1

That said, it should also be noted that some of those who said "yes" were very sure of their answer. One philosopher remarked

I was in line for a tenure-track position at a Jesuit university before I wrote a pro-life article for a student paper and criticized the administration's decision to allow a pro-abortion student group on campus.

Another at a Jesuit university commented,

A year ago my contract was almost terminated. Among other things, our Faculty Council stated that they were deeply concerned by student reports that I am not "open to the views of others."

Two of those who did not know cited other factors that made it hard to decide:

I did not achieve the professor rank last year–was told that it was based on my undergraduate teaching evaluations–who knows if there was any bias because I am pro-life–it would all be just speculation.

I do not know, except that perhaps listing so many paper presentations dealing with a pro-life topic makes my resumé look weighted. I think my inability to obtain a full-time position in academia is based on affirmative action policies which discriminate against white heterosexual males.

On the other hand, someone from Catholic University of America wrote, "I have always found support, even when I was arrested outside an abortuary." The survey also asked for a prose response to the question, "If your career has been hurt, do you believe there is any way you could have spoken out so forcefully without harming it?" The answer was negative. Ten of the twelve responding answered "no." One of the others said, "Dubious," and the last said, "I don't think I've spoken out so forcefully."

The question naturally arises: If it wouldn't have helped a respondent's career to speak out less forcefully, would it hurt to speak out *more* forcefully? The survey posed this question, with the results shown in Table 5.

TABLE 5. HOW LIKELY DO YOU BELIEVE IT IS THAT YOUR PRO-LIFE ACTIVITIES WOULD HURT YOUR CAREER-ADVANCEMENT PROSPECTS IF YOU WERE MORE OUTSPOKEN (WITHOUT DOING ANYTHING INFLAMMATORY OR ILLEGAL)?

	Very likely	Likely	Neither	Un-likely	Very un-likely	Avg.
All schools	6	7	14	13	7	2.8
Public	3	3	6	3	4	2.9
Private secular	2	0	2	1	0	3.6
Church-related	1	4	6	9	3	2.6
Protestant	0	1	0	2	1	2.3

| Catholic | 1 | 2 | 5 | 7 | 2 | 2.6 |
| Other | 0 | 1 | 1 | 0 | 0 | 3.5 |

Scale: Very likely = 5, ... , Very unlikely = 1

It can be seen that people at non-church related schools thought damage to their careers was slightly more likely than people at church-related schools. Within those two categories, differences between denominations and state affiliation should be discounted because of the small numbers reporting. However, there were two interesting comments on the influence of church affiliation. First, this observation from someone who recently left a Jesuit university for a state university:

My feeling is that I am much more free with respect to pro-life activities at the State university where I now teach than I was at the Catholic universities where I taught for a number of years. (I taught at five such institutions in the past 20 years). Perhaps the size of the school makes a difference, and the fact that here I am viewed as just another oddity (in a large class of other eccentrics). In that sense, it was a relief to leave the world of Catholic higher education so that I could promote Catholic teaching on the value of life. Odd, isn't it?

And this comment from someone at a masters-level Catholic institution:

Since we are a "Catholic" institution, making too much of a stink over a faculty member being pro-life would upset various members of the Board of Directors. But on the other hand, few in the administration are committed to see the culture at the school be pro-Christian or pro-Catholic, so outspoken pro-Christian/Catholic faculty/staff are bothersome. So it is difficult for the administration to be direct about such issues, but not difficult for them to be indirect. It is hard to say for sure, but I do believe that if any damaging decision was done for those reasons, it would be made impossible to prove.

One might conjecture that the danger one perceives in speaking out depends more on the academic discipline than on the type of institution. After all, the right to life is much more controversial in obstetrics/gynecology than in civil engineering, for example. The responses to these two questions were retabulated according to discipline. But still there was little difference in perceived past damage to one's career, as Table 6 shows.

TABLE 6. DO YOU BELIEVE THAT YOUR PRO-LIFE ACTIVITIES HAVE
HURT YOUR ACADEMIC CAREER-ADVANCEMENT PROSPECTS?

	Yes	?	No	Avg.
All depts.	10	8	29	1.6
Theology	1	1	4	1.5
Humanities	3	4	6	1.8
Soc. science	0	0	4	1.0
Nat. science	2	1	4	1.7
Engineering	1	0	1	2.0
Management	1	0	1	2.0
Professional	0	1	0	2.0
Medical	2	1	2	2.0
Other	0	0	7	1.0

Scale: Yes = 3, ? = 2, No = 1

It is perhaps noteworthy that none of the four social scientists thought their career had been harmed, but the numbers per discipline are too small and the results too mixed to draw any clear conclusions. A somewhat different picture emerges, however, when one asks whether career prospects would be harmed by taking a more public stance (Table 7). The majority of respondents from medical schools think their career would be harmed; this is the only discipline where this is true (the relatively high average in engineering can be dismissed, as it came from only two respondents).

TABLE 7. HOW LIKELY DO YOU BELIEVE IT IS THAT
YOUR PRO-LIFE ACTIVITIES WOULD HURT YOUR CAREER-ADVANCE-
MENT PROSPECTS IF YOU WERE MORE OUTSPOKEN
(WITHOUT DOING ANYTHING INFLAMMATORY OR ILLEGAL)?
(BY DISCIPLINE)

	Very Likely	Likely	Neither	Un-likely	Very Un-likely	Avg.
All depts.	6	7	14	13	7	2.8
Theology	0	2	1	3	0	2.8
Humanities	2	2	4	3	2	2.9

Soc. science	0	0	3	0	1	2.5
Nat. science	2	1	1	2	1	3.1
Engineering	0	1	1	0	0	3.5
Management	0	0	1	0	1	2.0
Professional	0	0	1	0	0	3.0
Medical	2	1	1	1	0	3.8
Other	0	0	1	4	2	1.9

Scale: Very likely = 5, ... , Very unlikely = 1

One might also wonder if one could minimize career damage by "lying low" within one's department. To explore this, the results from the first career-damage question were correlated with the results of another question asking whether respondents informed colleagues of their pro-life views. Table 8 shows the results. Those who made an attempt to inform their colleagues tended to report less damage than those who didn't. It should not be surprising that those who thought it more dangerous to speak out were less likely to have done so. But an alternate interpretation is also possible: the reticence of the respondents to state their own positions may have caused their colleagues to view them in a more negative light, which could itself be damaging to their careers.

TABLE 8. DO YOU BELIEVE THAT YOUR PRO-LIFE ACTIVITIES HAVE HURT YOUR ACADEMIC CAREER-ADVANCEMENT PROSPECTS? (BY OUTSPOKENNESS TOWARD COLLEAGUES)

	Yes	?	No	Avg.
All respondents	10	8	29	1.6
I inform all colleagues	4	2	9	1.7
I inform when opportunity arises	4	4	18	1.5
No attempt to inform them	1	0	1	2.0
No, afraid to inform them	1	1	0	2.5

Scale: Yes = 3, ? = 2, No = 1

Note: One respondent didn't answer the question on informing colleagues.

A related question is how making one's views known to *students* affects one's career. The consensus is that it doesn't have much effect (Table

9). Damage to respondents' careers appears to be virtually unrelated to how much effort they invest in informing students of their pro-life views.

TABLE 9. DO YOU BELIEVE THAT YOUR PRO-LIFE ACTIVITIES HAVE HURT YOUR ACADEMIC CAREER-ADVANCEMENT PROSPECTS? (BY OUTSPOKENNESS TOWARD STUDENTS)

	Yes	?	No	Avg.
All respondents	10	8	29	1.6
I inform all students	3	4	10	1.6
I inform when opportunity arises	7	2	16	1.6
No attempt to inform them	0	2	1	1.7
No, afraid to inform them	–	–	–	–

Scale: Yes = 3, ? = 2, No = 1

Note: Two respondents didn't answer the question on informing students.

Another dimension of pro-life identification is the number of pro-life activities someone participates in. The survey asked which activities people had been involved in, activities like participating in marches or demonstrations, writing letters to the editor, working at a crisis-pregnancy center, and so forth. The results suggest that those who are involved in more activities may experience more of an effect on their careers (Table 10). This may be due to bias against prominent pro-lifers, but it may also be due to these activities taking time away from the respondents' careers.

TABLE 10. DO YOU BELIEVE THAT YOUR PRO-LIFE ACTIVITIES HAVE HURT YOUR ACADEMIC CAREER-ADVANCEMENT PROSPECTS? (BY NUMBER OF PRO-LIFE ACTIVITIES PARTICIPATED IN)

# of activities	Yes	?	No	Avg.
At least 5	2	2	4	1.8
3 or 4	3	4	10	1.6
Two	2	2	7	1.5
One	2	0	8	1.4

Scale: Yes = 3, ? = 2, No = 1

Finally, whatever the damage to one's career, the respondent might consider it worthwhile. A nurse from a prominent secular medical school wrote,

I am an orthodox Catholic and pro-life. I am anti-birth control, pro-natural family planning. My views are novel to some and a threat to others. I have been fired from one inconsequential job working at a candy counter in college because of my pro-life activities. A student reporter personally insulted my looks and another threatened our group with violence. ... My career is certainly threatened by being pro-life. But I cannot imagine the evil I would live in leading an apolitical life knowing what I know. Evil is real. I ask God to lead me each day.

SUMMARY

This survey is just a first step in exploring whether discrimination against pro-lifers is widespread in academia. The sample is too small to draw any statistical conclusions. Further, there is the possibility of self-selection bias, from the author's attempt to publicize the survey *via* a list-serve message. The author intends to expand the survey to explore this question further. It has established, however, that it is easy to find pro-life academics who believe they have been discriminated against, and who present credible reports of discrimination. It is also true that this number is a rather small minority of the total number of respondents.

Many of the most vivid reports of discrimination came from those fields that have something to do with abortion, notably medical schools and the biological sciences. From this, one might conjecture that pro-abortion orthodoxy feels itself challenged most seriously from academic experts in these fields. Respondents did feel, however, that academic freedom is an important value, so there was a strong tendency to allow pro-life academics to speak their mind even when their views were unpopular. It is also encouraging that respondents seemed most concerned about the actions of their colleagues, and their colleagues were seen as more respectful of pro-life views than their administrators were.

Hamlet and Human Rights:
Is the Choice to Be or Not to Be
Protected under International Law?

Winston L. Frost

S HOULD THE "RIGHT TO DIE" be recognized as an international human right? This question is being asked frequently as the issues of euthanasia and assisted suicide increasingly arise in the courts, legislatures, and press. Despite the increase in attention, there does not seem to be anything near a consensus on the appropriate role that international law should play in this difficult area.

Little has been written on the "right to die," most likely because the "right to die" is not clearly delineated in any of the international human rights documents. However, it has been argued that the 'right to die' can be found within these documents through a number of rights relating to the autonomy of the individual (*e.g.*, human dignity, privacy, and liberty).

In an article entitled "The Human Right to Die With Dignity: A Policy-Oriented Essay," University of Houston law professor Jordan J. Paust tries to make such a case.[1] This paper is a response to that essay. It is not the intent of this paper to demonize those who support a 'right to die,' but rather to expose the fallacies of their arguments and to present a view that is more in line with international norms.

Before looking to the article by Paust, a note must be made about the power of language and the significant role which word-choice plays in end-of-life discussions.

One of the most common problems in discussion of end-of-life issues is the use of language. This happens as a result of the misuse of basic terminology. In his book *Whatever Happened to the Human Race: Exposing Our Rapid Yet Subtle Loss of Human Rights*, Francis Schaeffer writes, "Language itself is a subtle indicator and a powerful tool.... Language has power. The language we use actually forms the concepts we have and the results these concepts produce." He goes on to recall the name which the Nazis used for the agency which transported people to killing centers: "The Charitable Transport Company for the Sick." Schaeffer then urges: "But let us not be naive. Exactly the same language power is being used when the unborn baby is called 'fetal tissue'." The same language power is being used when the terms compassion, mercy, right, and "death with dignity" are used in the context of the euthanasia debate.

George Orwell wrote of the power of language in his classic novel *Nineteen Eighty-Four*. He showed how language can shape reality and how it can be used as a tool to manipulate people and ideas. The power of words was demonstrated by Orwell in *Nineteen Eighty-Four* through the "Newspeak." The purpose of "Newspeak" was to shape language in such a way as to meet the ideological and philosophical needs of the ruling party. It was also intended to "provide a medium of expression for the world view and mental habits [of the ruling party and]...to make all other modes of thought impossible."[2] As a result, the classic formulation of this was embodied in three principles: (1) war is peace, (2) freedom is slavery, and (3) ignorance is strength.

Referring to Orwell in his essay, "The 'Right to Die' in the Light of Contemporary Right-Rhetoric," J. Daryl Charles had this to say:

"Newspeak," as presented in the Orwellian script, is not an imaginary concept; rather it embodies the human tendency to corrupt and control human beings...Euthanasia today depends on euphemisms. Orwellianisms such as "exit preference," "death with dignity," and a "right to die" are absolutely critical to its cultural legitimation. Empowered by sentiment, euthanasia rhetoric is dependent on images and symbols.[3]

With this idea of the power of language and the importance of clear definitions in mind, it is appropriate to define key terms before focusing on the subject of the "right to die" as an international human right.

EUTHANASIA
The word euthanasia comes from the Greek word for "good death."[4] It is commonly used today to refer to a deliberate act by a doctor which results in the death of his patient by artificial means (*e.g..,* administering

a lethal dose of drugs) as opposed to natural means (*e.g.,* death as a result of disease). Some writers would subdivide euthanasia into passive versus active euthanasia and voluntary versus involuntary euthanasia.

Passive euthanasia has been defined as "[t]he deliberate disconnection of life support equipment, or cessation of any life-sustaining medical procedure, permitting the natural death of the patient." Active euthanasia has been defined as "[d]eliberate action [by a doctor or other health care professional] to end the life of a dying patient to avoid further suffering."

Voluntary euthanasia simply refers to the consent or request of the patient in the doctor's actions. Involuntary euthanasia refers to a doctor deliberately ending the life of his patient without that patient's express consent.

PHYSICIAN-ASSISTED SUICIDE, ASSISTED SUICIDE, AND DOUBLE EFFECT
Physician-assisted suicide occurs when a doctor makes the means of killing oneself available to a patient. This usually takes the form of a prescription of a lethal dose of drugs and instructions on how to use the drugs for the desired result. Assisted suicide is similar, except that the assisting party is not a physician but often a relative, nurse, or friend. Although the terms have a clear distinction, they are used interchangeably in this paper.

Double effect refers to what sometimes happens at the end of a terminal illness when the pain of an individual is most acute. The doctor, in an attempt to lessen the acute pain, may administer pain killing drugs which have the double effect of lessening the pain and at the same time of hastening the death of the patient.

RIGHT TO DIE
The phrase "right to die" sounds reasonable, but it is important to understand its full implications. The "right to die" does not only include the right of a patient to refuse medical treatment and therefore die of natural causes. If this restricted view was all the "right to die" consisted of, few people would have a problem with it. In fact, the laws of the United States clearly allow for this limited right to die. However, those advocating euthanasia have a much broader understanding of what that

right should include.

DEATH WITH DIGNITY

The phrase "death with dignity" is one of the more frequently used expressed by those who favor a "right to die." It has played a subtle role in allowing the word euthanasia to become an acceptable part of everyday vocabulary. As discussed above, the power of language is compelling and is often used in controversial areas with an aim to sway public opinion. What better word to use than "dignity" when referring to the purposeful termination of a life?

"Death with dignity" usually refers to a peaceful death without a great deal of pain. If that was all the phrase included, the concept would hardly be controversial.

Unfortunately, the concept involves the idea that a peaceful death with little or no pain includes, and often necessitates, the option of physician-assisted suicide, assisted suicide, or euthanasia. This concept of dignity is directly related to personal autonomy and the belief that individuals have an almost absolute right to choose the way they end their life.[5]

The term "death with dignity" was first coined in a book published in Germany in 1920 called *The Release of the Destruction of Life Devoid of Value*. "There was no doubt what the authors meant by the term. They made it the motto of the movement to legalize the killing of a person who had the 'right to complete relief of an unbearable life'." But, it must be asked, who is to define an "unbearable life"?[6]

Those who support assisted suicide and euthanasia would generally answer that question by saying that every individual has the capacity to determine when life becomes unbearable. That capacity is the logical result of the almost absolute autonomy that those supporting euthanasia grant to all. The consequences of this type of thinking are summarized by Dr. Nigel Cameron who writes:

What is it for a human to have dignity? It may be that the dignity of a dog is such that it should be killed in order that it should not suffer. Is human dignity that kind of dignity, or some other? That is, is a human being that kind of being whose dignity lies in death by contrivance, if it will avoid suffering of a certain character; or is it some other kind of being? To say that is, of course, to raise the question whether such questions have answers beyond the mere assertion that "it is for me to decide wherein my dignity lies"; that the storyline of every life should end in harmony with the way in which it has unfolded from its beginning, told by the one whose life it is. And while, as in other matters, this seems an appealing way of settling such controversial questions in an increasingly uncertain culture, since it leaves each one free to do that which is right in his or her own eyes, we have to face the fact that it seeks to resolve the question of the meaning of human life by allowing that it lies merely in the meaning that I choose to give it.[7]

MERCY KILLING

The final term which is important to this discussion is mercy killing. The issues it raises, much like the phrase "death with dignity" lie at the heart of this controversy. Mercy killing is defined by Derek Humphry as "ending another person' life without explicit request in the belief that it is the only compassionate thing to do." One of the obvious questions raised by this definition is: "Is it ever compassionate to end another's life, particularly without that other's consent?"

Mercy killing is often advocated in situations where a patient is in the final stages of a terminal illness and is either delirious or comatose. The word mercy is used to describe the act of the physician putting the patient "out of their misery" and therefore allowing them to "die with dignity."

One aspect often ignored by the promoters of euthanasia is the medical profession's ability to control pain almost completely. If this is in fact true, then much of the rhetoric about mercy killing and "death with dignity" is based on a false premise, namely, that the dying process *must* be filled with pain.[8]

The medical community should focus more on palliative care and the easement of pain, particularly in the training of new physicians. If the focus were shifted, the debate about euthanasia and physician-assisted suicide might also shift. If pain and suffering can be controlled until the time of natural death, much of the debate may be effectively subdued.[9]

After looking at some of the terms involved with the end-of-life discussion, it should be apparent that much of the controversy lies in the way certain words and phrases are used within the context of the discussion. With this in mind, let us consider how the "right to die" is dealt with under international human rights law.

The question "to be or not to be" is then whether there should be an internationally recognized human right to "death with dignity," or more specifically, whether there should be an internationally recognized human right to assisted suicide (physician or otherwise) and euthanasia.

DEATH WITH DIGNITY: AN INTERNATIONALLY RECOGNIZED HUMAN RIGHT?
As mentioned above, little has been written on end-of-life issues as they relate to international human rights law, but the article "The Human Right to Die With Dignity: A Policy-Oriented Essay" is a deadly exception. This article will be examined in detail below.

Paust divides his article into four sections. The first deals with his perceptions of the general problem of why a right to "death with dignity" is not internationally recognized. These problems include the contextual complexities involved in any discussion of end-of-life issues and the "overreaching" of domestic laws in the area.

The second section is devoted to the international policies and law, particularly international human rights law, which play an important role in the discussion of end-of-life issues. The third section deals with how the decision-making process involved in end-of-life issues should be approached, and the fourth section concludes the paper with a recommendation that the general "human right to die with dignity" be recognized.

In the second section of the article, Paust tries to show that the "right to a dignified death" is, or should be recognized as, a human right. It is the purpose of this paper to show that there is no international human right to euthanasia or physician-assisted suicide and that there is no right to "death with dignity." Paust begins his article with a host of questions and continues to ask them throughout.

Death and dignity, either alone or with others, is certainly preferable to death without dignity, whether it be lingering or rather sudden. When one can choose the time of one's death or knows of its impending inevitability, dignity seems all the more desirable. But what aspects of the process or experience of dying with dignity, certainly otherwise unique for each human being are most relevant to law, especially human rights law? *Is there and should there be a human right to die with dignity*? What might the content and contours of such a right involve? Choice, respect, recognition of the worth of each person, whether dying or a survivor?[10]

The title of Paust's article uses the illusive phrase "death with dignity." The phrase itself is loaded with controversy. What is human dignity? What does it mean to die with dignity? How much does that one phrase entail? All of these questions can be answered differently, depending upon which side of the discussion an individual happens to place him or herself. Paust lands squarely on the side of those who wish to legitimatize and legalize euthanasia and physician-assisted suicide.

Paust starts his discussion with that fact that "[domestic] laws...pose significant affronts to what should be recognized more generally as the human right to die with dignity." The domestic laws he is referring to are those relating to and prohibiting suicide, assisted suicide, and assisted death. Paust asks whether these laws serve human dignity, whether they can be dealt with on an individual basis. He holds that laws, not considerate of the contextual situation, are "too simplistic, too dangerous, and too inhuman."[11]

The assumption here is that there are only two options: A legal right to assisted suicide and euthanasia, or a death filled with suffering and pain which strips the individual of all human dignity.

This assumption, which lies behind so many arguments of those who promote the legalization of euthanasia and assisted suicide, is based on faulty reasoning. There are more than these two options. Simply because those who suffer a terminal illness would like to end their lives and are not legally allowed to does not necessarily imply that they will suffer a pain-filled death.

Paust discusses the goals of criminal laws which prohibit suicide and assisted suicide, calling them "supposed community goals of preserving life (of any quality) and assuring majority-oriented religious or moral preferences," whether these preferences are reasonable or not. In fact, he argues that when personal choice is exercised in contrast to these laws and criminal prosecution is brought, this is akin to oppression.[12]

Paust does allow that there may be situations where the community's interests will allow for some regulation of suicide and assisted suicide, but the examples he uses are quite obvious in their "reasonableness." For instance, an individual may be prohibited from committing suicide with a bomb in a crowded shopping center, or young people may have certain restrictions placed upon them as the state may have a legitimate interest as *parens patriae*.

According to Paust, these limited restrictions are reasonable but blanket restrictions prohibiting suicide and assisted suicide are not. These blanket restrictions consist of protecting "majority-oriented morality."[13]

This, of course, begs the question of what is, in fact, reasonable. It is clear from the controversy surrounding this issue that what is reasonable to one may not be reasonable to another. This is, in fact, just what Paust is arguing.

The "reasonableness" of the majority concerning end-of-life issues should not be forced on those who understand the issue differently and therefore have a different standard of "reasonableness." This places the discussion right back to the issue of individual autonomy, self-determination and community norms.[14]

Although there is no specific right to assisted suicide or euthanasia in any of the internationally recognized human rights instruments, Paust calls for assisted suicide and euthanasia as human rights. This call is based on rights (found within the applicable human rights documents) which are more general in nature and which, if read broadly enough, Paust argues, may support the right to assisted suicide and euthanasia.

Of these more general and established human rights, the one most important to Paust's argument for "death with dignity" is, quite logically, the right of every individual to human dignity.[15] Other general rights important to his argument include the rights to privacy,[16] liberty and security of person,[17] and adequate health care (both mental and physical).[18] Surprisingly, Paust also refers to the right to freedom from torture and cruel and degrading treatment[19] and the right to life[20] as indicative and supportive of the rights to assisted suicide and euthanasia.[21]

Paust states that because these rights and freedoms are found within all of the major human rights instruments they document "persistent and widespread patterns of expectation relevant to the identification and clarification of normative content."[22] While acknowledging that the rights themselves are certainly normative in character, it is clear that the expectations concerning the content of those rights are not at all consistent when they are placed within the context of the end-of-life debate.[23]

The concept of the inherent dignity of all humans is the foundation of the modern human rights movement. The international instruments spawned by this movement were "largely inspired by the need to protect the right to life... Moreover, [they] were formulated with the atrocities and genocide of the Nazi-period fresh in mind." And now, ironically, some fifty years later, those same instruments, created in response to the horrors of the holocaust are being used to defend a "right to die."[24]

Paust argues that the human right to live with dignity necessarily infers a human right to die with dignity.[25] Again, "death with dignity" is an important concept, but Paust's understanding of *dignity* differs significantly from many others and certainly could not be considered the norm.[26]

In his discussion of "liberty" as a human right, Paust cites the U.S. Supreme Court case *Cruzan v. Director, Missouri Department of Health*, 110 S. Ct. 2841 (1990), as an example of the importance of liberty in end-of-life issues. *Cruzan* dealt with a young woman, who was being artificially kept alive after being involved in a serious accident. Her parents wanted to unplug the machines and allow her to die but the state would not allow them to do it. The main issue was whether Ms. Cruzan had previously clearly indicated her desire to consent to such a move if she were ever put in such a position. Paust quotes Justice O'Connor's concurring opinion: "[A] state that forces a competent adult to endure such procedures against her will burdens the patient's liberty, dignity, and freedom to determine the course of her own treatment."[27]

Again, Paust cites *Cruzan* when discussing the importance of dignity in end-of-life issues. What is important to note here is that Paust has not differentiated in his discussion between the rights of assisted suicide and euthanasia and the right to end medical treatment. He is using a case dealing with the right to refuse medical treatment in support of his position on assisted suicide and euthanasia.

Indeed, there is a qualitative difference between an individual deciding to forego medical treatment and an individual who requests assisted suicide. One who forgoes medical treatment dies of natural causes (the underlying disease) and one who requests assisted suicide is killed, either by himself or another. Many of those who support assisted suicide and euthanasia insist that there is no real distinction between these two options.

In discussing this distinction in his article "Against Assisted Suicide –Even a Very Limited Form," Yale Kamisar quotes Daniel Callahan, the director and co-founder of the Hastings Center:

[T]here must be an underlying fatal pathology if allowing to die is even possible. Killing, by contrast, provides it own fatal pathology. Nothing but the action of the doctor giving the lethal injection is necessary to bring about death....

[A judgment that further life-extending treatment is futile]...is not principally a judgment about a patient's life at all. It is, instead, a judgment about the limits of medical skills in providing further patient benefit. It is a way of saying that, because the limits of those skills have been reached, the patient may be allowed to die.

To call these judgments, and the ensuing omission of treatment, "intending" death distorts what actually happens... [I]f I stop shoveling my driveway in a heavy snowstorm because I cannot keep up with it, am I thereby intending a driveway full of snow?

Since death is biologically inevitable sooner or later, not a consequence of our actions but outside of them, we can hardly be said to "intend" death when we admit we can no longer stop it.[28]

This distinction is crucial in any discussion of the liberty interests of the individual. Individuals are granted the liberty to refuse medical treatment, but at this point they are not granted the liberty actively to involve others in their death. This distinction is also important in the discussion concerning the human right to be free from cruel and unusual punishment and torture.

Another way that these two manners of dying, refusal of medical care and assisted suicide/euthanasia, may be distinguished, is that one has to do with a negative right and the other has to do with a positive right.

Negative rights "require only forbearance on the part of others" where positive rights "require others to provide goods or services if they are to be implemented."[29]

In the context of end-of-life issues, the right to forego medical treatment could be considered a negative right. It is a right *not* to have medical equipment or procedures used to artificially prolong life. The call for a right to assisted suicide or to euthanasia could be considered a positive right. In this sense, others must provide a service of either prescribing or administering a lethal dose of drugs. It is a claim, not "to be let alone" but to a "specific type of medical care–death-hastening treatment under certain circumstances."[30]

A well-established element of Canadian, English, and American tort law is that "medical treatment of a competent adult without the adult's informed consent...is a battery."[31] A consequence of this and now also a well established proposition in the countries mentioned above is that in "normal circumstances an informed competent adult may refuse to consent to medical treatment and may demand the cessation of medical treatment, even if the failure to administer the treatment will hasten or lead to the patient's death." This negative right is a protection against unwanted intrusion into the individual's life; it requires the state to forebear from intruding and requiring an individual to undergo unwanted medical treatment.[32]

There is direct historical and jurisprudential support for a negative right to refuse medical treatment, but there is no parallel historical or jurisprudential support for a positive right of assisted suicide or euthanasia. As noted above, Paust has used a case dealing with the right of refusal of medical treatment as support for a right of assisted suicide and euthanasia. The two are related but represent very different ways of dying.

There has also been some debate as to the overall legitimacy of positive rights claims as opposed to negative rights claims. Historically, civil and political rights have been considered negative in nature and economic and social rights have been considered positive in nature. The argument is that positive rights (like the right to medical care) are only aspirational and therefore cannot be enforced. If they are not rights with correlative duties but only "aspirations or dictates of justice" and therefore cannot be enforced, then *per se* they must not be rights.[33]

Next, one of the more remarkable claims made by Paust is that the human right to be free from cruel and degrading treatment and torture is instructive in the call for a new human right to "death with dignity." He again quotes Supreme Court Justice O'Connor in her concurring opinion in the *Cruzan* case. O'Connor wrote that "[a] seriously ill or dying patient whose wishes are not honored may feel a captive of the machinery required for life-sustaining measures." Paust adds that "such captivity might amount to violations of the right to be free from 'cruel, inhuman or degrading treatment,' if not 'torture'."[34]

If this argument were based only on the need for a right to refuse medical treatment by a competent adult, a right against intrusion, as was the focus of the *Cruzan* case, it would appear to have more validity. To be hooked up to life sustaining equipment against one's will could be considered cruel and degrading treatment. Paust seems to conclude that cruel and degrading treatment might also include being denied the right to assisted suicide. But the right to be *free from* cruel and degrading treatment and torture does not infer a right to assisted suicide and euthanasia.

The final human right that Paust argues is instructive in the recognition of a new human right to "death with dignity"; it is the human right to life. It seems strange at best to defend a human "right to die" with the human right to live. Paust contends that "[i]n context, many of the claims to a right to 'die with dignity' actually reaffirms a more general commitment to life (including life shared, love, and humanity)...."[35] This sounds very much like the Orwellian double speak. A right to death affirms a right to life? Clearly, Paust's definition of life has more to do with quality of life than with life itself. The human right to life certainly is concerned with the quality of life as can be seen through a variety of other human rights relating to quality of life (*i.e.*, health care, freedom from torture, *etc.*) but to argue that a "right to die" is reaffirming of a right to life is creative at best and a clear manipulation of language at worst.[36]

Paust continues by stating: "Clearly...death is a part of life and choice concerning life must necessarily include choice concerning the end and ending of life."[37] While it is clear that death is a part of life, it is not so clear that choice concerning life necessarily means a choice concerning death.[38]

In short, Paust has put forward a number of arguments for a more generally recognized human right to "death with dignity" based on international human rights instruments and the established human rights found within those instruments.

Paust's assertions concerning a right to assisted suicide and euthanasia are based partially on a claim to freedom of choice in these matters. Whenever the subject of choice comes into discussion, particularly a moral discussion involving end-of-life issues, the matters of subjectivity and relativity must also be considered. The concept of choice is by its nature subjective, and as such relative, relative to whatever is acceptable to the person making the choice.

It is accepted that human rights are inherent, inalienable, and universal. In discussing the nature of human rights, the first paragraph of the Vienna Program and Declaration of Action states that "[t]he *universal* nature of these rights and freedoms is beyond question."[39] And the Preamble to the Universal Declaration of Human Rights recognizes the "*inherent* dignity and...*inalienable* rights of all members of the human family..." (emphasis added).[40]

It would appear then that the question to be asked is whether the concept of "choice" as it applies to end-of-life issues is compatible with human rights law. Do not subjectivity and relativity of choice fly in the face of the inherent, inalienable and particularly the universal nature of human rights? If human rights are inherent, inalienable, and universal, can they at the same time be subjective in nature? Can an individual "choose" to accept or reject certain human rights?

Paust contends that choice concerning life must also include choice concerning death. He dismisses the text of the (European) "Convention for the Protection of Human Rights and Fundamental Freedoms" which states that no one shall be "deprived of his life intentionally" (Art. 2) by simply stating that the "choice to end life and to allow others to participate is still protected within the matrix of dignity, liberty, and other rights. One is not 'deprived' if one chooses."

But the very nature of the right to life as an inalienable and nonderogable right conflicts with Paust's explanation. An inalienable right is a "right which one can not give up."[41] If the right to life is in fact inalienable, then choosing to give this right up is not an option.

Likewise, Article 30 of the Universal Declaration of Human Rights states: "Nothing in this Declaration may be interpreted as implying for any state, group, or person any right to engage in any activity or to perform any act aimed at the destruction of any of the rights and freedoms set forth herein." The right to life is set forth in the Declaration, and Paust argues that a "right to die" is implied from other rights found within it.

Assisted suicide and euthanasia are overt acts aimed at the destruction of life and are the implied rights Paust finds within the Declaration and other instruments. Article 30 clearly prohibits these implied rights because they are aimed at the destruction of the right to life.

Human rights are "universal, indivisible, interdependent and interrelated," (Vienna Declaration, Para. 5) and therefore have no real hierarchical order. But it is argued that because some rights are derogable in times of national emergency and others are not, those nonderogable rights are the most fundamental in nature:

As a norm of *jus cogens*...the right to life may not be derogated from in any circumstances whatsoever. As a norm of *jus cogens*, no government may deny the existence of the right to life and a higher duty and standard of protection of the right is imposed upon governments.[42]

As the right to life is a nonderogable right, governments have a high standard of duty to protect that right. The same problem arises here as with inalienability. If the right to life may not be derogated in any circumstances, then how could it be asserted that an individual has the right to ask someone else to assist them in ending their life, or to end it for them?

Although not all individuals who choose assisted suicide or euthanasia are elderly, the topic obviously relates very specifically to them as a class of persons at risk. A number of human rights documents have specific provisions concerned with the protection of the elderly. Interpretive problems arise with these provisions when discussing the possible recognition of a human "right to die."

Article 17 of the Additional Protocol to the American Convention on Human Rights in the area of Economic, Social, and Cultural Rights declares: "Everyone has the right to special protection in old age." This protection includes but is not limited to specialized medical care for those who are unable to obtain it for themselves. Article four of the Additional Protocol to the European Social Charter recognizes the "right of elderly persons to social protection." Included in this right is the right to "health care and the services necessitated by...[the elderly's] state." Article 18, paragraph 4, of the African Charter on Human and Peoples' Rights claims: "The aged and the disabled shall also have the right to special measures of protection in keeping with their physical or moral needs."

The interpretive problems involved revolve around what type of medical care is appropriate for the elderly. Those in favor of assisted suicide and euthanasia argue that the right to health care would include assisted death and euthanasia (as Paust does). Those opposed to assisted suicide and euthanasia see these provisions as protective of the elderly against the inevitable *decline* of their autonomy. It is very much within the realm of possibility to see some family members and caretakers scramble to eliminate those who do not have an adequate "quality of life" to justify their existence (and who might also be draining precious family resources).

Even though international norms are not always reflective of a basic human right, they can be indicative of one. In the case of assisted suicide and euthanasia, there is nothing close to a consensus on the matter, let alone developed norms. "Large parts of the world's population find the idea of the right to die totally unacceptable."[43]

In 1976, the Council of Europe adopted "Recommendation 779 on the Rights of the Sick and Dying." This recommendation was mainly concerned with the right of terminally ill patients to terminate care. The Recommendation noted "that the doctor must make every effort to alleviate suffering, and that he has no right, even in cases which appear to him to be desperate, intentionally to hasten the natural course of death" (Para. 7). Admittedly, this recommendation was made twenty years ago and many changes have occurred since then. It does, however, show the lack of support assisted suicide and euthanasia had just a short time ago.

In relation to Europe and end-of-life issues, the Netherlands' liberal response to these matters is in the forefront of the controversy. But, "traditionally, euthanasia has not been popular in Europe outside the Netherlands." One of the main reasons for this unpopularity is the strict opposition the medical associations of Europe have taken to assisted suicide and euthanasia. "Although the European Code of Ethics represents an ambivalent view regarding euthanasia, the European Community Medical Association and its Standing Committee strongly rejected efforts by Dutch pro-euthanasia physicians who sought to gain European support."[44]

The American Medical Association has strongly opposed a "right to die" and issued a statement that said in part: "The American Medical Association (AMA) feels very strongly that physician-assisted suicide is against the Code of Medical Ethics and incompatible with the physician's role as healer and caregiver. It is not a Constitutional right."[45]

CONCLUSION

As we have seen, there are fatal flaws in the arguments supporting the recognition of a "human right to die." First and foremost, a "human right to die" is inconsistent with already recognized human rights and established international norms. Although recent developments in the U.S. and abroad indicate that public opinion about the "right to die" is slowly shifting toward a more casual acceptance of the right, this acceptance is more the result of the continual efforts made to legitimize assisted suicide and euthanasia by those who support a "right to die" and cannot be clearly attributed to humanitarian concerns.[46]

On the other hand, very little has been written on the relationship between human rights law and a "right to die." Those opposed to euthanasia, particularly those in the human rights community, must write about and discuss the human rights related grounds of why a "human right to die" should not be recognized. These discussions must not only involve moral and legal arguments in opposition to assisted suicide and euthanasia, but must also involve suggestions on how to make the dying process more humane. One such suggestion made here is that the focus on hospice care must be increased in all end-of-life discussion. Hospice meets the stated demands of a "death with dignity" without resorting to assisted suicide and euthanasia. As such, it is a viable alternative to the legalization of assisted suicide and euthanasia.

Dirk J. van de Kaa concluded in his 1989 report ("Human Rights, Terminal Illness and Euthanasia") to the United Nations Expert Group Meeting on Population and Human Rights by stating:

Good arguments can be advanced for a theoretical justification of a "right to die with dignity" but the arguments in favor do not go unchallenged. There is, similarly, no agreement on the question whether the current liberal practice of euthanasia in some countries should be legalized. Recognition of a "right to die with dignity" as a (basic) human right appears to be far away.[47]

However, it will take an ongoing legal and moral vigilance to keep it at bay. Those in favor of life need to counter the arguments for a "human right to die" or offer viable alternatives like hospice and palliative care to insure the recognition of the "right to die" as a human right never occurs.

NOTES

1. Jordan J. Paust, *The Human Right to Die With Dignity: A Policy Essay*, *Human Rights Quarterly* 17 (1995), pp. 463-487.

2. George Orwell, *Nineteen Eighty Four* (New York: Albert K. Knopf, 1992).

3. J. Daryl Charles, *The Right to Die in Light of Contemporary Right Rhetoric: An Essay*.

4. Dirk J. van de Kaa, "Human Rights, Terminal Illness and Euthanasia" in *United Nations Expert Group Meeting on Population and Human Rights* (3-6 April 1989) [ST] IESA/P/AC.28/10 (22 March 1989) p. 1.

5. *Ibid.*, p. 10.

6. Francis Schaeffer, *Whatever Happened to the Human Race: Exposing Our Rapid Yet Subtle Loss of Human Rights* (Old Tappan: Fleming H. Revell Co., 1978), p. 90.

7. Nigel Cameron, *The New Medicine: Life and Death after Hippocrates* (Wheaton: Crossway Books, 1996), pp. 5-6.

8. Connor Reardon, *A Time to Kill* (New York: Albert Knopft, 1936).

9. Scott Rae and Paul Cox, *Bioethics* (Grand Rapids: Wm. Eerdmans, 1999), pp. 232-33.

10. Paust, p. 463.

11. Paust, p. 467.

12. Paust, pp. 470-75.

13. Paust, p. 476.

14. Paust, p. 476.

15. *Human Dignity*: The preambles to the UN Charter, the Universal Declaration of Human Rights (UDHR), the International Covenant on Civil and Political Rights (ICCPR), the International Covenant on Economic, Social and Cultural Rights (ICESCR), and the American Declaration of the Rights and Duties of Man (American Declaration), all recognize the inherent dignity in every individual.

16. *Right to privacy*: Article 12, IDHR. Article 17, ICCPR (interestingly, the right to privacy in both of these instruments is stated as a qualified negative right of freedom from arbitrary interference with one's privacy). Article 5, American Declaration (right to protection against attacks upon private life). Article 11, American Convention on Human Rights (American Convention). Article 8, Convention for the Protection of Human Rights and Fundamental Freedoms (European Convention).

17. *Right to liberty and security of person*: Article 3, UDHR, Article 9, ICCPR. Article 1, American Declaration. Article 7, American Convention. Article 5, European Convention. Article 6, African Charter on Human and Peoples' Rights (African Charter).

18. *Right to health care*: Article 25, UDHR (right to adequate standard of living which includes adequate medical care). Article 12, ICESCR. Article 11, American Declaration (right to preservation of health). Article 10, Additional Protocol to the American Convention on Human Rights in the Area of

Economic, Social and Cultural Rights. Articles 11 & 13, European Social Charter. Article 16, African Charter.

19. *Right to freedom from torture and cruel and degrading treatment*: Article 5, UDHR. Article 7, ICCPR. Article 5, American Convention. Article 3, European Convention. Article 5, African Charter.

20. *Right to life*: Article 3, UDHR. Article 6, ICCPR. Article 1, American Declaration. Article 4, American Convention. Article 2, European Convention. Article 4, African Charter.

21. Paust, pp. 476-79.

22. Paust, p. 478.

23. Paust, p. 478.

24. Van de Kaa, p. 8.

25. Paust, p. 480.

26. Paust, p. 480.

27. Paust, p. 479.

28. Yale Kamisar, "Against Assisted Suicide–Even a Very Limited Form" in *University of Detroit Mercy Law Review* 72 (1995), p. 735.

29. Jack Donnelly, *Universal Human Rights in Theory and Practice* (Ithaca: Cornell Univ. Press, 1989), p. 33.

30. Neil Milton, "Lessons from *Rodrigues v. British Columbia*" in *Issues in Law and Medicine* 11 (1995), pp. 123-48.

31. Milton, pp. 123-48.

32. Milton, pp. 126-27, 135.

33. Milton, pp. 33, 100-01.

34. Paust, p. 481.

35. Paust, p. 480.

36. *Ibid.*

37. *Ibid.*

38. *Ibid.*

39. Clarke S. Austin and Rita Cartwright, ed., *Vienna Declaration and Programme of Action: A Basic Guide to International Human Rights*, App. 1, Vol. 1 (Santa Ana: The Center for Human Rights and Freedom, 1997), p. 87.

40. Preamble to *The Universal Declaration of Human Rights: Final Authorized Text* (New York: United Nations Dept. of Public Information, 1952).

41. Van de Kaa, p. 15.

42. Van de Kaa, p. 15.

43. Van de Kaa, p. 14.

44. Mark DiCamillo, *Strong Public Support for 'Passive' and 'Active' Euthanasia: Doctor Assisted Suicide in Certain Instances* (San Francisco: Field Institute, 1995), p. 808 n. 10.

45. Van de Kaa, p. 10.

46. Van de Kaa, p. 21.

47. *Ibid.*, p. 21.

Interpreting the Pro-Life Movement: Recurrent Themes and Recent Trends

Keith Cassidy

THE FACT THAT CONTROVERSY ABOUT the nature and value of human life has been a major and recurrent element in the social and political conflicts in the United States, at least since the 1973 decision in the case of *Roe v. Wade,* is hardly disputable. The various manifestations of that controversy–debates about abortion, infanticide, euthanasia, and assisted suicide–are of considerable significance in understanding recent American history, and it is therefore not surprising that a huge literature exists dealing with abortion, as well as a lesser but still substantial one on euthanasia and related topics. What of the contending social movements which have kept these issues in the public arena?

It is here that we encounter a puzzle. While there is a large and growing literature on the pro-life movement, the literature on its opposition, the pro-choice and pro-euthanasia movements, is much more limited.[1] Why this disparity of attention? Several reasons are possible. For one thing, the pro-life movement has been arguably a far larger, grassroots phenomenon which has mobilized the energies of millions of Americans.[2] Further, since the pro-life movement has been fighting for 25 years to change the *status quo*, it has of necessity been more pro-active than its opponents and consequently more visible. Still, the disparity is so great that there is clearly something else at work.

That something, I would suggest, is the fact that the communities most likely to describe and interpret social movements–journalists and academics–are far from neutral on the issues under dispute, and not even divided into roughly equal contending camps. Overwhelmingly they are pro-choice, and this colors not only what they say when they write but, even more fundamentally, what they write about.[3] The value commitments of both journalists and academics predispose them to see the pro-life movement as problematic in a way that the pro-choice movement is not, and hence in need of explanation and interpretation. The disproportionate attention paid to the pro-life movement is in large measure a product of the world-view dominant among those who, by vocation, interpret public affairs: to be pro-choice on abortion sounds so reasonable and natural that it requires little reflection, while opposition to abortion seems so clearly wrongheaded that an explanation for it seems necessary. This attitude in turn powerfully affects the questions asked about the pro-life movement and the answers given.

These predispositions–biases–of the great majority of social commentators are not likely to be corrected by contact with those of a different view. Pro-choice academics and journalists rarely encounter pro-lifers as colleagues in their work. They are seen as "other," and to them can be ascribed a number of negative traits. They are dismissed as religious fanatics, with little prospect of having to be encountered at a department meeting or a social function. There is no suggestion here of conscious bias, but only of the not so unusual human tendency to see as either fools or knaves people with whom you disagree and with whom you rarely have contact as social equals.[4] One way of describing the process at work is to speak of "social distance." It is this process which accounts for the fact that so much of the literature on the right-to-life movement sees it as deviant or pathological. While not true of all of the literature, it is an undercurrent in much of it. Because so many researchers have begun with the assumption that the pro-life movement is marginal to American society, it is hardly surprising that so many of them reach that conclusion.

Another factor shaping the treatment of the movement has been the disciplinary backgrounds of the academics studying it: overwhelmingly they are sociologists, anthropologists, or political scientists. In consequence, most of those writing about it have tended to reflect the strengths and weaknesses of those fields. A conscious use of theory, particularly social movement theory, and a heavy reliance on opinion polling data have typified this research. One striking feature has been the absence of a good sense of change over time. In fact, it is precisely this weakness which has drawn the attention of the most astute sociological observer of the pro-life movement, James R. Kelly, who notes the admission of the leaders in the field of social movement theory that "we know comparatively little about the dynamics of collective action over time."[5]

Many of the works reviewed here have the same interpretive themes. They see the movement as narrowly anti-abortion, and not more broadly pro-life. They argue that its opposition to abortion is rooted in other cultural interests, such as the defense of a conservative sexual morality or traditional gender roles. It is frequently characterized as a "right wing" movement, sometimes specifically as a part of the "New Right." Some see the crusade against abortion as largely symbolic, while others see substantive interests at stake, but in either case it is not "really" a defense of unborn life but only a façade–whether consciously or not–for other interests. Characteristically they stress the role of religion in the pro-life movement and often see it as a creation of the Catholic Church. These works tend to downplay or ignore the religious and political diversity of the movement, finding in it a single set of motives and a membership derived from a limited range of groups.

Early in the history of the movement several book-length journalistic accounts of it appeared. Andrew Merton's 1981 *Enemies of Choice: The Right to Life Movement and Its Threat to Abortion* voiced several themes which even that early had become staples in the interpretation of the movement. While there was "no doubt" that pro-lifers were sincere in believing abortion to be murder, it was "likely that they have other motives–perhaps hidden even from themselves–which drive them...." For one thing, they "are appalled by what they see as the rampant sexuality of today's society, and...they view the outlawing of abortion as a means of restoring a more repressive sexual climate." Secondly, "most oppose the gains of the feminist movement....They openly yearn for a return of women to the traditional role of wife and mother–something that is not likely to happen as long as abortion remains easily available." Merton added that "there are also considerable elements in the movement which are anti-democratic, anti-intellectual, and anti-humanist...."[6] This is in keeping with his earlier declaration that "most anti-abortionists, whether Catholic or Protestant, are fundamentalists."[7] However, Merton later argues that "the struggle over abortion is not primarily a religious struggle. It is a class struggle." By this he means that pro-lifers were members of the middle and lower middle classes, hostile to the ruling elite of "the Kennedys, the Rockefellers, the Fords," and were loyal to traditional values.[8]

Merton's account is relatively short and has a limited account of the movement's history. While it is based on a number of interviews, he brought to them a firm set of presuppositions which guided his conclusions. The sociologist James Kelly re-analyzed his taped interviews and described the process as one of turning "liberals into fascists"[9].

Another early work on the movement, Connie Paige's 1983 *The Right to Lifers: Who They Are, How They Operate, Where They Get Their Money*, is a more substantial account. Her dislike of the movement is obvious but less blatant than Merton's, and she makes some real efforts to be fair. This leads to a curious tension in the book, whose criticisms are sometimes quickly modified by concessions that right-to-lifers were indeed correct on important points. While the movement is sometimes spoken of as a single entity, significant divisions within it are recognized. She sees it as originally an offshoot of the Catholic Church, declaring that "the Roman Catholic Church created the right-to-life movement."[10] She attributes opposition to abortion to concerns about sexual conduct and to a desire by the Church to retain its power.[11] A major weakness of the book is its failure to understand that the movement was not, in fact, a simple creation of the Church but in many cases arose from the activity of individuals. Nor does it explain why so many members of the laity became passionately devoted to the cause.

Crucial to the book is the connection of the movement to the New Right: "Although many within the right-to-life movement remained uncertain about or unsympathetic to the rest of the New Right program, they would allow its leadership to call the shots."[12] The two appendices, one on "The New Right's Money Tree" that lists donors to "new right causes," the other a lengthy inventory of "Fundamentalist Donors" (a term which she uses interchangeably with "evangelical") seem intended to create the impression of a vast right-wing conspiracy of which right-to-life is a part. This is undercut, however, by Paige's clear account of the tensions between the pro-life movement and the New

Right. The book does not present a clear and coherent theory of the emergence of the movement, and its attempts to force it into a framework of the New Right have only limited success, but it is still a mine of useful information on the events of the late 1970s and early 1980s.

Also appearing in the late 1970s and early 1980s were a series of articles by the sociologist Donald Granberg and his research associates. They were based both on national public opinion data and on surveys mailed to members of pro-life and pro-choice groups. Granberg stressed two main themes in this literature: first, that pro-lifers were not truly pro-life but rather held views on capital punishment, war, and so on, inconsistent with a true pro-life orientation. Secondly, the real source of anti-abortion activism was moral conservatism.[13] While Granberg's data was, and is, of considerable value, his conclusions are questionable. In order to prove that pro-lifers were not really pro-life, he listed a series of issues as tests of consistency: however, there is no reason to believe that this is reflective of anything other than Granberg's ideological preferences. Thus, the failure of pro-lifers to oppose military spending or to support lower highway speed limits is held to count against pro-life consistency. Intriguingly, his data showed that on the issue of capital punishment pro-life activists were significantly more likely than members of the general public to oppose it; however, he does not list this as a sign of consistency.[14] The creation of consistency tests for pro-lifers has been a staple theme in critical comment on the movement: implicit in it is the assumption that pro-lifers need to be certified as sincere by their social betters. It is hard to recall media comment which calls into question the sincerity of those opponents of capital punishment or supporters of animal rights who are also pro-choice on abortion.[15]

That pro-lifers are motivated by a fear of changes in women's roles has been a recurrent theme. One version of it sees the movement as misogynist and repressive. As Susan Faludi argued, "So often in the battle over the fetus's 'right to life' in the 1980s, the patriarch's eclipsed ability to make the family decisions figured as a bitter subtext, the unspoken but pressing agenda of the anti-abortion campaign."[16]

The argument that the pro-life movement is male-dominated and misogynist has several interpretive problems, not least of which is the large number of women in its leadership ranks. The most influential of all interpretations takes a very different line while still maintaining that the movement is fundamentally devoted to the defense of traditional gender roles. More than fifteen years after its appearance, Kristin Luker's *Abortion and the Politics of Motherhood* continues to shape perceptions of the movement. Exhaustively researched and clearly written, it offers as a central thesis the proposition that "*the abortion debate is emotionally charged because new political constituencies–primarily women–have vested social interests in whether the embryo is defined as a baby or as a fetus.* Although both sides can fairly claim to be altruistic..., their involvements also reflect personal vested interests."[17] Luker claims that the abortion debate is primarily one between women with different life experiences: pro-choicers are better educated, more likely to work outside the home, and less likely to see motherhood as a defining characteristic of their lives than their pro-life opponents. Their different backgrounds and life experiences predispose them to different worldviews, and it is through these that the abortion issue is evaluated. For pro-life women the defense of the fetus is a defense of the value of their own lives: the acceptance of abortion will degrade the value of motherhood, an institution central to their self definition. Hence, pro-life activism is both a symbolic defense of their own values and a defense of a real material interest. Luker is thus able to be sympathetic to pro-lifers but is ultimately dismissive of them: far from being the disinterested defenders of the most vulnerable members of society, they are in reality protecting their own situation in life and validating the choices they have made.

A similar analysis to Luker's can be found in Faye Ginsburg's *Contested Lives*, a study of the abortion conflict in Fargo, North Dakota. Speaking of pro-lifers she says

In their view, social changes that could be interpreted as casting reproduction and childbearing as a liability are anti-woman. Abortion is thus a condensed symbol for the devaluation of motherhood, and the central attribute assigned to it in this culture.... Abortion represents, in addition, a threat to the social guarantees that a woman with children will be supported by the child's father.... In this conflict, then, one sees a struggle taking place over the meaning attached to reproduction and its place in American culture.[18]

That the pro-life movement is the defense–both symbolic and actual–of a social status is a common theme, though none of the other studies promoting it have achieved the prominence of Luker's and Ginsburg's.[19]

Several scholars have been more aware of the complexity of the pro-life movement and have approached it more objectively. Mary Jo Neitz argued that it contained two very different orientations: one "pro-life," espoused by more elite members of the Church, that links abortion to "liberal peace and justice issues," the other "pro-family," advocated by the "masses of the right-to-life movement."[20] A much more substantial account is Michael Cuneo's *Catholics Against the Church*, which although it is a study of the pro-life movement in Canada, provides significant insights into the American movement. Cuneo argues that the movement has, in fact, three components: those for whom abortion is an issue of civil rights and equal protection of the law for the unborn; those whom he calls "family heritage activists," who see in abortion a threat to traditional family values; and those who he calls "revivalist Catholics," who link it to a struggle over the nature of the Church.[21] Cuneo is sharply critical of Luker's "monocausality" respecting the movement and suggests that her thesis "perhaps conceals an ideological bias. In locating the roots of anti-abortionism in the sociocultural circumstances of activists, it seems to imply that the question of abortion itself cannot or should not carry sufficient moral weight to arouse people to activism."[22]

A scholar of particular significance is the sociologist James Kelly. His numerous articles, over nearly two decades, provide a shrewd and sympathetic (although not uncritical) analysis of changing trends, both in the abortion debate and in the pro-life movement. He is clearly aware of the complexity of the movement and the tensions within it. He astutely notes and refutes the claims that it is simply a Catholic operation and that it can be readily dismissed as a reactionary force. For Kelly a central theme is the struggle within the movement between the tendencies to be only an anti-abortion movement or to be a wider pro-life movement, linked to issues of peace and justice. Clearly sympathetic to the latter tendency, he has in recent years described the involvement of some pro-lifers in the "common ground" movement, in which they join with pro-choice supporters in a dialogue to find areas of agreement and common action.[23] As a social scientist, Kelly is ideally positioned to both understand and to criticize the limitations of most social science research on the topic. As a scholar who has conducted numerous interviews with pro-lifers and who has followed the movement's literature and activities, he brings a wealth of information and insight to his writings, which form an indispensable resource for anyone studying the topic.[24]

Another sociologist who has paid considerable attention to the movement and who is, like Kelly, a sympathetic but not uncritical observer is James Davison Hunter. A central theme in his writing on the subject is to locate the contending parties to the abortion dispute within the parameters of a "culture war" over America's fundamental values. His analyses of public opinion are invaluable, both on the abortion issue and on the movements mobilized around the topic, as is his account of the rhetoric employed by each side.[25]

Many of the works mentioned so far make extensive use of social movement theory. It is worth mentioning that a large and sometimes impressive literature dealing with social movements has arisen over the last four decades, with a significant maturation of the field occurring in recent years. These works offer students of the pro-life movement a number of suggestions for research and lines of analysis.[26] Over the years several of these works have used the pro-life movement to illustrate their larger theoretical conclusions. The pitfalls of this approach were apparent as early as 1975 when an early attempt by Armand Mauss to apply social movement theory led to the prediction of the "fragmentation and eventual demise" of the pro-life movement, with the last section of the chapter speaking somewhat prematurely of "the legacy of the abortion movements.[27]

More useful was Peter Leahy's early study of the movement, which contained some valuable insights into the rise and fall of support for the cause.[28] A widely cited study by John McCarthy, which focused on the "social infrastructures" available to social movements, saw the church structures–particularly the Catholic Church–available to pro-lifers as the key to their greater degree of grass-roots organization.[29] While McCarthy correctly identified the pro-life movement as far more "grass roots" than its opposition, his stress on the Church as a resource for the movement was greatly exaggerated. The cross-national comparison of pro-life groups has also drawn some attention, with useful comparisons of the United States both with Britain and Canada.[30] One work, Dallas Blanchard's *The Anti-Abortion Movement and the Rise of the Religious Right: From Polite to Fiery Protest*, attempts an overview account of the movement from a social movement theory perspective but fails to advance our knowledge of the topic.[31] It is marked by a deep-seated and open hostility and can fairly be described as superficial.[32] The same hostility is evident in Victoria Johnson's study of Operation Rescue, where she insists that pro-life is a "countermovement," not a movement. While such a distinction can be legitimately argued, Johnson does so on the extraordinary grounds that social movements "challenge groups higher up in the stratification hierarchy, while countermovements are oriented against changes from below."[33] The notion that the pro-life movement represents the elite and has easy access to wealth and power will be a revelation to its members. While social movement theory has uses for understanding the pro-life movement, many of its practitioners have been as susceptible to interpretations arising from bias as any other group of interpreters.

In the past few years a number of books have appeared dealing with the abortion controversy. They are a fascinating mix, with some repeating older and polemical themes while others break new ground. Leslie Reagan's *When Abortion Was a Crime* gives an account of the period from the passage of the restrictive laws of the nineteenth century to their repeal. Although a book with significant strengths, it fails utterly to understand the nature of the pro-life movement, portraying it as "a backlash in reaction to the expansion of women's reproductive rights and sexual freedom" and connected to a "New Right ...conservative political agenda hostile to feminism, sexual freedom, freedom of speech and religion, and civil rights."[34] No advance over Merton's early interpretation is visible here.

Another book with a wide scope–Donald Critchlow's *Intended Consequences: Birth Control, Abortion, and the Federal Government in Modern America*–provides a very useful framework within which the movement can be understood. Far from regarding it as a marginal or deviant phenomenon, he sees it as a legitimate participant in the public debate. He makes it clear that the pro-life movement, while often Catholic in composition, was not solely so, and included a number of members of other religious traditions. He notes as well that "Although the institutionalized Catholic Church supported the anti-abortion movement as it grew in the mid-1960's, groups emerged on the local level, often without official endorsement by the church hierarchy."[35] Critchlow offers heavily qualified support to Hunter's theory of a "culture war" over abortion by suggesting that, while the "concept 'culture war' exaggerates the political differences within the American polity, the term captures the nature of the polarized debate over abortion and gender-related issues in contemporary America."[36]

A promising work, but one with some significant limitations, is Kerry Jacoby's *Souls, Bodies, Spirits: The Drive to Abolish Abortion since 1973*. Originally a doctoral thesis in political science, it brings to bear on the movement the theoretical apparatus derived from social movement theory. Some of her insights are sharp, and her criticism of Dallas Blanchard's approach is particularly good. Her recognition of the complexity of the issue, which she describes as "not a single issue at all," and her desire to go beyond the "caricature" of the pro-life movement so often encountered, are commendable.[37] Her division of the history of the movement into three phases in which it was successively a "moral crusade" in the 1970s, then a "social movement" in the 1980s, and then in the late 1980s and 90s an "adjunct phenomenon to religious revivalism" is less useful and seems forced.[38] She ignores the years before 1973, apparently unaware of the crucial role of the decisions taken in that period.

The direct action wing of the movement, best known to the public in the form of Operation Rescue, has long had limited, and usually unsympathetic, coverage.[39] In *Wrath of Angels: The American Abortion War* James Risen and Judy Thomas, both journalists, have shed considerable light on this topic.[40] Their research was extensive—more than two hundred interviews—and they brought to their work good journalistic instincts. The writing is vivid, and there are a number of acute insights into the personalities involved.

A major contribution of the book is to make clear to the public that the roots of pro-life direct action lie not with Operation Rescue and Randall Terry, but rather with John Cavanaugh-O'Keefe and others who came out of the anti-war movement of the 1960s. They go on to discuss other exponents of direct action, such as Joe Scheidler, and they set out clearly the background to the emergence of Operation Rescue. They then trace that group's rise and decline and argue that the anti-abortion violence of the 1990s was a product of Operation Rescue's failure. The book's greatest weakness is its willingness to accept at face value the claim of some of the proponents of direct action that they constitute the real pro-life movement. The exclusive focus on this wing means that the mainstream institutional pro-life movement, as represented by the National Right to Life Committee, is largely ignored. It means as well that they treat the demise of Operation Rescue as the demise of the pro-life movement: "The violence of the 1990s spelled the end of anti-abortion activism as a significant political and cultural force in American society."[41] The continued presence of abortion as a political issue in the 2000 Presidential election makes that reported demise particularly unconvincing.

The most impressive of the recent books on the pro-life movement is Cynthia Gorney's *Articles of Faith: A Frontline History of the Abortion Wars.*[42] Asked by *The Washington Post* to write an article on the background to the Supreme Court's 1989 *Webster v. Reproductive Health Services* decision, she went to Missouri where the case originated. Struck by the inadequacy of the literature on the abortion controversy, she undertook a lengthy examination of both the pro-life and pro-choice movements in that state. After five hundred interviews and the examination of numerous archival holdings and of a large published literature, she came to understand both sides with a breadth, depth, and sympathy never before achieved.

The choice of Missouri was excellent since it has had a major influence on national developments and its opposing movements accurately reflect national trends. She chose to tell the story through the eyes of individuals: Judith Widdicombe, a pro-choice nurse who founded an abortion clinic (the Reproductive Health Services which acted as plaintiff in the *Webster* case) and on the pro-life side, first Dr. Matt Backer and then, at greater length, Sam Lee. Switching from one side to the other, she gives a detailed account of events in Missouri while stopping every once in a while to recount national developments. What is most striking about this book is the author's ability to set out, clearly and convincingly, the arguments of both sides. To a quite extraordinary degree she gets inside the minds of the adversaries: their arguments are not caricatured but presented as well as any partisan could. She is alert to conflicts within the movements as well as between them. In short this account, while not a scholarly one, does a far better job of making the actions, thoughts, and passions of the adversaries comprehensible than any other. It will not substitute for a true national history of either movement, but it represents a splendid resource for the writing of one.

As we look at 25 years of accounts of the pro-life movement, we are struck by several features of the literature. One is the frequent death notices, from Mauss's in 1975 to Risen and Thomas's in 1998. What these betray is a continued failure to realize that the pro-life movement is not a temporary reaction to a passing issue but rather represents a deep-seated belief by a large section of the public that human life–of anyone, at any time–is unique, invaluable, and sacred. The abortion issue is but one manifestation of the conflict generated when this belief is challenged, as the growing debate over euthanasia testifies.

This points to another characteristic: the movement's longstanding opposition to various forms of euthanasia tends to be ignored by those who wish to see it solely in terms of abortion. Seeing it that way, of course, permits theories to be advanced that the movement is "really" about motherhood, or the preservation of traditional sexual morals, or the subordination of women. As well, the presence from the beginning of pro-lifers who are clearly on the "left" politically has been ignored by those who wish to see it solely as a "right wing" movement.

That the movement is a longstanding, mainstream player in American political and social life would not be guessed solely by reading much of the literature on it. The distorted view of reality much of this literature advances is a testament to the power of personal bias to shape social research. Fortunately much of the recent literature points to a more mature understanding. Critchlow and Gorney, and to a lesser extent Jacoby as well as Risen and Thomas, represent significant additions to our knowledge. It should not be forgotten, however, that an alternative to the conventional–and wrong–wisdom has long existed. The work of James Kelly and others has for nearly twenty years offered an alternative. The decision for so long to ignore that alternative view represents not so much a failure of social science as of social scientists.

NOTES

1. Suzanne Staggenborg, *The Pro-Choice Movement: Organization and Activism in the Abortion Conflict* (New York: Oxford Univ. Press, 1991) is a full length scholarly study of the pro-choice movement; a compendious survey of the movement to legalize contraception and abortion, heavily focused on legal affairs, is David Garrow, *Liberty and Sexuality: The Right to Privacy and the Making of Roe v. Wade* (New York: Macmillan, 1994). See also Nanette J. Davis, *From Crime to Choice: The Transformation of Abortion in America* (Westport: Greenwood Press, 1985). An account of the right-to-die movement is found in Peter G. Filene, *In the Arms of Others* (Chicago: Ivan R. Dee, 1999).

2. Theda Skocpol, "The Tocqueville Problem: Civic Engagement in American Democracy," *Social Science History* 21/4 (Winter 1997) comments on the fact that the National Right to Life Committee is one of the few organizations created in recent years to have the "federal" structure of local, state, and national organizations, in contrast to those groups which are New York- or Washington-based lobbying groups which rely on a mailing list membership. It is also on her list of organizations which have succeeded in recruiting at least 1% of the population as members. No pro-choice group is on the list. John D. McCarthy, "Pro-Life and Pro-Choice Mobilization: Infrastructure Deficits and New Technologies" in *Social Movements in an Organizational Society*, ed. Mayer N. Zald and John D. McCarthy (New Brunswick: Transaction Books, 1987), p. 53, notes: "It can be safely said that pro-life is more dense in numbers, more grass-roots in nature, more variegated in organizational form, and more widely populated with single-issue groups than is pro-choice."

3. The issue of media bias has long been a source of concern to pro-lifers. That their concern had a basis in fact was confirmed by David Shaw in a series of articles in *The Los Angeles Times*, July 1-4, 1990. James Davison Hunter, "Partisanship and the Abortion Controversy," *Society* 34/5 (July/Aug 1997) observes "Through the 1970s and 1980s, the professions of history, psychology, and sociology became fully committed subsidiaries of the pro-choice establishment." See also the comments in James R. Kelly, "Seeking a

Sociologically Correct Name for Abortion Opponents," in *Abortion Politics in the United States and Canada*, ed. Ted G. Jelen and Marthe A. Chandler (Westport: Praeger, 1994).

4. Carole Joffe offers an interesting confirmation of this point. In a review of Kristin Luker's *Abortion and the Politics of Motherhood* (discussed below), she states: "Given that most academics have little firsthand knowledge of this group, and tend to be biased against them, it is a powerful revelation to see these "others" emerge as compassionate human beings...." Carole Joffe, "The Meaning of the Abortion Conflict," *Contemporary Sociology* 14/1 (January 1985) 27.

5. Kelly, "Sociologically Correct," p. 18.

6. Andrew Merton, *Enemies of Choice: The Right to Life Movement and Its Threat to Abortion* (Boston: Beacon Press, 1981) pp. 8-9.

7. Merton, *Enemies,* p. 6.

8. Merton, *Enemies,* p. 31.

9. James R. Kelly, "Turning Liberals Into Fascists: A Case Study in the Distortion of the Right to Life Movement," *Fidelity* (July/August, 1987).

10. Connie Paige, *The Right to Lifers: Who They Are, How They Operate, Where They Get Their Money* (New York: Summit Books, 1983), p. 51

11. Paige, *Right to Lifers*, pp. 30, 53.

12. Paige, *Right to Lifers,* p. 32.

13. Donald Granberg, "Pro-Life or Reflection of Conservative Ideology? An Analysis of Opposition to Legalized Abortion," *Sociology and Social Research* 62/3 (April 1978); "Comparison of Pro-Choice and Pro-Life Activists: Their Values, Attitudes, and Beliefs," *Population and Environment* 5/2 (1982); "The Abortion Activists," *Family Planning Perspectives* 13/4 (July/August 1981); Donald Granberg and Donald Denney, "The Coathanger and the Rose," *Society* (May/June 1982).

14. Granberg and Denney, "The Coathanger and the Rose," pp. 44-45.

15. This point has been discussed very effectively in James R. Kelly, "AIDS and the Death Penalty as Consistency Tests for the Prolife Movement," *America* (26 September 1987).

16. Susan Faludi, *Backlash: The Undeclared War Against American Women* (New York: Crown, 1991), p. 403. A similar refrain can be heard from Marilyn French, *The War Against Women* (New York: Summit Books, 1992), p. 90: "The real motivation of the campaign to criminalize abortion is to establish the principles that women's bodies belong to the state and that women bear the responsibility for sex."

17. Kristin Luker, *Abortion and the Politics of Motherhood* (Berkeley: Univ. of California Press, 1984), p. 7. Italics in the original.

18. Faye D. Ginsburg, *Contested Lives: The Abortion Debate in an American Community* (Berkeley: Univ. of California Press, 1989), p.7.

19. Stephen L. Markson, "The Roots of Contemporary Anti-Abortion Activism" in *Perspectives on Abortion*, ed. Paul Sachdev (Metuchen: Scarecrow Press, 1985), p. 41 declares that "the crusade against abortion has come to represent to its participants the defense of traditional conceptions of morality and conventional values against the threat posed not simply by the legality of abortion but also by the normative realignment in American culture that was its forerunner." See also Peter J. Leahy, David A. Snow and Steven K. Worden, "The Antiabortion Movement and Symbolic Crusades: Reappraisal of a Popular Theory," *Alternative Lifestyles* 6/1 (Fall 1983); Amy Fried, "Abortion Politics As Symbolic Politics: An Investigation Into Belief Systems," *Social Science Quarterly* 69/1 (March 1988).

20. Mary Jo Neitz, "Family, State, and God: Ideologies of the Right-to-Life Movement," *Sociological Analysis* 42/3 (1981).

21. Michael W. Cuneo, *Catholics Against the Church: Anti-Abortion Protest in Toronto, 1969-1985* (Toronto: University of Toronto Press, 1989). More recently Cuneo has focused on the latter group in the United States. See his *The Smoke of Satan: Conservative and Traditionalist Dissent in Contemporary American Catholicism* (New York: Oxford University Press, 1997), pp. 59-79

22. Cuneo, *Catholics*, p. 82.

23. Information on the Search for Common Ground "Network for Life and Choice" can be found at: http://www.sfcg.org/networkm.htm.

24. Kelly, "Sociologically Correct"; Kelly, "Liberals Into Fascists"; James R. Kelly, "Beyond the Stereotypes: Interviews with Right to Life Pioneers," *Commonweal*, 20 November 1981; "Toward Complexity: The Right to Life Movement," *Research in the Social Study of Religion*, no. 1 (1989); "Learning and Teaching Consistency: Catholics and the Right-To-Life Movement" in *The Catholic Church and the Politics of Abortion: A View From the States*, ed.

Timothy A. Byrnes and Mary C. Segers (Boulder, 1992); "Beyond Some Stereotypes: An Empirical Study of Some Right-to-Life Activists" in *Proceedings of Association for the Sociology of Religion 1981* (n.d.); "Truth, Not Truce: 'Common Ground' on Abortion, a Movement Within Both Movements," *Virginia Review of Sociology* 2 (1995); "AIDS and the Death Penalty"; "Consistency and Common Ground in the Post-Casey Abortion Era," in *The Politics of Abortion in the American States*, ed. Mary C. Segers and Timothy Byrne (Armonk: M. E. Sharpe, 1995); "The Vanishing Middle in Abortion Politics," *The Christian Century* (August 1988); "Ecumenism and Abortion: A Case Study of Pluralism, Privatization and the Public Conscience," *Review of Religious Research* 30/3 (March 1989); "Pro-Life and Pro-Choice After Reagan-Bush," *America* (30 January 1993); "A Political Challenge to the Prolife Movement," *Commonweal* (23 November 1990); "Abortion: What Americans Really Think and the Catholic Challenge," *America* (2 November 1991); "Common Ground for Pro-Life and Pro-Choice: Joining Forces to Challenge New Jersey Family Cap," *America* 180/2 (23 January 1999); "Why Republican and New Democrat Welfare Changes Need Legal Abortion," *America* 173 (6 January 1996); "A Dispatch From the Abortion Wars: Reflections on 'Common Ground'," *America* 171 (17 September 1994); "Abortion Politics: The Last Decades, the Next Three Decades and the 1992 Elections," *America* 167 (11 July 1992); "The Koop Report and a Better Politics of Abortion," *America* 162 (2 June 1990); "Beyond Slogans: An Abortion Ethic for Women and the Unborn," *The Christian Century* 107 (21 February 1990).

25. James Davison Hunter, *Culture Wars: The Struggle to Define America* (New York: Basic Books, 1991); *Before the Shooting Begins: Searching for Democracy in America's Culture War* (New York: The Free Press, 1994); "What Americans Really Think About Abortion," *First Things*, June/July 1992. For a critique of the "culture war" thesis, see Michele Dillon, "The American Abortion Debate: Culture War or Normal Discourse?" *Virginia Review of Sociology* 2 (1995).

26. Jo Freeman and Victoria Johnson, eds., *Waves of Protest: Social Movements Since the Sixties* (Lanham: Rowman and Littlefield, 1999); Mayer N. Zald and John D. McCarthy, eds., *Social Movements in an Organizational Society: Collected Essays* (New Brunswick: Transaction Books, 1987); Anne N. Costain and Andrew S. McFarland, eds., *Social Movements and American Political Institutions* (Lanham: Rowman and Littlefield, 1998); David S. Meyer and Sidney Tarrow, eds., *The Social Movement Society: Contentious Politics for a New Century* (Lanham: Rowman and Littlefield, 1997); Doug McAdam, John D. McCarthy and Mayer N. Zald, eds., *Comparative Perspectives on Social Movements: Political Opportunities, Mobilizing Structures, and Cultural*

Framings (New York: Cambridge Univ. Press, 1996); Sidney G. Tarrow, *Power in Movement: Social Movements, Collective Action and Politics* (New York: Cambridge Univ. Press, 1994).

27. Armand L. Mauss, *Social Problems As Social Movements* (Philadelphia: J.B. Lippincott, 1975), p. 471.

28. Peter James Leahy, "The Anti-Abortion Movement: Testing A Theory of the Rise and Fall of Social Movements" (Doctoral Dissertation, Syracuse University, 1975).

29. McCarthy, "Pro-Life and Pro-Choice."

30. J. Christopher Soper, "Political Structures and Interest Group Activism: A Comparison of the British and American Pro-Life Movements," *Social Science Journal* 31/3 (1994); David S. Meyer and Suzanne Staggenborg, "Countermovement Dynamics in Federal Systems: A Comparison of Abortion Politics in Canada and the United States," *Research in Political Sociology* 8 (1998).

31. Dallas A. Blanchard, *The Anti-Abortion Movement and the Rise of the Religious Right: From Polite to Fiery Protest* (New York: Twayne, 1994).

32. Indeed one expert in the field described it as such; see Clyde Wilcox, review of *The Anti-Abortion Movement and the Rise of the Religious Right: From Polite to Fiery Protest*, by Dallas A. Blanchard, in *Social Forces* 74/4 (June 1996). Blanchard's reference work on the movement, *The Anti-Abortion Movement: References and Resources* (New York: G.K. Hall & Co., 1996) is also of limited use. The work he co-authored on the clinic bombings in Florida is of more value: Dallas A. Blanchard and Terry J. Prewitt, *Religious Violence and Abortion: The Gideon Project* (Gainesville: Univ. Press of Florida, 1993).

33. Victoria Johnson, "The Strategic Determinants of a Countermovement: The Emergence and Impact of Operation Rescue Blockades" in *Waves of Protest: Social Movements Since the Sixties*, ed. Jo Freeman and Victoria Johnson (Lanham: Rowman and Littlefield, 1999), p. 241.

34. Leslie J. Reagan, *When Abortion Was A Crime: Women, Medicine, and Law in the United States, 1867-1973* (Berkeley: Univ. of California Press, 1997), p. 248.

35. Donald T. Critchlow, *Intended Consequences: Birth Control, Abortion, and the Federal Government in Modern America* (New York: Oxford Univ. Press, 1999), p. 138, 137.

36. Critchlow (1999), p. 8.

37. Kerry N. Jacoby, *Souls, Bodies, Spirits: The Drive to Abolish Abortion Since 1973* (Westport: Praeger, 1998), pp. xiii-xiv.

38. Jacoby, *Souls, Bodies, Spirits*, p. xiv.

39. See, for example, Marian Faux, *Crusaders: Voices From the Abortion Front* (New York: Birch Lane Press, 1990). For a scholarly account see Faye Ginsburg, "Saving America's Souls: Operation Rescue's Crusade Against Abortion" in *Fundamentalism and the State: Remaking Polities, Economies, and Militance*, ed. Martin E. Marty and R. Scott Appleby (Chicago: Univ. of Chicago Press, 1993). This literature is discussed in Keith M. Cassidy, "Pro-Life Direct Action Campaigns: A Survey of Scholarly and Media Interpretations" in *Life and Learning VI: Proceedings of Sixth University Faculty for Life Conference in Georgetown University June 1996*, ed. Joseph W. Koterski, S.J. (Washington, D.C.: University Faculty for Life, 1997), pp. 235-44.

40. James Risen and Judy L. Thomas, *Wrath of Angels: The American Abortion War* (New York: Basic Books, 1998).

41. Risen and Thomas, *Wrath*, p. 273.

42. Cynthia Gorney, *Articles of Faith: A Frontline History of the Abortion Wars* (New York: Simon and Schuster, 1998).

Horatio Robinson Storer, M.D. and the Physicians' Crusade Against Abortion

Frederick N. Dyer

MOST PEOPLE ARE SURPRISED to learn that induced abortion was common among married Protestant women in America in the middle of the 19th Century. This is testament to the effectiveness of the campaign against abortion that began in 1857. Dr. James Mohr in his *Abortion in America: The Origins and Evolution of National Policy, 1800-1900* described how this "physicians' crusade against abortion" changed state laws and public attitudes, with the result being a substantial reduction of abortion by 1900, at least among married women.

Mohr singled out one man as the driving force behind this successful American crusade against abortion. This was the Boston physician, Horatio Robinson Storer (1830-1922), but even Mohr was not fully aware of his efforts. Storer was not the first physician to point out the high prevalence of abortion or to call for physician efforts to curtail it. Professor Hugh L. Hodge did this in 1839 and 1854 in lectures at the Pennsylvania Medical School. Horatio's father, David Humphreys Storer, gave a similar Introductory Lecture to the new Harvard medical students in November 1855, and this was a key factor in Horatio's campaign less than two years later. However, Horatio Storer's efforts went well beyond those of his father and Hodge.

Although induced abortion was common in 1857, almost all physicians were strongly opposed to it unless the mother's life was threatened. The frequent abortions in this period were performed by quacks who called themselves doctors, by some midwives and women physicians, by friends or acquaintances of the pregnant woman who had learned how to induce abortion, and by the women themselves. Only a very small number of these unnecessary abortions could be attributed to the graduates of medical schools.

There were physicians in Boston who were against any public discussion of abortion and who particularly opposed the reform of Massachusetts laws on abortion. James Mohr may have interpreted such opposition as physician *support*, or at least, *tolerance* of induced abortion. However, Horatio Storer's most vocal Boston opponent, Dr. Charles Edward Buckingham (a.k.a. "Student" and "B."), did *not* claim that a "large proportion of the medical profession" believed that early abortions were not a crime, even though Buckingham's words in an editorial appeared to say just this. And Buckingham himself was no exception to the rule that physicians in 1857 strongly opposed induced abortion and believed that even early induced abortions were criminal. Buckingham's opposition to Horatio Storer and recent misinterpretations of this opposition are discussed below.

The Boston opposition actually began before Horatio became strongly involved. Dr. Henry J. Bigelow, probably with his father Jacob persuaded David Humphreys Storer to omit the abortion portion of his November 1855 Introductory Lecture when the lecture was published a few weeks later. Henry J. Bigelow was Professor of Surgery and Jacob Bigelow was Professor of Materia Medica at the Harvard Medical School where David Humphreys Storer was Professor of Obstetrics and Medical Jurisprudence. The Bigelow objection to publication of the anti-abortion segment apparently was concern that attendance at the medical school would drop as a result of such additional attention to the high rate of criminal abortion in Boston and New England. The suppressed portion of the 1855 Introductory Lecture was finally published 17 years later and it was no coincidence that this was in Horatio Storer's *Journal of the Gynaecological Society of Boston.*

David Humphreys Storer's November 1855 anti-abortion segment sounded like the start of the physician's crusade against abortion and Horatio later credited it as a key reason for his own efforts. It began:

I should feel that I had been guilty of an unpardonable neglect were I to omit to glance at a subject the importance of which, each succeeding year, has been more forcibly impressed upon my mind. I had hoped that, long ere this, some one of the strong men of the profession,—strong in the affections of the community, strong in the confidence of his brethren,—would have spoken, trumpet-tongued, against an existing, and universally acknowledged evil. I have waited in vain. The lecturer is silent, the press is silent, and the enormity, unrebuked, stalks at midday throughout the length and breadth of the land. It is time that this silence should be broken. It is time that men should speak. It is no presumption in the humblest individual to point out a much-needed reformation, however others may doubt the expediency of his course, if he thinks by thus doing he shall awaken in any mind the slightest attention to the subject; particularly if he sincerely believes that anything which can be found to be wrong can be rectified, that anything which ought to be done *can be* done sooner or later, whether it affects an individual, a community, or a race.

However, following this, David Humphreys Storer also became silent on the "universally acknowledged evil," *i.e.*, forced abortion. The same faculty pressure that caused him to withhold publication of this portion of his lecture probably caused him to cease public speaking and writing on the issue.

Horatio Storer was hardly a wallflower. The same egotism that Horatio's friend Hermann Jackson Warner noted in college and medical school days and that Dr. Oliver Wendell Holmes was later to mention, no doubt helped Horatio decide that he was the "trumpet-tongued" "strong man of the profession" who should speak out against abortion. Horatio would devote much of his enormous talent and energy to anti-abortion work for a decade and a half.

Horatio Storer not only started the physicians' crusade against abortion, he probably did more to found gynecology as a science and medical specialty than any other American physician. Horatio obtained his M.D. from Harvard in 1853 and then studied women's diseases in Europe and Scotland for a year and a half. Most of the time abroad was spent with Edinburgh's Dr. (later Sir) James Young Simpson, the discoverer of chloroform and the first to use anesthesia during child-birth.

Horatio returned to Boston in June 1855 and began his own medical practice about November 1855. He joined the American Medical Association and attended their June 1856 Annual Meeting in Detroit. Shortly afterwards, he began a tabulation of his patients who reported medical histories of induced abortion. This is the first indication of Horatio's decision to engage in an anti-abortion crusade of his own.

The campaign commenced formally on February 28, 1857 at the regular meeting of the Suffolk District Medical Society, the society of all regular physicians in Boston. The published minutes included:

[David Humphreys Storer] had since been repeatedly called upon for a reiteration of his views; many months had, however, now elapsed, and as there seemed little or no probability of such being done at present, if at all, his son, after duly ascertaining this fact, had no hesitation in at once bringing the subject before the Society; it being acknowledged by all, in the least degree conversant with this matter, that immediate action was necessary.[1]

At that meeting, Horatio cited the statistics on the frequency of induced abortion he had been collecting in his personal practice as one means to show that abortion was prevalent among married Protestant women in Boston. This led Jacob Bigelow to claim that he had never in his fifty years of practice "known such an act to be committed by a married woman." Horatio later wrote:

To my request if in his long experience he had ever asked the question which alone could elicit the truth, and to his reply "No. I should have insulted a lady by putting such a question," was attributable much of the sympathy and co-operation that I afterwards received.[2]

At the same Society meeting, Horatio indicated his concerns about the Massachusetts laws. The minutes are not specific, but he no doubt objected that the laws viewed the mother rather than the fetus as a victim of abortion and did not consider the mother culpable. Horatio also made reference to the "ignorance prevalent in the community respecting the actual and separate existence of foetal life in the early months of pregnancy" as a key reason for the rise of the crime. This had been noted by the editors of the *Boston Medical and Surgical Journal* in December 1855 when they wrote an editorial strongly protesting the suppression of the abortion section of David Humphreys Storer's Introductory Lecture when it was published. Horatio later would give editors William W. Morland and Francis Minot as well as his father credit for starting him on his crusade. Horatio then proposed:

That a Committee be appointed to consider whether any further legislation is necessary in this Commonwealth, on the subject of *criminal abortion*, and to report to the Society such other means as may seem necessary for the suppression of this abominable, unnatural, and yet common crime.

Horatio consented to adding: "And that said report, when accepted by this Society, shall by it be recommended to the Massachusetts Medical Society as a basis for its further action." The amended resolution passed unanimously, and the Chair appointed Horatio Chairman of the new Committee that included Dr. Henry Ingersoll Bowditch and Dr. Calvin Ellis.

Horatio interpreted the resolution as calling for a report dealing with legislation on criminal abortion and would give little attention in this report to "other means as may seem necessary for the suppression" of criminal abortion. It was this wish to modify Massachusetts statutes that produced opposition from Jacob Bigelow, probably from Henry J. Bigelow, and most vocally from Dr. Charles Edward Buckingham, who communicated his and Jacob's views to the New Jersey-based *Medical and Surgical Reporter* and to the *Boston Medical and Surgical Journal*. For example, the April 1857 *Medical and Surgical Reporter* contained the following as part of a letter from Buckingham which was signed "Student."

At the last meeting of the Suffolk District Medical Society a resolution was passed concerning criminal abortions. It is a great pity that the moral sense of the community cannot be brought to bear upon this subject, but it is not possible, that the interference of the law should succeed in putting a stop to it. The laws we now have cannot be enforced, and anything more stringent will only feed the operators. I would like to have the profession make a public protest against the practice. Anything beyond this will overshoot the mark. But they owe it to themselves to let the public understand that they in no way countenance it.

The opposition of Buckingham and Jacob Bigelow to change of the abortion laws may have reflected concern that some activities that regular physicians regularly engaged in, such as attempts to restore "stopped" menstruation, would become illegal. On the other hand, Jacob Bigelow almost certainly had been involved when the Massachusetts legislature revised the statutes on abortion a decade earlier, and probably Buckingham, as well. The changes Horatio proposed might have been viewed as meddling with their own products.

Shortly after the February meeting of the Suffolk District Medical Society, Horatio began a large letter-writing effort that obtained information about abortion laws in the other states and territories. Armed with this information on the various statutes, Horatio wrote his long Suffolk District Medical Society Committee Report on Criminal Abortion. He had completed a draft by April 20, 1857 when fellow-Committee-member Bowditch recommended minor revisions. Horatio included most of these, included a draft abortion statute, despite Bowditch's objection, and read the report at the regular Society meeting on April 25. It was ordered to be printed and a special meeting of the Society was set for May 9 to consider it.

The Report[3] echoed Buckingham's request that "the profession make a public protest against the practice," and even specified how to do this: "In private, among his families; in public from his professor's desk, from the pages of his journal, or from the witness' stand,–the physician is called upon by every dictate of humanity and religion to condemn it." However, the major thrust of Horatio's Report was revision of the Massachusetts abortion laws. Although these laws were as sophisticated as any state's, Horatio found serious faults in them, not the least of which was that they had led to few indictments for abortion and even fewer convictions. Horatio recommended that pregnancy need not be proved, only the attempt to end it; that the fetus rather than the mother be recognized as the victim; that assisting in abortion become a felony instead of the current misdemeanor with medical men penalized more than non-medical men; that women be guilty of a misdemeanor if they sought abortions with a higher penalty if they were married than single; and even that anyone advocating abortion be punished. When abortion actually was necessary to save the life of the woman or the child, he called for the requirement that another physician agree that this was the case. The draft statute added the new provisions and dropped such things as the requirement to prove pregnancy to which the Committee (at least, Horatio) objected.

The minutes of the May 9 Special Meeting[4] indicate that Dr. Jacob

Bigelow and Dr. Charles Buckingham were the principal speakers against the report. Bigelow first objected to the Committee's relaxation of a requirement that pregnancy be proven. He argued that pregnancy had to exist or there could be no crime of abortion, even as there had to be a murder victim for murder. Horatio countered by pointing out that it often was impossible early in pregnancy to prove its existence. He "thought it much easier and much more apt to promote the ends of justice, that the government should be obliged merely to prove the deed, and the prisoner be made to show its necessity."

Bigelow also noted that a physician by himself away from the city would not be able to provide a necessary abortion because there was no other physician around to agree to its necessity. Horatio pointed out that in this case, as when an operation is performed by someone other than a surgeon when a surgeon is unavailable, "necessity must be its own law."

Buckingham indicated his agreement with the objections of Jacob Bigelow. In addition, he objected to the increased penalties for married women and "that the tendency of this Section if carried out would be bad." "If a woman has made up her mind to have a miscarriage, she will have it some way or other;" he continued, "if she can't get drugs she will operate on herself as in Dr. Moore's case, with a piece of whale-bone or some other instrument."

Buckingham also objected to the Report's taking "the ground that the child's life is equal in importance to the mother's; this is going back too far, to the Roman Catholic laws,[5] making an excuse for the operation of Cesarean Section, a capital and very dangerous operation." He claimed the profession in Massachusetts would not support these ideas. The minutes recorded that Horatio

said that the Committee thought it their duty to report the paragraph objected to, and was surprised that Dr. Buckingham should object to it. In cases of deformed pelvis, abortion is frequently produced in order to save the life of the mother; it has sometimes been done as often as five times in the same patient. He thought that the lusts of man or woman should not be pandered to in this way. The man should be castrated or the child have a chance. The mother is responsible if she puts her own life in danger and the crime is against the child. In regard to Dr. Buckingham's statement that if a woman can't get drugs she will operate on herself, Dr. Storer said that was her own risk; the Committee act for the child; the mother is a willing agent and must answer for herself.

These statements by Horatio, particularly the last sentence, show the falsity of recent claims that the early physician opponents of abortion were primarily concerned about the dangers of abortion to the mother and that "concern for the alleged life of the fetus 'became a central issue in American culture only in the late twentieth century.'"[6] It might be argued that Horatio Storer was atypical in his views, but Storer contributed more to the successful "physicians' crusade" than any other physician and, as has been and will further be shown, he was hardly alone among physicians in acting "for the child."

Another meeting to deal with the Report was scheduled for May 30, 1857. A guest editorial highly critical of the Report appeared in the May 28 *Boston Medical and Surgical Journal*. It also was by Buckingham, although he did not indicate his identity, signing the editorial as "B." It was available for Boston physicians to read at least two days before the May 30 meeting of the Society was held and (Horatio claimed) was aimed at "foreshadowing a hostile demonstration to the" Report. Buckingham's editorial included:

The affair was too hastily got up, and ought not to pass in its present form. The writer of it seems to have thrown out of consideration the life of the mother, making that of the unborn child appear of far more consequence, even should the mother have a dozen dependent on her for their daily bread. It cannot be possible that either the profession or the public will be brought to this belief. Argue as forcibly as they may, to their own satisfaction, the Committee will fail to convince the public that abortion in the early months is a crime, and a large proportion of the medical profession will *tacitly support* the popular view of the subject.[7]

This guest editorial did not prevent the acceptance of the Committee Report, although the draft abortion statute was dropped. However, the meeting was a stormy one. David Humphreys Storer severely rebuked the editors of the *Boston Medical and Surgical Journal* for publishing the lie that "a large proportion of the medical profession" believed that "abortion in the early months" was not a crime. He also criticized the unknown "B." for not signing his name to his editorial.[8]

This led journal editor William W. Morland to claim that the "Argue as forcibly..." statement, despite appearances, was *not* a libel on the profession. Morland surely claimed (as was done explicitly in a June 11, 1857 editorial) that "B." had poorly chosen the words "tacitly support" when he really meant that the bulk of the profession would not make any attempt to *change* the public's false perception that early abortion was not a crime. David Humphreys Storer's criticism also led Buckingham to identify himself as the author of the anonymous editorial, and Buckingham claimed that his editorial "contained no such sentiments as Dr. S. had tried to make it contain."[9] In a subsequent letter published in the *Boston Medical and Surgical Journal* on August 13, 1857, Buckingham reinforced this.

"B." has not heard that he has lost caste with the profession here, nor does he think that the readers of the New Hampshire Journal would look upon him as such a monster of iniquity, if that Journal would re-publish his whole article, in place of the mere sentence which has given so much trouble.

Discussion of this issue in the June 11, 1857 *Boston Medical and Surgical Journal* indicated that "the denuciator," *i.e.*, Horatio's father, apparently came to accept that Buckingham was not actually implying what the "tacitly support" statement so readily implied. Similarly, an editorial in the August 1857 *New-Hampshire Journal of Medicine* indicated that once Buckingham had been identified as the author of the controversial sentence, they (the Editor and his Massachusetts "friend," *i.e.*, Horatio Storer) could accept that Buckingham meant to say that most physicians would not try to change the public view, not that most physicians themselves accepted the public view.

The fact that Buckingham believed that the bulk of the profession opposed abortion and viewed abortions as criminal, including early abortions, is important. Mohr was to write in *Abortion in America* (p. 154) that "B." "was finally driven to claim that his statements had been misinterpreted and that he had been a long-time personal foe of abortion." Readers of this might incorrectly conclude that Buckingham had been "finally driven" to claim something *counter* to his beliefs. Readers of Mohr's statement also might incorrectly conclude that "a large proportion" of the profession at that time was not opposed to early abortion or did not view it as criminal, and thus the common current view of some physicians (and many non-physicians) that there is little or nothing wrong with induced abortion is just a return to physicians' beliefs in 1857 before Horatio's crusade began to change these beliefs. If today's current defenders of induced abortion really believe that physicians' attitudes toward abortion in 1857 are the proper model for current attitudes toward abortion, they must become opponents of induced abortion.

As mentioned, the Committee Report was accepted after the draft statute was dropped. Two resolutions were adopted by the Society:

"*Resolved*, That the subject of criminal abortion demands the attention of the medical profession of the State. (Adopted–16 to 13.)
"Resolved, That [blank] be a committee to urge upon the Massachusetts Medical Society, to take action in the premises, and if it deem expedient, to present the subject for the consideration of the legislature. (Adopted–14 to 13.)"

The same Committee (Storer, Bowditch, and Ellis) was appointed to present the subject to the parent Massachusetts Medical Society at its meeting in New Bedford three days later. The Resolution that Horatio presented at that meeting was a stronger call for legislative action than the above. It read:

"*Resolved*, that a Committee be appointed by the Chair to bring before the next Legislature the alarming increase of criminal abortion in this Commonwealth, and to request in the name of this Society a careful revision of the Statutes upon that crime."

Although well received by many of the Massachusetts physicians at the New Bedford meeting, this Resolution was not well received by Jacob Bigelow and Jacob's supporters. After considerable discussion, a Committee of seven was appointed to report back to the Massachusetts Medical Society on the issue. Horatio and Jacob Bigelow were on the committee. The Committee made its report seven months later while Horatio was out of the state. Although resolving "That the Fellows of the Massachusetts Medical Society regard with disapprobation and abhorrence all attempts to procure abortion, except in cases where it may be necessary for the preservation of the mother's life," their Report echoed Jacob's earlier view "that they do not recommend any application to the Legislature on the subject, believing that the Laws of the Commonwealth are already sufficiently stringent, provided that they are executed." Horatio was not contacted by the Committee before they made their report and he later protested their action. However, there would be no reconsideration and the Massachusetts legislature would not be contacted until three years later after the American Medical Association got into the crusade and prevailed on the Massachusetts Medical Society to contact the legislature.

A day after the New Bedford meeting, Buckingham (as "Student") provided another "Letter from Boston" to the *Medical and Surgical Reporter* dealing largely with the proceedings of the May 30 Suffolk District Medical Society meeting and highly critical of Horatio and his Report. It included:

At the meeting of the Suffolk District Medical Society last month, a report, written by Dr. H.R. Storer, of this city, was under discussion. The subject of the report was the prevention of criminal abortions. It contained some of the most uncalled for insinuations, concerning the practice of Boston physicians; a few wild propositions for the protection of morals; and it closed with a law, such as could not be passed, and if it could be passed, would be an abortion of itself. This it was proposed to force down the throats of the Council of the Massachusetts Medical Society, bring before the Massachusetts Legislature, and give to the world as the recommendation of the physicians of Boston. The matter was discussed at two meetings.... At the second meeting...some gentlemen got exceedingly warm, and one indulged himself in the luxury of calling by abusive epithets, a correspondent of the *Boston Medical and Surgical Journal*, whose opinion, concerning the report alluded to, differed from his own, after misrepresenting that opinion.

It ended:

The end was not yet. The Massachusetts Medical Society were treated to a dose of abortion, yesterday, and one of the committee from Boston informed them, in a very forcible speech, that they *should* take notice of this subject, or he would for them. As they will undoubtedly do nothing, he will have employment enough.

By one of those remarkable coincidences which we sometimes hear of, the American Medical Association appointed a committee upon this same subject, with the same gentleman chairman.

Details on this "remarkable coincidence," *i.e.*, the American Medical Association Special Committee on Criminal Abortion and Horatio's Chairmanship of it, were provided in a letter Dr. J. Berrien Lindsley of Nashville wrote to Horatio in July 1857. It included:

The Nominating Committee objected to raising so large a special committee as you wished, but very cordially appointed you Chairman. As such you have the privilege of selecting such Co-adjutors as you may wish. The subject *is* very important as well as interesting, and the Washington meeting will be a good time to bring it up.[10]

When Horatio had contacted various physicians around the country in March 1857, his letter to Dr. Lindsley apparently had requested a large Committee on Criminal Abortion be formed at the May 1857 meeting of the Association in Nashville. The response from Tennessee at that time indicated that "Your letter is filed & will be attended to duly at the meeting though we shall expect you at the Association." Horatio did not make it to the Nashville meeting, but Lindsley's July letter indicates that most of what Horatio had requested had been granted.

Horatio was not to make the 1858 Annual Meeting of the American Medical Association in Washington and no Committee Report would be presented until 1859 in Louisville. Illness which Horatio apparently feared was tuberculosis sent Horatio to Texas for six months or more. Horatio returned to Boston in the summer of 1858, resumed his medical practice, and also resumed the frenetic pace of medical publication that had begun while he was in Scotland in 1855. In December 1858, Horatio presented a paper at the prestigious American Academy of Arts and Sciences, of which he was a Fellow. It described the key role played by induced abortion in the recent sharp decrease in the rate of increase in the population in New England and America. His statistics showed the rate of such abortions in Massachusetts to be so embarrassingly high that key Boston physicians and educators, including Harvard President Josiah Quincy, persuaded him not to publish the paper.

Horatio withheld his American Academy paper from the general scientific community for nine years, but he had no qualms about immediately addressing his fellow physicians on the topic of criminal abortion. He commenced research for and writing of a series of nine papers which were published in the *North-American Medico-Chirurgical Review* from January through November 1859. The first began:

By the Common Law and by many of our State Codes, foetal life, per se, is almost wholly ignored and its destruction unpunished; abortion in every case being considered an offence mainly against the mother, and as such, unless fatal to her, a mere misdemeanor, or wholly disregarded.

By the Moral Law, THE WILFUL KILLING OF A HUMAN BEING AT ANY STAGE OF ITS EXISTENCE IS MURDER.

This first article also laid out the rest of the sequence.

I shall accordingly proceed to prove, so far as possible, the truth of every premise as yet stated, and to show the real nature and frequency of the crime: its causes; its victims; its perpetrators and its innocent abettors; its means and its proofs; its excuses, the deficiencies and errors of existing laws, and the various other obstacles to conviction; and, above all, so far as the present series of papers is concerned, the duty of the profession toward its general suppression.

The following second-to-last paragraph of the January installment summarized what had been "proved."

If we have proved the existence of foetal life before quickening has taken place or can take place, and by all analogy, and a close and conclusive process of induction, its commencement at the very beginning, at conception itself, we are compelled to believe unjustifiable abortion always a crime.

It was followed by:

And now words fail. Of the mother, by consent or by her own hand, imbrued with her infant's blood; of the equally guilty father, who counsels or allows the crime; of the wretches who by their wholesale murders far out-Herod Burke and Hare;[11] of the public sentiment which palliates, pardons, and would even praise this so common violation of all law, human and divine, of all instinct, of all reason, all pity, all mercy, all love,–we leave those to speak who can.

As will be seen, this passage was a favorite of Horatio's and would appear three more times in his writing over the years.

In March 1859, Horatio began the effort of locating his seven "co-adjutors" for the American Medical Association Committee and began or continued writing the Committee's Report. Seven influential physicians from around the country agreed to join the Committee, uniformly praised Horatio's draft Report, and agreed to sign their names to it.[12]

The American Medical Association Report on Criminal Abortion began by describing the problem of frequent criminal abortion in the country and the three major reasons for this: public ignorance about the nature of the fetus, physicians' innocent abetment of abortion, and defective abortion laws. Horatio then called on physicians to help change the ignorance, to avoid the errors that led people to believe physicians "negligent of the sanctity of foetal life," and to urge needed changes in legislation as well as to aid legislators in these efforts. The following three resolutions were offered in his Report and unanimously adopted by the Association:

Resolved, That while physicians have long been united in condemning the act of producing abortion, at every period of gestation, except as necessary for preserving the life of either mother or child, it has become the duty of this Association, in view of the prevalence and increasing frequency of the crime, publicly to enter an earnest and solemn protest against such unwarrantable destruction of human life.

Resolved, That in pursuance of the grand and noble calling we profess, the saving of human lives, and of the sacred responsibilities thereby devolving upon us, the Association present this subject to the attention of the several legislative assemblies of the Union, with the prayer that the laws by which the crime of procuring abortion is attempted to be controlled may be revised, and that such other action may be taken in the premises as they in their wisdom may deem necessary.

Resolved, That the Association request the zealous co-operation of the various

State Medical Societies in pressing this subject upon the legislatures of their respective States, and that the President and Secretaries of the Association are hereby authorized to carry out, by memorial, these resolutions.

Horatio was too ill to travel to Louisville to present his Report. It was presented by Dr. Thomas Blatchford of New York, who wrote Horatio "Your report was highly spoken of, not a dissenting voice in any direction."

In the *North-American Medico-Chirurgical Review* articles on abortion that followed the May American Medical Association Report, Horatio noted that "its perpetrators" often were women and he spelled out the various roles of friends, midwives, nurses, and female physicians. "Its Innocent Abettors" was another key article in Horatio's series. "Innocent abettors" included physicians who were apt to resort to craniotomy or premature labor when there was a good chance of a normal birth. Horatio also admonished physicians to perform Caesarean section immediately to extract every foetus old enough to survive in cases of maternal death; to make every effort to prevent threatening miscarriages and resuscitate still-born children; and to avoid "operations of any kind on pregnant women, even tooth-drawing, that might be delayed." He argued that to do otherwise would not show the highest valuation of the unborn and newly born and some who observed this would conclude that unnecessary abortion was no crime.

The nine articles of Horatio in the *North-American Medico-Chirurgical Review* were published as a book entitled *On Criminal Abortion in America*. On February 16, 1860, the new *Boston Medical and Surgical Journal* editors, Dr. F. E. Oliver and Dr. Calvin Ellis, published an editorial which made reference to the new book "from the pen of one of our most painstaking and careful investigators...." "This paper contains much interesting information,"" the editors continued, "and if it do as much for poor humanity as might be fairly expected, from the ability and good intentions of the author, he will have much reason for pleasant reflection."

Those who may currently believe that physicians at that time opposed abortion only or primarily because of concern for the health of the mother, or who perhaps regard Horatio's many expressions of concern for the "sanctity of foetal life" as an aberration among physicians of his day, should take note of the following final sentence of the Oliver-Ellis editorial:

The physician may do much by warning his patients against the dangers and guilt of this awful crime, and using the "greater vigilance lest he become its innocent and unintentional abettor"; and the moralist may do more by the inculcation of those principles in the young, that shall lead them to regard with abhorrence such a violation of the positive laws of God, involving, as it does, the guilt of murder, and a total indifference to the most sacred privileges with which woman is endowed.

As specified in the last two of the three 1859 resolutions on Criminal Abortion, the American Medical Association requested the state legislatures to revise their abortion statutes and requested the state medical societies also to pressure their legislatures for this purpose. Horatio wrote the two memorials and also arranged for his series of articles to be provided along with them to state legislatures and state medical societies.

The memorial reached the New York State Medical Society sometime before early February 1860 when, at its annual meeting, the following Resolution was provided by the Committee appointed to consider the recommendations of the American Medical Association:

Resolved, That this Society cordially approves of the action of the American Medical Association in its efforts to exhibit the extent of the evils resulting from the procuring of Criminal Abortions, and of the means which are adopted to prevent its commission, and cheerfully comply with the request to a 'zealous co-operation' for furtherance of more stringent legislation in regard to this most destructive and revolting crime, committed almost with impunity, and with appalling frequency.

The New York Society also appointed a committee to present the American Medical Association memorial to the State Legislature. Other state medical societies responded similarly to the memorial from the American Medical Association, even Massachusetts.

Horatio was absent from the American Medical Association

Annual Meetings not only in 1857, 1858, and 1859 but again in 1860 when Dr. Henry Miller lavished praise in his Presidential Address on Horatio for his yeoman efforts in preparing the Committee Report, its supporting research, the resolutions, and the memorials to legislatures and state medical societies.

David Humphreys Storer *was* present at the 1860 meeting in nearby New Haven, Connecticut and was appointed with two Connecticut physicians to meet a request from the Judiciary Committee of the Connecticut Legislature to "frame a suitable bill to serve as a guide for their action" in compliance with the Association's Memorial. No doubt, had Horatio been present, he instead of his father would have been chosen for the Committee that provided assistance to the Connecticut Legislature. It is possible, even probable, that Horatio assisted his father and the two Connecticut physicians in this effort.

Whether Horatio was part of the process or not, the Connecticut Legislature produced a unique piece of legislation that combined "into a single forceful act the denial of the quickening doctrine, the notion of women's liability, and anti-advertising principles." "This 1860 Connecticut law, which remained virtually unchanged for over a century," Mohr continued, "set the tone for the kind of legislation enacted elsewhere in the United States during the succeeding twenty years."[13]

The Civil War, the commencement of his wife's mental illness, and/or other factors left any anti-abortion efforts of Horatio in the early 1860s undocumented, if there were such. Female insanity became a major research interest of Horatio in 1863, and Horatio claimed in his writing on this new topic that abortion sometimes precipitated insanity. One reason was the guilt associated with the crime, but another was pelvic disease caused by the abortion which Horatio believed acted reflexively on the mind.

Abortion again became part of the business of the American Medical Association at their annual meeting in New York in 1864. They adopted a resolution to "offer a premium for the best *short and comprehensive tract* calculated for circulation among females, and designed to enlighten them upon the criminality and physical evils of forced abortion." Horatio submitted the "tract" which won the special premium the next year when the American Medical Association met in Boston.

Horatio signed his essay with a Latin motto and also concealed his identity by using the third person when referring in the essay to his 1859 research and its researcher. The Prize Committee, three Boston physician friends of Horatio plus his father who was Chairman, may not have been fooled, however. On the other hand, Horatio's research was the primary information available on criminal abortion and, if there were other entries, Horatio's no doubt would have been the major contender for the prize, even with strangers judging it.

Horatio began the essay by testifying to its importance, noting that this was the first time that the Association had ever directly addressed a lay audience. He then provided a historical account of the medical profession's long silence on abortion; the efforts of Hodge and the two Storers to break that silence; the American Medical Association's outstanding performance after being enlisted in the campaign; and the fine support to the campaign provided by medical journalists and medical text book writers.

The next section of his Prize essay discussed inappropriate intentional abortions. "Physicians have now arrived at the unanimous opinion," he wrote, "that the foetus in utero is *alive* from the very moment of conception." "The law, whose judgments are arrived at so deliberately, and usually so safely, has come to the same conclusion," he continued, "and though in some of its decisions it has lost sight of this fundamental truth, it has averred, in most pithy and empathic language, that 'quick with child, is having conceived.'" "By that higher than human law, which, though scoffed at by many a tongue, is yet acknowledged by every conscience," Horatio continued and then quoted himself, "'the wilful killing of a human being, at any stage of its existence, is murder.'"

Horatio then became a biology teacher, noting that before the egg leaves the ovary and is impregnated "it may perhaps be considered as a part and parcel of herself, but not afterwards." He compared the temporary attachment of the fertilized egg to the womb to the attachment of the born child to the breast, throwing in the interesting and somewhat intermediate case of the tiny kangaroo fetus "born into the world at an extremely early stage of development" and placed by its mother in the external pouch to spend weeks attached to a teat therein before "in reality to be born." He continued:

Many women suppose that the child is not alive till quickening has occurred, others that it is practically dead till it has breathed. As well one of these suppositions as the other; they are both of them erroneous.

"Quickening" was discussed with the major point that it is but a sensation of the mother and that the movement of the fetus occurs much earlier. "These motions must be allowed to prove life," Horatio continued, "and independent life." He then asked: "In what does this life really differ from that of the child five minutes in the world?" Horatio's own answer is implicit in the following:

In the majority of instances of forced abortion, the act is committed prior to the usual period of quickening. There are other women, who have confessed to me that they have destroyed their children long after they have felt them leap within their womb. There are others still, whom I have known to wilfully suffocate them during birth, or to prevent the air from reaching them under the bed-clothes; and there are others, who have wilfully killed their wholly separated and breathing offspring, by strangling them or drowning them, or throwing them into a noisome vault. Wherein among all these criminals does there in reality exist any difference in guilt?

Although much of this essay was taken verbatim from Horatio's earlier articles for physicians, the following new paragraph was written for his female audience *and* for physicians:

I would gladly arrive at, and avow any other conviction than that I have now presented, were it possible in the light of fact and of science, for I know it must carry grief and remorse to many an otherwise innocent bosom. The truth is, that our silence has rendered all of us accessory to the crime, and now that the time has come to strip down the veil, and apply the searching caustic or knife to this foul sore in the body politic, the physician needs courage as well as his patient, and may well overflow with regretful sympathy.

Horatio recognized that moral arguments would not sway some of his audience and provided a section, "The Inherent Dangers of Abortion to a Woman's Health and to her Life." Horatio described the short-, medium-, and long-term consequences of induced abortion to women's health, including the very real possibility of immediate death. The non-fatal problems were due to premature interruption of the numerous preparations of the woman's body for birth and nursing, to incomplete abortion, and to the damage of tissues associated with invasion of the womb. This long section detailing the many adverse health consequences, including Horatio's belief in the risk of insanity, probably caused many women to accept Horatio's earlier statement:

barring ethical considerations, and looked at in a selfish light alone, [induced abortions] are so dangerous to the woman's health, her own physical and domestic best interests, that their induction permittal, 'or solicitation by one cognizant of their true character, should almost be looked upon as proof of actual insanity.

Horatio then proceeded with a section titled "The Frequency of Forced Abortions, even among the Married." He noted the sharp differences in abortion rates between Protestant and Catholic women, hoping to utilize the typical anti-Catholic sentiment of his Protestant women readers and induce them thereby to bear their children to do their part to prevent the population from becoming increasingly Catholic.

The next section was "The Excuses and Pretexts that are given for the Act." One-by-one Horatio refuted the excuses of ignorance, ill health, fear of childbed, and effects on living children. Fear of childbed was particularly stressed, since Horatio had another ongoing crusade which was for use of anesthesia during childbirth.

Horatio then asked, "Is there no alternative but for women, when married and prone to conception to occasionally bear children?" His answer was that this was certainly in their best interests "for length of days and immunity from disease." Horatio also indicated the need for foundling hospitals. Not only would this prevent infanticide and abortion by the unwed mother, "they would save her from one element of the self-condemnation and hatred which so often hurries the victim of seduction downward to the life of the brothel." For the wed who would seek abortion, Horatio wrote:

But for the married, who have not this strong stimulus of necessity, and the excuse of having been led astray or deceived, there need be no public channel provided, through which to purchase safety for their children. Is it not, indeed, inconceivable that the very women who, when their darlings of a month old or a year are snatched from them by disease, find the parting attended with so acute a pang, can so deliberately provide for and congratulate themselves, and each other, upon a willful abortion? Here words fail us.

This then was the cue for Horatio to quote the statement which had ended the first article of his 1859 series on criminal abortion, "Of the mother, ...we leave those to speak who can."

One of the last pieces of business of the 1865 Boston meeting of the American Medical Association was a resolution that "the Committee on Publication be requested to adopt such appropriate measures as will insure a speedy and general circulation of the Prize Essay on Abortion, provided this can be done without expense to the Association." This seemingly contradictory request to do something in a hurry without spending any money was the authorization of Horatio to publish the Prize Essay himself. This he did under the controversial title, *Why Not? A Book for Every Woman.* The little book was extremely successful and editions with dates 1866, 1867, 1868, and 1871 were published.

Horatio was requested from various sources, including a happy publisher, to produce a second book for men. This he did in 1867 calling it, *Is It I? A Book for Every Man.* It was aimed at inconsiderate husbands whose ill treatment of their wives, including forced sexual intercourse, was a major factor in the unwanted pregnancies that led to many abortions.

Horatio took a very circuitous route to the message that men needed to shape up in their marital relations, discussing the dangers of masturbation, prostitutes, and mistresses, and even discussing the proper age to marry (early). He finally got to this topic in the fourth chapter, "The Rights of the Husband." Horatio noted that these rights "are usually considered total and indisputable. Till now they have seldom been challenged; certainly seldom of men by men." Horatio then called for "loosing...woman's present chains, ...to increase her health, prolong her life, extend the benefits she confers upon society." This would "selfishly enhance her value to ourselves," but Horatio also argued that this be done out "of gratitude to her for the love with which she has solaced us, as mother, and sister, and wife, and daughter, –all of which I have myself possessed; unhappy he who has not."

Horatio went on to discuss women's slave status in primitive times, the frequent killing of wives for disobedience or infidelity in "former days," and the possession of multiple wives "in by-gone times, and among heathen, as at present in a remote valley of our own great land," following which Horatio introduced the subject of abortion. He described the slaughter of new-borns by the Spartans and asked whether this was less wicked than

the pre-natal murders of the present day, daily in occurrence, fashionable even, and be-praised by professing Christians, repeated over and over again by the same married woman and mother? You will exclaim with horror that it is not! And yet, in a very large proportion of instances, this shocking and atrocious act is advised and abetted, if not compelled by the husband–by us men. Who enjoys asking now, "Is it I?"

Horatio went on to indicate that the woman had a "certain measure of excuse" for abortion. "For her husband none." He continued with a crusade progress report and the phrase already used twice in his earlier writing:

This is a matter concerning which the public mind is now undergoing a radical change. Slow to set in motion, but every day gaining more rapidly in force, the world's revival proceeds. In "Why Not?" or "Why should women not commit this crime?" I have sounded almost a trump to wake the dead. Would, indeed, that it might arouse a better life in every man who reads these words: "Of the mother, by consent or by her own hand, imbrued with her infant's blood...."

Although not as popular as *Why Not?*, the book *Is It I?* also went into another edition. Both books no doubt greatly influenced popular opinion on abortion, causing women to continue pregnancies that they would otherwise have ended and to take additional measures to avoid unwanted pregnancies.

At about the same time as Horatio's second book was published, he was called on by the New York State Medical Society to assist them in drafting recommendations to the New York legislature for changes in the state's abortion laws. The recommended changes were eventually adopted and New York joined Connecticut in legislation treating the fetus as a victim of abortion and the mother as a culprit.

The summer of 1868 marked a "new" book written by Horatio and a Boston lawyer, Franklin Fiske Heard. However, Horatio's "Book I" of *Criminal Abortion: Its Nature, Its Evidence, and Its Law* was changed little from the out-of-print *On Criminal Abortion* of 1860, except for the final chapters dealing with abortion statutes which became the province of lawyer Heard's "Book II." One addition of Horatio was another progress report for the decade-old anti-abortion campaign. He described it as culminating in "an agitation which is now shaking society, throughout our country, in its very centre."

Early in 1869, Horatio and a handful of other Boston gynecologists formed the Gynaecological Society of Boston which was the first medical society devoted exclusively to the diseases of women. Six months later Horatio started the *Journal of the Gynaecological Society of Boston* which was the first medical journal devoted exclusively to gynecology and which obtained a large circulation in the U.S. and abroad. During its three-and-one-half-year existence, the *Journal of the Gynaecological Society of Boston* frequently expressed the anti-abortion views of its major editor, Horatio Storer.

A notorious abortionist in nearby Lynn, Massachusetts was an early target of the Gynaecological Society's biweekly meetings and of Horatio's monthly "Editorial Notes" in the Journal and within a year the man was expelled from the Massachusetts Medical Society. The Journal also published articles by other physicians on the subject of criminal abortion. Not the least of these was the March 1872 publication of the suppressed abortion portion of David Humphreys Storer's November 1855 Introductory Lecture which had started Horatio on his successful crusade.

The major story of Horatio Storer and the physicians' crusade against abortion draws nearly to an end in the Spring of 1872 and this corresponds to the severe illness Horatio contracted at that time from a surgical wound. This nearly killed Horatio and it produced a deep infection of his knee joint leading to life-long invalidism from an unbending knee. Mohr reported:

By the end of the 1860s Storer's health began to fail badly, and in 1872 he finally left the country for sunnier climates abroad. Though this removed him from medical politics in the United States, the crusade he had launched never foundered.[14]

Mohr followed this by the footnote: "Storer did return on occasion, but only rarely and never long enough to reinvolve himself in the anti-abortion crusade he had launched."

Mohr is correct in saying that "the crusade he had launched never foundered." Laws on abortion were changed or adopted in virtually every state and territory. The new laws recognizing the rights of the fetus helped educate the public about the origins of human life and probably produced even larger attitude change in the general public than all of the direct attempts at such change which constituted the second thrust of the physicians' crusade. A sharp reduction of the common practice of abortion resulted, at least among married women, as already noted.

However, Mohr's "By the end of the 1860s Storer's health began to fail badly," is incorrect. Horatio's health was not a major problem at the end of the 1860s, but deteriorated suddenly in the first or second week of April 1872. Horatio was at the April 2, 1872 meeting of the Gynaecological Society of Boston where he discussed two operations he had performed in the previous two weeks and, at the same meeting, was designated the Society's representative to attend the upcoming Annual Meeting of the American Medical Association in Philadelphia.

Mohr's "Storer did return on occasion, but only rarely..." is also wrong. Horatio went abroad in October 1872 seeking a cure and returned in August 1877 to Newport, Rhode Island, where he remained for the rest of his life except for a brief trip to Europe in the summer of 1899. Mohr's "this removed him from medical politics in the United States," also is incorrect. Among other offices, Horatio was elected Vice President of the Gynecological Section of the Ninth International Medical Congress held in Washington in 1887. He hosted the American Medical Association in his city of Newport in 1889 and appears to have been almost chosen President of the American Medical Association the following year.

The claim that Horatio "never...reinvolve[d] himself in the anti-abortion crusade he had launched" is another error. Mohr himself referred in his *Abortion in America* to an 1897 paper of Horatio's, "Criminal Abortion: Its Prevalence, Its Prevention, and Its Relation to the Medical Examiner–Based on the 'Summary of the Vital Statistics of the New England States for the Year 1892' By the Six Secretaries of the New England State Boards of Health." Horatio presented this paper at the Rhode Island Medico-Legal Society on August 12, 1897 and presented it again to the Newport Medical Society on August 18. It was published in the October 1897 *Atlantic Medical Weekly*, reprinted, widely distributed as a pamphlet, and referred to favorably by a number of medical journals. As a result of Horatio's presentation, the Newport Medical Society set up a Committee "to obtain through correspondence with medical societies and otherwise such action by the profession as may tend to lessen the occurrence of criminally induced abortion." This Committee probably was responsible for the widespread distribution of Horatio's address.

Horatio was to live until 1922 and even became Harvard's oldest living graduate. Dr. James Joseph Walsh, Dean of the Fordham Medical School, was a close friend of Horatio and provided at least three sketches of Horatio.[15] In the last year of his life, Horatio provided a number of autobiographical letters to assist Walsh in his biographical efforts, noting in one of these that "one does not like to have part in his own obituary." The last letter to Walsh, written two weeks before Horatio's 92nd birthday, and eight months before his death, included:

Since writing, I have been more than ever impressed by the great influence the Am. Med. Association has exerted, ... The Association, by speech, the printed word, & by action, showed that life did initiate from the very beginning, & that "therapeutic abortion" was therefore very generally murder. Protestant pulpits were compelled to preach Catholic doctrines. Will it then be too much, for you to insert in your Cyclopedia something like the following: Every single word helps in this crusade, & even a mouse may aid a lion like yourself.

> For nearly seventy years, Dr. Storer has written much upon the real time of commencement of foetal life, & of its sanctity. He has been supported, frequently and most authoritatively, by the concerted aid of the American Medical Association, the great body of reputable physicians, of

> which his father was a president and himself a vice-president. That action of the Association has been the most beneficent of its existence, and for the fact that he was to a small extent enabled to take a part, Dr. S. will be held in grateful remembrance, rather than as a progressive and successful surgeon.

Horatio was aware when he wrote this sketch of himself in 1922 that he and the American Medical Association had initiated a crusade that saved many thousands from an unnecessary uterine death. In an earlier letter to Walsh, Horatio also had discussed his own and the American Medical Association's effective roles in opposing abortion which "produced a very general change in belief and practice," and had instructed Dr. Walsh, "Think this over seriously, and then appreciate with me the character and universal extent of the change." This strongly suggests that Horatio recognized the ramifications of "the change" on the offspring of these survivors, and the offspring of offspring for the three generations he monitored from 1857 to 1922. He may have also appreciated the expanding ramifications on every succeeding generation as long as human beings survive on the planet.

It is not farfetched to indicate that the reader can thank his or her existence to this man, since the effects of even a small increase in surviving pregnancies exponentially increase on succeeding generations, and there is evidence that this increase in surviving pregnancies was not small.[16] Even if each ancestor of the reader would have been in place without Horatio, some key teachers, coaches, mentors, friends, would not have been around to make their contribution to that existence. Is Dr. Horatio Robinson Storer thus the most important figure in America in the 19th Century? Only decades of reluctance to discuss the taboo topic of criminal abortion may have prevented recognition of this long ago.

NOTES

1. *Boston Medical and Surgical Journal* (1855) 56, 282-84, p. 283.

2. 1901 letter of Horatio to his son Malcolm which is among Family Papers.

3. The only known original copy of the Report is located at the Harvard Countway Library of Medicine.

4. Minutes of Special Meetings of the Society are located at the Harvard Countway Library.

5. Horatio Storer, like his father, was a Unitarian in 1857. Horatio became an Episcopalian about 1870 and converted to Catholicism in 1879.

6. See the discussion of a brief submitted to the Supreme Court on behalf of over 400 professional historians for *Webster v. Reproductive Health Services* (1989) in "Academic Integrity Betrayed" in *First Things* (Aug./Sept. 1990) and in "Aborting History" in *National Review* (October 23, 1995).

7. *Boston Medical and Surgical Journal* (1857) 56, 346. Stress added.

8. Regular Meeting Minutes of the Society apparently have been lost. Much of the information about the May 30 meeting came from a report, "Suffolk District Medical Society," in the short-lived Boston-based journal *Medical World* (1857) 211-12. This included the identification of "B." as Dr. Buckingham.

9. *Medical World* (1857), p. 211.

10. Countway Library: Storer Abortion File.

11. The "Burke and Hare" reference refers to William Burke and William Hare who were indicted in 1828 for 16 murders they carried out in Edinburgh, Scotland within a single year. The Burke and Hare murders no doubt were highly salient to Horatio because of his year in medical training at the same Edinburgh University Medical School which had innocently bought the bodies of the murder victims so they could be dissected by medical students.

12. Thomas W. Blatchford, of New York; Hugh L. Hodge, of Pennsylvania; Charles A. Pope, of Missouri; Edward H. Barton of South Carolina; A. Lopez, of Alabama; Wm. Henry Brisbane, of Wisconsin; and A. J. Semmes, of the District of Columbia were the seven with Horatio on the Committee. The letters are at the Harvard Countway Library of Medicine.

13. *Abortion in America*, p. 202.

14. *Abortion in America*, p. 159.

15. The major one was in the Catholic publication *Ave Maria* (Nov. 11, 1922), pp. 619-24.

16. If only one generation showed an increase in surviving pregnancies amount to 3% of children, this would provide a parent (or two) for 5.9% of the next generation, for 11.5% of the second generation, for 21.6% of the third generation, *etc.*

Out of Respect for Life:
Nazi Abortion Policy
in the Eastern Occupied Territories

John Hunt

THIRTY YEARS after World War II, West Germany legalized abortion-on-demand for the first three months of pregnancy. On February 25, 1975, the Federal Constitutional Court of that country (Bundesverfassungsgericht) struck the law down as being unconstitutional. In its decision, it stated that "abortion is an act of killing (Tötenshandlung) that the law is obligated to condemn," and that the "bitter experience" with Nazism had led the Court to value life highly.[1] The beginning of the decision also showed the connection between abortion and Nazism in this way: "...the Constitution protects life being developed in the mother's womb as an independent legal entity. The express inclusion of the right to life [of the unborn] in the Constitution...is to be explained primarily as a reaction to...the 'final solution' and to 'liquidations' carried out by the National Socialist [Nazi] regime...."[2]

In other words, according to the German Supreme Court, the Nazis had no respect for human life, and to insure human life's protection for the future, we have to respect all human life, including life in the womb. The decision came to apply to all Germany after unification in 1990 and was re-affirmed by a second decision in mid-1993.[3]

The 1975 decision by the German High Court was completely the opposite of the U.S. Supreme Court decision in *Roe v. Wade* two years earlier, which had allowed abortion throughout all nine months of pregnancy. Was the German Court correct in labeling abortion killing and linking it to the Nazi mentality? This paper will now delve into day-to-day minutes, letters, bulletins, and newsletters among the Nazis, before and during World War II, to try and answer this question.

Hitler and the Nazis came to power in Germany in early 1933. From the start, Hitler took many initiatives in foreign and domestic policy.

In foreign policy, 1933 saw Germany re-arm and withdraw from the League of Nations. In early 1934, Germany signed a Non-Aggression Pact with Poland, deliberately lulling that country into a false sense of security. In mid-1935 came an agreement with Britain, then mistress of the seas, which helped Germany build its navy. In March 1936, Germany marched into the Rhineland, something forbidden by the peace treaty that had ended World War I. In March of 1938, Germany annexed Austria, and March 1939 saw Czechoslovakia go under to the Nazis. Finally, in September 1939, Germany attacked and quickly conquered Poland, beginning World War II.

A careful listening (or reading) indicates that, during the pre-war years of 1933 to 1939, 1937 was a quiet year on the international scene. Hitler, during this year, was digesting gains made and preparing for new ones, but also concentrating on domestic questions. One of the domestic questions discussed among top Nazis on June 15, 1937, which has received little if any attention to this day, concerned the questions of unmarried motherhood and illegitimate children.

A Ministerial Director named Dr. Volkmar spoke of the difficulty of reconciling the providing for illegitimate children the same advantages as for legitimate children. Questions about the identity of the father occur (for this is prior to DNA testing), which can offset the purity of German blood.[4] The Director of the Statistics Office, a Dr. Burgdorfer, stated that illegitimate children must be treated equally in order to continue the existence of the *Volk*, since the birthrate of married couples was low. Care must be taken that a child, whether legitimate or illegitimate, be born and that the mother not fall into the hands of an abortionist. For the good of the *Volk*, every conceived child must be brought to birth.[5] A third opinion came from a Dr. Astel, who presided over the lengthy meeting. According to him, whether to give unmarried mothers and children the same status as married mothers and legitimate children, should be decided on a case-by-case basis and that racial purity must be established.[6] Then a professor, Dr. Ley spoke. He claimed he was a racial hygienist (Rassengygieniker), that the morality of the past could no longer help Germany, and that law has no purpose; it is the servant of the German people. In referring to the large number of abortions before Nazism, Ley went on to say that there was no advantage in increasing births *per se*; that while abortion should remain illegal, Germany still had to measure quality against quantity, and that abortion was a necessary evil that Germans had to accept *out of respect for life* [emphasis mine] ("...es ist ein notwendiges Übel, das wir hinnehmen müssen aus Achtung vor dem Leben").[7]

The mixed views of these four professionals illustrated in general the dilemma facing Nazis: the desire for births to serve as the proverbial "fodder" for the re-arming of the military ("quantity") and the desire for the pure, perfect German ("quality").

The views of Dr. Ley in particular, illustrated true Nazi attitudes, namely, that the old morality is irrelevant and that the law does not exist outside of us. Law is what you make it; it is an extension of ourselves. As some historians have noted, down deep the Nazis believed in nothing and held that relations among people were to be settled through exercise of power.[8]

Heinrich Himmler, head of the infamous SS, one of the chief architects of the Holocaust and personal friend of Adolf Hitler, then spoke. Himmler stated that the evil of abortion lay not in the loss of an individual life, but more in the fact that many women through abortion lose their ability to have children later. Here we see Nazi contempt concerning the sanctity of life, but we see also an admission that the unborn have life, that they are children ("...nicht in dem einen Kind das einmal getotet wird...").[9] Echoing the "fodder" or "quantity" argument, he bemoaned the fact that 100,000 children were being lost each year through abortion, that in twenty to thirty years each 100,000 could produce an army of 400,000 men, which could alter the fate of Germany and the world. Here we see how this domestic question affected foreign policy considerations in the Nazi mindset. Himmler continued, it made no difference if the children here were legitimate or illegitimate. Young people are ready to reproduce at age 15 or 16, and it is only "bourgeoisie morality" that makes them wait. Himmler, however, also voiced concern about the *Volk* or "quality" argument. He maintained that many noble coats-of-arms had a bastard stripe because many right-blooded forefathers gave their blood outside of marriage as well as within, passing on the good stuff. He further maintained that there should be registration of illegitimate children so that the true bloodline could be known officially.[10] This tension among the Nazis of reconciling "quantity" and "quality" as described in this meeting continued into the future at later meetings.[11]

The attitudes in the sexual area expressed at this 1937 meeting during a lull in German foreign policy initiatives would surface with a vengeance after World War II began. As Germany conquered other European states, it took harsh measures to keep the conquered from reproducing, particularly in the Slavic east, most particularly in Poland. I have treated this in another paper.[12] Here, I would like to focus upon some day-to-day statements and actions by the Nazis during World War II that illustrate how they knew that abortion was the taking of a life at its earliest stages.

The Nazis used forced labor wherever they went. In the fall of 1939, after the conquest of Poland was over, one-half million foreigners (Czechs, Slovaks, and Poles) found themselves as laborers for the Third Reich, and by the end of 1942 the number had risen to four million. Involved also now were Ukrainians, Russians, Serbians, and Bulgarians. During the same period the number of women in this total went from slightly under 200,000 to 1,200,000.[13] Almost immediately, the Nazis began a policy of using birth control and abortion to keep eastern females available as slave laborers and, at the same time, to weaken eastern nations by hampering the reproduction of Slavic peoples.[14] The organization through which the Nazis carried out this policy was known as the Race and Resettlement Office, commonly known by the German acronym RuSHA.[15] Its first head was Heinrich Himmler, and from July 1940 to April 1943 it was headed by Otto Hofmann. Hofmann became SS Senior Police Commander in the occupied territories from April 1943 to the end of the war. On January 20, 1942, Hofmann, along with Reinhard Heydrich, Adolf Eichmann, and twelve others, made the decision at the Wannsee Conference House just outside Berlin, to begin the mass extermination (The Final Solution) of Jews and others, by gassing and cremation, commonly known today as the Holocaust.[16]

Hence, abortion was one of the tools of the Holocaust, used by the very same men who engaged in the mass killing that was so much a part of World War II. This was the broad picture of the Nazis and abortion.

Looking at some of the specifics of their activity in the occupied territories, particularly Eastern Europe, we can also see that the Nazis knew that abortion was killing. The Nazis took over the Sudetenland, a German-speaking area of Czechoslovakia, in September 1938 as the result of the infamous Munich Conference. In March 1939 they marched into the rest of Czechoslovakia without opposition. A year later the Reich Security Service, in a confidential newsletter-bulletin, complained that abortions among Germans in the Sudetenland were not being punished properly due to less stringent Czech laws. Specifically, it bemoaned the fact that a woman abortionist convicted of doing three abortions in a two-week period received only a year and three months in prison, and that this had to stop.[17] Here we see the desire by the Nazis *not* to have abortions done on German people. They would, however, encourage abortions on non-German peoples.

Shortly after taking over Czechoslovakia, Nazi Germany conquered Poland in September 1939, beginning World War II. A few months after the conquest, the Reich Security Service, again in its confidential newsletter-bulletin, expressed concern about the influx of Polish workers into Germany (it was forced, slave labor), how it was leading to sexual trafficking between Germans and Poles, and how this would contaminate "the body of the *Volk*." Nazis frequently expressed concern about an "eastern look."[18] In a letter to SS head Heinrich Himmler by a Nazi official,[19] the official stated that Hitler, in order to prevent offspring by foreign women in the occupied territories, to prevent the spread of venereal disease, and to reduce the number of children of native inhabitants, demanded that Himmler push condoms and any other form of birth control.[20]

Concern with not enough German reproduction in places like the Sudetenland but too much Slavic reproduction in the occupied eastern territories led the Nazis to go far beyond birth control. If both parents of an unborn were non-German, and the pregnancy prevented the woman from coming to work, the child of that couple could be aborted.[21] One should note that the word "parent" is used here before birth. Himmler claimed that, on the authority of Hitler, he could allow the abortion of the children of Polish women workers if the woman was "especially inferior," which was to be determined by a racial test. Again, one should notice that, concerning pregnancy, the word "child" is used twice here ("...wenn sie von einem besonders minderwertigen Ausländer ein Kind empfangen haben, das Kind in der Schwangerschaft bereits abnehmen lassen").[22] Himmler stated to Reinhard Heydrich and a Dr. Conti in March 1942, that abortion among the Poles themselves should not be punished.[23] In the same month, in another letter, informed by the Reich Health Minister that Poles engaged in abortion had been severely punished in German courts, Himmler protested, stating that Germans had no interest in protecting the passing on of Polish blood.[24] Ever ready to protect German unborn from the same fate, however, a decree from the German government issued in the middle of the war (1943) threatened those doing abortions on German unborn with the death penalty, since this activity "infringe[s] upon the vital forces of the German people."[25] This decree was carried out, in some cases even after pleas for clemency from other physicians.[26]

Jewish women were also the victims of Nazi abortion, but the abortions in these cases were often done by Jewish physicians, since a Jewish woman found to be pregnant meant immediate gassing for both her and her unborn. Doctors and the affected women here believed that in this way at least one life was saved.[27] The overwhelming use of abortion by the Nazis during World War II, however, was done on eastern Slavic women, particularly Polish women. While only 523 cases of abortion on eastern female workers have been authenticated, these cases stretch only from May 1943 to January 1945. The documented cases thus cover only one and one-half years and one small area of Poland.[28] Since the Germans, however, had been in Poland at least five years (September 1939 to early 1945), and virtually all of the rest of eastern Europe for periods longer than a year and one-half, abortions were, without question, in the thousands, probably the tens of thousands.

The science of obstetrics has long told us that there are two lives involved in every pregnancy:

investigations of the nature of human life *in utero* have been, and will continue to be, among the most fascinating and rewarding in all biological research. This obtains, in large measure, because the findings of these inquiries are of momentous impact to all mankind.... The status of the fetus has been elevated to that of a patient who... can be given the same meticulous care that physicians long have given the pregnant woman.[29]

During the past two decades [1970s, 1980s], remarkably detailed knowledge of the human fetus and his or her environment has accumulated.... Indeed, the fetus is no longer regarded as a maternal appendage ultimately to be shed at the whim of biological forces beyond its control. Instead, the fetus has achieved the status of the second patient, a patient who usually faces much greater risks of serious morbidity and mortality, than does the mother.[30]

Science thus forcefully states that there are two lives (patients) in every pregnancy. The Nazis seemed to have understood this also:
•We have Himmler's remark that the tragedy of abortion was that women often could not later have children after an abortion, not in the loss of an "individual life," as he put it.
•We have the word "parent" used to describe pregnant women and the fathers of the unborn.
•We have the word "child" used to describe the unborn.
•We have the forbidding of abortion to preserve German unborn but allowed, even encouraged, to destroy non-German unborn.

Without question, the German Supreme Court was correct in 1975 in labeling abortion as an act of killing, which belonged with so many other Nazi atrocities.

The Nazis were experts in killing. It is for that very reason that they certainly knew what human life was. Their obsession with racial superiority and "pure blood" has at least a rough affinity with many believers in legalized abortion today. Today we have the desire among many for the "planned," "wanted," "quality" child. It reminds one of the comments of Dr. Ley at the 1937 meeting, who, in trying to balance "quality" with "quantity" was reluctantly willing to tolerate abortion "out of respect for life."

ABBREVIATIONS

PSR–Persönlicher Stab Reichsführer-SS (Personal Staff Files of SS Head, Heinrich Himmler. German National Archives, Berlin, Germany).

RSH–Reichsicherheitshauptamt (Reich Security Headquarters, German National Archives, Berlin, Germany.

NOTES

1. Donald Kommers, "Abortion and the Constitution: The Cases of the United States and West Germany," *Abortion: New Directions For Policy Studies*, eds., Edward Maier, William Liv, and David Solomon (Notre Dame: Univ. of Notre Dame Press, 1977), pp. 97-98.

2. Translated by Dr. O. J. Brown, *The Human Life Review* (Summer 1975), pp. 77-78. The Kommer article (note 1) hits high points in the decision, and the Brown translation (here) covers in detail the first half of the decision. For the complete text, see *Neues Juristisches Wochenblatt* 13 (1975) 573-87. *Tötenshandlung* ("an act of killing") is mentioned on p. 576.

3. For the 1993 decision, see *Europaische Grundrechte Zeitschrift* (EuGRZ), 9/10 (June 4, 1993) 229-75. There is no connection made with Nazism in this 1993 decision.

4. Volkmar's complete remarks are found in PSR, R320/N518, pp. 27-49.

5. *Ibid.*, pp. 63-65.

6. *Ibid.*, pp. 81-83.

7. *Ibid.*, pp. 85-88.

8. See Koppel Pinson, *Modern Germany: Its History and Civilization*, 2nd ed. (New York: Macmillan, 1966), Chap. 21, sec. 2: Ideology and "Macht," esp. pp.488-90; Ernst Nolte, *Three Faces of Fascism: Action Française, Italian Fascism, National Socialism*, tr. Leila Vennewitz (New York: Holt, Rinehart and Winston, 1966), p. 422.

9. PSR, R320/N518, pp. 89-90.

10. Himmler also blamed homosexuals for luring men away from marriage, and, therefore, procreation. He stated that early marriages would prevent homosexuality; early marriage was the reason why homosexuality was not found among farmers and workers! See *ibid.*, pp. 91-92. Himmler's entire remarks cover pp. 89-99, 108.

11. *Ibid.*, pp. 107-08, 115-16, 179-80, 183.

12. "Nuremberg Revisited: Abortion As a Human Rights Issue," *Life and Learning: Proceedings of the Third University Faculty For Life Conference*, ed. Joseph Koterski, S.J., Washington, D.C.: University Faculty For Life, 1993.

13. See statistics and graph in PSR, NS19/2844, p. 66. See also a letter from Gauleiter in Czechoslovakia to Himmler, July 15, 1942, in *ibid.*, NS19/3596.

14. *Trials of War Criminals before the Nuremberg Military Tribunals*, October, 1946-April, 1949, Vols. IV-V: "The RuSHA Case" (Washington, D.C.: U.S. Gov't. Printing Office, 1949). IV, 685-86.

15. *Ibid.*, pp. 611-12.

16. The beautiful Wannsee Conference House on a lake outside Berlin has become a Holocaust museum. The minutes of the meeting in which the decision was made are there for all to see, as are fifteen portraits and biographies of the men who made the decision. Everything is in German. Hofmann at this meeting was charged specifically with sterilizing "half-breeds." He was convicted in 1948 for abortions, sterilizations and a number of other offenses at the Nuremberg War Crimes Trials, and was sentenced to 25 years. He was released from Landsberg Prison in 1954. He died in 1982 at the age of 86. Visit to Wannsee Conference House by the author, November 1, 1997.

17. RSH, R58/148, February 16, 1940, pp. 92, 100-01. The search for "quality" Germans can be seen in the guidelines issued by the Reich Ministry of the Interior on July 18, 1940, for hereditary health: "An especially high-grade hereditarily healthy person to note is one who is bodily and spiritually healthy and in whose blood connection (grandparents, parents, siblings, and other children) one cannot find a case of psychosis which would lead to social decline, criminality, drugs, and so forth." See Bundesarchiv File in the German National Archives, Berlin, German, R018/003252, folder 1, pp. 1520-22.

18. RSH, R58/148, February 28, 1940, p. 195. The "eastern look" is mentioned in a letter from an author, whose name is indiscernible, to a Dr. Brandt, August 15, 1942, in PSR, NS19/3207.

19. The name cannot be made out on the document.

20. PSR, NS19/1986, November 9, 1942, pp. 1-3.

21. Letter from Obersturmführer Meine to Himmler, December 23, 1942, in *ibid.*, NS19/940.

22. Himmler to Gauleiter Eigrüber, October 9, 1942, *ibid.*, NS19/3596.

23. Letter from Himmler to Dr. Conti, *ibid.*, NS19/3438.

24. Letter from Himmler to Kruger (first name and position unknown). *Ibid.*

25. West German Federal Republic, Press and Information Office, *Bulletin 6, May 27, 1980* (Bonn: Deutsche Bundesverlag GmBH), p.13. See also PSR, NS19/456 and NS19/1913.

26. Proceedings against a Polish doctor Siegmund Walczynski; for an abortion which he performed on a German woman, April ?, 1943, PSR, NS19/3180.

27. Robert Jay Lifton, *The Nazi Doctors: Medical Killing and the Psychology of Genocide* (Basic Books, 1986), pp.149, 224. See also Raul Hilberg, *The Destruction of European Jews* (Chicago: Quadrangle Books, 1961), pp. 664-65.

28. Records of the United States Nuremberg War Crimes Trials, *United States of America v. Ulrich Greifelt, et al.* (Case VIII), October 10, 1947-March 10, 1948; The National Archives, Washington, D.C., Microfilm Publication 894, Roll 31, p. 11. This is the complete record, on microfilm of the RuSHA Trial mentioned in note 14.

29. Gary F. Cunningham, Paul C. Macdonald, Norman F. Grant, eds., *William's Obstetrics*, 18th ed. (Norwalk: Appleton & Lang, 1989), p. 87 (from Chapter 6: "Morphological and Functional Development of the Fetus").

30. *Ibid.*, p. 277 (from Chapter 15: "Techniques to Evaluate Fetal Health").

The Empty Promise of Contraception

Teresa R. Wagner

IN JUNE JAPAN MOVED one step closer to legalizing what was
introduced into the United States nearly forty years ago, the oral
contraceptive, when her Ministry of Health and Welfare deemed the
oral contraceptive safe enough for Japanese women. While the decision
was hailed by feminists, physicians, and pharmaceutical companies as
one that will push the Asian economic powerhouse into the modern–meaning Western–world, the pending legalization of the Pill by the
government of Tokyo may be more ominous for this traditional and
family-center country than public officials realize. As reflection and
deliberation tend to be in short supply in the public policy-making
process, Japanese government officials probably did little to assess what
the Pill has conceived on this side of the Pacific Ocean. Had they
carefully looked at the legacy of the Pill in the United States, they might
have though twice before embracing this seeming wonder of medical
technology.

The American experience with the Pill, and with contraception in
general, tells a complex but nevertheless revealing story. Since 1960,
when the Pill was introduced, and since 1965, when the Supreme Court
limited the ability of the states to regulate contraceptive sales, public
accessibility to contraceptive drugs and devices has increased dramatically among married and single Americans alike. In the old days,
accessibility to contraceptives was largely limited to vending machines
in seedy public bathrooms. Today, federal and state programs, led by
Title X of the Public Health Service Act and Title XIX of the Social
Security Act (Medicaid), spend more than $715 million dollars annually
promoting and distributing contraceptive drugs and devices under the
guise of family planning to women, specially teenagers.[1] Not only are
Americans now far more familiar with contraception but also the advent
of sex education in many public schools includes explicit instructions
on contraceptive technique/ According to Donald Critchlow, approxi-

mately 80% of all adults in the United States now practice some form of contraception, including sterilization.[2]

The widespread acceptance and use of contraceptives has occurred in part because many in the medical and public health field perceived during the 1970s and 1980s that contraception was the answer for the rising rates of out-of-wedlock pregnancy, abortion, and illegitimacy, especially among teenagers.[3] While this perception may have been reasonable 25 years ago, the record a generation later suggests that the heavy dose of contraception pitched to the American public since then has not reduced those rates but actually intensified the problem. According to the U.S. National Center for Health Statistics, out-of-wedlock births jumped dramatically from 202,000 in 1957 to 1.3 million in 1994, the same period during which contraceptives became common-place in America. Relative to all births, the portion of out-of-wedlock births increased from 4% in 1950 to 24% in 1987.[4] The number of abortions continued to climb during the 1970s and 1980s, rising from an estimated 744,600 abortions in 1973 to an estimated 1,608,600 abortions in 1990.[5] The actual numbers may even be higher, given that not all state health departments collect or report abortion data while others provide only partial data.[6]

Nor has the country experienced a decline in unwanted pregnan-cies. *Family Planning Perspectives* reports that one-half of all pregnancies in the United States today remain "unintended" as 18% of couples who use condoms and 12% who take the Pill become pregnant within two years.[7] Data compiled by the Alan Guttmacher Institute, the research arm of Planned Parenthood, confirm that reality, finding that nearly 50% of women seeking abortions were using some form of birth control.[8] In addition, whatever declines in adolescent pregnancy, abortion, and birth rates have been documented between 1988 and 1995 have occurred because of the increased number of teenagers choosing to postpone sexual relations, not because of increased contraceptive use, according to the Consortium of State Physicians Resource Councils.[9]

THE FAILURE OF CONTRACEPTION

One reason contraception has not been able to reduce rising illegitimacy and abortion significantly is that contraception has not been nearly as reliable or effective as its promoters and marketers have led Americans to believe. Not only is contraception less effective than originally assumed,[10] but abortion is now demanded precisely because contraception–which Americans were told would eliminate the need for abortion–fails. As the National Abortion Rights Action League claims: "The need for abortion will never go away until we... can achieve... better access to more effective contraception."[11] Indeed, the United States Supreme Court re-affirmed the right to abortion in the 1992 *Planned Parenthood v. Casey* decision on the same grounds: "Abortion is customarily chosen as an unplanned response... to the failure of conventional birth control.... [P]eople have organized intimate relationships... in reliance on the availability of abortion in the event that contraception should fail."[12]

Even in its most reliable form–the oral contraceptive–birth control has not altered the biological reality; sexual relations continue to result in pregnancy. In fact, the Pill today prevents even fewer pregnancies than it prevented thirty years ago. Originally, the Pill was designed to suppress ovulation through a heavy dose of synthetic estrogen. Because the original Pill often caused weight gain and nausea, pharmaceutical companies have over time reduced its estrogen component and added progesterone. Consequently today's Pill produces three fertility-related actions, of which one alters the uterine lining so that the womb cannot sustain newly conceived and developing life, prompting an early abortion. In this respect, the current oral contraceptive acts more like an abortifacient than a true contraceptive, resulting in more actual pregnancies than are recorded and therefore factored into evaluations of the Pill's effectiveness.[13] Technical difficulties, however, are not the main factors that have contributed to the failure of contraception. Contraception, in general, and the Pill in particular, fueled nothing less than a revolution in the way Americans understand human sexuality that directly reinforced the very pathologies that contraception was meant to contain. While failing as a matter of biology to prevent pregnancy, contraception ironically succeeded in separating sex from children in the minds of most Americans. Even as millions of women faced unplanned pregnancies or suffered abortions, the contraceptive mentality took hold and persists to this day.

In the days before the Pill, human sexuality was more than simply orgasmic pleasure–it was part of a coherent understanding of human nature and family relations. Sex and children were so closely linked that those who chose to ignore that ontological reality did so at great risk: the risk of bearing children. Human sexuality was considered a sacred gift, binding husband and wife together. Whether or not spouses consciously intended children–who were also considered sacred gifts–sexual intercourse by its very nature, as George Gilder notes, anticipated or celebrated progeny.[14]   Widespread contraception, however, helped to render this older vision obsolete, offering the grand illusion that one could engage is sexual relations without considering children. Reinforced by popular magazines, music, motion pictures, and television programming, the contraceptive mentality has so effectively persuaded Americans that children will not result from sex that many Americans remain psychologically unprepared for what is now called an "accidental pregnancy." As Janet Smith of the University of Dallas has observed, teenagers and often health clinic workers wonder, "How did this happen?" when faced with a pregnancy.[15]

THE DISTORTION OF HUMAN SEXUALITY

While some Americans, particularly Roman Catholics and Mormons, have fought hard to resist the contraceptive mentality, the dominant public culture in America no longer upholds the view that sexuality is a gift to be shared exclusively between husband and wife anticipating or celebrating children; sexual relations outside the context of marriage have become a societal norm. Notwithstanding a popular abstinence movement that has emerged in primary and secondary schools as an alternative to sex education, the new norm is reflected in the findings of the National Marriage Project of Rutgers University: more than half of young American women not only lose their virginity by age seventeen but are also sexually active for eight years before getting married. The same study also discovered that nearly 50% of Americans between the ages of 25 and 40 years have at some point set up housekeeping with a member of the opposite sex outside marriage.[16] Even among conservatives who publicly champion traditional values, pre- and extra-marital sex is more common than assumed. As Danielle Crittenden of the

Independent Women's Forum writes: "The most politically conservative young women I know–women who say they oppose abortion and yearn to marry and have families–would never disavow their right to sleep with whomsoever they please."[17]

By severing the connection between children and sexuality, the contraceptive mentality has fostered new visions of human sexuality. No longer accepted or received as a gift, sex is now demanded as a constitutional right; no longer viewed as a mystery latent with meaning, sex is now considered a bodily, medical function like eating and drinking; no longer considered a marital privilege, sex is now considered a recreational activity for all. Sex now exists for the benefit of the individual for personal satisfaction, therapy, and enrichment; self-fulfillment, not self-giving, stands at the heart of the new ethic. Provided sex does not "hurt" anyone, sexuality itself carries no moral dimension invoking transcendent questions of right and wrong aside from the legal claim that all persons have a right to engage in sexual acts. Consequently, legal, religious, and social conventions that seek to maintain traditional sexual norms are perceived as limitations of that right–whether between individuals of the same sex, between unmarried individuals, or even between teenagers–are called repressive. As Richard Cohen of *The Washington Post* recently framed it: "Mature, responsible people are *entitled* to an erotic life [emphasis added]. It is preposterous to suggest that it should be saved for marriage."[18]

The new ethic has not thrown out all the rules, but has rather adopted another set. Modern moralists, in contrast to traditionalists, insist upon the elements of consent and privacy. *Consent* is the sole moral prerequisite; *privacy* means that society cannot and should not attempt to impose any norms regarding sexual conduct, which theoretically occurs in private. Reaction to the President Clinton and Monica Lewinsky scandal from many commentators and media representatives is illustrative. As Bill Press wrote in *The Washington Times*: "The President had sex... and denied it. So what? [L]ying about sex... as long as it's between consenting adults, has never been prosecuted."[19]

THE CONTRACEPTIVE CULTURE UNFOLDS

The ethic of consent and privacy would never have been possible without the Pill, which provided the focus of legal and constitutional claims about the right to privacy in the 1965 Supreme Court case, *Griswold v. Connecticut*. Once the contraceptive right to sex was established, additional sexual rights followed, including the right to divorce through no-fault divorce, beginning in California in 1970, and the right to abortion in 1973 in *Roe v. Wade*, which was based upon the same rationale of privacy discovered in the Griswold case. Now, almost all sexual conduct except forcible rape (because it lacks consent) is fair game, or is at least on its way to becoming legitimate. While illegitimacy, abortion, adultery, and divorce constitute the first wave of the contraceptive culture, homosexuality, pedophilia, "consensual" incest, necrophilia, and bestiality may be the next. Already, homosexuality enjoys public acceptance unimaginable just thirty years ago. A growing number of Fortune 500 companies now offer employment benefits to homosexuals on par with married couples; courts have even awarded homosexual couples parental rights over children.[20] The series *Ellen* may have been forced off television after the main character identified herself as a lesbian in April 1997, but the incident, like the Oscar-winning 1993 film *Philadelphia* reflects the long-standing and formal acceptance of homosexuality in Hollywood.

The advance of pedophilia is less known. An essay published last year in the journal of the American Psychological Association, not only called for the abandonment of the pejorative term, pedophilia, in favor of the more value-neutral phrase "adult-child sex" but also called for the removal of pedophilia from the catalogue of psychiatric disorders. Sexual relations between adults and children, the essay claimed, are "far less damaging" than previously thought.[21] Although the American Psychological Association has since renounced the essay, observers have noted that the normalization of homosexuality began exactly the same way.[22] The age of consent has already been lowered in Canada to age fourteen for heterosexuals. While the consent age in Holland is sixteen, in some cases twelve-year-olds can consent to sexual relations. Although initially defeated, an effort was launched earlier this year to lower the age in Great Britain.[23] As minors have historically been deemed unable to consent to anything legally, such efforts to lower the age of consent indicate either that the promoters do not accept this longstanding legal doctrine or do not care that consent be obtained. In keeping with the modern notion of sex, advocates for a lower age of consent argue that minors have the same right to sex as everyone else and claim that the legal creation of an age of consent violates that right.[24]

Both pedophilia and incest have made recent appearances in novels and in motion pictures as well. Filmmakers remade *Lolita* in 1998, a movie that celebrates a man's relationship with a twelve-year-old girl, based upon the 1955 novel by Vladimir Nabokov that now constitutes popular reading material in English classes throughout American colleges and universities.[25] In 1997, Random House published *The Kiss*, Kathryn Harrison's account of a daughter and father who begin a sexual relationship after meeting as adults.[26] While Americans may continue to harbor instinctual reservations about pedophilia and incest, these examples suggest that such perversions, as well as homosexuality, are simply by-products of a culture that separates sexuality from children. If privacy and consent are the only moral components left to mediate sexual relations, all manner of sexual behavior will follow. In essence, the entertainment and publishing industries are pressing very logical questions: If sexuality has nothing to do with marriage and children, what is wrong with "consensual" incest and why *not* "consensual" pedophilia?

THE DENIGRATION OF LIFE

As the contraceptive promise has persuaded them that they can engage in sex without children, Americans are now considering the reverse of that paradigm: that they might be able to bear children without sex. This development may represent the most tragic outgrowth of the contraceptive culture. While contraception has sought to suppress fertility, a corresponding panoply of services called reproductive technologies, including *in vitro* fertilization, has emerged to help those couples who want conception, not contraception. Originally intended to help create life and to fight disease, these sophisticated services are assumed to be *pro-life*, yet they often constitute new assaults upon human life, involving the blatant destruction of human beings in both the embryonic and fetal stages. For example, some scientists are now experimenting upon and actually killing the surplus embryos from *in vitro* fertilization clinics under the guise of stem cell research. Consequently, reports of frozen embryos, discarded blastocysts, as well as the destruction of some lives within the womb in order that others may live (called fetal reduction) are commonplace. Books and articles about surrogate mothers, ownership of human embryos, and the rights of a widow to her deceased husband's sperm are also numerous.[27]

Because of the speed with which new technologies have become available, and because of their promised benefits, Americans have not reflected upon the ethical questions they raise. Cloning is perhaps the only reproductive technology to which the public has registered resistance; thirty-two efforts have been introduced in seventeen states to regulate human cloning, and Michigan has banned all forms of it.[28] On the other hand, none of the three bills introduced into Congress in 1998 that would have prohibited some type of human cloning passed. To what extent Americans can, in the long run, resist the promises of cloning is not clear, as no one has yet framed a compelling argument against it.

Leon Kass of the University of Chicago has developed a case against human cloning, contending that it will transform starting a family into a manufacturing process, will reduce children to products, and will put family relations into disarray.[29] While these points have merit, they are not compelling in the present contraceptive culture: family relations are already very much in disarray; *in vitro* fertilization has already transformed starting a family into a manufacturing process with children as its products. For good or bad, Americans now accept most of these reproductive technologies and therefore may not be persuaded that cloning is wrong on these grounds. The initial resistance to cloning can probably be attributed to residual public distaste. Early efforts to normalize homosexuality also provoked an emotional reaction, but that negative response receded once Americans grew accustomed to the idea and became familiar with homosexuals. The ambivalence toward human cloning may very well foreshadow a similar course, just as many Americans have grown more comfortable with homosexuality, *in vitro* fertilization, and frozen embryos.

Like the relationship between contraception and abortion, the relationship between reproductive technologies and embryo experimentation confirms the larger link between human sexuality and human life (children). While *in vitro* fertilization does not necessarily lead to embryo destruction–just as contraception does not necessarily lead to abortion–the mentality to manipulate or destroy human sexuality clearly can lead to a mentality to destroy or manipulate human life. Indeed, the United States in the late 20th century has experienced unprecedented denigration of human life, not only though the rise of infanticide (including abortion), euthanasia, and assisted suicide, but also in the areas of child abuse, teen suicide, substance abuse, criminal activity, and medical experimentation upon the disabled. These examples of increased violence against the human person have occurred alongside the advent of widespread contraception.

Contraception, of course, is not the sole culprit behind these ills. The denigration of human life is largely the product of secularism, which denies and neglects the role of a personal God within the world and consequently within the human person. Human beings, the Creator's crowning achievement and the embodiment of the sacred on earth, become casualties along the way. Yet secularism's most insidious affront to human life has come within the realm of human sexuality in the form of contraception. By seeking to remove children from sex, contraception has taken the sacred out of sex. This degradation of human sexuality has encouraged the degradation of human beings to which human sexuality is biologically linked. Therefore, to the degree that contraception represents the manipulation and mistreatment of sexuality–the *means*–it has contributed to the manipulation and maltreatment of human beings–*the end*.

RESPONDING TO THE CONTRACEPTIVE CULTURE

Reversing the effects of the contraceptive culture will not be easy. With good intentions, socially conservative Americans have tended to lift up the importance of sexual abstinence, encouraging young people with the same chorus that first lady Nancy Reagan sang in her war against drugs, "Just say no." While the abstinence campaign has value, its ability to challenge the contraceptive culture is limited. By focusing solely on sexual purity in marriage, the campaign unintentionally plays into the hands of the sexual revolutionaries, in particular homosexuals who now seek legitimacy by saying that they too affirm marriage and purity. The abstinence and purity campaign also obscures the extent to which traditionalists have made peace with contraception–welcoming without reservation contraceptive use in marriage–making them vulnerable when asked: "Heterosexuals engage in sexual relations without children; why not homosexuals?" As Ramesh Ponnuru observes in *National Review*, many conservatives are reluctant "to spell out their case against homosexual conduct because it would condemn the practices of most heterosexuals."[30] Even if they were able to respond to such arguments, conservatives face significant hurdles in the nation's courthouses, which, since the 1965 *Griswold v. Connecticut* decision, have generally sided with those seeking to advance the modern sexual agenda. This puts traditionalists, at a strategic disadvantage. Traditional or religious arguments simply do not carry weight with a legal establishment that is more enamored with modern, procedural notions of rights and privacy than with ontological discussions about the nature of human sexuality.

Given these cultural and legal realities, how should traditional Americans respond to the contraceptive culture? For starters, conservatives need to develop a more coherent and compelling philosophy of human sexuality, one that looks at sex not narrowly as a right for married couples to enjoy, but as a divine gift that goes hand-in-hand with the divine gift of children. They need to recognize that tying sexuality exclusively to marriage can only work when sex is equally connected to children. In doing so, conservatives may need to think more critically about contraception, acknowledging that the same convenience that the Pill may provide for married couples has at the same time wreaked havoc in the broader culture. This does not necessarily mean that all conservatives must accept the Roman Catholic distinction between "artificial" contraception and "natural" family planning, but they should at least be open to the merits of the Catholic affirmation of children over contraception as a serious alternative to the sexual pathologies of the age.

Armed and chastened with a more coherent understanding of human sexuality, conservatives could achieve more in the political and legal realms, where they face an uphill battle. As no federal law currently forbids cloning, efforts to create the first human clone continues apace; homosexual activists continue to press for greater rights and recognition; and Title X of the Public Health Act and Title XIX of the Social Security Act, while modified by a predominantly Republican Congress since 1994, remain the law of the land. While contraception is no longer a legal issue, Planned Parenthood succeeded in securing contraceptive coverage for the Federal Employee Health Benefits Plan in the 105th Congress and is currently lobbying Congress to mandate contraceptive coverage as a benefit in all health insurance plans.[31]

The proposed federal mandating of contraceptive health coverage may be a battle not worth fighting at this time, since many health plans in the corporate and private sectors already cover oral contraceptives. However, the issue provides an excellent opportunity to start questioning the presumed desirability of contraception, not simply in medical insurance but also in Title X, Title XIX, and the congressional appropriations for the United Nations and its Population Fund, which dispenses contraception in global doses. At the same time, the seemingly minor issue of framing contraception as a medical health benefit is far more revealing than it appears. Contraceptive literature has for years typically referred to the woman as a patient, to fertility as the condition or sickness, and to contraception as the prescription or medication. On the other hand, courts have increasingly found that *infertility* is a disability for which health plans must also provide treatment.[32] The question remains: What precisely is the disease or disability that needs treatment?

This ambivalence about fertility reflects the ambivalence about women, to whom most contraception is directed. While the Pill and other devices have been successfully marketed as offering emancipation and increased control for women, the alleged freedom comes with a high price: tampering with a woman's natural condition of health and inherent fertility. At a deeper level, this ambivalence reflects the ambivalence about the identity, role, and status of women in American society, the ultimate contradiction of the contraceptive culture. Coupled with all the unintended pathologies which contraception itself has conceived in America, this reality may not encourage Japan to rethink her pending legislation of the Pill. On the other hand, it might sound the alarm needed to waken Americans to the fundamental realities of "the birds and the bees" to which nearly four decades on the Pill have anaesthetized them. Americans might then be able to direct their sexual passions toward truly productive ends, conceiving once again not only children, but also a culture where children, more than the sexual act that reaps them, inspire the human imagination.

NOTES

1. Jacqueline Darroach Forrest and Renee Samara, "Impact of Publicly Funded Contraceptive Servies on Unintended Pregnancies and Implications for Medicaid Expenditures" in *Family Planning Perspectives* 28/5 (1996) 188-95.

2. Donald T. Critchlow, *Intended Consequences: Birth Control, Abortion, and the Federal Government in Modern America* (New York: Oxford Univ. Press, 1999), p. 10.

3. Rochelle A. Turetsky, M.D., and Victor C. Strasburger, M.D., "Adolescent Contraception: Review and Recommendations" in *Clinical Pediatrics* 22 (1983) 337-34; and M. Zelnick and J. F. Kantner, "Sexual Activity, Contraceptive Use, and Pregnancy among Metropolitan Area Teenagers 1971 to 1979" in *Family Planning Perspectives* 12 (1980) 230-37.

4. *Statistical Abstract of the United States: 1998* (Washington, D.C.; U.S. Bureau of the Census, 1998), chart 101, p. 81; and "Infant Mortality by Marital Status of Mother" in *Morbidity and Mortality Weekly Report* 39/30 (1990) 521.

5. Stanley Henshaw, "Abortion Incidence and Services in the United States, 1995-1996" in *Family Planning Perspectives* 30/6 (1998) 263-70 at 264. See Table 1: Number of Reported Abortions, 1973-1996.

6. Janet E. Gans Epner et. al., "Late Term Abortion" in *Journal of the American Medical Association* 290/8 (1998) 725-29.

7. Haishan Fu *et al.*, "Contraceptive Failure Rates: New Estimates from th3 1995 National Survey of Family Growth" in *Family Planning Perspectives* 31/2 (1999) 56-63. See Table 1, p. 60.

8. Stanley K. Henshaw, "Unintended Pregnancy in the United States" in *Family Planning Perspectives* 30/1 (1998) 24-29.

9. *The Declines in Adolescent Pregnancy, Birth, and Abortion Rates in the 1990s: What Factors Are Responsible?* (Rahwah: The Consortium of State Physicians Resource Councils, 1999).

10. Alan O. Otton, "Contraceptive Problems Cause More Pregnancies" in *The Wall Street Journal* (May 25, 1993), p. B1.

11. National Abortion Rights Action League, "An American Right at Risk" (June 1999), www.naral.org.

12. *Planned Parenthood v. Casey*, 505 U.S. 833, 856 (1992).

13. *The Physician's Desk Reference*, 53rd ed. (Montvale: Medical Economics Co., 1999), p. 2222; Nicholas Tonti-Filippini, "The Pill: Abortifacient or Contraceptive?" in *Linacre Quarterly* (Feb. 1995), pp. 5-28; and Marc A. Fritz *et al.*, "The Effect of Oral Contraceptive Pills on Markers of Endometrial Receptivity" in *Fertility and Sterility* 65/3 (1996) 484-88.

14. George Gilder, *Sexual Suicide* (New York: Bantam Books, 1975), pp. 33-38.

15. Janet Smith, "*Humanae Vitae*: Part II," lecture delivered at the University of Notre Dame (June 1991).

16. David Popenoe and Barbara Dafore Whitehead, *The State of Our Union: The Social Health of Marriage in America* (New Brunswick: National Marriage Project, 1999).

17. Danielle Crittenden, *What Our Mothers Didn't Tell Us: Why Happiness Eludes the Modern Woman* (New York: Simon & Schuster, 1999), p. 36.

18. Richard Cohen, "The Abstinence Candidate" in *The Washington Post* (June 24, 1999), p. A27.

19. Bill Press, "All About Sex" in *The Washington Times* (July 29, 1998), p. A21.

20. Andy Soltis, "New Jersey's Gay Couples Win the Right to Adopt" in *The New York Post* (Dec. 18, 1997), p. 5.

21. Bruce Rind *et al.*, "A Meta-Analytic Examination of Assumed Properties of Child Sexual Abuse Using College Samples" in *Psychological Bulletin* 124/1 (1998) 22-53.

22. Robert H. Knight and Frank V. York, *Homosexual Activists Work to Lower the Age of Consent* (Washington, D.C.: Family Research Council, 1999).

23. Dirk Kruithof, "Dutch Law on Ages of Consent Since 1991," Dutch Association for the Integration of Homosexuality, www.x54all.nl/nvihoe/history.html; Joe Woodward, "Victims at Last" in *Alberta Report/Western Report* (June 12, 1995), p. 28; and Terence Neilan, "Lords Defeat Gax Sex Bill" in *The New York Times* (April 15, 1999), p. A10.

24. Mark Blasius, "Sexual Revolution and the Liberation of Children," www.namle.org.

25. Vladimir Nabokov, *Lolita*, Second Vintage International Edition (New York: Random House/Vintage Books, 1997).

26. Kathryn Harrison, *The Kiss* (New York: Random House, 1997).

27. For example, see Julian Duin, "Brave New World of Cloning Spawns Ethical Nightmares" in *The Washington Times* (May 19, 1999), p. A2.

28. Clarke D. Forsythe, "Human Cloning and the Constitution" in *Valparaiso Univ. Law Review* 32/2 (1998) 469-541.

29. Leon R. Kass, "The Wisdom of Repugnance" in *The Ethics of Human Cloning* (Washington, D.C.: American Enterprise Institute, 1998), pp. 3-59.

30. Ramesh Pannuru, "Sexual Hangup" in *National Review* (Feb. 8, 1999), p. 42.

31. Senate Bill 1324, Equity in Prescription Insurance and Contraceptive Coverage Act, introduced June 10, 1999. For Planned Parenthood's lobbying efforts in support of the legislation, see its recent newspaper advertisement, "The Ol' Boys' Double Standard... For Fairminded People It's a BITTER PILL" in *The Washington Post* (June 25, 1999).

32. Randy Kennedy, "U.S. Agency Says Employer Should Pay for a Woman's Infertility Treatments" in *The New York Times* (April 29, 1999), p. B1.

An Argument for Continuing a Pregnancy Where the Fetus Is Discovered to be Anencephalic

Bridget Campion

LITERALLY, ANENCEPHALY means to be without a brain. In fact, the anencephalic fetus, although severely compromised, is not entirely brain absent.[1] Rather, he is without much of his forebrain, or "higher" brain; that is, he is without the part of the brain thought to be responsible for human consciousness, for human awareness and reflection. However, the anencephalic fetus has "lower" brain or brainstem activity. It is this part of the brain that governs the basic functions of circulation, digestion, respiration and other vital activities of the body.

Current research suggests that anencephaly is preceded by exencephaly: early in the fetus's development, sometime in the first three weeks of life, the neural tube fails to close.[2] The skull fails to form, leaving the developing brain tissue exposed to amniotic fluid. This fluid is hostile to brain tissue and causes it to degenerate. Given the lengthy gestation of the human fetus, the degeneration can be so severe as to render the fetus anencephalic.

The incidence of anencephaly is 0.3/1000 births, or approximately 1100 babies born yearly in the U.S.[3] Although there have been many theories, the causes of anencephaly are unknown.[4] The condition is so physically distinctive as to be detected quite reliably through ultrasound by the 14th to 16th week of pregnancy. Because anencephaly is a defect of the neural tube (as is spina bifida), it can be detected by measuring alphafetoprotein levels in the mother's blood and in the amniotic fluid. These tests are usually done between the 15th and 20th week of pregnancy, with the results available a few weeks later.

Anencephaly is a fatal condition. According to one source, 65% of the afflicted fetuses die *in utero*.[5] For the fetus who survives to term, birth is very traumatic. Because they are without a skull to protect them, many anencephalic fetuses are stillborn. For those who survive birth, most are likely to die within hours. In one study, half of the babies died within twenty-four hours of birth; the remainder, within fifteen days.[6] Because the infants have no higher brain function, many researchers believe that the live-born babies have no awareness and experience nothing. Anencephaly is a grim and tragic diagnosis.

THE DILEMMA

During my practice as a clinical ethicist in Catholic hospitals, I was confronted with the question: once anencephaly is detected, can physicians induce labor early–sometime between 15 and 22 weeks gestation?[7] Some of the physicians considered the pregnancy futile because the baby would die so soon after delivery, if not before birth. The fetus was so compromised neurologically that he could be neither harmed by termination of the pregnancy nor benefitted by its continuation. With early induction of labor, couples could get started sooner on a "normal" pregnancy and put this abnormal one behind them. Some practitioners pointed out that in non-Catholic hospitals, termination of this pregnancy was seen as "good medicine." Furthermore, this would not be an abortion because Catholic hospitals do not do abortions; rather, it would be an early delivery of the baby.

Interestingly, the nursing staff had some difficulties with the procedure. They were afraid that women carrying the afflicted babies were being rushed into the procedure. Because the diagnosis of anencephaly is not made until the second trimester of pregnancy, time is often of the essence. Nurses wondered whether women were able to make a truly informed choice while still reeling from the shock of the diagnosis. More to the point, they were concerned about the infant. For the fetus with anencephaly, birth, whenever it should come, means almost immediate death. The nurses wondered why they were assisting in a procedure that seemed to lead to the death of the infant. Were they in fact assisting in an abortion?

A meeting of moral theologians was called to examine the issue. The group considered the moral status of the fetus. Without higher brain function, or the possibility of it, could the fetus be considered a person? Was the death of the infant the intended or unintended outcome of early induction of labor? Would it make a moral difference if the procedure were postponed until 22-24 weeks of pregnancy, when an unafflicted fetus would have achieved viability?

The participants acknowledged that, according to Catholic teaching, human life begins at conception. While we may not know precisely when "personhood" begins, the teaching is that we must give that life the benefit of the doubt and that we must treat and respect the life as a person from conception.[8] For most of the group, the question seemed to be: does anencephaly change this? Is the anomaly simply so severe that personhood is compromised even if the life is human?

Frankly, I was not concerned about the possible personhood of the anencephalic fetus. It seemed to me that if we would baptize the anencephalic infant (and I could not imagine anyone suggesting that baptism be withheld), then we were implicitly acknowledging the moral status of the baby and, consequently, of the fetus. A very different question occupied me. Because the anencephalic fetus suffers severe neurological impairment and faces imminent death, many practitioners see little point in continuing the pregnancy. They consider the pregnancy "futile."

To label a pregnancy "futile" implies that pregnancy has value only outside of itself. It has worth because of what it can do. It is a means to an end. Pregnancy is meant to yield a viable infant and when it cannot achieve this goal–as when the fetus is anencephalic–the pregnancy is judged to be futile. For some of the moral theologians at the table, this was a crucial point and I wondered if this was the only way to view pregnancy. Was it possible that pregnancy had value in itself independent of outcome? If so, could pregnancy continue to have value when the fetus is anencephalic? These questions formed the basis of my thinking and research.

THE VALUE OF PREGNANCY

In 1975, Reva Rubin, a professor of nursing actively engaged in research, published "Maternal Tasks in Pregnancy," an article which would become a seminal work for those trying to understand the developmental work of pregnancy and prenatal attachment in particular.[9] According to Rubin, pregnancy is not simply a time of fetal physiological development and accompanying physical changes in the woman. Rather, "Pregnancy is also a period of identity reformulation, a period of re-ordering interpersonal relationships and interpersonal space, a period of personality maturation."[10] Rubin found that, in pregnancy, women were actively engaged in specific developmental tasks. Among them was what she termed "binding-in to her unborn child."[11] Rubin observed women becoming attached to their babies prenatally.

This was a rather startling claim to have made in light of the work done by Marshall Klaus and John Kennell. In the early seventies, these researchers published findings that indicated that the period immediately following birth was crucial to the bonding of mother and child.[12] The researchers' belief in the importance of post-natal bonding influenced practices around post-natal care.

Rubin's observations led her to believe that attachment begins prior to birth. As she wrote:

The bond between a mother and her child that is so apparent immediately after the birth of her child is developed and structured during pregnancy. At birth there is already a sense of knowing the child, within the limitations of not having had perceptions through the usual sensory modalities. At birth there is already a sense of shared experiences, shared history, and shared time on an intimate and exclusive plane. There is a sense of 'We-ness,' a sense of 'I-and-you.'[13]

Other researchers noticed that women were relating to their children before birth, naming the unborn babies with names that might not be used after birth, describing their personalities and talking to them. This interaction was occurring prenatally. According to Mecca S. Cranley, "women described interaction and communication with their unborn children. They ascribed individual characteristics to them and reported feelings of love."[14]

The women and their partners were also grieving their unborn children. Studies indicate that miscarriage or stillbirth often leads to a grief as intense as the sorrow one might feel at the death of a beloved adult.[15] When a baby or a fetus dies, there is much to be grieved. There is the loss of the child and the dreams that go with her. But there is the loss of *this* unborn baby as she is–as someone who was known and loved and experienced in a very private and intimate way. The unborn baby is herself irreplaceable.

The studies done on prenatal attachment were meant to lead to a better understanding of the impact of fetal and infant loss, too often treated as a non-event. With knowledge, researchers believed, practice could be improved. For the purposes of this paper, the important point is that for the woman, pregnancy has its own work and its own identity. It is not a time of suspended animation, of holding one's breath while waiting for "real" life to resume. It possesses an identity of its own and experiences unique to it. While it is preparation for life after birth, it is also a busy and meaningful state in itself.

Of course pregnancy is an active time for the fetus as he grows and develops and lays the foundations for life after birth. Before birth, the fetus is far from passive. Researchers in fetal psychology contend that in pregnancy the unborn child is actively interacting with his uterine environment.[16] He is actively engaged in his own development–and not just physical development. The fetus is also coming to "know" something of the woman who carries him, becoming familiar with her voice and heartbeat, perhaps even her emotions through the changing biochemistry they evoke, all the while learning something of the rhythms of life. This familiarity will aid the baby after birth as he recognizes his mother even though she exists for him in a very different way. This familiarity will aid him as he and his mother continue to bond.

Researchers are finding that the neonate is surprisingly capable. Norman A. Krasnegor and Jean-Pierre Lecanuet write: "We now know that human babies are sentient beings who are aware of their surroundings, can learn within hours of birth, are responsive to their environment at sensory, behavioral, and psychological levels."[17]

This discovery emerged as researchers stopped measuring the abilities of newborns against standards appropriate for children or adults and began to appreciate the infant's own capabilities. Adopting this perspective, researchers found that newborns actively engage in attachment. According to Krasnegor and Lecanuet, "research has convincingly documented that newborn babies are capable of adaptation, of identifying caregivers, and of eliciting behavior from them."[18]

It is unlikely that these complex behaviors emerge spontaneously with birth; researchers believe that they may have their origins in the prenatal period. If so, it appears that *in utero* existence may be a very rich time for the fetus. In other words, it seems that the fetus not only prepares for attachment after birth but is herself "an integral part of the prebirth experience of relating."[19] It seems that the unborn baby and the woman who carries her exist in a relationship prenatally.

Clearly pregnancy is not a passive time for either the woman or for the fetus. Not is it solely a means to an end. While it certainly prepares the woman and the fetus for birth and life afterwards, pregnancy is also a state in itself with its own identity and work. Pregnancy is a time of intimate human relationship–perhaps the most intimate humanly possible. While this is one way of understanding pregnancy, the question remains: is such an understanding applicable when the fetus is anencephalic?

THE ANENCEPHALIC FETUS

Anecdotal evidence suggests that anencephalic infants who survive birth are capable of responding to a variety of stimuli. They cry when they are hungry or uncomfortable, can suckle, swallow, and startle, and will settle when they are held.[20] Anencephalic infants, despite other defects of blindness or deafness, may be capable emotional partners eliciting and responding to behaviors from their caregivers.

How is this possible, given their severe neurological anomaly? According to research done by Alan Shewmon and Peter McCullagh, there appears to be more similarity between an anencephalic infant and unafflicted newborn than was previously thought.[21] There is a reason for this: while an unafflicted infant may be born with an intact forebrain, the higher brain is relatively immature. Both the anencephalic and non-anencephalic infant rely largely on brainstem function for the first weeks of postnatal life. It is also possible that neuroplasticity plays a part in the phenomenon. Given the deficiencies in the cerebral cortex at such an early stage, the brainstem may "assume somewhat more complex integrative activity than would ordinarily be the case, as has been suggested in some animal studies."[22] As time goes on, the non-afflicted infant's higher brain will become more operative but, during those first weeks of life, the two infants are functionally similar.

If it is true that babies do not spontaneously emerge with their complex capabilities intact but actively develop them prenatally and if the anencephalic infant and non-afflicted newborn are functionally similar, it would seem that the anencephalic fetus, like the non-afflicted fetus, is actively engaged in developing those abilities despite his severe anomalies while he is in the womb. In other words, the case can be made that the rich *in utero* life of the unafflicted fetus is in some sense available to the anencephalic fetus. He is nourished and grows, is exposed to stimuli and reacts, comes to know as much as he is able about his environment and the woman who carries him. There is one important difference, however. Unlike the unafflicted fetus, the anencephalic fetus suffers from a condition that is fatal. More than likely this fetus will not be born alive. Death is an inevitable part of this young life. It is in light of this fact that the challenge exists to find meaning in the pregnancy where the fetus is anencephalic.

THE POSSIBILITY OF MEANING

Until just decades ago, the anencephalic infant was technically classified as a monstrosity.[23] We know now that such a baby is deserving of comfort and care and love during his short life, whether that life is *ex utero* or, I would argue, *in utero*. Still, how could this pregnancy have meaning? If we believe that pregnancy has value not simply as a means to an end but generally as a state in itself and particularly as a relationship, and if we view the anencephalic fetus not as a monster but as a dying individual, then we may be able to under-stand the pregnancy as a way of caring for the fetus in her dying, as a way of ministering to her in the only relationship she may ever know or experience.

Continuation of the pregnancy may thus be very important to the fetus. It may also be important to the woman and her partner. Health care professionals caring for women who have had miscarriages or had their babies stillborn recognize that the grieving process may be facilitated when the fetus is made as real as possible for the parents. Having the parents see the baby and hold him even if he is dead, having the parents name the baby and keep a picture of him are becoming common practices after perinatal death. To have this connection is very important. In her studies, researcher Alice Lovell found that "acceptance [of the loss] was linked to the way that the baby's existence, though short, had been acknowledged and made tangible."[24]

Usually, interventions to facilitate this connection happen once the baby has died. Continuing the pregnancy when the fetus is known to suffer from a fatal condition may initiate this process while the fetus is still alive and ease the grieving that the parents inevitably face. Each day lived consciously sustaining this life and allowing the process of attachment to continue and deepen will make the fetus more real to the woman and her partner. They in turn can draw those around them into this ministry to the very fragile life that lies within her. When the end should come, they will have the satisfaction of knowing that they loved this baby as best they could. The parents will still grieve and need support but "grief is the price which we must all pay for our experience of loving."[25]

Once it has been diagnosed, there is nothing that will make anencephaly not have happened. Not even terminating the pregnancy can do that. However, if the woman and her partner can continue the pregnancy as a way of caring for their dying baby and of sustaining him in the only relationship he may ever know, perhaps they will begin to find worth and meaning in the pregnancy. Perhaps they will begin to find healing. Viewed this way, it seems to me, that the pregnancy is far from futile.

NOTES

1. David A.Stumpf, Ronald E. Cranford, Sherman Elias, Norman C. Fost, Michael P. McQuillen, Edwin C. Meyer, Ronald Poland and John T. Queenan, "The Infant with Anencephaly," *New England Journal of Medicine* 322 (1990) 669.

2. Louise Wilkins-Haug and Walter Freedman, "Progression of Exencephaly to Anencephaly in the Human Fetus–An Ultrasound Perspective," *Prenatal Diagnosis* 11 (1991) 227, 231-232.

3. D. Alan Shewmon estimates that 1125 infants with anencephaly are born yearly while Stumpf and others place the number of births at 1050 yearly. See D. Alan Shewmon, "Anencephaly: Selected Medical Aspects," *Hastings Center Report* 18 (Oct.-Nov. 1988) 12; and Stumpf *et al.*, 671.

4. Current thinking links anencephaly to a deficiency in folic acid in the pregnant woman. See Howard S. Cuckle and Nicholas J. Wald, "Recent Developments in the Prevention of Neural Tube Defects in the United Kingdom" in *Alpha-Fetoprotein and Congential Disorders*, ed. Gerald J. Mizejewski and Ian H. Porter (Orlando: Academic Press, Inc., 1985), p. 277. Earlier theories linked the anomaly to influenza and to women eating blighted potatoes. See B.C. McGillivray, "Anencephaly–the Potential for Survival," *Transplantation Proceedings* 20 (1988) 9; Stuart Campbell, E.M. Holt, F.D. Johnstone and Pamela May, "Anencephaly: Early Ultrasonic Diagnosis and Active Management," *Lancet* 2 (1972) 1226.

5. Stumpf *et al.*, 670.

6. Sheldon T. Berkowitz, "A Committee Consults: The Case of an Anencephalic Infant," *Hastings Center Report* (June 1986) 18.

7. The issue was not limited to my own practice but posed a dilemma in other Catholic health care institutions. See, for instance, Kevin O'Rourke, "Ethical Opinions in Regard to the Question of Early Delivery of Anencephalic Infants," *Linacre Quarterly* 63 (1996) 55-59. See also National Conference of Catholic Bishops Committee on Doctrine, "Moral Principles Concerning Infants with Anencephaly," *Origins* 26 (Oct. 10, 1996) 276; Peter J. Cataldo, "The NCCB on Anencephaly," *Ethics and Medics* 22 (1997) 3-4.

8. Sacred Congregation for the Doctrine of the Faith, "Declaration on Abortion" in *Official Catholic Teaching: Love and Sexuality*, ed. Odile M. Liebard (Wilmington.: McGrath Publishing, 1978), pp. 413-14.

9. Reva Rubin, "Maternal Tasks in Pregnancy," *Maternal-Child Nursing Journal* 4 (1975) 143-53.

10. *Ibid.*, p. 143.

11. *Ibid.*, p. 145.

12. Marshall H. Klaus and John H. Kennell, "Mothers Separated from their Newborn Infants," *Ped. Clin. North Am.* 17 (1970) 1015-37.

13. Rubin, p. 149.

14. Mecca S. Cranley, "The Origins of the Mother-Child Relationship–A Review," *Physical and Occupational Therapy in Pediatrics* 12 (1992) 41. See also Ramona T. Mercer, *Becoming a Mother: Research in Maternal Identity from Rubin to Present* (New York: Springer, 1995), p. 130.

15. Rosemary Mander, *Loss and Bereavement in Childbearing* (Oxford: Blackwell Scientific Publications, 1994), p. 121. Patricia Witzel and Brian M. Chartier, "The Unrecognized Psychological Impact of Miscarriage," *Canada's Mental Health* 37 (1989) 18.

16. See, for instance, William P. Smotherman and Scott R. Robinson, "Dimensions of Fetal Investigation," in *Behavior of the Fetus*, ed. William P. Smotherman and Scott R. Robinson (Caldwell: The Telford Press, 1988), pp. 19-34; and Myron A. Hofer, "On the Nature and Function of Prenatal Behavior," pp. 3-18 in the same volume. See also Peter G. Hepper, "Fetal Psychology: An Embryonic Science," in *Fetal Behavior: Developmental and Perinatal Aspects*, ed. Jan G. Nijhuis (Oxford: Oxford Univ. Press, 1992), pp. 129-56.

17. Norman A. Krasnegor and Jean-Pierre Lecanuet, "Behavioral Development of the Fetus" in *Fetal Development: A Psychobiological Perspective*, ed. Jean-Pierre Lecanuet, William P. Fifer, Norman A. Krasnegor and William P. Smotherman (Hillsdale: Lawrence Erlbaum Associates, 1995), p. 3.

18. *Ibid.*, pp. 3-4.

19. M. Colleen Stainton, "Commentary by Stainton," *Western Journal of Nursing Research* 16 (1994) 619.

20. See J.M. Nielsen and R.P. Sedgwick, "Instincts and Emotions in an Anencephalic Monster," *Journal of Nervous and Mental Disease* 110 (1949) 387-94. Although fifty years old, this seminal study continues to have relevance.

21. D. Alan Shewmon, Alexander M. Capron, Warwick J. Peacock, and Barbara L. Shulman, "The Use of Anencephalic Infants as Organ Sources," *Journal of the American Medical Association* 261 (1989) 1773-81; Peter McCullagh, *Brain Dead, Brain Absent, Brain Donors: Human Subjects or Human Objects* (Chichester: John Wiley and Sons, 1993), pp. 118-19.

22. Shewmon *et al.*, p. 1776.

23. J. Mark Elwood and J. Harold Elwood, *Epidemiology of Anencephaly and Spina Bifida* (Oxford: Oxford Univ. Press, 1980), p. 8.

24. Alice Lovell, "Some Questions of Identity: Late Miscarriage, Stillbirth and Perinatal Loss," *Social Science and Medicine* 17 (1983) 759.

25. Mander, p. 11.

Multifetal Pregnancy Reduction (MFPR): The Psychology of Desperation and the Ethics of Justification

Elizabeth Ring-Cassidy

It is hurt that drives the growing fertility industry in Canada.... A market has been built around the patients' desperation without acknowledging their vulnerability.

S. Fine, *The Globe & Mail*, May 27, 1999

You can't have a baby–a numbness beyond desperation. Baby Lust. Do you know how it feels to want a baby so much that every other activity in life, everything you've worked for and planned for–jobs, friends, family, marriage, seem hollow as a tin can? To be in emotional pain so extreme that when you see a pregnant woman's stomach or a newborn baby that the pain becomes physical.

K. Blomain, Review, Amazon Books on Line 1997

JUST AS REPRODUCTIVE technologies have changed obstetrical practice, so too have they led to a type of abortion which affects a different population of pregnant women. It is an irony that couples suffering problems of infertility must often come face to face with abortion.

There is a large literature detailing the psychological distress experienced by couples who wish children but who cannot conceive naturally (Stanton *et al.* 1991, Greil 1997, Lukse & Vacc 1999). Laffont and Edelmann (1994) concluded that long term infertility that is treated by *In-vitro-fertilization* (IVF) superimposes cycles of hope and disappointment on the already depressed and vulnerable psyche of such couples. The IVF interventions can occur in as many as nine menstrual cycles since few couples conceive on the first attempts. Indeed the overall success rate is a matter of continuing controversy in

331

both the academic literature and the public media. Oddens *et al.* (1999) found that for those women involved in this treatment "psychological well-being may deteriorate subsequent to unsuccessful treatment cycles." Both partners experience psychological peaks and troughs during treatment as Bouvin *et al.* (1998) note: "Spouses appeared equally to respond with ambivalent feelings involving emotional distress and positive feelings of hope." However, the recent literature also suggests that women report greater negative reactions to IVF failures. The coping mechanisms utilized by some women to deal with these cycles of failure have been identified by Lukse & Vacc (1999) as denial and desensitization strategies like those often seen in post-abortion psychopathology.[1]

It is following this cyclical, emotional roller coaster that the fortunate couple find themselves 'pregnant,' and in increasing numbers these pregnancies are higher order with three or more implanted fetuses. "The international rates of triplet or higher order pregnancies after assisted reproduction are 7.3% at conception." In order to deal with such pregnancies women must put themselves in the care of the high risk obstetrical experts. Practitioners in this specialty know the latest research and utilize, the most up-to-date technologies in the management of multiple pregnancies.

One of these new and highly recommended management techniques is Multifetal Pregnancy Reduction(MFPR),[2] a form of abortion in which the most accessible fetus(es) or those with some identifiable genetic disorder, are terminated and the overall pregnancy numbers reduced to twins or singletons. This approach was developed by researchers, some of whom are active participants in the prenatal diagnostics aspects of the Human Genome Project.

MFPR: PRACTIONERS AND ADVOCATES

While many researchers end their studies with a call for curbs on the number of originally implanted embryos (Cohen 1998), their studies continue to show their continued commitment to the improvement of the techniques for MFPR. In fact, the words of one of the main proponents of this technique show just how committed these practitioners are to the procedure:

Evans, M., Dommergues, M., Wapner, R., Lynch, L., Dumez, Y., Johnson, M., Boulet, P., Berkowitz, R. *et al.* (1993): "the authors of the publication view MFPR as a *temporary need* (emphasis theirs) until such time as better assisted reproductive techniques obviate the need for its use."

Evans, M. (1998): " Multifetal pregnancy reduction has emerged as a staple of infertility therapy...."

Evans, M., Hume, R.F., Yaron, Y., Kramer, R., Johnson, M. (1998): "Multifetal pregnancy reduction has become a mainstay of infertility therapy...."

From the change of language over time, it is clear that MFPR is not a temporary technique which will be abandoned when new approaches are developed. It is now entrenched and institutionalized as the management approach of choice for high risk multiple pregnancies. As this paper will demonstrate, the procedure has also been given ethical probity by the same researchers and is shifting from a voluntary decision based intervention to a 'necessary' medical procedure. As MFPR has mutated from the merely tolerated to the fully accepted, the studies which provide the supporting data are characterized by the same methodological flaws (Cassidy *et al.* in press) and the same self-referral or "incestuous citations" (Crutcher 1996) that are so prevalent in the general abortion literature. As an illustration of this phenomenon, Chart I shows the publication relationships between the main researchers in this field. As in the other abortion areas, the vast majority are themselves practitioners of the procedure and some, such as Evans, have the distinction of being practitioners, advocates, and the source of ethical justification for the procedure.

CHART I: COLLABORATION OF MAIN RESEARCHERS IN MFPR

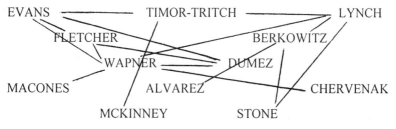

-------Connecting lines indicate co-authorships of published research---------

The approach has been improved and expanded to the point that all major teaching hospitals in North America and Western Europe now routinely offer couples MFPR for management of multiple pregnancies. But, as in many other life issues, the option is well on its way to becoming what the Automobile Dealers now call a Mandatory Option.

The research literature in this area discusses the cases in relation to the number of mothers who participated in the study. An extrapolation from the raw data, however, gives a clearer picture of what is actually occurring in this abortion procedure. Table 1 gives a breakdown of some of the foundational studies with dates of publication, the time the abortion was done, the number of cases reported, and the actual numbers of aborted fetuses. As the Table shows, the gestational age at which these abortions are occurring has steadily increased to the point that Evans *et al.* (1999) support the use of the technique into the third trimester or after 28 weeks of pregnancy.

TABLE I: MFPR–WHAT THE STUDIES REPORT

Study	Date	Fetal Age (Weeks)	Sample Size (Mothers)	# Aborted (Fetuses)
Timor Tritch*	1993	9.5–?	134	237
Boulet *et al.*	1993	8–13.5	16	32
Tabsh	1993	11–13	131	279
Evans *et al.*	1993	10.8	463	832
Kanhai *et al.*	1994	9–13	21	48
Hartoov *et al.*	1998	20.2	28	32
Evans *et al.*	1999	(see below)	321	375
		TOTAL	1094	1845

*   "at or after 9.5 to be able to make observations of fetal anatomy."
** "3rd trimester cases, where legal, can be performed with good outcomes."

It is with the use of MFPR that the psychology of desperation, so clearly identified in the women undergoing IVF intersects with the Ethics of

Justification equally clearly articulated by Berkowitz et al. (1996):

The medical justification for performing multifetal pregnancy reduction is philosophically similar to the 'Lifeboat Analogy'...it is justifiable to sacrifice some innocent fetal lives to increase the changes of survival or decrease the risk of serious morbidity in the survivors of the procedure.

In an attempt to make the use of MFPR a more readily accepted part of obstetrical practice, the literature has attempted to link the procedure to the already well tolerated abortion for reasons of genetic or fetal abnormality known as selective abortion. The proponents of this technique believe this linkage addresses two important concerns. First, they conclude that patients will not tolerate multiple births and MFPR offers a method of avoiding the 'trauma' (Evans 1996) of abortion of a wanted pregnancy since, if faced with the risk of delivering and having to parent several babies, some with abnormalities, the parents will choose to abort all of the fetuses. Thus by aborting some, particularly the defective, the doctors are actually saving others. This convoluted rationale was earlier used to justify prenatal testing by doctors who concluded that couples want only healthy children, and so without prenatal testing, high risk couples would abort all pregnancies. This flawed logic has now become the basis for all new prenatal interventions. Second, the researchers accept the assumption that since these couples' only goal is one healthy child, prenatal wastages will be well tolerated in the quest for the one baby.

These assumptions are intrinsic to the overall principle of "Ethical Justification," which is based on three possible goals: "(1) achieving a pregnancy that results in a live birth of one or more infants with minimal neonatal morbidity and mortality, (2) achieving a pregnancy that results in the birth of one or more infants without antenatally detected anomalies, (3) achieving a pregnancy that results in a singleton live birth" (Chervenak *et al.*, 1995).

THE PSYCHOLOGY OF DESPERATION

Individuals acting out of desperation are not psychologically free, and without such freedom there is no true choice. The psychological impact of coercive choice is well documented in the decision-making literature. Miller (1992) delineated seven psychological models that apply to the abortion decision and Cassidy (1997) expanded upon these in relation to the decision-making in fetal abnormality abortions. Regardless of the models applied, the overwhelming consensus among psychologists is that major life decisions based on perceived or overt coercion have the following characteristics: (1) they lack the qualities of free choice, (2) they lack informed consent, and (3) they result in significant psychological distress.

In North America the prevailing medical decision model is based on "personal autonomy" (Beckwith 1997) and informed consent has become the cornerstone for the ethical acceptability for any and all medical procedures. In the case of MFPR, many of the decisions taken by couples to reduce the number of fetuses can be seen as lacking true informed consent for the following reasons: (1) the compromised psychological state of the couples involved and (2) the degree of subtle or overt medical coercion the couples experience.

IMPEDIMENTS TO INFORMED CONSENT:
   (A) COMPROMISED PSYCHOLOGICAL STATE

Most couples lack the capacity to give full assent due to the pre-existing psychological trauma brought on by long term infertility and the IVF process itself. As the numbers of MFPR abortions increase, the families involved are now beginning to come forward and their cases are being discussed in the clinical therapy and post-abortion healing literature. Kluger-Bell (1998) describes the family of triplets whose IVF resulted in a quad pregnancy. As her client notes, "I really didn't feel like I had a whole lot of choice about reducing it. And I was pretty much told by the doctors, 'Oh, well, you're not going to carry that many babies.' And most likely it would have to be reduced to two. And not knowing anything about it, we thought that was just the way it was." It was only when this family firmly expressed their desire to have all four babies that the doctors agreed to leaving three. The (MFPR) was successful "but emotionally there's still an ache that will probably always be there. We had been trying for so many years to create life, it was very contradictory and painful...no one ever said we could *consider* keeping all four...why wasn't that an option?"

Since 99% of the women involved in this procedure have achieved pregnancy through infertility treatment, they represent a group which Tabsh (1993) characterizes as "highly motivated to have successful pregnancy outcome. They tend to be compliant with the medical plan for their care..." and will therefore, as Macones and Wapner (1994) report, assent to whatever "approach that will most likely assure them of a heathy child." Women seeking such an outcome have little control over the process and will do whatever the medical experts deem necessary.

What is ironic about this issue is that, up until 1995, "paradoxically, the attitude of infertility patients towards multiple births has never been investigated" (Gleicher *et al.* 1995). When these researchers did study the attitudes of couples seeking treatment for infertility, they found that the medical profession's implementation of MFPR was undertaken without input from patient populations:

[I]t can therefore be no surprise that the survey reported here about patients is in strong conflict with the rather universally accepted practice patterns of minimizing multiple pregnancy rates...infertile patients express a considerable desire for multiple births...the medical profession so far has assumed that the decision to minimize multiple births...was reflective of patient desires. This study suggests otherwise.

The Ethical Justification of MFPR is posited on the desperation of infertile couples to be parents to a healthy baby. When desperation is the psychological motivator, the avenue that promises the greatest hope may appear to be morally legitimate. Campion (1999) discussed the status of pregnancy as a feminine life event that has saliency regardless of the birth status of the fetus(es). It is suggested here that this metaphysical understanding of pregnancy is diminished by the psychological distress of infertility, is compounded by the mechanization of IVF conception and is further sublimated by the desperation for a baby. Since for these couples the process of conception is doctor-driven, so too are the decisions that are made toward the ultimate goal of 'a born child.' Thus, if pregnancy reduction is presented as the medically best option to guarantee birth, then to refuse such advice requires that the couple take control of a pregnancy over which they have had no control from the outset.   Such a refusal would necessitate freedom from coercion, a well developed personal philosophy of life, and access to information on alternative management approaches.   Couples who have entrusted their reproductive lives to technologists would seldom meet these criteria for freedom of choice and informed consent.

(B) COERCION

The level of coercion placed on parents to undergo this procedure is not addressed in the actual MFPR literature.   Timor-Tritsch *et al.* (1992) reported that only 6 of 146 "withdrew after the counseling session."   It would seem that those who are willing to undergo the invasiveness of IVF represent a unique cohort of couples who are willing to allow the abortion because, as Tabsh notes (1993), they "are concerned with the chance that they could lose the entire pregnancy." Most studies begin after the decision is taken, and the few that do look at psychological outcome do not analyze the medical or counseling information upon which the decision is based.

Because so few studies address the decision-making process or detail the specific information that is given to patients, it is impossible to evaluate any biases or subtle influences that may be inherent in the pre-procedure counseling. However, some clues are provided in studies such as Kanhai *et al.* (1994), who report that, following reduction, two-thirds of the parents in their sample "disclosed that at the time they were unaware of the risks and the consequences of infertility treatment." Similarly in studies of the psychological sequelae McKinney *et al.* (1995) found that post MFPR regret was associated with feeling pressure to undergo the procedure. The mothers whom Garel *et al.* (1997) studied two years following MFPR were asked why they had undergone the intervention. All responded that the decision was taken out of necessity: "I would have lost them all" and "I had no choice." Beyond this, however, it is difficult to determine the content of counseling interviews.

In fact, it is in the recent research literature on 'surrogacy' that one finds glimpses of how reproductive medicine specialists view MFPR, and it is here also that one sees just how value-laden and coercive the counseling can be. Odden *et al.* (1999) report that women who volunteer to be surrogate mothers must agree to MFPR for pregnancies of triplets or higher level gestations. In the pre-pregnancy counseling these women are "educated to the necessity" of reduction. Given that North America has no regulatory laws controlling the number of embryos initially introduced, and given that surrogate mothers are, by their participation in such a program, gynecologically healthy, they are likely to be faced with a multiple gestation. Parkinson *et al.* (1998) states that "an average of 4.1 embryos are transferred to the surrogates" and notes that these women must therefore be told of "the necessity for reduction in surrogacy." If MFPR is necessary for healthy, fertile, surrogate mothers, 'necessity' will soon replace 'choice' for all women with higher order pregnancies. In its transformation from 'temporary need' in 1993 to 'mainstay' and 'necessity' in 1999, MFPR has become a perfect example of top-down medicine. Its widespread acceptance underscores just how so many medical researchers, in experimenting with new reproductive technologies, operate without legislative guidance or public policy control.

MFPR: OUTCOME MEASURES
   (A) MEDICAL OUTCOMES

If MFPR is so necessary, then the medical outcomes of the procedure must offer significant improvement in care for both mothers and babies. The main rationale for this procedure is the birth of at least one healthy child. Does MFPR guarantee this? The answer to this seems to be a matter of debate in the literature. Groutz *et al.* (1996) found that, "contrary to previous studies, we found a higher incidence of pregnancy complications after MFPR compared with spontaneous twins...." Souter and Goodwin (1998) did a meta-analysis of all 83 articles published on the procedure since 1989 and found that:

there is a general consensus that reducing triplets to twins results in significant secondary benefits: lower cost and fewer days in hospital and a decrease in a variety of moderate morbidities associated with prolonged hospitalizations and preterm delivery for mother and baby. However, it is not clear that couples are more likely to take home a healthy baby if they undergo multifetal pregnancy reduction.

A recent Swedish study also identified the presence of post-procedure full miscarriage in 21% of the cases undertaken in that country (Radestad *et al.* 1996) while analysis of the data from Kanhai *et al.* (1994) shows that 19% of their sample couples remained without a surviving child on follow-up (9 mos.–6 yrs.) Similarly, Elliott (1994) has suggested that studies of properly managed triplet pregnancies "show equal or better outcomes with non-reduced triplets compared with selective reduction."

The benefits of MFPR remain in question but the primary research practitioners continue to advocate the procedure. Their report on the *International Collaboration on MFPR: Improved Outcomes with Increased Experience* (Evans, Wapner, Dumez, Johnson, Timor-Tritsh, Berkowitz *et al.*) to the International Symposium on Maternal & Fetal Health in January of 1999 contained several interesting findings. Based on the 3037 procedures studied,[3] 9.2% of the pregnancies ended in full miscarriages while premature delivery of the remaining fetuses occurred in a further 38.7% of the cases managed by MFPR. In all, 48% experienced post-procedure complications. There are no statistics on the number of children who may have died the first year after birth.

What is noteworthy is the authors' conclusion that, regardless of the number of fetuses remaining following reduction, the chances of a positive outcome to the pregnancy are linked to the number of fetuses before MFPR. In other words, "higher starting numbers do worse." If two out of five fetuses remain following the procedure, their chances of morbidity and mortality are higher than for original twin pregnancies. But why? Is it the very presence of multiple gestations to which the mother's body adapts and that she cannot readjust to having fewer, or does the process of the multiple abortions make the medical intervention more intrusive?[4] The published studies of MFPR do not adequately address these issues.

(B) PSYCHOLOGICAL

Given the ethical ramifications of MFPR, it is not surprising that, even with the goal of parenting achieved, couples who have participated in reduction-decisions experience grief and emotional distress concomitant with the loss of a child. Follow-up studies on these families stress the normal physical and cognitive development of the surviving children and usually conclude that, regardless of the level of psychological stress produced, reductions are "well tolerated" (Schreiner-Engel 1995). Most studies conclude that women accept the procedure to achieve parenting goals (Garel 1997, McKinney 1995,1996, Shreiner-Engel 1995). What then are the psychological outcomes that are tolerable for these families?

TABLE II: PSYCHOLOGICAL OUTCOMES IDENTIFIED IN MFPR LITERATURE

Grief & Mourning Reactions:

% of Sample Reporting Grief	Study
12	Kanhai *et al.* 1994
70	Schreiner-Engel *et al.* 1995
80 (miscarriage group)	Schreiner-Engel *et al.* 1995
20	McKinney *et al.* 1995,1996
50	Garel *et al.* 1997

Depressive Reactions:

% of Sample Reporting Depression	Study
33	Garel *et al.* 1997
20	Schreiner-Engel 1995
17.4	McKinney *et al.* 1995
100 (miscarriage group)*	McKinney *et al.* 1995
7**	Boulet *et al.* 1993

*   75% met clinical criteria at 1-year follow-up
**   "severe depression requiring psychotherapy"

It is clear that the couples who have participated in these research initiatives have been severely impacted by the procedure. Beyond the actual symptomology, Garel *et al.* (1997) were struck "by the medical and rational language used by many women who expressed no emotion."[5] They conclude that there is a significant lack of knowledge of long-term psychological complications for both parents and children.

METHODOLOGICAL FLAWS IN PSYCHOLOGICAL STUDIES

Little emphasis is placed on the methodological problems inherent in follow-up research of sensitive, reproductive issues such as MFPR. A careful analysis of the study designs and the raw data from existing published research suggests the following. There are significant rates of attrition and refusal in study samples. Individuals involved in the initial interview may not participate in later interviews, while some parents refuse to cooperate at all. This is particularly true of couples who experienced a miscarriage of the whole pregnancy following MFPR and have no child to show for their decision. Of those eligible to take part in the Garel *et al.* (1997) research, 45% refused to participate. Although their specific psychological status remains unknown, the researchers recognized that without these women their results led to an underestimation of the negative reactions. This finding is consistent with the results from general post-abortion research where it is known that those who refuse to take part in studies represent a separate cohort within the sample population, a cohort far more damaged by the experience than participants (Rogers *et al.* 1989).

To date there have been no studies on the impact of MFPR on the parent-child unit or on the children who are described by practitioners as "the surviving fetuses."

Given these limitations, the studies that do address the psychological outcomes find that a significant proportion of their sample experiences psychological distress following the procedure. The affective reactions most often reported are immediate and intense grief characterized by repetitive and intrusive thoughts and images of the terminated fetus(es). Schreiner-Engel *et al.* (1995) report that 20% of those willing to participate in follow-up experienced long-term dysphoria. "Their continued feelings of guilt appeared due to a wishful belief that some better solution should have been found."

Consistent with the findings from other post-abortion research are the pre-existing factors that Schreiner-Engel *et al.* (1995) have isolated among post-MFPR women. The most disturbed women are those who are young, from larger families, are open to more than two children, and who view the ultrasound of the pregnancy more frequently. The authors conclude that "seeing multiple viable fetuses on repetitive sonograms may interfere with the ability of women to maintain an intellectualized or emotionally detached stance toward the multifetal pregnancy." What is most interesting about this quote is the assumption that women who have undergone the stress and emotional impacts of infertility and *IVF* treatment can, and somehow should, be able to be detached from the one thing that has been a driving force in their lives–pregnancy.

It is also of concern that the psychological impact of MFPR will have long term effects on parenting style and parent-child interactions. Women experiencing postnatal depression are known to have difficulty bonding with their infants. Golombi (1998) studied the principles of "Attachment Theory" in relation to families achieved through reproductive technology and found that in his sample "maternal depression can lead to increased risk of difficulties." This is consistent with the comments of Garel *et al.* (1997), who not only found that a number of post-MFPR women experience depressive symptomology but also that "conscious and unconscious responses to the procedure included ambivalence, guilt, and an sense of narcissistic injury, increasing the complexity of their attachment to the remaining babies." No research has been done on the long-term implications of the psychological development and maturation of these children. Indeed future studies of these families may well place the surviving children within the ten categories of Post-Abortion Survivors identified by Ney (1993).

REFERENCES

Beckwith, F. "Absolute Autonomy and Physician Assisted Suicide: Putting a bad idea out of its misery" in *Life & Learning VII*, ed. J. Koterski (Washington, D.C.: UFL 1998).
Berkowitz, R.L. "Ethical issues involving multifetal pregnancies" in *Mt. Sinai Journal of Medicine* 65/3 (1998) 404-08.
Berkowitz, R., Lynch, L. *et al.* "The Current Status of Multifetal Pregnancy Reduction" in *American Journal of Obstetrical Gynecolology* 174/4 (1996) 1265-72 .
Beutel, M. , Kupfer, J., *et al.* "Treatment-Related Stresses and Depression in Couples Undergoing Assisted Reproductive Treatment by IVF or ICSI" in *Andrologia* 31/1 (1999) 27-35.
Blomain, K. "Infertility Review" Amazon.com online, 1997.
Boulet, P., Hedon, B. *et al.* "Effects of Selective Reduction in Triplet Gestation: A Comparative Study of 80 Cases Managed with or without This Procedure" in *Fertility and Sterility* 60 (1993) 497-503.

Bouvin, J., Anderson, L., *et al.* "Psychological Reactions During *In Vitro Fertilization:* Similar Response Patterns in Husbands and Wives" in *Human Reproduction* 13/11 (1998) 3262-67.

Campion, B. "An Argument for Continuing a Pregnancy where the Fetus Is Discovered to be Anencephalic" – pp. xxxx-xxxx of *UFL IX*

Cassidy, E., Crean, M. *et al. Literature & Research in Abortion's Aftermath: Published Results/Methodological Issues* (Toronto: deVeber Institute (Winter 2000).

Cassidy, E. "Psychological Decision-Making Models: An Extension of Miller's Abortion Decision Models to Miscarriage and Genetic Abortion in Light of the Human Genome Project." Paper presented at University Faculty for Life Conference VII at Loyola College, Baltimore (June 1997).

Chervenak, R., McCullough, L., *et al.* "Three Ethically Justified Implications for Selective Termination in Multifetal Pregnancy: A Practical & Comprehensive Management Strategy" in *Journal of Assisted Reproductive Genetics* 12/8 (1995) 531-36.

Cohen, J. "How to Avoid Multiple Pregnancies in Assisted Reproduction" in *Human Reproduction* 13/3 (1998) 197-214.

Crutcher, M. *Lime 5* (Denton: Life Dynamics, 1996).

Dommergues, M., Nisand, I, *et al.* "Embryo Reduction in Multifetal Pregnancies after Infertility Therapy: Obstetrical Risks and Perinatal Benefits Are Related to Operative Strategy" in *Fertility and Sterility* 55:4 (1991) 805-11.

Elliott, J.P. "Letter" in *American Journal of Obstetrics and Gynecology* 171 (1994) 278.

Evans, M., Hume, R. *et al.* "Multifetal Pregnancy Reduction." *Baillares Clin Obstet Gynaecol* 12/1 (1998) 147-59.

Evans, M., Dommergues, M., *et al.* "Efficacy of Transabdominal Multifetal Pregnancy Reduction: Collaborative Experience Among the World's Largest Centers" in *Obstetrics and Gynecology* 82 (1993) 61-66.

Evans, M., Wapner, R. *et al.* "International Collaboration on MFPT." Paper presented at the International Symposium on Maternal Fetal Medicine (January 1999).

Evans, M., Johnson *et al.* "Ethical Issues Surrounding Multifetal Pregnancy Reduction and Selective Termination." *Clinical Perinatology* 23/3 (1996) 437-51.

Fine, S. "Living Quietly with the Pain of Infertility" in *The Globe & Mail*, Toronto (May 27, 1999) p. A4.

Garel, M., Star, B. *et al.* "Psychological Reactions after Multifetal Pregnancy Reduction : A 2-Year Follow-up Study" in *Human Reproduction* 12/3 (1997) 617-22.

Gleicher, N., Campbell, D. *et al.* "The Desire for Multiple Births in Couples with Infertility Problems: Contradictions in Present Practice Patterns" in *Human Reproduction* 10/5 (1995)1079-84.

Groutz, A., Yovel, I., *et al.* "Pregnancy Outcome after Multifetal Pregnancy Reduction to Twins Compared to Spontaneously Conceived Twins" in *Human Reproduction* 11/6 (1996) 1334-36.

Hartoov, J., Geva, E. *et al.* " A 3-Year Prospectively Designed Study of Late Selective Multifetal Pregnancy Reduction" in *Human Reproduction* 13/7 (1998) 1996-98.

Kanhai, H., deHaan, M. *et al.* "Follow-up of Pregnancies, Infants and Families after Multifetal Pregnancy Reduction" in *Fertility and Sterility* 62/5 (1994) 955-59.

Kluger-Bell, K., *Unspeakable Losses: Understanding the Experience of Pregnancy Loss, Miscarriage, and Abortion* (New York: W.L. Norton, 1998).

Laffont, I., Edelmann, R.J., "Psychological Aspects of *In Vitro* Fertilization: A Gender Comparison" in *Journal of Psychosometrics and Obstetrical Gynecology* 15/2 (1994) 85-92.

Lukse, M. & Vacc, N., "Grief, Depression and Coping in Women Undergoing Infertility Treatment" in *Obstetrics and Gynecology* 93/2 (1999) 245-51.

Lynch, L., Bertowitz, R.L. *et al.* "Preterm Delivery after Selective Termination in Twin Pregnancies" in *Obstetrics and Gynecology* 87 (1996) 366-69.

Macones, G., Schemmer, G. *et al.* "Multifetal Reduction of Triplets to Twins Improves Perinatal Outcome" in *American Journal of Obstetrics and Gynecology* 169 (1993) 982-86.

McKinney, M., Tuber, S., "Multifetal Pregnancy Reduction: Psychodynamic Implications" in *Psychiatry* 59/4 (1996) 393-407.

McKinney, M., Downey, J. *et al.* " The Psychological Effects of Multifetal Pregnancy Reduction" in *Fertility and Sterility* 64/1 (1995) 51-61.

Miller, W. "Psychological Antecedents and Consequences of Abortion" in *Journal of Social Issues* 43/3 (1992) 67-94.

Ney, P. "Emotion and Physical Effects of Pregnancy Physical Effects of Pregnancy Loss on the Woman and Her Family: A Multi-Centred Study of Post-Abortion Syndrome and Post-Abortion Survivor Syndrome" in *Post Abortion Aftermath*, ed. M. Mannion (Kansas City: Sheed & Ward, 1994).

Oddens, B.J., der Tonkelear, I., *et al.* "Psychosocial Experiences in Women Facing Fertility Problems–A Comparative Study" in *Human Reproduction* 42/1 (1999) 255-61.

Parkinson, J., Tran, C., *et al.* "Perinatal Outcome After *In Vitro* Fertilization Surrogacy" in *Human Reproduction* 31/1 (1999) 27-35.

Radestad, A., Buis, T. *et al.* "The Utilization Rate and Pregnancy Outcome of Multifetal Pregnancy Reduction in the Nordic Countries" in *Acta Obstetrica et Gynecologica Scandinavia* 75/7 (1996) 651-53.

Rogers, J., Stoms, G., *et al.* "Psychological Impact of Abortion" in *Health Care of Women International* 10 (1989) 347-76.

Schreiner-Engel, P., Walther, V. *et al.* "First Trimester Multifetal Reduction: Acuate and Persistent Psychological Reactions" in *American Journal of Obstetrics and Gynecology* 172/2 (1995) 541-47.

Souter, I. & Goodwin, T. "Decision Making in Multifetal Pregnancy Reduction for Triplets" in *American Journal of Perinatology* 15/1 (1998) 63-71.

Speckhard, A. & Rue, V. "Post-abortion Syndrome: An Emerging Public Health Concern" in *Journal of Social Issues* 42/3 (1992) 95-119.

Stanton, A., Tenmen, H. *et al.* "Cognitive Appraisal and Adjustment to Infertility" in *Women's Health* 7/3 (1991) 1-15.

Stone, J. & Lynch, L. "Multifetal Pregnancy: Risks and Methods of Reduction" in *Mt. Sinai Journal of Medicine* 87 (1994) 366-69.

Tabsh, K. "A Report of 131 Cases of Multifetal Pregnancy Reduction" in *Obstetrics and Gynecology* 82/1 (1993) 57-60.

Timor-Tritch, I., Peisner, M., *et al.* " Multifetal Pregnancy Reduction by Transvaginal Puncture: Evaluation of the Technique Used in 134 Cases" in *American Journal of Obstetrics and Gynecology* 168 (1993) 799-804.

NOTES

1. See Speckhard & Rue 1992 for a discussion of the many symptoms they have isolated in Post-Abortion Stress Disorder.

2. Some medical researchers also use the term "embryo reduction" (Garel 1997, Groutz 1996, Dummerguez 1991), an interesting euphemism since these procedures are undertaken after 8 weeks gestation and continued into the third trimester with studies reporting reductions at 29 weeks gestation (see Table I).

3. No mention is made of the total number of fetuses involved in the procedure. This would require extrapolation from the raw data which was not provided in the Conference report.

4. This may also have a metaphysical context that is not amenable to statistical analysis. This may be the point at which the meaning of pregnancy, diminished but not lost in the technological construction of a pregnancy, asserts itself.

5. This numbing or lack of affect is identified as a main post-abortion outcome and part of the psychopathology of "disenfranchised grief" (Rue 1994).

Adolescent Fiction on Abortion: Developing a Paradigm and Pedagogic Responses from Literature Spanning Three Decades

Jeff Koloze

I. JUSTIFICATION FOR THIS STUDY AND CRITERIA FOR NOVELS

Consider these following possible first lines:

"It was a dark and stormy night...."
"The inspector looked at the knife protruding from the back of the deceased...."
"Tiffany wondered whether she would ever meet the man of her dreams...."

Each opening line indicates in what genre the work of fiction can be categorized. For Gothic fiction, for example, the paradigm seems to be that there must be a dark, ruined castle. There must be a heroine or some other damsel in distress. There must be a sinister presence. The opening section, if not the opening paragraph or the opening line, must address certain meteorological circumstances (accounting for the derivative line ridiculed in much fiction "It was a dark and stormy night..."). And there must be love.[1]

A detective novel will situate the reader immediately so that he or she will be hooked into reading about how someone has been murdered.

For a romance—whether it is a Harlequin or a Danielle Steel or a paperback which features a Fabio-type[2] stud on the cover holding a sweet, virginal, and buxom young woman lest she fall—certain other criteria of the paradigm must be met (including some already facetiously stated here).[3] Although feminism has empowered women to unparalleled degrees in the last thirty years, the contemporary romance is still much fashionable with young American women and appeals to them for

347

a variety of reasons. Perhaps the appeal of the glossy-covered paperback romances indicates just how successful the romance paradigm is in the marketplace of ideas. Women buy these books or borrow them from the libraries because they follow a basic pattern: girl meets boy; boy and girl fall in love; girl and boy fall out of love; boy and girl are tortured for a time; and finally girl and boy fall in love again and live happily ever after (whether that living is done in a sacramental union or not is up to the individual writer's tastes and religious and moral persuasions).

Before analyzing details of a possible paradigm for the typical adolescent abortion novel, we must consider an important presumption of this paper. Why should we even care what our college and university students read when they were teens? After all, we who are on the faculties of colleges and universities have much more important matters to lecture about and cannot worry about what our students read when they were still teens. While there are definite matters of civil rights and biological rights involved in answering this question, I will propose a more pedagogic response, based on some recent classroom experiences with adult abortion fiction. The following example of literature discussion will demonstrate why we should care.

Recently, while teaching Ernest Hemingway's short story "Hills Like White Elephants," the inability of the students to sympathize with the female main character, Jig, was striking. First, of course, few students know on an initial reading that the story is about abortion. Secondly, even after a traditional New Critical close reading, few students came to understand how tortured Jig feels about being coerced into having an abortion. This inability to appreciate Jig's anxiety is further complicated for the student because there are no "stage directions"–no markers to indicate, for example, with what tone of voice a line of dialogue should be read–to help the student understand certain key passages. Consider the following lines from the story.

"You don't have to be afraid. I've known lots of people that have done it."
"So have I," said the girl. "And afterward they were all so happy...."
"Do you feel better?" he asked.
"I feel fine," she said. "There's nothing wrong with me. I feel fine."
    (Hemingway 322, 324)

These lines can be read in multiple ways, especially because, although the prime marker is the hyberbaton used in the first sequence but not in the last two lines of the passage, the author himself gives no indication what words should be emphasized more so as to indicate the tone of the character's voice. For example, Jig's last line can be read so that emphasis is placed on the first-person pronoun: "*I* [meaning not you, American man, but I, your lover] feel fine" or "There's nothing wrong with *me* [meaning this pregnancy is a problem for you, American man, but not for me; I want the child]." With such emphasis, the entire result of this story moves from life-negating to life-affirming.

Some mechanism prohibiting satisfactory interpretation similarly operated in my literature classes. Nearly every student presumed that Jig acquiesced in the American man's effort to force her into abortion.[4] When I asked my students if they have ever read anything like Hemingway's story before, the inevitable negative answer made me ask further: what did these new college students, most of whom are just out of high school, read before?

I realize that this was a loaded question. As we know not only from our own experience in the classroom but also from Hirsch's seminal work, the databank of "common knowledge" is disappearing among American students.[5] $E=mc^2$? Huh? The Madonna as opposed to Madonna? Wha? When did World War II begin for the British Empire? Duh... Similarly, while it can be argued that what most of my students, especially those from government schools, said to me may be true (that they never read a book through all of high school), I thought that they must be reading something. The libraries continue to buy paperback novels geared for teens. These novels enjoy high circulation. And many of these novels are about abortion. And so I began to investigate abortion as a topic in adolescent fiction.

The novels which I will discuss in this paper have been selected on the basis of four criteria. First, the novels must primarily concern abortion as an actuality or potentiality within the plot development. This necessary condition excludes many other novels which may happen to include teens as subordinate characters but whose true protagonists and antagonists are adults whose actions affect (and may even effect) the actions of young people.

Secondly, these novels must be established teen fiction. The novels I have selected have satisfied perhaps the most important criterion which demarcates whether a work is to be canonized, the test of time. Granted, while the issue of abortion has a relatively longer history in the adult American literary canon (one thinks of Fitzgerald's novel *Tender Is the Night* published in 1934 or of William Faulkner's *The Wild Palms* of 1939), for teenagers the abortion issue did not hit young adult fictional concerns until the early 1970s. It is striking that adolescent fiction should have had such a delayed reaction from the swarm of controversy as represented in adult novels on abortion. And yet there may be definite reasons to account for this delayed reaction. As Zena Sutherland, a commentator on children's books writes:

Many children today have seen more violence and more sexual titillation on television and in the news than children knew of in the past; almost every child has heard rough language that earlier generations never heard–or didn't hear until they were adults. Not all of these issues affect every child directly, but almost every child knows about them. These facets of contemporary society have appeared in adult literature and, following a pattern of long standing, after a time, they began to appear in books for adolescents, then in books for younger children. Beginning in the late 1960s, one taboo after another was broken in children's literature. (15)

Thus, whatever is meant by "a pattern of long standing," it seems that the world of adult fiction was the testing ground for explosive issues which eventually filtered into the adolescent category. Furthermore, Ramsdell affirms that reading interests of teens changed in the late 1960s:

During the 1940s, 1950s, and well into the 1960s, most of the female teenage population was eagerly devouring the light romances.... Many of them, of course, also dealt with the more substantial issues.... However, the general tone was always innocent and upbeat, and serious topics such as divorce, pregnancy, sex, marriage, drug and alcohol abuse, or death were rarely discussed.

m(0 advent of the "problem novel" in the late 1960s, things did an about-face. Romance was out and reality was in. Typically, these realistic, often urban-set novels reflected the turbulent times, and social themes such as alienation, isolation, abuse, pregnancy, death, drugs, prejudice, poverty, divorce, injustice, and sex were the rule. (212)

Thirdly, the novels to be discussed are popular not only with the library community (especially young adult librarians whose recommendations often determine whether the books will be purchased for public and school library collections).[6] These novels are also popular with the readers themselves in terms of theme. Teen readers want to read about the lives of such experientially based characters. As Diana Tixier Herald indicates in her study of teen reading preferences in her recent book, *Teen Genreflecting*: "Even with the escalating rate of teen pregnancy and the prevalence of teens keeping their babies, teens still want to read about how others cope with the situations caused by early parenthood" (86). A subdivisional point of this criterion is that, with one significant exception, all novels had to be American in production or authorship. If the United States is the greatest advocate of keeping abortion legal throughout the nine months of pregnancy, then studying how American teens respond to abortion fiction may suggest what tone future voters will bring to political resolution of this biological rights question.[7]

Finally, the titles I will examine will be what I consider the best either for the span of years they cover in the real world of abortion politics or for the subject matter.

II. PARADIGM FOR TEEN ABORTION NOVELS

To begin a discussion of the novels, I propose that a template can be helpful. As there are various genres of fiction addressing adult reading interests, each of which has a necessary template, I argue that adolescent fiction on abortion has a template, a paradigm, which orders the novel, the world being depicted, and the characters who move within that world.[8] More importantly, perhaps, my paradigm will convey some common themes in teen abortion fiction to which we in higher academia can respond.

PARADIGMATIC ELEMENTS OF ADOLESCENT ABORTION FICTION

1. A teenaged girl (unmarried, seventeen years old, and irreligious) reluctantly discovers that she is a mother.
2. The young mother usually can recount several previous sexual adven-

tures with the father of the child.
  a. She has difficulty telling not only the father of the child (who is usually the same age and equally irreligious) but also her family about the pregnancy.
  b. She expresses fears that she will be rejected by the father of the child and by her family.
3. The reaction of the teen father to the pregnancy has three immediate effects.
  a. He usually accuses the mother of not having used contraception effectively.
  b. Either not thinking or not aware about alternatives to abortion, he may renounce his child completely; he may also renounce the mother herself.
  c. The teen father will either encourage or pressure the mother of his child to have an abortion.
4. The mother agonizes over deciding whether to abort or to give birth.
  a. She sees concrete instances of young mothers who are burdened with their newborns and few examples of young mothers who are happy.
  b. She thinks that her decision on abortion is constrained by medical or legal limits regarding when abortions can be performed.
5. The decision regarding abortion can generate two significant outcomes for the mother.
  a. If the mother aborts, especially if the abortion was arranged by either her parents or others, the mother immediately regrets the choice; the relationship with the father inevitably deteriorates, and the novel will end either clearly negatively or ambiguously.
  b. If she does not abort, the mother will become more mature (whether she decides to keep the baby or put him or her up for adoption); novels which depict that this choice has been exercised will invariably end positively.

Two points must be remembered here. I will group all subdivisional aspects from a given level of my outline together for easier discussion. Moreover, the functions of each primary level of the outline could be collapsed into four dependent phrases: I. The Teenaged Girl Becomes a Mother; II. The Father's Reaction; III. The Mother's Decision; and IV. Possible Outcomes of Decision. While there are details in individual novels which I will consider which do not fit the paradigm exactly, most novels on abortion for adolescents which I have read and researched generally reinforce the structure presented above to a surprising degree. Now to analyze specific fictional works.

III. ANALYSES F THE N VELS

While the decade of the 1960s offers few examples of fiction solely devoted to teenagers dealing with abortion, there are several good examples which can be considered a prelude to the format of most other teen abortion novels. One of these is Shirley Ann Grau's *The House on Coliseum* de icts hat can ha en to a oung oman ho is ealth a are that she can attract man men and ho is se uall romiscuous

THE H USE N C LISEUM STREET

I. *The "teen" mother.* Although she is twenty-years-old (27), three more years than what the paradigm would suggest is the standard, Joan's behavior is reminiscent of an adolescent. She is unable to develop social contacts, even to the point of taking an obscure job in the library far away from other people where she attends college (71). In fact, Joan's self-esteem is so low that she manifests masochistic tendencies (51-52). She is unmarried, a lapsed Catholic (8), and reluctant to acknowledge that she might be pregnant. Joan has had a variety of sexual experiences: not only does she engage in intercourse with her steady boyfriend (83), but she also becomes attracted to a wilder type of man, whom she later discovers is a professor at the college she attends (115). Although her mother asks her if she is being "careful" (86), the reader discovers much later in the story that Joan had been using a diaphragm as her main means of contraception (219).

II. *The father's reaction.* When Joan becomes pregnant, Michael places blame for the pregnancy on her, saying that he thought she would be "careful" (124). In many ways, their conversation about the three ways to handle the pregnancy is presented on the page in ways similar to Hemingway's story. Using clipped dialogue, the man is for the abortion while the woman expresses some doubts (125-27).

III. *The mother's decision.* Although there is little to suggest that she suffers agony in the decision regarding abortion, Joan is able to personalize the unborn child, even though dehumanizing terms are simultaneously used. While she refers to the unborn baby as "the child" in one place, she later says, "it would look something like a shrimp, or a piece of seaweed" (119). Joan acknowledges that the unborn baby is "another generation inside of me. A tiny point of life, a floating point of life" (138).

IV. *Possible outcomes of decision.* Since this novel is written *in medias res*, the reader learns early on that Joan's mother arranged for the abortion (9); Joan herself derisively thinks how organized her mother became to make arrangements for it (132-33). Although the problems attending the abortion decision seemed to have been lessened for her since her mother and aunt were the ones who planned the abortion, Joan suffers greatly after the abortion is performed.

Amazingly, once the abortion had been performed, Joan "had forgotten to tell Michael," the father of the child (141); later, however, he was happy that she had the abortion (153).

With the beginnings of what we would now call post-abortion syndrome, Joan minimizes the effect of the abortion by literally minimizing the aborted child: he or she becomes "a tiny speck of a child" (154). A few pages later she is having regrets about the abortion (156). Elsewhere, she wonders what would have been done "with the little shrimp child" (174). She cannot eradicate the memory of the child, though. Joan still recalls the baby (204) and assumes that "the hurt will stop when I'm pregnant" (217); many pages later she still thinks of the aborted child (241).

Joan's social life deteriorates considerably. She skips classes and ceases to be interested in her steady boyfriend Fred (176), who later confronts her about the abortion (178-80). Joan tries to get Michael fired from his teaching position at the college by saying that he arranged for the abortion (235-38). She does this to get revenge against Michael, who now has not merely one new girlfriend (a younger student), but also a second one, Joan's younger sister. The ending of the story shows Joan's life destroyed: after she tells the dean of the college about Michael's supposedly urging her to have an abortion, she knows she has to "leave"; at the novel's end Joan is symbolically locked out of her house, sitting on the porch (242).

GROWING UP IN A HURRY

Winifred Madison's *Growing Up in a Hurry* (1973) is the story of sixteen-year-old Karen, who develops a romance with Steve, a Japanese-American boy. Published in the same year as the infamous *Roe v. Wade* decision, this novel clearly illustrates the paradigm in action.

I. *The teen mother.* The circumstances of the protagonist in this novel are worth examination. Karen is a sixteen-year-old (3) who is on a first-name basis with her parents, her slightly aggressive mother, Martha, and her more congenial father, Ross (5-6). Karen has a stutter (8) and probably because of this suffers low self-esteem (11). Karen's older sister is using the pill (40) and her mother is too busy socially to be involved with her (65-66). Steve, Karen's boyfriend, is depicted as an enlightened individual who has seen more of the world than the sheltered Karen. He brings her to visit his friends as they do drugs (76-77); he even encourages her to attend a "population control" talk in their community (83). Halfway through the novel they engage in sexual intercourse (96-97). Karen's sense of religion is displayed when she thanks "Whoever" that her period came (99). Unfortunately, however, Karen later realizes that she is pregnant and calls it a "Terrible Discovery" (120-21).

II. *The father's reaction.* Before their sexual encounter, Steve suggests that Karen go to a "clinic" for "protection" (97). She lacks the courage to enter it, however (99-100). Although she asserts that she is using "the rhythm thing" (109), Karen is careless about "marking calendars" (118).

When informed about the pregnancy, Steve at first feels male pride in being a father, but immediately thereafter suggests that she have an abortion (124-25). Steve commands Karen to go to a clinic for a pregnancy test; if positive, she should get an abortion.

III. *The mother's decision.* Karen's experience with babies is not positive; she sees a sad sixteen-year-old with a baby (47). Later in the novel, there is a scene of a mother and her child intruding on the conversation (126-27).

And yet, Karen's language describing the unborn child shows her ambiguity regarding the humanity of the unborn. Often Karen will identify the unborn child as a baby (125). In contrast, the child is called "a Thing, an Encumbrance," or simply "it" (131). At one point Karen admits that "it" is "my baby" (159).

Karen decides on abortion and calls an abortionist (133-34). She recalls stories and stereotypes about "abortion butchers" (138). Significantly, the first abortionist she goes to avoids the word "abortion" (142). The first estimate she receives is that the abortion will cost $300. Unable to pay such a large amount, she contemplates suicide (144). A second abortionist talks about "wanted" life (161) and ultimately convinces her to have one. She is helped in her decision by her mother who, although personally against abortion, thinks that it is the right decision for Karen, probably because news of Karen's pregnancy would be a social embarrassment if it reached the mother's circle of friends (151). At another point, Karen presumes she may need to go to a psychiatrist to get approval for the abortion. It is this fact in the novel which can indicate that either the action is pre-1973 or the characters think that lack of a psychiatric barrier could prohibit an abortion being done on a teenager (161).

More importantly, after deciding on abortion, Karen thinks that Steve will fade from her life (148). She states that she would have turned back from going to the abortionist if Steve had been there to stop her (157).

IV. *Possible outcomes of decision.* After Karen has the abortion, the immediate reaction is sorrow, not even the presumed joy that the "problem" has been resolved. In fact, a couple of pages later, the novel ends with this note of dejection (166-68).

MIA ALONE

Originally published in Sweden in 1973 and then published by Viking Press, Gunnel Beckman's *Mia Alone* (1975) has enjoyed continuous popularity since its debut, perhaps for two reasons. First, the cultural milieu of *Mia Alone* does not differ as radically as another multicultural novel would. Secondly, coming onto the publishing scene so soon after *Roe v. Wade* made the subject matter of the novel contemporary, meaningful, and interesting for young readers.

I. *The teenaged girl becomes a mother.* Seventeen-year-old (56)

Mia is faced with the difficult situation of not knowing but only presuming that she is pregnant. Her attraction to her lover Jan is based on physical attributes primarily. Mia had slept with him five times (29-30). Several pages later, the reader discovers that they had used condoms (49). Much later in the progression of the novel, Mia's mother asks her daughter whether she even knows about contraceptives (120).

The indicators for Mia's religious sense are clear. Mia views the ban against sex before marriage as sanctimonious (37) and later in the novel she even questions the existence of right and wrong (39). Similarly, to match her lack of a religious sense, Jan is described as an atheist, even though his father is a minister (75). The closest one comes to determining the ethics and morals by which these young people operate is in a statement contrasting two world views: Mia refers to "the Christian's talk" in distinction to her family's ethics (106). One presumes that the family's ethical sense is devoid of a Christianizing influence. Thus, for example, Mia is able to assert that using contraceptives was "a sin" in a time which she designates only as "before," but that now financial and social exigencies not only suggest contraceptive use but require it (40).

II. *The father's reaction.* Jan has little to say about the possible pregnancy. Although he (and presumably Mia) have had sex education since age five (35-36), Jan had been specifically taught that abortion was murder (51-52). Jan's purported sense of respect for the unborn child, then, functions in this novel only to be an agent of distress to the young mother.

III. *The mother's decision.* Babies are not a good subject or influence for Mia. Since her agony over being pregnant occurs around the Christmas season, the holy day itself takes on an emblematic function in the novel. Since Mia's exclamation "If only it hadn't been Christmas" is repeated twice (16), the reader's attention is drawn to the importance not only of the season, but also of the main character's reaction to it; the reader would thus question such a seemingly hopeless response. It is significant that the author has Mia note someone else's screaming baby (15). It is even more interesting that Mia says that she hates Christmas (43) and doesn't say what Christmas is all about when she relates her "distaste" of it (78).

Family influences further complicate Mia's thinking about abortion. Mia's parents are separating. Her father is openly anti-life (103), and Mia's mother specifically states that she thought about abortion when she was carrying her (21). Her mother's negativity extends to the condition of all women; she says that women are in a "rat trap" (15). Moreover, Mia's grandmother, whom she respects greatly, asserts that women's liberation for her does not include abortion (64-65).

Mia displays the ambivalence which is typical for young mothers in these novels. A three-week fetus is described as looking "horrid" (42). Mia's response to a classroom situation-ethics type question regarding the survival of a human baby is "God, what a mess" (40). Abortion for Mia is equated with "having it taken away" (94). Only the mother is viewed as "the living person" (106). However, despite her lack of a religious sense, Mia identifies the unborn child with distinctively humanizing terms which the omniscient narrator supplies to help the reader understand what's going on in Mia's mind. Mia, or so the narrator reports, calls the possible unborn baby "a child, which was perhaps already inside her" (21) or a "possible child" (53). Not only does Mia's family compound her agony, but it seems as though this same omniscient narrator also aggravates her: the narrator asks Mia questions about abortion similar to those offered in clinic situations (41). In this way, the narrator of the novel functions as the catalyst for dialogue on the issue of abortion.

IV. *Possible outcomes of decision.* Fortunately for Mia, however, a possible untimely pregnancy is ruled out, almost like a *deus ex machina*: Mia's period comes a month late (113).[9] One of her first reactions is happiness that she doesn't have to make a decision about abortion (114). However, Mia is committed not to make the same mistake (whether that is getting involved sexually or merely risking becoming pregnant again) in a passage which is strikingly repetitious and adamant in its resolution: "It was as if she would never again be as she had been before, childish like that, and unaware and credulous. Never, never ever again would she expose herself to this. Never. Never ever take a single risk again. That's what it felt like" (117). As a final consequence of her possible pregnancy, Mia turns against Jan (121).

EDITH JACKSON

Although Rosa Guy's *Edith Jackson* (1978) contains writing which drags in some places (92-93), the novel provides insights into the factors which may persuade an African-American teen mother to abort, including financial, familial, and distorted sexual concerns.

I. *The teen mother.* Written in first-person, Edith is a seventeen-year-old African-American (4) whose mother died from tuberculosis and whose father abandoned the family shortly before (29-30). Edith plans to quit school to raise her siblings (35). One other important figure in her life, her minister Reverend Jenkins, sexually assaults her (41-42). Edith's sister Bessie is similarly being sexually aroused by "Uncle" Daniels, the boyfriend or live-in lover of Mother Peters, who is Edith's foster mother (60-61).

Another woman who shows great interest in Edith is Mrs. Bates, who tells Edith that she doesn't "count" (53). It is Mrs. Bates who introduces the idea of "choice" to Edith–but here choice merely means intellectual progress (54-55). Later in the novel, Mrs. Bates says that Edith should be "a person who can make choices and fight for them" (57).

Edith's attitudes toward sex and children are displayed in a few key utterances. She says that her parents should not have had more kids after her sister Bessie was born (74). And, although Edith helps with the abandoned children in the institution to which she is ultimately sent after her stay with another foster family is terminated (98-100), her positive caring attitude toward one particular abandoned child is tempered by a social worker at the institution who says that the "luxury of choices" is denied to black children (103-04). This nuance of "choice" can be balanced by another statement of Mrs. Bates regarding Edith's sister's being adopted by white Jews–it is a "wise choice" in her opinion (129-30).

Edith's first sexual encounter with any man is with James, the thirty-two-year-old nephew of Mrs. Bates (139-41). Even after he returns to his aunt's house after an extended absence, his first thought seems to be to get physical with Edith (134). Edith becomes pregnant by him (145).

II. *The father's reaction.* When she discovers she is pregnant,

Edith wants to tell James in order to share the good news with him, hoping that he will want to marry her (154). James's response is anything but altruistic. While Edith just wants to talk with him about getting married, James rushes her to a friend's apartment where he tries to force sex with her (156).

III. *The mother's decision.* In the absence of a strong moral foundation, Edith can rely only on the opinions of others regarding abortion. Mrs. Bates's daughter Debra thinks that Edith should have an abortion (145); in fact, Debra asserts that abortions are common among her college friends (147). Ruby, the sister of Edith's best friend Phyllisia, is sick in bed, but the friend casually comments that she "only had an abortion" (175). When she goes to a welfare office to seek financial help with having the baby, Edith is faced with a couple of episodes of children who are certainly not angelic. A belligerent child in the office waiting room disturbs her (182). More negative images of children immediately follow this scene (184).

IV. *Possible outcomes of decision.* This novel ends with Edith deciding to have an abortion; she calls Mrs. Bates, who will be with her during it (186-87). However, her decision to kill the unborn child is obviously negative: when she makes the fateful phone call to her lover's aunt, Edith does so haltingly, stuttering and stammering in her attempt to get the words out.

LAUREN

Harriett Luger's *Lauren* (1979) is a good example of teen abortion fiction closing out the first decade of legal abortion in the United States.

I. *The teen mother.* Lauren's home life presents great difficulties for the heroine of this novel. Her parents fight a lot (6); later in the novel, in one particularly demeaning argument, they suggest that they have other romantic involvements. In fact, Lauren's mother intimates that she got married because she was pregnant (147-48).

II. *The father's reaction.* Lauren's male friends are typical adolescents ogling sex pictures who claim to be familiar with sex. The reaction of Lauren's boyfriend Donnie on hearing that she is pregnant is to command her to go to Planned Parenthood (19). He has a chance to obtain an academic scholarship; since he does not want to jeopardize his chances at obtaining it and she hasn't followed through with his first recommendation, he commands her again to do something (23-24). Donnie asserts that he will "stick by" Lauren (39). They fight, however, when she thinks he's more concerned about his chemistry test than her or the baby (40-1).

III. *The mother's decision.* Lauren's terminology for describing the unborn child is typically ambivalent as in other adolescent novels. Abortion is described euphemistically as "taking care of" the pregnancy (4). She calls the baby a "worm" (21-22). During an exam, Lauren thinks that the baby could be a "monster" in retribution for her "sin" (34). Lauren calls the unborn child a "ghost" and an "it" (67). At one point she calls the baby a "little bastard." To "get even" with it she thinks she will "let [the baby] be born" (104). Despite such dehumanizing language, she knows that the unborn child is a baby (29). Not only that, but she thinks of the baby as a person: "a *me*, an *I*" (154). After an attempted suicide, Lauren's changing attitude is expressed through the omniscient narrator, who calls the fetus a "tiny creature," a positive sign that the humanity of the unborn child is secure now that Lauren has chosen life for herself and, by implication, saved the child from death as well (128).

Lauren made the decision to give birth to the child after some difficult forces tried to persuade her to do otherwise. Not only was she urged to abort by Donnie; even the first thought of her two best friends was that she should get an abortion (25). An abortion counselor tries to dissuade her against abortion for half an hour (36-37). Her mother wants her to have an abortion (43-44). Donnie's parents want her to have an abortion (47). When she leaves her house, planning to have an abortion, she simultaneously thinks of the possibility of raising the child herself (53). Lauren wonders if she is too far along in the pregnancy, "too late," to have one performed (62).

Fortunately, if it were not for the positive experience of meeting two poor mothers who decided to give birth to their babies instead of having abortions, Lauren could have been just another abortion statistic (56). Liz, one of the two mothers who befriend her and with whom she stays after she leaves home, says that Lauren "didn't do anything wrong" and asserts Lauren's right to keep the baby (69). After a long interlude (the second "book" within the book) with the poor women Liz and Dawn, she attempts suicide by drowning (105). After Lauren returns home, the reader learns that she had been away a month.

IV. *Possible outcomes of decision.* As incredible as it sounds, coming so soon after her suicide attempt, Lauren's parents (and Donnie's parents) still want her to have an abortion (111-12). What is even more incredible is that Lauren falls in love with Donnie again (122-23). Donnie is adamant, however, in not wanting their baby (123-24). Donnie's response to Lauren's query ("how can you love me and not our baby?") is matched by his saying that he feels forced into marriage (124).

Eventually, Donnie loses the scholarship (143). Although Lauren eventually decides to give the baby up for adoption, she does this because she has matured: she wants what's best for the baby (156-57). Moreover, it is suggested that Lauren, no longer an adolescent girl, has now found her own self, has become a woman (156). This new mature attitude is manifested when she chastises her younger sister for engaging in premarital sex; Lauren reacts furiously, telling her sister that she should not engage in such behavior (151-52).

UNBIRTHDAY

A. M. Stephensen's *Unbirthday* (1982) continues the trend of teen abortion novels whose characters have a definite pro-abortion bias.

I. *The teen mother.* Although the teen mother in this novel and her boyfriend had used condoms "religiously" (8), Louisa Billingham discovers she is pregnant when her period is late (7). Louisa describes herself in this largely first-person narrative as a girl who is "as popular as a python with acne" (14). The opinion which she and Charlie have about sex is easy to summarize: they think sex should be for immediate gratification (22); she even mocks her parents' cautions against engaging in sex and other rash behavior (26).

II. *The father's reaction.* Charlie does not seem to have any significant role in this novel except to engage in sex with Louisa and to crack frequent jokes. In fact, the title of the novel can be found in one such joke: having an abortion is an "unbirthday" (82). Driving her to the abortion, Charlie's humor distracts Louisa from the reality of what she will do (89-90). After she has her abortion, Charlie and Jane (see below) sing "happy unbirthday" to her (107).

III. *The mother's decision.* Louisa ridicules books in her library which espouse a pro-maternal position (29). Unlike other abortion novels, where images of babies are skewered so that the main character can see how bad it would be to become a mother, in this novel Louisa purposely denigrates the positive images of babies she comes across (51).

Louisa ruminates over her abortion decision clandestinely. The baby is "the biggest secret" in her life (53); she rejects and ridicules the advice to tell her parents about the pregnancy (54-55). Both she and Charlie think that abortion is the best solution to this untimely pregnancy; moreover, he suggests that they not use the word "killing" to denote abortion since the baby is an "it" (56).

Louisa's secrecy is accomplished with help from a Women's Center staffperson at a college in the area, significantly named Jane. This affable feminist activist plays an important role in the novel. She relates her own abortion episode to Louisa. According to Jane, the word "abortion" is strictly negative and the alternative "termination of pregnancy" is to her even worse–an honest comment from such a strident feminist activist (63). Jane describes the pre-*Roe* period as bad because women did not have the option of abortion (65). Jane distorts the views of her pro-life mother (65-66). She relates how she thought that she "could get help from Planned Parenthood" (72) and how euphoric she was over her abortion (72). Jane's narrative regarding her abortion ends with the phrase "The End," and it seems to the reader as though the abortion is the same as a fairy tale or as innocent and simple as any piece of fiction (73). It is shortly after this that Louisa decides on having an abortion (77-78). The abortion itself is "secret": the actions of the aspirator are described, not the actual killing (101).

IV. *Possible outcomes of decision.* Louisa herself says at first that there were no problems after the abortion. She then qualifies that by saying that there may be one: Charlie resents her friendship with Jane. After more narratorial thought, Louisa thinks that there might even be another: the secrecy involved regarding her abortion (108-09). By the last lines of the novel, the reader can presume that her affection for

Charlie is slipping as she becomes involved in feminist activism; she records that she is working against "a powerful local congressman" who is "one of the sponsors of a constitutional amendment to ban abortion" (112).

The last one-line paragraph in the novel is one of those statements which proverbially speaks volumes in four words. Speaking about the congressman she's trying to unseat, Louisa says, "He says it's immoral" (111-12). Such a statement, being in third person, not only shows that Louisa has now distanced herself from moral and ethical statements, but also makes it seem that she herself can no longer argue the morality of abortion.

BEGINNERS' LOVE

Norma Klein's *Beginners' Love* (1983) is one of many novels which depicts the abortion decision from the unique perspective of the father.

I. *The teenaged girl becomes a mother.* While the focus of this first-person novel is the hero's reaction to his girlfriend's pregnancy, the reactions of the young mother are reflected in the leading male character. A seventeen-year-old young man named Joel, who thinks that he is in some way "being like Leda" (172), may be voicing the projection of the lead female character through a male body.[10] Thus, for example, the attitude that Joel has toward diverse sexual matters is replicated in Leda. Joel cannot withstand the temptation to masturbate; he does so at least three times in the novel, not only while thinking about his girlfriend Leda but also about another woman (21, 112, 194). Joel is masturbated at one point by Leda (63) and on another occasion she oral-sexes him (92-93). When she notices that he is having an erection, Leda's response ("Let's just take our clothes off and get it over with") makes it seem as though sex is a chore for these young people, not a pastime of delight (125). Joel's attitude toward sex in general can be summarized in one maxim: he thinks girls want boys who are sexually experienced (35). With such a sexual philosophy Joel finds nothing wrong with having sexual intercourse with Leda at least four times (88, 126, 143, and 162).

Joel is ostensibly Jewish (46), although he affirms that he is not religious (78). His best friend, Berger, who is also irreligious (104), makes snide comments about celibacy (133).

Although Joel's father discourages him from having sex with Leda (106), he asks Joel whether he is using birth control (130). Joel expresses some fear about their not using birth control (91), but it seems clear that the woman is supposed to be the one who is in charge of that. It is only when Leda says that her period is late that she admits she hadn't regularly used her diaphragm (142). Joel, too, assumes some responsibility for the pregnancy, saying that he had some condoms that he "could have used" (144).

II. *The father's reaction.* Joel is certain that, if Leda is pregnant, she'll "just get rid of it" (144). Perhaps in reference to the anti-life feminist joke, Joel finds out by a Father's Day card from Leda that he is a dad (172). Joel accuses Leda of not having been "careful" (174). When asked, Joel thinks she should not have the baby (180). Regarding the baby's future, Joel says "it's better not to think about it" (182). Although he had never thought about babies before, Joel now sees them all over (155).

III. *The mother's decision.* There is no anxiety over an abortion decision between the two young people. Leda is shown on several occasions as having already made up her mind for abortion: she is adamant that, if she is pregnant, she will have an abortion (163) because, for her, "it was just a little clump of cells" that could become "a real baby" with the passage of time (180). Perhaps one factor which led her to accept abortion–in a reversal of what most other male characters experience in other adolescent novels–Leda is accepted into Yale and being pregnant would prevent her from fulfilling her educational career (176).

IV. *Possible outcomes of decision.* When Leda has her abortion, the other mothers in the abortion clinic look dejected, even though many of them, as in Leda's case with Joel, have with them their boyfriends or the fathers of the babies (197). After the abortion, Leda wants to "celebrate" (203). However, when she and Joel invite another brother-and-sister couple from the abortion clinic over her apartment to smoke some marijuana, almost immediately into the celebration she cries over "our babies" (205). Leda's plaintive "we're all going to be fine," spoken almost immediately after her breakdown over the aborted babies, sounds too similar to the famous lines from Hemingway's story (205). Just as saying "fine" for Jig meant the opposite, so too for Leda, it can be argued, matters will not be satisfactory.

As the novel reaches its denouement, Leda's and Joel's relationship deteriorates after the abortion (207). They grow apart, especially after he goes off to a Texas college (209). The novel ends with a group of characters wanting to see the film *Endless Love*. This was the film which Joel and his best friend saw when they double dated and Joel first met Leda. Joel's final comment about seeing the movie is telling, symbolic as it is of the main characters' now broken relationship: "I saw it already" (216).

LUCY PEALE

From this point on in the paper, I will depart from one of my necessary criteria to analyze three teen novels which show a growing concern, not so much for abortion in contemporary teen fiction but for how a mother or her lover, the father of the child, react to the mother's decision in choosing life over abortion for the unborn child.

Colby F. Rodowsky's *Lucy Peale* (1992), chronologically the first in this new set, is a unique departure from most adolescent fiction. While this novel may depict a lead female character who is responsible for her act of fornication, the culpability is lessened by two factors: Lucy Peale's father is an ultra-strict fundamentalist Christian who wants his recently-graduated from high school daughter to confess her sin publicly at a revival; secondly, the boy who impregnates her is depicted as one who forced his will on her. Instead of confessing her sin, she runs away (26) and eventually meets another young man, Jake, who harbors her in his apartment, cares for her food and clothing needs, and, most importantly, does not take sexual advantage of the young woman who just happened to come across his path. Jake is a very respectful young man who wants to reserve his sexual powers for marriage with his ideal woman. If this novel merges with the genre of a romance, then *Lucy Peale* is both a novel depicting the lives of two tortured young people caught up in teen pregnancy and simultaneously a novel of mature romance.

I. *The teen mother.* In retrospect, Lucy recalls how she became pregnant. Wanting to get out of her father's stifling environment, Lucy meets a gang of young men which includes Phil, the father of her future child by one act of sexual intercourse (35). She discovers she is pregnant when she vomits from morning sickness (7). When she decides to run away to avoid confessing her sin in public, Lucy realizes that her father is not going to come after her to bring her back home (31).

Lucy's ambivalent thoughts and low self-esteem are detailed in a series of uncomplimentary similes: her thoughts are "like fiddler crabs" (37) or "like burrs on a dog's ear" (43). Other girls whom she sees walking with confidence are "like flies on sticky paper" (39). Lucy is immature and cannot function socially (41). The reader presumes that she is seventeen-years-old since she graduated from high school "this year" (69).

II. *The father's reaction.* Jake, her boyfriend, is a former college man (59). Although he has numerous classic books scattered all over his typically-messy bachelor apartment (61), he found working on the beach more interesting than college. He is not to be considered a beach bum, however; his ambition is to be an assistant to a British author, Adrian Blair, who will be a writer-in-residence at Johns Hopkins (68).

III. *The mother's decision.* Lucy's father is an evangelist who calls her baby a "sin"; she retorts: "my baby's no sin" (11). She doesn't want "to get rid of it" (77). Much later in the novel, there is a curious reference to the baby as an "it," but in a humanizing way (116). When the baby kicks, Lucy then "knew" that she was carrying a child (96-97). Lucy says she can't think of the baby as an "it" after she and Jake discuss things about their life together (116-18). More importantly, Jake provides the necessary moral support for Lucy by reacting happily to news of the baby's quickening (98-99). Unlike most other teen abortion novels, Lucy experiences a pleasant encounter with some children (87-89). She hopes to marry Jake and be happy with him forever.

IV. *Possible outcomes of decision.* If the abortion portion of the novel seems resolved [Lucy will not have an abortion; she and Jake seem to be the "perfect couple"–they even argue as agreeably as married people do (100-03)], then the problem for the reader over the final sixty pages is to consider whether they can succeed in their ambitions. Fortunately, and, once again, unlike most other teen abortion novels, Lucy and Jake are genuinely religious (94-95). Even though Lucy comes from a family which distorts Christian ideals, they both want the baby to know about God (118). Their "living together" is asexual (100). When Lucy gets into bed with him one night, thinking that the only way she can repay him for his kindness is to offer him what her rapist, the father of her child, took from her, Jake jumps out (106). Sex "counts for too much" for Jake, he tells her (115). Jake considers the baby his (107), he wants to marry her, and (putting most men to shame) he is a perfectly romantic young man (108).

This happiness, which may seem saccharine to most jaundiced readers, is too much for Lucy, however. She plans to leave him so that he will not be burdened with a wife and a baby as he pursues his chance at working for Blair (110, 148-49). Just when it seems this incredibly happy resolution will fall apart, the end of the novel has a virtual *deus ex machina* when Lucy's sister Doris leaves her strict family and decides to help with the baby (162). Jake goes to Baltimore to become an assistant to Blair. In short, what one would never find in most teen abortion novels, this story ends happily. The final statement ("it's going to be okay") conveys none of the ambiguity or despair found in novels where the mother has aborted (164-67).

TOO SOON FOR JEFF

Marilyn Reynolds achieved success not only with her print version of *Too Soon for Jeff* (1994), but also with the made-for-television film adaptation of the novel as well as with her Hamilton High series of stories for teens.[11] Like other novels of the early 1990s, this one reflects the anxieties of the father of the child. In a first-person narrative, Jeff Browning relates his experiences with the pregnancy of his lover. Jeff is a seventeen-year-old who has an excellent chance not only at winning his high school's debate competition but also a scholarship to a university just when he discovers that he is a father.

I. *The teen mother.* Christy Calderon, a Mexican-American (35), is Jeff's lover. Although she is depicted as having had a Catholic grade school background (Jeff for some reason laughs when he first hears this fact) (40), Christy is as irreligious as Jeff. Jeff is halfway between being an atheist and being a believer (73). All we know about Christy at the beginning of the novel is that, when she announces her pregnancy to Jeff, she is happy about the baby (13-14).

II. *The father's reaction.* Jeff's reaction to the pregnancy should be understood in the context of his sexual understanding. He is not a virgin (10); presumably, he had used condoms with Christy (16). His mother, who is studying to be a nurse, had talked with him about condoms (17). Jeff's father had abandoned him and his mother when he was little (18). He is unable to control his sexual impulses and masturbates when thinking about Christy (45-46). Jeff was enrolled at a human sexuality class at Planned Parenthood (57). Jeff reports that his friend Jeremy says that abstinence "is the wave of the future" (183). Lest this be interpreted as a statement that he has learned from his sexually explicit ways and will reserve his sexual powers for marriage, the reader is immediately hit with a qualification of this fact about his abstinence history: Jeff couches it negatively by saying that his friend "may be telling the truth about virginity, or he may be following another of his old-fashioned codes..." (183). Even after his experience with Christy, when he eventually goes out-of-state to college, Jeff meets another young woman, for whom he buys condoms, and with whom he has sex at least three times (198, 200-01, and 212).

With this type of sexual background, it should be no surprise that Jeff is angry at the baby. He accuses Christy of being lax about birth control (14); he wants her to have an abortion (15). Even though his mother says that abortion "makes sense" to her (57), Christy calls Jeff a "baby killer" (63).

III. *The mother's decision.* At one point, while Jeff wonders if it is too late for an abortion (36), Christy is adamant that she will not abort, saying "It's my body, it's my choice, and I choose NO ABOR-TION!" (36). Eventually, Jeff wins the debate competition for his high school and is accepted into a Texas university later that fall (112). Jeff later learns that Christy has given birth to a son (145), whom he later calls "my son"" (160). Jeff's father, however, urges him to disavow anything to do with the child, viewing the pregnancy as a trap on the part of Christy (165).

IV. *Possible outcomes of decision.* Although Jeff and Christy go their separate ways at the novel's conclusion, Jeff ends the novel with a limp paternal directive: he tells his newborn son not to have sex without a condom (222).

Sheila Cole's *What Kind of Love? The Diary of a Pregnant Teenager* (1995) follows a category of teen fiction which depicts the anxieties of teen mothers who have exercised their reproductive rights by choosing to give birth to their unborn babies.[12]

I. *The teen mother.* Valerie is a fifteen-year-old who describes her sexual relations with her lover Peter early in the novel (7-9). Even though she immediately thought of "protection" because she wanted to have sex with Peter (22), Valerie discovers she's pregnant (36).

II. *The father's reaction.* Since he is Harvard- or Stanford-bound (27), Peter suggests she has "to do something" (40). Several pages later it is clear what he wants her to do: ask about abortion at Planned Parenthood (44). Because of perceived time limits on abortion, Peter blames Valerie for waiting so long (57). When Peter proposes marriage to her, the unborn child who was called an "it" suddenly becomes *"Our Baby"* (61). While Valerie progresses in the pregnancy, Peter advances toward his college goals (140). Eventually, Peter reneges on his promise to marry her (170).

III. *The mother's decision.* Valerie is confronted with an image of a sixteen-year-old girl carrying a baby (43). She calls the baby an "it" (46). Valerie assumes Planned Parenthood is the place to go for birth control (48). Since she's four months pregnant, abortion must be done in a hospital; it will cost her more (52-54). Her parents want her to abort (68). Peter's and Valerie's elopement plans are halted (83-84). Despite an ultrasound, which enables her to bond with her baby (91-92), Valerie calls the baby an "it" (103) or "this thing growing inside me" (107). The unborn child is dehumanized with a direct simile: he or she is "like an alien invader" (112). Eventually, while she still calls the baby an "it," Valerie is able to humanize the child in a direct metaphor which culminates in her first positive emotional statement for the child: he or she is a "little astronaut floating inside...I love you" (127).

IV. *Possible outcomes of decision.* Although she had hoped for marriage and a happier resolution about the problems of parenthood, Valerie, seeing that Peter is more interested in his college career than his fatherhood, renounces him and decides to offer the baby for adoption (190-92).

IV. CRITICAL EVALUATION AND PEDAGOGIC RESPONSES: ATTACKING THE PARADIGM

Now that several works have been scanned for paradigmatic elements, it may be helpful to consolidate some general criticism before engaging in a pedagogic response. First, it should be noted that adolescent fiction on abortion in the 1960s seemed to be "masked" or, better yet, "encased" in a larger, more comprehensive plot which involves the adult characters of the novel. For example, Romulus Linney's 1965 novel *Slowly, by Thy Hand Unfurled* depicts the anguish of a mother who comes to realize two brutal truths: first, that her daughter had an abortion and died of it; second, that the daughter seems to have had the abortion at her mother's insistence. Similarly, the concerns of Carla, the young mother who seeks an abortion in Violet Weingarten's 1967 novel *Mrs. Beneker*, occupy only a small portion of the plot. Even though 1967 is a decisive year in abortion history in the United States, the more dominant concern in the novel is a feminist one: the emergence of Lila Beneker, who in her middle age is finally developing her talents as a liberated woman.

The situation is similar in another novel in this pre-*Roe* period, B. J. Chute's *The Story of a Small Life* (1971). Richard Harris, the narrator, is concerned not so much that a seventeen-year-old young man whom he admires gets his girlfriend an abortion as that the young man get out of the ghetto. Even though abortion permeates this novel, the function of the narrator is clear: he is distant from the actors in the abortion subplot; the novel is his spiritual quest, at which, of course, he dismally fails.[13]

A period of less than a decade spans the earliest of the novels I have read before abortion was legalized in the United States throughout the nine months of pregnancy. Adolescent novels in the years immediately preceding and following *Roe* were strong in their support for abortion; this pro-abortion bias continued until the decade's end. Although an uncomfortable decision for teen mothers, abortion is never questioned as an inappropriate course of action in Gunnel Beckman's 1973 novel *Mia Alone*. Jeannette Eyerly's 1972 novel *Bonnie Jo, Go Home* is an extremely hostile account of a mother who wants to abort. Abortion is the social-worker's cure for the poverty and for the apparent hopelessness of the African-American lead character in Rosa Guy's 1978 novel *Edith Jackson*.

And yet, despite the stridency of some of the characters in firmly pro-abortion novels, the 1970s can boast of a life-affirming trend as well. Evelyn Minshull's 1976 novel *But I Thought You Really Loved Me* is one of many novels which explore the situation of a young mother who has decided to give birth to her baby. Korie, who is not a sexually-promiscuous young woman, happened to fall for the very attractive Ron who impregnated her. When Ron not only rejects the baby but also rejects her, Korie turns to the people who love her the most: her family.

The theme of mothers who return to the safety of their families after the difficult experience of being rejected in love (and maybe even abandoned by their lovers as in Korie's case) continues throughout the 1980s and into the 1990s. These novels show a growing trend toward the principle that abortion is a negative solution to an untimely pregnancy. According to Jane S. Bakerman and Mary Jean DeMarr, who studied adolescent fiction in the two decades from 1961 to 1981, some fiction began this life-affirming trend in the late 1970s. Joyce Carol Oates's 1978 novel *Son of the Morning* depicts a teen mother who wants to keep her baby after her lover abandons her. They also categorize Joyce Maynard's 1981 novel *Baby Love* as a novel about teen mothers who want to keep their babies.

A new trend developed in the 1990s, however, that proved not only commercially acceptable but appealing to the mass of the teen reading audience: consideration of the role and reaction of the unwed father to an untimely pregnancy. This decade saw a variety of fictional accounts of young teen fathers who may at first have been strongly unwilling to have anything to do with their unborn children but who ultimately become their born children's best defenders. Such is the case in

Marilyn Reynolds's 1994 novel *Too Soon for Jeff.*

This trend toward the father's view of life-affirming options may indicate that abortion itself as subject matter may be submerging itself under a more prominent one, just as it was a subordinate issue for fiction in the 1960s. The interest in abortion as a prime factor in the plot is waning even more significantly within the general view against fiction with life-affirming themes. Norma Klein's 1988 novel *No More Saturday Nights* may be one of the earliest novels to connect the dramatic tension of an unwed teen father and the trend to look beyond abortion as a dilemma which seems unsurmountable. The bibliographic summary for this novel reads: "A seventeen-year-old unmarried father wins the rights to custody of his son in court; goes off to college in New York City, where he finds an apartment with three girls as roommates; and improves his relationship with his own father, always knowing his baby is the most important thing in his life." Terry Farish's 1990 novel *Shelter for a Seabird* is summarized in its bibliographic record as: "At a time when her stern father seems determined to sell the island home where her family has lived for generations, sixteen-year-old Andrea is swept into a doomed romance with a nineteen-year-old AWOL soldier." Kimberly M. Ballard's 1991 novel *Light at Summer's End* is concerned not with an abortion decision to be made by the fourteen-year-old lead character but by the decision to abort which her mother made. Ballard's novel shows how excruciating the abortion decision is for other persons involved: siblings, the father of the child, and grandparents.[14] Berlie Doherty's 1992 novel *Dear Nobody* is summarized as a story where "Eighteen-year-old Chris struggles to deal with two shocks that have changed his life, his meeting the mother who left him and his father when he was ten and his discovery that he has gotten his girlfriend pregnant." Another 1992 novel, Geraldine Kaye's *Someone Else's Baby*, makes it clear that abortion for the young mother involved is not a serious option; deciding whether to keep the baby or not is the real concern: "Seventeen-year-old Terry, single and pregnant, decides to keep a journal to help herself come to terms with an unhappy homelife and poor self-image as she tries to decide whether or not to keep her baby." This is also the case in Marilyn Reynolds's 1993 novel *Detour for Emmy*, which is summarized as an exploration of a young mother of a child already born: "Emmy, whose future had once looked so bright, struggles to overcome the isolation and depression brought about by being a teen mother who gets little support from her family or the father of her child."[15] C. B. Christiansen's 1994 collection of short stories, *I See the Moon*, is summarized in its bibliographic record thus: "Twelve-year-old Bitte learns the answer to the question, 'What is love?' when her older sister decides to place her unborn child for adoption." Abortion as an issue is certainly of secondary importance in Doran Larsen's 1997 novel *Marginalia*, which is primarily concerned with abused children and adolescents in the Buffalo area. The latest contribution to the body of adolescent abortion fiction is James Wilcox's 1998 novel *Plain and Normal*, which seems to merge the popular fascination with homosexual and lesbian issues with the plight of teens dealing with untimely pregnancy. It is obvious, however, that the issues which were once most characteristic of teen fiction (untimely pregnancy or serious thoughts about abortion) are relegated in this novel to the exploits of homosexual men in Manhattan and in an imaginary place in Louisiana.

THE LEGITIMACY OF THE PARADIGM

After having gone through several key works of teen abortion fiction, it may be helpful to demonstrate how one can attack the legitimacy of the paradigm as used as a template for such fiction. Just because an author may adapt his or her story to such a tight outline does not mean that the outline itself is beyond question. In fact, it is our duty to attack it in order to demonstrate that abortion novels need not follow such a pro-abortion bias. If we are in the business of encouraging our students to think positively about life, to surmount whatever problems are thrown their way, and to encourage them to become fully human, then we must guide them in the dissolution of some of the nastier elements of the outline. It is our task to demonstrate to our students that sometimes the fiction which they have read can be severely questioned—as strongly as anti-lifers would question the value of human life. Therefore, I would like to offer some "speed bumps" to help our students understand that they need not necessarily adopt the elements of this paradigm as a contemporary decalogue to guide their reading or their lives.

One counter to the validity of the outline is to ask students why an irreligious attitude seems necessary for modern life. Why are so many characters not so much seemingly tolerant of others' religion but openly anti-religion? More acutely, why are Roman Catholics so reviled in contemporary teen fiction on abortion?[16] In Grau's *The House on Coliseum Street,* Joan is a lapsed Catholic (8). When she arrives at the abortion clinic, strongly anti-life Bonnie in Eyerly's *Bonnie Jo, Go Home* is suspicious that the cab driver is Catholic (26). Bonnie has a supposedly Catholic friend who helps to arrange the abortion for her (59). Leda, the heroine in Klein's *Beginners' Love,* and her friend dress up as nuns in one episode, only to mock them (114-15). Christy, the mother in Reynolds's *Too Soon for Jeff* who is later shown to be manipulative, had a Catholic grade school background (40). This is the same young woman who yells at her father that "All you care about is what your stupid old church says!" (64).

A review of sexuality can assault the integrity of the outline as well. What is sex? It might be helpful to encourage students to discuss whether they truly believe in the merely secular rendition of the definition. If a secular view of the term is accepted among today's students, then it can be pointed out that the characters in these novels demonstrate how sex, which was perceived as something purely stimulus-driven and seemingly beautiful between a young man and a young woman, can become selfish and demeaning.

Moreover, why should a young person immediately think of Planned Parenthood when discussing birth control and abortion? Planned Parenthood immediately comes to Peter's mind when he suggests the abortion of his child in Cole's *What Kind of Love? The Diary of a Pregnant Teenager* (44); the mother of his child, Valerie, assumes Planned Parenthood is the place to go for birth control (48).[17] The lead character in Eyerly's *Bonnie Jo, Go Home* sees a child in a baby stroller pasted with a "Planned Parenthood" sticker (6). On hearing that his girlfriend is pregnant, Donnie (in Luger's *Lauren*) commands her to go to Planned Parenthood (19). The Women's Center staffperson in Stephensen's *Unbirthday* who relates her own abortion experience to the protagonist of the novel automatically thinks that she "could get help from Planned Parenthood" (72). Jeff's inability to control his sexual promiscuity in Reynolds's *Too Soon for Jeff* can perhaps be attributed to the fact that he was enrolled at a human sexuality class at Planned Parenthood (57).

Where are the abstinence courses and programs? Where is Birthright? Where are any of the crisis pregnancy support groups around the country that have served the maternal, legal, and financial needs of mothers with untimely pregnancies since before the *Roe* decision? Why don't these pregnancy-support groups appear in teen abortion fiction? And, in true Marxist literary critical fashion, if they do not appear, then students should examine why they do not. Their absence may be evidence of the oppressive power of an anti-life feminist distortion of matriarchy.

The outline can also be attacked from a feminist viewpoint in another manner. If today's young woman is truly the feminist society supposedly makes her to be, then she should assert her right over the father's non-compliance with her choice to give birth.

Some feminist writers argue that such teen fiction liberates teens–female teens, especially, of course, since female teenagers are women in an expansively denotative and connotative definition of "woman." Proposing an alternative feminist view is not only politically-incorrect in today's academic world but also revolutionary since the standard party-line feminist thinking is that sexuality liberates pure and simple; there is no discussion of the responsibilities which go along with sexual rights. These feminist writers are absolutely positive that teen sexuality has solely empowering tendencies whose primary function is to overcome the much-aligned and difficult-to-define term "patriarchy."[18] What does this really mean, however? Does it mean that party-line feminist thinking is so deeply entrenched in a view of sexuality that it obscures the fact that sometimes young women who engage in sexual activity face certain "dire consequences" of a failed sexual interest when the boyfriend leaves her when she's pregnant? Does it mean that the party-line feminist thinking is blind to the presence of a third party–the unborn child–who is often sacrificed as the teen sexual partners debate how they should live the rest of their lives? Could it also mean that party-line feminist thinking is bankrupt–as is the fiction which embodies such thinking–and that readers must therefore turn to creative authors like Ballard, Cole, Luger, Minshull, and Rodowsky to provide that alternative feminist envisioning?

More importantly, for purposes of examining the fourth aspect of the analysis in the classroom, students should be asked about the relative merits of each of the two outcomes. The first outcome is clearly the result of a bad choice. Abortion–despite any of its linguistic masks as "freedom of choice" or "pregnancy termination" or the exercise of a tenuous "right to choose"–is still absolutely negative. It is significant that none of the teen novels which end with the mother aborting the child end "happily"–not in the saccharine kind of happiness typical of a gushy romance novel, but in the aesthetically pleasing sense of fiction which involves romance between two teen partners and which ends with love between the partners rather than ambiguity. The novels which are resolved by abortion end in a loss of romance, a loss of individual strength for the mother, and a loss of certainty. Of course, no student would object to the pleasing ending of a life born and a young woman who, in true feminist fashion–matures to adulthood when she makes the best choice for herself and her child.

I began this paper with sample opening sentences from particular genres. Maybe the dominant feature of adolescent fiction on abortion is best characterized by the ending statements. If an adolescent abortion novel ends in the killing of the unborn child, then the ending will be as sad as that in Eyerly's *Bonnie Jo, Go Home*: "Leaving New York eleven days after she had arrived, her face seemed to have aged a year for every day she had been there" (114); or it will be as ambiguous as the ending in Klein's *Beginners' Love*: "I saw it already" (216). If, however, the adolescent abortion novel ends with a life-affirming statement, then that which ends Rodowsky's *Lucy Peale* may have already set the standard for what a young mother with low self-esteem can do in her life and that of her unborn child:

I'm ready now, and I'll go and get Doris and she'll come home with me and we'll put my stuff in the bedroom, where the crib's already set up, and her stuff in the living room, and then maybe we'll go out and I'll show her the library and the laundromat and what the beach's like in wintertime.

I'll go now and this time I'll drive right up to the house, only Pa won't be there, 'cause Doris said he had to see a man over Salisbury way. But Ma'll be there and maybe she'll come out. Or maybe I'll get brave and go inside and see Warren and Liddy and where I used to live, and even that moldy old parrot.

And maybe I'll get to see the quilt. The one Ma's making for the baby.

And as far as the rest–everything else–it's going to be okay. One way or another, it's going to be okay. (166-67)

WORKS CITED

Bakerman, Jane S., and Mary Jean DeMarr. *Adolescent Female Portraits in the American Novel, 1961-1981*. New York: Garland, 1983

Ballard, Kimberly M. *Light at Summer's End*. Wheaton.: Harold Shaw, 1991

Beckman, Gunnel. *Mia Alone*. Trans. Joan Tate. New York, Viking, 1974. Trans. of *Tre veckor over tiden*. Stockholm: Albert Bonniers Forlag, 1973

Christiansen, C. B. *I See the Moon*. New York: Atheneum, 1994. Electronic. Cuyahoga County Public Lib., OH. 3 May 1999

Chute, B. J. *The Story of a Small Life*. New York: E.P. Dutton, 1971

Cole, Sheila. *What Kind of Love? The Diary of a Pregnant Teenager*. New York: Lothrop, Lee & Shepard Books, 1995

Doherty, Berlie. *Dear Nobody*. New York: Orchard Books, 1992. Electronic. Cuyahoga County Public Lib., OH. 3 May 1999

Doty, Carolyn. *A Day Late*. New York: Viking, 1980

Eyerly, Jeannette. *Bonnie Jo, Go Home*. New York: Bantam, 1972

Farish, Terry. *Shelter for a Seabird*. New York: Greenwillow Books, 1990 Electronic. Cuyahoga County Public Lib., OH. 3 May 1999

Faulkner, William. *The Wild Palms*. New York: Random House, 1939

Fitzgerald, F. Scott. *Tender Is the Night*. New York: Charles Scribner's Sons, 1934

Grau, Shirley Ann. *The House on Coliseum Street*. New York: Knopf, 1961

Guy, Rosa. *Edith Jackson*. New York: Viking, 1978

Hemingway, Ernest. "Hills Like White Elephants" in *Literature and the Writing Process*. 5th ed. Eds. Elizabeth McMahan, Susan X. Day, and Robert Funk. Upper Saddle River: Prentice Hall, 1999, pp. 321-24

Herald, Diana Tixier. *Teen Genreflecting*. Englewood: Libraries Unlimited, 1997

Hirsch, E. D. *Cultural Literacy: What Every American Needs to Know*. Boston: Houghton Mifflin, 1987

Kaye, Geraldine. *Someone Else's Baby*. New York: Hyperion Books for Children, 1992. Electronic. Cuyahoga Cty. Public Lib., OH. 3 May 1999

Klein, Norma. *Beginners' Love*. New York: Hillside Books/E.P. Dutton, 1983

_____. *No More Saturday Nights*. New York: Knopf, 1988. Electronic. Cuyahoga County Public Lib., OH. 3 May 1999

Larsen, Doran. *Marginalia*. Sag Harbor: Permanent Press, 1997. Electronic. Cuyahoga County Public Lib., OH. 3 May 1999

Lee, Joanne. *I Want to Keep My Baby*. New York: NAL, 1977

Linney, Romulus. *Slowly, by Thy Hand Unfurled*. New York: Harcourt, Brace & World, 1965

Luger, Harriett. *Lauren*. New York: Viking, 1979

Madison, Winifred. *Growing Up in a Hurry*. Boston: Little, Brown, 1973

Maynard, Joyce. *Baby Love*. New York: Knopf, 1981

Minshull, Evelyn. *But I Thought You Really Loved Me*. Philadelphia: Westminster, 1976

Murfin, Ross, and Supryia M. Ray, eds. *The Bedford Glossary of Critical and Literary Terms*. Boston: Bedford Books, 1997

Oates, Joyce Carol. *Son of the Morning*. New York: Vanguard, 1978

Ramsdell, Kristin. *Happily Ever After: a Guide to Reading Interests in Romance Fiction*. Littleton: 1987

Renner, Stanley. "Moving to the Girl's Side of `Hills Like White Elephants'" in *The Hemingway Review* 15:1 (1995):27-41

Reynolds, Marilyn. *Beyond Dreams: True-to-Life Series from Hamilton High*. Buena Park: Morning Glory, 1995

_____. *Detour for Emmy*. Buena Park: Morning Glory, 1993. Electronic. Cuyahoga County Public Lib., OH. 3 May 1999

_____. *Too Soon for Jeff*. Buena Park: Morning Glory, 1994

Rodowsky, Colby. *Lucy Peale*. New York: Farrar, Straus and Giroux, 1992

Rossner, Judith. *Emmeline*. New York: Simon and Schuster, 1980

Spencer, Pam. *What Do Young Adults Read Next? A Reader's Guide to Fiction for Young Adults*. Vol. 2. Detroit: Gale, 1997

Stephensen, A. M. *Unbirthday*. New York: Avon Books, 1982

Sutherland, Zena. *Children & Books*. 9th ed. New York: Longman, 1997

Too Soon for Jeff. By Marilyn Reynolds. Perf. Freddie Prinze, Jr., and Jessica Alba. 1994. Videocassette. Films for the Humanities, 1996

Tolman, Deborah L. "Doing Desire: Adolescent Girls' Struggles for/with Sexuality." *Through the Prism of Difference: Readings on Sex and Gender*. Eds. Maxine Baca Zinn, Pierrette Hondagneu-Sotelo, and Michael A. Messner. Boston: Allyn and Bacon, 1997, pp. 173-85

Weingarten, Violet. *Mrs. Beneker*. New York: Simon and Schuster, 1967

Wilcox, James. *Plain and Normal*. Boston: Little, Brown, 1998. Electronic. Cuyahoga County Public Lib., OH. 3 May 1999

NOTES

1. With language as similarly connotative as mine, the more scholarly literary critics Ross Murfin and Supryia M. Ray corroborate my extemporaneous definition when they define the Gothic novel as: "a romance typically written as a long prose horror narrative that exhibits the Gothic qualities of doom and gloom as well as an emphasis on chivalry and magic. Dark, mysterious medieval castles chock full of secret passageways and (apparently) supernatural phenomena are common elements used to thrill the reader. Gothic heroes and heroines tend to be equally mysterious, with dark histories and secrets of their own. The Gothic hero is typically a man known more for his power and his charisma than for his personal goodness; the Gothic heroine's challenge is to win his love without being destroyed in the process" (149).

2. That is, with all due respect to the (young?) man Fabio before his aviary mishap.

3. Again, Ross and Ray record the contemporary understanding of the romance novel not only as "a fictional account of passionate love prevailing against social, economic, or psychological odds, but any plot that revolves around love" (346).

4. However, this conclusion was not the final one reached by the disproportionately large number of students who found this story so interesting that they culminated their final research project on an analysis of this short story. Apparently, this story is resilient enough to withstand a feminist literary critical attack as much as it is malleable to a biographical or a masculinist interpretation. What is most surprising is that many students were able to discover in the course of their research Stanley Renner's fine critical article, which argues that, since the characters do not explicitly suggest that the abortion is definitely going to occur, an easy anti-life extrapolation of the plot of the story may be faulty–a position which refutes most students' initial reading of the story.

I would also like to point out that I presume that at least one student was painfully aware of the message of the story. It was difficult for me during one class to press on with an explication of the story when one young woman became visibly upset while discussing it–to the point of needing to leave the room for the balance of the class time, a full forty minutes. Granted, this is a subjective comment on my part and the student herself did not confide anything to me. Unfortunately, however, we who are faculty can often gauge whether a student who becomes distressed over this one story and not others which might be more graphic, more sexual, or more politically-charged may have had an abortion and is now suffering the emotional symptoms of post-abortion syndrome.

5. See especially his commentary on SAT scores (4-5) and the lack of "shared information" in American education (19-25).

6. Sometimes, even the library community may not be helpful in collating titles on the subject of abortion. Abortion as a subject entry does not appear in Spencer's massive 692-page bibliographic compendium *What Do Young Adults Read Next? A Reader's Guide to Fiction for Young Adults* (Detroit: Gale, 1997). Many authors who are considered in this paper, however, are featured as are other titles which they have written.

7. Of course, I am aware that only a fraction of the total number of teens who are eligible to vote do so and that this lack of civic pride in electing quality candidates will remain at a plurality level when the teens become young adults in their twenties. After all, this is the decade when the United States elected someone as president on a plurality vote not once but twice in the span of four years.

8. In the course of my reading I discovered two intertextual references to schemes or paradigms of teen abortion fiction. Both passages ridicule the simplistic plot development of such fiction. The first passage, from A. M. Stephensen's *Unbirthday* (1982), has the main character recount her analysis of the teen abortion fiction she has read when she herself must decide whether or not to have an abortion:

> "I thought back on stories I'd read. The ones I could remember were always about a girl who lost her head in the heat of passion and went all the way with some guy in the backseat of a car. Usually at a drive-in. Usually with a guy she really didn't give a damn about. Always without a contraceptive. And–surprise!–she got pregnant.
> "Then she had the baby. If she married the guy, she'd end up staying home, cooking supper, washing bottles, changing diapers, and waiting for her husband to return from a long day pumping gas, after which he'd take out his frustrations on her and the kid. Or if she didn't get married, she'd leave school and put the tyke up for adoption, and since she was known to one and all as a 'bad girl,' she'd move to another part of town and after much effort find a dead-end job answering phones or selling shoes. Once in a while, she'd keep the baby. Then she'd move in with her alcoholic mother and, after trying valiantly to support her child, end up on welfare. And whiskey.
> "There was only one book I could remember where a girl got an abortion. It was so badly botched she ended up puking blood all over the upholstery of her boyfriend's car on the way home, and when she got into her house and puked more blood on the rug before collapsing to the floor, her exceptionally swift parents suddenly realized what was going on and virtually disowned her." (51-52)

Another passage, in Norma Klein's *Beginners' Love* (1983), similarly reduces the simplistic plots of most teen abortion novels to set patterns. The lead female character in Klein's novel comments about teen abortion novels with her boyfriend, suggesting that a standard set of steps in plot development has made the classification trite:

> "God, don't you hate those books for teen-agers where they *have* to get married and she drops out of school and they live over a garage and he works in some used car lot. And there's always some scene where some girl who had an abortion comes to visit and she's gone insane and becomes a Bowery bum, just in case you didn't get the point."
>
> "I never read a book like that," I said.
>
> "You're lucky.... Every other book I've read since I was *ten* is like that. The girl's a moron, the guy's a moron, they never heard of birth control. What I love are the scenes where the father takes the guy aside and says, 'Son, if you marry Betsy, you'll have to give up your football scholarship to Oklahoma State.' They're *always* going to some godforsaken place like Oklahoma State! And the guy says, 'But, Dad, I love her!'... And then there's a scene where the mother says, 'Dear, you haven't let him take advantage of you? You know what boys are like.' Quote unquote.... God, I think writers must be really dumb! Or else they're living in the Stone Age." (163-64)

9. The argument that a pregnancy is better described as "untimely" instead of being a "problem" is more accurate in its specificity, at least in the literary sense. The novels I have considered show that the pregnancies which result from faulty or non-existent contraception or from a hedonistic view towards sexuality are not problems to the young people involved. The characters do not so much doubt the existence of the human entity over whose life they think they have jurisdiction, but rather are much more concerned with how to continue their lifestyles–their educational choices, their career choices, and their romantic or sexual choices. The term "difficult" when used to refer to pregnancy, seems more proper when used in medical contexts.

10. The study of transgendered characterizations may be helpful here, especially in the emerging branches of gender criticism called masculinist and queer theory.

11. Interested persons may be interested in her *Beyond Dreams: True-to-Life Series from Hamilton High* (1995). Moreover, they may find the performances of Freddie Prinze, Jr. and Jessica Alba in the video adaptation of the novel under analysis convincing.

12. Bakerman and DeMarr have identified other titles which fall into this category of fiction written from the perspective of the mother who wants to give birth to her baby. Readers may be interested in the following: *I Want to Keep My Baby* (1977) by Joanna Lee (92-93); *Son of the Morning* (1978) by Joyce Carol Oates (125); *Emmeline* (1980) by Judith Rossner (155); and *Baby Love* (1981) by Joyce Maynard (107).

13. The situation of an abortion subplot in a larger adult-theme work does not dissolve after *Roe*, of course. Carolyn Doty's 1980 novel *A Day Late* uses the stereotype of a seventeen-year-old pregnant runaway to reflect (and deflect) the middle-aged crisis of Sam the protagonist. A traveling salesman, Sam finds the youth of Katy, the mother, disturbing to the point that he becomes violent against her and the young man who had befriended her. He also becomes violent against himself by spending a night with a whore. The climax in the novel is not abortion-related at all: Sam "finds himself" by engaging in a male-bonding dance with his Greek friend. The denouement, however, does return to the abortion subplot: Katy miscarries a malformed unborn child and this is considered "a blessing" (230).

14. Ballard is one of the bold breed of writers who are clearly identified with the pro-life movement. More importantly from a literary standpoint, her novel is not preachy or didactic, which some critics of evangelical and pro-life fiction have claimed are dominant characteristics of such life-affirming material. While there certainly are titles which are preachy (if not hostile to religious diversity), Ballard's book contains a few pages (by my estimation three) where one of the main characters, an elderly woman named Vellie, summarizes Christian principles for the other main character, fourteen-year-old Melissa (138-40). It would be interesting to see how anti-life critics or critics hostile to evangelical or pro-life fiction would evaluate the final chapter of the book. Melissa suggests holding a "service" for the aborted child which seems more pagan in liturgical setting than Christian: the service is to be conducted at dawn in the woods; while she expresses her anger and sorrow, Melissa moves stones in certain formations (143-47). Is this Wicca practice or Christian didacticism? Perhaps this is the author's intent: to frustrate those critics who would categorize her novel as merely "one of those" pro-life books.

15. In fact, one could even argue that the title signals to the reader (the teen in the public library or the school library or in the bookstore) that the option of abortion is never entertained seriously: if unwed motherhood were so disastrous for the teen heroine, then it would be metaphorically described as a "halt" in her life, not a "detour." This connotatively implies that, while one option has been closed, another option is available.

16. At least one religious reference is non-denominational. Mia in Beckman's *Mia Alone* contrasts "the Christian's talk" about sanctity of human life in contrast to her family's ethics (106).

17. Whatever her personal position regarding this abortion organization, the author is fair when she thanks "the staff of Planned Parenthood of San Diego and Riverside Counties," among others, "for their help in understanding what it is like to be young and pregnant" (Cole; opposite title page).

18. Consider the following analysis of interviews of teen girls regarding sex and related issues: "To be able to know their sexual feelings, to listen when their bodies speak about themselves and about their relationships, might enable these and other girls to identify and know more clearly the sources of oppression that press on their full personhood and their capacity for knowledge, joy, and connection.... Asking these girls to speak abut sexual desire, and listening and responding to their answers and also to their questions, proved to be an effective way to interrupt the standard 'dire consequences' discourse which adults usually employ when speaking at all to girls about their sexuality. Knowing and speaking about the ways in which their sexuality continues to be unfairly constrained may interrupt the appearance of social equity that many adolescent girls (especially white, middle-class young women) naively and trustingly believe, thus leading them to reject feminism as unnecessary and mean-spirited and not relevant to their lives. As we know from the consciousness-raising activities that characterized the initial years of second-wave feminism, listening to the words of other girls and women can make it possible for girls to know and voice their experiences, their justified confusion and fears, their curiosities. Through such relationships, we help ourselves and each other to live in our different female bodies with an awareness of danger, but also with a desire to feel the power of the erotic, to fine-tune our bodies and our psyches to what Audre Lord has called the 'yes within ourselves'." (Tolman 183-84)

Writing a Play about Virtue:
The Way to *Evolution Valley*

Bernadette Waterman Ward

T HE PLAY I PRESENTED at this conference, *Evolution Valley*,[1] was
written entirely in verse, partly because I had learned playwriting
from a poet. It was reading my teacher William Alfred's work
that revealed to me the reasons for writing in verse rather than in
prose–and those reasons go deeper than the mere beauty of the sound of
it, important though that is. For one thing, I have not yet the grace with
meter which one would need to create a play whose verse was beautiful
in every moment; nor do I think that such delicacy is what is needed in
this hour in the American theater. But I must go the long way round to
explain why it seems necessary to write in verse, rough though it be,
when one takes the side of life in the artistic climate of our culture of
death.

My old teacher, the playwright William Alfred, died on May 19,
1999. About three weeks before that I had read his play *Hogan's Goat*
for the first time. Its remarkable run of 607 performances, followed by
a televised version and a musical revival, began in 1966. I had taken a
couple of courses with Alfred and visited him whenever I got to
Boston–we had kept in contact for more than twenty years–but I knew
him as a teacher rather than as a writer. I found the play in the stacks at
Stanford while researching something else. I could not resist opening
it, and then I tasted Alfred's verse: rich upon the tongue, yet sharp with
the ironic tang of remembered injustice that flavors Irish speech. (Are
there any English dialects besides Irish and Black American in which
"wicked" means "good"?) I saw him employing in the play all sorts of
things of which he had told us in playwriting class: rhythmically paced
scenes, characters' lives that well up from an immense imagined past
into a few words on the stage, gestures captured in speech so unmistakable that they cannot be done wrongly if the line is to be said at all.

385

These were all good things. But when I finished reading *Hogan's Goat*, I wrote him a letter about its language, telling him that he had brought back into my ear the cadence of my Irish mother's voice as she spoke of the politics in some of the very parishes in which he set the play. I had not known he was any sicker than usual, but he died within the month, and I was glad that I wrote him that last note about the poetry in *Hogan's Goat*.

The more I think about it, the more it seems that the verse was the proper thing to praise. I met Alfred in his course on Anglo-Saxon poetry, which was the way he taught beginners the language. His scholarship in Anglo-Saxon was impeccable and vividly communicated. He illustrated the instrumental case-ending by beginning, in a calm professorial tone: "This is the case-ending you would use for 'stone' when you said" –he then drew his tall stooped frame to its feet and backed away from the desk, his face upraised with a look of mounting panic, cringing so that we all looked at the empty air above him with alarm– "What are you doing with *that stone?*" He looked back down at our anxious countenances. "*Thē stāne,*" he finished mildly, smiled, and went on to the next case ending. There was a bit of theater in the class, and more than a bit of poetry, and, of course, they went together. It was that class which showed me more than anything that in fact memory exerts a stronger pull in the presence of both poetry and drama. We learned *thē stāne* by enacting it with Bill Alfred; and we learned much about courage and cowardice, deprivation and necessity and loyalty and terror, by indwelling the old poems and learning to speak their language. *Hogan's Goat* brought home to me again the knowledge that a scrap of rhythmic speech remembered is immensely more powerful than any number of wise thoughts couched in language that strives to be bold and innovative. The play held history in its cadences, and Alfred knew it–I could only hear the words he wrote in the voices of my mother and my uncle from the Irish parishes across the river from Brooklyn.

Bill Alfred was a philologist concerned with what people use language for and how people have used it–language mostly from a long time ago. He loved the old heroic poetry, and he showed us how even poetic catalogues of warriors' names–not an ordinary way to induce students to love a language!–allow us to touch and taste the rhythms by which honor and disrepute were communicated. Those rhythms are still the rhythms of such things in English; that he knew too. For in his class I learned the beat of speech that returns to my ear in hearing rap, or the flourishes of graduation speeches, or the words of the liturgy. He showed us how these rhythms are the bones of the language, the way memory is held through generation after generation. The meters of our nursery-rhymes were familiar to West Saxon poets–and for the same reason they are familiar to our children. They hold the memory, and they hold deep within them some wisdom about repetition, about dependability, about the sharing of a world from generation to generation. The very strangeness of the ancient words–what Alfred called the "subtle Germanics" of the syntax and word-formation–made it all the clearer that the very sound of the language, still recognizably our own, has a pointedness that strikes at the memory and the emotions.

Because meter is about the return of something we have heard before, it is about trust. And it is about trust in people, for the rhythm of a language is given by one person to another, not by a book. It was because he understood the practice of the spoken word, even–no, especially–at its most formal, that Alfred was able to draw from his playwriting students a deep attention to the hearts and memories of their characters. A play is an enactment of a certain kind of life; it has its origins in liturgy, and its function is still, in a way, liturgical: we, to some degree, become what we participate in.

I say "liturgy" designedly, for one of the reasons Bill Alfred understood tradition so well was that he lived thoroughly and deliberately within it. Liturgy was essential to his life; he went to the St. Paul Choir School Mass every morning at eight. And, following the dictates of his Catholic tradition, he was also, straightforwardly and simply, a good man. He was generous with hospitality and scholarly courtesy; he lived among little marble-topped tables teetering with stacks of things people had sent him to read and recommendations to be written; but he was generous beyond the circle of his students. His financial generosity was legendary, both among institutions and among local vagrants. He wore second-hand suits so that he could commit more of his income to those in need. I myself have unexpectedly received charity at his hand, and I know that I was not the first person of his wide acquaintance who found that Alfred had some mysterious way of discovering who might be sick and finding his way to the hospital bedside with gifts. And his piety was likewise most incomprehensibly simple and easily discovered, rather unnervingly so in a university town where sophistication was the rule. He was willing to talk to people about converting to Catholicism, and he prayed for those who had fallen away. I recall one supercilious student deliberately writing a snide, obscene, anti-religious play for the fun of shocking and wounding Alfred. But he got no bitter response. The old professor knew exactly what kind of an oddity he was in academia; he was not afraid to leave himself open to contempt, nor surprised when he found it.

The secret power of the very rhythm of *Hogan's Goat* is in that public piety which made its author an inevitable object of ridicule. The protagonist, Matthew Stanton, barters his chastity for political advantage and destroys his political and his personal life together at a stroke. The causal structure of stories was not Alfred's central concern; there are improbably preserved documents in *Hogan's Goat*, and there is at least one very convenient death. The plot, set in the political backrooms of turn-of-the-century New York, did not strain the bounds of the possible, but it was rather symbolic than naturalistic. Matthew Stanton desires to set up a good government, one free of corruption, but his ambition has cost him his loyalty to his wife. His scorn of religious ceremony—carefully, ironically, couched in verse—finally swallows in public shame his own advancement and the good he had hoped to do for his city.

Intimately as *Hogan's Goat* communicates the Augustinian truth that sin lies in the choice of the lesser good, it was not Alfred's knowledge of sin but his knowledge of virtue that gave the play its grip. The play fascinates by its vision of a calmly acknowledged possibility of real spiritual freedom flourishing in the seamy but unshakably Catholic culture of New York's Irish immigrants. Most fail to reach out for true virtue, but some succeed in reaching that level of freedom at which good can be loved calmly for itself, and one's personal cupidity and fear have no control over whose good one serves. In short, some of the people in his corrupt Irish ghetto have put on the mind of Christ; and one of them, the penitent Ag Hogan, allows the world to continue to think of her as a whore, willing to die under the calumny for the good of her community. She stands as a foil to Matthew Stanton, who repudiates her but who fears for his political reputation as a clean-living Catholic too much to face the disrepute he might garner from his own legally recorded actions.

Matthew Stanton is a strong man, able to pursue his desires with great singleness of purpose and in the face of great difficulties. Nevertheless, he is not free. To have a life ruled by fear or sex, power or money, or especially (as Stanton does) by the craving for admiration, is to twist and cramp the fullness of one's humanity. Now, Matthew Stanton is not limited to envisioning only what is good for himself; he has risen to such a level of virtue as to make him desire to see his whole community happy and prosperous–but he is still tied to his own pride. He desires to have an honest community but discovers that he will be hampered in establishing one if he himself is honest about his past–so he does not choose powerlessness and honesty. He cannot take the general good as a good to be pursued when it costs him his public name. He does indeed have some vision of the general good. But his vision is not wide enough; he is willing to lie to come at the good–a little lie, he thinks, a harmless lie; only one woman suffers for it, and a whole city will benefit. He tells the lie because he is not willing to bear shame; his public image will suffer, he thinks, and with it the whole city.

But he is a Catholic, and his tragedy comes as priests, acting the part of prophets, show him his own venality and the narrow road of personal integrity that he cannot bear to take–to be in the image of God, completely free to choose among loves, without subjection to either the pleasures or the insecurities of unstable worldly fortune. The human capacity for desire is infinite; to limit our desire to the good of some finite thing–self, tribe, country–is finally to do to oneself what Alfred's protagonist does: destroy his very self through seeking to assuage his infinite desires with the finite good of himself and his political party, rather than the infinite good of faithfulness to the truth. His wife, who is not a rebel against her religious tradition, although she has strayed from it, finally seeks the good in God. She is more free and, though she dies, is not left in the deep devastation that attends Matthew Stanton.

It is perhaps startling that in the American culture of the Sixties,

Hogan's Goat located the beauty of freedom in a tradition encrusted with rote habit passed on through the ages and bound by seemingly senseless religious rules about Easter duty and approved venues for marriage. For the sentiment of the day was shot full of Romanticism which placed all hope in breaking conventions and setting free the purity of youthful feeling. Alfred found the sentimentality of *The Graduate*, for instance, both funny and sad. "A little child shall lead them," he used to say. "That is the great myth of our time." And he lived to see the myth, in the way of such things, turn itself inside out and become bitter, as rebellion against conventionality ultimately left the rebels to be victims of the sheer voracity of their own desires–what we now so often dignify as "needs." What is kept in check by rules and hierarchies is a restless, fundamentally ruthless rivalry, a desire to be endowed by others with "superior being."[2] Social structures are cumbersome and violent; but only because the humans who need them are prone to seek for their good in all the wrong places and to kill each other on the way there.

Having discovered that the loosening of traditional restraints has led, rather predictably, to predation and insecurity, the American artistic intelligentsia has become increasingly fascinated with evil. Only such works as explore and confront and reveal evil are considered to have depth. Today the premise of rebellion against tradition–religious and family structures in particular–is still *de rigueur*; "Ozzie and Harriet are dead," goes the derisive refrain. It is unquestioningly assumed in the reigning artistic community that the old rules were violent, constricting, and warping to the health of human desires. Nevertheless, the real fascination among playwrights today is with the failure of what came to replace the old rules: the optimism about the fundamental goodness of humanity, the sense that desire set free is healthy.

Like Dickens's Podsnap, twentieth-century American high culture loves to see itself as the culmination of all civilization–and what it sees is "not a very large world, morally." So, after having assumed that Original Sin does not exist, the artists of our day nevertheless feel compelled to attack, in relentlessly bleak productions, the culture in which everyone is to be seen as basically good and no one really does anything inexplicably wrong. Certainly that optimistic culture still exists; there were many sympathetic editorials about the pitiable isolation imposed upon the teenage mass-murderers at Littleton High, teens who had jobs and girlfriends and numerous people who liked them. Much of the soul-searching aimed itself at breaking down the oppressive structures of high-school culture. It is so hard for Americans, even now, to see that youth is not identical with virtue, and that respect for traditional virtue is not identical with evil oppression. Therefore, the artists perhaps are justified in seeking to shock their audiences with vice more and more triumphant, unpunished and gleefully inflicting undeserved misery whose injustice is never compensated by any alleviation of the victims' suffering. And most of all, perhaps, they are justified in making the criminals more and more like us.

The high culture has great respect for anyone willing to rip off the blinders of the sentimentalists who claim, over and over again, that people are fundamentally good if they are allowed to develop freely. Therefore, in any review which doesn't involve a restaurant, "gritty" is an unquestioned term of praise. Artists are praised for their courage in confronting the compulsive violence–a violence that, in fact, is the logical outgrowth of the breaking of traditional structures. For tradition gives us boundaries; without them competition for attention is all-consuming. To follow one's heart, truly, is to discover the truth of Jeremiah 17[9]: "The heart is deceitful above all things, and beyond cure. Who can understand it?"

Sometimes a reviewer will wish for something different. *The New York Times* recently printed a long lament that most plays which focus on sex seem to deal with how loveless, mechanistic, and competitive promiscuity is. But the old assumptions were still in place. Reviewer Sylviane Gold longed for more plays like the profoundly dishonest *Cloud Nine* by Caryl Churchill, where "sex is at once funny, serious, and good for you."[3] (Has any woman outside of a Caryl Churchill play ever been transformed from a withered drudge into a joyous, self-confident achiever by masturbation?) The reviewer was reluctant to recognize that the reason playwrights write constantly about shattered trust and lovelessness and various sorts of violence in sexual matters is because they want to tell the truth about it "as a chaotic and destructive element in life rather than a wholesome one." The underside of our freedom to fornicate where we please is indeed sheer violence: abandoned women killing their children, mostly before but sometimes after birth, and the shattered trust of their surviving offspring.[4] There is good reason why the latest fad among the children of *Roe v. Wade* is self-mutilation and "extreme" games: one can depend only upon oneself, upon one's own capacity for enduring pain, for a sense of anything permanent and stable about one's life. Thence comes the understanding of faith articulated solemnly in *The San Francisco Examiner and Chronicle* in an article on the religion of Generation X: "'My piercings and tattoos are more sacred than any faith could be because they are permanent markings that I can identify with,' she says. 'My family doesn't understand this. And yet they are the ones who wanted me to choose my own way'."[5] Written all over this woman's body is our culture's collapse of trust and desperate need for some direction. Unworthy obsessions are eating us alive and, therefore, in an economy built on advertising, we are prosperous. The language of salesmen is properly transformed in our plays into the language of murderers. *The New York Times* respectfully affirms that the mark of a good playwright is that he "hunts out the sinister in sunny American imagery."[6]

But to find evil—even to condemn the evil earnestly—is not necessarily to serve the good. There is often (though not always) a genuinely high-minded motive in facing unpleasant truths about our own corruption. But there is a trap in much praising iconoclasm, even if the icon being smashed is indeed an idol. What too often garners critical admiration is the artist's boldness—the proof of how little this artist is trammeled by convention. The breaking of convention soon becomes a form of self-deception too—the great fraud of independence from the opinion of others. And this need to be different is only a most subtle form of dependence. Needing to shock someone, and finding that the capacity for shock becomes fatigued with each imitation, creates a macabre rivalry for the darkest and most horrific vision. One can easily see why crossover audiences are drawn to tinny fantasies of cheery domesticated homosexual bliss, falser than *Ozzie and Harriet* ever attempted to be: the other revulsions they have to face are worse.

Outside the gay subculture, prestigious theater has become "insistently brutal"–another term of praise–and often actively seeks to exploit the audience's horror at its own sympathy for or even admiration of the miscreants on stage. Sometimes this tactic is meant to reveal our own hypocrisy in condemning sinners, but it is more jarring, and therefore bolder and more surely evidence of the artist's superior courage, when it leaves the audience mired in its moral unease and refuses to condemn the evil. As our theater explores the ordinariness not only of murder but of various kinds of sexual victimization, including incest and the sexual use of children; business practices that verge on the same level of viciousness (*Glengarry Glenn Ross*); suicide; family and racial hatreds; and gleeful or banal heartlessness on the part of characters whose authors earnestly seek to make them seem as ordinary as possible–our capacity for outrage is dulled. It may be that sometimes the depiction of vice as it is restrains some people from sin. But the message of the theater of brutality is not merely that we risk a life that imitates the art; it is that we have not recognized that we are already living in that hell.

No less blind than the hopeful sentimentality it seeks to debunk, the theater of brutality faces us with an utterly unyielding vision of evil, intimately threatening each soul; no one is immune. By mere repetition–and sometimes by interactive participation–we learn to accept, to mentally practice, meaningless sexual couplings, aggressive physical revenge, cynical humor. As John Henry Newman put it, those who habituate themselves to evil

are very skeptical about the existence of principle and virtue; they think all men are equally swayed by worldly, selfish or sensual motives, though some hide their motives better than others, or have feelings and likings of a more refined character. And having given in to sin themselves, they have no higher principle within them to counteract the effect of what they see without... and they use their knowledge to overreach, deceive, seduce, corrupt, or sway those with whom they have to do.[7]

Again, look to the ancient traditions of good that founded the work of Bill Alfred: freedom consists of being able to conceive of good that is not oriented to oneself, because then it becomes possible to be attracted to something besides what instinct commands. Of course, the understanding of others' goods need not be used to serve them. We can feed someone else who is hungry—or we can exploit his hunger to make him do something we want. Because of our ability to corrupt even our perceptions of good, we also understand—and become suspicious—when we see that someone wants attention, or wants money, or wants power. Our intensely cynical popular culture constantly confirms the fear that exploitation is the real secret to anyone's actions. We expect all manner of lies and oath-breaking as normal behavior, in private and public.

The theater of brutality feeds this fear. A great motivator of the violence, for instance, in American abortion clinics, is in fact lack of faith that there is anyone who really is motivated by something good for another person rather than in their own sense of control. The Caring Foundation has uncovered that, overwhelmingly, to women who seek abortions

there is simply no question here of the woman viewing pro-lifers as altruistically and selflessly defending the good of her child. Recall, the woman has not been able to adopt any point of view from which the child looks to be her good. How can she accept, then, that someone else really takes the child to be his good? .... It would be precisely in dismissing the claims of pro-lifers that she would find some way of affirming her actual and greater "concern" or authority in the matter.[8]

A diminishing capacity for establishing social categories that create status through obligations creates a deep insecurity about one's place in the social and spiritual world and a tremendous need to defend one's own personal position of power. Less and less permanent relationships are demanding recognition as equivalent to marriage, for the sake of the perceived privileges of that state—and without the penalties and sacrifices that come with a real covenant whose good must be put above the obvious good of each party. And the sick have become convinced that no one really will find any good in caring for them when they become disabled—the assisted suicide movement. Our culture of death breaks down every permanent commitment even among human beings, so that the imagination has nothing but its own darkest fears to feed upon. Thus virtue becomes incomprehensible and every tradition and moral precept seems merely a complex form of betrayal.

That everyone is actually acting from some warped sense of self-aggrandizement is the foundational conviction of the theater of brutality, and in pursuit of it the playwrights of our day are quite right in rendering their characters' horrific actions in the flattest and ugliest language. If you want to communicate that absolutely everyone is likely to be evil, it is best to chill the heart with horror "imprinted with the rhythms and clichés of pop psychology, televangelism, and business pep talk... couched in the sort of everyday, lazy language that you routinely overhear in train stations or diners."[9] The dull normality of the language has precisely the effect of making what the audience would prefer to encounter as the strangeness of evil an intimate and unsettling experience.

But what of the artist who would encourage in an audience some vision of the good? What of the artist who would make faith possible in the audience, who would prefer to enable the hearers to believe that those who speak of morality are not necessarily hypocrites? The dilemma of a playwright who is committed to the defense of life is that it is difficult to enable our hearers to understand that it is possible for people to love what the Scholastics called "some good not oriented to self." It has become a project of some subtlety to convince audiences that they are not required to seek for the secret ugliness of the people we present as virtuous. In a culture habituated to mistrust, I believe it does a writer good to invoke the security of a set of rules that is known and trusted. William Alfred required his audience to understand the by-then alien culture of unquestioned loyalty to the Catholic system of ecclesiastical discipline; but he also chose another device. He used verse.

Verse creates its own atmosphere of trust. That's what we are teaching children when we teach them nursery rhymes: so many beats in this line, so many beats in that, and they'll rhyme. What you heard before, you'll hear again. No matter if they're nonsense; the ancient rhythms of nursery rhymes are meant to create trust. And rhythms have an emotive power familiar to preachers everywhere–listen hard to Jesse Jackson, or listen to a tape of Martin Luther King delivering any of his great discourses. In the theater, the rhythm becomes actual, as in music. Within that atmosphere of trust, that predictable rhythm, things which are strange and powerful can seem to be held in check. That is why our most formal language falls naturally into rhythm, and why it is used on such perilous occasions as weddings and deaths. The very formality of the speech, a familiarity thrust in the face of the uncontrollable, helps us to bear the terror and to trust that we can emerge whole from the risk.

Therefore, rhythmic speech is best for the establishment of two things: first, that unconscious sense of familiarity which breeds trust; and, second, the sense that we are facing mystery. Evil has much less mystery about it than good; the desires oriented to self have, in the end, a maddening repetitiveness, and the possibilities of goodness for others are as infinite as the realities we encounter. The language of goodness should be beautiful; but Americans shy away from beautiful language, democratically suspicious, even envious, of pomposity. Every day one hears people speaking poetically, if one listens, but our art has insistently convinced us that such things do not happen. In order to prevent such language from seeming false, it is necessary to build up the trust of the audience. It was for this reason, I think, that William Alfred chose to render even the backroom political meetings in *Hogan's Goat* in blank verse, though the characters have such flattened sensibilities that it sounds to the ear like prose. Once the ear trusts the rhythm, its power can be employed to allow the hearers to trust a vision of beauty and discipline in verse of a higher level of diction. Certainly it seemed so to me as I followed Alfred's example and set the entire text of *Evolution Valley*, financial transactions included, in blank verse. I knew that only something poetic in force could convey the intensity of emotion felt by the character who became Edmund when he rejected his own suicidal act; the line "I cannot sin against life again" is the germ of the whole play. It was Alfred's work that convinced me that I could best prepare for that moment by enabling the audience to accept rhythmic language as something natural to the character. I had to make room for beauty, and therefore had to forge a language–whether successfully or not–in which beauty would not seem like mere window-dressing.

The important things that must be said about suicide in *Evolution Valley* have, of course, already been said: "He who would save his life will lose it; he who loses his life will save it." I wished to make a commentary on this text for our times as we face pain in a cowardly culture. I envisioned an audience that would dislike the self-righteous-ness that is almost inevitably associated with Christian characters. I therefore determined that the self-righteous representatives of the culture of death would have to constantly browbeat a representative of the culture of life, and here I got frumpy but compassionate Corey, named for Cordelia in *King Lear*. I had to make virtue believable so that my audience would not be looking constantly for the hidden vice of those who take the side of life. For this I settled on the need for the vices of the character to be obvious and for him to be a penitent: thus Lancelot's personal history came into being. My generation has little sense of the glory and risk of matrimony, of sex, of any commitment, yet they long for it, counterfeit it with money, buy houses together. Somehow I had to bring my audience, as Alfred did, inside a way of life in which ceremony is not despised and agreements ultimately mean something. I decided to do it in a way that my audience would understand, a very physical way: Lancelot's fornication and careless-ness about obligations must be given grave effects, and his marriage must be seen as a reparation–by both spouses– of his sin. I knew from the first moment when I imagined his paternity that his child must be handicapped and despised by the proponents of the death culture, and yet worth loving. But even Lance had to be educated into loving little Sofia, whose name I chose specifically to assert that the life of such a child is the foolishness of men but the wisdom of God.

The culture of death had to be represented in its bold, brash, attractively take-charge incarnation as well as its dry, respectable, PBS version: these considerations shaped the characters of Mona and Edmund. The terrible fear that makes people desire death instead of life controls Goldie; both her suicide and her earlier abortion are products of her submission to someone else's perceived will rather than an assertion of any desire of her own. This follows the classic pattern of women who have abortions and, I suspect (for there are never going to be exit interviews to confirm this) of people who agree to suicide. But Mona, the great proponent of asserting her autonomy, is actually as dependent as Goldie–Goldie directly, upon the will of husband or boyfriend, and Mona upon the admiration of others. Her strong appetites are undirected–her rapid consumption of boyfriends is one of the running jokes of the play—and her strongest need is to have someone to envy her or to triumph over, to assure herself of her own worth.

Lancelot could be made attractive to the audience as a mere underdog, the victim of Mona's envy, but I was not seeking to create condemnation. What I wanted was to establish faith that heroic charity is possible. I had to create in my audience an understanding of a sensibility which is willing to forego personal good and even allow the evil committed by another person to have its consequences upon himself rather than on the culprit. And the family pride was the key: Lance begins the play as dependent upon his father's opinion as his mother is. Gradually Lance learns to face humiliation for the evil he has done rather than try to escape it. By the time he meets his father in Evolution Valley (a real place, by the way), he has learned something about Christian freedom centered in the Cross. To have him die in place of his father would have turned the play into mere melodrama, meaningless in my hearer's lives; so I made Lancelot learn courage in relation to patience, responsibility, and obedience to law. Such milder forms of submission to the greater good could be made, I thought, free of bombast. And in the speeches in which the characters who sought virtue told about their motives, there had to be dignity as well as the wisdom of the love of life. Although her role in the action was not large, longer and more formally poetic speeches had to be given to the one who has learned faith and courage already, Corey.

I remember once listening to a poet I knew in graduate school as he railed about how heroism is impossible, how there are no heroic deeds left to do, and how those who might have been heroes in the past were the muttering madmen who lived in trash heaps and slept on gratings. I felt abashed and unsophisticated, and I did not raise my voice to contradict. But at that very moment my heart leapt with the knowledge that I could, within five miles, point to a priest who had stood up to his neighborhood's crack dealers; to a rock climber who had paid with the flesh on his hands—palms and fingers burnt to the deep structures on both hands—in order to save his partner from a fall; to two undergraduate boys who bicycled down into the local slum twice a week to teach English, unpaid, to refugees in a neighborhood where automatic machine-gun fire punctuated every single night. My poet friend had simply and irrationally become unable to perceive the very things he saw before his eyes. It is because of such dulled sensibilities that we are expected to believe that chastity, fidelity, parenthood, and many other fine patterns of behavior have become impossible. Great care must be taken to foster the full flowering of the imagination, that most human of capabilities, by which we recognize another being's desires as like our own. It is all too easy to constrict it, to make it an instrument of fear. To elevate the spirit and enable our hearers to understand virtue is a project requiring the resolution of the psalmist: "keep no vile thing before thy eyes." Our audiences must not be drawn to participate in the narrowed world of evil, for that is what they will learn. I learned Anglo-Saxon declensions by vicarious participation. Yet how can we have stories if no vile thing is presented? I think that as those who set themselves to honor life as a good thing in itself, the answer is that we must treat all things, including the vile things, from the point of view of those who sensibilities are not yet dead. Nothing must make us so cynical as to expect vice when virtue is possible, or willing to laugh at those who do not understand the degree of corruption of our fellow human beings. Seeing evil, we must nevertheless act from our knowledge of the beauty of virtue. We must never take the point of view that evil is the norm and that the only profound thing is evil, but must seek to demonstrate that virtue is as intimate and possible as malice; we must not be ashamed of goodness.

To remove the shame and the terror of that mystery, I chose verse. To reveal the working of good in our world, I chose penitence as my subject. And I hope that the resulting drama shall serve the cause of life.

NOTES

1. Not yet in print, but those wishing to obtain copies may apply directly to the author, c/o The English Dept., University of Dallas, 1845 E. Northgate Dr., Irving TX 75062-4736.

2. René Girard, *Violence and the Sacred* (Baltimore: The Johns Hopkins Univ. Press, 1979), p. 146.

3. Sylviane Gold, "One Place Sex Is Seldom Taken Seriously" in *The New York Times* (Sunday, June 27, 1999), p. AR5+.

4. In "Every Child a Wanted Child" (in *The Newman Rambler* 3/2, Spring-Summer 1999, p. 17) Daniel Cere cites a 1999 study by Dr. Philip Ney, "Abortion and Family Progress" in *The Canadian Journal of Diagnosis*, which points out that children who learn that their parents have aborted a sibling "often suffer from disorientation, depression, and guilt."

5. Christa Palmer, "Boomers, Kids often at Odds over Religion" in *The San Francisco Sunday Examiner and Chronicle* (March 14, 1999), p. W12, col. 3.

6. "The Face of Evil, All Peaches and Cream" in *The New York Times* (Friday, June 25, 1999), p. B14:5.

7. John Henry Newman, "Ignorance of Evil" in *Parochial and Plain Sermons* (Westminster: Christian Classics, 1968), vol. VIII, pp. 262-63.

8. Michael Pakaluk, "Abortion, Self-Love, and Virtue: The Work of the Caring Foundation" in *Life and Learning VIII: Proceedings of the Eighth University Faculty for Life Conference, June 1998, at the University of Toronto*, ed. Joseph W. Koterski, S.J. (Washington, D.C.: UFL, 1999).

9. "The Face of Evil, All Peaches and Cream" in *The New York Times* (Friday, Jun 25, 1999), p. B14:5.

About Our Contributors

Frank Beckwith is Associate Professor of Philosophy, Culture, and Law at Trinity Graduate School, California Campus. He holds a Ph.D. from Fordham University. Besides numerous articles, he has authored several books, including *Doing the Right Thing* and *Politically Correct Death*.

Rev. W. Jerome Bracken, C.P., received his doctorate in Systematic Theology from Fordham University in 1978. For the last ten years he has been teaching Ethics at Immaculate Conception Seminary at Seton Hall University.

Bridget Campion is Assistant Professor of Moral Theology at St. Augustine's Seminary in Toronto. Formerly a clinical ethicist, she has a special interest in health care ethics and serves on the Board of the deVeber Institute for Bioethics and Social Research.

Elizabeth Ring Cassidy, M.A., is a psychometrist and researcher who lives in Guelph, Ontario, and does social science research for the deVeber Institute. She has published numerous papers, many of which are included in past proceedings of University Faculty for Life conferences.

Keith Cassidy is a full-time member of the History Department of the University of Guelph, Ontario, where he has served as president of the Faculty Association. He is at work on a full-length study of the Right-to-Life Movement.

Rev. John J. Conley, S.J. is Associate Professor of Philosophy at Fordham University in New York. He received his Ph.D. from Louvain and has published many articles on bioethics, including publications in *America, Inquiry, Society*, and *Thought*.

John F. Crosby, Ph.D., has taught at the University of Dallas, the International Academy of Philosophy, and is now Professor of Philosophy at Franciscan University of Steubenville. Among his recent publications is *The Selfhood of the Human Person* (Catholic University of America Press, 1996).

401

Frederick N. Dyer obtained his Ph.D. in Experimental Pscyhology from Michigan State University in 1968. He has published numerous scientific articles and two books during four years as a university professor and more than twenty years as a research psychologist at the Army Medical Research Laboratory and elsewhere.

Winston L. Frost is the Dean of Trinity Law School and founding director of the Center for Human Rights and Freedom. He teaches courses in constitutional law, legal history, ethics, and human rights. He received his J.D. *cum laude* from O. W. Coburn School of Law at Oral Roberts University.

Jorge Garcia is a Professor of Philosophy at Rutgers University. His primary teaching and research interests are normative ethical theory, action theory, applied ethics, and African-American philosophy. Currently teaching in Boston, his most recent book is entitled *The Heart of Racism: Studies in Social, Political and Legal Philosophy.*

Ed Gehringer received his Ph.D. from Purdue University in 1979 and has been on the faculty of North Carolina State University since 1994, where he currently is Associate Professor of Electrical and Computer Engineering and Computer Science.

John Hunt received his Ph.D. from Georgetown University in 1966. Since 1965 he has taught history at St. Joseph College. His primary field of study has been modern European history, and he is currently interested in the subjects of human rights, definitions of humanity, and truth in academe and media.

Mitchell Kalpakgian, Ph.D., is a Professor of English at Simpson College in Indianola, Iowa, where he teaches the Great Books, classics of children's literature, and courses in Chaucer, Milton, Shakespeare, Renaissance and 18th century literature, and the English novel.

Jeff Koloze is completing his dissertation (tentatively titled "Right to Life Issues in American Fiction") at Kent State University. Besides teaching English literature, research writing, and business courses at

Kent, he also teaches similar courses at other educational institutions in the metropolitan Cleveland, Ohio, area. He has presented and published many papers on the application of various critical theories to literature.

Rev. Joseph W. Koterski, S.J., is Associate Professor of Philosophy at Fordham University in New York. He received his Ph.D. from St. Louis University. He serves as the Editor-in-Chief of the *International Philosophical Quarterly* as well as the editor of the annual proceedings of the University Faculty for Life Conferences.

Kevin Miller, Ph.D. cand., is Instructor of Theology at the Franciscan University of Steubenville. He has previous degrees in molecular biology and political science. His primary interests are issues in social, sexual/family, and medical ethics, especially as explored with the help of the thought of Pope John Paul II. He is writing a dissertation on John Paul's position on capital punishment.

David C. Reardon, Ph.D., is the Director of the Elliot Institute. He has specialized in research and education regarding the effects of abortion on women since 1983. He is the author of numerous books, including *Making Abortion Rare: A Healing Strategy for a Divided Nation, The Jericho Plan: Breaking Down the Walls which Prevent Post-Abortion Healing,* and *Aborted Women: Silent No More.*

Charles E. Rice has been Professor of Law at Notre Dame since 1969. He earned his A.B. from the College of the Holy Cross, his J.D. from Boston College, and his LL.M. and J.S.D. from New York University. His areas of academic interest include constitutional law, jurisprudence, legislation, real property, restitution and torts. From 1970 to 1997 he served as co-editor of the *American Journal of Jurisprudence.*

Fr. Peter F. Ryan, S.J., received his doctorate in moral theology from the Gregorian University in Rome. He now teaches theology at Loyola College in Maryland, his *alma mater.* He serves on the executive board of the Fellowship of Catholic Scholars and the Cardinal Newman Society.

Michael A. Scaperlanda teaches administrative law, constitutional law, contracts, immigration law, and professional responsibility at the Law School of Oklahoma University. His publications include articles in such journals as *Wisconsin Law Review, Iowa Law Review, Stanford Law & Policy Journal, Connecticut Law Review*, and *Georgetown Immigration Law Journal*.

Thomas W. Strahan is a Minnesota attorney who concentrates on medical-legal issues, particularly as related to abortion. He has written numerous articles on abortion and serves as Editor of the *Research Bulletin*, a publication of the Association for Interdisciplinary Research in Values and Social Change (Washington, D.C.).

Teresa Wagner, a domestic policy analyst, joined the Family Research Council in 1998. A philosophy graduate of St. Michael's College at the University of Toronto, she earned a law degree with honors from the University of Iowa and a master's degree in European history from Washington University in St. Louis. Her essay was prepared with the research assistance of Katherine Ann Steers, a Witherspoon Fellow at the Family Research Council.

Bernadette Waterman Ward's first play was produced at Harvard, where she took her B.A. in English. Her Ph.D. in English and Humanities is from Stanford. She serves on the Board of Directors of the Venerable John Henry Newman Society. Her book *World as Word: Philosophical Theology in the Poetry of Gerard Manley Hopkins* is forthcoming from Catholic University of America Press. Until June 2000 a member of the faculty of SUNY Oswego, she has accepted a position as Associate Professor of English at the University of Dallas, beginning August 2000. She is a member of Feminists for Life and the Association of Literary Scholars and Critics.

UFL Board of Directors, 1999-2000*

UFL Board of Advisors, 1999-2000*